1-2-3® Release 3
Made Easy

Mary Campbell

Osborne **McGraw-Hill**
Berkeley New York St. Louis San Francisco
Auckland Bogotá Hamburg London Madrid
Mexico City Milan Montreal New Delhi Panama City
Paris São Paulo Singapore Sydney
Tokyo Toronto

Osborne **McGraw-Hill**
2600 Tenth Street
Berkeley, California 94710
U.S.A.

For information on translations and book distributors outside of the U.S.A.,
please write to Osborne **McGraw-Hill** at the above address.

A complete list of trademarks appears on page 513.

1-2-3® Release 3 Made Easy

1234567890 DODO 898

ISBN 0-07-881541-X

Acquisitions Editor: Elizabeth Fisher
Technical Reviewer: Scott Tucker
Copy Editor: Kay Luthin
Word Processor: Bonnie Bozorg
Proofreaders: Barbara Conway, Julie Anjos
Production Supervisor: Kevin Shafer

1-2-3® Release 3 Made Easy

DEDICATION

I dedicate this book to my husband, Dave

CONTENTS

ACKNOWLEDGMENTS

I wish to thank the following individuals for their contributions to this book:

Gabrielle Lawrence, who helped with all phases of this book, including a last-minute change requiring a different format for all the artwork.

Scott Tucker, for taking time from his busy schedule to review the manuscript.

Kristy Fordham, who helped in many ways, including creating all the worksheet examples and double-checking my keystrokes.

Liz Fisher, Ilene Shapera, and all the other staff members at Osborne McGraw-Hill for their help with the project.

Kevin Shafer, who always does a wonderful job on production.

Susan Erabino, Chris Noble, Mary Beth Rettger, Alexandra Trevelyan, Scott Tucker, and all the other people at Lotus that were so helpful during the testing phase of the new release.

INTRODUCTION

1-2-3 has been one of the most popular software packages since its introduction. Its flexibility makes it a powerful business tool in a wide range of disciplines. With the introduction of Release 3 of this popular package in the summer of 1989, business users have an even wider range of spreadsheet features to work with, including new three-dimensional capabilities, file linking, a macro recorder, and an Undo capability. Even if you are new to computing, you can master the features of 1-2-3 with this book as your guide. If you are working with an earlier release of the package, you can still build financial models to handle all of your projections and other computations with the directions in this book.

Uses of This Book

1-2-3 Release 3 Made Easy is designed to meet the needs of the new 1-2-3 user. You will find everything you need, from installation instructions to step-by-step examples for creating complex tasks like macros. If 1-2-3 is already installed on your system, you can start with Chapter 1 and proceed sequentially through the chapters. You will want to cover at least the first six chapters in this manner to ensure that you have mastered the basic skills that will be needed in all of your model building. After the first six chapters, the sequential approach is still the best way to gradually build your skills, but you can feel free to jump ahead if you have a specific need in a particular area.

If you have not installed 1-2-3 on your system, Appendix A will provide all the help you need to install your copy of 1-2-3. You will need to tell 1-2-3 the exact type of equipment you have so it can conform to your hardware.

If you have already mastered the basics of 1-2-3 with a trial and error approach, you can start at the beginning if you want a logical progression though the package features. You should also feel free to allow the table of contents to be your guide to learning as you have a need to explore topics like data management or graphics or Release 3's new features, like Undo and the macro recorder.

Organization of This Book

This book is divided into 13 chapters. In most cases, each chapter contains just the right number of new features to cover in a single session. The first few chapters provide the building blocks for your first model. After you have mastered these, you will probably want to progress through the remaining chapters sequentially as they lead you to more advanced topics. If there is a particular topic you need to learn immediately, the models in the latter chapters are self-contained and do not require the entries from other chapters. A practice exercise at the end of each chapter can help you monitor your progress. The review section at the end of each chapter can provide a quick refresher when you have not used a feature for some time.

Chapter 1 will get you started with the package. It explains the important features of 1-2-3's display. It also introduces you to the entry of numbers and labels on the worksheet. Release 3's new screen display and the Undo feature are introduced in this chapter.

Chapter 2 provides an introduction to the use of formulas on the 1-2-3 worksheet. You will learn how formulas add power to the worksheet through what-if capabilities. You will also learn how to utilize 1-2-3's new Release 3 note option.

Chapter 3 provides information to tailor the format of your entries to meet your needs. You will learn how to select currency, percent, fixed, scientific notation, date, or other formats for cells on the worksheet. You will also learn how 1-2- 3's new Release 3 format options can improve the appearance of your output.

Chapter 4 shows you how to protect your investment in model building through the use of files that can be stored on your disk permanently. You will learn how easy it is to store or retrieve this data on your disk. The new backup feature of 1-2-3 is covered here.

Chapter 5 covers everything you need to know to copy entries you have already made on the worksheet to other locations. In this chapter you will learn techniques for rearranging the data on your worksheet so that 1-2-3 can share the work required to create or change models. You will also learn how to use Release 3's search and replace features.

Chapter 6 provides explanations and examples of 1-2-3's print features. You will learn how to do everything from printing a draft of your worksheet to adding headers and other sophisticated options.

Chapter 7 introduces you to 1-2-3's @functions. These are formulas and features that are part of the package and available for your immediate access. You will learn about the different categories of functions 1-2-3 offers and can select those that are of interest based on your needs.

Chapter 8 introduces 1-2-3's graphic features so you will have a tool for presenting numeric information in an understandable fashion. You will learn how to create pie charts, line charts, and pie graphs. You will learn to use 1-2-3's new graph settings sheet and options for creating a graph quickly.

Chapter 9 covers the data management features of the package. You can use these to create a simple database. You will also find examples that show you how to sort the information in the database and selectively copy information to another area of your worksheet to create a quick report. New Release 3 options like extra sort keys are covered here.

Chapter 10 focuses on advanced @functions—more sophisticated than the ones in Chapter 7. They can add the power of logic and sophisticated business calculations to your models with minimal work.

Chapter 11 expands the basic file features and teaches you how to combine the data in several files into the current worksheet. You will also learn how to create external links to data in worksheets stored on disk.

Chapter 12 introduces 1-2-3's new multisheet environment that allows you to use 256 sheets in one file or to place 256 different worksheet files in memory at once. You will learn new ideas for organizing information with the multiple sheet concept.

Chapter 13 examines the basics of 1-2-3 macros. With these macro features you will learn how to record keystrokes for execution at a later time. The new Release 3 recorder features make macro creation easy.

Appendix A provides step-by-step directions for installing 1-2-3. This must be your starting point if 1-2-3 is not installed on your system.

Appendix B provides a glossary of spreadsheet terms.

Appendix C provides a list of all the @functions 1-2-3 provides. You can use this to explore functions that parallel the examples presented in Chapters 7 and 10.

Conventions Used in This Book

Several conventions have been used throughout this book to expedite your mastery of 1-2-3 and to make the process as easy as possible.

- Entries that you must make to duplicate examples within the book are shown in boldface within numbered steps.

- The word *enter* is used to precede options that you must choose from 1-2-3's menus.

- The word *type* is used to indicate other information that you must type in from the keyboard.

- Uppercase letters are used when filenames are entered, although either upper- or lowercase will produce the same results.

1

WORKSHEET BASICS

You are about to enter the world of 1-2-3 Release 3. This world will give you a new way of working with everyday business problems—a way that is both efficient and flexible. Traditionally, business problems were worked out on the green-bar columnar pads used by accountants and business managers to evaluate financial decisions. 1-2-3 replaces the paper versions of these worksheets by turning your computer into a large electronic version of the columnar pad.

You will learn to use 1-2-3's worksheet features to handle the same types of problems that were previously solved on columnar pads. Applications such as budgeting, financial planning, project cost projections, break-even analysis, and cost planning are some of the applications you might consider. You also will learn to pattern calculations after real-life situations and lay out models representing the problem to be solved on the electronic worksheet.

The electronic paper that 1-2-3 places in your computer's memory has a structure organized to help you construct these models. The electronic worksheet is arranged into rows and columns, and with Release 3 there are even multiple sheets that you can use to better organize your data. This structure allows you to enter numbers, text entries, and formulas representing computations in many locations. Making entries on 1-2-3's worksheet offers significant advantages over making them on paper. For example, once you have entered a calculation on paper, it is difficult to make a change, but 1-2-3 provides a number of features that facilitate change. On a paper worksheet, you must update calculations every time you change a number; because 1-2-3 can remember calculations, however, it recalculates the worksheet automatically when you update a number.

In this chapter you will look at beginning and ending a worksheet session, worksheet organization, entering numbers and labels on the worksheet, correcting data-entry errors, using the new Undo feature, and accessing 1-2-3's Help feature. Since this chapter covers some of the basic building blocks of worksheet-model construction, you will want to master it completely before progressing to more advanced topics.

Although you probably are eager to start using 1-2-3's features right away, you may have to complete some preliminary work first. Before you begin, assess your current knowledge of the PC and whether your copy of 1-2-3 is ready to use. If you are a new PC user, read Appendix A before proceeding. If 1-2-3 has not yet been installed on your system, follow the instructions in Appendix A before proceeding. Then, once you have filled in the gaps, continue reading and working with this chapter.

LOADING 1-2-3 TO BEGIN A SESSION AND QUITTING WHEN YOU ARE FINISHED

You cannot begin to use 1-2-3 until you have loaded it into the memory of your computer system. The procedure provided here is for users loading 1-2-3 from their own hard disk. Network users will use different procedures, depending on where 1-2-3 has been installed, and will need to follow the specific instructions supplied by the network administrator for activating 1-2-3.

Starting 1-2-3

To start 1-2-3 from your hard disk, you need to activate the directory that contains the 1-2-3 files. If you have installed the files in a directory on drive C named 123, you need to follow these steps:

1. Activate drive C by booting the system from drive C.

   If your system is already on with DOS loaded but another drive is active, you can activate drive C by typing **C:** and pressing ENTER. Once drive C is active, the DOS prompt will display as C>.

2. Activate the subdirectory containing the 1-2-3 files. To activate the 123 directory, type **CD \123R3** and press ENTER. If your files are in another directory, substitute the name of your directory for 123R3 in this entry.

3. Type **123** and press ENTER to start the 1-2-3 program.

A Lotus copyright screen will be displayed. After a brief delay, it will be replaced by an empty worksheet screen.

Quitting 1-2-3

When you have finished all your 1-2-3 tasks for the day, you will want to return to the operating system to work with other programs. To end your 1-2-3 session and return to the operating system, type **/QY** to activate 1-2-3's menu and select the commands Quit and Yes. 1-2-3 understands your entry as a request to clear memory and end the program unless there is data in memory that has not been saved. 1-2-3 keeps track of whether or not you have changed any cells. If you have made changes but they have not been saved, 1-2-3 will prompt you with the following before it allows you to quit the program and erase any data in memory:

WORKSHEET CHANGES NOT SAVED! End 1-2-3 anyway?

1-2-3 expects you to respond with the letter "Y" or "N." Typing **Y** causes 1-2-3 to end immediately. Once you are back at the operating system you can run another program

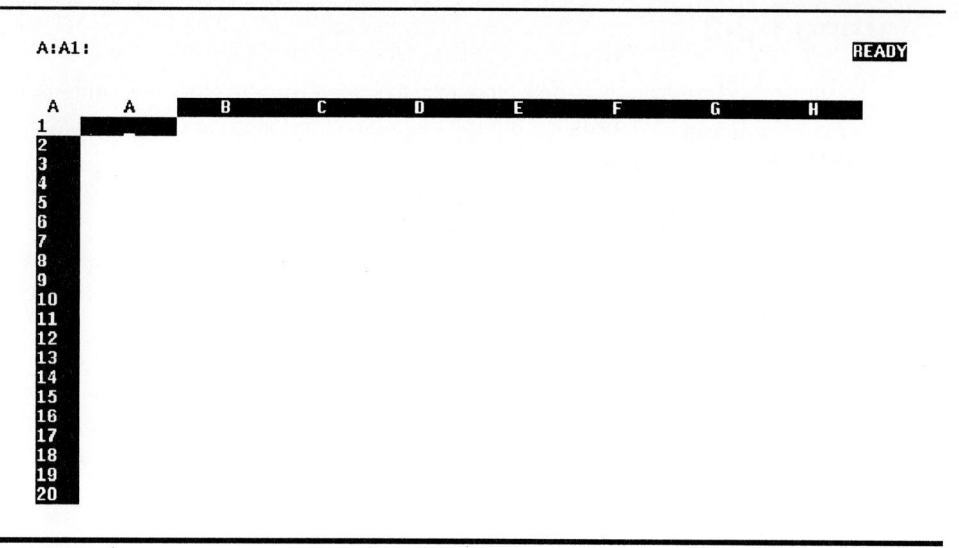

FIGURE 1-1.   Left corner of worksheet visible on the screen

or enter direct operating system requests. You can start 1-2-3 again by typing **123** and pressing ENTER.

If 1-2-3 prompts you about unsaved changes and you decide that you do not want to lose them, type **N** in response to the prompt. 1-2-3 will not end, and this will allow you to save the data in memory if you wish. Later in this chapter you will learn the procedure for saving entries in the worksheet.

WORKSHEET ORGANIZATION

When you load 1-2-3 into the memory of your computer, you will see only the upper-left corner of the first sheet in your worksheet file. Your display should match the one shown in Figure 1-1. This initial display lets you see the 8 leftmost columns and the first 20 rows of the first worksheet. (Depending on the screen you selected in Install, you may have as many as 38 rows.) The worksheet is much larger than it first appears. There are 256 columns in the worksheet, named A to IV. Single alphabetic letters are used first; then AA to AZ, BA to BZ, and so on. Rows are named with numbers rather than letters. Release 1A of 1-2-3 had only 2048 rows, but all versions from Release 2.0 onward have 8192 rows.

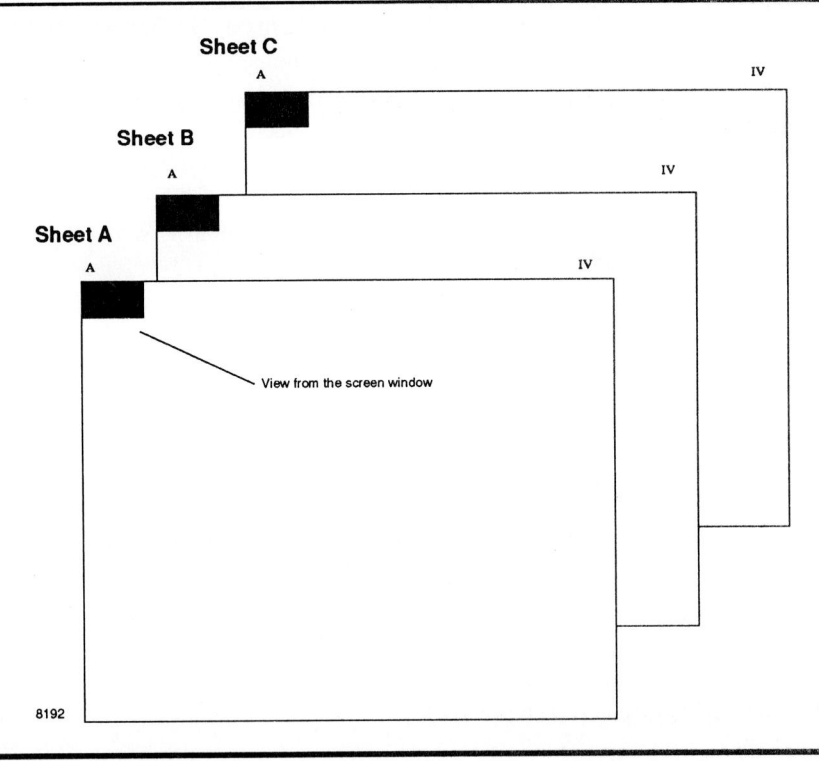

FIGURE 1-2.   Worksheet file containing several sheets, with the small screen window highlighted

Release 3 is unique in that it allows you to insert extra sheets into a worksheet file, just as you might add extra sheets to a folder or notebook. Although a new worksheet file has only one sheet, you can add as many as 255 additional sheets for a total of 256 sheets in a Release 3 worksheet file. You can think of each sheet as a gigantic piece of electronic paper that can help you record and organize computations. Figure 1-2 shows several sheets from a worksheet file, compared with the small portion of one sheet that is visible when you first load the package. You do not need to concern yourself with additional sheets just yet; you will want to explore all the possibilities one sheet offers before adding additional sheets.

The Cell Pointer

Each location on the worksheet is referred to as a *cell*. Each cell is uniquely identified by its *worksheet level* and its *column* and *row location*. The worksheet level refers to which sheet of a multiple-sheet file the cell is located on. The first worksheet level is A, and the last is IV. Sheets are named like columns, with single alphabetic letters used first and then double-letter combinations beginning with AA and ending with IV. A new worksheet will only have an A-level sheet.

Telling 1-2-3 which level you are referring to is similar to telling someone which page of a notepad you have used for recording information; if both of you are looking at the same page, there is no need to specify the page number. With 1-2-3, if you do not specify a level when you specify the address for a cell, 1-2-3 assumes that you are referring to the current sheet. Since you will only be working with sheet A initially, specifying a cell address without a sheet level will cause 1-2-3 to assume that it is on this sheet.

The column is always specified after the level. It is followed immediately by a row number to create cell locations such as A:A1, A:C10, D:IV8192, A:Z1025, and A:IJ850. A *cell pointer* always marks the current location with a small highlighted bar. In a new worksheet, such as the one in Figure 1-1, the cell pointer is located in cell A:A1. The location of the cell pointer is extremely important; it marks the location of the *active cell,* the only cell into which you can make an entry without first moving the cell pointer.

Other Important Indicators

The top three lines of the screen are called the *control panel.* You can see this panel in Figure 1-1; it is used to monitor most of your 1-2-3 activities. As you make entries on the worksheet, these entries will appear in the control panel. If the entries you make are longer than one line, 1-2-3 will automatically expand the control panel area to allow you to see your complete entry. The panel also monitors 1-2-3's activities and tells you when 1-2-3 is ready to proceed with new activities. In addition, it functions as a place keeper, letting you know your current location on the worksheet and giving you specifics about that location.

THE TOP LINE   The top line of the control panel almost always displays the location of the cell pointer in the left corner. This location is referred to as the *cell address;* it always matches the location of the cell pointer in the lower portion of the worksheet. The cell address displayed in the top line always shows the sheet level in addition to the row and column location. As you begin to make worksheet entries, you will find that this location also displays the contents of the cell, as well as any width or formatting changes that you have applied to this cell. Figure 1-3 shows a 1-2-3 screen with $5 in cell C6. Here, the control panel tells you that the cursor is in C6, that a format of currency with zero decimal places is used for the format (C0), and that the column has been assigned a width of 3 [W3]. The last piece of information in the

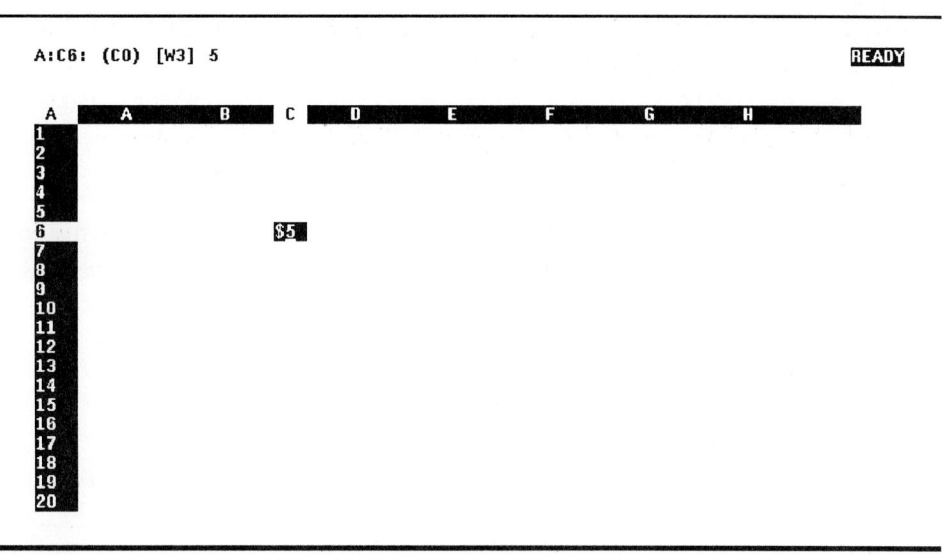

FIGURE 1-3. Control panel entries for cell format, width, and contents

control panel is the contents of the cell, which is represented by the numeral 5. All these special entries will be discussed in detail in later chapters.

THE MODE INDICATOR The right corner of the top line of the control panel contains a *mode indicator*. When you first load 1-2-3, this indicator will display READY, indicating that 1-2-3 is ready to respond to whatever you enter. The mode indicator can tell you either that 1-2-3 is busy with your previous request or that it is ready to do something new. It can also tell you to correct an error, point to a worksheet location, or select a menu choice. Once 1-2-3's mode indicator changes from READY to another mode, you must either follow along with 1-2-3 or find a way to change the indicator. Many new users become frustrated at this point, but you can avoid frustration by watching the mode indicator and staying in sync with the current mode. Table 1-1 lists all the modes you will encounter, along with their meanings. They will also be pointed out in later chapters as new activities cause mode changes.

OTHER CONTROL PANEL LINES Lines two and three of the control panel will take on special significance as you begin to alter cell entries and begin to use 1-2-3's features. When you use 1-2-3 commands, line two lists all your options at any point. Line three gives an explanation of each choice. The use of these lines to alter cell entries will be covered later in this chapter, and displaying options in this area is discussed in Chapter 3.

Indicator	Meaning
EDIT	The cell entry is being edited. EDIT can be generated by 1-2-3 when your cell entry contains an error. It can also be generated by pressing F2 (EDIT) to change a cell entry.
ERROR	1-2-3 has encountered an error. The problem will be noted in the lower-left corner of the screen. Press ESC to clear the error message, and correct the problem specified in the error message at the bottom of the screen.
FILES	1-2-3 wants you to select a filename to proceed. This message is also shown when you request a list of the files on your disk.
FIND	The /Data Query Find command is active.
HELP	A Help display is active.
LABEL	1-2-3 has decided that you are making a label entry.
MENU	1-2-3 is waiting for you to make a selection from the menu.
NAMES	1-2-3 is displaying a menu of range, print, external table, @ function, or graph names.
POINT	1-2-3 is waiting for you to point to a cell or a range. As soon as you begin to type, POINT mode will change to the EDIT mode.
READY	1-2-3 is currently idle and is waiting for you to make a new request.
STAT	Worksheet status information is being displayed.
VALUE	1-2-3 has decided that you are making a value entry.
WAIT	1-2-3 is processing your last command and cannot begin a new task until the flashing WAIT indicator changes to READY.

TABLE 1-1.   Mode Indicators

THE BOTTOM LINE OF THE SCREEN   The bottom line of the display can also provide a variety of information, as shown in Figure 1-4. In Release 3, the lower-left corner displays the date and time until the worksheet is saved to disk. Once a name is assigned to a file with the Save operation, the filename is displayed in this area, rather than the date and time. If you prefer to see the date and time instead, you can have 1-2-3 display it in this area. When the date and time are displayed, 1-2-3 updates them constantly. You will learn how to change the display for this area in Chapter 3.

If an error occurs in any release, the contents of this area are replaced temporarily with an error message such as "Disk Full," "Printer Error," or "Disk Drive Not Ready." Whenever an error message is displayed in the lower-left corner, the mode indicator displays ERROR in the upper-right corner. The ERROR indicator will blink, and your

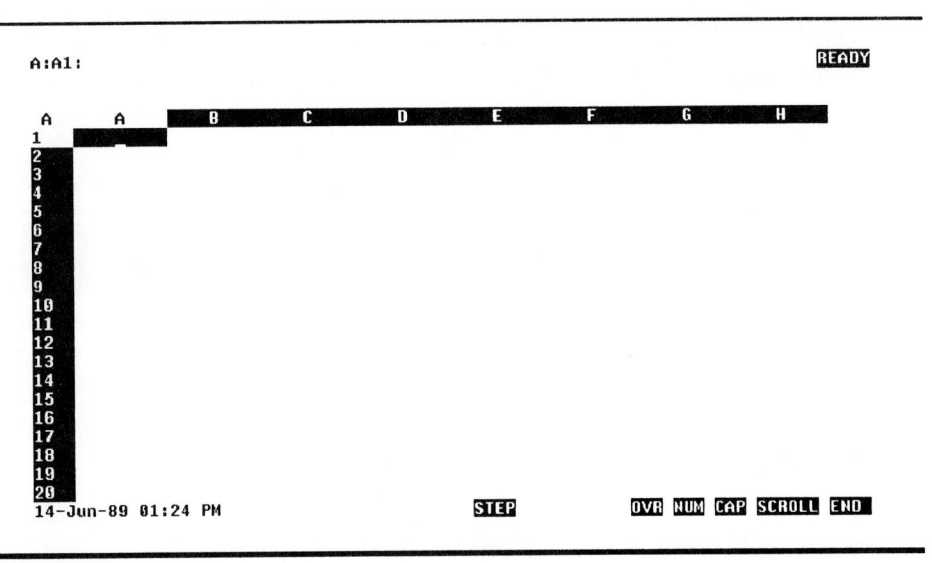

FIGURE 1-4. Indicators in the bottom line of the display

computer will sound a warning beep. You will not be able to proceed until you press the ESC (ESCAPE) key to acknowledge the error.

The area to the right of the date and time (or error message display) lets you know when certain keys have been pressed. It also tells you if 1-2-3 has encountered a special situation. The five indicators designed to inform you that a certain key or key sequence has been pressed are as follows:

CAP	This indicator lights up at the bottom of the screen when the CAPS LOCK key is pressed; pressing CAPS LOCK causes the alphabetic keys to produce capital letters.
END	This indicates that the END key has been pressed. The END key is used to move the cursor to the end of entries in a given direction or to the end of a group of blank cells in a given direction. After using the END key, you must use an arrow key to indicate the direction. The END indicator reminds you to press an arrow key.
NUM	This indicates that the NUM LOCK key has been pressed and that you can enter numbers from the keyboard's numeric keypad. This provides an alternative to using the top row of keys.
SCROLL	This indicates that the SCROLL LOCK key has been pressed. It affects the way in which information scrolls off the screen.

	Without SCROLL LOCK, information scrolls off your screen one row or column at a time. With SCROLL LOCK, the entire window shifts each time you press UP ARROW or DOWN ARROW.
OVR	This indicates that the INS (INSERT) key has been pressed. When editing cell entries, you will sometimes want to use the overstrike method. This lets you replace the characters in the original entry with new characters, rather than adding new characters onto the original entry.
RO	This indicates that you are working in a network environment and you have *read-only access* to the file. While you have read-only access to a file, you cannot save changes that you make. If you see this indicator and want to save your changes, retrieve the file until the RO indicator disappears.

There are other indicators that monitor advanced features and have broader meanings. They will be covered as they occur later in this book.

MOVING AROUND ON THE WORKSHEET

Now you are ready to learn about navigating 1-2-3's worksheet. This will prepare you for constructing models with entries in worksheet cells. You will look at the basic features as well as at the more advanced options that let you to travel long distances quickly.

Basic Options

1-2-3's basic pointer movements within a sheet are accomplished with the arrow keys. These keys may be on the numeric keypad or in another location, depending on the age and model of your computer system. Figure 1-5 shows the enhanced keyboard (standard for AT's and newer computers) with the arrow keys highlighted. Even if your keyboard is slightly different, you should find it relatively easy to locate the keys with the arrows on them. If the arrow keys on your keyboard also house other functions, be careful that the keys are set for the arrow key function. For example, when the arrow keys are on the numeric keypad keys, pressing NUM LOCK causes these keys to enter numbers rather than to move the cell pointer. You can tell if NUM LOCK has been pressed by the NUM indicator in the bottom line of the display panel; press

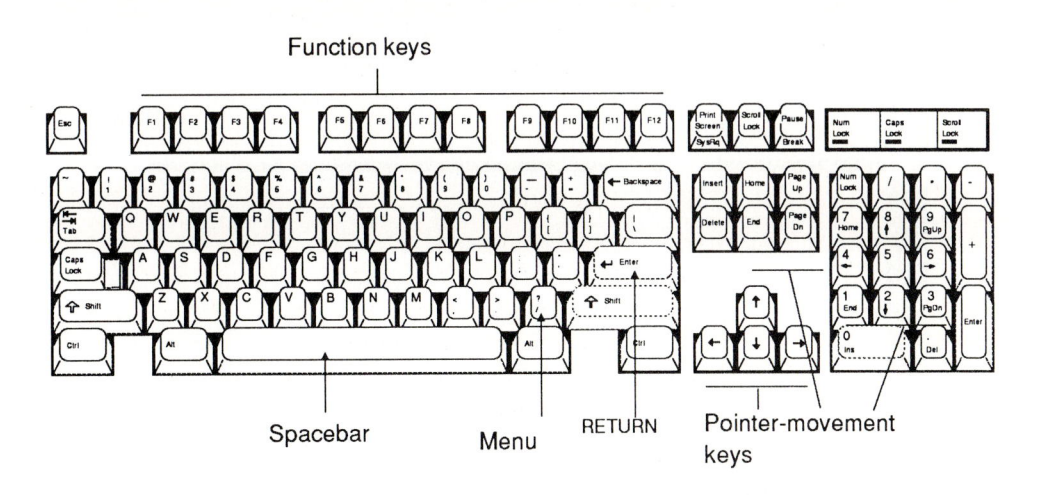

Function keys

Spacebar   Menu   RETURN   Pointer-movement keys

FIGURE 1-5.   IBM's enhanced keyboard

NUM LOCK a second time to remove the indicator from the screen before using the arrow keys to move the cell pointer.

MOVING WITH THE ARROW KEYS   Each of the arrow keys moves the cursor one cell in the direction indicated by the arrow. Your computer's keyboard will record multiple presses for a key, so if you hold down the arrow key, be careful to press it only once and to remove your finger if you want to move the cursor only one cell at a time. Try the following exercise with the arrow keys to become expert in their use.

1. With your cursor in the starting A1 location, press the RIGHT ARROW key once. Your cursor should now be in B1, as follows:

A:B1:   READY

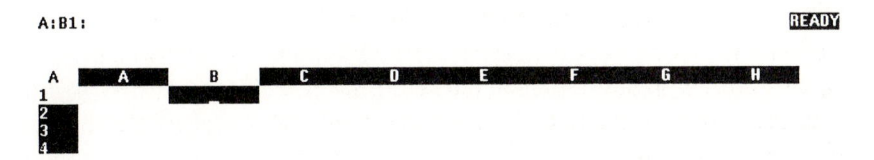

2. Press the RIGHT ARROW key a second time to move your cursor to C1.

3. Press the DOWN ARROW key twice to move your cursor to C3.

4. Press the DOWN ARROW key a few more times until your cursor reaches C20, as follows:

If you hold the DOWN ARROW key down and move too far down the screen, row 1 will scroll off the screen. You can move your cursor back up to line 20, but line 1 will not reappear until you move your cursor all the way back up to the top.

5. Press the RIGHT ARROW until your cursor is in H20; then press it again to scroll a column off the screen as you move to I20. Your screen will look like this:

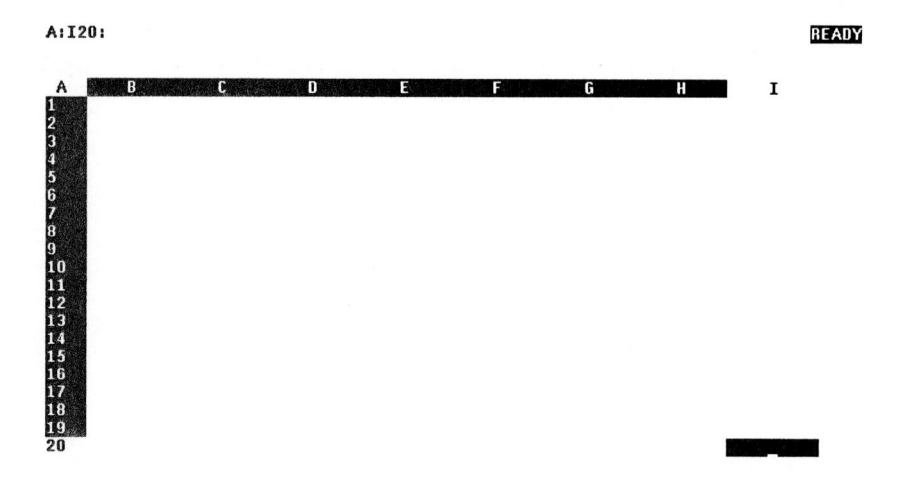

6. Press UP ARROW until your cursor is in I1; then press LEFT ARROW until the cursor returns to A1.

7. Press the LEFT ARROW key again.

    1-2-3 will beep unless someone has disabled the beep feature in your copy of 1-2-3. The beep tells you that the cell pointer cannot be moved.

You may want to practice with these keys a little more to ensure that you are comfortable with them. You can use them to move to any worksheet location. Clearly, however, some shortcuts will be required. The arrow key method would take too long to move you to cell IV200, for example, and to then return to A1.

Quick Steps

A variety of methods let you for move the cursor more quickly. Some methods use special keys to make the move to a new location; others use a combination of keys. The HOME key is the quickest way to return to A1, the *home position* or beginning location on a worksheet. As soon as you press this key, the cell pointer moves from its current location to A1.

PGUP AND PGDN   PGUP moves the cursor up 20 rows without moving it from its current column. Of course, this key works effectively only when the cursor is in row 21 or greater. If the cursor is in B1 and you press PGUP, 1-2-3 will beep at you and will not move the cursor at all, since the cursor is already at the top of the worksheet. If the cursor is in B5, PGUP will move it to B1; if the cursor is in B26, PGUP will move it up 20 rows to B6. PGDN does the exact opposite: it moves the cursor down by 20 rows. However, if you are fewer than 20 rows from the bottom edge of the sheet, it will take you to the bottom. When the screen displays more than 20 rows, PGUP and PGDN operate on the number of rows that appear on the screen instead of the 20 used in this discussion.

THE END KEY   The END key can be used in combination with the arrow keys to move you to the end of the worksheet in the direction specified. When a worksheet contains data, END functions differently and moves you to the last blank cell or to the last cell containing data in the direction you specify. END will stop at the last cell with an entry in it or the last blank cell, depending on whether it was resting on a blank cell or a cell containing data when you pressed it.

To use the END key and arrow key combination, follow these steps:

1. Move the cell pointer to A1, and then press the END key.

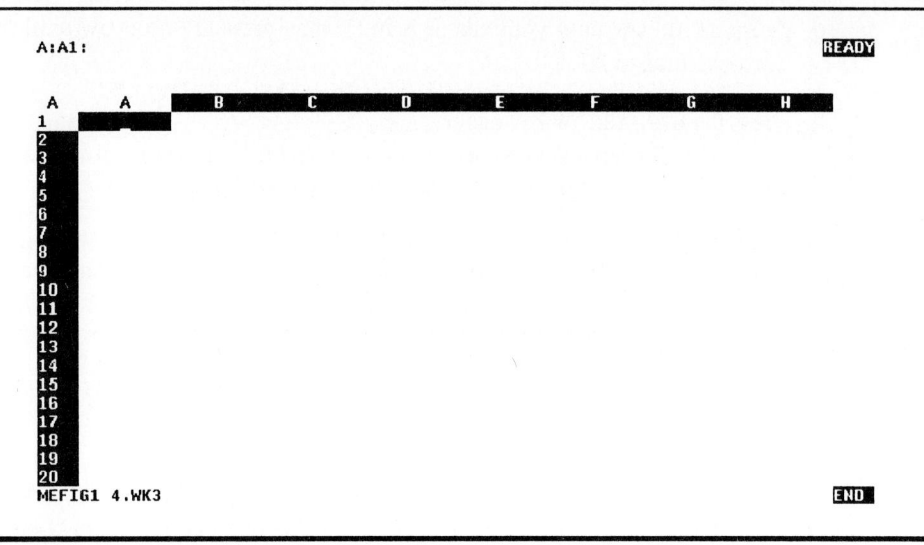

FIGURE 1-6.   END indicator at the bottom of the screen

Verify that the END indicator has appeared in the lower-right corner of the worksheet, as shown in Figure 1-6. Next, you will press the arrow key that specifies the direction in which you wish to move.

2. Press the RIGHT ARROW key.
   The cell pointer will move to the last cell on the right, IV1.

3. Press END followed by the DOWN ARROW key.
   The cell pointer is now in IV8192.

Once you have placed entries on the worksheet, the END key can take on a different function—it will move the cell pointer to the last entry in the direction you indicate. Figure 1-7 shows a worksheet containing data with the cell pointer originally located in A2. In this example, if you press the END key and then the DOWN ARROW key, the cell pointer will be relocated to A10, the last cell in column A that contains data. END searches for the first blank cell in the specified direction, so it is important that the data be contiguous if you want to move to the end of the data with this method. If you press the END key again and then the RIGHT ARROW key, the cell pointer will be relocated to E10, the last cell in row 10 that contains data.

```
A:A2:  'Part_No                                                          READY

     A      A        B        C        D        E        F      G      H
1
2          Part_No     Price  Quantity    Bin  Warehouse
3          AX-8976      4.67     100        7      15
4          BY-8761      8.90      75        6       1
5          CD-7865      7.75     100        8       6
6          ER-5412      6.60      50        2       3
7          FG-6611     12.98      65        1       4
8          GT-8811     15.89      76        7       1
9          NB-6512      3.56     150        5      15
10         RT-8976     10.95     100        4       4
11
```

FIGURE 1-7.   Sample data and the END key

Press the HOME key to move to A1 again, and use this quick method for moving to E10. First press the END key, and then press HOME. When this sequence is used, 1-2-3 moves the cell pointer to E10, the last worksheet cell that contains an entry.

THE CTRL KEY   The CTRL (CONTROL) key can be used with the arrow keys to move one screen's width to the right or left. Once you learn to insert additional sheets in Chapter 3, you can use the CTRL key in combination with PGUP and PGDN to move from sheet to sheet. Unlike the END key, CTRL is not pressed before the arrow key, but simultaneously with it. To move the cell pointer from A1 to I1, press CTRL and hold it down while pressing the RIGHT ARROW key. The notation used for this action is CTRL-RIGHT ARROW. To move the cell pointer back to A1 again, press CTRL with the LEFT ARROW key (CTRL-LEFT ARROW).

THE GOTO KEY   Your last option for moving the cursor quickly is to use the GOTO option provided by the F5 key. To use this direct cell-pointer movement, follow these steps:

1. Press F5.

2. Type **Z10** and press ENTER.

1-2-3 immediately positions your cell pointer in Z10, regardless of the pointer's beginning location.

USING ALL THE BASIC CURSOR-MOVEMENT FEATURES   The following example uses a variety of the quick pointer- movement features to reinforce your understanding of the various options. First press HOME to position your cursor in A1. Then follow this sequence of entries:

1. Press PGDN twice to position the cursor in A41.

2. Press END followed by the RIGHT ARROW key to position your cell pointer in IV41.

3. Press CTRL-LEFT ARROW twice to move two screens to the left and position your cell pointer in HY41.

4. Press END followed by the LEFT ARROW key to position the cell pointer in A41.

5. Press END followed by the UP ARROW key to position your cursor in A1.

6. Press F5, enter **S2**, and press ENTER to place your cell pointer in S2.

7. Press HOME to return your cursor to A1.

CORRECTING ERRORS

You may wonder why you are already learning about error correction when you have not even made any cell entries yet. Everyone makes at least a few mistakes, and it is impossible to predict when you will make your first one, so it is best to be prepared before you begin to explore cell entries. 1-2-3 offers several error-correction methods. Which one you use depends on whether you are still entering the entry you want to correct, or whether you have already finalized the entry by pressing ENTER or by moving the cell pointer to a new location.

Fixing an Entry
Before It Is Finalized

To make a correction while making an entry into a cell, you can press the BACKSPACE key to delete the last character you entered. Suppose that you intend to enter "SALES" but that you leave out the "E." To correct this, try these steps:

1. Move your cursor to A1.

2. Type **SALS**, and then press the BACKSPACE key to delete the last "S."

3. Type **ES**.

Do not press any additional keys. You will use this partially completed entry in the next example.

The ESC key is a more dramatic way to eliminate characters. It eliminates all the characters you have typed in a cell, as long as you have not finalized the entry. Try it now by pressing the ESC key. The entire SALES entry will disappear, and 1-2-3 will be ready to accept a new entry.

One more error-correction method allows you to edit an entry while you are making it. Since it functions the same whether or not the cell entry has been finalized, it will be discussed in the next section.

Fixing a Finalized Entry

You can finalize and display entries in the cells in which you want to enter them by pressing ENTER or by moving the cell pointer to a new location. Once the entry is finalized in this way, you must use other methods for correcting mistakes.

RETYPING ENTRIES   One way to change a cell entry that has been finalized is to retype it. Follow these steps to create and correct finalized entries:

1. Enter **SALS** in A1 and press ENTER.
   This time you will find that neither BACKSPACE nor ESC will affect the entry. One method of changing the contents of A1 is to retype your entry.

2. With the cell pointer in A1, type **SALES** and press ENTER to make the correction.

This method gets the job done but requires a considerable amount of unnecessary typing.

EDITING A FINALIZED ENTRY   A better method, especially for longer entries, is to edit the entry and change only the mistakes. You must be in EDIT mode to make this type of change. To place yourself in EDIT mode, press F2 (EDIT). Later, you will find that 1-2-3 will sometimes automatically place you in EDIT mode when it is not happy with the cell entry you are trying to finalize. Regardless of how you get there, once you are in EDIT mode, the entry in the cell will be placed in the second line of the control panel, just as it was when you originally entered it.

Within EDIT mode, the special keys that you used to move the cell pointer around on the worksheet function differently. Now the RIGHT and LEFT ARROW keys move you a character to the right or left each time you press them. This allows you to position your small flashing cursor on a letter that you want to delete, or to move it where you want to make an insertion.

The HOME key also takes on a new function within EDIT mode: it moves you to the front of the entry. If the correction you need to make occurs at the beginning of the entry, HOME moves you to that location quickly. The END key moves in the opposite direction. It places the flashing cursor at the end of the entry.

Within the entry, two different keys can be used to eliminate characters. You can press the BACKSPACE key to delete the character to the left of the flashing cursor, and you can press the DEL key to delete the character above the cursor.

If you type a character from the keyboard, it will be added to the right of the cursor location unless you first press the INS key to start the overstrike setting (overstrike replaces characters already in the entry). Let's try an example using each of these keys.

1. Type **SELRS** in B2, as follows:

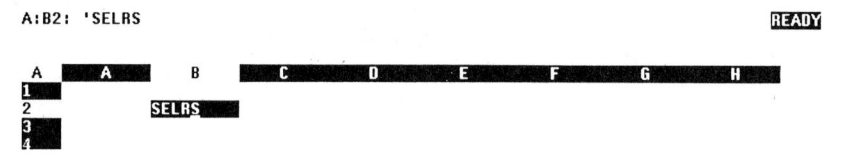

2. With the cell pointer still in B2, press F2 (EDIT).

1-2-3 will display the entry in the cell in the second line of the control panel with a small cursor at the end, like this:

3. Press the BACKSPACE key to move the cursor one position to the left to delete the "S." Then type **Y**.

4. Press the LEFT ARROW key again to position the cursor under the "R", and then type **A**.

Since 1-2-3 was in its default INSERT mode, the A was added to the left of the "R."

5. Move the cursor until it is under the "E" and press the INS key once to go into OVERSTRIKE mode. Then type **A**.

1-2-3 will replace the "E" and the control panel will look like this:

6. Press the ENTER key.

The entry will be finalized in the cell and will disappear from the edit line of the control panel.

THE NEW UNDO FEATURE

Release 3 offers a new Undo feature that allows you to reverse the effect of the last menu command in most cases and can eliminate the last entry you finalized. The secret to using the Undo feature effectively is to make sure you invoke it before taking any other actions, since it can only change the last action performed.

The Undo feature reverses the effect of the actions taken since the last time 1-2-3 was in READY mode. If you just made an entry in a cell, pressing ALT-F4 (UNDO) would eliminate this entry. If you just performed an action requiring multiple steps and 1-2-3 did not return to READY mode between steps, UNDO would eliminate all the steps.

In Chapter 3 you will learn about the use of ALT-F4 (UNDO) for reversing menu commands. For now, you can use it to eliminate your last cell entry. First, let's take a look at the way you turn the Undo feature on and off. Make sure your worksheet is blank. If it is not blank, enter **/WEYY** to clear the worksheet from memory. Next, enter **/WGDOUE** for /Worksheet Global Default Other Undo Enable. These are the keystrokes needed to enable Undo if it is not on. Then type **Q** for Quit to return to the worksheet. If you ever want to turn Undo off, you can use the same key sequence, except you should change the last character to a "D" to disable it. Once Undo is on, all you need to do is press the ALT-F4 (UNDO) key after completing an action and respond with **Y** when 1-2-3 prompts you about undoing the action. If Undo is not enabled when you try this, an error message at the bottom of the screen will tell you that Undo cannot undo your last action. At this point, enabling it will not allow you to make the correction, since Undo must be enabled before taking an action that you can undo.

TYPES OF WORKSHEET ENTRIES

1-2-3 has two basic types of entries for worksheet cells: *labels* and *values*. Labels are text characters that can be used to describe numeric data you plan to place on the worksheet or to store character information. Label data cannot be used in arithmetic calculations even if the labels contain numbers, without converting the labels to values by using advanced functions covered in Chapter 10. Value data, on the other hand, consists of either numbers or *formulas*. Formulas result in numbers but are entered as a series of calculations to be performed. The numeric digits, cell addresses, and a limited set of special symbols are the only entries that can be made in those cells categorized as value entries. 1-2-3 attempts to distinguish label entries from value entries by looking at the first character you enter into a worksheet cell. As long as this first character is not one of the numeric digits or characters that 1-2-3 considers numeric, it will be treated as a label. 1-2-3 generates a default label prefix for any entry it considers to be numeric.

Let's look at some examples. If you were to enter **Sales** in a cell, 1-2-3 would treat the entry as a label, since the first character in the entry is an alphabetic character. Because 1-2-3 always makes its determination from the first character, entering **15 Johnson St.** causes 1-2-3 to reject your entry when you attempt to finalize it; the first character is numeric, and 1-2-3 attempts to treat the entire entry as a value.

1-2-3 is also very stubborn once it determines the type of entry it thinks you planned for a cell. The only way you can change its mind is by editing the cell contents or by pressing ESC to start over. After a little practice with the label entries in your first few models, however, you will know all the tricks that will put you in command of how your entries are interpreted.

Entering Labels

Label entries in 1-2-3 cells must all begin with one of the acceptable label prefixes. These are an apostrophe ('), a double quotation mark ("), and a caret (^). Each of these three symbols causes 1-2-3 to align the contents of the cell differently. Beginning with an apostrophe is the default option and causes the label entry to be left aligned in the cell. 1-2-3 will even generate this label prefix for you if your entry begins with an alphabetic character or a special symbol that is not considered part of the value entry options. Using the double quotation mark causes the entry to be right aligned in the cell, and using the caret symbol causes the entry to be centered. If you want right or center justification, begin your label entry with the special symbol and follow it immediately with the text that you wish the cell to contain. If you want to begin a label entry with a character that 1-2-3 considers to be a value, you may start your entry with one of the three label prefixes to trick the package into treating it like a label. There are two other symbols that can be used to start labels in exception situations; these are the \ and the | symbols. Before starting an actual model, try each of these exercises:

1. Move your cell pointer to A1 with the arrow keys, type **AT**, and press ENTER.
   AT appears in the display of the worksheet. However, when you observe the entry in the control panel, you will notice that it reads 'AT. 1-2-3 generated the label prefix for you. Because of this prefix, your entry should also appear as left-aligned within cell A1 and will match this:

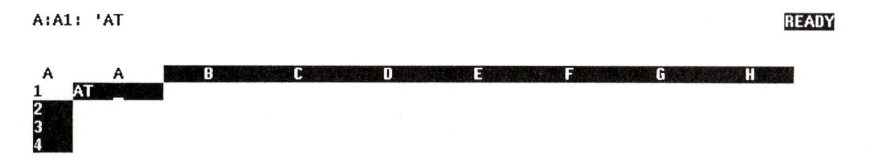

2. Use the DOWN ARROW key to move the cursor to A2. Type **"AT** and press ENTER. Your entry should be right aligned in the cell display.

3. Use the DOWN ARROW key to move to A3. Enter **^AT** and press ENTER.
   The entry should be centered in the cell, as follows:

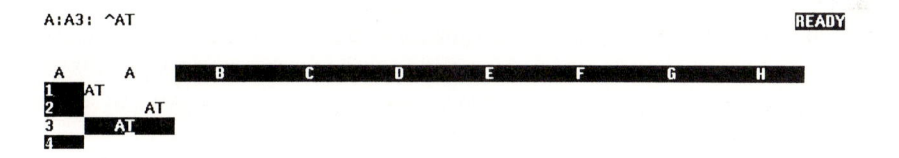

4. Use the DOWN ARROW key and move to A4. Type **3AT** and press ENTER.
   Notice that 1-2-3 beeps at you, does not accept this entry, and places you in EDIT mode.

5. Press the HOME key and add an apostrophe at the front of the entry. Then press ENTER again.
   This time, 1-2-3 accepts the entry. By placing a label prefix at the front of the entry, you have asked 1-2-3 to treat the entry as a label, even though the first character is a number. Your worksheet should now look like this:

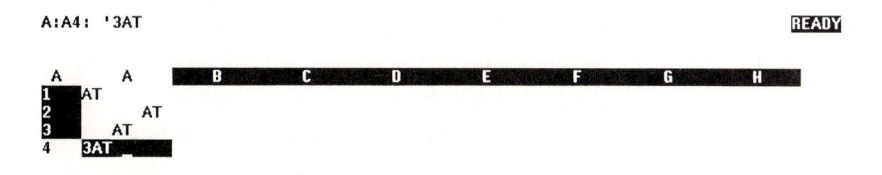

A:A1:   READY

```
 A       A        B        C        D        E        F        G        H
 1
 2                    Real Estate Investment Analysis
 3
 4                               Surfer I Meadows
 5      Cost                      1500000  2000000
 6      Rent Revenue               500000   550000
 7      Number of Units                60       60
 8      Square Footage              80000    98000
 9      Number of Parking Spaces      100      125
10      Acreage                        20       30
11      Rent to Cost Ratio           0.33     0.28
12      Cost per Unit              25,000   33,333
13      Cost per Square Foot        18.75    20.41
14      Rent per Square Foot         6.25     5.61
15      Units per Acre                  3        2
16      Parking Spaces per Unit      1.67     2.08
17
```

FIGURE 1-8.   Real estate investment model

6. To have a blank screen displayed, enter **/Worksheet Erase Yes Yes** by typing the slash (/) and the first letter of each word.

This was just a practice exercise, so you can clear everything you have entered. You will find the commands required to erase an entire worksheet on 1-2-3's menus. For now, you need to take the required key sequence on faith, but you will learn all the details in a later chapter.

Now you will put your newly acquired label-entry techniques to work by building the model shown in Figure 1-8. This model compares two investment properties. You could easily modify the model to compare two potential stock or bond investments, or two departments, or two sales managers. All you need is the information pertinent to the subjects being compared. All the entries you make in this section of the chapter will be entered as labels. These labels can be used to describe the data the model will contain and the calculations the model will perform, as well as to provide an overall description of the model's purpose, so you can see the versatility of label entries. You will continue to build this model by adding numeric entries in the next section of this chapter, and you will complete it in Chapter 2 by adding formulas.

Follow these steps to create the model shell shown in Figure 1-9:

1. Move the cell pointer to A5 with the arrow keys, and type **Cost.**
   This step enters a label that describes the detail entries in column A. You may wonder why you are not entering the title or heading line first. It is often

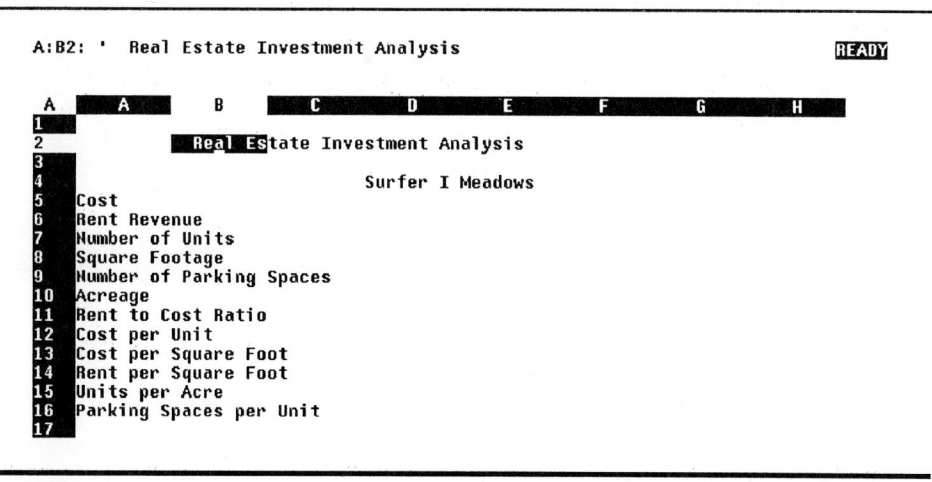

A:B2: ' Real Estate Investment Analysis `READY`

```
   A        A         B        C        D        E        F        G        H
1
2                     Real Estate Investment Analysis
3
4                            Surfer I Meadows
5  Cost
6  Rent Revenue
7  Number of Units
8  Square Footage
9  Number of Parking Spaces
10 Acreage
11 Rent to Cost Ratio
12 Cost per Unit
13 Cost per Square Foot
14 Rent per Square Foot
15 Units per Acre
16 Parking Spaces per Unit
17
```

FIGURE 1-9. Label entries that build the shell

easier to choose an appropriate location for the title or heading after you have positioned the detail below it.

A few rows are skipped to allow for the eventual addition of a heading and entries, which begin in row 5.

2. Press the DOWN ARROW key to move to A6 and finalize your entry in A5.

There are two methods for finalizing cell entries: you can use the arrow keys to move to a new location, or you can press the ENTER key. The DOWN ARROW key is a better method, since you need to position your cursor for the next entry anyway and it lets you both finalize and position with a single keystroke.

3. With your cursor in A6, type **Rent Revenue** and press ENTER.

This time you are using the ENTER key rather than the DOWN ARROW key so you can examine the label entry in the cell in which you entered it. Notice the label prefix generated automatically for you at the front of the entry; this was also added at the front of your last entry. This label entry is different from the last one: it is longer than the default cell width of nine characters, which means that it is too long to fit in cell A6. However, 1-2-3 borrows display space from cell B6 rather than shortening the label entry to fit in A6. Had B6 contained data, its space would not have been available; 1-2-3 would then have truncated the display to fit within the nine-character width for column A.

Even though the label entry may be truncated when displayed, 1-2-3 will always retain the complete entry in memory. This means that complete label entries are always available for display if the cell width is increased or if the cell to the right no longer contains an entry. Remember that these long label entries are always stored in the original cell where you entered them. If you choose to go back and edit the entry, you must edit this cell regardless of where the entry is displayed.

4. Move to A7 with the DOWN ARROW key. Type **Number of Units** and press the DOWN ARROW key again.

5. Complete the remainder of vertical label entries by making sure that your cell pointer is in the cell specified and making the entries shown here:
   A8: Square Footage
   A9: Number of Parking Spaces
   A10: Acreage
   A11: Rent to Cost Ratio
   A12: Cost per Unit
   A13: Cost per Square Foot
   A14: Rent per Square Foot
   A15: Units per Acre
   A16: Parking Spaces per Unit

6. Press F5, type **D4**, and press ENTER. Type **Surfer I** and finalize the entry by pressing the RIGHT ARROW key.

   Step 6 added a column heading, which represents the name of the first apartment house you are evaluating. The F5 (GOTO) key is the quickest way to position the cell pointer.

7. Type **Meadows** and press ENTER.

8. Use UP ARROW and LEFT ARROW keys to move to B2.

9. Type **Real Estate Investment Analysis** and press ENTER.

   The heading is a little too far to the left. Using C1 for the entry would not work, since it would be too far to the right. A useful method is to add a few spaces at the front of the entry to position it exactly as you wish.

10. With your cursor in B2, press F2 (EDIT). Then press the HOME key to move to the front of the entry.

11. Press the RIGHT ARROW key once to move the cursor to the right of the label prefix. Press the spacebar twice to add two spaces at the front. Then press ENTER.

These extra spaces make your model look better by moving the heading toward the center.

The entry of the title should complete the label entries and lay the groundwork for the numeric data, which you will add in the next step.

Entering Numbers

Numbers are one of the two types of value entries that 1-2-3 permits. As value entries, they follow much more rigid rules than do label entries. Like labels, numbers are constant at a given moment in time; they do not change as the result of arithmetic calculations. They are placed in a cell and will remain as you enter them unless you take some direct action to change them.

Numbers can contain any of the numeric digits from 0 through 9. Other characters allowable in value entries are

^ . + @ $ ( ) E / * -

The only characters used in entering regular numbers are the . (used to separate the whole number portion of the entry from the decimal digits), the + (used to indicate a positive number), and the - (used to indicate a negative number). A percent sign can be used at the end of a numeric entry to indicate a percentage, but it is not allowed in other positions within the entry. Spaces, commas, and other characters cannot be added to numeric entries except by using the formatting options discussed in Chapter 3. The exceptions to this rule are the use of the letter "E" (or "e"), which can be used to represent numbers in powers of 10 (referred to as *scientific notation*) and the entries made in worksheet cells when using 1-2-3's Automatic format, which includes many additional characters including abbreviations for the months of the year when you are entering month numbers. The Automatic formatting options and the special rules that apply to them are covered in Chapter 3. An example of an entry in scientific notation is 3.86E-05, which is equivalent to .0000386. This number can also be represented as (3.86*10^-5) or 3.86E-05. The caret symbol represents exponentiation, or the power of 10 that this number is raised to.

You will only enter the numbers for the constant numeric data on the worksheet. Even though numeric entries are considered constants, there is nothing to prevent you from updating any of these numbers once they are entered by typing a new number or editing the existing entry. For this model, the numbers you will enter are the first six entries in the column. The other entries will be the results of formulas added in the next chapter; these cells will remain blank initially. As you enter the first numeric digit in each cell, you will notice that the READY mode indicator is replaced by VALUE. The first character is all that 1-2-3 needs to determine the type of cell entry. Here are the steps to follow:

1. Move the cell pointer to D5 with the arrow keys. Type **1500000** and press ENTER.

   Notice that you did not enter any commas or other characters. You can have 1-2-3 add them at a later time as a formatting option if you wish. Also, notice that 1-2-3 did not add a label prefix in front of this number since it considers it a value.

2. Move the cell pointer to D6 with the DOWN ARROW key. Type **500000** and then press the DOWN ARROW key.

3. Type **60** and then press the DOWN ARROW key.

4. Type **80000** and then press the DOWN ARROW key.

5. Type **100** and then press the DOWN ARROW key.

6. Type **20** and then use the UP ARROW and RIGHT ARROW keys to move to E5.

7. Complete these entries for the Meadows building with the following entries:
   E5: 2000000
   E6: 550000
   E7: 60
   E8: 95000
   E9: 125
   E10: 30

The result of entering each of the numbers is shown in Figure 1-10.

   Remember, it is easy to change any of the entries. You can type a new number or edit a cell. Try a few changes, following these steps:

1. Move to E8 and press F2 (EDIT).

2. Press the LEFT ARROW key to move your cursor under the 5.

3. Press the DEL key to remove it.

4. Type **8**.

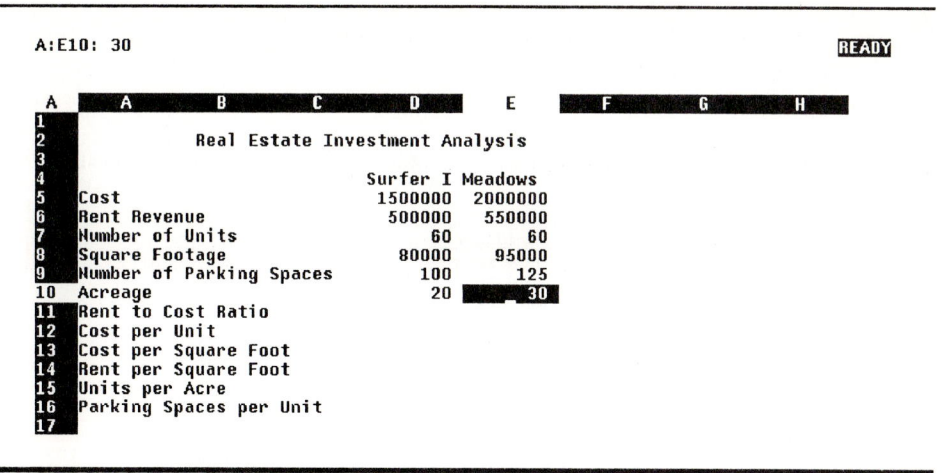

```
A:E10: 30                                                    READY

A      A         B         C         D       E       F       G       H
1
2                      Real Estate Investment Analysis
3
4                                     Surfer I Meadows
5     Cost                             1500000  2000000
6     Rent Revenue                      500000   550000
7     Number of Units                       60       60
8     Square Footage                     80000    95000
9     Number of Parking Spaces            100      125
10    Acreage                              20       30
11    Rent to Cost Ratio
12    Cost per Unit
13    Cost per Square Foot
14    Rent per Square Foot
15    Units per Acre
16    Parking Spaces per Unit
17
```

FIGURE 1-10.   Adding numbers to the shell

5. Finalize your entry by pressing ENTER.

You also could have finalized with UP or DOWN ARROW. However, the RIGHT and LEFT ARROW keys are not options for finalizing while you are editing, since they move you within the cell entry.

This is the last entry that you will make in the model, so save a copy of the model to disk. The commands that handle saving files are covered in Chapter 4 in detail. For now, all you need to know is that you need a menu command in order to save a file. You must enter /**File Save** followed by the name of the file you wish to save. If the file is already stored on the disk, you must confirm your desire to save by entering **R** for Replace. You can enter each of these commands by typing the first letter of the command, but you must enter the filename in full. Enter /**File Save**, type **REALEST**, and press ENTER.

GETTING HELP

Navigating your way around the worksheet and entering numbers and labels in worksheet cells probably has seemed quite simple. That is because you have taken everything a step at a time. As you begin to add more skills to your toolkit of 1-2-3 options, you may find that you need a quick refresher of an earlier topic. Although you can always look back to the particular chapter or to your 1-2-3 reference manual,

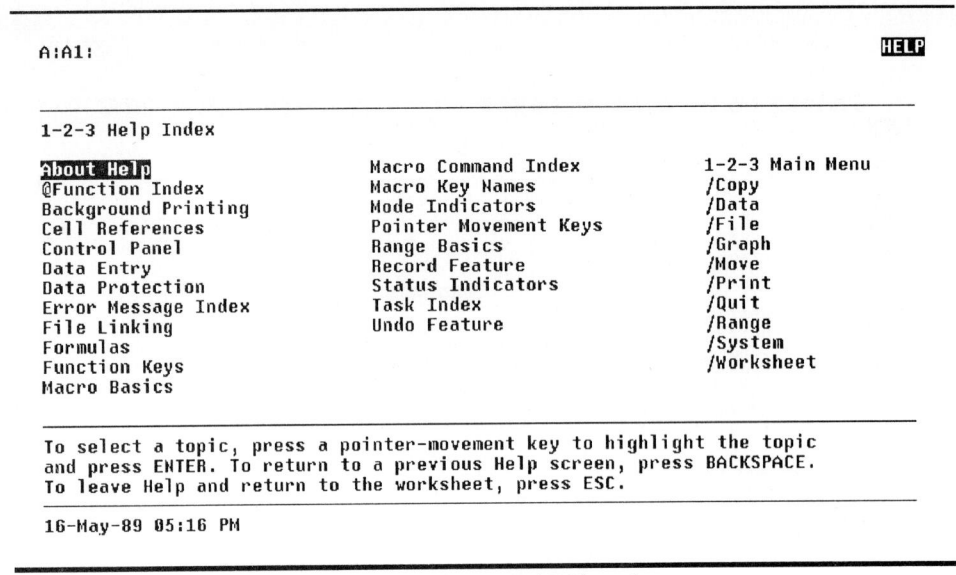

```
A:A1:                                                                    HELP

1-2-3 Help Index

About Help           Macro Command Index       1-2-3 Main Menu
@Function Index      Macro Key Names           /Copy
Background Printing  Mode Indicators           /Data
Cell References      Pointer Movement Keys     /File
Control Panel        Range Basics              /Graph
Data Entry           Record Feature            /Move
Data Protection      Status Indicators         /Print
Error Message Index  Task Index                /Quit
File Linking         Undo Feature              /Range
Formulas                                       /System
Function Keys                                  /Worksheet
Macro Basics


To select a topic, press a pointer-movement key to highlight the topic
and press ENTER. To return to a previous Help screen, press BACKSPACE.
To leave Help and return to the worksheet, press ESC.

16-May-89 05:16 PM
```

FIGURE 1-11.   HELP screen presented from READY mode

1-2-3's onscreen Help facility will often provide just the hints you need to complete your planned task. Accessing the Help feature is as easy as pressing F1 (HELP). You can do this even if you are in the middle of a task, such as entering a label in a cell. 1-2-3 will not disrupt the task in progress; instead, it will set it aside temporarily to let you review help information on the screen.

If you press F1 (HELP) before starting a task, 1-2-3 will display a Help Index screen from which you can choose a topic relating to your current needs. Assuming that you are in READY mode, try this right now and press F1. If you are using Release 3, your screen should match the one in Figure 1-11. (The HELP screens for other releases of 1-2-3 are similar but not always exactly the same, since some of the features of Release 3 are different.) To select information on any topic, just place the highlighted bar on the desired topic and press ENTER. If you choose Formulas, additional information will be presented as in Figure 1-12. There may be additional levels of help that you can select in the same manner, depending on the topic. When you are through, leave the Help feature by pressing ESC. This returns you to the 1-2-3 task where you left off.

If you request help with F1 after beginning a task, 1-2-3 tries to provide appropriate options. This is 1-2-3's "best guess" as to the type of help you need, based on the entries you have made so far. Assuming that you were entering a label and wanted additional information on 1-2-3's label-entering rules, you could press F1 before finalizing. Try this by entering the label **Salaries** in a worksheet cell and pressing F1

```
A:A1:                                                                    HELP
```

```
Types of Formulas --  1-2-3 has four types of formulas:
  Numeric      Performs calculations with numbers. For example, +B5*5
               multiples 5 times the value in B5.
  String       Performs calculations with strings (text enclosed
               in quotation marks or labels in a worksheet). For example,
               the formula +"Mr. "&B2 concatenates (joins together) Mr.
               (space) and the label in cell B2.
  Logical      Performs true/false tests on numeric or string values and
               returns 1 (for true) or 0 (for false). For example, +A1>500
               returns 1 if the value in cell A1 is greater than 500 and 0
               if the value in A1 is less than or equal to 500.
  @Function    Performs specific database, date-and-time, financial, logical,
               mathematical, statistical, scientific, or string calculations.
               For example, the formula @SUM(B10..F10) calculates the sum
               of the values entered in the range B10..F10.
```

```
Entering Formulas                                          Operators
@Function Index                                            Help Index
16-May-89 05:24 PM
```

FIGURE 1-12.   Requesting additional help for entering formulas

before finalizing your entry. You still have the option of selecting help on less-specific topics by choosing the Help Index at the bottom of the screen. You can also choose Task Index from the Help Index screen to select from an alphabetical list of tasks. This index provides a whole list of topics like the ones shown in Figure 1-13.

When you have finished using the Help feature, you can press ESC again to return to the worksheet. Everything will be exactly as you left it. 1-2-3 places a marker in your current location and records your actions up to that point before displaying the HELP screen, so it can put things back exactly as you left them. Even the partially completed label entry will be waiting for you to finalize it. You do not wish to actually make another entry at this time, so you can press ESC again to eliminate it.

1-2-3 can assist you when you encounter an error message. Just press F1 (HELP), select the Help Index, and choose Error Message to see an explanation of each, as well as actions that you can take to correct the error.

REVIEW EXERCISE

You have had a chance to look at the basic entry features for numbers and labels. Before you enter formulas in the next chapter, you can put your new skills to work by

A:A1:   **HELP**

Task Index

Change display of data   -- see **/Range Format**
Change formulas to numbers   -- see /Range Value
Change global default settings   -- see /Worksheet Global Default
Change the column width   -- see /Worksheet Column
Create a text file   -- see /Print File
Create a multiple-sheet file   -- see /Worksheet Insert Sheet
Create a "what-if" table   -- see /Data Table
Display three worksheets at once -- see /Worksheet Window Perspective
End a 1-2-3 session   -- see /Quit
Enter characters not on a keyboard -- see COMPOSE(ALT-F1) Key
Enter dates   -- see Date Formats
Enter formulas   -- see Entering Formulas
Enter information in a worksheet   -- see Entering Data
Erase worksheet data   -- see /Range Erase
Erase a file on disk   -- see /File Erase

Continued   Help Index
16-May-89 05:28 PM

FIGURE 1-13.   Looking at the task index

entering some basic information about a company's assets. Figure 1-14 shows the completed entries.

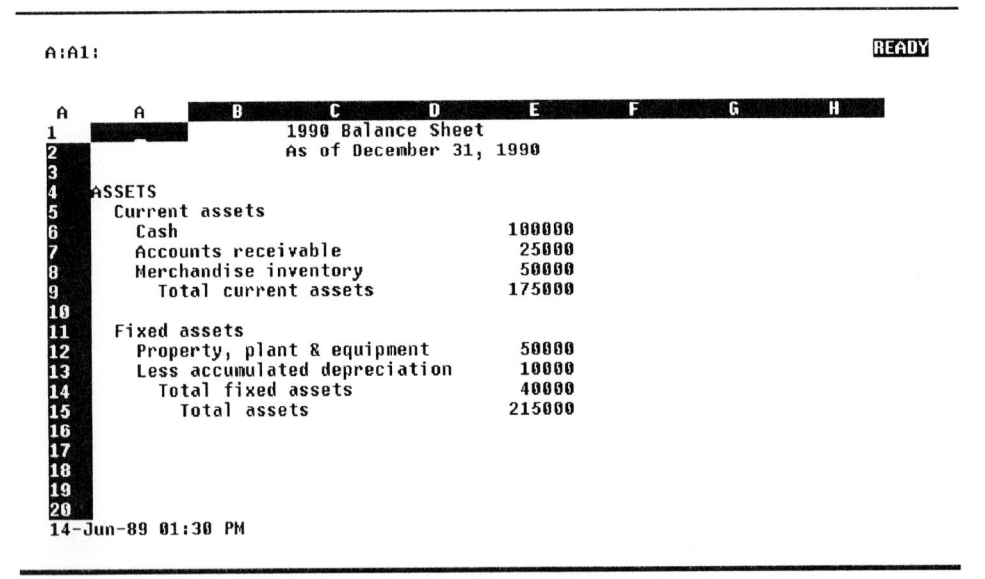

FIGURE 1-14.   Entries to record a company's assets

1. If your worksheet contains entries, enter /**WEY** to select /Worksheet Erase Yes from the menu and clear the screen. If the data on the screen has not been saved, you will have to type a second **Y** to erase the screen.

2. Use the RIGHT ARROW key to move to C1 and place the first heading entry in the cell. (*Hint:* Since the entry begins with a number and contains label characters, you will want to type a label prefix first, as in '.) Complete the entries in C2 and A4.

3. Complete the remaining label entries as shown in cells A5..A15. (*Hint:* Use the spacebar to add two spaces for each new level of indentation.)

4. Use the arrow keys to move to E5 and complete the numeric entries shown.

5. Save the worksheet by entering /**FS**, typing **ASSETS**, and pressing ENTER.

6. To erase your screen and begin a new model, enter /**WEY**.

REVIEW

- To start 1-2-3, you must first load the operating system into the memory of your computer. All you need to do is turn the system on with drive A empty. Next, respond to any date or time prompts, and then activate the 1-2-3 directory. For example, if 1-2-3 is stored in the 123 directory, you would type **CD \123** and press ENTER, and then type **123** and press ENTER to begin the program.

- The highlight that marks your place on the worksheet is called the cell pointer. Use the keys in Table 1-2 to move it around.

- The control panel at the top of the screen provides valuable information about 1-2-3. Look at the mode indicator in the upper-right corner of the screen to determine 1-2-3's current mode. The upper-left part of the screen shows the current cell's contents, format, and width.

- The bottom line of the screen displays the date and time or the filename. It also displays indicators for several keys and other options that can tell you what to expect from 1-2-3.

- How you correct worksheet entries depends on whether or not they were finalized. One set of techniques works for active entries, and another set is most useful for entries that were not finalized.

- The Undo feature can eliminate an entry just finalized or reverse the result of a 1-2-3 command if Undo is enabled. Just press ALT-F4 (UNDO) and type **Y** to use it.

Key	Meaning
UP ARROW	Moves the cell pointer up one cell.
DOWN ARROW	Moves the cell pointer down one cell.
RIGHT ARROW	Moves the cell pointer one cell to the right in READY mode. In EDIT mode, moves one character to the right.
LEFT ARROW	Moves the cell pointer one cell to the left. In EDIT mode, moves the cell pointer one character to the left.
CTRL-LEFT ARROW	Moves one screen to the left.
CTRL-RIGHT ARROW	Moves one screen to the right.
CTRL-PGUP	Moves you to the next sheet when a worksheet contains multiple sheets.
CTRL-PGDN	Moves you to the previous sheet when a worksheet contains multiple sheets.
PGUP	Moves up one screen.
PGDN	Moves down one screen.
END	Causes the arrow key pressed next to move the cell pointer to the last blank cell or the cell containing the last contiguous entry in the specified direction. When pressed with EDIT mode in effect, takes you to the end of the entry.
HOME	Moves the cell pointer to A1. When EDIT mode is in effect, places the cursor at the front of your entry. When pressed following END, moves the cell pointer to the last cell on the spreadsheet that contains an entry.
ESC	Eliminates an entry that is not finalized. Exits from the 1-2-3 Help system. When pressed repeatedly, allows you to escape from a menu selection made in error.
F1 (HELP)	Activates the 1-2-3 Help system.
F2 (EDIT)	Places you in EDIT mode to allow the correction of entries without retyping. The arrow keys, HOME, and END all function differently when EDIT mode is in effect.
F5 (GOTO)	When followed by typing a cell address and pressing ENTER, moves the cell pointer to the specified address.
ALT-F4 (UNDO)	When no intervening actions have occurred, eliminates the last finalized cell entry. Can also eliminate the effect of most menu commands.

TABLE 1-2.   Special Keys

- Cells can be empty or contain labels or values. Labels are treated as characters by 1-2-3. Depending on the label prefix they may be left aligned ('), right aligned ("), or centered (^).

- One type of value is a number. You can use the digits 0 through 9 or special symbols like . + - in number entries.

- To save the current worksheet, enter **/FS**, type a name of no more than eight characters with no spaces, and press ENTER. If there is a file with that name on the disk, you can type **R** if you wish to replace the existing file with the current worksheet.

- To access 1-2-3's Help feature, press F1 (HELP).

- To erase the current worksheet without saving it, enter **/WEYY**.

- To quit 1-2-3, enter **/QY** and confirm by entering another **Y** if you have not saved the worksheet and still wish to quit.

2

DEFINING YOUR CALCULATIONS

Formula Basics
Arithmetic Formulas
Using Logical Formulas
Using String Formulas
Performing More Complex Calculations
Using Cell Names in Formulas
Review Exercise
Review

Calculations are an important part of many of the business tasks that you perform. Some calculations are simple. If you get a 10% discount when you purchase from a given vendor, it takes no great effort to calculate your savings. It is also simple to calculate the total number of employees in your group if the headcount increases by 5. In fact, these calculations are so easy that you can compute them without even writing them down.

However, not all computations are this simple. For example, if you want to determine the most economic quantity to order for each item in your inventory, you will need to perform a much more complex calculation, one that is difficult to compute without writing it down. Even when you do write complex computations down on paper, mistakes are easy to make. And if conditions change slightly, the numbers in your computations are likely to change as well, requiring you to redo the calculations. Evaluating a series of conditions would cause you to spend a considerable amount of time redoing calculations.

1-2-3 provides a solution that eliminates the need for you to perform calculations yourself. You simply define the calculations you wish to perform, and 1-2-3 handles the computations. To do this you must determine each step in the computational process and record these instructions in a cell on 1-2-3's worksheet. Recorded instructions for handling calculations are known as *formulas*. Once the formulas are entered, 1-2-3 will handle all the work required for computing your results.

Entering formulas is really quite simple and is not too different from entering numbers and labels as you did in Chapter 1. The formulas will tell 1-2-3 what data to operate on and which of the operators will be used. A sample formula for profit might be Sales - Cost of Goods Sold; a sample formula for net payable on an invoice might be Amount - (Amount * Purchase Discount).

This chapter will show you how to enter any of these formulas, using references to the worksheet cells that contain your data. 1-2-3's formulas are very powerful; they allow you to reuse applications even when significant changes occur. Such flexibility makes formulas a valuable addition to your worksheet models.

In this chapter, you will look at all the features provided by 1-2-3 to handle your calculations. You will find that they have wide applicability: the same methods are used to calculate interest expense, budget projections, salary increases, and any other calculation. In addition to the basics, you will also explore 1-2-3's full set of features for building more complex formulas, including string formulas that manipulate text data rather than numeric values.

FORMULA BASICS

Formulas, like the numbers you entered in Chapter 1, are value entries. Unlike numbers, however, they produce results that vary, depending on the entries they reference. This variability makes formulas the backbone of spreadsheet features: it allows you to make *what-if* projections based on changing entries on your worksheet. You can update the formula results without changing the formula itself. The only thing required is new entries for the variables referenced by the formula.

The Basic Rules of Entry

To enter a formula in a cell, you must define to 1-2-3 the location of the variables involved and the operations you wish performed on them. 1-2-3 has three types of formulas it supports: *arithmetic* formulas, *logical* formulas, and in Release 2 and higher, *text* or *string* formulas. A few rules apply to all formulas, and some special conventions apply to types of formulas. The special rules will be discussed when each type of formula is discussed, and the general guidelines will be presented here.

The first and perhaps most important rule is that the first character in a formula entry must always come from the following list of value characters:

+ - (@ # $. 0 1 2 3 4 5 6 7 8 9

The second rule is that formulas cannot contain extraneous spaces except within names or text. As you type the examples presented here, be careful not to separate the formula components with spaces. The third and last rule pertains to the length limitation for a formula: as with other cell entries, it cannot exceed 512 characters in Release 3. Unless you are building some extremely complex calculations, this last rule is not likely to restrict you.

ARITHMETIC FORMULAS

Arithmetic formulas are nothing more than instructions for certain operations: addition (+); subtraction (-); multiplication (*); division (/); and exponentiation (^), which represents raising a number to a specific power, such as 3 cubed or 2 squared. These are the same types of operations you can compute by hand or with a calculator. When you record these formulas on the worksheet, you can build the formula with the arithmetic operators and references to the numbers contained in other worksheet cells. The result of the calculation will be determined by the current value of the worksheet cell referenced.

You can see the advantage of recording these formulas on a worksheet more clearly when you wish to change one of the numbers. All you need to do is change the number in the referenced cell. Since the formula has already been entered and tested, it will be available on a permanent basis. Anytime you wish the same set of calculations to be performed, you can enter the numbers involved without having to reenter the formula; the sequence of required calculations will be stored on the worksheet in the cell that contains the formula.

Entering Simple Arithmetic Formulas

1-2-3's formulas can be entered with numeric constants, as in 4∗5 or 3+2. However, numeric constants within formulas are limiting; you have to change the formulas as conditions change. A better method is to store the constants in a worksheet cell. When you wish to use the value in a formula, you can use its cell address within the formula. Then, if the value changes, you need only enter a new number where it is stored; the formula will use it automatically.

Using cell addresses in formulas requires an additional rule. Since cell addresses begin with non-numeric characters, an entry's initial alphabetic character (as in A2+B3) causes it to be treated like a label entry. Thus, the entry appears in the worksheet cell just as you typed it, rather than performing any calculations. Try this with the following entries:

1. Move the cell pointer to A2, type **3**, and press ENTER.

2. Move the cell pointer to B3, type **2**, and press ENTER.

3. Move the cell pointer to D2, type **A2+B3**, and press ENTER.

No calculation is performed for you. 1-2-3 decided that the cell entry was a label, since its first character was alphabetic. This approach produces the following display, which does not perform any calculations:

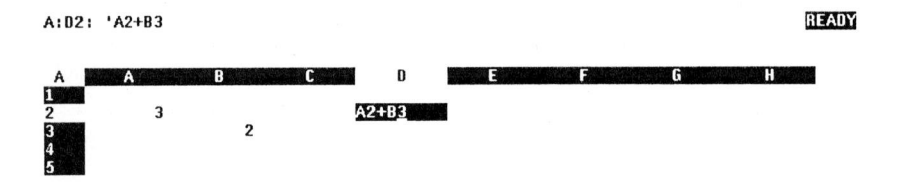

Several numeric characters can be used to begin a formula. The + sign is a logical choice as a character to add to the front of the formula; it requires only one keystroke and will not affect the contents of A2. Try it now to see the results. Type **+A2+B3** in D2. This time, 1-2-3 interpreted your entry as a formula and computed the result of adding the current contents of A2 to the current contents of B3. Since A2 contains 3 and B2 contains 2, after the formula is entered D2 displays 5, as follows:

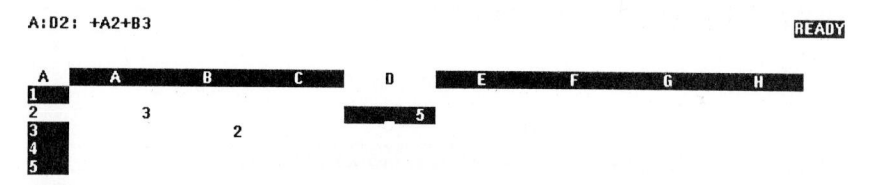

When you point to D2 you still see the formula you entered in the control panel. If you decided to change A2 to 10 later on, the result displayed in D2 would change to 12 as evidence that the formula was still doing its assigned task.

When you enter formulas by using their cell address, 1-2-3 is not fussy and will accept either upper- or lowercase. The formula +A2*AB3 is equivalent to +a2*ab3 or +a2*Ab3 and computes the same results.

Adding Notes to Formulas

Release 3 allows you to document a formula as you enter it. Although the formula is likely to be perfectly clear to you on the day that you enter it, when you want to change the formula after a period of time has elapsed, it can be difficult to remember the logic behind your entries.

You can place the note in the same entry as the formula calculation as long as you enter a semicolon after the formula and the combined length of the entry does not exceed 1-2-3's 512-character limit. You are not restricted in the entries that follow the semicolon, since they are not part of the calculation and do not need to conform to 1-2-3's rules for value entries. You can also use 1-2-3's editing features to add notes at the end of existing formula entries.

Complete the following steps to add a note at the end of a formula:

1. Move the cell pointer to D2, and press F2 to edit the entry in the cell.

2. Type ; and then type this note:

    This formula adds the contents of cell A2 to B3

3. Press ENTER to finalize the addition of the note to the formula.

4. Move the cell pointer to D4 and type

    +A2*B3;This formula multiplies the contents of A2 by B3

5. Press ENTER to finalize the results:

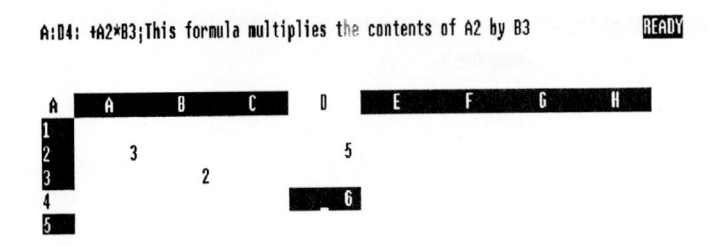

Adding Formulas to
The Real Estate Model

You will use your new formula techniques to add formulas to the real estate investment model that you started in Chapter 1. If the model is still in the memory of your computer, you are ready to begin. If you have just started a new 1-2-3 session and wish to recall your copy of the model from your disk, type **/FRREALEST** and press ENTER. The model shown in Figure 2-1 should be displayed on your screen in preparation for adding the formulas.

The first formula you need to enter is the rent-to-cost ratio, which you compute by dividing the rent by the cost. Each investment will be evaluated separately; you will enter the computations for Surfer I first. Follow these instructions to add the formulas:

1. Move the cell pointer to D11.

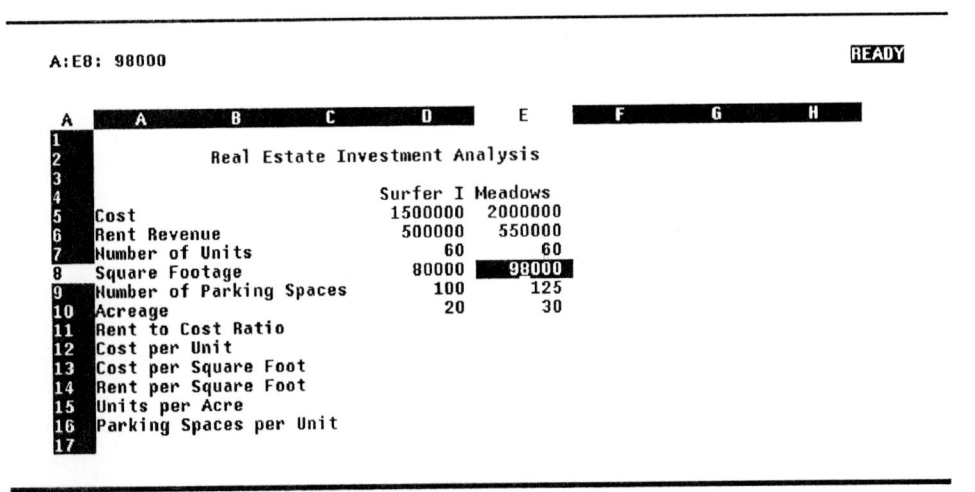

FIGURE 2-1.   Real estate model from Chapter 1

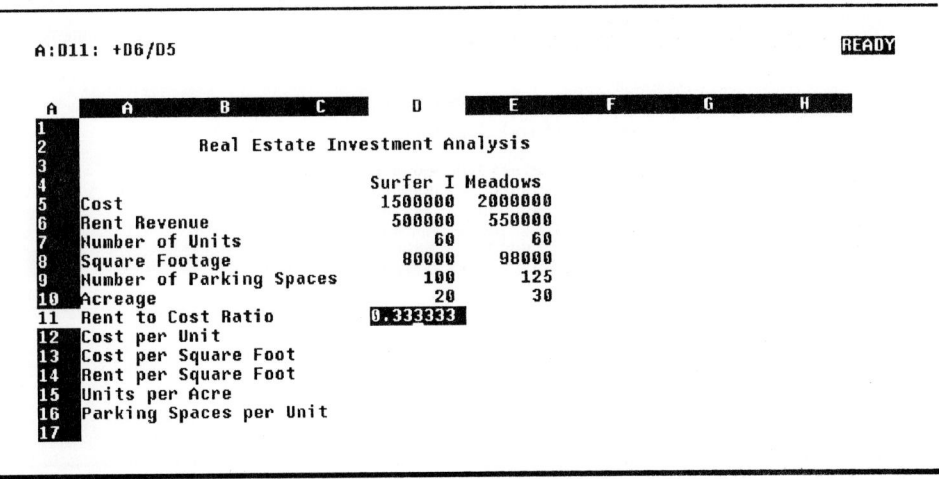

A:D11: +D6/D5   READY

	A	B	C	D	E	F	G	H
1								
2	Real Estate Investment Analysis							
3								
4				Surfer I	Meadows			
5	Cost			1500000	2000000			
6	Rent Revenue			500000	550000			
7	Number of Units			60	60			
8	Square Footage			80000	98000			
9	Number of Parking Spaces			100	125			
10	Acreage			20	30			
11	Rent to Cost Ratio			0.333333				
12	Cost per Unit							
13	Cost per Square Foot							
14	Rent per Square Foot							
15	Units per Acre							
16	Parking Spaces per Unit							
17								

FIGURE 2-2.   Formula entered in D11

This is an appropriate location for the first Surfer I calculation.

2. Type **+D6/D5;Rent divided by cost** and press ENTER.

Since the rent revenue for this property is stored in D6 and the cost is in D5, the formula will calculate the ratio you need and the note will document your entry. The results should look like those in Figure 2-2, with the formula and note you entered displayed in the control panel and the results of the calculation shown in the cell. You may add notes to the remaining formula entries if you wish; they are not required entries and in the interest of focusing your attention on the formulas, they are not shown for the remaining entries.

The next computation is cost per unit. This calculation splits the total cost evenly across all units to give you an estimate of what one unit costs.

3. Move the cell pointer to D12 with the DOWN ARROW key. Type **+D5/D7**.

This formula divides the cost by the number of units. The next formula will allocate the cost on a square-footage basis.

4. Move the cell pointer to D13 with the DOWN ARROW key. Then type **+D5/D8** and press the DOWN ARROW key.

The remaining three formulas for Surfer I follow the same pattern.

5. Type **+D6/D8** and press DOWN ARROW.

6. Type **+D7/D10** and press DOWN ARROW.

7. Type **+D9/D7** and press ENTER.

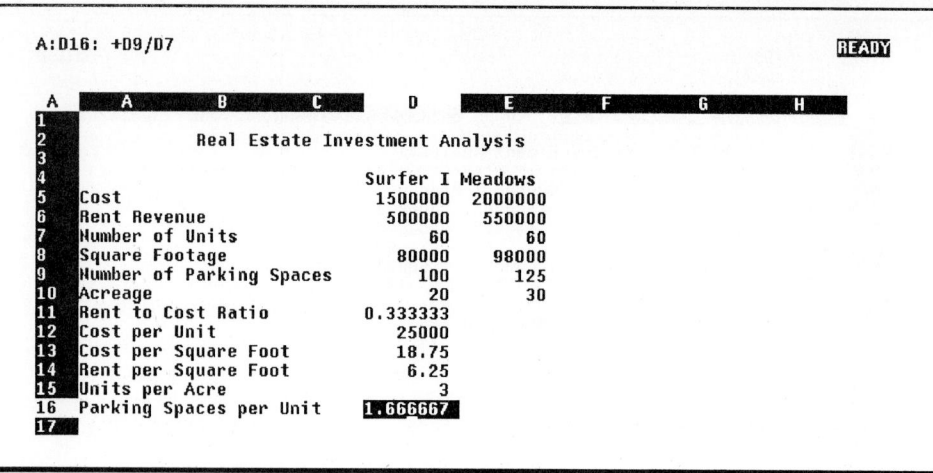

A:D16: +D9/D7   READY

A	A	B	C	D	E	F	G	H
1								
2		Real Estate Investment Analysis						
3								
4				Surfer I	Meadows			
5	Cost			1500000	2000000			
6	Rent Revenue			500000	550000			
7	Number of Units			60	60			
8	Square Footage			80000	98000			
9	Number of Parking Spaces			100	125			
10	Acreage			20	30			
11	Rent to Cost Ratio			0.333333				
12	Cost per Unit			25000				
13	Cost per Square Foot			18.75				
14	Rent per Square Foot			6.25				
15	Units per Acre			3				
16	Parking Spaces per Unit			1.666667				
17								

FIGURE 2-3.   All of the formulas entered for Surfer I

This completes the entries for Surfer I and produces the results shown in Figure 2-3.

Later, you will learn techniques for copying formulas like these to other locations rather than reentering a set of similar formulas for the Meadows property. For now you need practice with formula entry, and the second set of formulas lets you look at another formula-entry method.

Entering Arithmetic Formulas With the Point Method

The formulas in the last section were all built by typing both the arithmetic operators and the cell addresses they referenced. This method works fine if you are an average typist and if all the referenced cells are within view on the worksheet. However, if neither of these conditions is true, typing the formulas may lead to a higher error rate than necessary. 1-2-3 provides a second method of formula entry that can reduce the error rate. With this method, you type only the arithmetic operators, and you select the cell references by using the arrow keys to position the cell pointer on the cell you wish to reference. 1-2-3 adds the cell address to the formula being built in the control panel and changes the mode indicator from VALUE to POINT. This method provides visual verification that you are selecting the correct cell and eliminates the problems of typing mistakes.

Follow these steps to add the first formula for the Meadows property, using the pointing method of formula entry:

1. Move your cell pointer to E11 and type +.

   You can use the + sign on the key next to the pointer movement keys or the one over the = sign.

2. Move your cell pointer to E6.

   This will cause the cell address A:E6 to appear in the control panel:

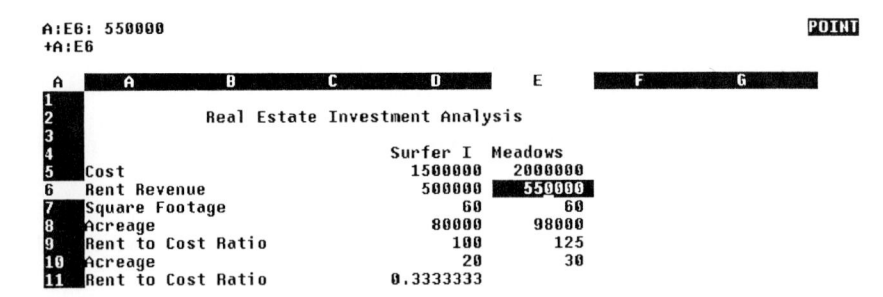

```
A:E6: 550000                                                    POINT
+A:E6

A    A         B         C         D      E        F        G
1
2              Real Estate Investment Analysis
3
4                                   Surfer I  Meadows
5    Cost                           1500000   2000000
6    Rent Revenue                    500000    550000
7    Square Footage                      60        60
8    Acreage                          80000     98000
9    Rent to Cost Ratio                 100       125
10   Acreage                             20        30
11   Rent to Cost Ratio          0.3333333
```

   Note that the indicator in the upper-right corner of the screen has changed to POINT and the sheet level is included as part of the address.

3. Type /.

   Notice that the cell pointer returns to the cell where the formula is being recorded.

4. Move your cell pointer to E5. The control panel will now contain the complete formula:

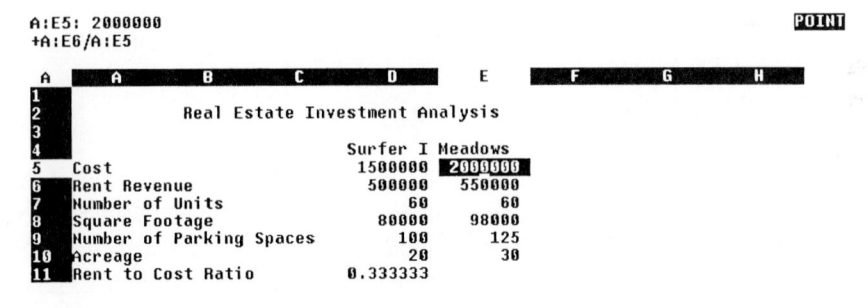

```
A:E5: 2000000                                                   POINT
+A:E6/A:E5

A    A         B         C         D      E      F      G      H
1
2              Real Estate Investment Analysis
3
4                                   Surfer I Meadows
5    Cost                           1500000  2000000
6    Rent Revenue                    500000   550000
7    Number of Units                     60       60
8    Square Footage                   80000    98000
9    Number of Parking Spaces           100      125
10   Acreage                             20       30
11   Rent to Cost Ratio          0.333333
```

5. Press ENTER to finalize the formula.

   The following result will appear:

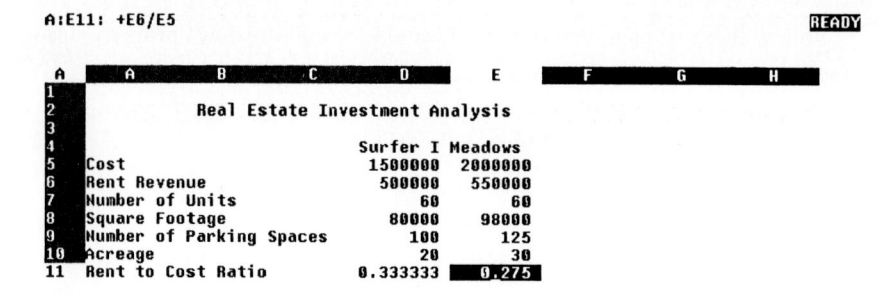

```
A:E11: +E6/E5                                                    READY

  A     A          B         C          D         E       F       G       H
  1
  2                 Real Estate Investment Analysis
  3
  4                                 Surfer I Meadows
  5   Cost                          1500000  2000000
  6   Rent Revenue                   500000   550000
  7   Number of Units                    60       60
  8   Square Footage                  80000    98000
  9   Number of Parking Spaces          100      125
  10  Acreage                            20       30
  11  Rent to Cost Ratio            0.333333    0.275
```

Completing the Meadows Formulas

The remaining Meadows formulas can be completed by using the pointing method, following these steps:

1. Move your cell pointer to E12 and type +. Then point to E5 with the UP ARROW key and type /. Next, point to E7 and press ENTER.

2. Move your cell pointer to E13 and type +. Point to E5 with the UP ARROW key and type /. Point to E8 and press ENTER.

3. To enter the formula for rent per square foot, begin by moving the cell pointer to E14 and typing +. Use the UP ARROW key to move to E6. Then type /, move to E8, and press ENTER.

4. Move the cell pointer to E15 and type +. Use the UP ARROW key to move to E7. Type / and then move to E10 and press ENTER.

5. Move the cell pointer to E16 and type +. Use the UP ARROW key to point to the number of parking spaces in E9. Then type /, move to the number of units in E7, and press ENTER.
    The completed model is shown in Figure 2-4.

Notice that ENTER was used to finalize each of the formulas. If you had attempted to finalize by pressing an arrow key, the last reference in the cell would have been changed by the movement of the cell pointer. With the pointing method of formula construction, ENTER will always be your only way of finalizing a formula. Other than the differences in the entry method, these two sets of formulas will perform identically.

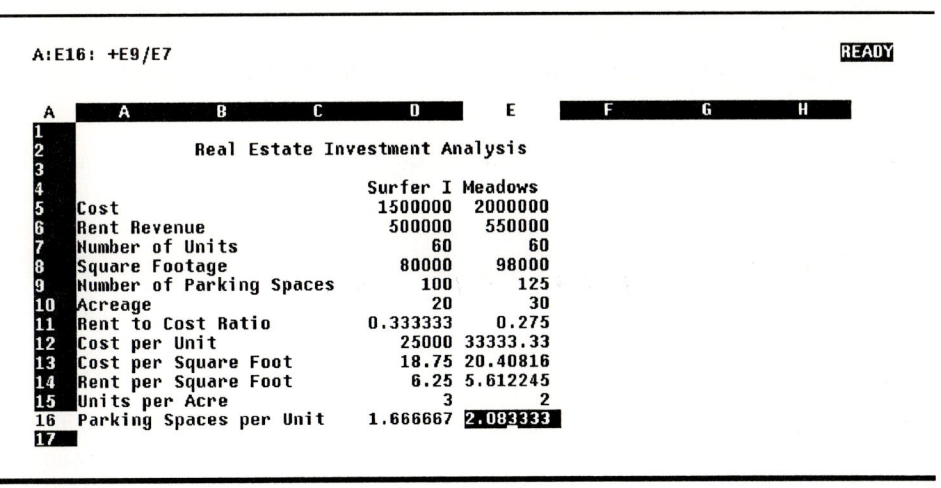

A	B	C	D	E	F	G	H
			Real Estate Investment Analysis				
				Surfer I	Meadows		
Cost			1500000	2000000			
Rent Revenue			500000	550000			
Number of Units			60	60			
Square Footage			80000	98000			
Number of Parking Spaces			100	125			
Acreage			20	30			
Rent to Cost Ratio			0.333333	0.275			
Cost per Unit			25000	33333.33			
Cost per Square Foot			18.75	20.40816			
Rent per Square Foot			6.25	5.612245			
Units per Acre			3	2			
Parking Spaces per Unit			1.666667	2.083333			

FIGURE 2-4.   Remaining formulas entered for Meadows

Once a formula has been entered, it is not possible to determine which entry method was chosen; the results are the same.

Using Formulas to Perform A What-If Analysis

Now that you have entered the basic formulas, your investment analysis model is complete. It will help you compare the two properties; in addition, it can assist you in your negotiations. You might feel that the price of one unit has more flexibility than the other; or perhaps the seller might be willing to add additional parking spaces or to include vacant land that is adjacent to the apartment complex. All these factors can change your evaluation of the properties. If you were performing your computations manually, each of these possibilities would require a new set of calculations and would be time-consuming. Now that you have automated the calculations, however, each option requires only that you enter a new number on the worksheet to have the package perform a new comparison immediately.

Let's look at how easy it is to evaluate changes in conditions. Suppose that you were able to negotiate a new price of $1,600,000 for the Meadows building. To add the updated data to your model, follow these steps:

1. Move the cell pointer to E5.

2. Press F2 (EDIT) to enter EDIT mode.

3. Press the HOME key to move to the beginning of the entry.

4. Delete the first two digits by pressing the DEL key twice.

5. Type **16** to replace the digits you just eliminated.

6. Press ENTER to finalize your entry.

After entering these new entries, you will find that the results of formula calculations have been updated. They indicate that the rent-to-cost ratio and the cost per unit for the two properties are much closer than you might have thought.

Use the same process to add the updates for the Surfer I building. If you feel that the owners will agree to add 50 more parking spaces and include another 15 acres of land at the same purchase price, you will want to make the following changes:

1. Move the cell pointer to D9.

2. Type **150** and press ENTER.

3. Move the cell pointer to D10.

4. Type **35** and press ENTER.

This time, the new figures were retyped rather than editing the original entries. You will have to evaluate each situation to see which is the quickest method. For very short entries, it is often just as easy to type the new entries.

As these last entries show, what-if analysis is quite simple once you have the formulas entered. The result of the most recent changes are shown in Figure 2-5. You could easily use these techniques to evaluate potential changes in purchase price or other factors with only a minimal investment of time.

Now that you have updated your model with formulas and the results of what-if analysis, you should save the updated copy on disk to reflect the current status of the worksheet. Enter **/FS** and press ENTER. You did not have to type the file name this time because it was saved previously. To ensure that the copy on disk is replaced with the current copy in memory, take one additional step: when 1-2-3's prompt message asks if you wish to cancel the request, replace the copy on disk, or back up the file and save the old copy with a .BAK extension and the current model with a .WK3 extension, respond by entering **R** to replace the file.

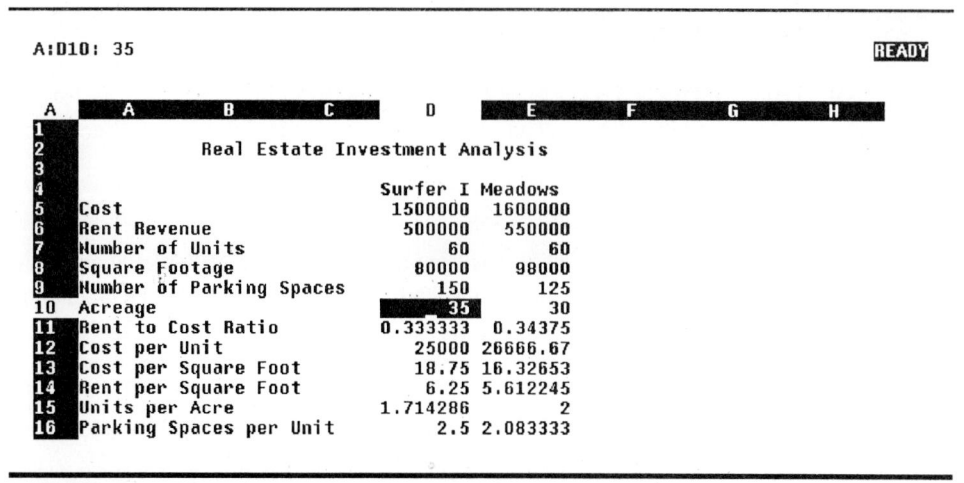

A:D10: 35   READY

A	A	B	C	D	E	F	G	H
1								
2			Real Estate Investment Analysis					
3								
4				Surfer I	Meadows			
5	Cost			1500000	1600000			
6	Rent Revenue			500000	550000			
7	Number of Units			60	60			
8	Square Footage			80000	98000			
9	Number of Parking Spaces			150	125			
10	Acreage			35	30			
11	Rent to Cost Ratio			0.333333	0.34375			
12	Cost per Unit			25000	26666.67			
13	Cost per Square Foot			18.75	16.32653			
14	Rent per Square Foot			6.25	5.612245			
15	Units per Acre			1.714286	2			
16	Parking Spaces per Unit			2.5	2.083333			

FIGURE 2-5.   Changing acreage to see updated formula results

Using Other Arithmetic Operations

The model you just completed used only the division operator in all of the formulas. Now let's look at another calculation that uses other operators to perform the computations. Erase the real estate calculations—you have saved them to your disk. Then enter **/WEY**.

You will use the blank worksheet to lay out a model that computes an employee's gross pay, given an hourly rate of pay and regular and overtime hours worked. 1-2-3 does not assign the same priority to each of the arithmetic operators. You can use this to your advantage in constructing the formula. 1-2-3 evaluates formulas from left to right, but it completes all of the multiplication and division operations before coming back through the formula to perform addition and subtraction. Use a multiplication process to calculate regular pay, and then use another multiplication process to calculate overtime pay before adding the results of the two operations together. 1-2-3 will automatically do the two operations in this sequence, due to their priorities. The precedence of operators will be covered in greater detail later in this chapter, along with a solution for altering the normal precedence sequence. Keep this model simple for now; enter just the basic information for one employee, following these steps:

1. With the cell pointer in A1, type **Employee** and press the RIGHT ARROW key.

2. Type **"Hours** and press the RIGHT ARROW key.

3. Type **"Rate** and press the RIGHT ARROW key.

4. Type **"O. Hrs** and press the RIGHT ARROW key.

   Use the letter "O" instead of a zero in your entry, or 1-2-3 will not allow you to finalize it.

5. Type **"Gross Pay** and press ENTER.

   Notice that the " symbol was used at the beginning of the label entry. As you will recall from Chapter 1, this causes 1-2-3 to right-align the label entry in the worksheet cell, so the column labels will line up with the first value in the database.

6. Move the cell pointer to A2 with the HOME and DOWN ARROW keys, type **J. Smith**, and press the RIGHT ARROW key.

7. Type **40** and press the RIGHT ARROW key.

8. Type **3.75** and press the RIGHT ARROW key.

9. Type **10** and press the RIGHT ARROW key. Your entries should look like this:

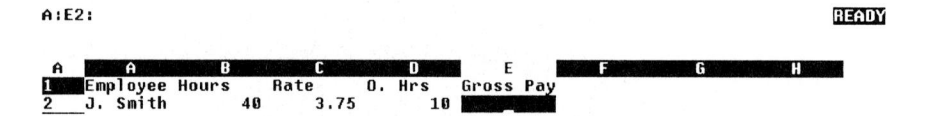

The next formula must calculate gross pay by multiplying regular hours by the rate of pay and then multiplying overtime hours by 1.5 times the rate of pay. The result of these two multiplication operators will be added to obtain the gross pay. This sounds complicated but can be represented succinctly in the formula.

10. Type **+B2*C2+D2*1.5*C2** and press ENTER to have 1-2-3 compute these results:

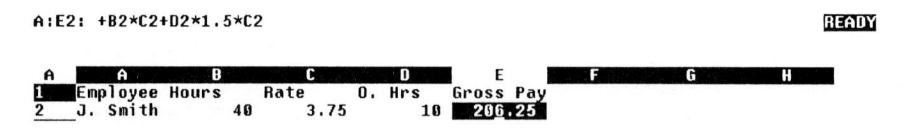

You could add still more employees to this model, but for now, save it as PAY by entering **/FSPAY** and pressing ENTER. You can always retrieve it again after you have learned how to duplicate formulas in Chapter 5. For the time being, continue to look at other types of formulas. Clear the entries from your worksheet by entering /**WEY**. Since you saved the model, you only need to enter one **Y**. If you had not saved the model, you would need to enter a second **Y** to confirm that you wanted to clear the unsaved entries.

USING LOGICAL FORMULAS

Logical formulas are used to compare two or more worksheet values. They use the logical operators = for equal, <> for not equal, > for greater than, >= for greater than or equal to, < for less than, and <= for less than or equal to. Logical formulas can be entered with the same methods used for arithmetic formulas, but unlike arithmetic formulas they do not calculate numeric results. Instead, they produce a result of either a zero or a one, depending on whether the condition that was evaluated is true or false. If the condition is true, 1 will be returned; if the condition is false, 0 will be returned. For example, if D4 contains a 5, the logical expression +D4<3 will return 0, since the condition is false. This capability can be used to evaluate a series of complex decisions or to influence results in other parts of the worksheet.

If an expression contains both logical operators and arithmetic operators, the expression containing the arithmetic operators will be evaluated first. For example, the logical expression +D4*2>50 will be evaluated by first multiplying the current value in D4 by 2 and then performing the comparison.

Creating a Model to Calculate Commissions

One application of logical operators in a spreadsheet might be the calculation of a commission bonus. In your example, sales personnel are paid a quarterly bonus, which includes a regular sales commission and a bonus paid for meeting sales quotas. The regular commission is computed as 10% of total sales. The bonus is calculated by product. A bonus of $1000 is paid for each product for which the sales quota is met. A salesperson could thus gain $3000 by meeting quotas for three products.

Look at the steps required to build the commission model shown in Figure 2-6. First, follow these directions to add the labels that are required:

1. Move the cell pointer to B1, type **Commission Calculation**, and press ENTER.

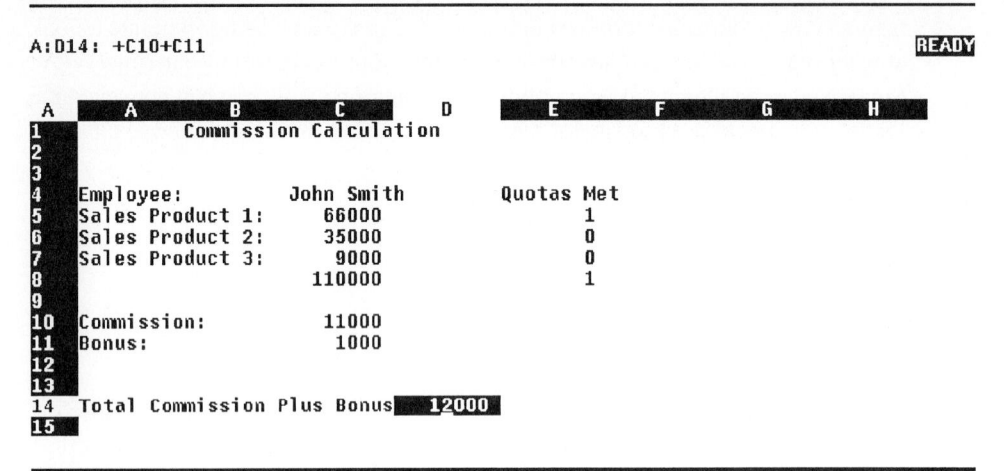

A:D14: +C10+C11   READY

```
A      A         B         C        D        E        F        G        H
1                Commission Calculation
2
3
4    Employee:             John Smith        Quotas Met
5    Sales Product 1:         66000              1
6    Sales Product 2:         35000              0
7    Sales Product 3:          9000              0
8                            110000              1
9
10   Commission:              11000
11   Bonus:                    1000
12
13
14   Total Commission Plus Bonus    12000
15
```

FIGURE 2-6.   Commission model

2. Move the cell pointer to A4, type **Employee:**, and press the DOWN ARROW key.

3. Type **Sales Product 1:** and press the DOWN ARROW key.

4. Type **Sales Product 2:** and press the DOWN ARROW key.

5. Type **Sales Product 3:** and press the DOWN ARROW key three times to place the cell pointer in A10.

6. Type **Commission:** and press the DOWN ARROW key.

7. Type **Bonus:** and press the DOWN ARROW key three times to place the cell pointer in A14.

8. Type **Total Commission Plus Bonus** and press ENTER.
   Notice that a colon (:) has not been added at the end here. This is for convenience, since you do not wish the entry to display beyond column C. It means you do not have to widen the column to show more than the default of nine characters.

9. Press F5 (GOTO), type **C4**, and press ENTER. Type **John Smith** and press the DOWN ARROW key to enter the name of the employee for whom you will be calculating commissions.

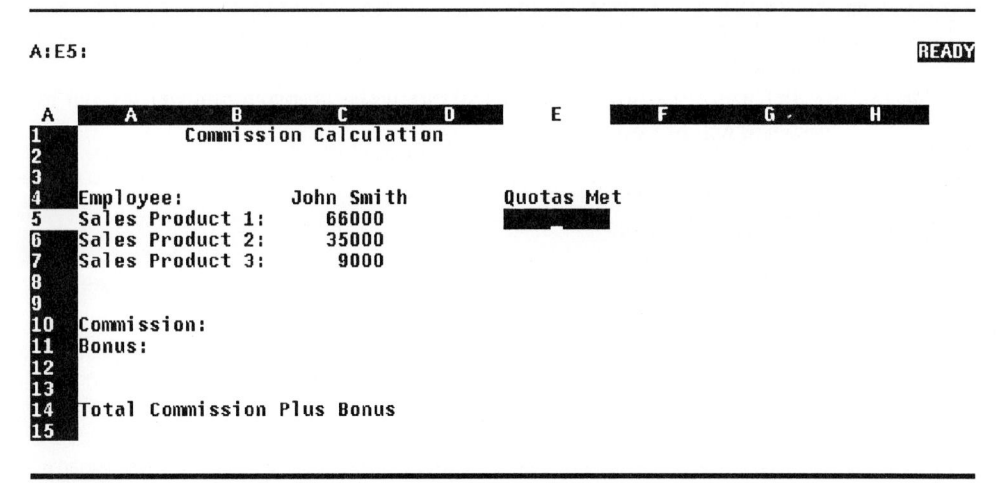

A:E5:   READY

A	A	B	C	D	E	F	G	H
1		Commission Calculation						
2								
3								
4	Employee:		John Smith		Quotas Met			
5	Sales Product 1:		66000					
6	Sales Product 2:		35000					
7	Sales Product 3:		9000					
8								
9								
10	Commission:							
11	Bonus:							
12								
13								
14	Total Commission Plus Bonus							
15								

FIGURE 2-7. Labels and numbers for the commission model entered

10. Type **66000** and press the DOWN ARROW key. Type **35000** and press the DOWN ARROW key. Type **9000** and press the DOWN ARROW key.

11. Position the cell pointer in E4 and type **Quotas Met**. Then press the DOWN ARROW key.

Adding Formulas to The Commission Model

The number and label entries for this model are now complete. Your model should match the one shown in Figure 2-7. At this point it is time to add the formulas for calculating the regular and bonus commission. For computing the bonus, assume that the quota is $50,000 per product. Use the following steps to enter the logical formulas for determining whether the sales quota in each category was met:

1. Type **+C5>50000** and press the DOWN ARROW key.
   This formula will produce 1 if the Product 1 quota is met and 0 if it is not.

2. Type **+C6>50000** and press the DOWN ARROW key.

3. Type **+C7>50000** and press the DOWN ARROW key.

4. Total the number of quotas met by adding the result of each of the logical formulas: type **+E5+E6+E7** and press ENTER.

   In Chapter 7 you will learn a shortcut method for summing entries, but for now you will use simple addition.

5. Total the sales of all three products in the same fashion: move the cell pointer to C8, type **+C5+C6+C7**, and press the DOWN ARROW key two times.

6. Enter the formula for commission in C10 by typing **+C8∗.1** and pressing the DOWN ARROW key.

7. Type **+E8∗1000** and press ENTER.

   This lets you calculate the bonus commission by multiplying the number of quotas met by 1000.

8. Position the cell pointer in D14, type **+C10+C11**, and press ENTER.

Your completed model should now match the one shown in Figure 2-6. The logical formulas it contains will respond to changes in the model's data. Let's try a few:

1. Move the cell pointer to C7.

2. Type **73000** and press ENTER.

You will find that a new commission and bonus of $19,400 is calculated immediately, as shown in Figure 2-8. Notice that the result does not display the dollar sign or the comma between hundreds and thousands. You will learn how to add these special characters in the next chapter.

Using Compound Operators

1-2-3 also has three compound operators that can be used with logical formulas. These operators are used either to negate an expression or to join two different expressions. The negation operator #NOT# has precedence over the two compound operators #AND# and #OR#. When the compound operator #AND# is used to join two logical expressions, *both* expressions must be true for the compound formula to return a true value. If the two expressions are joined by #OR#, *either one* can be true for the condition to return a true value.

You can add a second condition to your commission calculation by using the compound operators. Let's say that bonus commissions require a minimum of six

```
A:C7: 73000                                                              READY

A      A        B        C        D        E        F        G        H
1               Commission Calculation
2
3
4      Employee:          John Smith        Quotas Met
5      Sales Product 1:      66000              1
6      Sales Product 2:      35000              0
7      Sales Product 3:      73000              1
8                          174000              2
9
10     Commission:          17400
11     Bonus:                2000
12
13
14     Total Commission Plus Bonus    19400
15
```

FIGURE 2-8.   Calculations after logical formulas for quotas are entered

months of service in addition to the minimum sales level for a product. Revise the model to allow for this new condition by following these steps:

1. Move the cell pointer to A9, type **Months in Job:**, and press the RIGHT ARROW key twice to move to C9.

2. Type **4** and press ENTER.

3. Move the cell pointer to E5.

4. Press F2 (EDIT), type **#AND#C9>6**, and then press the DOWN ARROW key.

5. Use the same procedure outlined in step 4 to revise the formulas in E6 and E7.
   You will find that the bonus commission in Figure 2-9 is now zero, since the employee has been on the job fewer than six months.

6. Move the cell pointer to C9 and type **8**. Then press ENTER to see the bonus commission calculated again.

7. Enter **/FSCOMM** and press ENTER to save this worksheet to disk.

8. Enter **/WEY** to erase memory.

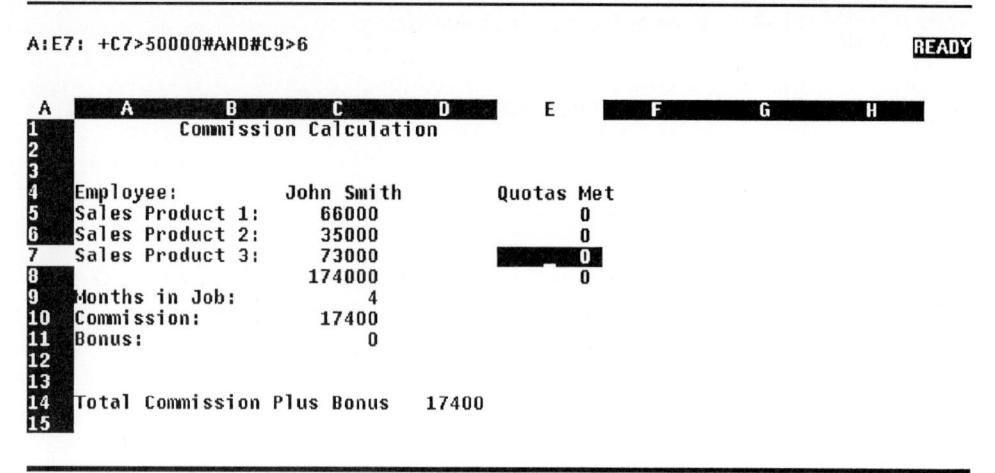

A:E7: +C7>50000#AND#C9>6

```
A    A        B        C        D      E        F      G        H
1              Commission Calculation
2
3
4   Employee:          John Smith        Quotas Met
5   Sales Product 1:      66000                 0
6   Sales Product 2:      35000                 0
7   Sales Product 3:      73000                 0
8                        174000                 0
9   Months in Job:           4
10  Commission:           17400
11  Bonus:                    0
12
13
14  Total Commission Plus Bonus    17400
15
```

FIGURE 2-9.　Using a complex logical formula to test two conditions

USING STRING FORMULAS

String formulas were added to 1-2-3 with the introduction of Release 2. Although they do not perform formula calculations as arithmetic formulas do, they let you join character strings together to create headings or other data elements for the worksheet. String formulas use only one operator, the ampersand (&), which is used to join variables containing character strings or string constants. For example, +"John"&"Smith" will result in JohnSmith, +"John"&" "&"Smith" will result in John Smith, and +A1&A2&A3 will result in abc if A1 contains an a, A2 contains a b, and A3 contains a c. As with the other types of formulas, with string formulas you can either type the complete formula or point to the cell addresses referenced and have 1-2-3 place them in the formula for you.

Let's use a string formula to build a part number. In this model, separate data elements provide all the different components of All Parts, Incorporated's part-number structure. The warehouse location, bin number, product type, and vendor are all combined to create a part number. Follow these steps to enter the data for the model:

1. Enter the worksheet heading by moving the cell pointer to B3, typing **All Parts, Inc. Inventory Listing**, and pressing ENTER.

2. Move the cell pointer to A5, type **Location**, and press the RIGHT ARROW key.

3. Type **Bin** and press the RIGHT ARROW key.

4. Type **Type** and press the RIGHT ARROW key.

5. Type **Vendor** and press the RIGHT ARROW key.

6. Type **Part No** and press ENTER.

7. Move the cell pointer to A6, type **'5**, and press the RIGHT ARROW key.
   The single quotation mark is required because labels will not join values. Using the single quote ensures that the number 5 is stored as a label.

8. Type **'12** and press the RIGHT ARROW key.

9. Type **AX** and press the RIGHT ARROW key.

10. Type **CN** and press the RIGHT ARROW key.

11. Verify that the cell pointer is in E6, type **+C6&"-"&D6&A6&B6**, and press ENTER.
    The part number for the first item will appear as shown in the following list:

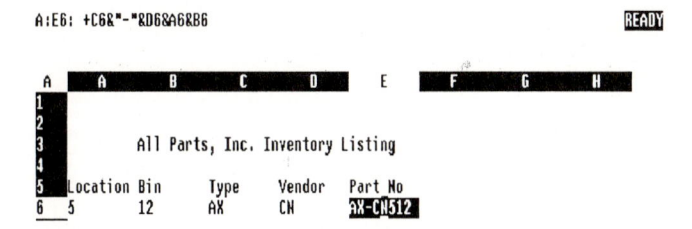

For practice, you may wish to enter the data and the required string formula to build several additional part numbers. Like the other formula types, changing the values for any of the variables will immediately change the results produced by the string formula. Once you have finished with your entries, you can save the model by entering **/FS** from the menu, typing **PARTNO**, and pressing ENTER. To clear the screen, enter **/WEY**.

The part-number display in the last example is useful if the model contains information on additional parts, as well as fields to the right that were also important to view. Using the string formula to build the part number, you could move the cell pointer to the right and view the other data without losing track of the part number, as follows:

```
A:E6: +C6&"-"&D6&A6&B6                                              READY
```

A	E	F	G	H	I	J	K	L
1								
2								
3	isting							
4			Quantity	Order		Freight	Delivery	
5	Part No	Price	On Hand	Quantity	Charge	Time		
6	AX-CN512	$11.00	100	250	95	30 days		
7	BY-TA432	$43.00	67	125	60	5 days		
8	ST-BC711	$67.00	32	50	120	10 days		
9	UY-KT255	$12.59	125	500	85	8 days		

The full power of 1-2-3's string formulas will be realized when you learn to combine the string concatenation features for joining label entries with special string functions that can extract a portion of a string entry. These special string functions can be used for complex combinations and are an excellent tool for correcting data-entry errors. Special string functions will be covered in Chapter 10.

PERFORMING MORE COMPLEX CALCULATIONS

When 1-2-3 encounters more than one operator in a formula, it does not use a left-to-right order to compute the result. Instead, it evaluates the formula based on a set precedence order for each of the operators. As you begin to build more complex formulas, you will see how important it is to understand 1-2-3's priorities in order to achieve the desired results.

When more than one operator is used in a formula, it is important to know which operation 1-2-3 will perform first. Table 2-1 shows the order of precedence for each of the operators. If more than one operator has the same precedence, they will be evaluated from left to right.

You will notice that parentheses are at the top of the list in Table 2-1. This indicates that any expression enclosed within them will be evaluated first. The other operators that may cause confusion are the + and - symbols shown in level 6 and level 4. The first set represents the positive or negative sign of a value. For instance, -5*3 indicates that 5 is a negative number that should be multiplied by a positive 3. On the other hand, in the expression 5-4*2 the minus symbol represents subtraction and has a lower precedence than the multiplication operation, which will be carried out first.

A short example will demonstrate this clearly. Suppose you wish to add the total number of pounds of books in a shipment by combining the 10-pound weight of the books ordered with 3 pounds of stationery items and then multiplying the total weight by the per-pound shipping rate of 25 cents. You would not get the correct result if you entered 10+3*.25, since 1-2-3 would perform the multiplication first and calculate 10

Precedence	Operator	Operation Performed
8	( )	Parentheses to override priorities
7	^	Exponentiation
6	+ -	Positive and negative indicators
5	/ *	Division and multiplication
4	+ -	Addition and subtraction
3	= <>	Logical operators
	< >	
	<= >=	
2	#NOT#	Compound NOT indicator
1	#AND#	Compound AND, compound OR, and the string
	#OR#	operator
	&	

TABLE 2-1.   Operation Priorities

plus 0.75, totaling 10.75 rather than the 3.25 you expected. To make 1-2-3 perform the calculation your way, you need to enter the data as (10+3)*.25. 1-2-3 will evaluate the expression within the parentheses first and carry out the multiplication second, resulting in the desired answer of 3.25.

Let's look at another salary model to demonstrate the importance of the precedence and controlling precedence with parentheses. This model will project a single employee's salary based on his or her current salary, the percentage of increase you choose to give the employee, and the month of the increase. Since a lengthy formula is required, you will perform only the computation for one employee. However, you will want to save it and add additional employees once you have learned how to copy entries from one cell to another.

To enter the data for the salary computation model, follow these steps:

1. Type the following entries in the worksheet cells specified:

   A2: Name
   B1: '1989
   B2: Salary
   C1: Increase
   C2: Month
   D1: Increase
   D2: Percent
   E1: '1990
   E2: Salary

This completes the entry of the column labels and produces these results:

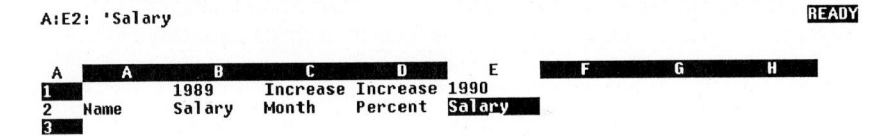

A:E2: 'Salary   READY

A	A	B	C	D	E	F	G	H
1		1989	Increase	Increase	1990			
2	Name	Salary	Month	Percent	Salary			
3								

2. Type **J. Brown** in A3 and press ENTER.

3. Move the cell pointer to B3, type **35900**, and press ENTER.
   To look at the effect of giving the increase in month 5, you would need to enter a new number in C3. Try this now:

4. Type **5** in C3 and press ENTER.

5. Type **.06** in D3 and press ENTER.
   This .06 entry represents the amount of the increase.

The last step is the most complicated. The formula must compute the current monthly salary and multiply it by the number of months that the individual will continue to receive this salary. The result of this first computation must then be added to the figure computed for the amount paid at the new salary level. The total dollars paid at the new salary level are computed by multiplying the current monthly salary by 100% plus the increase percentage by the number of months that the individual will receive the increased salary amount. Predictably, the formula is quite long when it is recorded in the worksheet cell, as shown in Figure 2-10. The parts of the formula are as follows:

(B3/12)	Represents the annual salary divided by 12 to compute the monthly salary
(C3-1)	The month of the increase minus 1 or the number of months the employee receives his or her current salary
(1+D3)	Indicates that the employee will receive 100% of his or her existing salary, plus an increase represented by a decimal fraction in D3
12-(C3-1)	The number of months that the employee receives the increased salary amount.

6. Combining all these, enter the following formula in E3:

   ((B3/12)*(C3-1))+((B3/12)*(1+D3)*(12-(C3-1)))

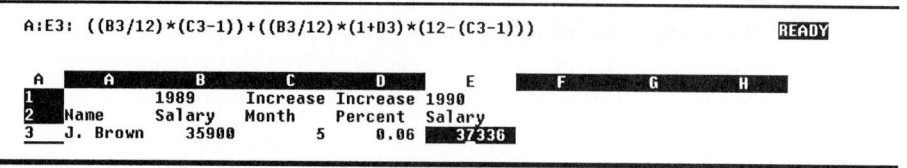

FIGURE 2-10. Projecting next year's salary

Type carefully and give yourself a pat on the back if you manage to complete the entire entry successfully on your first attempt. If you do make a few mistakes, you can always edit your entry to make the necessary corrections. If your mistakes are serious enough, 1-2-3 will place you in EDIT mode without requiring you to press the F2 (EDIT) key.

A few extra parentheses have been added to the formula expression to make it more readable. For example, the result would be the same if the parentheses were omitted from (B3/12), since multiplication and division have the same precedence. Using an extra pair of parentheses does not change the value of the expression as long as the parentheses do not change the order of operations. Feel free to add parentheses in this manner whenever they improve the readability of the formula without altering it. In this example, you have entered the data for only one employee, but this model could be expanded easily.

In a later chapter, you will use this model to add additional employees, but for now, save a copy of it to disk by entering /**FSSALARY** and pressing ENTER.

USING CELL NAMES IN FORMULAS

Meaningful names are often easier to remember than cell addresses. If you have sales stored in B10 and a discount rate in Z2, it will be easier to remember the name of the type of information you have stored than it is to remember the cell addresses, especially when you have a model with many items of data. 1-2-3 lets you name the data stored in worksheet cells. Although you will not want to make the extra effort for every model, names can be especially helpful in some situations. Before learning how to assign names to your data, however, you need to know about 1-2-3 ranges.

Range Basics

In 1-2-3, a *range* is a group of one or more cells that form a contiguous rectangle. You can use ranges in 1-2-3 to tell the package to take the same action on each of the cells in the group. Using ranges saves a substantial amount of time compared to making separate requests to change each cell in the group. You will see more about the use of ranges in Chapter 3. For now, we will use ranges to assign names to individual worksheet cells.

A cell reference consists of the column location followed by the row location, as in A10 or C4. Since a range can include a rectangular area of cells, a range address is always expressed as two separate cell addresses separated by a period. Even if the range consists of only one cell, both the beginning and end of the range must be expressed as in A1..A1. The standard method of entering a range address is to first supply the upper-left cell in the range, then type a period as a separator, and then supply the lower-right cell in the range, as in A1.B10 or C3.G20. Although you only need to type one period as a separator, 1-2-3 always converts it to two, as in A1..B10 or C3..G20. You can assign a name to any range so that you can refer to the range by the name rather than by its cell addresses.

Later in the book, you will look at applications for applying names to ranges that include more than one cell. For now, you will only need to assign range names to individual cells, since the formulas you have used so far only operate on one cell at a time. Even though you are interested in naming one cell, you will still need to refer to that cell as a range rather than attempting to use its individual cell address, because the command that you will use is designed to accept range addresses rather than cell addresses. The proper way of expressing a range consisting of one cell is to use the cell address for both the beginning and the end of the range. When A1 is treated as a range, the range address is expressed as A1..A1. Although A1 and A1..A1 refer to the same data on the worksheet, range names are only appropriate for ranges and should not be used for a single unanchored cell reference like A1. You will have an opportunity to see how 1-2-3 treats the two entries differently in the next example.

Naming a Range

To name the range, you will need to use a command from 1-2-3's menu. You will learn more about the various menu options in Chapter 3, but for now all you need to do is use a slash (/) whenever you need to invoke the menu and type the first letter of the commands that you need to execute. The complicated salary formula you entered in Figure 2-10 will be a good place to try out the benefits of range names.

As you name each of the cells in the model, you will be limited to 15 characters for the range name. Range names cannot begin with numbers. Each range name must be unique and can only refer to one cell if you want to use it in the types of formulas entered so far. 1-2-3 does not distinguish between upper- and lowercase and will display all range names in uppercase when you see them in formulas.

To name the three cells used in computing the 1990 salary figure for J. Brown, follow these steps:

1. Move the cell pointer to B3 as show here:

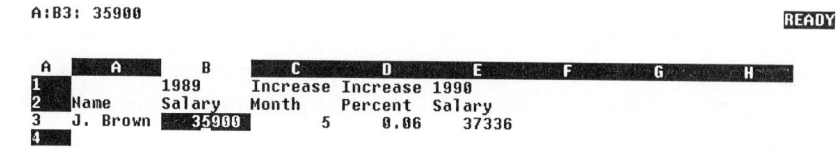

2. Type / to invoke the menu. Type **R** to select the Range command. Type N to select the Name option from the Range menu. Type C to select Create from the Name menu. Your screen will look like this:

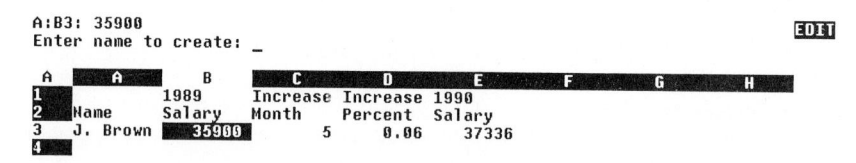

3. Type **SALARY_89** and press ENTER.

4. Press ENTER a second time to accept 1-2-3's suggested range designation of the current cell.

   If you forget to position the cell pointer before requesting the /Range Name Create command, 1-2-3 will suggest a different range address. You can replace its suggestion by typing your own in the format B3.B3.

5. Move the cell pointer to C3 and enter **/RNC** followed by **INC_MO** and press ENTER twice.

   Again, the keystrokes **/RNC** are requesting an action through 1-2-3's menus. You will learn more about these menus in Chapter 3.

6. Move the cell pointer to D3, enter **/RNC** followed by **INC_%**, and press ENTER twice.

7. Move the cell pointer to E3 to see this formula:

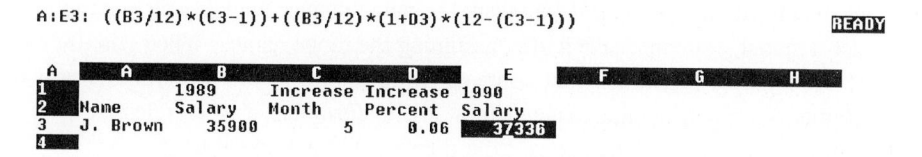

Your formula will not show the range names despite all your hard work to enter them correctly. This is because the original formula used cell references like D3 rather than a range address of D3..D3. At this point retyping the formula with range references would still not complete the conversion to a formula that displayed range names; 1-2-3 will make the conversion to an existing formula at the time you add the name, but it will not automatically make the conversion if you enter a new formula by referencing a name that is already named. The solution for incorporating names in formulas is to use the F3 (NAME) key as you are entering the formula to select the name from the list of names. Try it now by reentering the formula with these steps:

1. With your cell pointer still in E3 type ((.

2. Press the F3 (NAME) key.

3. Highlight SALARY_89 in the list and press ENTER.

4. Type /12)*(.

5. Press F3 (NAME), highlight INC_MO in the list, and press ENTER.

6. Type -1))+((.

7. Press F3 (NAME), highlight SALARY_89, and press ENTER.

8. Type /12)*(1+.

9. Press F3 (NAME), highlight INC_%, and press ENTER.

10. Type)*(12-(.

11. Press F3 (NAME), highlight INC_MO in the list, and press ENTER.

12. Type -1))) and press ENTER.

Although this is still a complex formula, it is a little easier to understand when you do not need to make the mental comparison between cell address and cell contents for each entry in the formula. If you want the range names available the next time you use a model, you must save it after assigning the range names. When you use the F2 (EDIT) key to edit a cell that contains range names in the formula, the edit line continues to display the range names in the formulas; earlier releases of 1-2-3 converted them to cell addresses. Your display will look like this:

```
A:E3: ((SALARY_89/12)*(INC_MO-1))+((SALARY_89/12)*(1+INC_%)*(12-(INC_MO-1))  EDIT
      ((SALARY_89/12)*(INC_MO-1))+((SALARY_89/12)*(1+INC_%)*(12-(INC_MO-1)))_
```

```
  A       A         B        C        D        E        F        G        H
1                  1989    Increase Increase  1990
2       Name       Salary   Month   Percent   Salary
3       J. Brown   35900       5      0.06     37336
4
```

Range names are not a good solution in all models. If you expand this model to show the salary computations for a department of 100 individuals, with each individual shown on a different row, range names would be impractical—you would need to assign a unique range name to each of the entries in each of the rows. In such a situation it is best to continue to use cell addresses in your formulas. On the other hand, a model containing a financial statement that will be used to prepare ratios would be a good application for the assignment of range names, because similar data items would not be repeated and range names would make the formulas much more readable.

Using Range Names When Building Formulas

The last example showed you how a formula does not change to display range addresses once they have been assigned. You must assign names to a cell before you reference it in a formula or use the same reference as in the formula in your definition. In other words D3 and D3..D3 are different entries. This will allow you to specify the name with the F3 (NAME) key when you build a formula. To try an example, save the model currently in memory by entering /**File Save**, press ENTER to select Salary, and type **R** to replace the copy on disk with the model currently in memory. Then enter /**Worksheet Erase Yes** to clear memory. Follow these steps to try the new approach:

1. Make the following entries:

    A2: Cost
    A3: Accumulated Depreciation
    A4: Book Value
    D2: 5000
    D3: 1000

2. Move the cell pointer to D2 and enter /**Range Name Create** by typing the first letter in each word after typing the slash (/).

3. Type **COST** and press ENTER twice.

4. Move the cell pointer to D3 and enter /**Range Name Create**.

5. Type **ACCUMULATED_DEP** and press ENTER twice.

Note you are limited to 15 characters and can use spaces, although you might want to consider using the underscore as a separator (it makes it clearer that there is only one name).

6. Move the cell pointer to D4. Type + and then press the F3 (NAME) key. Your display will look like this:

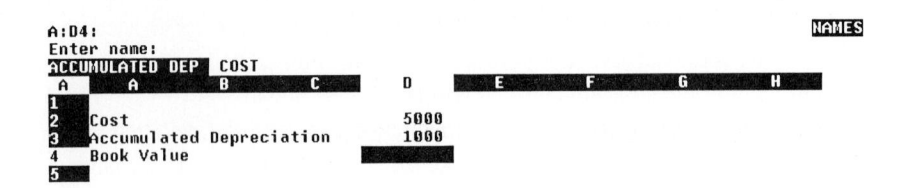

7. Move the highlight to COST and press ENTER.

8. Type - and press F3 (NAME). Press ENTER with the highlight on ACCUMU-LATED DEP. Your display will look like this:

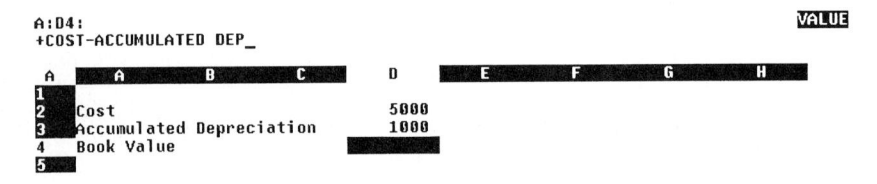

9. Press ENTER to finalize the formula entry. Your display will look like this:

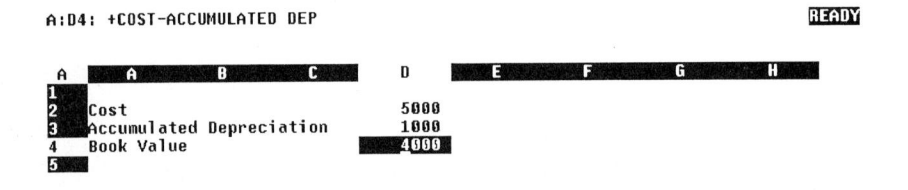

Deleting Range Names

You can delete range names that you no longer need. The command that eliminates them is on the /Range Name menu that you have been using to create them. When you eliminate a range name, you will not eliminate the worksheet data with the name. The formulas with references to the range names that you delete will revert to displaying the address of the cell, rather than its name.

To delete the range name ACCUMULATED_DEP from the previous example, follow these steps:

1. Enter /**Range Name Delete**.

2. Highlight ACCUMULATED_DEP and press ENTER.

When you move the highlight to D4, the formula will look like this and will no longer display the deleted range name, since it is replaced by the range address D3..D3:

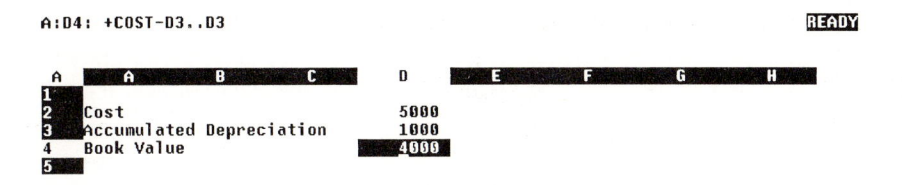

REVIEW EXERCISE

Formulas are the building blocks of all 1-2-3 models. A little practice with formula entry will soon make you think of yourself as a model construction expert. Before beginning to practice on your own application, you can try the model shown in Figure 2-11. This model will allow you to compute the cost of another type of construction project as you look at the cost of adding a deck to your house as a weekend project. You can estimate the amount of each supply that you will need and enter the unit cost of each item after checking at the nearest lumber supply yard. The model will show

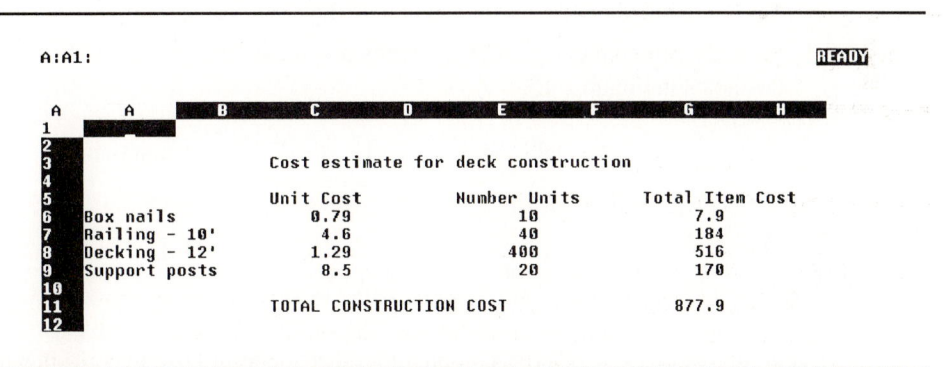

FIGURE 2-11. Model for creating construction estimates

you the total cost of the project. If you revise your estimate, you can change the number of units required for any item. If you decide to shop around for the lowest price, you may also want to revise some of the unit costs shown in the model. You can also revise the model to prepare cost estimates for all sorts of other projects.

Follow this sequence in creating the model:

1. Enter /**WEYY** to clear the screen of data that has not been saved. Type the description of the model in C2. Enter the column headings in C4, E4, and G4. Enter the labels representing the required supplies in A5 though A8.

2. Enter the unit cost figures in C5 through C8.

    Note that even though you enter **.79**, 1-2-3 will display the entry as 0.79. Also, entering **4.60** will display as 4.6. In Chapter 3 you will learn how to improve the appearance of these model entries.

3. Enter the units in E5 through E8.

4. Enter the formulas for the total cost of each item in G5 through G8. (*Hint:* The formula for the total cost of the nails can be computed by entering +**C5∗E5.** The other formulas are similar but refer to entries on different rows.)

5. Type the label **TOTAL CONSTRUCTION COST** in C10, and then enter the formula to compute it in G10. (*Hint:* You can add each of the entries in G5 through G8 to compute the proper total, and your formula will look like +G5+G6+G7+G8.)

6. Although naming the cells used in the model may not be required to understand the formula, go ahead and name each of the entries in G5 through G8 for practice. (*Hint:* Use the /Range Name Create command.) Be sure to choose unique and meaningful names like TOT$_NAILS, TOT$_RAILING, TOT$_DECKING, and TOT$_POSTS. If you use these range names and then move the cell pointer to G10, your formula will look like the one at the top of the model in Figure 2-12.

7. Save the model as CONSTRCT. (*Hint:* Use the /File Save command.)

REVIEW

- Formulas allow you to define computations that you want 1-2-3 to perform with the contents of worksheet cells.

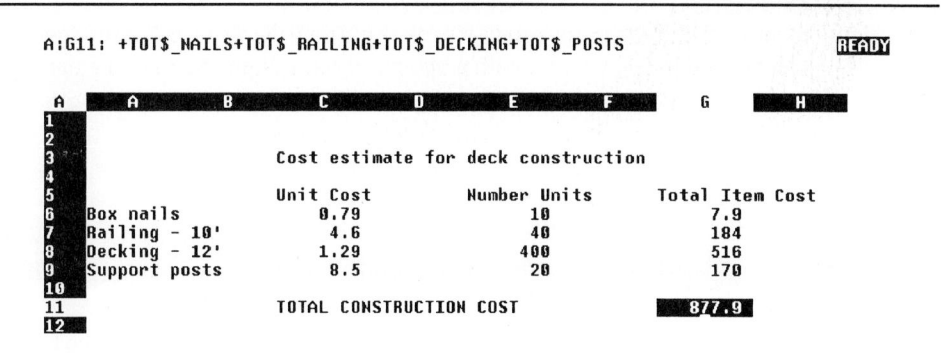

FIGURE 2-12.   Formula showing range names

- Formulas must always start with a value character and cannot exceed 512 characters.

- In Release 3 you can add documentation to a formula entry by ending the formula with a semicolon (;) and then typing the comments you wish to add to the end of the formula.

- Arithmetic formulas are the most popular type of 1-2-3 formulas; they support typical business calculations like computing purchase discounts, invoice extensions, and sales projections. They use operators for addition (+), subtraction (-), multiplication ($*$), division (/), and exponentiation ($\wedge$).

- String formulas use only one operator, the ampersand (&), which allows you to join two character strings.

- Logical formulas use the logical operators equal to (=), not equal to (<>), less than (<), less than or equal to (<=), greater than (>), and greater than or equal to (>=).

- All formula operators do not have the same order of precedence. You can use parentheses to raise the precedence of an operation; 1-2-3 evaluates entries in parentheses first. Table 2-1 lists the normal precedence of the operators.

- A range name can be assigned to any cell on the worksheet. Formulas referencing this cell will automatically display the range name in the formula. To access an existing range name when building a formula, use the F3 (NAME) key and select it from the list presented.

- A range name that is no longer needed can be deleted without deleting the data in the referenced cell. After the range name is deleted, the formula will display the cell address rather than the range name. Another option with Release 3 is redefining the range for a range name by using the /Range Name Undefine command and following it with a another /Range Name Create command for the new range reference.

Commands and Keys

/FR	Accesses /File Retrieve to allow you to read a file from disk into memory
/RNC	Allows you to name a worksheet cell with /Range Name Create
/RND	Allows you to delete a range name with /Range Name Delete
/RNU	Allows you to remove the current definition for a range name with /Range Name Undefine
/WEY	Invokes the /Worksheet Erase command and responds with Yes to clear memory
F3 (NAME)	Allows you to access a list of range names

3

CHANGING THE WORKSHEET APPEARANCE

Until now, you have accepted 1-2-3's choices for how to present your entries. You have used the package's default for the format in which the data has been displayed. It is great to have this default available; it lets you build a model that produces completely accurate results without having to concern yourself with how your entries should be displayed. But it is also good to know that 1-2-3 provides a set of powerful formatting options and commands that let you change the default settings for the display of your entries. 1-2-3 commands let you select a new display format for all the values on the worksheet or change the format for the value entries in a small section of the worksheet. Other 1-2-3 commands allow you to affect the alignment of labels, either before or after you enter them, change the number of characters that can be displayed in a column, or hide certain columns from view.

In this chapter you will look at examples of each of these techniques. You will find that the 1-2-3 commands are easy to use and provide significant improvements in the appearance of your worksheet models. First, let's address how you access these commands, since they can be accessed only when 1-2-3's menu is on the screen.

1-2-3's MENU

1-2-3's menu system is designed to make commands easy to access and remember. Only one keystroke is needed to access the menu system, and Lotus has used descriptive command names to represent each command's function in building the menu. Each menu option also includes a description of the tasks that you can use it for, which makes it easier for you to select the correct command as you are learning to use the package.

Activating the Menu

1-2-3's menu is activated by pressing the slash key (/) from READY mode. The slash key is located on the lower-right side of your keyboard near the SHIFT key. If the mode indicator is WAIT, POINT, ERROR, or something other than READY, it means that 1-2-3 will not be ready to accept your request. If you type a slash when 1-2-3 is not ready to respond, the menu will not appear onscreen. Instead, in most cases, 1-2-3 will make a beeping noise to let you know that it cannot process your request to view the main menu selections.

If 1-2-3 is in EDIT mode when you enter the slash, it adds the slash to the current entry. You must take an action to return the indicator to READY before entering the slash. This action may be completing the entry you have already started, waiting for 1-2-3 to finish its current task, or pressing ESC to acknowledge that you saw an error message.

The Menu Structure

You will want to examine the menu structure that 1-2-3 presents. Type / to activate the *main menu* and produce this display:

```
A:A1:                                                              MENU
Worksheet  Range  Copy  Move  File  Print  Graph  Data  System  Quit
Global  Insert  Delete  Column  Erase  Titles  Window  Status  Page  Hide
  A      A      B        C        D        E      F        G        H
1
2
```

Notice that the mode indicator changes to MENU; it will remain this way as long as one of 1-2-3's menus is displayed on the screen. The second and third lines in the control panel are devoted to the menu display. The second line in the control panel shows the various menu choices; the line beneath it provides an explanation of the types of tasks that you can do from the currently highlighted selection in the top row. All menu selections must start from the top row of menu choices. When you select one of the commands in the top row, you are often shown a submenu of choices that allow you to refine your choice. Most of the main menu entries provide many options, and you may be given as many as six levels of menus to select from before you get to your final choice. You need not be concerned with the complexity of the menus, however—the options are organized logically. With a little practice, it is easy to decide which path to select at any point.

The third line of the control panel describes each of the menu choices onscreen. This line helps you make a selection. If you make an inappropriate choice, there is an easy way to retreat and start over to reach the exact command you are seeking. Again, do not be discouraged by the complexity; you will not need to learn all the menu commands. You can accomplish 90% of your work by using only a small percentage of the total menu. The other commands are there to provide sophisticated options for 1-2-3's power users.

Before examining any particular menu choice in further detail, let's take a look at each of the main menu selections to get an overview of the types of features each of them provides:

Menu Selection	Type of Task Handled
Worksheet	Think of the Worksheet menu anytime you wish to make a change that will affect the worksheet. Options include globally setting the format of value entries in the worksheet cells, inserting and deleting worksheet rows or columns, and erasing the entire worksheet.
Range	Think of the Range menu when the changes you wish to make are less extensive and will affect only a section of the worksheet. Options in the Range section include formatting a section of the worksheet, assigning a name to a group of worksheet cells, and erasing a section of the worksheet.

Copy	Use the Copy selection whenever you wish to duplicate the information in one group of worksheet cells into another group of cells. With this menu choice you do not have to select from additional submenus; you need only specify which cells you need to copy and where you want them copied to.
Move	Move is similar to Copy, but it relocates data rather than copying it. Choose Move whenever this is the task you wish to perform. As with Copy, Move requires you to respond to its prompts rather than selecting from additional submenus.
File	Consider selecting File whenever you wish to perform tasks that relate to saving or retrieving data stored on the disk. Options include saving a file, retrieving a file, and listing the directory of the current disk drive.
Print	Use the Print selection whenever you wish to obtain a hard copy of the worksheet that is currently in memory.
Graph	Graph is the option to select when you wish to create a graphic representation of data stored on the worksheet. Some of the options include defining the type of graph you wish to create, defining the data to be shown on the graph, and viewing the graph that is currently defined.
Data	The Data commands provide data-management features and some special arithmetic features. The two most frequently used Data options are the Sort option, which allows you to resequence your data, and the Query option, which allows you to locate and extract specific information from your model.
System	The System option provides access to the basic operating system commands without having to exit 1-2-3.
Quit	Quit exits 1-2-3 without saving the worksheet currently in memory. Use this selection only when you have completed your 1-2- 3 session and have already saved your work.

Each of these main menu selections will be discussed in more detail as you proceed through this book. Next, you will look at how you can select the options from 1-2-3's menus.

Making Selections

You can select an option in any menu that is displayed by typing the first letter of the menu selection, using either upper- or lowercase. In other words, to select the first option, Worksheet, you can type **w** or **W**. If you type a letter that is not used on the menu, 1-2-3 will beep at you and will not respond until you enter a valid menu selection. A second way to make your selection is to use the RIGHT or LEFT ARROW key to move the menu pointer to the menu item you want and then press ENTER. The latter approach is best while you are learning the menu, because it causes 1-2-3 to display a description of the command you are about to choose in the third line of the control panel. If after reading the description you decide you have not made the correct selection, you can continue to move to new selections until the desired description is displayed. No action will be taken until you activate a menu choice by pressing ENTER.

Sometimes just pointing to a menu selection will cause you to change your mind. As an example, move the cursor to the Quit selection. The description will tell you to use it to end your current 1-2-3 session. Since you do not want to end the current session, reading this description should convince you not to select Quit.

Often, a series of menu selections are needed to complete a task with 1-2-3. Each selection helps to refine the description of your needs to 1-2-3 and selects an option deeper in 1-2-3's menu hierarchy. You can think of your selection as creating command sentences, with a word selected from each level of the menu hierarchy that further refines the meaning of your command. After making your first selection, you may need to choose from a submenu of additional choices to make your request clearer. A selection from the submenu may complete the process or it may invoke yet another menu level for your selection. If you think of the process as building a command sentence, you might choose File from the main menu to tell 1-2-3 that the command you want to enter involves files. You might choose Save from the File submenu to refine the file operation,. Finally you might enter **REALEST** to complete your command sentence by supplying the name under which 1-2-3 should save the file.

Try a few selections so you can see how the process works:

1. Type / to activate the menu.

2. Select Worksheet by typing **W** or by pressing ENTER, since the highlight is already positioned on that selection.

The menu that appears shows all the options you have for affecting the worksheet:

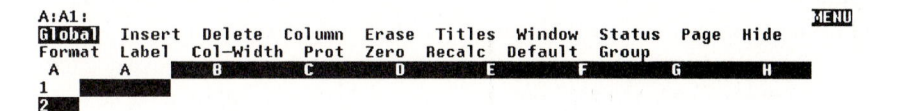

Press ENTER to select Global from the submenu that is presented. When you select Global, a third-level menu is presented:

```
A:A1:                                                                    MENU
Format  Label  Col-Width  Prot  Zero  Recalc  Default  Group
Fixed   Sci   Currency  ,   General  +/-   Percent  Date  Text  Hidden  Other
  A       A          B            C         D         E           F         G        H
1
2
```

You are just examining the menu structure, so do not make any additional selections at this time. Instead, examine the methods for backing out of menu selections to return to the previous menu and eventually to the READY mode. This is useful when you accidentally make an incorrect menu selection and want to back out of it to make a new choice.

The ESC key is used to back out of one level of menu selection. Try this key to see how it works:

1. Press ESC once.

   The menu of worksheet selections returns to the screen.

2. Press ESC again.

   The main menu appears with the second press.

3. Press ESC a third time.

   The READY mode indicator appears. If you had made four menu selections, you would have had to press ESC four times to return to READY mode.

An easier way to return to READY mode is to press the CTRL-BREAK key combination. Hold down the CTRL key while you press the PAUSE or SCROLL LOCK key, and then release both keys. Regardless of the number of menu selections you have made, you will immediately be taken out of MENU mode and placed back in READY mode.

CHANGING THE FORMAT OF VALUE ENTRIES

The default format that 1-2-3 uses for all value entries is called the *General format*. It is somewhat unusual in that it does not provide consistent formats for all entries. The display it provides is affected by the size of the number that is entered in the cell. Some numbers are displayed exactly as they are entered, while others have a leading zero added or are rounded to the number of decimal digits that will fit in the cell width you have selected. (1-2-3 stores the number you entered, even though all of the digits do not appear.) The General format also suppresses trailing zeros after the decimal point; if you enter them, they will not appear in the display. Very large and very small numbers are displayed in *Scientific format,* which means that exponential notation will be used. *Exponential notation* is a method of representing a number in abbreviated form by including the power of 10 that the number should be raised to. If **100550000** is entered in a cell when the General format is in effect, 1-2-3 will use exponential notation to display it as 1.0E+08.

Format	Cell Entry	Display
Fixed	5678	5678.00
2 decimal places	-123.45	-123.45
Scientific	5678	5.68E+03
2 decimal places	-123.45	− 1.23E+02
Currency	5678	$5,678.00
2 decimal places	-123.45	($123.45)
,(Comma)	5678	5,678
2 decimal places	-123.45	(123.45)
General	5678	5678
	-123.45	-123.45
+/-	4	++++
	3	− − −
	0	.
Percent	5	500%
	.1	10%
Date (D1)	31679	24-Sep-86
Time (T1)	.5	12:00:00 PM
Text	+A2*A3 +	A2*A3
Hidden	35000	
Automatic	$5,678.00	$5,678.00
	24-Sep-86	24-Sep-86
Label	679-34-7898	679-34-7898

TABLE 3-1.   1-2-3's Format Options

General format handles a wide variety of formats but often results in a display whose results have varying numbers of decimal places. This makes it less than desirable for many business models because of the inconsistencies in the display of decimal numbers, as you saw in the investment model in Chapter 2. However, this inconsistency does not mean that this format is useless—it provides an ideal format in many situations. General format is useful when you want to minimize the space used to display very large or very small numbers. Exponential notation ensures that these numbers will be shown in a minimum amount of space and that the conversion will be handled for you automatically if required. It simply is not the format to use when you need to control the number of decimal places shown.

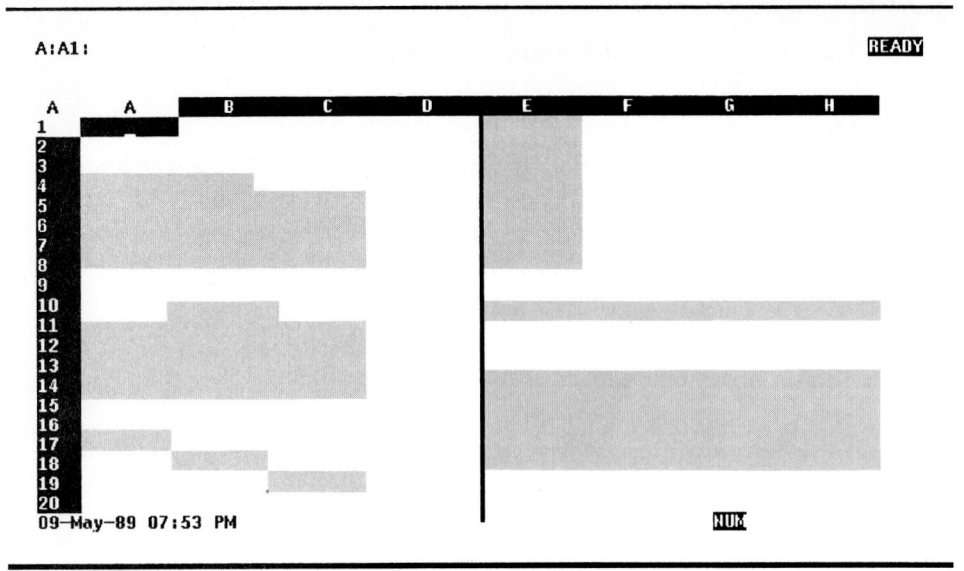

A:A1:   READY

09-May-89 07:53 PM   NUM

FIGURE 3-1.   Invalid and valid ranges

Formatting Options

1-2-3 provides many alternatives to the general display format. A wide range of formatting options allow you to display your data with everything from dollar signs and commas to percent symbols. You can even specify the number of decimal places for most of the formats. The specific formats supported by 1-2-3 and their effect on worksheet entries are shown in Table 3-1. You will apply some of these formats to models you have already created.

Scope of the Formatting Change

You can also choose how extensive an impact you want a particular format command to have by formatting the entire worksheet or a range of cells in one area of the worksheet. Let's first examine the procedure for changing the default format for a section of the worksheet.

CHANGING THE FORMAT FOR A RANGE OF CELLS   Everything you have accomplished with 1-2-3 so far has focused on individual cells. However, 1-2-3 also allows you to work with any contiguous rectangle of cells—a range—to accom-

A:A1:   READY

09-May-89 07:53 PM   NUM

FIGURE 3-2. Range selected by providing two opposite corners

plish tasks such as formatting. You were introduced to ranges in Chapter 2 when you assigned names to ranges consisting of a single cell reference. Figure 3-1 shows groups of cells that are valid ranges as well as some groups that are not. The cell groups on the left are invalid ranges because they do not form one contiguous rectangle. The cell groups on the right are valid ranges because they form a contiguous group. As long as this rule is met, the range can be as large as you wish or as small as one cell.

You can use several methods to specify cell ranges. You can type them in like a cell address or highlight them with the cell pointer. Any two diagonally opposite corners can be used to specify the range as long as they are separated by one or more decimal points. For example, the range of cells shown in Figure 3-2 can be specified as B4.C8, B4..C8, B8.C4, B8..C4, C8.B4, C8..B4, C4.B8, or C4..B8.

The most common way to specify a range is to use the upper-left cell first and the lower-right cell last. Also, since 1-2-3 will supply the second period, you might as well save a keystroke and just type **B4.C8**. If you plan to specify a range by highlighting it, you can save yourself some time by positioning the cell pointer in the upper-left corner of the range before beginning.

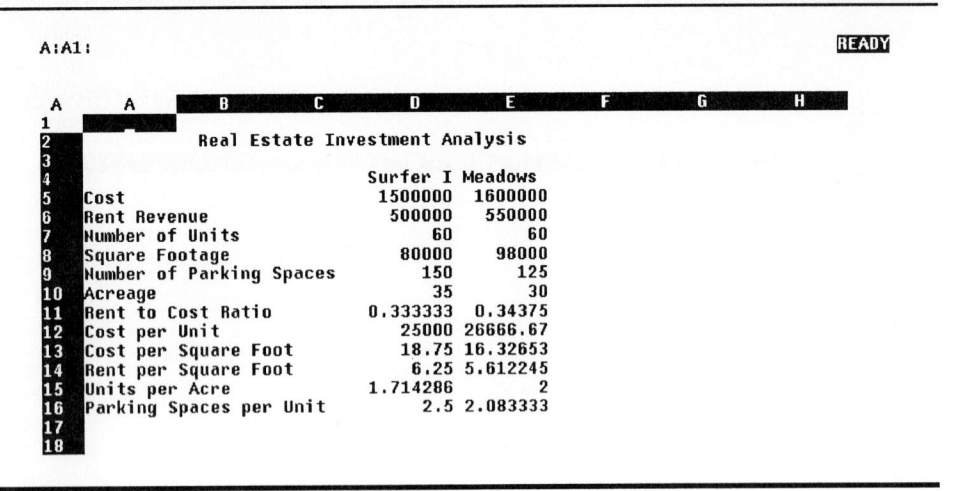

A:A1:   READY

	A	B	C	D	E	F	G	H
1								
2			Real Estate Investment Analysis					
3								
4				Surfer I	Meadows			
5	Cost			1500000	1600000			
6	Rent Revenue			500000	550000			
7	Number of Units			60	60			
8	Square Footage			80000	98000			
9	Number of Parking Spaces			150	125			
10	Acreage			35	30			
11	Rent to Cost Ratio			0.333333	0.34375			
12	Cost per Unit			25000	26666.67			
13	Cost per Square Foot			18.75	16.32653			
14	Rent per Square Foot			6.25	5.612245			
15	Units per Acre			1.714286	2			
16	Parking Spaces per Unit			2.5	2.083333			
17								
18								

FIGURE 3-3.   Real estate investment model created in Chapter 2

Retrieve your investment model by typing **/FRREALEST** and pressing ENTER.
The model should match the one shown in Figure 3-3. To try out the range specifications as you add some formats to this model, follow these steps:

1. Move the cell pointer to D13, the upper-left cell in the range you will format.

2. Type / to activate the menu.

3. Use the RIGHT ARROW key to move the cursor to the Range menu option, and
   press ENTER.

4. Press ENTER to select the Format option that is currently highlighted.

5. Select the option for *Fixed format* by typing **F**.

6. Press ENTER to select the default of two decimal places.

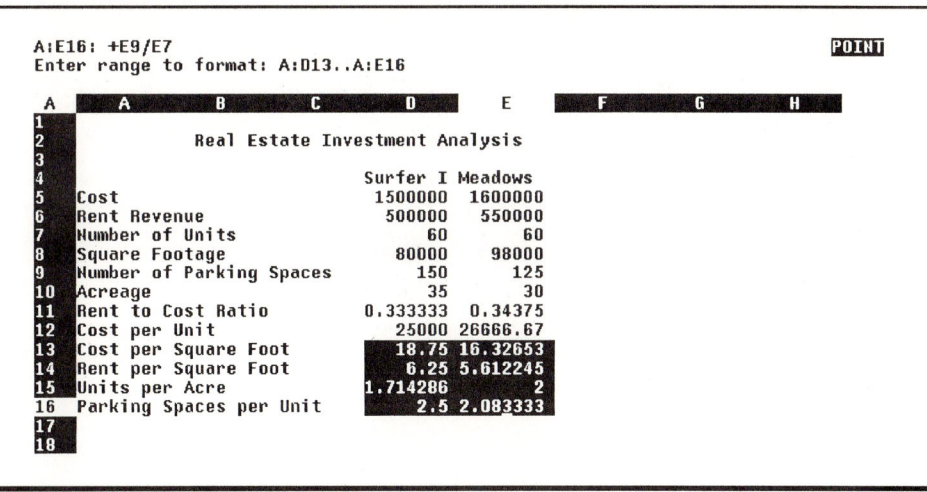

FIGURE 3-4.   Highlighting a range to be formatted

7. Use RIGHT ARROW and DOWN ARROW to position the cell pointer in E16, highlighting the entire area to be formatted as shown in Figure 3-4. Then press ENTER.

   The format should immediately change to two decimal places for each of the entries in this section and match the display in Figure 3-5. The other range that needs to be formatted is D11..E11. This time, you will not position the cell pointer first so that you can experience the extra steps involved.

8. Enter **/Range Format Fixed** and press ENTER.

   This command sequence will accept the default of two decimal places. You cannot expand the range at this point, since it has an incorrect beginning location. You must first free the beginning of the range.

9. Press ESC. Now you will find that you can move the cell pointer to D11 without altering a range specification.

10. Type . (a period).

    This will anchor the beginning of the range again.

```
A:D13: (F2) +D5/D8                                              READY

A      A         B         C         D      E      F      G      H
1
2                   Real Estate Investment Analysis
3
4                                     Surfer I Meadows
5   Cost                               1500000 1600000
6   Rent Revenue                        500000  550000
7   Number of Units                         60      60
8   Square Footage                       80000   98000
9   Number of Parking Spaces              150     125
10  Acreage                                35      30
11  Rent to Cost Ratio                0.333333 0.34375
12  Cost per Unit                        25000 26666.67
13  Cost per Square Foot                 18.75   16.33
14  Rent per Square Foot                  6.25    5.61
15  Units per Acre                        1.71    2.00
16  Parking Spaces per Unit               2.50    2.08
17
18
```

FIGURE 3-5.   Result of format operation

11. Expand the range by moving the cell pointer to E11 and pressing ENTER to finalize the range selection.

If you move the cell pointer to any cell that has been formatted with a /Range command, you can determine the format that has been assigned to the cell even if it is empty. This information is displayed as a single character representing the format type in the control panel. Table 3-2 shows some of the most common format abbreviations. These format specifications are enclosed within parentheses and are placed immediately after the cell address. The following cell, for example, is formatted as Text, causing the formula entry to be displayed instead of the result of the formula:

```
A:A3: (T) +A1+A2                                               READY

A      A         B         C         D      E      F      G      H
1                3
2                5
3   +A1+A2
```

For formats that allow you to specify the number of decimal places, a numeric digit follows, as shown here:

```
A:A1: (C2) 3                                                   READY

A      A         B         C         D      E      F      G      H
1       $3.00
2
```

Abbreviation	Format in Effect
(P2)	Percent with two decimal places
(T)	Text, to display formulas as they are entered
(G)	General
(C0)	Currency with zero decimal places
(,2)	Comma with two decimal places
(D1)	Date format 1
(D6)	Time format 1
(H)	Hidden format
(A)	Automatic format

TABLE 3-2.   Examples of Format Abbreviations

The model still is not presented in the optimal format. The numbers in the cells at the top would be easier to read if they had commas inserted after the thousands position. There are two formats that will add these commas; one is the *Comma format* (,) and the other is the *Currency format*. The only difference between the two is whether or not a dollar sign is inserted at the front of the entry. Either of these two formats could be added with another range request, but since the cells that you wish to change include all of the remaining value entries on the worksheet, you will use the Global formatting option.

MAKING A GLOBAL FORMAT CHANGE   When you wish to alter the format of the entire worksheet or even most of it, a *Global format* change is the ideal solution. A Global format change alters the default format for every cell on the worksheet, including both cells with entries and cells that are currently empty. As long as the worksheet cells have not had their formats altered with /Range Format commands, the new default format will take effect. For an empty cell, this format will be used as soon as a value entry is placed in the cell. The Global formatting option is especially useful when most of the worksheet is formatted with the same option. You can choose a Global format that meets the requirement for most of the cells, and then go back and format the exceptions with a /Range Format command.

To alter the Global format for the model, follow these steps:

1. Type / to activate the menu.

2. Press ENTER to select the Worksheet option.

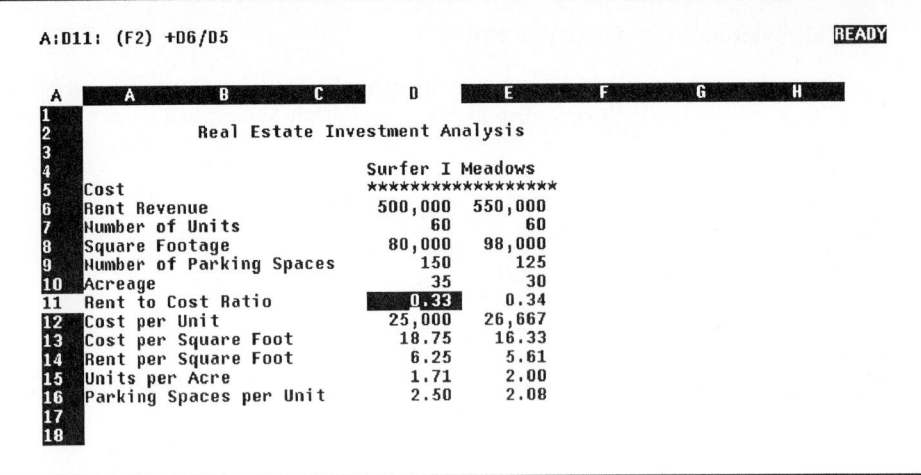

A:D11: (F2) +D6/D5   READY

	A	B	C	D	E	F	G	H
1								
2			Real Estate Investment Analysis					
3								
4				Surfer I	Meadows			
5	Cost			*****************				
6	Rent Revenue			500,000	550,000			
7	Number of Units			60	60			
8	Square Footage			80,000	98,000			
9	Number of Parking Spaces			150	125			
10	Acreage			35	30			
11	Rent to Cost Ratio			0.33	0.34			
12	Cost per Unit			25,000	26,667			
13	Cost per Square Foot			18.75	16.33			
14	Rent per Square Foot			6.25	5.61			
15	Units per Acre			1.71	2.00			
16	Parking Spaces per Unit			2.50	2.08			
17								
18								

FIGURE 3-6.   Column width too narrow for the format selected

3. Press ENTER to select the Global option.

4. Press ENTER to select the Format option.

5. Type , to select the Comma format.

6. Type **0** to specify zero decimal places, and press ENTER to finalize the entry.

   The display will change to match the one in Figure 3-6. Everything looks fine, except the two Cost figures are now displayed as asterisks. The values that were stored there are still in memory and are replaced only by the asterisks to indicate that once the new formats are used, the numeric values in these cells require more space than the column width allows. You can correct this quickly by increasing the Global width. This command will be explained later in the chapter; for now, the command will be entered as shown.

7. Enter **/WGC10** and press ENTER.

   The columns will be widened to ten characters, producing the display shown in Figure 3-7. The columns are now wide enough to display the Cost figures with commas.

8. Type **/FS** and press ENTER.

9. A prompt message will be displayed. Type **R** in response.

   This will replace the file on disk.

```
A:D11: (F2) +D6/D5                                                    READY

   A     A          B          C         D        E        F        G
1
2                   Real Estate Investment Analysis
3
4                                     Surfer I  Meadows
5     Cost                           1,500,000 1,600,000
6     Rent Revenue                     500,000   550,000
7     Number of Units                       60        60
8     Square Footage                    80,000    98,000
9     Number of Parking Spaces            150       125
10    Acreage                              35        30
11    Rent to Cost Ratio                  0.33      0.34
12    Cost per Unit                     25,000    26,667
13    Cost per Square Foot               18.75     16.33
14    Rent per Square Foot                6.25      5.61
15    Units per Acre                      1.71      2.00
16    Parking Spaces per Unit             2.50      2.08
17
18
```

FIGURE 3-7.   Global width changed to 10

AUTOMATICALLY FORMATTING A WORKSHEET   Release 3 introduces the *Automatic format,* which converts a formatted entry into one of the formatting options 1-2-3 supports. For example, an automatically formatted cell will format the entry of $5,432.09 as currency with two decimal places. Once you make an entry, 1-2-3 formats the cell using one of 1-2-3's formats. When the format is selected, the format remains with the cell. The Automatic format option is available with the /Range Format and /Worksheet Global Format commands. To try this new formatting option, follow these steps:

1. Enter /**Worksheet Erase Yes** to erase the worksheet.

2. Enter /**Range Format Other** to display these options:

```
A:A1:                                                                 MENU
Automatic  Color  Label  Parentheses
Automatically format cell when data is entered
```

3. Enter **Automatic.**

4. Type **A1..D10** as the range to format and press ENTER. 1-2-3 returns to the worksheet.

5. Make the following entries so the resulting worksheet looks like Figure 3-8:

A1: Date
A2: Time
A3: Old Sales
A4: Growth %
A5: New Sales
A6: Units Sold
A7: Price
C1: 12/31/90
C2: 12:41 PM
C3: $671,500
C4: 8.0%
C5: C3*(1+C4)
C6: 170,000
C7: 3.95

6. Move the cell pointer to each of the entries in column C and notice how the cell is formatted.

The control panel entries for C1 and C2 will appear as numbers that may not mean anything to you, but they represent how 1-2-3 stores the date or time. (Dates and times are covered in fuller detail in Chapter 7.) When you move to the cells in column C, the format description in the control panel may include L, D4, D7, C0, P1, a comma and a zero, or F2. For each of the cells, 1-2-3 used your entry to determine the format you want to use. 1-2-3 performed a /Range Format command for each of the cells in which you made an entry. Once 1-2-3 selects a format for a cell, the format does not change unless you execute another /Range Format command. The only cell that retained the (A) for automatic was C5, since entering a formula does not provide 1-2-3 with the characters it uses to determine how you want the data formatted.

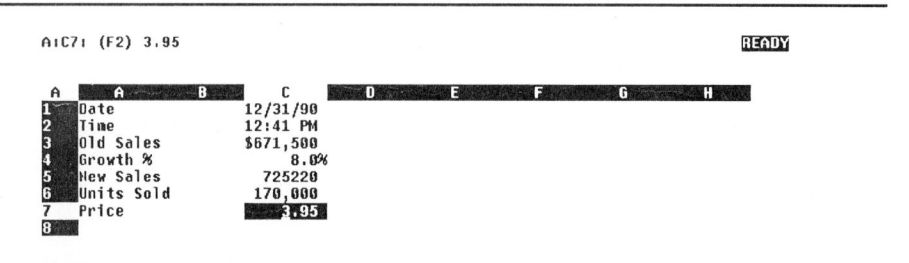

FIGURE 3-8.   Automatic format for values

```
                                                              STAT

    Available memory: 2362584 of 2363224 Bytes (100%)

    Processor: 80286
    Math coprocessor: None

    Recalculation:
      Method.......... Automatic
      Order........... Natural
      Iterations....... 1

    Circular reference: (None)

    Cell display:
      Format.......... (G)
      Label prefix..... '
      Column width..... 9
      Zero setting..... No

    Global protection: Off
```

FIGURE 3-9.   Worksheet Status screen

7. Enter **$60.3** in C7 and press ENTER.

   Even though the entry has a dollar sign and only one digit after the decimal, 1-2-3 formats the number as Fixed with two decimal digits; that is how 1-2-3 formatted the cell when you made the first entry.

CHECKING A FORMAT SETTING   If you move the cell pointer to one of the cells that has been formatted with the Global option, you will notice that there is no format code in the control panel. Only /Range formats will display in the control panel. To check the Global format setting, you have to check the worksheet status. The Worksheet status screen provides information on all the worksheet default settings. Check it now by following these directions:

1. Enter /**W** to select the Worksheet menu.

2. Type **S** to display the status.

   Your screen will look like the one in Figure 3-9. Notice that the indicator has changed to STAT. Don't be concerned if your screen is slightly different; the display for the available memory, the processor, and the math processor will vary from computer to computer.

3. Press ESC or ENTER.

   This step will return you to the worksheet and READY mode.

You can use a format option to look at the formulas within worksheet cells by using the Text display format. This means that you can review all of the formulas at once instead of having to move the cell pointer to each cell and view the control panel to see the formula. The Text format displays formulas in the cells where you entered them, rather than showing the result of the formulas within the cell. To make this change, you must use both the Global format change and a /Range format change. The Global change will alter the default setting for all worksheet cells; however, since /Range formats take priority, some of the cells will ignore the default. This means that you must reset the format of these cells with the /Range Format command before the cells use the default setting.

Before beginning, replace the formatted numbers in the current worksheet with a copy of the investment model on disk:

1. Type **/FRREALEST** and press ENTER.

   Retrieving a copy of the file keeps the original data intact while you reformat the worksheet. If you later save the worksheet, you will eliminate the Fixed and Comma formats that you added before.

   Since you are becoming familiar with menu selections, from now on you will be given only the entries that you should make for each exercise. Directions will no longer tell you to point to a selection and press ENTER or type the first letter of the selection. You can use whatever method you prefer, as long as you enter the menu selections specified.

2. Enter **/Worksheet Global Format** to select the Global Format menu, or press ENTER as each menu is presented until you are looking at the menu that provides format options.

3. Select **Text** as the format option.

4. Move the cell pointer to D11. Then enter **/Range Format Reset** to reset the range format to the Global default.

5. Move the cell pointer to E16 and press ENTER to view a display of the formulas like the one in Figure 3-10.

Since the formulas in this particular model are short, you can view the complete formula within each cell. If the formulas were longer, the columns would need to be widened to see the entire formula. In the next section you will learn all about tailoring the column width to meet your particular needs.

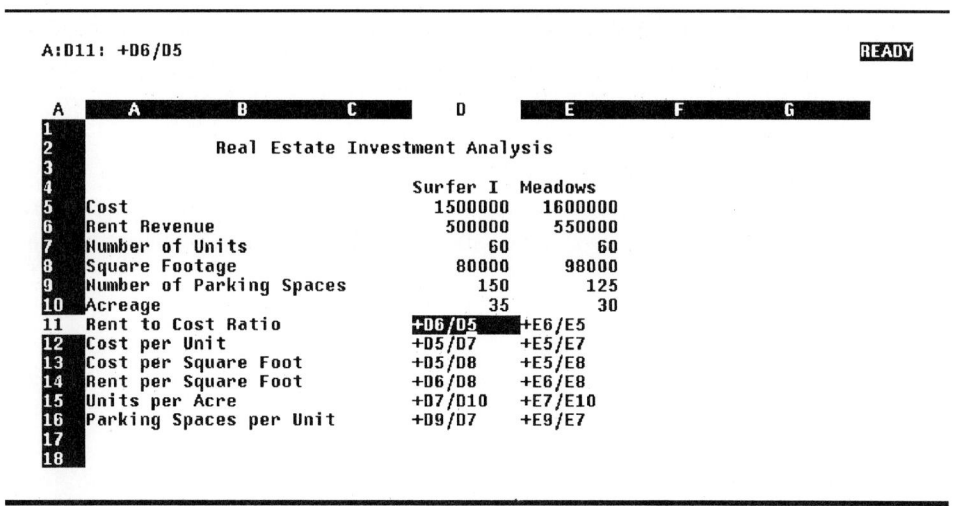

A:D11: +D6/D5   READY

	A	B	C	D	E	F	G
1							
2	Real Estate Investment Analysis
3							
4				Surfer I	Meadows		
5	Cost			1500000	1600000		
6	Rent Revenue			500000	550000		
7	Number of Units			60	60		
8	Square Footage			80000	98000		
9	Number of Parking Spaces			150	125		
10	Acreage			35	30		
11	Rent to Cost Ratio			+D6/D5	+E6/E5		
12	Cost per Unit			+D5/D7	+E5/E7		
13	Cost per Square Foot			+D5/D8	+E5/E8		
14	Rent per Square Foot			+D6/D8	+E6/E8		
15	Units per Acre			+D7/D10	+E7/E10		
16	Parking Spaces per Unit			+D9/D7	+E9/E7		
17							
18							

FIGURE 3-10.   Formula display

CHANGING WORKSHEET COLUMNS

You have examined some of the changes you can make to the appearance of individual entries in cells. There are also several commands that allow you to make changes to one or more columns at one time. 1-2-3 provides options that let you determine the width you wish to use for columns. With Release 3, you can change the width of a range of columns with one command. With other options, you can also hide or display columns on your worksheet.

Altering Column Widths

The default width of columns is nine when you begin a new 1-2-3 worksheet. This is adequate for values displayed with the General format; often, however, it is not wide enough when you want to display numbers with commas, dollar signs, decimal places, labels, or most of the formulas you wish to display with the Text format option. At other times, the opposite might be true. Even though you may have a column that never contains more than one character, the full width of nine is always reserved for the column. If you could make some columns narrower, you might be able to view a few more columns on the screen.

1-2-3 will let you handle both types of changes by altering the column width. In fact, it even lets you choose whether to change the width of all the columns at once or to alter the width of a single column.

CHANGING THE WIDTH OF ONE COLUMN   Altering the width of individual columns lets you tailor your display to meet your exact needs. This is the preferred approach when you only have a few columns to change, since columns are neither wider nor narrower than the requirements of your data. Any change you make for single columns will take precedence over the Global default column width setting that you establish. This means that you can make both types of changes to your worksheet.

The investment model created in Chapter 2 provides an opportunity for changing a column width. Follow these steps for making the changes:

1. Enter **/File Retrieve REALEST** and press ENTER.

2. Move the cell pointer to column A.
    Notice the list of long label entries in that column. They extend beyond the boundaries of column A and borrow space from column B. You can widen column A so that the entries will fit completely within the column.

3. Enter **/Worksheet Column Set-Width**.

4. Press the RIGHT ARROW key until column A is wide enough to display the entire entry, as in Figure 3-11. A width of 25 is a good selection.

5. Press ENTER.
    This finalizes the width change. Column A will remain at a width of 25 unless you make another change.

Adjusting the width of this column makes it clear where the data is entered. Adjusting the column width can also be important if you ever print a copy of the worksheet. 1-2-3 will only print data that displays within the columns selected to print.

CHANGING THE WIDTH OF A RANGE OF COLUMNS   Release 3 allows you to alter the width of a range of columns. 1- 2-3 changes the width of the range of columns with a single command; the changes are applied to the individual columns as if you had changed each one individually with the /Worksheet Column Set-Width command. This means that settings will override any changes made with the /Worksheet Global Col-Width command.

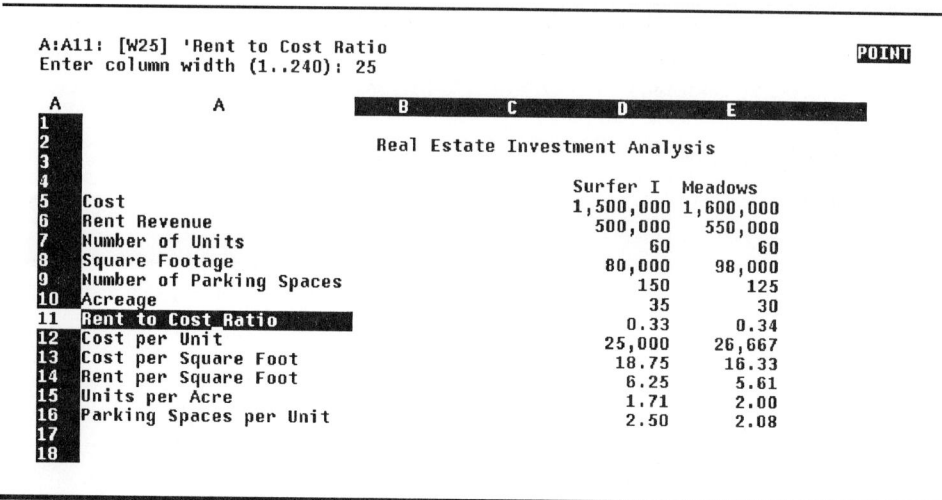

FIGURE 3-11. Column A widened to 25

Clear the screen with /WEYY. Enter the data in Figure 3-12 as the first step in trying this command. Note that the heading in row 1 is actually entered as a long label in B1. Also, the name entries in column A are truncated when you originally enter them; the full names will appear again later when the column width is altered. After completing the entries, follow these steps:

1. Move the cell pointer to A1.

2. Enter **/Worksheet Column Set-Width**.

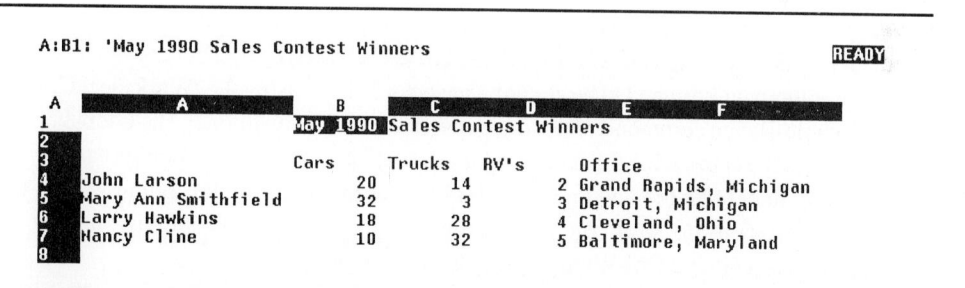

FIGURE 3-12. Sales contest winners

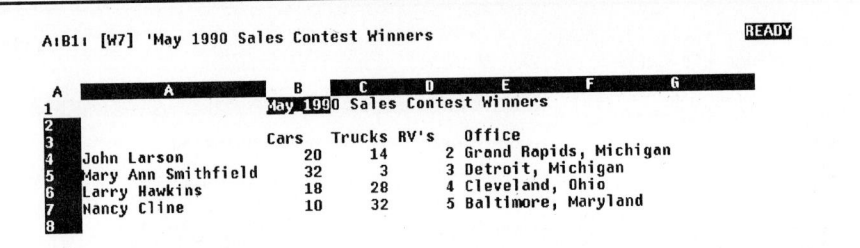

FIGURE 3-13.   Model after Worksheet Column Column-Range was used on columns B through D

3. Type **20** and press ENTER.
   This changes the column width for column A to 20.

4. Position the cell pointer in column B.

5. Enter /**Worksheet Column Column-Range Set-Width**.

6. Press the RIGHT ARROW key twice to expand the range to include column C and column D, and press ENTER.

7. Press the LEFT ARROW twice to shrink the width to 7.

8. Press ENTER.
   Steps 4 through 8 change the width of the three columns with one command sequence. Your revised model will match Figure 3-13.

9. Save this model as VEHICLES by entering /**File Save**, typing **VEHICLES**, and pressing ENTER.

CHANGING THE WIDTH OF ALL THE COLUMNS   For certain models, all of the column widths need to be altered. One possibility is using the /Worksheet Column Column-Range command, but it only covers the range you define. The Global option changes the entire worksheet, making model expansion for similar entries easy. If you have a model like the one in Figure 3-14 and wish to narrow the column width, it is also tedious to do so a column at a time or for a range of columns, making the /Worksheet Global Col-Width option the method of choice.

```
A:A1:                                                                    READY

    A       A        B         C         D         E         F         G         H
1                                   Employees Hired By Month
2
3                    Jan       Feb       Mar       Apr       May       Jne       Jly
4       Region 1      1         7         7         6         0         3         8
5       Region 2      4         3         8         6         4         6         9
6       Region 3      5         0         5         6         8         5         6
7       Region 4      6         7         4         6         4         2         0
8       Region 5      2         3         0         9         0         6         8
9       Region 6      9         3         7         8         4         4         4
10      Region 7      4         5         2         8         8         8         5
11      Region 8      5         3         3         7         6         2         2
12      Region 9      3         8         8         6         8         9         2
```

FIGURE 3-14.   New employees by month

Since each entry under the "Month" heading is so small, it is better to narrow the columns and view all the months on the screen at once. The /Worksheet Global Col-Width command can make this change for you easily: only one command is required to change all the columns. After entering the command sequence, you can type the new width or use the LEFT ARROW key to make the width narrower by one each time you press it. When you have adjusted the column to the desired width, you just press ENTER to finalize the current selection.

When you change the Global column width, column widths set with /Worksheet Column Set-Width and /Worksheet Column Column-Range Set-Width are not affected. Changing the Global column width will alter the preceding report so that all the months can be viewed. Follow these steps to make the change:

1. Enter /**Worksheet Global Col-Width.**

2. Enter **5** for the width. Press ENTER.

    This produces the results shown in Figure 3-15. The only problem with this display is that column A has also become smaller and will not display the region numbers. To fix this problem, do the following:

1. Move the cell pointer to column A.

2. Enter /**Worksheet Column Set-Width 9** and press ENTER.

```
A:A4:  'Region  1                                                    READY
```

A	A	B	C	D	E	F	G	H	I	J	K	L	M	N
1				Employees Hired By Month										
2														
3		Jan	Feb	Mar	Apr	May	Jne	Jly	Aug	Spt	Oct	Nov	Dec	
4	Regio	1	7	7	6	0	3	8	6	7	3	6	7	
5	Regio	4	3	8	6	4	6	9	2	8	6	5	5	
6	Regio	5	0	5	6	8	5	6	5	0	1	5	1	
7	Regio	6	7	4	6	4	2	0	9	5	8	8	0	
8	Regio	2	3	0	9	0	6	8	5	3	4	5	8	
9	Regio	9	3	7	8	4	4	4	8	2	1	6	6	
10	Regio	4	5	2	8	8	8	5	6	5	1	1	8	
11	Regio	5	3	3	7	6	2	2	0	6	1	7	6	
12	Regio	3	8	8	6	8	9	2	0	7	9	3	1	

FIGURE 3-15.   Column width narrowed globally

This change to an individual column width fixes the problem and produces the result shown in Figure 3-16.

A /Worksheet Global Col-Width change can also be used to make all the columns wider. This is often useful when you are displaying the model as text to view its formulas. If all the formulas are approximately the same length, you may want to widen the column width to accommodate the longest formula entry.

If you want to check the default column width, you cannot point to one of the cells and see it displayed. The width is displayed in the control panel only when the change has been made to a single column with the /Worksheet Column Set-Width command. You must give the same status instruction used to check the format by entering

```
A:A4:  [W9]  'Region  1                                             READY
```

A	A	B	C	D	E	F	G	H	I	J	K	L	M
1				Employees Hired By Month									
2													
3		Jan	Feb	Mar	Apr	May	Jne	Jly	Aug	Spt	Oct	Nov	Dec
4	Region 1	1	7	7	6	0	3	8	6	7	3	6	7
5	Region 2	4	3	8	6	4	6	9	2	8	6	5	5
6	Region 3	5	0	5	6	8	5	6	5	0	1	5	1
7	Region 4	6	7	4	6	4	2	0	9	5	8	8	0
8	Region 5	2	3	0	9	0	6	8	5	3	4	5	8
9	Region 6	9	3	7	8	4	4	4	8	2	1	6	6
10	Region 7	4	5	2	8	8	8	5	6	5	1	1	8
11	Region 8	5	3	3	7	6	2	2	0	6	1	7	6
12	Region 9	3	8	8	6	8	9	2	0	7	9	3	1

FIGURE 3-16.   Individual column change overrides Global change

/Worksheet Status. Remember that you can always change this default; or, if you prefer, you can use the /Worksheet Column command to alter the width of one column.

Inserting and Deleting Columns

No matter how thoroughly you plan your worksheet applications, sometimes you need to make substantial changes to a worksheet model. You might need to add an employee to a model, to delete accounts that are no longer used, or to add some blank space to make the worksheet more readable. 1-2-3 will accommodate each of these needs by means of commands that let you insert or delete blank rows or columns in the worksheet.

INSERTING ROWS AND COLUMNS
You can insert blank rows and columns at any location in the worksheet you choose. Before beginning your request, tell 1-2-3 where to place the blank rows or columns by positioning the cell pointer. If you will be adding rows to the worksheet, they will be placed above the cell pointer's location. If you will be adding columns, they will be placed to the left of the cell pointer.

When 1-2-3 inserts rows into a worksheet, the cell addresses of the data below this location are changed. It is as though 1-2-3 pushes the data down on the worksheet to make room for the new blank rows. Under normal circumstances, 1-2-3 automatically adjusts all the formulas that reference this data. The same is true for data that resides to the right of the location at which columns were inserted.

The insert request is invoked by entering /**Worksheet Insert Row.** 1-2-3 prompts you for the number of rows to insert but does not use a straightforward question such as "How many rows would you like to add?" Instead, it asks for the range where you want the insertion to occur. It does not use this range to control the placement of the insertion, only to control the number of rows to insert. If you need to move the cell pointer to where you want to add rows, press ESC, move to the first row where you want a new row added, and type a period. If you specify a range that includes three rows, three rows will be inserted. If you specify a range of one row, only one row will be inserted. Seeing this in action will clarify the way it works.

Let's add a few blank rows to the commission calculations you created in Chapter 2. Follow these steps to complete the changes:

1. Enter /**File Retrieve**.

2. Type **COMM** and press ENTER.

3. Move the cell pointer to C8.

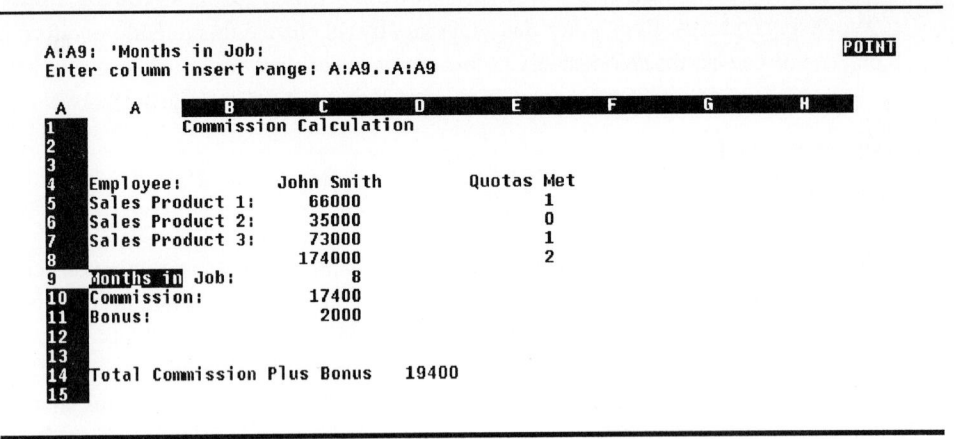

FIGURE 3-17.   Inserting a column

Notice that the formula that totals sales is entered as **+C5+C6+C7**. Look at this formula again after inserting a column, and notice how 1-2-3 has automatically adjusted it for you.

4. Position the cell pointer in A9 (anywhere in column A would work just as well).

5. Enter /**Worksheet Insert Column** to produce the display in Figure 3-17.

6. Press ENTER to restrict the insertion to one column.

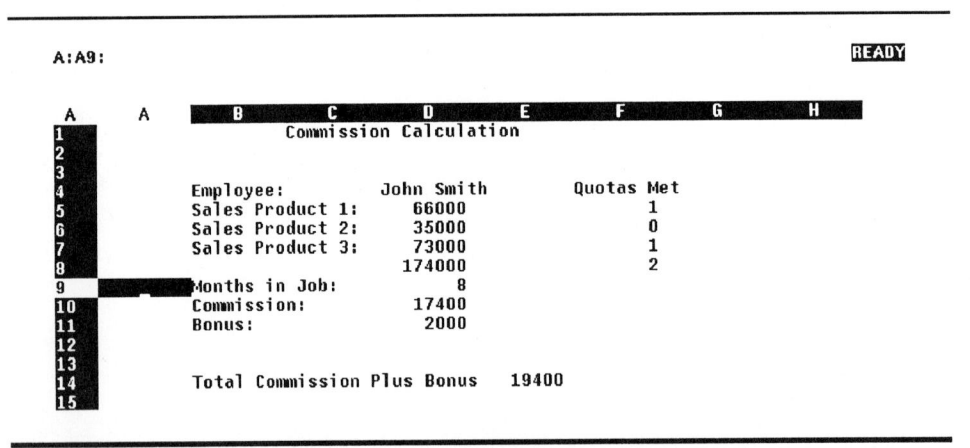

FIGURE 3-18.   New column added for column A

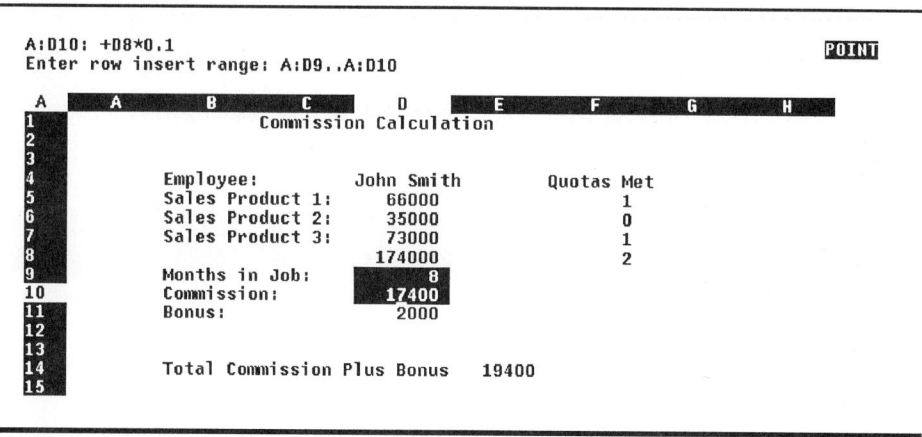

```
A:D10: +D8*0.1                                              POINT
Enter row insert range: A:D9..A:D10
```

FIGURE 3-19. Inserting a row

The results are shown in Figure 3-18. If you move the cell pointer to D8, you will find that the formula has been changed, and the formula for summing sales is now +D5+D6+D7 to reflect its new location in the worksheet.

Inserting rows is just as easy. Let's insert two blank rows above the section that begins with "Months in Job" to separate the sections of the model:

1. Move the cell pointer to D9 (any place in row 9 would work just as well).

2. Enter /**Worksheet Insert Row** and expand the range to include two rows, as shown in Figure 3-19.

3. Press ENTER.

    You will find that two blank rows have been added, producing the results shown in Figure 3-20. Notice that the addition of empty space on the side and between the two sections makes the model more appealing.

4. Save these changes by entering /**File Save**, pressing ENTER, and typing **R**.

DELETING ROWS AND COLUMNS   You can delete rows and columns at any location in a worksheet. This allows you to eliminate blank rows and columns or rows and columns that contain entries you no longer need.

When 1-2-3 deletes rows or columns in a worksheet, the cell addresses of the data below and to the right of the deleted rows or columns are changed. It is as though 1-2-3

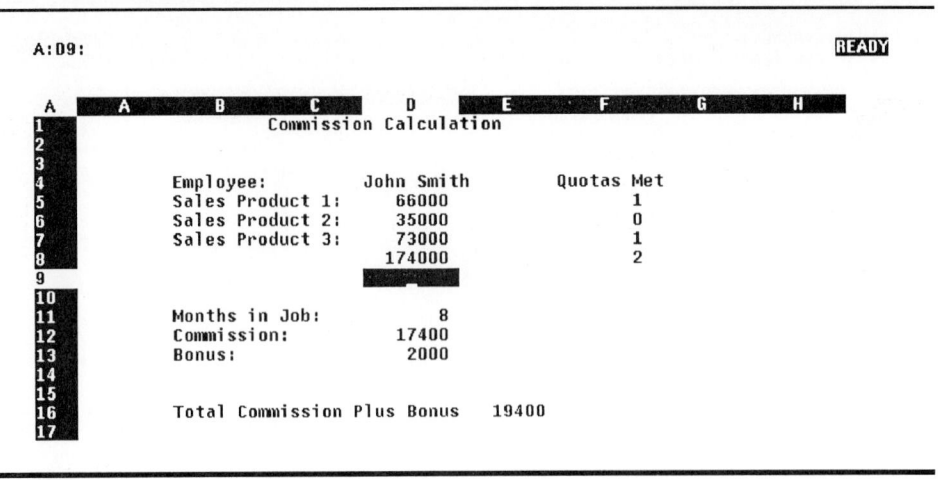

FIGURE 3-20.   Two new rows added

pushes the data up on the worksheet to replace the deleted rows or columns. Under normal circumstances, 1-2-3 automatically adjusts all the formulas that reference this data. Formulas that reference a cell in the deleted rows or columns will return ERR. If a formula references a range that spans the deleted rows or columns, the formula uses the range values with the original beginning and end cells of the range, although the range itself is smaller because it does not include the deleted rows or columns.

Before beginning your delete request, tell 1-2-3 where to start deleting rows or columns by positioning the cell pointer on the first row or column that you want to delete. The delete command is invoked by entering /**Worksheet Delete Row**. 1-2-3 asks for the range containing the rows or columns that you want to delete. If you forget to position the cell pointer before requesting the delete command, press ESC, move to the first row or column you want to delete and type a period. If you specify a range that includes three rows, three rows will be deleted. If you specify a range of one row, only one row will be deleted.

Seeing this in action will clarify the way it works. Let's remove the blank rows added to the commission calculations to try the /Worksheet Insert Row command. Follow these steps to complete the changes:

1. Move the cell pointer to D13.

    The formula in D13 is +F8*1000. Look at this formula again after deleting two rows, and notice how 1-2-3 automatically adjusts the formulas for you.

2. Position the cell pointer to D9 (anywhere in row 9 would work just as well).

3. Enter /**Worksheet Delete Row**.

4. Press the DOWN ARROW to highlight one cell from rows 9 and 10.

5. Press ENTER to delete the rows.
   The results are shown in Figure 3-18. If you move the cell pointer to D8, you will find that the formula has not changed, even though the relative number of rows between D13 and the cells it uses has decreased.

Deleting columns is just as easy. To delete a column, use the /Worksheet Delete Column command and select a range containing at least one cell from each column you want to delete before pressing ENTER.

Hiding and Displaying Columns

Release 3 allows you to temporarily conceal columns from view on the display screen. The data in these columns is not altered in any way and can be displayed again at any time with the entry of another command. This feature is particularly useful if you are working with sensitive information like salary data and do not wish it to be visible onscreen, in plain view of anyone who walks by your PC.

Use an expansion of the salary data you entered in Chapter 2 to take a look at how this feature works. The data for several employees is shown in Figure 3-21.

A:B3: (C0) 35900   READY

A	A	B	C	D	E	F	G	H
1		1989	Increase	Increase	1990			
2	Name	Salary	Month	Percent	Salary			
3	J. Brown	$35,900	1	6.00%	$38,054			
4	M. Smith	$56,000	3	5.00%	$58,333			
5	J. Harris	$18,750	4	7.00%	$19,734			
6	S. Jacobs	$23,450	1	3.00%	$24,154			
7	P. Morris	$56,400	10	6.00%	$57,246			
8	H. Frank	$19,800	2	7.00%	$21,071			
9	J. Peters	$45,300	12	4.00%	$45,451			
10	F. Dean	$49,600	6	5.00%	$51,047			
11	L. Parks	$51,250	5	5.00%	$52,958			
12								

FIGURE 3-21.   Model displaying salary data

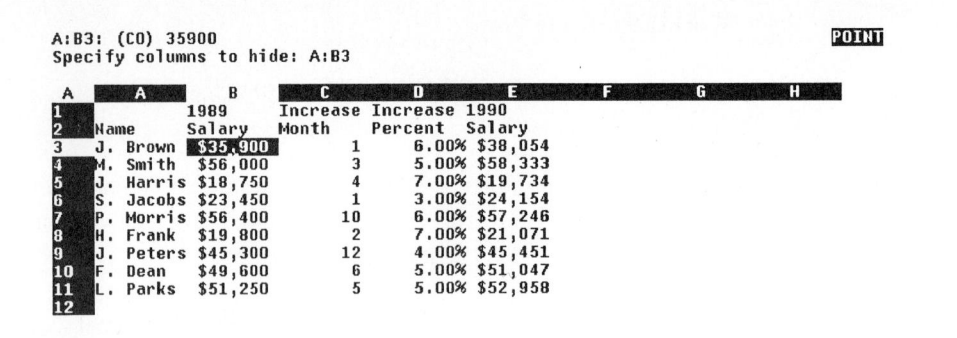

FIGURE 3-22.   Hiding a column

If you want to correct misspellings in the name entries, you might want to temporarily remove the salary information from the screen. This can be accomplished by following these steps:

1. Enter /**File Retrieve**.

2. Type **SALARY** and press ENTER.

3. Enter /**Worksheet Column Hide**.

4. Point to column B as shown in Figure 3-22, and press ENTER.
   Your model will not match this exactly because you have only one row of salary entries and you have not formatted your entries. You will be able to see the column disappear from view.

5. Enter /**Worksheet Column Hide**.

6. Move to column E.

7. Press ENTER.
   The result is a worksheet with both salary columns temporarily hidden as shown in Figure 3-23. To bring these columns back into view, another set of menu entries is required:

8. Enter /**Worksheet Column Display**.
   Notice that all the hidden columns are marked with an asterisk. Since you did not specify a range of columns to display, another command sequence is required to restore the other salary column.

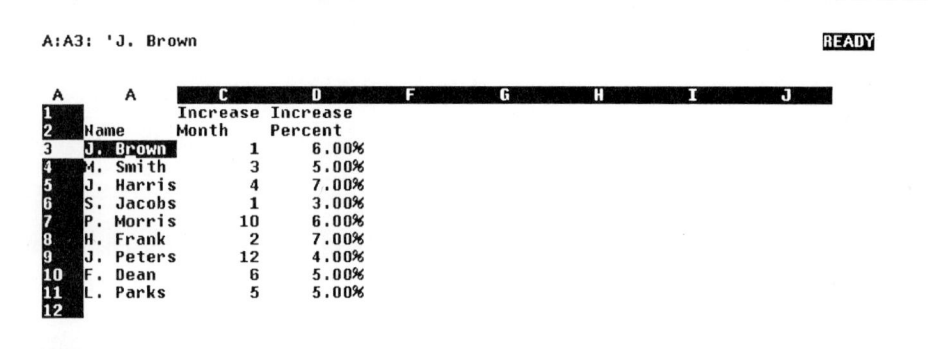

```
A:A3:  'J. Brown                                                    READY

     A      A        C        D       F       G       H       I       J
  1         Increase Increase
  2  Name   Month    Percent
  3  J. Brown    1      6.00%
  4  M. Smith    3      5.00%
  5  J. Harris   4      7.00%
  6  S. Jacobs   1      3.00%
  7  P. Morris  10      6.00%
  8  H. Frank    2      7.00%
  9  J. Peters  12      4.00%
 10  F. Dean     6      5.00%
 11  L. Parks    5      5.00%
 12
```

FIGURE 3-23.   Columns B and E hidden

9. Point to column B and press ENTER.

10. Enter **/Worksheet Column Display**, point to column E, and press ENTER.

CHANGING THE ALIGNMENT OF LABEL ENTRIES

You already learned one method for changing the alignment for a label in Chapter 2, when you entered a few of the labels by beginning them with a " symbol. If you have a large number of labels to enter, however, this is a time-consuming method. It also requires you to edit the entries and replace the label indicator at the front of the label if you want to change its alignment. Fortunately, there are several alternatives that can be real time-savers. One option allows you to change the alignment of labels that are currently on the worksheet; the other changes the default for the current worksheet so that any new labels you enter will use the new alignment setting.

Changing Previously Entered Labels

1-2-3 has two methods for altering the alignment of labels that are already recorded on the worksheet. You can use the EDIT method, or you can use a /Range command that alters the label alignment of the rows in the range. The EDIT method follows these simple rules for editing the entry in any cell:

1. Move the cell pointer to the cell whose alignment you wish to change.

2. Press F2 (EDIT) followed by HOME to move to the front of the entry.

3. Press the DEL key to eliminate this label indicator. Then type the indicator that corresponds to the type of alignment you want to use.

The second method requires less work; many cell indicators can be changed with a single command. When you enter the /Range Label command, it presents the following menu:

You can choose the type of alignment you want and specify the range of entries that

```
A:A1:                                                    MENU
Left  Right  Center
Left-align labels in cells
```

are affected. The major differences between this approach and a Global format change is the scope of the change and the fact that the /Range Label command affects only the cells that contain entries. Empty cells do not retain this information. If you subsequently place entries in these empty cells, the entries will be aligned in accordance with the default label prefix. To check this default, enter /**Worksheet Status** to view the by now quite familiar display screen.

Look at the effect of altering the alignment of the labels in this example:

1. Clear your screen with /WEYY; then Move your cell pointer to A1.

2. Type **Jan** and press the RIGHT ARROW key.

3. Type **Feb** and press the RIGHT ARROW key.

4. Type **Mar** and press the RIGHT ARROW key.

5. Continue making these entries until you enter **Aug** in H1.

6. Move the cell pointer to A1.
   Your display should look like this:

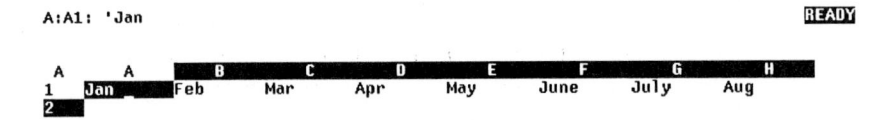

```
A:A1:  'Jan                                              READY

   A      A        B         C        D        E        F        G        H
1  Jan      Feb       Mar      Apr      May     June     July     Aug
2
```

The labels are currently left aligned in accordance with the default.

7. Enter **/Range Label Right**.

8. Use the RIGHT ARROW key to move to H1, and press ENTER.
    Each of the entries in row 1 is now right aligned in its cell, although subsequent entries in these cells would not be affected.

9. Enter **/Worksheet Erase Yes Yes** to erase this example.

Changing Alignment Globally Before Making Entries

If you change the default label alignment, any new entries you make on the spreadsheet will use this setting. Existing entries will not be affected. This is especially useful when you wish to enter a series of column headings or some other information with a different alignment: you can alter the default alignment without concern for the data already on the worksheet, and then make your entries and change the alignment back to its original setting.

Let's enter some month names as column headings, using center alignment to see how this works:

1. Enter **/Worksheet Global Label Center**.

2. Move the cell pointer to B2 and type **Jan**. Then press the RIGHT ARROW key.

3. Enter **Feb** and press the RIGHT ARROW key.

4. Continue entering the month abbreviations across until you have entered **July** in H2.
    Each of your entries will be center aligned in its cell, as shown here:

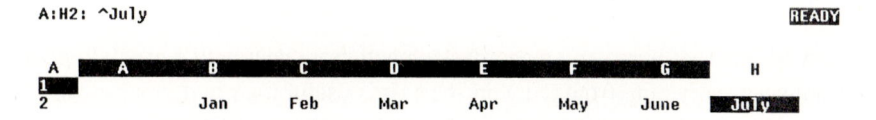

The caret symbol at the front of each entry is generated automatically by 1-2-3. Erase these entries by entering **/WEYY**.

ERASING WORKSHEET DATA

You have learned how to change worksheet entries and completely replace them with other data. However, there are times when you will want to eliminate the entries completely; they may be mistakes or old data that is no longer required. Whatever your reason for wanting to eliminate them, 1-2-3 provides a quick solution. 1-2-3 does not even care what type of entry the cell contains; it erases labels, numbers, and formulas with equal ease. The most common way to eliminate data is to erase a range of cells, which eliminates all their contents. A second approach is more extensive and thus more dangerous, since it eliminates all the entries on the entire worksheet.

To erase a range of cell entries, move the cell pointer to the upper-left cell you wish to erase and enter **/Range Erase**. In response to the prompt, move the cell pointer to the lower-right corner of the range you wish to erase and press ENTER. This eliminates not only the cell entry but also any label prefix assigned to the cell with a /Range command. Formats assigned with a /Range command are retained when the cell contents are erased and will be applied to any new entries placed in the cell. To eliminate Range formats use /Range Formet Reset.

The following data shows two entries that were made on the worksheet and finalized:

Pressing ESC will not help you eliminate either entry; both have been finalized. To eliminate the "x" that was entered in error, do the following:

1. Place the cell pointer in B1.

2. Enter **/Range Erase**.

3. Press ENTER to erase the single cell entry.

A /Worksheet Erase command packs much more destructive capability, since it eliminates everything from the worksheet. It is useful mainly if you have saved the file or have made a complete mess and want to start over. In that case, you can enter **/Worksheet Erase Yes** to effectively remove the entire worksheet from memory and start over with your entries on a blank worksheet. If the file contains entries that have not been saved, a second confirming Yes is required.

UNDOING APPEARANCE CHANGES

You have looked at 1-2-3's Undo feature for eliminating an entry from a worksheet cell, but Undo has even more power than the ability to eliminate an entry. When the Undo feature is enabled, 1-2-3 keeps track of all the activities that occur from the time that 1-2-3 is in READY mode until the next time it is in READY mode. As long as these activities only involve the current worksheet or its settings, they can be undone. External activities like printing or writing a file to a disk cannot be undone.

If you retrieve a file, format a range, or alter the width of a range of columns, 1-2-3 will be able to undo these actions as long as the Undo feature is enabled and you invoke it before performing any new activities. Once you invoke another command or make a new entry, that action is the latest action, and it would be undone when you press the ALT-F4 (UNDO) key. You must first enable Undo. If it is still at its default setting, enter **/WGDOUE**.

When you press ALT-F4 (UNDO), this selection appears:

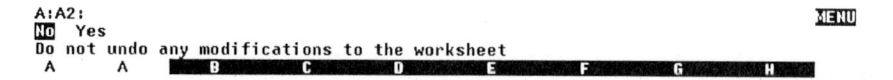

```
A:A2:                                                                    MENU
No  Yes
Do not undo any modifications to the worksheet
    A        A        B        C        D        E        F        G        H
```

1-2-3 prompts for confirmation that you want to undo the last task you performed. Type **Y** to undo the last task or **N** to return to READY mode without making the change. If you change the width of a column and press ALT-F4 (UNDO), 1-2-3 will eliminate the change in the column width.

When Undo is enabled, 1-2-3 can undo most changes that you can make to a worksheet. If you want Undo's "safety net" to protect you from mistakes like erasing the wrong range or erasing the worksheet, enter **/Worksheet Global Default Other Undo Enable** to enable it. Later, if you want to disable it, you can enter the same command sequence except for the last step, where you would choose Disable rather than Enable. Since Undo requires extra memory to undo an action, you may not be able to keep it enabled on very large worksheets.

To see how the Undo feature can help you, first check to make sure Undo is enabled and then follow these steps:

1. Retrieve the VEHICLES file created earlier in the chapter by entering **/File Retrieve**, typing **VEHICLES**, and pressing ENTER.

2. Move the cell pointer to column B. Then enter **/Worksheet Column Column-Range Set-Width**, highlight columns B through D by using the RIGHT ARROW key, and press ENTER. Then type **20** and press ENTER.

Notice that the columns become much wider.

3. Press ALT-F4 (UNDO).

4. Type **Y** for Yes.

    The columns return to the width they had before you executed the last command.

5. Enter **/Worksheet Erase Yes Yes**.

    1-2-3 clears the screen, and the model is removed from memory.

6. Press the ALT-F4 (UNDO) key to have 1-2-3 restore the worksheet in memory.

7. Type **Y** for Yes.

The Undo feature prevents you from accidentally performing a step you do not want. Remember, however, that 1-2-3 can only undo one step.

MAKING A
WORKSHEET MAP

Earlier in the chapter, you used the /Worksheet Status command to display worksheet settings. Release 3 can also display information about the worksheet cells, telling you which cells contain values, labels, and formulas. You can use this feature to see the types of data in various worksheet cells or to correct errors. By seeing the types of data stored in cells, you can find any labels that should be values or any values that should be formulas.

The /Worksheet Window Map Enable command quickly provides a *map view* of the worksheet. Figure 3-24 shows a map view of the REALEST worksheet. The double quotes (") represent cells containing labels, the # represents cells containing numbers, and the + represents cells containing formulas or annotated numbers. While the worksheet appears like this, you cannot continue working on it; 1-2-3 does not update the map. If you prefer the normal display, you can return to it by pressing ENTER, ESC, or CTRL-BREAK. 1-2-3 then returns to READY mode and changes the map display to the normal display.

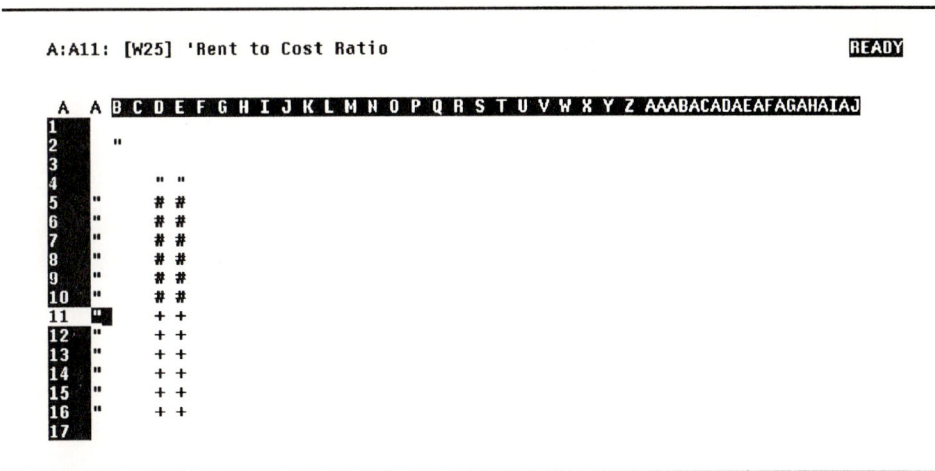

A:A11: [W25] 'Rent to Cost Ratio   READY

FIGURE 3-24.   Map view of REALEST worksheet

REVIEW EXERCISE

You can practice some of the techniques covered in this chapter by completing the price update model shown in Figure 3-25.

1. Enter the labels in column A exactly as shown. *Hint:* Use /Worksheet Column Set-Width to widen column A to accommodate your entries.

2. Enter the labels in row 2.

A:A1: [W25]   READY

	A	B	C	D	E
1		1989		1990	
2	Item	Price	%Chg	Price	
3	Transparencies (50)	$37.95	5.15%	$39.90	
4	Felt-tip pens (12)	$6.75	7.00%	$7.22	
5	Walnut credenza	$189.50	12.00%	$212.24	
6					

FIGURE 3-25.   Review exercise model to record price changes

3. Set 1-2-3 to format the worksheet cells automatically. *Hint:* You might use /Range Format Other Automatic and select A1..D5 as the format range, or use /Worksheet Global Format Other Automatic.

4. Enter the numbers shown in columns B and C. *Hint:* The first percent entry is entered as **5.15%**.

5. Change the width of column B through D to 10.

6. Change the alignment of the entries in B1..D2 to right aligned. *Hint:* Use the /Range Label command.

7. Enter the formulas for the price changes for 1989. *Hint:* The formula in D3 should be +B3*(1+C3). You will need to use /Range Format.

8. Hide the column containing the percentage change. *Hint:* Use the /Worksheet Column Hide command and select column C.

REVIEW

- Other than basic entries and function-key options, all of 1-2-3's features can be accessed with selections from a series of menus. The main menu is invoked by typing /.

- You can select an option from any menu by highlighting your selection and pressing ENTER. Typing the first letter of the menu selection works the same way.

- Use the ESC key to back out of the menu by one level.

- You can format numeric entries to match your needs. The /Range Format command will format a contiguous group of cells. The /Worksheet Global Format command sets the default format and will format any numeric entry not formatted with the /Range Format command. Formats established with the /Range command are shown in the top line of the control panel. Release 3 adds an Automatic format where 1-2-3 determines the appropriate format for every cell based on the formatting characters you include in the entry.

- You can change the column width of one or more worksheet cells. Use the /Worksheet Global Col-Width command to change the width of any cells for which an individual width is not set. Use /Worksheet Column to change the width of the current column. Use /Worksheet Column Column-Range to change the width of a group of columns. A column width established for an individual column is shown in the top line of the control panel.

- You can insert and delete rows and columns. When you delete a row or a column, you delete the contents of all the cells in the row or column.

- You can hide columns of data and redisplay them. Use this feature to remove confidential information from the worksheet area of the screen.

- You can erase a group of cells with /Range Erase and the entire worksheet with /Worksheet Erase. With Undo enabled, you can undo either of these actions with ALT-F4 (UNDO).

- Use /Worksheet Global Label to change the alignment for entries you are about to make. Use /Range Label to alter the alignment of existing label entries.

- Use /Worksheet Status to review the current Global settings.

- Use the /Worksheet Window Map command to quickly see which cells in a worksheet contain labels, values, and formulas.

Commands and Keys

/	Invokes the menu
ESC	Backs you out of the menu by one step
CTRL-BREAK	Backs you all the way out of the menu to READY mode, no matter how many levels deep you are in the menu
/RE	/Range Erase eliminates entries from a contiguous group of worksheet
/RF	/Range Format allows you to change the appearance of numeric entries in a contiguous group of worksheet cells
/RL	/Range Label allows you to change the alignment of a contiguous group of label entries on a worksheet
/WCCS	/Worksheet Column Column-Range Set-Width changes the width of a contiguous group of worksheet columns
/WCS	/Worksheet Column Set-Width changes the width of the current worksheet column
/WCH	/Worksheet Column Hide removes a column from display, although the column remains in the worksheet
/WD	/Worksheet Delete allows you to delete a contiguous group of worksheet rows or columns
/WGC	/Worksheet Global Col-Width changes the width of all columns that have not been set individually with the /Worksheet Column or /Worksheet Column Column-Range commands

/WGF   /Worksheet Global Format changes the format of all worksheet
              cells whose formats have not been set with the /Range Format
              command
/WI   /Worksheet Insert allows you to insert blank rows and columns
              on a worksheet
/WWME   /Worksheet Window Map changes the display to show " for label
              entries, # for numeric entries, and + for formula entries and use
              ESC, ENTER, or CTRL-BREAK to return to the normal display

4

WORKING
WITH FILES

New computer users always find the concept of files a little difficult to understand. This is partly because you cannot *see* a file the way you can see entries that you place on the worksheet. But computer files are really quite simple to work with. They are very similar to the files you use every day for storing written documents in your office. The main difference is that computer files are stored on a disk instead of in a drawer.

In this chapter you will learn about basic file concepts and explore the basic file commands that 1-2-3 has to offer. You will then learn about a 1-2-3 command that allows you to exit 1-2-3 temporarily and access the file-handling features of your computer's operating system. Although Release 3 can have several files open at once, this chapter focuses on using one file at a time. After you master the basics of working with files, you can refer to Chapter 12 to learn how you can use multiple files at once.

FILE CONCEPTS

Every day, you undoubtedly work with a number of different pieces of paper. Periodically, you probably place some of these papers into file folders in a cabinet or desk drawer to make space for new information on your desktop. Then, when you want to review these papers again, you search for them in the cabinet or you ask your secretary to bring you the file folder you wish to see. Assuming that you have an organized filing system, the papers you want will arrive back on your desk.

Your computer uses very similar procedures to maintain its information. Taking a look at the similarities and differences will help you understand the important role that files can play for you.

Storing Information on Disk

When you store information in your computer, you provide the machine with an organizational challenge similar to the one faced by you or your secretary. In the computer's case, the "desktop" is *RAM memory,* the temporary memory of the system; and like your desktop, it has a limited amount of space. How much space is available in memory will dictate how much information you can place in memory at any one time. Part of this space can be used for a program such as 1-2-3; another part can be used to store worksheets that you are building with the package.

Just as you use file folders to store papers, your computer uses disk files to store information. The computer's files are maintained on disk rather than in a cabinet. When you build a model, it will be stored in the computer's desktop—its temporary memory. You generally will want to store a copy of this model in a file on your disk before you exit 1-2-3 or before you start creating a second model. This will make it possible for the computer to recall the first model another time so that you can work on it again.

TEMPORARY NATURE OF MEMORY   When working with a computer, you need to save your model before you complete it; 1-2-3 does not automatically maintain a permanent record of your model. As soon as you turn your system off or exit 1-2-3 (whether deliberately or accidentally), the model is lost from memory. In order to use this model again, you must already have stored a copy of it in a file on your disk. The disk provides more permanent storage because its contents are not lost when the power is off in your computer. As long as you store the file on disk, you can retrieve a copy of the file from disk and place it in the memory of your computer system again. The addition of a prompt message when you attempt to exit from 1-2-3 will remind you if you have not as yet saved changes to the current worksheet.

DISK COPIES When you are working with data in the form of papers stored in your office files and you retrieve those papers so you can work with them again, the file no longer contains them. But storing data in computer disk files works differently. Once you store a model on disk, it remains there until you take some special action to remove it from the disk. Even when you retrieve a copy of the model to place it in memory again, the original is maintained on the disk. This feature offers a tremendous advantage over paper storage methods: if you accidentally destroy the copy in the computer's memory, you can always retrieve another copy of the model from the disk.

Organizing the Disk Data

When you create file folders for your office, you probably have a system—even a rudimentary one—for labeling these files. One rule of your system is probably that no two folders should have exactly the same label. If they did, you would have a lot of difficulty finding the papers you need once they were filed. Perhaps your system for labeling file folders is quite organized. It may include color coding or some other scheme that makes it easy to categorize your files.

Storing files on disk also requires a system. Part of this system involves rigid rules you must follow; there is also room for some flexibility, however, so that you can personalize the system to suit your needs. You need not be concerned with the specifics of how the data is stored on disk. Your only concern is the rules that you need to follow when working with these files, especially rules that center around the names you use for your files and the location of these files when they are stored.

FILENAMES Before you can store a file on your disk, you must determine what to name it. Since the naming process follows particular, although somewhat flexible, rules, first review the options before considering the mechanics for storing the file.

Each file on a disk must have a unique name. This name will consist of from one to eight characters. You can create a name using the alphabetic characters, numeric digits, and some of the special symbols. Since it can be difficult to remember which symbols are permissible and which are not, it is best to limit your use of special symbols to the _ (underline) symbol, which is particularly useful as a separator in a filename. For example, the name Sales_87 might be used to store the sales data for 1987. Be aware even though 1-2-3 will let you include spaces in a filename, the spaces will cause confusion with some DOS commands. Sales 87 is a valid filename, but Sales_87 is a better one.

Although there is no flexibility in the rules just discussed, you can assign the eight allowable characters any way you like. It is best to develop some consistent rules for naming your data, because consistency can help you determine a file's contents when

Extension	Use
.WK3	Worksheet file in Release 3 format
.WK1	Worksheet file in Release 2, 2.01, and 2.2 format
.WKS	Worksheet file in Release 1A format
.BAK	Backup of Release 3 or 2.2 worksheet
.CGM or .PIC	1-2-3 graph files
.PRN	Print files
.ENC	Print files containing printer codes
.COM or .EXE	Executable program files
.BAT	DOS batch files

TABLE 4-1.   Common Filename Extensions

you see the filename later on. If you are storing sales data for a number of years, keeping one year's worth of data in each file, you could use the method already described and create names such as Sales_89 and Sales_90. You could also use names such as 90_Sales or Sls1990. It really does not matter what pattern you select for your names; what is important is that once you decide on a naming pattern, you apply it consistently for each file that you create. Naming files 88_Sales, Sales_87, Sls_1990, and Sales91 is not a good strategy; the pattern is too inconsistent. It is also best not to begin a filename with a number to insure upward compatibility with later mainframe versions of the package. You can enter filenames in either uppercase or lowercase letters or in a combination of the two. Regardless of which type of entry you make, it will be translated into uppercase. All filenames are stored in uppercase on the disk.

You can also add filename *extensions*. An extension consists of one to three optional characters added at the end of a filename. They too can be entered in upper- or lowercase. They are separated from a filename by a period. For example, in Sales_87.WK3, the filename extension is .WK3. Extensions can be used to categorize files or to provide an extra three characters of description. Some programs automatically add extensions for you. 1-2-3 does this. Table 4-1 shows some of the most common filename extensions that you will encounter and the types of files they are used for.

The file extension 1-2-3 assigns to a file depends on the release you are using. 1-2-3 assigns a .WK3 file extension to Release 3 worksheet files. Previous releases use .WK1 for Release 2 worksheet files and .WKS for Release 1A worksheet files. With Release 3, you can create a backup copy of a worksheet file with the extension .BAK.

1-2-3 has other filenames that it uses when data other than models are stored in files. Later in this book you will learn that you can create a graph on the screen and save a copy of this image on disk. Such files are automatically assigned the filename extension .CGM (or .PIC if you execute the /Worksheet Global Default Graph PIC command). You will also learn that you can print a copy of your model to the printer or to the disk if you prefer. When you print to the disk, the print output is stored in a file with the extension .PRN. You do not need to memorize this information; 1-2-3 handles it all for you. You only need to realize what these extensions are when you want to work directly with the data stored on your disk, using commands from your operating system. The filename extensions appear when you use operating-system commands. They could cause confusion if you were not at least aware that 1-2-3 was creating them and using them to distinguish different types of files.

LOCATION OF YOUR DATA   Files can be stored on either hard or floppy disks. The lower-cost hard disks, thanks to today's technology, are popular storage media for business computer systems. A floppy disk holds from 360,000 to over 1,440,000 characters, depending on whether you are using the standard double-sided, double-density disks or the new high-density disks. Today's typical hard disk installed in a computer system has a capacity of over 20,000,000 characters of information.

When new files are added to floppy disks, their names are added to a *directory* on the disk that keeps track of every file on the disk. Although you could use a single directory to maintain a hard disk, such a directory could become so lengthy that it would be difficult to work with. This would be like having a single index to catalog a whole library of reference volumes; it would take a long time to read. It would be better if each book in the collection had its own index, and if books had chapter outlines that could be referenced for contents.

To lessen the burden of the main disk index, you can set up *subdirectories* for your hard disk. Subdirectories function as a second-level index to group files that are related. You can create these groupings on any basis you like, including for each individual that uses the system, for each application category on the system, or by application program. In all cases, common files such as DOS utilities are usually maintained in the *root directory* (the main directory on the disk). When subdirectories are added, their names are placed in the root directory; however, the names of the files they contain are kept in the subdirectory, not in the root directory. Subdirectories are organized in a hierarchical structure, as shown in Figure 4-1. Here, the entries in the main directory include two references to subdirectories. These subdirectories must be created through commands in your operating system. Although 1-2-3 cannot create the directories, it will use whichever directory is current on the hard disk, and it gives you commands that let you activate another directory.

1-2-3 always assumes that you want to work with files on the *current* or *default directory*. This means that if you are content to use the current directory, you do not need to specify it when saving your data. However, if you want to use a different disk drive or a directory other than the current default, you must either change the default

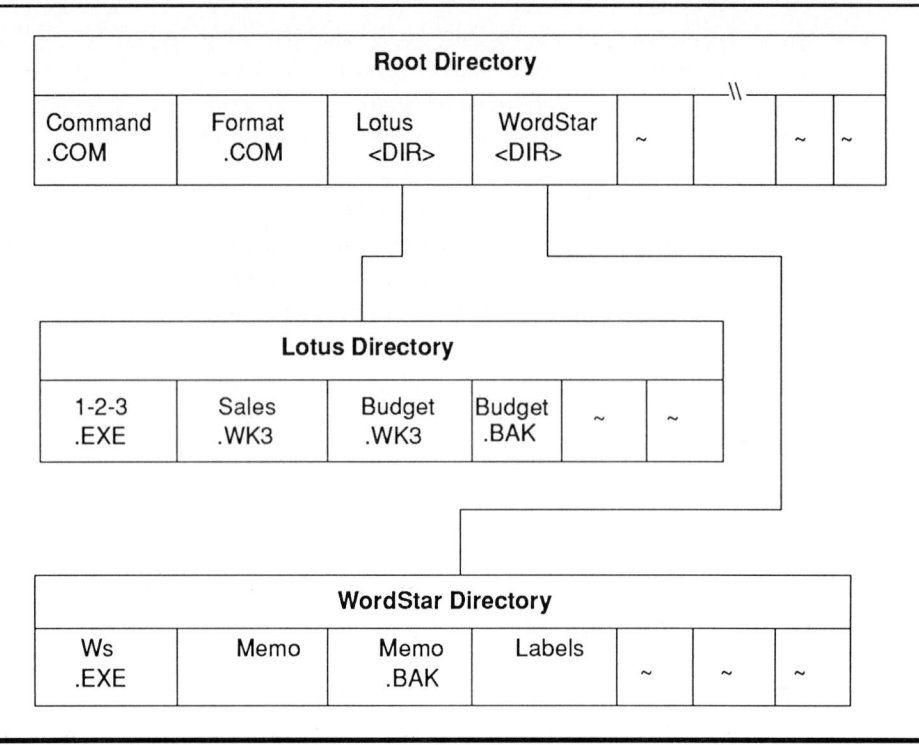

FIGURE 4-1.   Hierarchical directory structure

or enter the file location along with the filename. You will look at both of these possibilities in the following section on 1-2-3 commands.

1-2-3 FILE COMMANDS

The commands on 1-2-3's menu help you handle your file- management tasks. There are menu selections for saving your data into disk files and for retrieving copies of these files to place in memory. 1-2-3 has grouped each of the file-management commands under the selection File option in the main menu. You can bring this menu to your screen by entering /**File**. The following will appear:

```
A:A1:                                                             MENU
Retrieve  Save  Combine  Xtract  Erase  List  Import  Dir  New  Open  Admin
Replace the current file with a file from disk
```

You will have an opportunity to try many of these commands in the following sections.

Saving Files

1-2-3 does not save your files automatically—it is your responsibility to save the data you enter in memory. It is best to do this periodically; do not wait until you are ending your 1-2-3 session before you save data for the first time. A good guideline is to save every 20 to 30 minutes so you can never lose more than 20 to 30 minutes of your work, even if the power goes off unexpectedly.

SAVING THE FIRST TIME Saving a file for the first time is a little different with Release 3 than with other releases. 1-2-3 suggests a filename even though the file has not been saved before. The name suggested is FILE*xxxx,* where *xxxx* is replaced by the next unused sequential number (as in FILE0005). You can either accept this filename or provide one of your own. If you are saving onto floppy disks, you also need to ensure that a formatted disk is placed in the current drive. At this point, make a few entries on the current screen and then save the data.

1. Erase memory by entering /**Worksheet Erase Yes.** You will need to enter a second Yes if you have not saved the entries in memory.

2. Move the cell pointer to B2 and type **Qtr1.** Press the RIGHT ARROW key. Type **Qtr2** through **Qtr4** in C2 through E2, as follows:

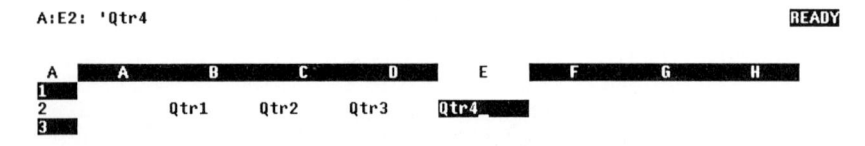

3. Enter /**File Save** to produce the following display:

FILE followed by four digits is 1-2-3's suggestion for a filename. You can use 1-2-3's suggestion or provide a more meaningful name for the file by typing a new name.

4. Type **QTRSALES** and press ENTER to supply the name to use when storing your data.

After you have completed the last entry, the disk drive light will come on momentarily while your data is being written to disk. When the file has been placed on the disk, the indicator light will change from its WAIT status back to READY. At this point you can continue to work on the model or start a new one, since you know that this one has been saved to the disk. For now, you will want to make some additions to it to see how the process differs for subsequent saves.

SUBSEQUENT SAVES   Each time you save a model that is already on disk, you have the choice of replacing the copy on the disk with the information that is currently stored in memory or of entering a new name. If you have saved the model previously, 1-2-3's default will be to save the model under this name. A new Release 3 option allows you to copy the old version of the file to a backup file before saving the file.

Make the following changes to the model and save the model again with these steps:

1. Move the cell pointer to A3 and type **Sales**. Press the DOWN ARROW key. Type **Expenses** in A4 and **Profit** in A5.

2. Enter /**File Save**. 1-2-3 will present this display:

Notice that 1-2-3 is suggesting that the file be saved under the same name you used previously.

3. Press ENTER. 1-2-3 will present this menu:

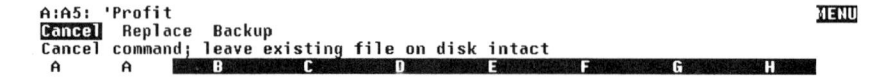

1-2-3 is asking if you wish to cancel the save request, replace the copy of the model stored on disk with the current contents of memory, or back up the original file, using the same filename but with a new filename extension (.BAK) for the original file and the same filename with a .WK3 extension for the current contents of memory.

4. Enter **Replace**. 1-2-3 will save the updated model under the name you used previously.

If you want to save a model under a new name, 1-2-3 also makes this possible. When 1-2-3 suggests that you use the original name, all you need to do is type a new name. Then, when you press ENTER, the file will be saved under the new name. This feature is especially useful when you need to create two similar copies of a model; you can create identical entries on both files and then save the model under two different names before entering the changes on the duplicate file.

You can also save a file to a directory other than the current one. To do this, specify the directory you want when you use /File Save. If 1-2-3 suggests that you use C:\LOTUS\QTRSALES but you wish to use A:SALES, when 1-2-3 presents its suggestion do the following:

1. Press HOME to move to the "C" at the beginning.

2. Press the DEL key until the filename is displayed as SALES.

3. Type **A:** to supply the drive.

4. Press ENTER to use the modified filename.

Another option is pressing ESC until 1-2-3 removes the filename, the directory, and the drive, and then entering the full drive, directory, and filename. (If you want 1-2-3 to save to the current drive, you can omit the drive and directory.) Using the example just described, you could press ESC three times to remove the directory and type **A:\SALES** before pressing ENTER.

MAKING A BACKUP COPY OF THE WORKSHEET   Sometimes when you revise a document, you keep the previous version of the document in the file cabinet along with the current version. If you revise a budget projection, for example, you may keep the previous projection until after the budget meeting for comparison purposes. You can then refer to the previous copy in case you want to revert to any of the old projections, or you can use it as a backup in case you lose the later copy.

Release 3 offers the same feature for your worksheet files. The third choice in the /File Save command is Backup. When you select this option, the worksheet file stored on disk with a .WK3 extension is copied to a file with the same name but with a .BAK extension. Then 1-2-3 saves the current worksheet with the .WK3 extension. As an example, make the following changes to the model and save the model again with these steps:

1. Move the cell pointer to A1 and type **ABC Company**. Press ENTER.

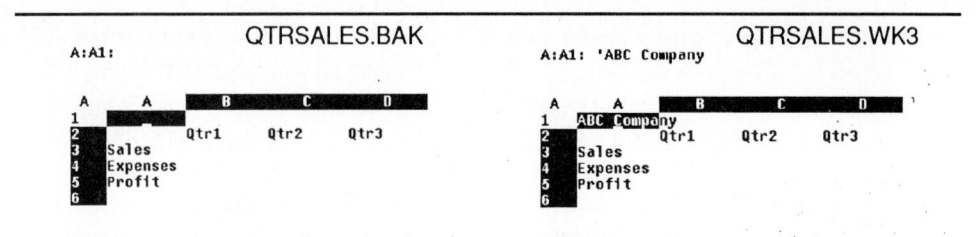

FIGURE 4-2.   Worksheet file and backup file

2. Enter **/File Save**. 1-2-3 suggests that the file be saved under the same name you used previously.

3. Press ENTER. 1-2-3 displays the Save, Backup, and Replace options.

4. Enter **Backup**. 1-2-3 saves the updated model under the name you used previously. The previous version of the file is saved with a .BAK extension.

For a closer look at what the /File Save Backup feature offers, imagine looking inside the QTRSALES.WK3 and QTRSALES.BAK files. Their contents are shown in Figure 4-2. On the left side, the QTRSALES.BAK file does not have "ABC Company" in the upper-left corner of the worksheet—this file contains the worksheet as it existed after the previous save operation. On the right side, the QTRSALES.WK3 file has "ABC Company" in the upper-left corner—it was created by the most recent save operation. If you ever need to use the backup version, you can use it just as you would use a normal worksheet file. Each time you backup the file, 1-2-3 replaces the .BAK file with the .WK3 file on disk, and then it copies the worksheet in 1-2-3's memory to disk using the .WK3 extension. Using the Backup option always allows you to access the current file and its most recent previous version.

Retrieving Files

A file-retrieve operation reads a worksheet file from disk and places it in the memory of your computer. When it places the model in memory, it erases the memory's previous contents. This means that you must always save a copy of your worksheets in memory in order to retain a copy before you bring another worksheet into memory. Of course, if the Undo feature is enabled, you can use it to eliminate a big mistake (like retrieving a file before saving the current file) as long as you remember to use it immediately after retrieving the file.

RETRIEVING FROM THE CURRENT DRIVE   When you want to bring a worksheet file into memory, you usually want to use the default drive, since this is the same drive you have been using for data storage. If you don't take any special action, 1-2-3 assumes that this is where it should look for worksheet files and automatically displays a list of all the worksheet files on the drive. Release 3 even displays the file list in alphabetical sequence to make it easy for you to find the file you want. You can press F3 (NAME) to see a full-screen listing of all the filenames.

You can select a file by pointing to it with the highlighted bar 1-2-3 provides. You can also type the name of the file from your keyboard, either before or after 1-2-3 displays its list. However, one thing you cannot do is use the first-letter entry method, since 1-2-3 is presenting a list of names instead of menu options. This feature will work with all of 1-2-3's other menus, but not with a /File Retrieve operation.

Follow these steps to retrieve the QTRSALES file from the disk in the current directory:

1. Enter **/File Retrieve**.

   A list of filenames similar to this will appear:

```
A:A5: 'Profit                                                    FILES
Enter name of file to retrieve: C:\123R3\*.WK*
7_11.WK3              7_11.WKS           7_12.WK3           7_9.WK3
```

2. Use the arrow keys to move the highlighted bar through the list until it is on QTRSALES. Then press ENTER.

If you need additional information about the files to make a selection, you can press F3 (NAME) before you make a selection. 1-2-3 expands the list to provide information on the size of each file and the date and time each file was created, as shown in Figure 4-3.

If you need to retrieve a backup file, you must type the filename and include the .BAK extension. For example, to retrieve the backup of QTRSALES.WK3 you would enter **QTRSALES.BAK** for the filename to retrieve. Typing the filename is required since 1-2-3 only displays files with a .WK3 extension.

```
A:A5: 'Profit                                                    FILES
Enter name of file to retrieve: C:\123R3\*.WK*
         7_11.WK3       27-Feb-90      07:32 PM      988
7_11.WK3              7_11.WKS           7_12.WK3           7_9.WK3
A.WK1                 A.WK3              BASS.WK3           BUDGET.WK3
B.WK3                 COMM.WK1           C.WK3              DEPREC.WK1
D.WK3                 EMP2.WK3           EMPLOYEE.WK1       EMP.WK3
E.WK3                 FC029A.WK3         FC5_1.WK3          FC6_18.WK3
```

FIGURE 4-3.   Expanding the list for files to retrieve

RETRIEVING FROM ANOTHER LOCATION   Release 3 lets you retrieve a file that is not on the current disk or in the current directory, but the retrieve procedure changes slightly. To change the directory for a retrieve operation, you must override the current directory setting for this one activity. The difference in the process is subtle: you begin and end the same way as usual, but you change the directory in the middle.

Assuming that you want to retrieve a file that is in a different directory on your hard disk or on a floppy disk that you have inserted in a disk drive, use these steps to try the procedure:

1. Enter /**File Retrieve**.

2. Press ESC twice to delete the reference to the current drive and directory. The following display appears:

```
A:A5: 'Profit                                                    EDIT
Enter name of file to retrieve: _
```

3. Type in the full name of your file, including its path and directory, and press ENTER.

Determining What Files Are On Your Disk

Just as you might look at the names of the different file folders in an office file cabinet, sometimes you may wish to look through the names of the files on your disk. The /File List command will handle this type of request for you. It lets you determine what types of files you want to view by offering this menu selection:

```
A:A5: 'Profit                                                    MENU
Worksheet  Print  Graph  Other  Active  Linked
List worksheet files
```

Since 1-2-3 stores worksheet, print, graph, and other types of files on the disk, these are your options when entering the command from Release 3. (Active files, new to Release 3, are covered in Chapter 12. Linked files, also new, are covered in Chapter 11.) 1-2-3 checks the files whose filename extension corresponds to the type of file you choose. Enter the following sequence of commands to view all the worksheet files on your disk:

1. Enter /**File List**.

2. Enter **Worksheet**.

```
A:A5: 'Profit                                                      FILES
Enter names of files to list: C:\123R3\*.WK*
        7_11.WK3        27-Feb-90      07:32 PM      988
7_11.WK3            7_11.WKS         7_12.WK3          7_9.WK3
A.WK1              A.WK3            BASS.WK3          BUDGET.WK3
B.WK3              COMM.WK1         C.WK3             DEPREC.WK1
D.WK3              EMP2.WK3         EMPLOYEE.WK1      EMP.WK3
E.WK3              FC029A.WK3       FC5_1.WK3         FC6_18.WK3
```

FIGURE 4-4.   Exploring the list of files on your disk

3. Move the highlighted bar around in the list to point to various filenames.

As each filename is highlighted, an expanded description of the file entry appears at the top of the screen, as shown in Figure 4-4. This extra information allows you to determine the date and time for the last file update. It also lets you see the relative size of the file.

4. Press ENTER to return to READY mode.

To list files on another disk or in another directory, use the approach described in the preceding discussion for retrieving from another disk. When you are presented with the list, press ESC twice to delete the reference to the current directory, and type in a new drive or directory designation before pressing ENTER.

Removing Files from the Disk

The files that you save on your disk are retained indefinitely. In fact, 1-2-3 never eliminates any of them; it will remove a file only if you make a specific request for it to do so. The command used for eliminating files is /File Erase. To remove a file from your disk, follow these steps. (Execute them only if you have a file you wish to eliminate—these steps work!)

1. Enter /**File Erase**.

This produces the following display, which lets you select the type of file you want to erase:

```
A:A5: 'Profit                                                      MENU
Worksheet  Print  Graph  Other
Erase a worksheet file
```

2. Enter **Worksheet** to produce a list of your worksheet files like this:

```
A:A5: 'Profit                                                      FILES
Enter name of file to erase: C:\123R3\*.WK*
7_11.WK3            7_11.WKS         7_12.WK3          7_9.WK3
```

If you wish to expand this list to include file sizes and date and time stamps, press F3 (NAME).

3. Use the arrow keys to position the highlighted bar on the file that you want to permanently remove from the disk, and press ENTER.

4. Enter **Yes** to confirm that you want to delete the file.

Once you have deleted a file, there is no practical way to restore it. There are utility programs that can restore a file that has been deleted in this fashion, but they are not part of 1-2-3 and most of them require some technical expertise to use effectively. Therefore, be extremely cautious when you are removing files from the disk.

Changing the Directory

1-2-3's dependence on a current directory—the drive and subdirectory you are using—saves you a considerable amount of time. Since you are working with a hard disk system, your data will probably be stored in a subdirectory. To work in it for a period of time, you need to be able to change to another one. A current directory means that 1-2-3 assumes that the directory you are referencing is the current default unless you specify otherwise. If you keep it set to the drive and directory containing your data, you will not need to enter the directory in order to make most of your file requests. However, 1-2-3 does provide capabilities that let you alter the directory setting. This means that when you want to work with worksheet files that are on the floppy disk in drive A, it will be easy to have the directory set at drive C and alter it to a floppy drive.

USING ANOTHER DRIVE   As computers and software technology increase, computers provide more data storage areas. You can store your data on a floppy disk or one or more hard drives. While Release 3 keeps its program information on a hard disk, you can use any disk drive to store the data. If you change the current drive to a floppy disk drive, you must insert a formatted disk into the drive before changing the current directory, since 1-2-3 will read the current directory before allowing you to change it. Before making the change, insert a formatted disk in drive A for data storage; 1-2- 3 will check this drive as it changes the directory. To make the directory change, follow these steps:

1. Enter **/File Dir**.

2. Enter **A:** and then press ENTER.

CHANGING HARD DISK DIRECTORIES   You have already seen how you can access data on another disk or in another directory on a one-time basis with the /File Retrieve and /File Save commands. Each time you wish to use a directory other than the current one, you must enter the complete *pathname* for the file. The pathname includes the disk drive and an optional subdirectory along with the filename. This approach is cumbersome if you have to use information in these other locations repeatedly.

A better solution is to make the other disk or directory the active one. You also use the /File Dir command to change the active directory on your hard disk. First you must enter **/File Dir**. The current directory is then displayed. In this example, the current directory is C:\123R3\:

```
A:A1:                                                         EDIT
Enter current directory: A:\_
```

Next, type the new directory. If the new directory were C:\ACCT\, you would type **C:\ACCT**. The new directory must already exist; 1-2-3 will not create a directory that does not already exist. You can also type in a drive designator if you want to start using one of the floppy disks for storage and retrieval.

A TEMPORARY EXIT TO
THE OPERATING SYSTEM

In Release 3, 1-2-3's /System command allows you to exit from 1-2-3 temporarily to perform file-management tasks directly with the operating system. Since 1-2-3 provides a number of file-management commands in its menu structure, it is easier to use 1-2-3's menu selection where these commands are available. However, DOS commands are useful for performing tasks that 1-2-3's menu does not support. Before examining how the system feature works, let's cover a few basics about your computer's operating system.

The Operating System

The operating system that your computer uses is in some ways similar to a foreman in a production environment. A foreman manages the operation of the production line and coordinates the resources required to complete a job. The operating system in your computer is a program that manages the tasks that your computer performs and coordinates the resources required to complete a task. It must always be in memory along with 1-2-3 or any other application program, to ensure that these programs can access the resources of the computer system.

The operating system you will be using on your computer is MS-DOS, PC-DOS, or OS/2. The letters in the "OS" or "DOS" portion of these names stand for "Operating System," and all of these systems are commonly referred to as DOS. Even though this is not accurate in some cases, since DOS has been the most prevalent operating system, most people will assume that is the operating system you are using.

BASIC FEATURES

Some of the basic tasks that the operating system performs are reading and writing data to and from the disk. The operating system also contains a variety of utility programs that copy files or disks, prepare disks for data storage, and check the directory of a disk. You can use these utility features before you enter a program like 1-2-3 to handle many tasks relating to file and disk information. After you place an application program like 1-2-3 in the memory of your machine, you usually cannot access the operating system features any longer. With Release 3 of 1-2-3, Lotus has provided a temporary exit from 1-2-3 that retains all of your current worksheet data in memory while you work with DOS tasks.

Types of DOS
Tasks to Perform

Once you are in 1-2-3, you usually want to forget about the operating system and enjoy the ease with which you can use 1-2-3's menu to handle tasks. But there are exceptions. One of the most important of these is when you want to save data on a disk and don't have a formatted disk available to save it on. Without the /System feature, if you do not have a formatted disk available, you cannot save files to a floppy disk. With the /System feature, you can exit temporarily and format another disk, and then use the newly formatted disk to save your data. You can also make a copy of a file on your disk to give to another business associate: you can remain in 1-2-3, temporarily switch to DOS to complete your task, and switch back again. The steps for each of these special uses are covered in the following sections.

USING /SYSTEM TO PREPARE A DISK   The DOS command for preparing a disk is FORMAT. In the following exercise, you will use this command to format a blank disk that you will place in drive A. Follow these steps to complete the exercise and return to 1-2-3:

1. Enter /**System**.

2. Type **FORMAT A:** and press ENTER.

3. Place a blank disk in drive A in response to the following prompt on your screen:

   Insert new diskette for drive A:
   and strike ENTER when ready

4. Press ENTER to begin formatting.

5. Type **N** and press ENTER to indicate that you do not want to format additional disks.

6. Type **EXIT** and press ENTER to return to 1-2-3.

A transcript of the entries for this process through step 5 is shown in Figure 4-5. Your display will look similar. However, if any bad sectors were encountered in your disk, FORMAT will skip them and notify you that it has done so with a message about the number of bad sectors excluded.

```
(Type EXIT and press [ENTER] to return to 1-2-3)


The IBM Personal Computer DOS
Version 3.30 (C)Copyright International Business Machines Corp 1981, 1987
              (C)Copyright Microsoft Corp 1981, 1986

C>format a:
Insert new diskette for drive A:
and strike ENTER when ready

Format complete

   1457664 bytes total disk space
   1457664 bytes available on disk

Format another (Y/N)?n
C>
```

FIGURE 4-5.   Using the /System feature to prepare a disk

When DOS formats a disk it uses the FORMAT.COM program, which is supplied on your operating system disk. The directory that contains FORMAT.COM must be the active directory when you type the format instructions or you must have a PATH statement active that points to the correct directory. If FORMAT.COM is not in the current directory, type **CD ** before executing step 2 in the instructions. This changes the directory to the root directory on your hard disk; presumably, you will have a copy of FORMAT.COM stored there.

USING /SYSTEM TO COPY A FILE   You can use the DOS COPY command to copy a file on your disk to another disk without leaving 1-2-3. To copy the SALES file from the disk in drive A to a formatted disk in drive B and return to your task in 1-2-3, follow these steps:

1. Enter **/System**.

2. Place the disk containing SALES in drive A and the formatted disk in drive B.

3. Type **COPY A:SALES.WK3 B:** and press ENTER.
    The filename extension .WK3 was used in this example. After 1-2-3 has completed the task, the screen will appear as follows:

```
C>copy a:sales.wk3 b:
        1 File(s) copied

C>
```

4. Type **EXIT** and press ENTER.

USING /SYSTEM TO CREATE A NEW DIRECTORY   You can create a new subdirectory for your hard disk without leaving 1-2-3. This option lets you create a *logical section* on the disk, which you can begin to use for specialized storage of worksheet data or other information. In the following example, the subdirectory will be added directly to the root directory of the disk, which is the main directory. In most cases, this is where directories should be added. Using too many levels causes confusion and makes it difficult to locate individual files. Follow these steps if you have a hard disk and wish to establish a subdirectory called BUDGET:

1. Save your current worksheet and clear memory with **/WEY** if data from a previous task remains on your screen. You may need to enter a second Y if the data in memory has not been saved.

2. Enter **/System**.

3. Type **cd ** to make the root directory active.

```
(Type EXIT and press [RETURN] to return to 1-2-3)


The IBM Personal Computer DOS
Version 3.30 (C)Copyright International Business Machines Corp 1981, 1987
                (C)Copyright Microsoft Corp 1981, 1986
C>cd\

C>md\budget

C>cd\budget

C>
```

FIGURE 4-6.   Creating a subdirectory

4. Type **md \budget** to create a subdirectory named BUDGET.

5. Type **cd \budget** to make your new directory active.
    Figure 4-6 shows the transcript of your DOS entries on the screen up to this point.

6. Perform any DOS tasks you wish in this directory.

7. Type **EXIT** and press ENTER to return to 1-2-3.

Note that the current 1-2-3 directory has not changed. To use this new directory, use the /File Dir command to change the current directory.

Returning to 1-2-3

You may have noticed in the previous examples that when you finished entering DOS commands, you returned to 1-2-3 by typing **EXIT** and pressing ENTER. When you exit to DOS and return, everything is the same as it was before you entered the /System request. The same worksheet will be on the screen, and 1-2-3 will be ready to continue where you left off.

REVIEW EXERCISE

In the following exercise, you will practice saving and retrieving a document. Then you will try other 1-2-3 commands like /File List and /System.

1. Clear any existing worksheet entries with the /Worksheet Erase Yes command.

2. Enter **Sales Report** in A1. Press DOWN ARROW twice to move to A3. Enter **Area** in A3, **East** in A4, and **West** in A5.

3. Enter **1988** in B3, **70000** in B4, and **50000** in B5.

4. Save the file using the /File Save command. Save the file as **AREASALE**.

5. Erase the worksheet in the computer's memory. (*Hint:* Use the /Worksheet Erase command.) The file that you just saved is still saved to the disk.

6. Retrieve the AREASALE worksheet. *Hint:* Use the /File Retrieve command. Highlight the filename or type **AREASALE** and press ENTER.

7. Find the file in the directories listing using the /File List Worksheet command. Move the highlight to your AREASALE worksheet file. Notice the date and time.

8. Find the file using the operating system. Use the /System command to exit temporarily to DOS. Type **DIR AREASALE**, and press ENTER. Find your file in the listing. If you have other files named AREASALE with a different extension, 1-2-3 includes them in the list.

9. Type **EXIT** and press ENTER to return to 1-2-3. Notice that the worksheet has remained in 1-2-3's memory.

10. Add new data by entering **1989** in C3, **85000** in C4, and **70000** in C5. The final results are shown in Figure 4-7.

11. Save the file again with the /File Save command, and replace the existing file copy with the current worksheet.

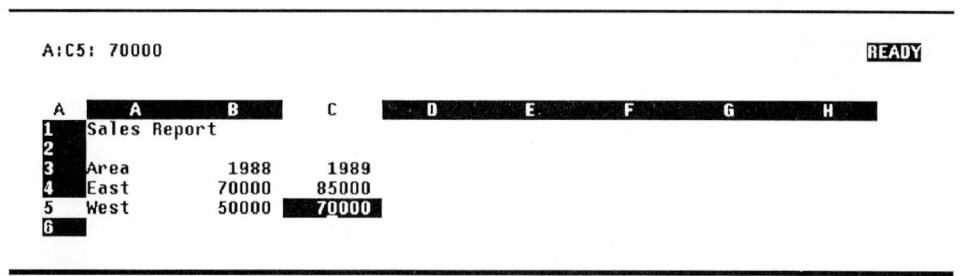

FIGURE 4-7.   AREASALE worksheet

REVIEW

- Files provide permanent storage for your worksheets. You can save and retrieve worksheets to a floppy or hard disk.

- You can save a worksheet with the /File Save command. When you save a file the first time, 1-2-3 displays a suggested name (FILE followed by a four-digit number). You can use this filename or type a new one to use instead. When you save the file again, 1-2-3 displays the filename to select. If you press ENTER to select the displayed filename, you must choose between Cancel, Replace, and Backup. You can also enter a new filename to save the worksheet in memory under the new filename.

- You can retrieve a worksheet with the /File Retrieve command. When you execute this command in Release 3, 1-2-3 lists the files you can select in alphabetical order.

- You can list files in a directory with the /File List command. With Release 3, you can list worksheet, graph, print, all, linked, or active files.

- You can select where 1-2-3 looks for the files that you work with by using the /File Dir command. When you use this command, you can provide a new directory before pressing ENTER.

- With Release 3, you can access the operating system with the /System command, while keeping 1-2-3 and the worksheet in the computer's memory. You can use this feature to format disks, copy files, and create subdirectories.

Commands and Keys

/FD	/File Dir allows you to change the current directory.
/FE	/File Erase eliminates a copy of a file on disk.
/FL	/File List displays a full screen list of all the files in the current directory or disk.
/FR	/File Retrieve retrieves a file from disk and places it in memory.
/FSB	/File Save Backup renames the .WK3 extension with a .BAK extension and saves the current version as .WK3.
/FSC	/File Save Cancel cancels a save request without saving when 1-2-3 prompts that the file already exists.
/FSR	/File Save Replace replaces the current copy on disk with the current contents of memory.

5

MAKING 1-2-3 DO YOUR WORK

Copying Worksheet Data
Rearranging the Worksheet
Generating Cell Entries
Other Worksheet Commands for Expanded Data
Searching and Replacing Worksheet Data
Review Exercise
Review

Until now, you have had to enter every worksheet entry that you needed for your models by yourself. While that is similar to using a columnar pad for your entries, it does not take advantage of the features offered by a package like 1-2-3. This chapter will introduce you to some of these features. Making only a few entries, you often can complete your model by putting 1-2-3 to work.

1-2-3 offers commands that can move worksheet data to a new location. This means that if the requirements of your application change, it will be easy to restructure the worksheet. You can also restructure the data stored in a column to row orientation, and vice versa. Again, this is quite an improvement over the "eraser method" that manual spreadsheets provide. This chapter also introduces you to a new command in Release 3 that allows you to search for characters in labels or formulas. The new command also offers a Replace feature that you can use to quickly modify labels and formulas.

1-2-3's /Copy command, also covered in this chapter, has more potential than any other command to increase your productivity with 1-2-3. You will learn the ins and outs of copying both label and formula data. You will also learn about other 1-2-3 features, such as repeating label entries and generating a series of numeric entries. Once you have mastered the Copy feature, you will want to master some of the tools that can help you monitor your expanded worksheet. For example, you will learn how to control the recalculation of formulas stored on the worksheet. In addition, you will be introduced to commands for splitting your screen display into two windows and for freezing certain information on the screen.

COPYING WORKSHEET DATA

Copying entries on a manual worksheet is a laborious task. To make an additional set of entries that duplicate existing ones, you must pick up your pencil and physically copy each entry that you wish to make. Naturally, duplicate entries take just as long to make as the original entries.

When you make duplicates with 1-2-3, this is not the case. For any entry that you wish to duplicate, 1-2-3 can complete 95 percent of the work for you. You just tell 1-2-3 what you want to copy and where you want it copied to, and 1-2-3 does all the remaining work. It can take a column of label entries and copy it to ten new columns. It can even take a row of formulas that calculate all your sales projections for the month of January and copy it down the page to the next eleven rows, thus giving you all the calculations for February through December. The truly amazing part of this process is that 1-2-3 even adjusts the formulas as it copies them.

This chapter uses a building-block approach to cover all of the features of the /Copy command. First, you learn to use /Copy to duplicate a label entry. Then you will look a little closer at /Copy's inner workings as you examine its ability to adjust formulas.

Copying Labels

There are many situations in which copying labels can save you time. Perhaps you want to create a worksheet that uses account titles or months of the year in two different locations. Rather than typing them in again, you can use the Copy option of the main menu. Not only does it save you time, but it also guarantees that both sets of entries are identical. /Copy is also useful when you have a number of similar entries to make; you can often copy your original entries and make minor editing changes in less time than it would take to type each of the complete entries.

INVOKING /COPY TO DUPLICATE LABELS   /Copy is a little different from the other menu commands you have used. It does not have a submenu like /Range Format Currency or /Worksheet Insert Rows. Instead of presenting multilayered menus, the /Copy command provides prompts. You must respond to these prompts in order to define the *source location* you wish to copy information from and the *target location* you wish to copy information to.

When you invoke the /Copy command by entering /**Copy**, this is the first prompt message you see:

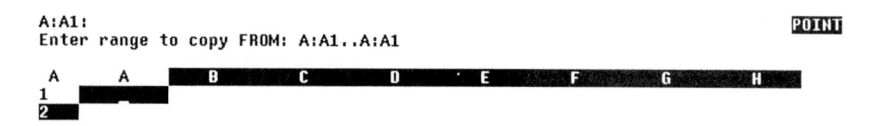

1-2-3 is asking what cells you wish to copy from. Think of this "From" range as the source of information to be copied. 1-2-3 suggests a range that encompasses only one cell, which is always the location of the cell pointer at the time you invoke /Copy. If the location that 1-2-3 suggests is acceptable, you can press ENTER to accept it. If you like the beginning of the range but wish to enlarge it to include a row or column of cell entries, you can expand it with your pointer-movement keys. If you don't want to accept the beginning of the range, you must unanchor the starting position by pressing ESC. You will then be free to move the beginning of the range. When you want to anchor it again, use the same strategy you used with the format commands, and type a period. You will then be free to expand the range with the arrow keys.

Once you have finalized the source selection, 1-2-3's interest shifts to the target location, which you can think of as the "To" range. The prompt displayed by 1-2-3 Release 3 for the target range looks like this:

You may want to do a little planning before invoking 1-2-3's /Copy command, since the cell address where you begin will be 1-2-3's suggested location for starting the copy operation. It will also be the cell to which 1-2-3 returns the cell pointer when you are through. If you forget to plan ahead, 1-2-3 still offers you the flexibility to successfully complete the copy operation.

1-2-3 again suggests the location of the cell pointer as the target range. The suggested location is not a range but a single cell, since you will almost always need to move the cell pointer to define the target range. And this is *all* you need to do, since it is displayed as a cell address rather than a range. You do not have to press ESC, because there is no range to unanchor.

With Release 3, you can even press the F3 (NAME) key to select a range name as the source for the copy operation. Once you select a location to start the copy, you must either press ENTER to finalize the location or you must modify it to represent a range. You can create a range with the standard method of typing a period and using the arrow keys to mark the end of the range.

Reviewing an example will help clarify how easy it is to copy a label entry. Follow these steps:

1. Move the cell pointer to A1 and type **Sales - Product A**. Then press ENTER.

2. Enter **/Copy** to generate this prompt message:

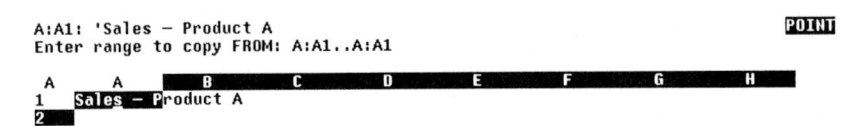

Notice that the suggestion for the source range is A1, the location of the cell pointer when you invoked the /Copy command.

3. Press ENTER.

The prompt generated next also suggests the original location of the cell pointer as the target range. However, you must change it:

4. Move the cell pointer to A2. Your screen should look like this:

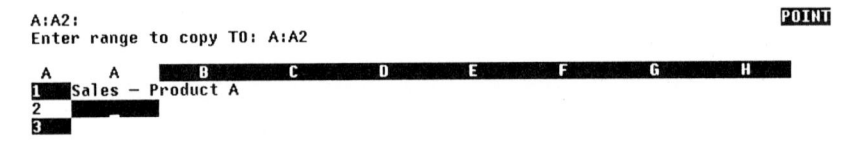

5. Press ENTER to generate these results:

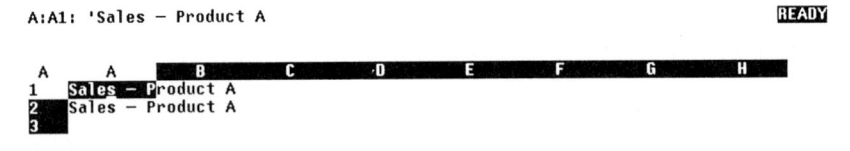

The new label you generated is identical to the original entry, but you used far fewer keystrokes to create it. Later, you will learn how to extend this productivity even further by copying to many locations with one command. For now, here are a few additional hints for the simplest case of copying—copying an entry to one new location.

Modifying Copied Labels   The entry in A2 is currently identical to the original. Sometimes this situation is exactly what you need; at other times, however, a slight modification might be required. If you wanted the label "Sales Product B" in A2, the /Copy approach is still best. However, fixing the label would require these extra steps:

1. Move the cell pointer to A2.

2. Press F2 (EDIT).

3. Press the BACKSPACE key, type **B**, and press ENTER to finalize.
   The results will look like this:

Keep this possibility in mind when you look for opportunities to copy; a /Copy followed by a quick edit can still be much quicker than making new entries. Since you can use this feature with numbers as well, one potential application of /Copy is to generate a list of numbers with only one digit different.

Making /Copy Work Smoothly   Because of the way in which 1-2-3 suggests a location for the source range, the most efficient way to work with /Copy is to position your cell pointer on the cell you wish to copy before requesting the command. If more than one cell is being copied, select the upper-left cell in the range being copied. This strategy will allow you to expand the cell range downward and to the right once you are prompted for the source range.

Copying Formulas

In one sense, copying formulas is no different from copying label or number entries. It is accomplished with the same /Copy command, and you respond to the prompts the way you do when copying label and number entries. With formulas, however, you need to be able to control how 1-2-3 copies the cell addresses in formulas. If you have one constant interest rate and want all formulas to refer to it, you must be able to direct

1-2-3 to carry out that direction. On the other hand, you need a different approach if you enter a formula for January profit that subtracts the cost of goods sold in January from the sales for January and you want to copy this formula to generate formulas that calculate profit for the other 11 months. You cannot calculate February's profit by subtracting the January cost-of-goods-sold figure from January sales—you need to subtract February's cost of goods sold from February sales. Fortunately, 1-2-3 can handle this type of situation as well. These different types of calculations are handled by the type of references contained in the original formula and are not an option selected after the copy operation begins. Let's examine an example of different reference types to help clarify this.

ADDRESS TYPES   All the cell addresses you have entered in formulas so far have contained a column name immediately followed by a row number (for example, A1, E4, and IV2000). This is the cell address specification that is used most frequently with 1-2-3. This type of address is called a *relative address*. There are two additional types of addresses: *absolute* and *mixed addresses*. These three types are distinguished by the way they are recorded in your formulas and the way in which 1-2-3 performs a copy operation for each of them. It is important to master the differences between these types of addresses; the type of address references you use is critical in determining how your formulas are copied to new worksheet locations.

Relative Addresses   Relative addresses are the only type of cell address you used prior to this chapter. They are easy to enter in formulas using the typing or pointing method of formula creation. When 1-2-3 records your entry, it appears to store the formula exactly as you entered it. If you move your cell pointer to any cell that holds one of the formulas you have entered, you will see the exact formula you entered in the control panel.

However, 1-2-3 remembers your instructions in a slightly different way from what it displays. If you store the formula +A1+A2 in cell A3, 1-2-3 will interpret your instructions in this way: "Take the value that is located two cells above the location that will store the result, and add that value to the value that is located one cell above the cell that will contain the result." When your formula contains relative references, everything is remembered in terms of relative direction and distances from the cell that will contain the result.

When you copy this type of formula to another location, 1-2-3 will adjust the formula in the new locations to reflect the same relative distances and directions. For example, if you were to copy the formula stored in A3 to B3, the formula you would see in the control panel for B3 would be +B1+B2. The cell addresses are different from the original, but the formula still records the same relative directions: "Take the value that is two cells above the cell that will contain the result, and add that value to the value that is one cell above the cell that will contain the results." This adjustment

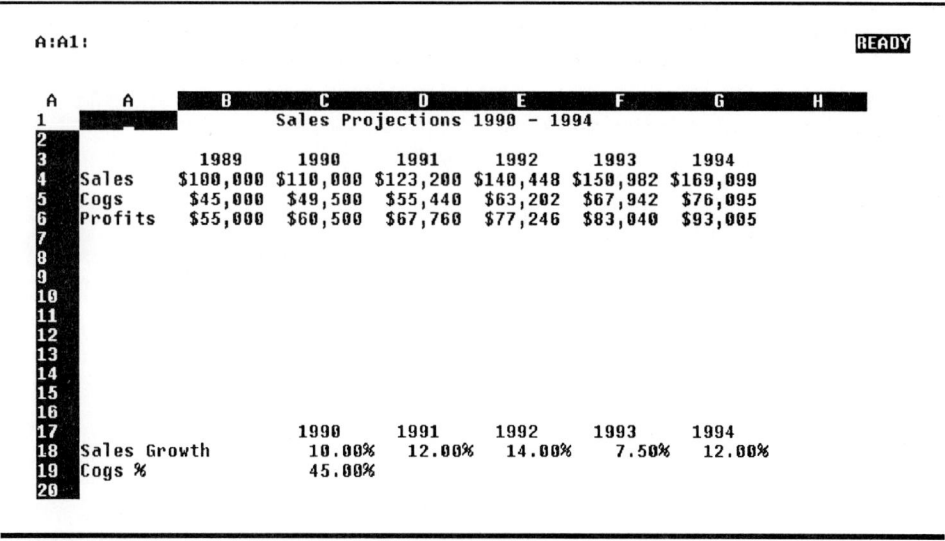

FIGURE 5-1.   Completed sales projection model

is made automatically as long as you use relative references when you build your formulas. Since you have not learned about other types of address yet, this should be easy.

Let's build a model that allows you to practice the formula copy process. This model records profits for the current year and projects them for the next five years. The final result of your entries will look like Figure 5-1. Follow these steps to create the model:

1. Enter /**Worksheet Erase Yes** to start with a clean worksheet. Enter Yes a second time if your data has not been saved to disk.

2. Move the cell pointer to C1 and type **Sales Projections 1990 - 1994**. Then press ENTER.

3. Move the cell pointer to A4 and make these entries:

   A4: Sales
   A5: Cogs
   A6: Profit
   B3: ^1989
   C3: ^1990
   D3: ^1991
   E3: ^1992
   F3: ^1993
   G3: ^1994

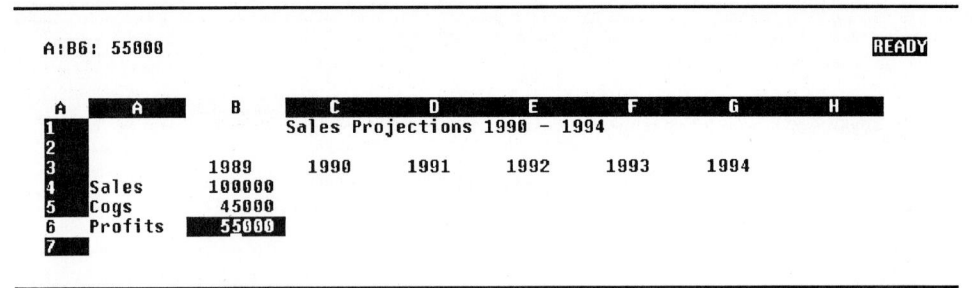

FIGURE 5-2.   Beginning sales projection model

The caret (^) symbols in front of the year entries will cause the numeric digits to be treated as labels and will center them within the cell.

4. Move the cell pointer to B4 and make these entries for 1989:

   B4: 100000
   B5: 45000
   B6: 55000

These entries are not computed, as they are assumed to be the actual numbers at the end of 1989. They will appear as shown in Figure 5-2.

It is time to think about how you want to project sales for the remaining years. You can use a constant growth rate that would apply to all years, or you can assume that sales will grow at varying percentages each year. There are also a number of choices for computing the cost of the goods sold each year. One method is to use a percentage of sales. Even if you select this method without evaluating your other options, you must again decide if one percentage rate will be used for all years or if the percentage will vary by year. The profit calculation does not require you to make a decision, since it is always equal to Sales minus Cost of Goods Sold.

This model assumes that sales will grow at varying rates but that cost of goods sold will be the same percentage of sales each year. You must enter these assumptions before projections can be made:

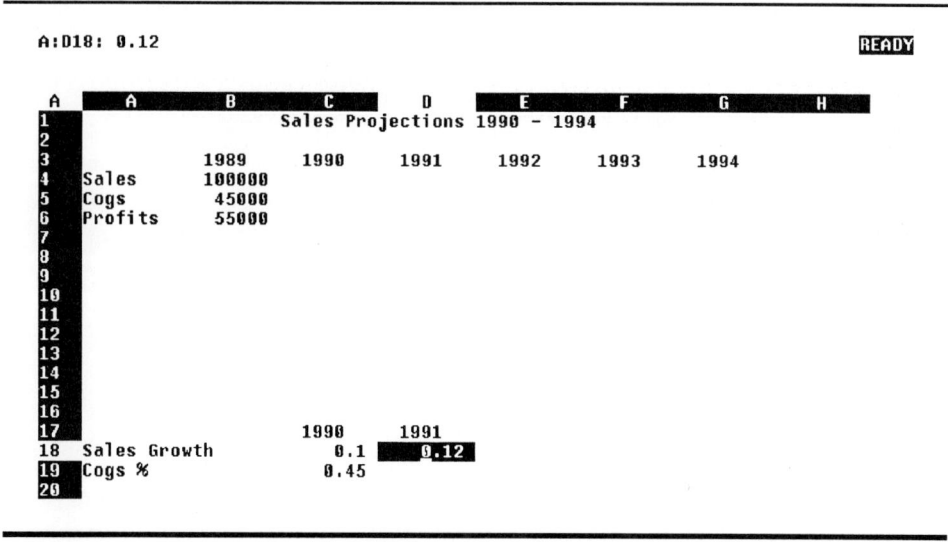

FIGURE 5-3.   Entering numbers and labels for the sales projection model

5. Complete these entries:

    A18: Sales Growth
    A19: Cogs %
    C17: ^1990
    C18: .1
    C19: .45
    D17: ^1991
    D18: .12

Your entries should look like those shown in Figure 5-3.

6. Enter **/Worksheet Global Format Currency**. Type **0** and press ENTER. The percentages will be displayed as zeros, like the ones in Figure 5-4.

    This instruction sets the Global format to Currency, but you will also need to use a /Range Format for the percentages that will be used in the model.

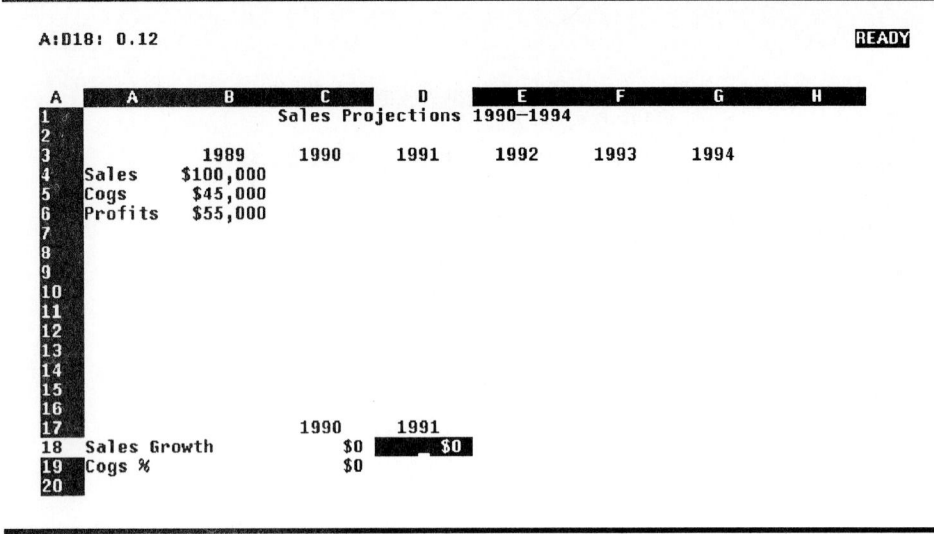

```
A:D18: 0.12                                                          READY

    A        A         B         C         D         E         F         G         H
1                            Sales Projections 1990-1994
2
3                 1989      1990      1991      1992      1993      1994
4        Sales    $100,000
5        Cogs     $45,000
6        Profits  $55,000
7
8
9
10
11
12
13
14
15
16
17                           1990      1991
18   Sales Growth              $0        $0
19   Cogs %                    $0
20
```

FIGURE 5-4.   Using a Global format

7. Move the cell pointer to C18. Then enter **/Range Format Percent** and press ENTER to accept two decimal places. Use the RIGHT and DOWN ARROW keys to move the cell pointer to G19, and then press ENTER.

   The range of cells you just selected includes all the values you want formatted as percentages. It also includes a few blank cells—but they have to be included, unless you wish to apply the format with separate commands for the sales growth and cost-of-goods-sold percentage. The reformatted percentage entries are shown in Figure 5-5.

8. Move the cell pointer to C4, type **+B4∗(1+C18)**, and press ENTER.

   This will compute the sales projection for 1990. Rather than typing this formula for each year, a better option is to copy it.

9. Enter **/Copy**. Press ENTER in response to the 1-2-3 prompt that appears, as shown in Figure 5-6.

10. Move the cell pointer to D4 and press ENTER. The cell pointer will remain in C4, which was the beginning of the source range.

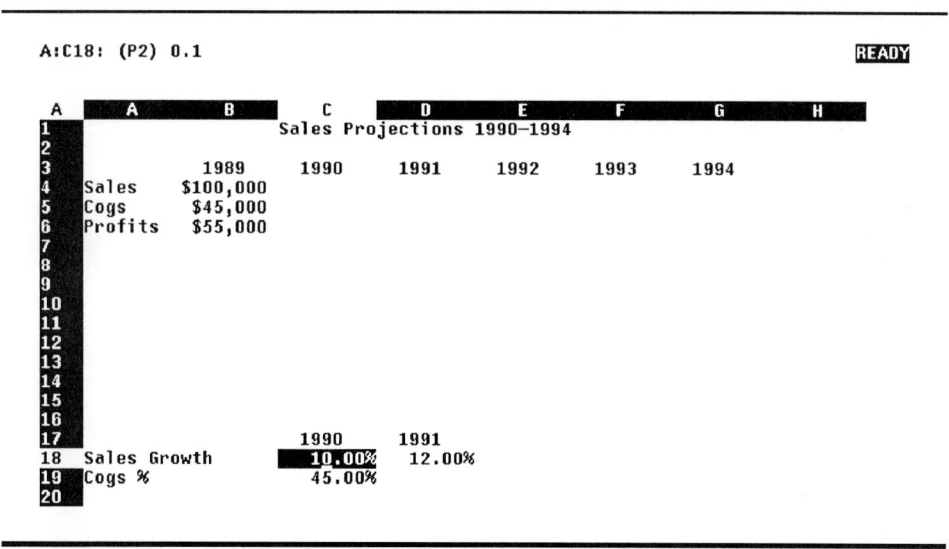

FIGURE 5-5.   Adding a Range format

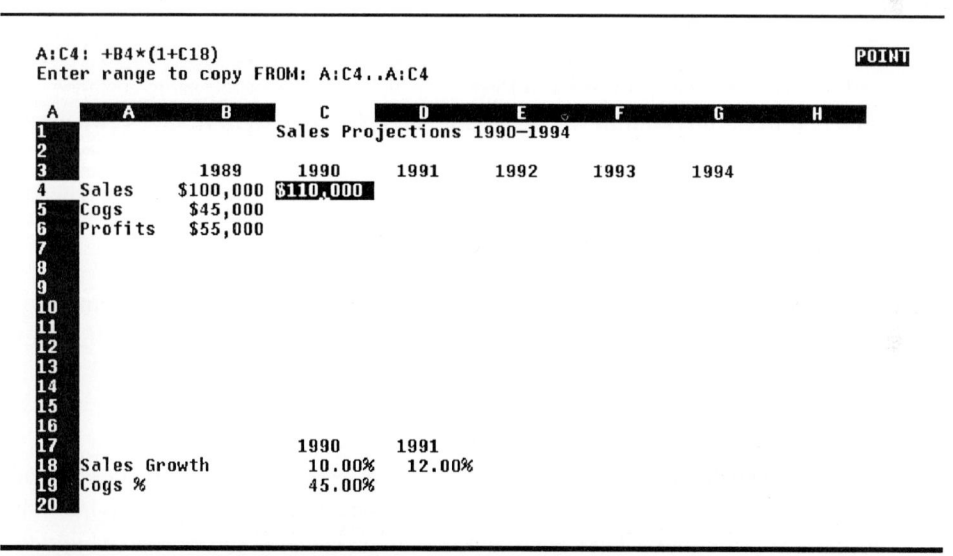

FIGURE 5-6.   Specifying the source or range for /Copy

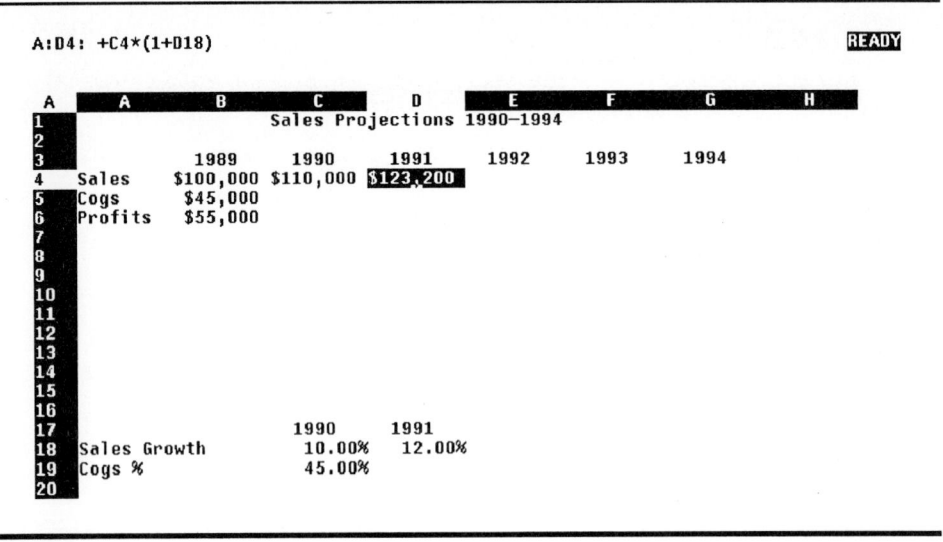

A:D4: +C4*(1+D18)   READY

A	A	B	C	D	E	F	G	H
1			Sales Projections 1990–1994					
2								
3		1989	1990	1991	1992	1993	1994	
4	Sales	$100,000	$110,000	$123,200				
5	Cogs	$45,000						
6	Profits	$55,000						
7								
8								
9								
10								
11								
12								
13								
14								
15								
16								
17			1990	1991				
18	Sales Growth		10.00%	12.00%				
19	Cogs %		45.00%					
20								

FIGURE 5-7.   The completed formula

11. Move the cell pointer to D4 to look at the new formula, shown in Figure 5-7.

Notice that 1-2-3 has adjusted each of the cell references to take the new location of the result into account. Each reference in the formula is the same distance and direction from the result in D4 as the original references were from C4, where the original result was computed. Before completing the copy process for sales, you will want to take a look at an absolute reference—a reference that will not be updated by a copy operation.

Absolute Addresses   Absolute cell references are references that remain the same regardless of where the formula is copied to. The formula reference is effectively frozen in place and is not allowed to change. To create these references, you must place the $ character in front of the row, column, and sheet portions of the address. $A8 or $D8 are examples of absolute cell references.

You can create an absolute reference in one of two ways: by typing or pointing. Both parallel the creation method for relative references. If you choose to build the formula by typing, you will need to type the dollar signs. If you choose to build the formula by pointing, you can press F4 (ABS); 1-2-3 will then add the dollar signs in front of the row, column, and sheet portions of the address.

Let's use this approach to build the cost-of-goods-sold data. Follow these steps to enhance the sales projection model you have been working on:

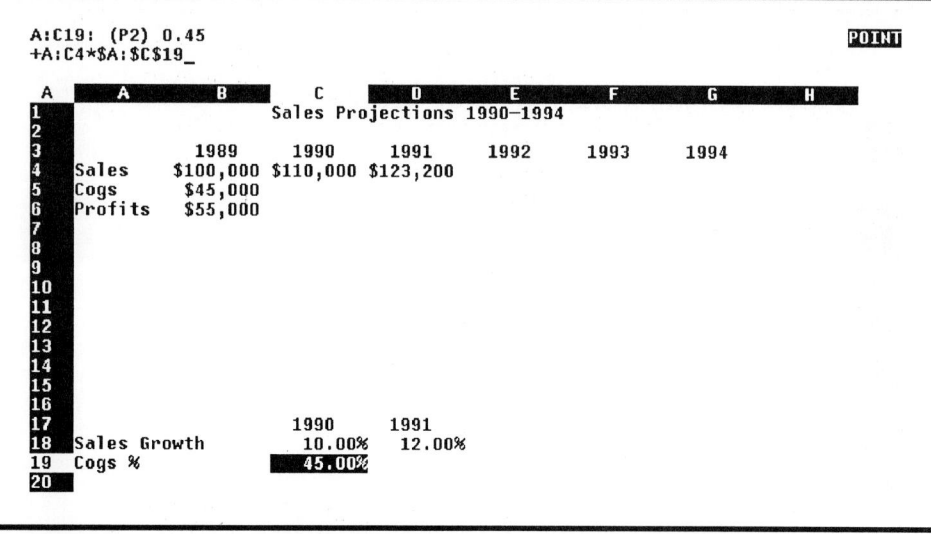

FIGURE 5-8.   Using an absolute reference

1. Move the cell pointer to C5.

2. Type +.

3. Move the cell pointer to C4 with the UP ARROW key.

4. Type *.

5. Move the cell pointer to C19 with the DOWN ARROW key.

6. Press F4 (ABS) once to add the $ signs.

   Your display should match Figure 5-8. Since you were in POINT mode, you could add the $ signs with F4 (ABS). If you want to type the cell address, you cannot use F4 (ABS) to add the $ signs, so you will have to type them. If you accidentally depress F4 (ABS) too long, the $ signs will not be placed correctly. Continue to press F4 (ABS) until there are three $ signs in the cell address.

7. Press ENTER to complete the formula.

8. Enter **/Copy** and press ENTER to accept C5 as the source range.

9. Move the cell pointer to D5 and press ENTER.

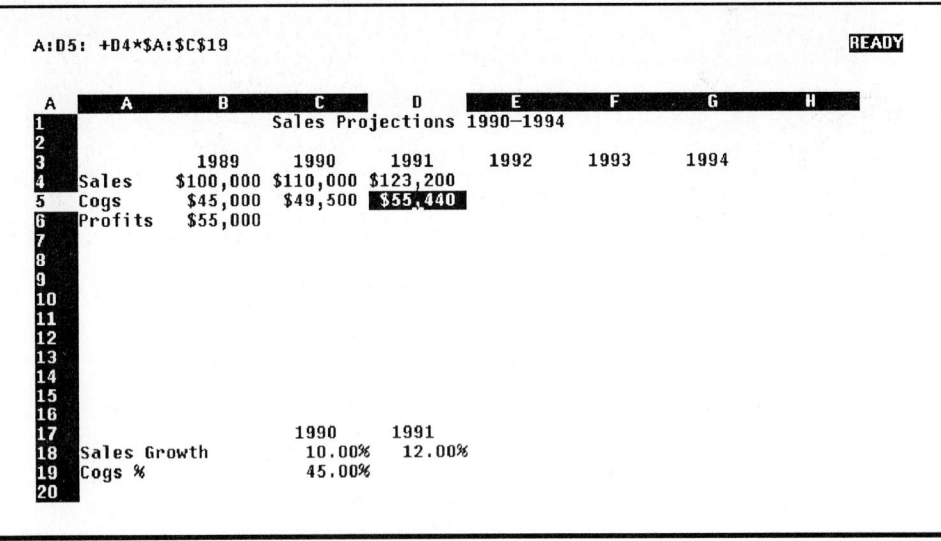

FIGURE 5-9.   Copy operation completed for the Cogs formula

If you move the cell pointer to D5, you will see that the new formula also references C19 for its cost-of-goods- sold percentage, as shown in Figure 5-9.

Mixed Addresses   Mixed addresses borrow something from each of the other two types of addresses. A mixed address is "mixed" in that one part is fixed and the other part is relative. This means that the row, the column, or sheet portion of the address can be fixed, but not all three. During the /Copy process the fixed portion behaves like an absolute address, and the other portion functions like a relative address and is adjusted based on the location it is being copied to.

A mixed address can be written as A$5 or $D7. In A$5, the column portion of the address will be adjusted as the formula is copied to different columns, but the row portion will remain fixed if the formula is copied to other rows. In $D7, the exact opposite takes place: the column portion of the address will always remain fixed, regardless of where the formula containing it is copied, and the row portion will be updated when the formula is copied to a different row.

Mixed addresses are used only if you are building complex models. Still, it is important to know that they are possible in case you ever see a mixed address in a formula. For now, it is enough just to know that this feature exists. A more productive way to spend your time is to put the relative and absolute address types to the test with additional /Copy commands.

THE SCOPE OF /COPY   You have learned how to copy a formula to a new location on the worksheet in the exercises you have completed so far. This is just one of the ways you can use /Copy. Other options are copying the contents of one cell to many additional locations, and copying many locations to many additional locations.

Copy One Entry to One New Location   You have already used this type of /Copy operation to copy the sales and cost-of-goods-sold projections for 1990 to create the same projections for 1991. Now you will use it one more time to copy the profit calculation from 1990. First, though, you must enter the formula for 1990 profit and complete the assumption area. Follow these steps to add a formula for profit and then to copy the formula to one additional location:

1. Move the cell pointer to C6.

2. Type **+C4-C5** and press ENTER.
    Since you wish both components of this calculation to be updated for the appropriate year when the formula is copied, both references are relative.

3. Enter **/Copy.**

4. Press ENTER to accept the source range generated by 1-2-3.

5. Move the cell pointer to D6 with the RIGHT ARROW key and press ENTER.

6. Enter the following in the assumption area:
    E17: ^1992
    F17: ^1993
    G17: ^1994
    E18: .14
    F18: .075
    G18: .12

The model should now look like the one in Figure 5-10. You have been making slow but steady progress in completing it. Now it is time to step up the pace and copy to more than one location at a time.

Copy One Entry to Many New Locations   1-2-3's /Copy command is not restricted to the single-copy approach we have been using. By expanding the size of the target range, you can copy the entry in one cell to a range that is as large as a row or column of the worksheet. You can put this expanded version of /Copy to use in completing the sales projections for the remaining years of the model:

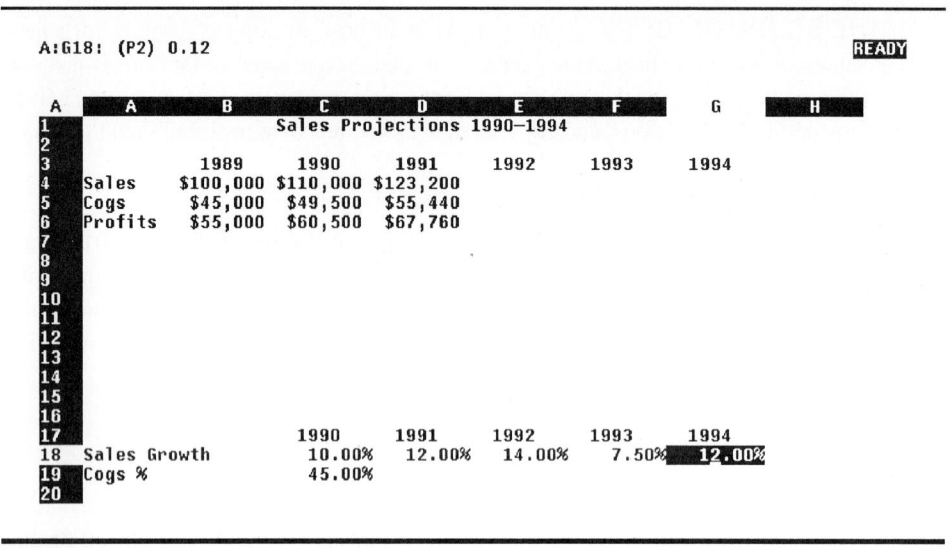

FIGURE 5-10.   Profit formula added and assumptions extended

1. Move the cell pointer to D4.

2. Enter /**Copy** and press ENTER to accept the source range.

3. Move the cell pointer to E4 in response to the prompt for the target range.

4. Type **.** (a period).
   The period will anchor the beginning of the range and allow you to expand it.

5. Move the cell pointer to G4.
   The target range you are copying to is highlighted, as shown in Figure 5-11. This one command will copy the sales projection formula into E4, F4, and G4.

6. Press ENTER to produce the results shown in Figure 5-12.

Copy Many Locations to Many New Locations   You can step up the pace a little more and copy a column or a row of formula to many columns or many rows all in one step. To accomplish this, you must expand both the source and target ranges to include a range of cells. You can use this approach to complete the formulas for your model. Although the column of formulas you need to copy includes only two cells, it

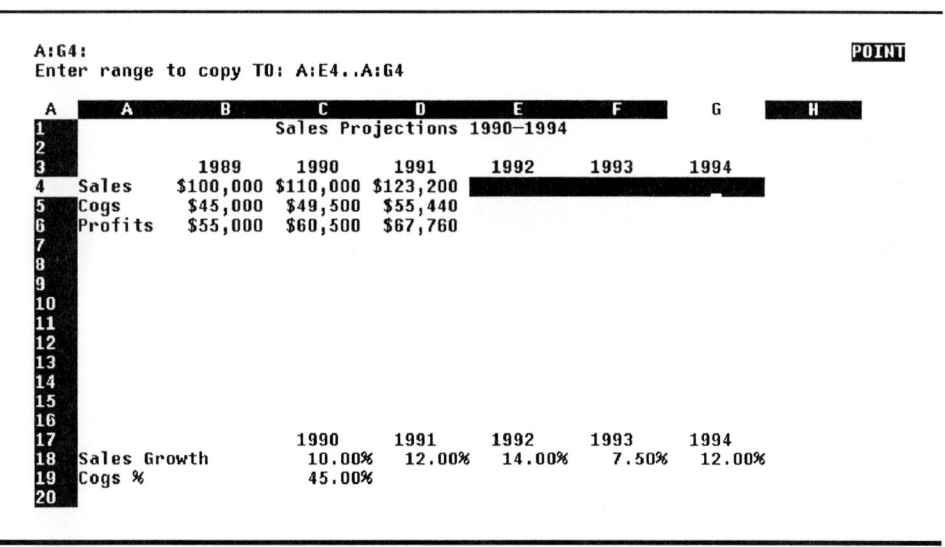

FIGURE 5-11.   Copying to a target range of more than one cell

is still a column. You will be able to copy this column of formulas to columns E, F, and G.

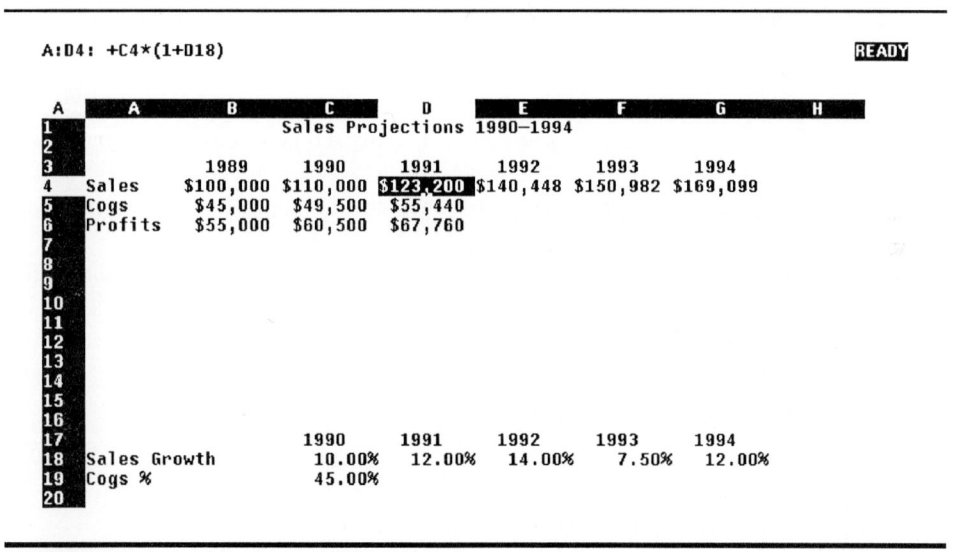

FIGURE 5-12.   Copy operation completed

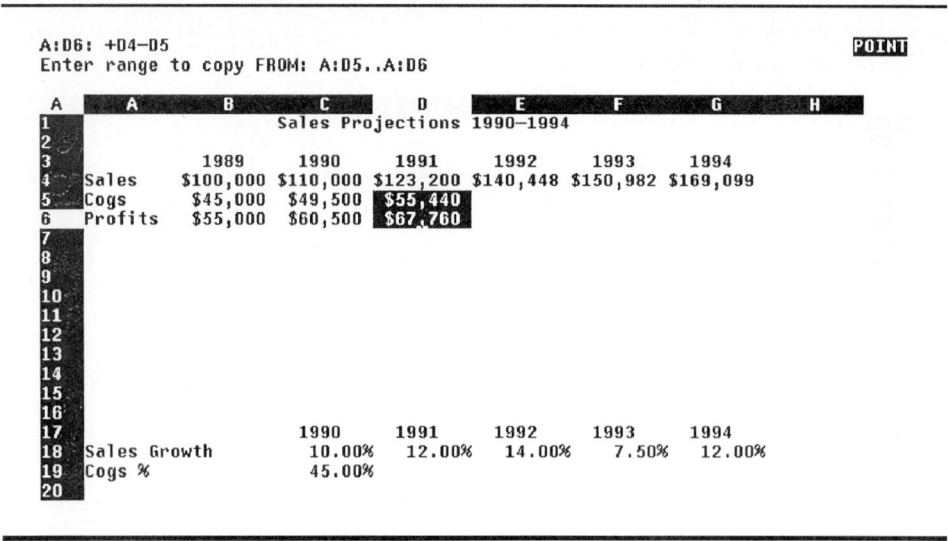

FIGURE 5-13.   Copying a source range of more than one cell

Follow these directions to complete the copy operation:

1. Move the cell pointer to D5.

    This is the upper-left cell in the range to be copied. As long as you remember to place the cell pointer in the upper-left cell in the range to be copied, the copying process will be easy to follow for either rows or columns.

2. Enter /**Copy**.

3. Expand the source range to D6 by moving the cell pointer with the DOWN ARROW key.

    The cells you are copying from should be highlighted, as shown in Figure 5-13.

    The location where you should place the cell pointer when expanding the source range is always the lower-right cell in the range to be copied. Again, keeping the lower-right cell in mind will make these directions work even when you wish to copy a row of data.

4. Press ENTER, move the cell pointer to E5, and type . (a period).

    This anchors the upper-left cell in the target range.

5. Move the cell pointer to G5.

    You are probably thinking that G6 would have been the correct location. Since 1-2-3 already knows from your definition of the target range that you

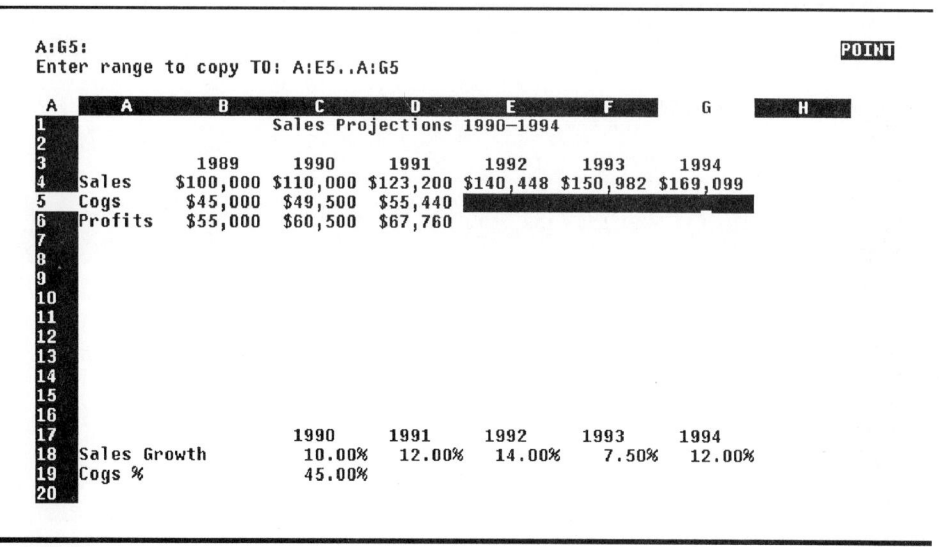

A:G5:   POINT
Enter range to copy TO: A:E5..A:G5

```
A      A         B        C        D        E        F        G        H
1                      Sales Projections 1990-1994
2
3                1989     1990     1991     1992     1993     1994
4      Sales   $100,000 $110,000 $123,200 $140,448 $150,982 $169,099
5      Cogs     $45,000  $49,500  $55,440
6      Profits  $55,000  $60,500  $67,760
7
8
9
10
11
12
13
14
15
16
17                        1990     1991     1992     1993     1994
18     Sales Growth      10.00%   12.00%   14.00%    7.50%   12.00%
19     Cogs %            45.00%
20
```

FIGURE 5-14.   Defining the target range for /Copy

are copying a column of formulas, it only needs to know how far across the worksheet you wish to copy this column. G5 answers that question. The target cells you are copying to should be highlighted and should match the display in Figure 5-14.

6. Press ENTER to see the results shown in Figure 5-15.

Copying a row of cell entries will follow the same basic pattern as this example. First, you must define which row of cells is in the source or from range. Next, you must tell 1-2-3 where to begin copying this row to and how far down the worksheet to copy it. Keep in mind that all these copy methods can be used for values and labels just as easily as for formula entries.

REARRANGING
THE WORKSHEET

Planning is the best assurance that your completed model will both look good and meet your business needs. But even when you plan, there still will be occasions when you want to rearrange the data contained in your model. 1-2-3 has commands that will

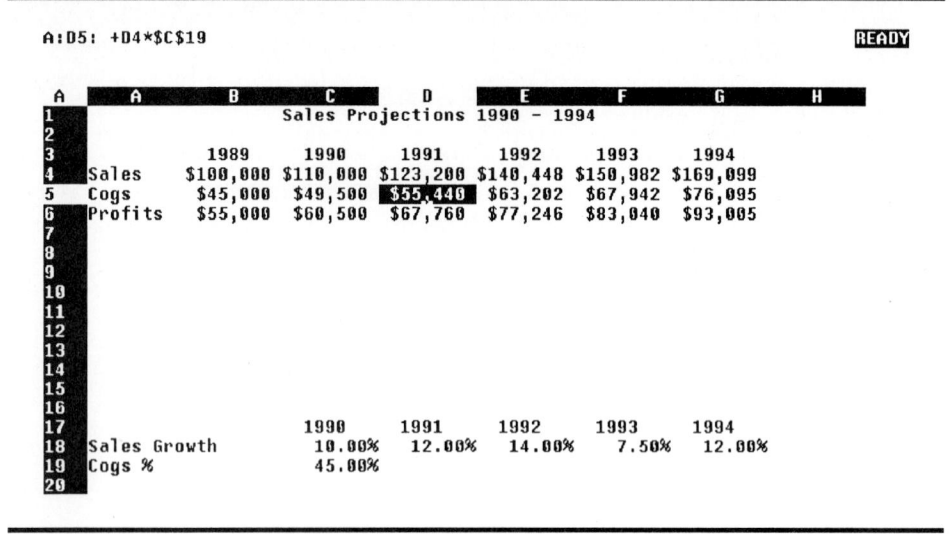

A:D5: +D4*$C$19   READY

	A	B	C	D	E	F	G	H
1		Sales Projections 1990 - 1994						
2								
3		1989	1990	1991	1992	1993	1994	
4	Sales	$100,000	$110,000	$123,200	$140,448	$150,982	$169,099	
5	Cogs	$45,000	$49,500	$55,440	$63,202	$67,942	$76,095	
6	Profits	$55,000	$60,500	$67,760	$77,246	$83,040	$93,005	
7								
8								
9								
10								
11								
12								
13								
14								
15								
16								
17			1990	1991	1992	1993	1994	
18	Sales Growth		10.00%	12.00%	14.00%	7.50%	12.00%	
19	Cogs %		45.00%					
20								

FIGURE 5-15.   Result of the copy operation

reorganize the worksheet for you, so you do not have to reenter and erase entries the way you would with a manual version of your model. These special commands include one that can move any range of data to another range that is the same size and shape. A second command allows you to take a row of data and place it in a column, or to take a column of data and place it in a row.

Moving Worksheet Data

The /Move command is used to move data in one range of the worksheet to another range. This range can be a single cell, a row of cells, a column of cells, or a rectangle with multiple rows and columns. The size and shape of the relocated data are determined by the original location of the data. This means that a row of data can only be moved to another row and cannot be placed into a column of cells.

You can use the /Move command to relocate labels, values, and formulas. When /Move relocates formulas, it adjusts the cell references in the formulas being moved to account for the new location of these formulas on the worksheet. /Move also adjusts absolute references to conform to the new worksheet location.

The /Move command is very similar to the /Copy command except that the original location of the data is not retained. To use this command, enter **/Move**. 1-2-3 prompts you for the source range. Just as with the /Copy command, it is easiest to specify the range if you position your cell pointer in the upper-left cell in the range before requesting /Move. Also like the /Copy command, the /Move command lets you press ENTER to specify a single cell as the source, or you can move the cell pointer to expand the size of the range.

After you finalize the source range with ENTER, 1-2-3 prompts you for the target range, the new location for your data. Unlike the /Copy command, the source range in a /Move command determines the size and shape of the data being moved. Therefore, all you need is a beginning location for the relocated data, which you can define by specifying the upper-left cell of the new area. Once you have specified the target range and finalized it with ENTER, the move operation is complete.

You can use /Move to relocate your assumptions on the current model by following these steps:

1. Move the cell pointer to A15.

    This is the upper-left cell in a rectangle that will include all the entries in the assumption section, including the label in row 15.

2. Enter /**Move**.

3. Move the cell pointer to G19.

    Everything to be moved will be highlighted, as shown in Figure 5-16.

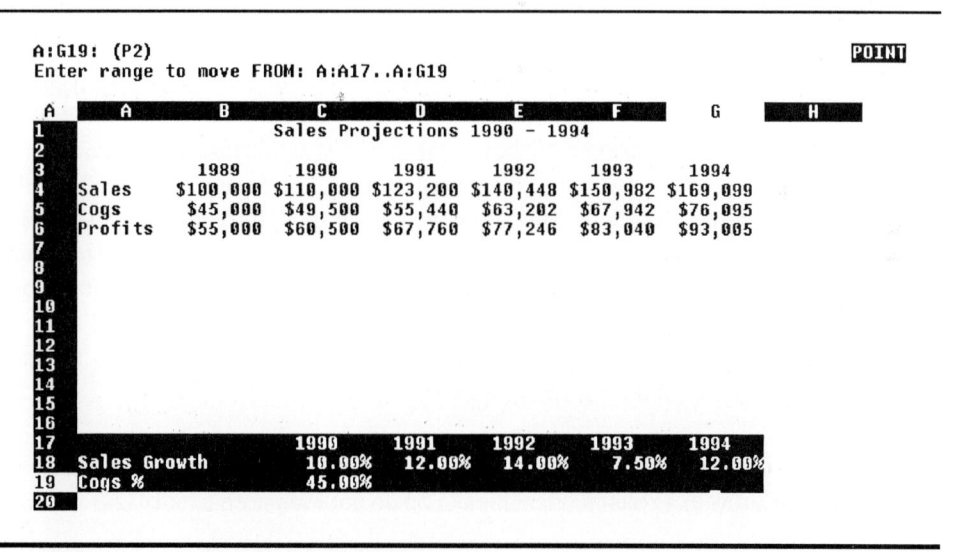

FIGURE 5-16.   Highlighting the area to move

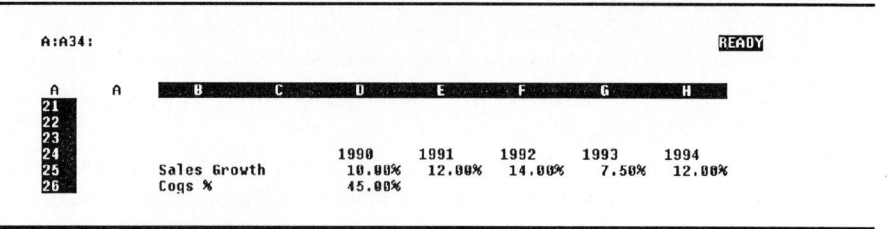

A:A34:   READY

A	A	B	C	D	E	F	G	H
21								
22								
23								
24				1990	1991	1992	1993	1994
25		Sales Growth		10.00%	12.00%	14.00%	7.50%	12.00%
26		Cogs %		45.00%				

FIGURE 5-17.   Move completed

4. Press ENTER to finalize the source range (or from range).

5. Move the cell pointer to B22 and press ENTER.

6. Press PGDN to see where the range was moved.
    The entire range of cells containing assumption data will be relocated to B22..H26, as shown in Figure 5-17.

7. Enter /**File Save**, type **SALESPRJ**, and press ENTER to save this worksheet.

Transposing Data

1-2-3's Transpose feature offers another way to rearrange your worksheet data. Not only does it copy data, but it also alters its orientation. Transpose places data with a row orientation into a column. It also places data with a column orientation into a row. The power of this feature will become apparent the first time you need to do major restructuring of a worksheet. You will have an opportunity to try both types of transposition.

Both versions of Transpose can be used with labels, numbers, and formulas. When you transpose rows or columns containing formulas, 1-2-3 copies the results of the formulas to the new locations. This allows you to transpose formulas without concern for whether or not the new orientation will damage the resulting entries. The resulting copy contains values but not formulas. In earlier releases, you could not transpose formulas because the results would reference cells that were not intended. When you transpose worksheet data, the original entries remain intact, allowing you to erase either these entries or the transposed entries.

ROWS TO COLUMNS   /Range Trans makes it easy to change data that was entered in a row to a column orientation. You do not even need to tell 1-2-3 whether the data you are transposing is in a row or column; 1-2-3 can figure it out from the range that you define. All you need to do is define the data to transpose and then tell 1-2-3 the upper- left cell of the area in which you wish to place the data. The following example illustrates how this command works:

1. Enter **/Worksheet Erase Yes** to clear the worksheet.

2. Enter **/Worksheet Global Col-Width**, type **20**, and press ENTER.

3. Make these entries in cells B2..K2:

> B2: Sales - Widgets
> C2: Sales - Kites
> D2: Sales - Wind Surfers
> E2: Sales - Rockets
> F2: Sales - Blocks
> G2: Sales - Sand
> H2: Sales - Jacks
> I2: Sales - Rafts
> J2: Sales - Balls
> K2: Sales - Dolls

4. Press the HOME key.
   A few of the entries appear as follows:

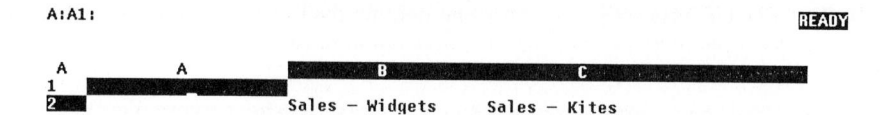

The entries are so wide that only a few are visible on the screen at once. You may decide to try a different orientation using the Transpose feature.

5. Move the cell pointer to B2 and enter **/Range Trans**.

6. Select B2..K2 as the source (from) range, and press ENTER. This selection can be accomplished quickly by pressing END followed by the RIGHT ARROW key.

7. Move the cell pointer to A4 and press ENTER.
   This will place the entries in column A, but the original entries are still in row 2.

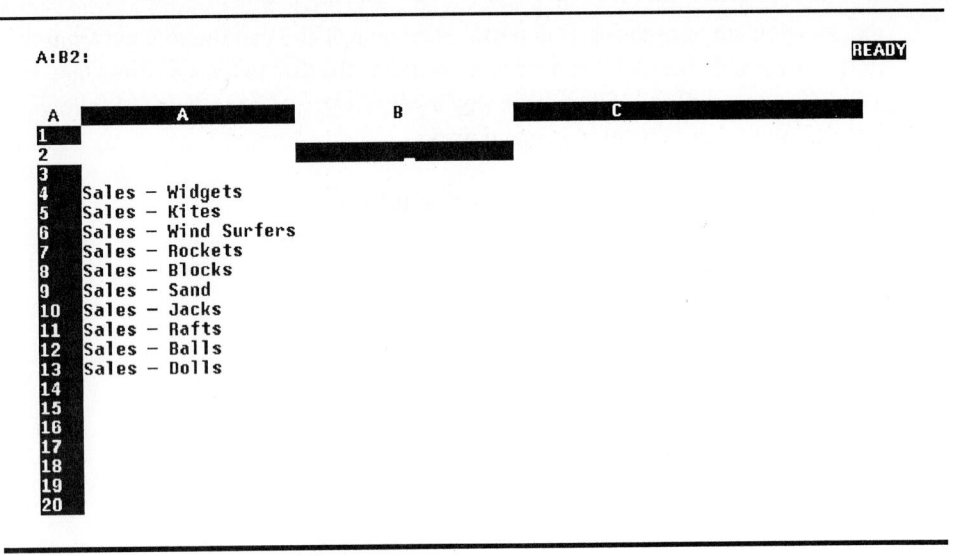

A:B2:   **READY**

	A	B	C
1			
2			
3			
4	Sales — Widgets		
5	Sales — Kites		
6	Sales — Wind Surfers		
7	Sales — Rockets		
8	Sales — Blocks		
9	Sales — Sand		
10	Sales — Jacks		
11	Sales — Rafts		
12	Sales — Balls		
13	Sales — Dolls		
14			
15			
16			
17			
18			
19			
20			

FIGURE 5-18.   Transposed data

8. Enter **/Range Erase** and expand the range by pressing the END key, followed by the RIGHT ARROW key, until the range reads B2..K2. Then press ENTER. Your screen should match the display shown in Figure 5-18.

COLUMNS TO ROWS   Transposing column data to a row is just as easy as the other way around. Try this example with the months of the year:

1. Clear the current worksheet by entering **/Worksheet Erase Yes Yes**. Using Figure 5-19 as your guide, enter abbreviations for each of the months in A5..A16.

2. Move the cell pointer to A5 by pressing the END key followed by the UP ARROW key. Then enter **/Range Trans**.

3. Select the range A5..A16 and press ENTER.

4. Move the cell pointer to B3 and press ENTER.

Although you can only see the first seven month names in Figure 5-20, the remainder have been transposed as well. The months are in the range B3..M3. The original entries will remain unless you use the /Range Erase command to remove them.

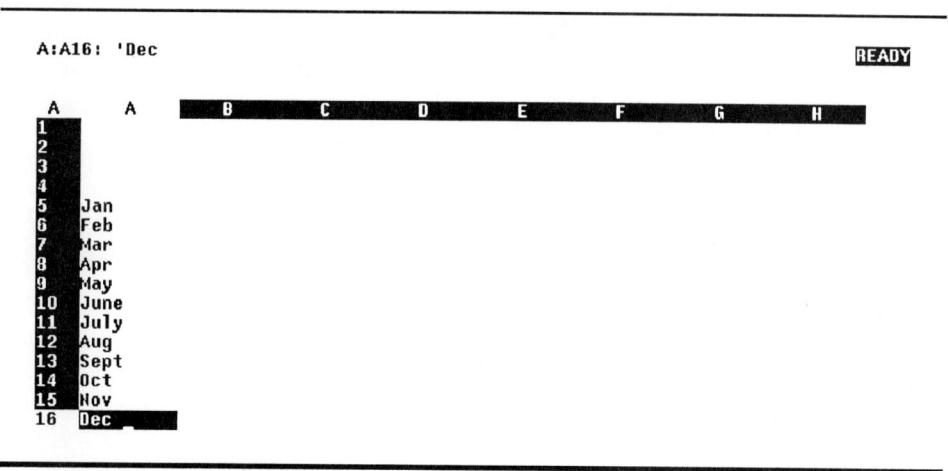

FIGURE 5-19.   Data entered in a column

GENERATING
CELL ENTRIES

1-2-3's generating features are so easy to use that it is like having someone perform data entry for you free of charge. The Repeating Label feature provided by 1-2-3 can

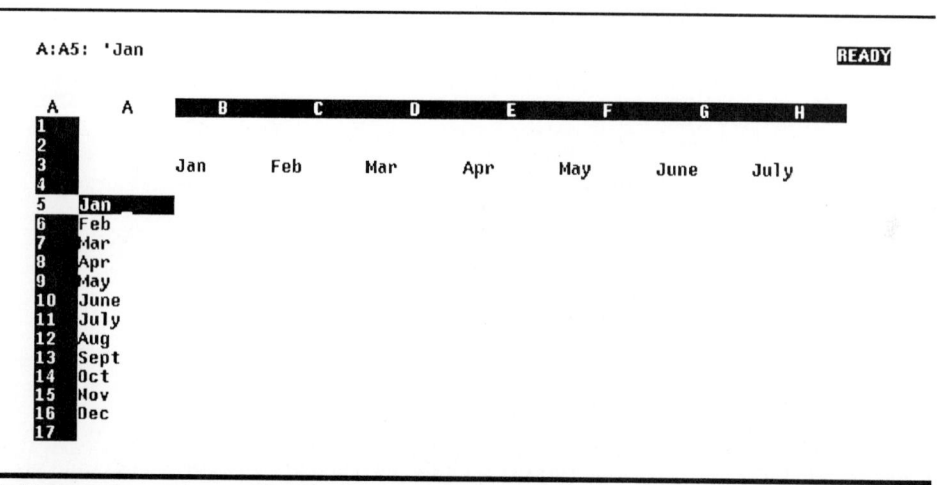

FIGURE 5-20.   The result of transposing data to a row

generate dividing lines and other quick entries in worksheet cells. The other feature, a series generator, can generate a series of numbers that have the same increment between each value in the series—for example, the series 1, 2, 3, 4 or the series 25, 50, 75, 100.

Creating Repeating Labels

You do not need a menu command to generate repeating labels. Instead, you accomplish it with the backslash (\) special label indicator followed by either a single character or a series of characters. Whichever you choose, 1-2-3 will duplicate your entry automatically to fill the complete width of the cell and adjust its width if you change the cell width.

You can use this feature to make a dividing line between sections of a worksheet or to create the top and bottom lines when you want to draw a box around your assumptions. Follow these steps to draw a box around the assumptions section of the worksheet:

1. Enter **/File Retrieve**, type **SALESPRJ**, and press ENTER.

2. Move the cell pointer to A22.

3. Enter * and press ENTER.
   Notice how the asterisks completely fill A22.

4. Enter \Copy and press ENTER.

5. Move the cell pointer to B22, type . (a period), move the cell pointer to I21, and press ENTER.

6. Move the cell pointer to A23 and type *. Then press ENTER.

7. Enter /Copy and press ENTER.

8. Move the cell pointer to A24, type ., and then move the cell pointer to A27 and press ENTER.

9. Move the cell pointer to A21 and then enter /**Copy**.

10. Move the cell pointer to I21 with the END and RIGHT ARROW keys, and press ENTER.

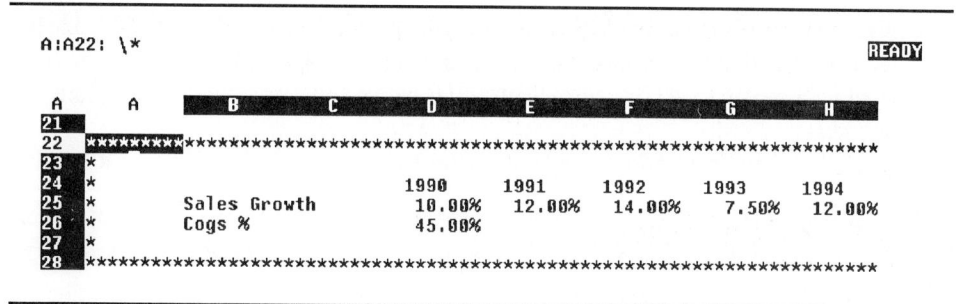

FIGURE 5-21.   Box generated with repeating labels

11. Move the cell pointer to A28 and press ENTER.

12. Move the cell pointer to I23 and type '   *.

    Leave eight spaces before the asterisk to form the right edge of the box. Since you are entering spaces, you can omit the label indicator; 1-2-3 will automatically consider it a label and add the ' symbol.

13. Enter **/Copy** and press ENTER.

14. Move the cell pointer to I24, type ., move the cell pointer to I27, and press ENTER.

15. Move the cell pointer to A22.

    The final result of your entries is a line of asterisks on all four sides of the assumptions. Since the display is wider than the screen width, you can view only three sides of this box, as shown in Figure 5-21.

16. Enter **/File Save**, press ENTER, and enter **Replace**.

17. Enter **/Worksheet Erase Yes**.

Generating a Series of Numbers

It can be tedious to enter a long list of numbers. In one special situation you can assign this task to 1-2-3: when the list of numbers is a series with equal intervals. The interval can be either positive or negative, but it must be the same between every number in the series. This means that lists such as 10, 20, 30, 40; 7, 9, 11, 13, 15; 52609, 52610, 52611; and 30, 29, 28, 27 can be generated by the package. A list such as 1, 3, 7, 15 could not be generated, because the intervals between the numbers in the list are not the same.

Follow these instructions to try this feature by generating a list of invoice numbers:

1. Type **Inv. No.** in A3.

2. Move the cell pointer to A4.

   This is the upper-left cell in the range where you will have 1-2-3 generate numbers.

3. Enter **/Data Fill**, type ., and use the DOWN ARROW key to highlight the fill range to A20, as shown in Figure 5-22. Then press ENTER.

4. Type **57103** and press ENTER in response to the prompt for the start number.

5. Press ENTER to accept 1 for the step increment number.

   This is the value that is added to each value in the list to create the next entry.

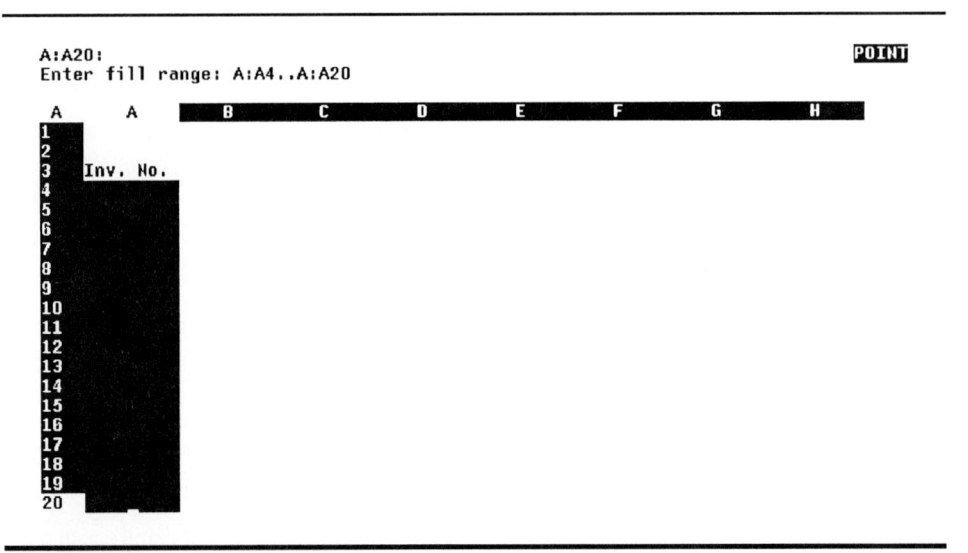

FIGURE 5-22.   Highlighting the fill range

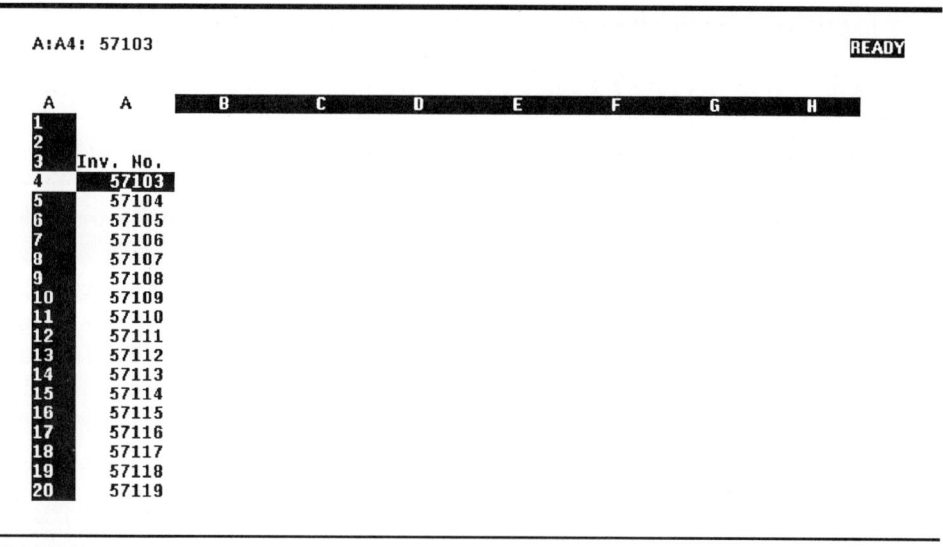

FIGURE 5-23.   Numbers generated by /Data Fill

6. Type **59000**.

    The entries in the control panel should look like this:

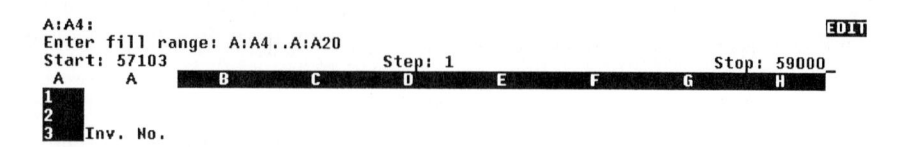

The stop value must always be as large as the last value in the list. This means that there are two factors that can end a list. The fill numbers stop being generated at the end of the range selected. They can also stop sooner if the stop value is not large enough to accommodate the numbers you are generating.

7. Press ENTER.

    The list of numbers generated is shown in Figure 5-23. Naturally, you can make your range larger to generate a larger list of numbers. You can also choose a horizontal range of cells and create an entry for each cell in the row.

8. Enter **/Worksheet Erase Yes Yes**.

OTHER WORKSHEET COMMANDS FOR EXPANDED DATA

Now that you have learned how to create these models quickly, you will find that you can create many more models as well. Some of the models you create will contain data for many months or years. You will also want to learn some of the tricks that make working with these models easier, such as controlling recalculation. This is a helpful trick, because as your models grow larger, 1-2-3 takes longer to recalculate after each of your entries. 1-2-3's speed seems quite good, compared to manual alternatives, when you do what-if analysis; but if you are entering a long list of account names or invoice numbers, it is annoying to have to wait for the package to finish recalculating. In this section you will learn how to put yourself in charge of the recalculation process.

You will also need additional tools to use for large models, since the entire model cannot be kept on the screen. You will learn in this section the technique of creating a second window and of freezing certain information on the screen.

Recalculation

1-2-3's recalculation options are accessed with the /Worksheet Global Recalc command. Actually, this is three commands in one, since it lets you change three different aspects of recalculation. You can select when the worksheet will recalculate, the order in which it will recalculate formulas, and how many times it will recalculate the worksheet. The latter two options are advanced features of recalculation that are seldom required. If you are curious about these, check your 1-2-3 manual. The first option affects when the recalculation occurs. This is a real time-saver that can be used with any large worksheet.

Release 3 uses a calculation method known as *minimal recalculation*. This method is more efficient than earlier methods, which recalculated every worksheet formula anytime you changed a worksheet entry. With minimal recalculation, 1-2-3 only recalculates values affected by worksheet changes. Another change in 1-2-3's recalculation is the addition of *background recalculation*, which means that 1-2-3 does not require 100% of the system resources to perform its calculations. Background recalculation allows you to continue editing and entering data as 1-2-3 updates the worksheet formula values. This makes 1-2-3 more efficient with all your calculations but reduces the time savings that you gain by changing 1-2-3's recalculation to the Manual setting.

To alter the timing of recalculation for the sales projection worksheet, follow these steps:

1. Enter **/File Retrieve**, type **SALESPRJ**, and press ENTER.

2. Enter **/Worksheet Global Recalc**.
   The following menu will be displayed:

```
A:A1:                                                                    MENU
Natural  Columnwise  Rowwise  Automatic  Manual  Iteration
Recalculate in natural order
```

   The first three options in this menu refer to the order of recalculation. The last option refers to the number of times the worksheet recalculates. The other two options, Automatic and Manual, let you determine whether the package will automatically update the model after a change or whether you wish to control recalculation.

3. Enter **Manual**.
   This selection means that 1-2-3 will not recalculate formulas after a worksheet change. To recalculate them you will need to press the F9 (CALC) key.

4. Move your cell pointer to C4, type **120000**, and press ENTER.
   Notice that this change does not affect the results in any category, although it does turn on the CALC indicator at the bottom of your screen. This indicator is a warning that changes have been made and the worksheet has not been recalculated.

5. Press F9 (CALC).
   Now you will see the results of the change.

6. Change the value in C4 back to 110000 by typing **110000**.
   Again, the results are not affected.

7. Press F9 (CALC).
   Your display should again show the results you started with.

8. Enter **/Worksheet Global Recalc Automatic**.

From this point on, every worksheet entry will cause recalculation. Keep this easy-to-make change in mind; it is a great option when you have a significant amount of data to enter.

Using Windows
To Help Monitor Data

1-2-3 allows you to split the screen into two different sections, called *windows,* and to view a different portion of the worksheet in each section. You have the option of splitting the screen vertically or horizontally; which method you use will depend on how your worksheet is arranged and which sections you want to view. If you want to see columns in two different areas, you will split the screen vertically. If you want to view rows from two different locations, you will want to choose a horizontal split.

The command that you use to create the split is /Worksheet Window. It is different from any other 1-2-3 command you have used: it requires you to position your cell pointer before invoking it. The location of the cell pointer determines the size of the two windows, and the window size cannot be changed while the menu is active.

After invoking the /Worksheet Window command, you must select Horizontal if you want two horizontal windows. The split will be made above the cell pointer at the time the command is invoked. Selecting Vertical will draw two vertical windows, the first of which ends immediately to the left of the cell pointer's location when the command was invoked.

Once the screen has been split into two windows, you can use the F6 (WINDOW) key to move to the other window. Regardless of which window you are in, F6 (WINDOW) always takes you to the opposite window.

The Worksheet Window menu has some additional selections. The only other command that is not an advanced option is the Clear selection, which allows you to return to a display with one window. Cell-pointer position is not important when you plan to choose Clear.

Try this exercise with your sales projection model to clarify how it works:

1. Press the HOME key.

2. Use the DOWN ARROW key to move the cell pointer to A10.

3. Enter **/Worksheet Window**.
   The menu shown in Figure 5-24 will appear.

4. Enter **Horizontal**.

5. Press F6 (WINDOW) to move the cell pointer to the lower window.

6. Move the cell pointer to A29 to view the assumptions in the lower window.
   Your screen should match the display in Figure 5-25.

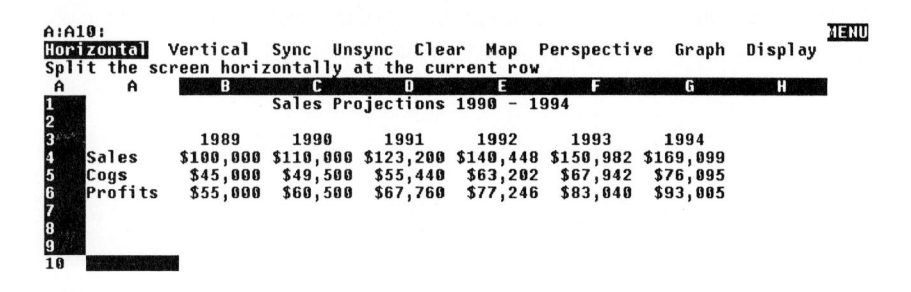

FIGURE 5-24.   Worksheet Window menu

7. Enter /**Worksheet Window Clear**.

The display will return to a single window.

Using Titles with
Large Worksheets

One of the problems with large worksheets is that you cannot see all the data on the screen at one time. This problem is magnified when you move your cell pointer to the

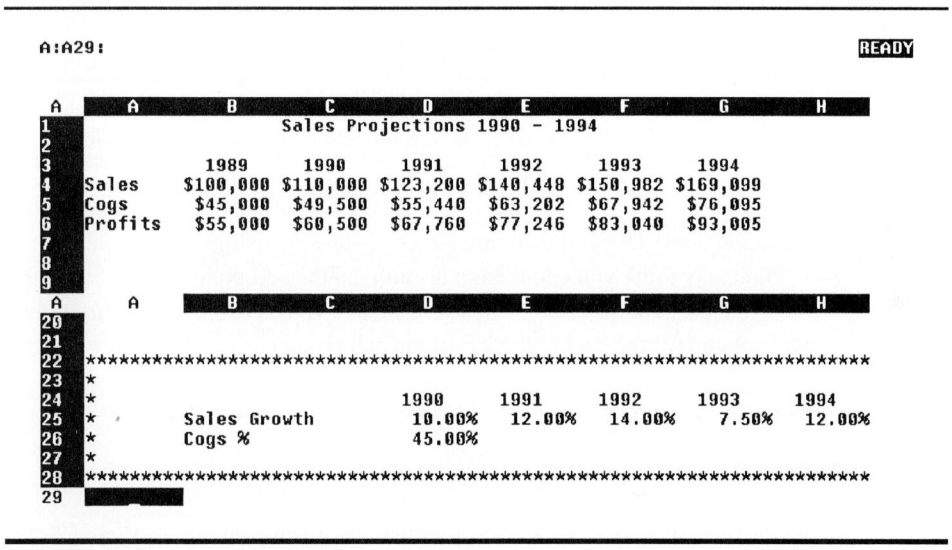

FIGURE 5-25.   Two horizontal windows

right or down and find that the labels at the left of the rows and the top of the columns scroll off the screen. You can find yourself in a sea of numbers with no visible indication of what each of these numbers represents. The solution in 1-2-3 is to freeze some of the label information on the screen.

The /Worksheet Titles command freezes label information on the screen. As with the /Worksheet Window command, the position of the cell pointer at the time you invoke this command is critical. If your cell pointer is in A1, you will not be able to create either vertical or horizontal titles—there is no information below or to the left of the cell pointer. The cell-pointer location defines what information will be frozen on the screen. The command has four options: to fix titles both vertically and horizontally; to fix them vertically; to fix them horizontally; or to clear all fixed titles from the screen. This last option does not eliminate the titles themselves, but it ensures that neither vertical nor horizontal titles are frozen any longer.

If you choose to freeze vertical titles with either the Vertical or Both options, when you invoke /Worksheet Titles any columns to the left of the cell pointer will become fixed on the screen. You will not be able to move your cell pointer into these columns with the arrow keys. If you move to the right of the point at which columns would normally scroll off the screen, only columns to the right of the fixed titles will scroll off the screen. The columns defined as titles will always be visible.

The situation is similar for horizontal titles, whether you choose Horizontal or Both. All rows above the cell pointer at the time /Worksheet Titles is invoked will remain frozen on the screen, even when the cell pointer moves far enough down on the worksheet to cause rows to scroll off the screen. The rows below the frozen titles can scroll off the screen, but not the titles you have fixed on the screen.

Looking at an example of this command with the sales projection worksheet will show you how it works. If you wanted to bring the right edge of the assumptions box into view, the left edge would scroll off the screen unless you first fixed the titles. Use these steps for fixing columns A through C:

1. Press the HOME key and then press PGDN. Move the cell pointer to D25.

   You may think you could have just moved the cell pointer to D25, but the step you just took is the only way to ensure that you have only the desired rows and columns above and to the left of the cell pointer.

2. Enter /**Worksheet Titles** to produce the menu shown in Figure 5-26.

3. Enter **Vertical**.

4. Move the cell pointer to K25 to produce the display shown in Figure 5-27. Notice that columns A, B, and C are frozen on the screen, yet columns D, E, and F scrolled off the screen.

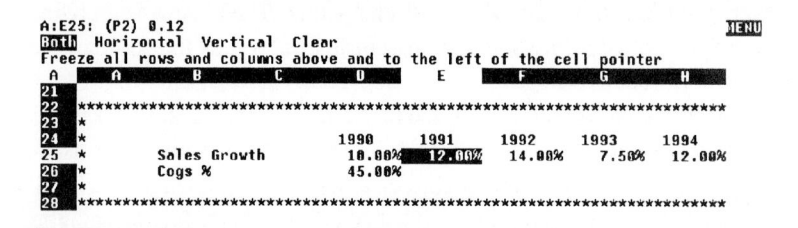

FIGURE 5-26.   Worksheet Titles menu

5. Enter **/Worksheet Titles Clear**.

    This will unfix the titles, and columns A through C will scroll off the screen.

These title-fixing features will be useful for situations in which the total is at the bottom of a long column or on the right side of a long row. By fixing the titles you can check the total and still keep the corresponding labels on the screen for readability.

SEARCHING AND REPLACING WORKSHEET DATA

Once you master 1-2-3's features, you will be creating large worksheets that model your business operations. Working with larger models can make it more difficult to find a particular entry; it will no longer be practical to scan the model for a particular entry. If you are working with Release 3, you can have 1-2-3 scrutinize entries for you. 1-2-3 can match a string of characters in either labels or formulas. Instead of just locating the matching characters, you can also use the Replace option to change one

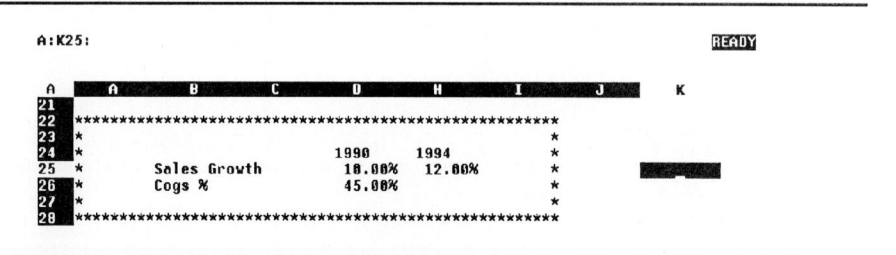

FIGURE 5-27.   Vertical titles displaying columns A, B, and C

or more occurrences to another set of characters. These new Search and Replace features can save you time in reviewing entries, as well as the editing time required for those you want to change.

The /Range Search command is used for finding and replacing worksheet data. You can find text in cell formulas and labels. Since 1-2-3 can replace text as well as find it, you can use this command to correct a misspelling, change a cell address that formulas use, or find a name in a worksheet. The options for replacing text or cell addresses allow you to make all of the changes at once. If you would prefer to move a little slower, you can skip a matching entry, find the next matching entry to replace, or replace the current matching entry and move to the next one.

Searching Worksheet Data

1-2-3 can find text stored in formulas and labels. This feature cannot be used to search a cell that contains only numbers. Using the Search feature with the sales projection worksheet will show you how it works. With the SALESPRJ file in memory from the previous example, use these steps to find the text "Sales":

1. Move the cell pointer to A1.

2. Enter **/Range Search**. 1-2-3 prompts you for the range to search.

3. Type a period to anchor one corner of the search range. Press the DOWN ARROW five times; then press END and RIGHT ARROW to highlight A1..G6. Press ENTER. 1-2-3 asks for the string to search for. You can use either upper- or lowercase letters when typing the search string, since 1-2-3 treats them as equivalent entries.

4. Type **Sales** and press ENTER.
   You can type **sales** or **SALES** for the same results. 1-2-3 then prompts you to determine what type of entries should be searched for with the search string:

5. Enter **Labels** to have 1-2-3 search all label cell entries for the string "Sales." 1-2-3 asks whether you want to find the string or replace the string with another string.

6. Enter **Find**.
   1-2-3 finds the word "Sales" in A4 (searching a column at a time) and creates the following display:

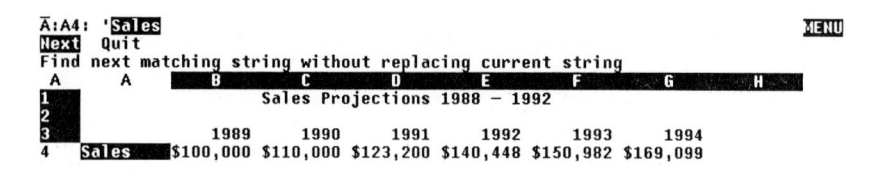

7. Select **Next**.

 1-2-3 continues the search, column by column, finds "Sales" in C1, and shows the same prompt.

8. Select **Quit**.

 1-2-3 returns to READY mode.

If you select **Next**, 1-2-3 will not find another Sales entry in the range selected but will beep to alert you to the lack of additional matching entries.

You can also use this command to find text in formulas. To find which cells use the 1992 sales-growth figure stored in F25, you can search for a cell reference to F25 in formulas within the model by using these steps:

1. Enter **/Range Search**.

 1-2-3 prompts you for the range to search and highlights the range you selected when you were attempting to find "Sales."

2. Press ENTER.

 1-2-3 prompts you for the string to search for and displays Sales.

3. Type **F25** and press ENTER.

 1-2-3 prompts you to determine what type of entries it should check for with the string.

4. Enter **Formulas**.

 1-2-3 then asks whether you want to find the string or replace the string with something else.

5. Enter **Find**.

 1-2-3 searches all cells containing formulas for the cell reference F25. It finds F25 in E4 and prompts you to determine if you want it to find the next occurrence or quit.

6. Select **Next**.

1-2-3 cannot find another formula that uses F25, which causes it to beep and display this error message on the bottom row of your screen:

```
No more matching strings — Press HELP (F1)
```

7. Press ESC. 1-2-3 returns to READY mode.

Replacing Worksheet Data

If you make a few mistakes when reentering labels and formulas, the Replace option of 1-2-3's /Range Search command can handle the corrections for you. Replace not only locates your text but changes it to whatever character string you specify. You can use the SALESPRJ file and follow these steps to replace the text "Profit" with "Gross Profit":

1. Enter /**Range Search**.

   1-2-3 asks for the range to search. It displays the range you selected for searching the worksheet earlier.

2. Press ENTER to select A1..G6.

   1-2-3 asks for the string to search for and prompts you with F25 from the last /Range Search command.

3. Type **Profit** and press ENTER.

   Since upper- and lowercase are equivalent in the search string, you can use either with identical results. 1-2-3 next prompts you for the type of entries you want to look for in the string.

4. Enter **Labels**.

   1-2-3 will search all label cell entries for the string "Profit." It then asks you whether you want to find the string or replace it with something else.

5. Enter **Replace**.

6. Type **Gross Profit** and press ENTER.

   1-2-3 finds "Profit" in A6 and creates the following display:

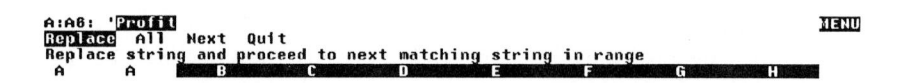

```
A:A6: 'Profit                                                          MENU
Replace  All  Next  Quit
Replace string and proceed to next matching string in range
   A       A       B       C       D       E       F       G       H
```

7. Select **Replace**.

1-2-3 replaces "Profit" in A6 with "Gross Profit" and then searches for the next occurrence of "Profit." Since 1-2-3 cannot find another label that contains "Profit," it beeps and displays an error message indicating that it cannot find the search string.

8. Press ESC.
   1-2-3 returns to the READY mode.

When you use the /Range Search command to replace text in formulas or labels, you must be careful about what you supply as a search string. If the text that you search for is not clearly defined, you may wind up replacing text that you did not want to replace. As an example of an unintentional replacement, suppose you want to use the sales-growth rate for 1992 in 1993. One method of doing this is to replace the G25 cell reference with F25. If you use a search string of **G** and a replacement text of **F**, 1-2-3 returns unexpected results, since it prompts you on many unexpected matches. To show how this happens, follow these steps:

1. Enter /**Range Search**.
   1-2-3 prompts you for the range to search and highlights the one you selected in the last /Range Search command.

2. Press ENTER to accept A1..G6.
   1-2-3 asks for the string to search for and displays "Profit."

3. Press ESC to remove the previous entry, type **G**, and press ENTER.
   1-2-3 prompts you for where it should look for the string.

4. Enter **Both**.
   1-2-3 asks whether you want to find the string or replace it with something else.

5. Enter **Replace**.

6. Type **F** and press ENTER.
   1-2-3 finds "G" in "Cogs" in A5 and prompts you for finding the next one or quitting.

7. Select **All**. 1-2-3 finds all occurrences of the letter "G" in the worksheet and replaces them with the letter "F."
   When 1-2-3 cannot find another "G," it returns to READY mode. The screen looks like Figure 5-28.

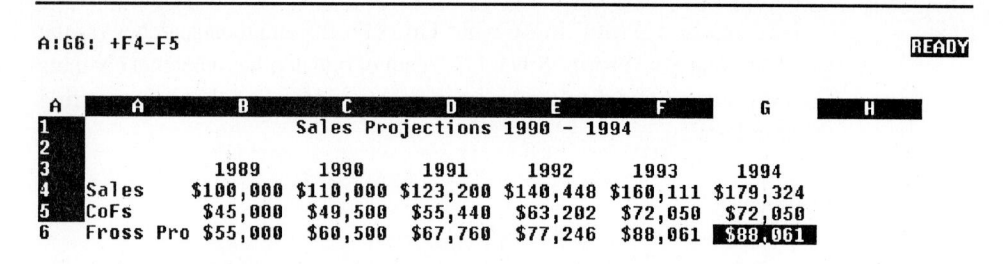

FIGURE 5-28.   Worksheet after supplying an inadequate search string

Since the search string is not specific enough, the /Range Search command replaced every "G" in the specified range. The entries in column G will highlight the error. A better solution is to enter **G25** as the search string and **F25** as the replacement string. Although you must type more characters, you exclude cells that you do not want to alter.

8. Enter /**Worksheet Erase Yes Yes** to erase the worksheet.

The second Yes is required because the worksheet changes have not been saved.

REVIEW EXERCISE

Now that you have had an opportunity to look at some of the commands that can save you time, you will want to practice them a bit. Pay special attention to /Copy and /Move, since you will use these commands repeatedly in your everyday model

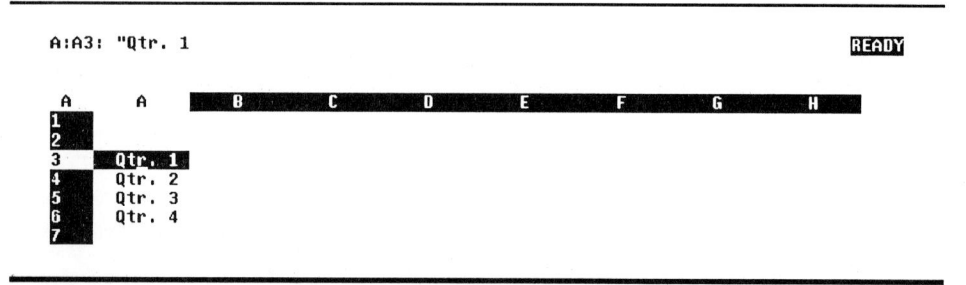

FIGURE 5-29.   Initial entries for each quarter

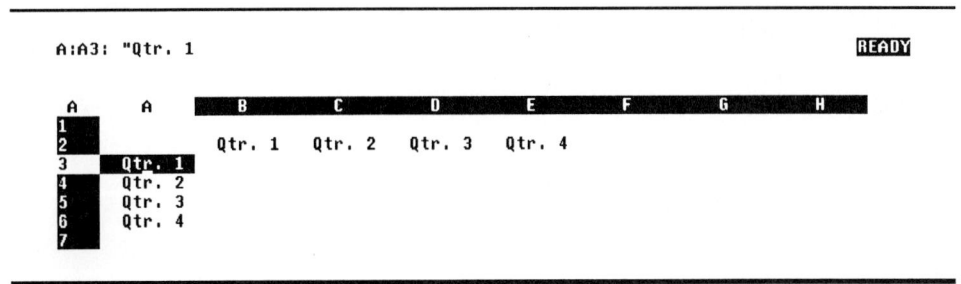

FIGURE 5-30.   Transposing column entries to row entries

building. Mastering them can make you a model construction expert. Follow these steps to create a model to record quarterly sales:

1. Enter /**Worksheet Erase Yes** to clear any existing worksheet entries if you have made entries since the last example.

2. Place **Qtr. 1** through **Qtr. 4** in A3 through A6. You can refer to the model in Figure 5-29. *Hint:* You might enter **"Qtr1** in A3 and copy the contents of A3 to A4..A6, then edit the contents of A4..A6 so the worksheet has labels for the four quarters.

3. Transpose the labels from A3..A6 to into column headings. *Hint:* Use /Range Trans, selecting A3..A6 as the from range and B2 as the to range. The worksheet looks like Figure 5-30.

4. Erase the column entries in A3..A6. *Hint:* /Worksheet Erase will eliminate all your entries; /Range Erase is the command you need.

5. Enter **Widgets** in A3, **Things** in A4, and **Total** in A5.

6. Move "Total" from A5 to A6. *Hint:* Use /Move and select A5 as the from range and A6 as the to range.

7. Create a line with a repeating hyphen in B5. *Hint:* Enter \\- and then copy the entry with /Copy.

8. Set recalculation to Manual. *Hint:* Use the /Worksheet Global Recalc Manual command, and remember that you will need to press F9 (CALC) when you want to see the effect of worksheet changes.

9. Enter the following numbers in these cells:

   B3: 50000
   C3: 60000
   D3: 55000
   E3: 40000
   B4: 35000
   C4: 55000
   D4: 60000
   E4: 70000

10. Enter a formula in row 6 that adds together Widgets and Things for each quarter. *Hint:* For Qtr. 1, you can enter **+B3+B4** in B6 and then use /Copy to place the formula in other cells on this row.

11. Move the column headings from row 2 to row 1, and add a dashed line below it. *Hint:* Use /Move to relocate the column headings and then use /Copy to copy the existing line of hyphens.

12. Set recalculation to Automatic to recalculate the worksheet. (*Hint:* Use the /Worksheet Global Recalc Automatic command followed by F9 (CALC).) The CALC indicator at the bottom of your screen will disappear.

13. Move to B3. Create a vertical window with /Worksheet Window Vertical. The screen now looks like Figure 5-31. Press F6 (WINDOW) key to switch between the two windows. Close the window with the /Worksheet Window Clear command.

14. Save the file as WIDGETS.

15. Replace "Things" with "Gizmos." *Hint:* Use the /Range Search command with the Replace option.

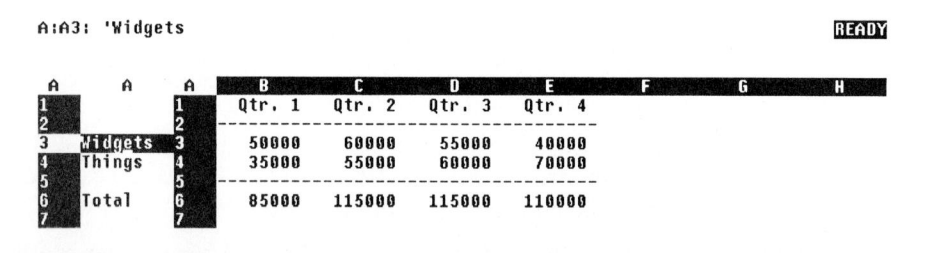

FIGURE 5-31.   Two vertical windows

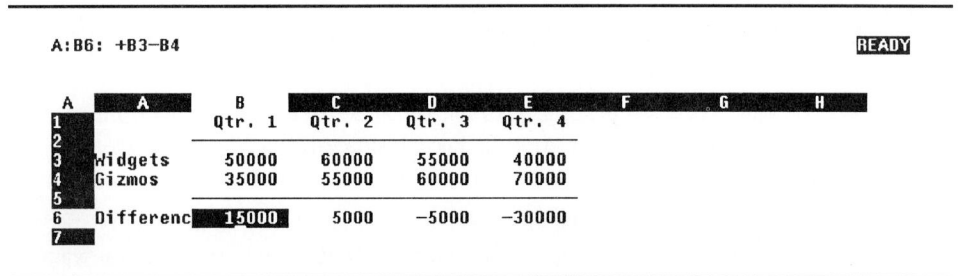

FIGURE 5-32.   Worksheet after replacing labels and formulas

16. Replace "Total" with "Difference." *Hint:* Use the /Range Search command with the Replace option.

17. Replace the formula that adds the total Widgets and Gizmos for each quarter with a formula that subtracts Gizmos from Widgets. *Hint:* You can even use /Range Search to make this change. Since it is a bit trickier than other replace operations, each of the steps are listed here for you. Press ESC and highlight the range B6..E6 as the search range. Enter 3+ for the search string. Select **Formulas** to search. Select **Replace**. Enter **3-** as the replacement string. Select **All** to replace the plus sign with the minus sign. 1-2-3 returns to READY mode. Including the 3 in the search and replace operation prevents the /Range Search command from prompting to see if you want to replace the plus sign at the beginning of the formula. The worksheet looks like Figure 5-32.

REVIEW

- The /Copy command can copy cells within a worksheet. You can copy one cell to one cell, or one cell to many cells. You can also make one copy of an entire range of cells, or make many copies of the same range. When you copy cells, 1-2-3 adjusts the formulas in the range depending on whether the formulas use absolute, mixed, or relative cell addresses.

- The /Move command can move cells within a worksheet. When you move cells, 1-2-3 adjusts the formulas so that all cell formulas reference the same cell contents as they did before cells were moved.

- The /Range Trans command copies a range of cells and changes the cells' orientation from row to column or column to row. If you transpose formulas, this command copies and transposes the values of the formulas, rather than the formulas themselves.

- You can create a repeating label by using the backslash (\) label prefix. The characters that you enter after the backslash are repeated for the width of the cell. This repeating label adjusts the label's length for the column's width.

- The /Data Fill command generates a series of numbers that are evenly spaced. To use this command you must provide the worksheet range that you want to fill with numbers, the number that you want to start the series, the increment between values (positive for ascending and negative for descending), and the last value that may appear in the series.

- The /Worksheet Global Recalc command determines whether 1-2-3 recalculates the worksheet whenever a worksheet entry is made or when you press the F9 (CALC) key. This command was more frequently used in earlier releases, which did not have the minimal and background recalculation that Release 3 features.

- The /Worksheet Window command lets you create vertical and horizontal windows. These windows divide the screen so you can see two sections of your worksheet at once.

- The /Worksheet Titles command locks rows and columns on the screen display so you can always see the column or row header. Options let you select horizontal titles (rows that always appear on the screen), vertical titles (columns that always appear on the screen), both titles (columns and rows that always appear on the screen), or clear titles (removing the titles from the screen).

- The /Range Search command can search for text in label or formula cell entries. The Replace option allows you to replace the text the command finds with different text.

Commands and Keys

\	As a label prefix character, repeats the string that follows until the column width is filled
F4 (ABS)	Converts the address at the cursor's location to an absolute, mixed, or relative address
F6 (WINDOW)	Switches between the active windows
F9 (CALC)	Updates the calculations in the worksheet
/C	Copies one or more cells to one or more locations
/DF	Generates a series of numbers a specific interval apart
/M	Moves one or more cells to another location
/RS	Finds, or finds and replaces, text in formulas and label cell entries

/RT	Copies one or more cells to a new location and changes the column and row orientation
/WGDRA	Sets 1-2-3 to recalculate the worksheet when an entry is made
/WGDRM	Sets 1-2-3 to recalculate the worksheet when F9 (CALC) is pressed
/WTB	Freezes the rows above the cell pointer and the columns to the left of the cell pointer as worksheet titles
/WTC	Clears worksheet titles created with the /WTB, /WTH, or /WTV command
/WTH	Freezes the rows above the cell pointer as a horizontal title
/WTV	Freezes the columns to the left of the cell pointer as a vertical title
/WWC	Removes a window created with the /WWH or /WWV command
/WWH	Splits the screen display in half with a horizontal line, allowing you to view different sections of the worksheet
/WWV	Splits the screen display in half with a vertical line, allowing you to view different sections of the worksheet

6

PRINTING YOUR WORKSHEET

Printing Basics
Adding a Few Options
Special /Print Options
Review Exercise
Review

In this chapter you will have an opportunity to explore 1-2-3's printing features. You can use them to create a quick draft copy of your worksheet with only a few instructions. When you are ready for a final copy, you can create a professional-looking report with a few new commands. These commands will allow you to control the print margins, access the special /Print options offered by your printer, and even add headers and footers to every page.

You will first learn to use the basic /Print options. Then you will learn more complex /Print options, via the building-block approach, until you have a full set of printing features that you can use. You will also have the opportunity to explore options for printing formulas and to use worksheet commands to further customize your print output. Additional enhancements, such as fonts, line spacing, size, and rotation, which are new to Release 3, are covered as well.

PRINTING BASICS

1-2-3's basic printing features are designed to give you quick access to a printed copy. This quick access is made possible by default values that 1-2-3 has set for options such as margins and page length. Later, you will learn to override these default settings, but for now you might as well appreciate their presence; they make it easy for you to print out your files.

Determining the Destination

What is the destination for 1-2-3's print features? At first the answer seems obvious. After all, if you are printing, you would expect to use the printer. But 1-2-3 offers you several choices: you can print to a printer, a file on disk with the printer codes, or to a file on disk without the printer codes. *Printer codes* are directions to the printer that tell the printer how to print your worksheet. The ability to capture print output on a disk adds considerable flexibility to the print features.

To select a destination, first access the printing features by entering **/Print**. This command displays the following submenu:

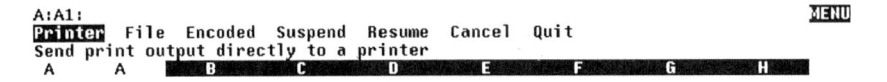

1-2-3 is asking if it should direct your output to the printer or write it to a file. If you want to create printed hard copy immediately, choose Printer. The last four options are for controlling when 1-2-3 sends printer information to the printer.

THE ENCODED OPTION   The Encoded option is designed to let you write your print output to a file. Unlike the files that contain worksheets, this file contains print data and the printer codes that instruct the printer how to print the worksheet. Encoded files are automatically assigned the filename extension .ENC. Once you have stored the information in the file, you can print it at a later time.

Because these files contain printer information, they are not designed to be used by other programs. The Encoded option is for printing to a file that you will later print. You print the encoded file by copying it to the LPT1 device. For example, to print the encoded file SALES.ENC, you enter **COPY SALES.ENC LPT1** from the operating system prompt. Although the focus of this chapter is on printing to a printer, you can use the same printing options with encoded files.

THE FILE OPTION   The File option lets you write your print output to a file. Unlike the files that contain worksheets, this file contains the values of the worksheet. The File option creates an *ASCII text file* that is automatically assigned the filename extension .PRN. Once you have stored the information in the file, you can do various things with it: you can modify it with a word processor or use it as input to some application programs.

It is good to be aware that you can print to a file, but you will usually want to print to a printer, so this chapter will focus on doing so. Unlike the Encoded option, some of the /Print options do not affect files created by selecting File. Most of the options that have no effect are for printer-specific features such as fonts, spacing, and character size.

THE PRINTER OPTION   When you select the Printer option, 1-2-3 assumes that the output device is the printer you selected when 1-2-3 was installed. As long as this printer is attached to your system and online when you tell 1-2-3 to begin printing, your print output will be sent to this device. Normally, the top or front of the printer has a series of small lights to indicate that the printer is ready to accept data. Verify that the printer is turned on and is online before you start to work with the /Print commands. It is also a good idea to understand the defaults that will apply to your output before you learn about the instruction that actually starts the printing.

THE DEFAULT SETTINGS   One of the things that simplifies printing the first time you use a worksheet is the default settings of some of the /Print options. These defaults affect the length of a page of output and the amount of white space, or the margin, on all four sides of a printed page. The defaults also apply to the printed pages you write to a disk.

The default page defined by 1-2-3 has several areas affecting the amount of data that prints on a page. The layout of a printed page is shown in Figure 6-1. Notice that a page of output is defined as 66 lines, but not all these lines will contain printed data. Some of them are reserved for top and bottom margins. Once 2 lines are deducted for a top margin and 2 more are deducted for a bottom margin, only 62 lines will print on a page. In addition to the top and bottom margins, 1-2-3 allows 3 lines at both the top and bottom for a header or footer, even if you choose not to use either one. This means that of the 66 possible lines, only 56 lines will be used for printing with the default settings.

Similarly, standard print on an 8 1/2- by 11-inch sheet of paper allows 80 characters to print across the page, but the default settings will reduce this number. 1-2-3 has a default left margin setting of 4 and a default right margin setting of 76. This means

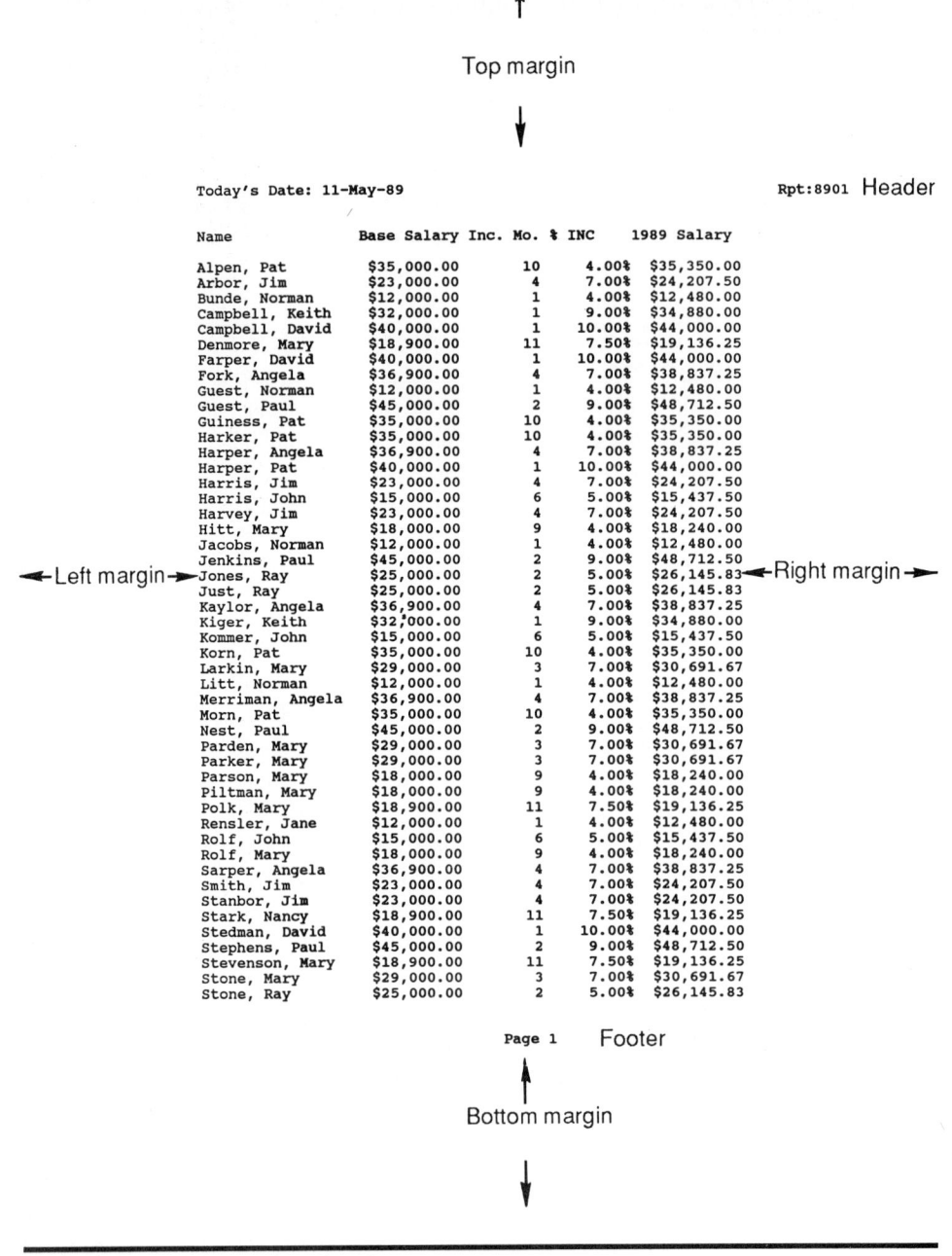

FIGURE 6-1.   Layout of a printed page

that without modifying the defaults you can print a maximum of 72 characters across the page. Initially, try the /Print operation without modifying any of these defaults.

The Basic /Print Options

The second level of the Print menu is the same, whether you have chosen Encoded, Printer, or File. It is actually the main Print menu, since it is the root from which all the other /Print options can be selected. It looks like this:

This menu is different from any of the other menus you have used, which all disappear as soon as you make your first selection. In contrast, this Print menu stays on your screen so you can make additional selections. For this reason, it frequently is referred to as a "sticky menu." You will find it a real convenience; most printing operations require more than one menu selection.

Another important distinction is that 1-2-3 can remember the results of any command that affects the print setting. To have 1-2-3 remember what you want to print or any changes that you make to the print settings, first complete the definition of your print specifications, and then save the worksheet.

DEFINING THE RANGE TO PRINT   At this point you want to tell 1-2-3 how much of the worksheet you wish to print. Therefore, select the Range option from the main Print menu. The next step depends on whether the worksheet already has a print range defined. If not, just move to the beginning of the print range, type a period, and move to the end of the print range. If the worksheet was printed previously, the range address used from that time will probably still be defined. Before you can move the cell pointer to a new beginning location, press ESC to unlock the beginning of the range. Whether you have printed previously or not, you can type a range reference by entering the address of the beginning of the range followed by a period and the cell address of the end of the range, as in B3.H15. If a current range exists, 1-2-3 will immediately replace it with the range you enter; you do not need to press ESC.

The size of the range you define will affect how 1-2-3 prints your data when you request printing. If your defined range contains more data than will fit on one page, 1-2-3 will break the data into more than one page when you print. If the width of the range selected exceeds the number of characters that will print across one page, 1-2-3 will print as many columns across the first page as possible without exceeding the right margin setting. It will then break the output into more than one page. If the number of rows in the selected range exceeds the number of rows that can print on one page, 1-2-3 will generate a page break when the data prints.

To enter some data for printing and try several options for specifying the print range, experiment with the following exercise. You could print worksheets you entered for other chapters, but you might not have one readily available. Therefore, this section offers instructions for creating employee data to be printed. You need to make quite a few entries to create this model, but it is designed to let you try each of the /Print options covered in this chapter without having to enter data again. You will use entries more than once to build a large file quickly, and you will use the /Copy command extensively to further reduce these entry requirements. Follow these steps to enter the model and define the print range:

1. Enter the following labels across row 1:

   A1: SS#
   B1: Last Name
   C1: First Name
   D1: Salary
   E1: Location
   F1: Phone
   G1: Position
   H1: Increase %
   I1: '1990 Salary

2. Enter **/Worksheet Global Col-Width**, type **11**, and press ENTER.

3. Move the cell pointer to column A, enter **/Worksheet Column Set-Width**, type **13**, and press ENTER.

4. Make these entries in the cells shown:

   A2: '516-75-8977
   B2: Jones
   C2: Paul
   D2: 45900
   E2: DAL
   F2: 980
   G2: 2301
   H2: .05
   I2: +D2*(1+H2)
   A3: '541-78-6754
   B3: Parker
   C3: Mary

```
D3: 32100
E3: CHI
F3: 541
G3: 1605
H3: .04
A4: '897-90-8769
B4: Smith
C4: Larry
D4: 61250
E4: ATL
F4: 342
G4: 1402
H4: .05
A5: '213-78-5412
B5: Appel
C5: Tom
D5: 22300
E5: BOS
F5: 219
G5: 1750
H5: .06
```

5. Move the cell pointer to I2, enter /**Copy**, and press ENTER. Move the cell pointer to I3, type **.** (a period), move the cell pointer to I5, and press ENTER.

   This completes the first four records. You need more rows of data to get the full effect of 1-2-3's printing features, but typing the entries would take too long. Instead, copy these entries until you have a sufficient number to print more than one page. You will have many duplicates, but you will have the opportunity to print more than one page.

6. Move the cell pointer to A2 and enter /**Copy**. Then press END and the DOWN ARROW key, followed by END and the RIGHT ARROW key. Press ENTER to finalize the source range. Next, move the cell pointer to A6 and press ENTER.

   This time you copied the first 4 rows of the worksheet to create another 4 rows. Next time, you will copy the 8 existing data rows. After that, you will copy the 16 entries and then the 32 entries (the number of records become larger each time you make a copy).

7. Proceed with the copy by entering /**Copy**. Then press END and the DOWN ARROW key, followed by END and the RIGHT ARROW key. Press ENTER, and then move the cell pointer to A10 and press ENTER.

A:A1: [W13] 'SS#   READY

```
    A          A            B            C             D          E          F
1   SS#                   Last Name    First Name  Salary       Location   Phone
2   516-75-8977  Jones        Paul          $45,900 DAL                   980
3   541-78-6754  Parker       Mary          $32,100 CHI                   541
4   897-90-8769  Smith        Larry         $61,250 ATL                   342
5   213-78-5412  Appel        Tom           $22,300 BOS                   219
6   516-75-8977  Jones        Paul          $45,900 DAL                   980
7   541-78-6754  Parker       Mary          $32,100 CHI                   541
8   897-90-8769  Smith        Larry         $61,250 ATL                   342
9   213-78-5412  Appel        Tom           $22,300 BOS                   219
10  516-75-8977  Jones        Paul          $45,900 DAL                   980
11  541-78-6754  Parker       Mary          $32,100 CHI                   541
12  897-90-8769  Smith        Larry         $61,250 ATL                   342
13  213-78-5412  Appel        Tom           $22,300 BOS                   219
14  516-75-8977  Jones        Paul          $45,900 DAL                   980
15  541-78-6754  Parker       Mary          $32,100 CHI                   541
16  897-90-8769  Smith        Larry         $61,250 ATL                   342
17  213-78-5412  Appel        Tom           $22,300 BOS                   219
18  516-75-8977  Jones        Paul          $45,900 DAL                   980
19  541-78-6754  Parker       Mary          $32,100 CHI                   541
20  897-90-8769  Smith        Larry         $61,250 ATL                   342
```

FIGURE 6-2.   The left side of the entries

8. Continue copying in this manner until you have entries in cells A1..I65, using the procedures described in the previous step.

9. Move the cell pointer to D2, enter **/Range Format Currency**, type **0**, press ENTER, and then press END followed by the DOWN ARROW key. Press ENTER.

10. Move the cell pointer to H2 and enter **/Range Format Percent**. Press ENTER, and then press the END key followed by the DOWN ARROW key. Press ENTER again.

11. Move the cell pointer to I2. Enter **/Range Format Currency**. Type **0** and press ENTER. Press the END key followed by the DOWN ARROW key. Press ENTER.
    The upper portion of your entries should match Figures 6-2 and 6-3.

12. Press the F5 (GOTO) key, type **A2**, and press ENTER to bring the left side of the worksheet into view on your screen.

13. Enter **/Print Printer Range** and press the HOME key. Type **.** (a period). Press END followed by the HOME key to highlight the range A1..I65, as shown in Figure 6-4. Press ENTER.

```
A:G1:  'Position                                                    READY

    A       G           H           I          J        K        L
1    Position     Increase %  1990 Salary
2        2301       5.00%      $48,195
3        1605       4.00%      $33,384
4        1402       5.00%      $64,312
5        1750       6.00%      $23,638
6        2301       5.00%      $48,195
7        1605       4.00%      $33,384
8        1402       5.00%      $64,312
9        1750       6.00%      $23,638
10       2301       5.00%      $48,195
11       1605       4.00%      $33,384
12       1402       5.00%      $64,312
13       1750       6.00%      $23,638
14       2301       5.00%      $48,195
15       1605       4.00%      $33,384
16       1402       5.00%      $64,312
17       1750       6.00%      $23,638
18       2301       5.00%      $48,195
19       1605       4.00%      $33,384
20       1402       5.00%      $64,312
```

FIGURE 6-3.   The right side of the entries

```
A:I65:  (CO) +D65*(1+H65)                                          POINT
Enter print range: A:A1..A:I65_

    A       D        E        F        G        H          I
46    $45,900 DAL            980      2301     5.00%     $48,195
47    $32,100 CHI            541      1605     4.00%     $33,384
48    $61,250 ATL            342      1402     5.00%     $64,312
49    $22,300 BOS            219      1750     6.00%     $23,638
50    $45,900 DAL            980      2301     5.00%     $48,195
51    $32,100 CHI            541      1605     4.00%     $33,384
52    $61,250 ATL            342      1402     5.00%     $64,312
53    $22,300 BOS            219      1750     6.00%     $23,638
54    $45,900 DAL            980      2301     5.00%     $48,195
55    $32,100 CHI            541      1605     4.00%     $33,384
56    $61,250 ATL            342      1402     5.00%     $64,312
57    $22,300 BOS            219      1750     6.00%     $23,638
58    $45,900 DAL            980      2301     5.00%     $48,195
59    $32,100 CHI            541      1605     4.00%     $33,384
60    $61,250 ATL            342      1402     5.00%     $64,312
61    $22,300 BOS            219      1750     6.00%     $23,638
62    $45,900 DAL            980      2301     5.00%     $48,195
63    $32,100 CHI            541      1605     4.00%     $33,384
64    $61,250 ATL            342      1402     5.00%     $64,312
65    $22,300 BOS            219      1750     6.00%     $23,638
```

FIGURE 6-4.   Selecting a print range

You can use the END-HOME approach to include all of the cells. Notice that the main Print menu is still in the control panel to let you make additional selections. Take advantage of its presence and enter the range specification a few different ways:

14. Enter **Range**, press ESC to unlock the beginning of the range, and then move the cell pointer to B1. Type . and press the END key followed by the DOWN ARROW key. Press the RIGHT ARROW key twice, and then press ENTER to select the range B1..D65.

15. Enter **Range**, type **A1.I65**, and press ENTER.

    When you type the address of a replacement range, you do not have to press the ESC key first.

TELLING 1-2-3 TO BEGIN PRINTING   Once you have defined the range, you simply select Go from the Print menu. To immediately send the range you just defined to the printer, be sure your printer is turned on and is online and then enter **Go**. This will cause 1-2-3 to print the worksheet row by row and increment its internal line count with each line printed. Since Release 3 uses background printing, you can immediately use 1-2-3 without waiting until 1-2-3 has finished printing. You can proceed to select the next range you want to print or use other Print Menu options. The printed output is shown in Figure 6-5.

If you want a second copy, you can enter **Go** again, but 1-2-3 will not move to the top of a page before it starts printing again. You cannot solve this problem by paging with the Formfeed or Linefeed button on your computer, since 1-2-3 maintains its own *line count* to tell it how much more space it has on a page. If you physically advance the paper in your printer without changing 1-2-3's line count, the printed output will have page breaks in the wrong places.

CONTROLLING THE PRINTING   Once 1-2-3 starts printing, it continues to print until it has sent all of the information. In prior releases of 1-2-3, you had few options if you changed your mind or wanted to stop printing temporarily. Release 3 introduces three new commands to control the printing process: the menu options you ignored earlier in the chapter when you entered **/Print**.

The Cancel option cancels the printing process. Once you select this option, you will need to realign the paper in the printer. Another possibility is to temporarily suspend printing. You may want to do this if you notice that the printer has a low paper supply and you are printing a lengthy document. To temporarily stop printing, use the Suspend option. 1-2-3 stops the printing process until you use the Resume option. The Resume option is also necessary when your printer uses a single-sheet feeder; you

```
SS#            Last Name  First Name Salary      Location  Phone
516-75-8977    Jones      Paul        $45,900 DAL              980
541-78-6754    Parker     Mary        $32,100 CHI              541
897-90-8769    Smith      Larry       $61,250 ATL              342
213-78-5412    Appel      Tom         $22,300 BOS              219
516-75-8977    Jones      Paul        $45,900 DAL              980
541-78-6754    Parker     Mary        $32,100 CHI              541
897-90-8769    Smith      Larry       $61,250 ATL              342
```

```
   541-78-6754    Parker     Mary        $32,100 CHI          541
   897-90-8769    Smith      Larry       $61,250 ATL          342
   213-78-5412    Appel      Tom         $22,300 BOS          219
   516-75-8977    Jones      Paul        $45,900 DAL          980
   541-78-6754    Parker     Mary        $32,100 CHI          541
   897-90-8769    Smith      Larry       $61,250 ATL          342
   213-78-5412    Appel      Tom         $22,300 BOS          219
   516-75-8977    Jones      Paul        $45,900 DAL          980
   541-78-6754    Parker     Mary        $32,100 CHI          541
                                          $61,250 ATL          342
```

```
Position    Increase % 1988 Salary
     2301       5.00%    $48,195
     1605       4.00%    $33,384
     1402       5.00%    $64,312
     1750       6.00%    $23,638
     2301       5.00%    $48,195
     1605       4.00%    $33,384
     1402       5.00%    $64,312
```

```
   1750       6.00%    $23,638
   2301       5.00%    $48,195
   1605       4.00%    $33,384
   1402       5.00%    $64,312
   1750       6.00%    $23,638
   2301       5.00%    $48,195
   1605       4.00%    $33,384
   1402       5.00%    $64,312
```

FIGURE 6-5. Output from the print operation

must use Resume after inserting the next sheet in the printer. Once you have done so, 1-2-3 starts printing where it stopped.

With the /Print Cancel and /Print Suspend commands, 1-2-3 stops sending information to the file or printer immediately. However, your printer may not stop immediately, since many printers have buffers that store the output until the printer can print it.

```
516-75-8977  Jones    Paul     $45,900
541-78-6754  Parker   Mary     $32,100
897-90-8769  Smith    Larry    $61,250
213-78-5412  Appel    Tom      $22,300
516-75-8977  Jones    Paul     $45,900 DAL        980
541-78-6754  Parker   Mary     $32,100 CHI        541
897-90-8769  Smith    Larry    $61,250 ATL        342
213-78-5412  Appel    Tom      $22,300 BOS        219
516-75-8977  Jones    Paul     $45,900 DAL        980
541-78-6754  Parker   Mary     $32,100 CHI        541
```

FIGURE 6-6.   Two ranges selected and printed

PRINTING MULTIPLE RANGES   A new feature of Release 3 is selecting multiple ranges to print instead of selecting and printing each range. To select multiple print ranges, select each range and type a semicolon (;) when you want to select another range. You can mix typing range addresses, pointing to the range, and typing range names to print. When 1-2-3 prints the ranges, it starts in the order in which they were provided. To see how this feature works, follow these steps to print two sections of the worksheet:

1. Enter **Range**.

2. Type **A2..D5** as the first range to print.

3. Type **;**.

4. Type **A10..F15** as the second range to print.

5. Press ENTER.

6. Enter **Go**. Your output looks like Figure 6-6.
   To try the other print settings in this chapter, you will want to reset the range to A1..I65 before trying the other Print menu options:

7. Enter **Range**, type **A1.I65**, and press ENTER.

ADVANCING A LINE   Sometimes you want to print more than one print range. Depending on the size of each range of data, you may want to place it on a single page or separate pages. If you placed it on the same page, it would merge together unless you added one or more blank lines after printing the first range. 1-2-3 will do this for you when you use the /Print Printer Line command. Normally, you need only enter **Line**, since the Print menu is likely to be on your screen. Each time you enter **Line**, 1-2-3 causes the printer to advance the paper one line and add 1 to its internal line count.

ADVANCING A PAGE   Advancing a line is fine for a small separation, but when you want data on separate pages you might have to use Line too many times to make this solution a practical one. Instead, use the /Print Printer Page command, which will quickly advance the paper to the top of the next page. Try it now by entering **Page** from the main Print menu.

SETTING 1-2-3'S LINE COUNT TO ZERO   When the paper in your printer is set at the top of a form, you will want 1-2-3's line count to be set to 0. The option for this is Align. Try it by entering **Align**. It looks like nothing has happened, but 1-2-3 has completed its housekeeping chore of zeroing the line count.

CLEARING THE PRINT SETTINGS   The Print menu has a special command for clearing /Print settings from a previous operation. If you select Clear from the Print menu, these options will appear:

```
A:A2: [W13] '516-75-8977                                              MENU
All  Range  Borders  Format  Image  Device
Return all printer settings to defaults
```

The first selection clears everything connected with the previous printing and is appropriately labeled All. It sets everything back to the defaults. This means that you must define the next /Print operation just as if you had never printed before.

The second option, Range, only eliminates the definition of the print range. After executing this command, you must define a print range again before printing. If you forget, nothing will happen when you tell 1-2-3 to begin printing since there are no default settings for the print range.

The next two options, Borders and Format, will be discussed along with the more advanced features they relate to. Like the other options, they eliminate any special settings that have been made and leave the worksheet as if these special features had never been invoked. The option, Image, is discussed in Chapter 8 with printing graphs. The option, Device, eliminates settings made with the /Print Printer Options Advanced Device command.

QUITTING THE PRINT MENU   Since the Print menus do not disappear after you make your selections, you need a way to let 1-2-3 know you are finished selecting /Print options. The Quit option in the Print menu is designed to do this. Once you select Quit, you will be back in READY mode. Selecting Quit is the same as pressing ESC until you are in READY mode. If you are printing to a file, leaving the Print menus closes the .PRN or .ENC file, whereas selecting Hold returns you to READY mode without closing the .PRN or .ENC file, in case you want to add additional information to the file.

Enter **Quit** now to let 1-2-3 know you have finished making Print menu selections.

SAVING PRINT SPECIFICATIONS   When you decide to print a worksheet, you probably will want to produce updated copies of the same report when your worksheet data changes. It is easy to print a report on subsequent occasions if you save the worksheet file after printing. The /File Save command saves any updates to worksheet data, as well as your print settings. This means that the print range and any special settings you may have entered for margins or page length will still be available the next time you need to print. You can then enter the /Print Printer Go command to produce the output.

ADDING A FEW OPTIONS

You have already mastered the basics of printing; you do not need any other commands to get a printed copy of your data. Soon, however, your expectations will increase and you will not be content with just any old printout of your data. You will want to improve it. This is where /Print options can assist you significantly. You can access them by entering **Options** from the main Print menu to produce this menu:

```
A:A2: [W13] '516-75-8977                                          MENU
Header  Footer  Margins  Borders  Setup  Pg-Length  Other  Name  Advanced  Quit
Create a header
```

This is another "sticky menu" like the main Print menu. It will stay around until you choose Quit or press ESC. To remove the settings created through this menu, you use the /Print Printer Clear Format command. It resets the margins, page length, the advanced menu settings, and the setup string to the default value. The only /Print option setting that this command does not reset is the borders, which you can reset with /Print Printer Clear Borders.

Margin Settings

To change margin settings, select Margins from the Options menu. You will be presented with a submenu that looks like this:

```
A:A2: [W13] '516-75-8977                                          MENU
Left  Right  Top  Bottom  None
Set left margin
```

Each option on this menu represents one of the four areas where margins can be specified. The None option, new to Release 3, removes the margins settings from the worksheet so 1-2-3 will use the widest area for printing your worksheet. This option is often used for printing to a .PRN file.

Whatever values you enter for margins will change the printing defaults for this one worksheet. If you save the worksheet file after making changes to the margins, the changed values will be in effect for the worksheet the next time you retrieve it. If you want to make a temporary change, don't save the worksheet after changing the margins.

The limits on top and bottom margins are from 0 lines to 240 lines for each of the margin choices. The range of acceptable values for the right and left margins is 0 to 1000 characters. To enter a new margin setting, select the type of margin you wish to specify, and then type a new value and press ENTER. If you select None, 1-2-3 sets the top, left, and bottom margins to 0 and the right margin to 1000.

Try the following exercise with the employee data to see how margins can affect the output:

1. Enter /**Print Printer Options Margins**.

2. Enter **Left**, type **10**, and press ENTER.

3. Enter **Margins Right**, type **70**, and press ENTER.

4. Enter **Quit**.
   This Quit option exits the Options menu and returns you to the main Print menu.

5. Enter **Go**.
   You should find that one fewer column prints across the page because you have reserved more space for the right and left margins.

6. Enter **Page Align**.

Defining Headers and Footers

Headers and *footers* are lines that appear at the top and bottom of every page of print output. Information placed in the header at the top of a page can include the date or time, an identifying report number, a report title, the preparer's name, or a page number. The most frequent entry in a footer at the bottom of the page is the page number.

Headers and footers can be up to 512 characters in length. However, do not make them any longer than the number of characters that will fit on a page bounded by your left and right margin settings, or else 1-2-3 will truncate the extra characters. Thus, if you use the default left and right margin settings of 4 and 76, do not enter a header longer than 72 characters.

USING SPECIAL SYMBOLS   Three special symbols can be used anywhere in a header or footer to add special information. The @ symbol makes 1-2-3 substitute the current system date at its location when the header or footer line is printed. The # symbol makes 1-2-3 insert the current page number at its location in the header or footer.

1-2-3 resets the page count when you leave the Print menus or when you select Align. Using ## symbols followed by a number makes 1-2-3 substitute the current page number at the location in the header or footer, but starts page numbers with the number following the double pound signs instead of 1.

These special symbols can be used alone or in combination with text characters. If you wanted the words "Page Number" to appear in front of the actual page number, you would enter **Page Number #** in the header. Likewise, if you wanted to label the date you could enter **Today's Date: @**.

THE THREE SECTIONS   1-2-3 allows you to define entries for the left, middle, and right sections of a header or footer. In other words, each header or footer has the potential to be divided into three sections. The sections are separated by the vertical bar symbol (|).

When you ask to enter a header with the /Print Printer Options Header command, this is the display you will see:

```
A:A2: [W13] '516-75-8977                                    EDIT
Enter header: _
```

Whatever you type will be left aligned in the header line. When you are finished entering information for the left section, type a vertical bar (|) to indicate that you would like to begin entering the center section. When you have completed the center section, type another vertical bar (|) to indicate the beginning of the entries for the right section.

You can omit any section by entering the vertical bar to end the section without entering anything in it. For example, entering **||Report Number: 3405** would leave the left and middle sections of the header empty and right-align "Report Number: 3405" in the header line printed at the top of every page. You can also enter everything on the left side by not using any vertical bar characters in your header.

Try this exercise to see how adding a header can affect your output:

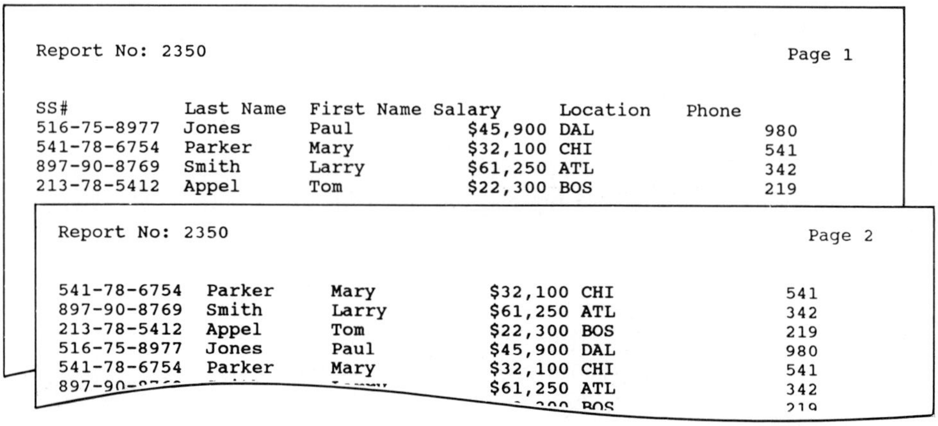

```
Report No: 2350                                              Page 1

SS#           Last Name  First Name Salary      Location   Phone
516-75-8977   Jones      Paul       $45,900 DAL            980
541-78-6754   Parker     Mary       $32,100 CHI            541
897-90-8769   Smith      Larry      $61,250 ATL            342
213-78-5412   Appel      Tom        $22,300 BOS            219

   Report No: 2350                                          Page 2

   541-78-6754   Parker    Mary       $32,100 CHI           541
   897-90-8769   Smith     Larry      $61,250 ATL           342
   213-78-5412   Appel     Tom        $22,300 BOS           219
   516-75-8977   Jones     Paul       $45,900 DAL           980
   541-78-6754   Parker    Mary       $32,100 CHI           541
   897-90-8769   Smith     Larry      $61,250 ATL           342
                                      $22,300 BOS           219
```

FIGURE 6-7.   Header at the top of two pages

1. Enter **Options Header**. Then type **Report No: 2350||Page #** and press ENTER.

2. Enter **Quit**.

3. Enter **Go**.

4. Enter **Page Align**.

Figure 6-7 shows the header at the top of the first two printed pages.

USING A CELL'S CONTENTS   In Release 3, you can use the contents of a worksheet cell for the header or footer. To refer to a cell's contents, enter a backslash and the cell address or range name that you want to use for the header or footer. If you enter a range name, 1-2-3 will use the cell in the upper-left corner of the range.

1-2-3 uses a cell's contents just as if you entered that cell's contents at the header or footer prompt. This means you can include the vertical bars and the special @ and # symbols in the cell. You may want to use this new feature if you want to select from one of several headings when you print a report. To change a heading, all you would do is type the cell address that contains the header that you want.

As an example, you can create the same header shown in Figure 6-7 by typing **Report No: 2350||Page #** in K1. Then, from the Print Options menu, you would enter

Header, type **\K1**, and press ENTER. If the header or footer contains a backslash and a cell address or range name, it cannot contain the other special header or footer characters, although the cell referenced in the header or footer can.

Using Borders

The labels you enter at the top and left side of a worksheet provide descriptive information on the first page of a printed report. When the rows in the worksheet exceed the length of one page, the rows at the top are not repeated automatically, and the second page contains data that is meaningless without labels. Similarly, when the rows in the worksheet exceed the width of one page, the columns at the left will appear only on the first page. Data further to the right will be printed on subsequent pages but will be meaningless without labels.

The Borders option allows you to select rows or columns that will appear at the top or left side of every page. Print borders are similar to worksheet titles, since they provide descriptions for what the columns and rows represent. The columns or rows you select as borders should not be included in the print range. Otherwise, this data will print twice on the first page of the report: once as part of the border, and once as part of the print range. An option new to Release 3, Frame, will print a different type of border. It puts a frame around the print range that displays the rows and column labels.

To use the Borders option, enter **/Print Printer Options Borders**. The following menu will display:

```
A:A2: [W13] '516-75-8977                                    MENU
Columns  Rows  Frame  No-Frame
Print border columns to the left of each print range
```

When you want to place information at the top of the worksheet on every page, choose Rows and select a range that includes at least one cell in each row you want to use. To use column information on each page, select Column and choose a range with at least one cell from every column you want to use. To include the row and column labels in the print range, select Frame. To remove the row and column labels in the print range, select No-Frame.

You can put the Borders option to use for the employee file you created earlier in the chapter; the worksheet has more rows than will fit on one page, and the second page has no labels. Follow these steps to add the top row as a border:

1. Enter **Range** from the main Print menu.

2. Type **A2.F65** and press ENTER.

```
Report No: 2350                                          Page  3

SS#              Last Name  First Name Salary      Location   Phone
516-75-8977      Jones      Paul         $45,900 DAL             980
541-78-6754      Parker     Mary         $32,100 CHI             541
897-90-8769      Smith      Larry        $61,250 ATL             342
213-78-5412      Appel      Tom          $22,300 BOS             219
516-75-8977      Jones      Paul         $45,900 DAL             980

  Report No: 2350                                        Page  4

  SS#              Last Name  First Name Salary      Location   Phone
  541-78-6754      Parker     Mary         $32,100 CHI             541
  897-90-8769      Smith      Larry        $61,250 ATL             342
  213-78-5412      Appel      Tom          $22,300 BOS             219
  516-75-8977      Jones      Paul         $45,900 DAL             980
                                           $32,100 CHI             541
```

FIGURE 6-8.   Borders option places labels on all pages

Notice that the row containing the labels is not included in the print range, since you will use it as a border row.

3. Enter **Options Borders Rows**.

4. Move the cell pointer to A1 and press ENTER.

5. Enter **Quit**.

6. Enter **Go** followed by **Page Align Clear All Quit** when the printing stops.

The output contains labels at the top of both pages 1 and 2, as shown in Figure 6-8. The Clear All command eliminated all of the /Print settings, including the print range and borders. If you only want to eliminate the border settings without affecting the other print settings, use the /Print Printer Clear Borders command.

Changing the Page Length

The page length is set at a default of 66 lines for most printers. This is perfect for 8 1/2- by 11-inch paper on most printers when you are printing at 6 lines to the inch. But if you change to 8 lines to the inch or use a different-size paper, you need to change the page length.

To make this change, enter **/Print Printer Options Pg-Length** and type any acceptable length before pressing ENTER. (Which length to choose depends on your printer. Release 3 supports page lengths of any size between 1 and 1000 lines.) This change in length affects only the current worksheet. If you bring a new worksheet into memory and want it to use a different page length, you need to invoke the command again.

Setup Strings

Setup strings are special character sequences that you can transmit to your printer to activate special features. These special features allow you to override standard settings such as printing six lines per inch or using standard typeface. Depending on the features of your printer, you can access alternate fonts, print can be eight lines to the inch, or it can be compressed to allow more characters per inch horizontally than the standard setting of 10 or 12. Many of the printer features that you activated with setup strings in prior releases of 1-2-3 can now be activated with menu settings through Advanced in the Options menu. Setup in the Options menu is for activating printing features that are unavailable through 1-2-3's menus.

Unfortunately, print setup strings are specific to different brands of printers. The commands that activate the features of one printer would not necessarily communicate the same information to another. The examples in this section use codes that will function for a Hewlett Packard LaserJet Series II, one of the most popular printers on the current market. Before you try any of the examples, first check the manual for your printer and substitute the proper setup strings.

To add a setup string, enter **/Print Printer Options Setup**. This display will be presented:

```
A:A2: [W13] '516-75-8977                                        EDIT
Enter setup string: _
```

The characters you enter are generally a three-digit number preceded by a backslash. Supposing that when you look in your manual, you find that the printer control code for your Gothic font cartridge is \027\040\115\049\050\072. In that case, type **\027\040\115\049\050\072** and press ENTER.

For some computer features, you can enter a combination of codes to activate a printer feature. Rather than entering a backslash and three digits for each code that activates the printer feature, you can often use a character that has the same code. For example, to activate proportional spacing, you can also enter **\027(s12H**. The "\072" in the first code is equivalent to the "H" in the second code. Your printer manual will provide both the codes and the character string that you can use instead.

The printer features generated by your setup string will be in effect for the entire worksheet when it is printed. They will also be used the next time you retrieve the file containing the worksheet, as long as you remember to save the file after entering the setup string. Also, since most printers have a memory feature, the printer features will be in effect until you turn the printer off or send a string that turns off compressed print.

Keep in mind that the size of characters affects the number that can fit across a line. If you choose an option that changes the character size, you might need to adjust your margin settings.

Try this example with the printer control codes to have your printer produce a different font:

1. Enter **/Print Printer Range**, type **A1..I65**, and press ENTER.

2. Enter **Options Setup**.
   You do not have to enter /Print Printer again, since you are already in the main Print menu.

3. Type **\027(s12H** or your control codes and press ENTER.
   You will need to substitute the proper code for your printer at this point.

4. Enter **Quit** and then **Go** to print.
   Your output should look like that in Figure 6-9.

5. Enter **Options Setup**.

6. Type **\027(s10H** and press ENTER.

```
Report No: 2350                                           Page 1

SS#            Last Name  First Name Salary      Location  Phone
516-75-8977    Jones      Paul       $45,900 DAL            980
541-78-6754    Parker     Mary       $32,100 CHI            541
897-90-8769    Smith      Larry      $61,250 ATL            342
213-78-5412    Appel      Tom        $22,300 BOS            219
516-75-8977    Jones      Paul       $45,900 DAL            980
541-78-6754    Parker     Mary       $32,100 CHI            541
897-90-8769    Smith      Larry      $61,250 ATL            342
213-78-5412    Appel      Tom        $22,300 BOS            219
```

FIGURE 6-9.   Using Gothic font cartridge

This setup string tells the printer to return to the default font (Courier). You will want to check your manual for the proper string for your printer.

7. Enter **Quit** and then **Go**.

8. Enter **Quit** to exit the Print menu.

To delete printer setup strings, enter **/Print Printer Clear Format**. Do not use the Clear All option; it does eliminate printer setup strings, but it affects other /Print settings as well.

SPECIAL /PRINT OPTIONS

The printing features you have worked with up to now are the backbone of 1-2-3's print capabilities. You will want to master them because you will use them every day to produce printed copies of all your models. A few additional printing features are used less frequently but are still important. They can help you solve the occasional problems for which the regular features offer no solution. The additional printing features include special commands for printing data to a file; printing cell formulas; embedding setup strings in a worksheet; using menu selections to activate printer features; selecting the font, size, spacing, and orientation of the output; and using printing options that are hidden away in the Worksheet menu.

Special Preparation
For Writing to a File

You can write all your print output to a file by entering **/Print File** rather than /Print Printer. When this is the only change you make, the file that is created is identical to the data printed by a printer except for some special printing features such as boldface. Since the file data is frequently used for a purpose other than printing, keeping the formatting may not be appropriate. When writing data to a file, ask yourself whether page breaks, borders, and other formatting options should be applied. If you decide that you do not want the format options included—that you want your data written to the file without regard to page breaks or any other formatting such as margins, headers, or footers—enter the following command:

/Print File Options Other Unformatted

Later, if you decide to again include formatting when you print the worksheet data to your printer, you will first need to enter

/Print Printer Options Other Formatted

to restore formatting for the worksheet.

Printing Cell Formulas

1-2-3 provides a quick way to print a list of the contents of worksheet cells. This means that what is displayed is not the result of a formula, but the formula you originally entered. Other attributes of the cell, such as width and format, will also be included in the list, and if a cell contains an annotated formula or value, the note attached to the cell's contents also appear in the output. Cells that are blank will be excluded from the list. Since 1-2-3 only prints the contents of one cell on a line, you can see how long this list might be for even a medium-sized worksheet.

You can try this technique for a section of the current worksheet. Follow these steps:

1. Enter /**Print Printer Range**.

2. Type **G2.I10** and press ENTER.

3. Enter **Options Other Cell-Formulas**.

4. Enter **Quit** to leave the Options menu, and enter **Go**.

5. Enter **Options Other As-Displayed Quit**.
   This command sequence will set the display back to the normal mode in which the printout of the worksheet matches the display you see on the screen.

6. Enter **Page Align Quit**.
   The list produced should look like the one in Figure 6-10.

Changing the Characters' Appearance

Most of your printed output will use 1-2-3's default settings for the characters' appearance. The new Advanced option in the /Print Printer Options menu can change

```
A:G2:   [W11] 2301
A:H2:   (P2) [W11] 0.05
A:I2:   (C0) +D2*(1+H2)
A:G3:   [W11] 1605
A:H3:   (P2) [W11] 0.04
A:I3:   (C0) +D3*(1+H3)
A:G4:   [W11] 1402
A:H4:   (P2) [W11] 0.05
A:I4:   (C0) +D4*(1+H4)
A:G5:   [W11] 1750
A:H5:   (P2) [W11] 0.06
A:I5:   (C0) +D5*(1+H5)
A:G6:   [W11] 2301
A:H6:   (P2) [W11] 0.05
A:I6:   (C0) +D6*(1+H6)
A:G7:   [W11] 1605
A:H7:   (P2) [W11] 0.04
A:I7:   (C0) +D7*(1+H7)
A:G8:   [W11] 1402
A:H8:   (P2) [W11] 0.05
A:I8:   (C0) +D8*(1+H8)
A:G9:   [W11] 1750
A:H9:   (P2) [W11] 0.06
A:I9:   (C0) +D9*(1+H9)
A:G10:  [W11] 2301
A:H10:  (P2) [W11] 0.05
A:I10:  (C0) +D10*(1+H10)
```

FIGURE 6-10.   Printing cell formulas

the style or font, the size, the spacing, and the orientation of the characters you print. For many of these features, 1-2-3 adds the appropriate setup strings for you. The new options provide features for which you would have had to use special add-in packages in prior releases of 1-2-3. These options are available when you are printing to the printer or to an encoded file.

To see how 1-2-3 will print these new features, enter **/Print Printer Sample Go**. 1-2-3 will print sample worksheets and graphs. The first part of the sample lists the current print settings. After printing two worksheets that show how your printer will print different features (such as label alignment), 1-2-3 shows how the printer will print different fonts, different character sizes or pitch, and different spacing. These samples show how such features are printed, even if your printer cannot print the features.

SETTING THE CHARACTER STYLE   Most printers have a default font, or style of the character, that 1-2-3 uses for printing your worksheets. Printers may include other fonts for features such as serifs (the lines that decorate the ends of a letter), boldface, and italics. Prior releases of 1-2-3 could only use font features like this if you provided the correct setup string; Release 3 has them as part of the menu, so you can use them without referencing a printer manual.

To try the font features, follow these steps:

1. Enter **/Print Printer Range**, type **A1..I40**, and press ENTER to select a new range to print.

2. Enter **Options Advanced**.
   1-2-3 displays the following options:

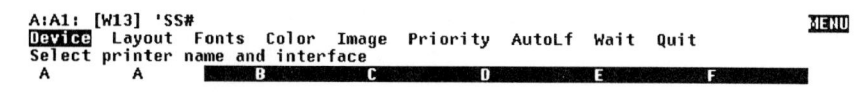

3. Enter **Fonts**.
   The following options appear:

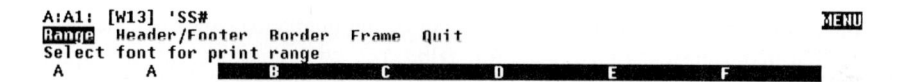

This option selects the portion of the printed worksheet that uses the new feature.

4. Enter **Header/Footer** so the header and footer will be in a different font than the rest of the worksheet.
   1-2-3 displays the numbers 1 through 8. Each number represents a different font selection. On the line below the numbers, 1-2-3 describes how 1-2-3 will print the font selected if it is available. To see how your printer will print this font, look at the sample printed earlier.

5. Enter **2**.

6. Enter **Quit** twice to return to the Print Options menu.

7. Enter **Header**, type **Today's Date: @**, and press ENTER.

8. Enter **Quit Go Page** to print the worksheet.
   The results are shown in Figure 6-11, which has a boldfaced header and the worksheet range in the regular font.

```
Today's Date: 11-May-89

SS#             Last Name  First Name Salary      Location  Phone
516-75-8977     Jones      Paul       $45,900 DAL            980
541-78-6754     Parker     Mary       $32,100 CHI            541
897-90-8769     Smith      Larry      $61,250 ATL            342
213-78-5412     Appel      Tom        $22,300 BOS            219
516-75-8977     Jones      Paul       $45,900 DAL            980
541-78-6754     Parker     Mary       $32,100 CHI            541
897-90-8769     Smith      Larry      $61,250 ATL            342
213-78-5412     Appel      Tom        $22,300 BOS            219
516-75-8977     Jones      Paul       $45,900 DAL            980
```

FIGURE 6-11.   Printing with boldface font

SETTING THE LINE SPACING   Many printers use a predetermined number of lines per inch. Dot-matrix and laser printers often allow you to change how many lines the printer prints per inch. When you change the number of lines per inch by using 1-2-3's menus instead of using a setup string, 1-2-3 will automatically adjust the page length for you.

To see how 1-2-3 will print with more lines per page, follow these steps:

1. Enter **Options Advanced Layout**.

    1-2-3 displays the following options:

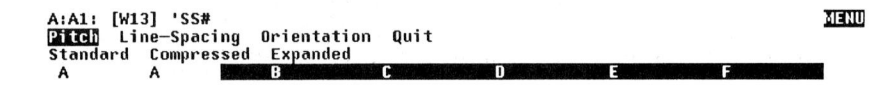

```
A:A1: [W13] 'SS#                                                      MENU
Pitch  Line-Spacing  Orientation  Quit
Standard  Compressed  Expanded
A         A         B         C         D         E         F
```

2. Enter **Line-Spacing**.

    1-2-3 displays the Standard and Compressed options, which represent the different line spacing available.

3. Enter **Compressed** to print more lines per inch. This will switch most printers from 6 lines per inch to 8 lines per inch, which changes the page length from 66 to 88.

4. Enter **Quit** three times to return to the main Print menu.

5. Enter **Go Page** to print the worksheet.

```
Today's Date: 11-May-89

SS#           Last Name   First Name Salary        Location   Phone       Position
516-75-8977   Jones       Paul          $45,900 DAL                 980          23
541-78-6754   Parker      Mary          $32,100 CHI                 541          16
897-90-8769   Smith       Larry         $61,250 ATL                 342          14
213-78-5412   Appel       Tom           $22,300 BOS                 219          17
516-75-8977   Jones       Paul          $45,900 DAL                 980          23
541-78-6754   Parker      Mary          $32,100 CHI                 541          16
897-90-8769   Smith       Larry         $61,250 ATL                 342          14
213-78-5412   Appel       Tom           $22,300 BOS                 219          17
516-75-8977   Jones       Paul          $45,900 DAL                 980          23
```

FIGURE 6-12. Printing with compressed lines spacing

Figure 6-12 shows the beginning of the printout. It contains the same information as Figure 6-11 but takes less space, since it prints more lines per inch.

SETTING THE CHARACTER SPACING Most printers have a default character spacing that 1-2-3 uses for printing your worksheets. Many printers print 10 characters per inch, which is adequate for most applications. If you want to print more or fewer characters on a line, however, you will need to change that number. Usually, as the number of characters per inch decreases or increases, the size increases or decreases. Earlier releases of 1-2-3 used setup strings to change the character spacing. In Release 3, you can change the character size with 1-2-3 menus instead of using your printer manual. Changing the character spacing is often combined with changing the line spacing so the printed output does not look too compressed or stretched out.

To try changing the character size, follow these steps:

1. Enter **Options Advanced Layout Pitch**.

   1-2-3 displays the Standard, Compressed, and Expanded options, which represent the different sizes available.

2. Enter **Compressed** so the worksheet will print using smaller letters but more characters per inch.

3. Enter **Quit** twice to return to the Print Options menu.

4. Enter **Quit Go Page** to print the worksheet.

   The result, shown in Figure 6-13, has smaller characters than in Figure 6-12.

```
Today's Date: 11-May-89


SS#           Last Name  First Name Salary    Location  Phone      Position   Increase % 1990 Salary
516-75-8977   Jones      Paul       $45,900 DAL          980        2301       5.00%     $48,195
541-78-6754   Parker     Mary       $32,100 CHI          541        1605       4.00%     $33,384
897-90-8769   Smith      Larry      $61,250 ATL          342        1402       5.00%     $64,312
213-78-5412   Appel      Tom        $22,300 BOS          219        1750       6.00%     $23,638
516-75-8977   Jones      Paul       $45,900 DAL          980        2301       5.00%     $48,195
541-78-6754   Parker     Mary       $32,100 CHI          541        1605       4.00%     $33,384
897-90-8769   Smith      Larry      $61,250 ATL          342        1402       5.00%     $64,312
213-78-5412   Appel      Tom        $22,300 BOS          219        1750       6.00%     $23,638
516-75-8977   Jones      Paul       $45,900 DAL          980        2301       5.00%     $48,195
```

FIGURE 6-13.   Printing with compressed character spacing

SETTING THE ORIENTATION   When you print a document, 1-2-3 initially prints from the top of the page to the bottom. An alternative is printing sideways. You may want to print sideways so you can print a wider document. To try it, follow these steps:

1. Enter **Options Advanced Layout Orientation**. 1-2-3 prompts you to select between Portrait (top to bottom) and Landscape (left to right).

2. Enter **Landscape**.

3. Enter **Quit** twice to return to the Print Options menu.

4. Enter **Pg-Length**, type **54** (the number of lines per page may vary from printer to printer), and press ENTER.

5. Enter **Margins Right**, type **150**, and press ENTER. A worksheet printed in landscape mode frequently fits fewer lines per page but more characters on each line.

6. Enter **Quit Go Page Clear Format** to print the worksheet and reset the /Print Option settings. You may need to realign the paper in the printer if the page length setting was incorrect.

   This command sequence prints the worksheet in landscape mode (if your printer has that capability) and sets the display back to the normal mode in which the printout of the worksheet matches the display you see on the screen.

Worksheet Features
To Enhance Control

All of the /Print options you have seen so far have been located within the Print menu, which is accessed with the /Print command. This is exactly where you would expect to look for printing features. Several additional options can significantly affect print results, but they are activated in unexpected ways. Two of the commands are found in the Worksheet menus; the other is entered directly in worksheet cells.

ADDING PAGE BREAKS   You can add a page break at any location within a worksheet to ensure that the information following the page break starts a new page. This feature can prevent awkward breaks that can occur, for example, between the last number in a column and the total for a column. Once 1-2-3 has processed the manual page break that you insert, it will again begin processing the automatic page breaks from the location of the manual page break to the end of the document. If you do not want this, you must insert additional manual breaks to again interrupt the automatic page-processing feature.

To insert a page break in the worksheet, move your cell pointer to the leftmost cell in the print range in the row that you want to force to the top of a new page. Then enter **/Worksheet Page**. This causes 1-2-3 to insert a blank line above the cell pointer and to place a double colon symbol (::) in the cell that contained the cell pointer. The cell pointer then moves down a line and stays on the line containing the data it was originally with. If the double colon symbol is anywhere but at the left edge of the print range, 1-2-3 will ignore the page-break request. If this symbol is at the left edge of the range and if you choose a range that is more than one page across, the break will occur across all pages in the range.

Follow these steps to insert a page break in the employee listing:

1. Move the cell pointer to A25.

2. Enter /**Worksheet Page**.
    The entries in row 25 and subsequent rows were moved down a row. Your command inserted a blank row and placed the page-break symbol in the cell where the cell pointer was located when you requested the command, as shown in Figure 6-14.

3. Enter /**Print Printer Go**.
    1-2-3 remembers your range from last time and automatically expands it by one row when you add the page break.

```
A:B26:  'Appel                                                              READY

   A        B            C          D          E          F          G
8       Smith       Larry      $61,250 ATL                342        1402
9       Appel       Tom        $22,300 BOS                219        1750
10      Jones       Paul       $45,900 DAL                980        2301
11      Parker      Mary       $32,100 CHI                541        1605
12      Smith       Larry      $61,250 ATL                342        1402
13      Appel       Tom        $22,300 BOS                219        1750
14      Jones       Paul       $45,900 DAL                980        2301
15      Parker      Mary       $32,100 CHI                541        1605
16      Smith       Larry      $61,250 ATL                342        1402
17      Appel       Tom        $22,300 BOS                219        1750
18      Jones       Paul       $45,900 DAL                980        2301
19      Parker      Mary       $32,100 CHI                541        1605
20      Smith       Larry      $61,250 ATL                342        1402
21      Appel       Tom        $22,300 BOS                219        1750
22      Jones       Paul       $45,900 DAL                980        2301
23      Parker      Mary       $32,100 CHI                541        1605
24      Smith       Larry      $61,250 ATL                342        1402
25      ::
26      Appel       Tom        $22,300 BOS                219        1750
27      Jones       Paul       $45,900 DAL                980        2301
```

FIGURE 6-14.   Inserting a page break

4. Enter **Page Align Quit**.

ADDING SETUP STRINGS IN THE WORKSHEET   You have already seen
how you can add a setup string through the Print Options menu. These setup strings
activate features on your printer and stay in effect while the entire worksheet is
printing. You can also embed the same setup strings within the worksheet. This allows
you to turn setup strings on and off in different parts of a document, and to use boldface
printing for a heading or important information.

Embedded setup strings must be in a row by themselves. Therefore, you must insert
blank rows above the area where you want the setup string activated. Place the
embedded setup string to the far left of the inserted row, and make sure that it starts
with two vertical bar symbols (ǁ). Follow these bars with the specific setup strings you
want to use. Use the same format for the setup strings that you use when you add a
single string through the Print Options menu. The string always starts with a backslash
(\) and is followed by a three-digit number that represents an acceptable setup string
for your particular printer.

Use the following instructions to boldface the heading for the employee listing.
When you enter the example, substitute the setup string for your particular printer.

1. Press HOME to move to A1 in the employee worksheet.

2. Enter /**Worksheet Insert Row** and press ENTER.

3. Type ||.

4. Continue typing \027(s3B and press ENTER.

   This is the control code for boldface printing on a Hewlett Packard LaserJet Series II printer. Substitute the correct control code for boldface printing on your printer; check your printer manual if you are not familiar with the codes.

5. Move the cell pointer to row 3.

6. Enter /**Worksheet Insert Row** and press ENTER.

7. Type ||\027(s0B and press ENTER.

   This entry represents the two vertical bars and the backslash that starts all setup strings, and the control code, which indicates that you want your printer to use its default setup string again. Only the control-code portion of this entry varies from printer to printer. You will need to select the correct code from your printer manual.

8. Enter /**Print Printer**.

9. Enter **Range** and type **A1.F25**.

10. Enter **Go**.

    A portion of the output showing the highlighted entries from row 1 appears in Figure 6-15.

11. Enter **Page Align Quit**.

HIDING COLUMNS   1-2-3's /Worksheet Column Hide command can enhance the features of the /Print commands by letting you define a wide print range and hiding columns that you do not want printed. The /Print Range command allows you to define only one contiguous print range. With the Column Hide option, you can effectively extend this to many separate columns of information by hiding the columns that lie between the areas you want to print.

This feature is especially advantageous when a worksheet contains confidential information. You can hide a column that contains salary information or a projected increase percentage, yet you can still create a list of employee names, locations, and

Today's Date: 11-May-89

SS#	Last Name	First Name	Salary	Location	Phone	
516-75-8977	Jones	Paul	$45,900	DAL		980
541-78-6754	Parker	Mary	$32,100	CHI		541
897-90-8769	Smith	Larry	$61,250	ATL		342
213-78-5412	Appel	Tom	$22,300	BOS		219
516-75-8977	Jones	Paul	$45,900	DAL		980
541-78-6754	Parker	Mary	$32,100	CHI		541
897-90-8769	Smith	Larry	$61,250	ATL		342
213-78-5412	Appel	Tom	$22,300	BOS		219
516-75-8977	Jones	Paul	$45,900	DAL		980
541-78-6754	Parker	Mary	$32,100	CHI		541
897-90-8769	Smith	Larry	$61,250	ATL		342
213-78-5412	Appel	Tom	$22,300	BOS		219
516-75-8977	Jones	Paul	$45,900	DAL		980
541-78-6754	Parker	Mary	$32,100	CHI		541
897-90-8769	Smith	Larry	$61,250	ATL		342
213-78-5412	Appel	Tom	$22,300	BOS		219
516-75-8977	Jones	Paul	$45,900	DAL		980
541-78-6754	Parker	Mary	$32,100	CHI		541
897-90-8769	Smith	Larry	$61,250	ATL		342
213-78-5412	Appel	Tom	$22,300	BOS		219
516-75-8977	Jones	Paul	$45,900	DAL		980
541-78-6754	Parker	Mary	$32,100	CHI		541

FIGURE 6-15.   Boldfacing by adding printer setup strings to the worksheet

phone numbers, even when the salary information is in the midst of the data columns you need. The Hide feature will not destroy the salary data—it will merely remove temporarily the unwanted data from view. When you want to restore hidden data, use the /Worksheet Column Display command and select one or more adjacent columns that are marked by asterisks to indicate their hidden status.

Follow these steps to print a copy of the employee data without the salary or social security number columns:

1. Move the cell pointer to column A.

2. Enter /**Worksheet Column Hide**.

   The control panel asks that you specify the columns to be hidden, as shown here:

```
A:A2:  [W13]  '516-75-8977                                        POINT
Specify columns to hide: A:A2
```

```
Last Name  First Name Salary      Location  Phone      Position
Jones      Paul         $45,900 DAL            980       2301
Parker     Mary         $32,100 CHI            541       1605
Smith      Larry        $61,250 ATL            342       1402
Appel      Tom          $22,300 BOS            219       1750
Jones      Paul         $45,900 DAL            980       2301
Parker     Mary         $32,100 CHI            541       1605
Smith      Larry        $61,250 ATL            342       1402
Appel      Tom          $22,300 BOS            219       1750
Jones      Paul         $45,900 DAL            980       2301
```

FIGURE 6-16. Hiding worksheet columns

3. Press ENTER to select column A.

4. Move the cell pointer to column D, where the salary information is stored.

5. Enter **/Worksheet Column Hide** and press ENTER.

6. Enter **/Print Printer Clear All** to remove any prior print settings.

7. Enter **Range**, press HOME, and type a period. Then move with the RIGHT and DOWN ARROW keys until the cell pointer is in G10, and press ENTER.

8. Enter **Go**.
   The printed report will appear like the one in Figure 6-16.

9. Enter **Page Align Quit**.
   This command will position the paper at the top of a form, zero the line count, and exit you from the Print menu, placing you back in READY mode.

10. Enter **/Worksheet Column Display** and position the cell pointer in column A before pressing ENTER.

11. Enter **/Worksheet Column Display** and select column D.
    The last two instructions prove that your original data is still intact, even though it was not visible on the screen.

REVIEW EXERCISE

Rather than creating a new worksheet to practice printing with, you can use a model created at the end of Chapter 5. You can follow these steps to test the basics, as well as a few enhancement options:

1. Retrieve the SALESPRJ file that you created in Chapter 5.

2. Specify the print range as A1..I28. *Hint:* Use /Print Printer Range. Press the HOME key, type **.** (a period), and then press END followed by HOME to highlight all of the worksheet area the file uses. Press ENTER to accept A1..I28.

3. Create a header with the date at the left preceded by "Date:" and "Sales Forecasting Report" in the center. *Hint:* Use Options Header and enter **Date: @|Sales Forecasting Report**; then press ENTER.

4. Add a footer by entering **Page :** on the right side followed by the page number. *Hint:* Enter **Footer**, type **||Page: #**, and press ENTER.

5. Print the worksheet. *Hint:* Be sure that your printer is turned on and is online. Then use Quit Go. This quits the Options menu and prints your worksheet with 1-2-3's default print settings.

6. Use 1-2-3 to form-feed the paper and print the footer at the bottom of the page. *Hint:* Use Page Align Quit.

7. Add a page break in A15. *Hint:* Use /Worksheet Page to insert a page break after positioning the cell pointer in A15.

8. Hide column F. *Hint:* Use /Worksheet Column Hide.

9. Specify row 1 as a border row. *Hint:* Use /Print Printer Options Borders Rows after positioning the cell pointer in row 1. Remember to check that row 1 is not part of your print range, or it will print twice on page 1.

10. Print the worksheet again. *Hint:* Use Quit Go Page Align.

11. Clear the Border setting. *Hint:* Use Clear Borders.

12. Print the cell formulas. *Hint:* Use Options Other Cell- Formulas Quit Go Page Align.

13. Set the Print Options display back to printing what is displayed on the worksheet, and then quit the Print menu. *Hint:* Use Options Other As-Displayed Quit Quit.

REVIEW

- The Print menus available with the /Print command provide the options that you use to print your worksheets. Your initial selection from the Print menu is the destination. You can print directly to the printer or to a file with an .ENC or .PRN extension. Once you select a destination, 1-2-3 displays the main Print menu.

- To print a worksheet, you must select the area of the worksheet to print with the Range option from the main Print menu and then select Go. Additional enhancements are selected before entering Go.

- Release 3 adds a feature that allows you to select multiple ranges within one print range. 1-2-3 prints multiple worksheet ranges one at a time, immediately after each other.

- Print settings are saved with the worksheet data.

- You can control the printer with options in the Print menus. These options include Line, to advance the printer one line; Page, to advance the printer to the next page; and Align, to reset the line count for the printer to zero. The Cancel option in the initial Print menu stops 1-2-3 sending data to the printer. The Resume option stops sending data to the printer until the Suspend option is selected.

- 1-2-3 makes several assumptions about how it should print a worksheet. These are the default settings. They include the margins and the page length, although selections under /Print Printer Options allow you to change these assumptions.

- The /Print Printer Clear command selects which of 1-2-3's print settings are removed or returned to the default setting.

- A report can contain headers and footers that appear on every page. Headers and footers can contain the at symbol (@) for the current date and the number sign (#) for the current page number. Vertical lines can divide the header or footer sections to left-align, center, and right-align header and footer text. As a new feature of Release 3, you can enter a cell address or range name to use the contents of the cell referenced.

- The /Print Printer Options Borders command selects the rows and columns that appear at the top and to the left of every page. Borders allow lengthy reports to retain their identification labels.

- You can activate printer-specific features by using setup strings. The /Print Printer Options Setup command activates printing features for the entire printing task. Embedded setup strings activate printing features for a section of the print range.

- You can prevent columns from printing by hiding them with the /Worksheet Column Hide command.

- You can document a worksheet by printing the cell formulas. Normally, 1-2-3 prints the worksheet data as it appears.

- The /Worksheet Page command inserts a page break into a worksheet. When 1-2-3 prints a worksheet with a page break, it advances to the next page when it reaches the page break.

- You can suppress the headers, footers, and page breaks when you print with the /Print Printer Options Other Unformatted. This command is often used to print to a file that you want to use in another computer package.

- With Release 3 you can change characters' appearance through options in the /Print Printer Options Advanced menu. These options let you change the font, line spacing, and character spacing. They have no effect when you are printing to a .PRN file.

Commands and Keys

/PP	/Print Printer sends print output to the printer
/PF	/Print File sends print output to a file with a .PRN extension that excludes printer formatting codes
/PE	/Print Encoded sends printer output to a file with an .ENC extension that includes printer formatting codes
/PPR	/Print Printer Range selects the worksheet area to print
/PPC	/Print Printer Clear removes all print settings, the range setting, the border settings, or the settings for margins, page length, and setup strings
/PC	/Print Cancel stops print output to the printer
/PS	/Print Suspend stops print output until the /Print Resume command is executed
/PR	/Print Resume starts printing after 1-2-3 has halted
/PPL	/Print Printer Line advances the printer one line

/PPP	/Print Printer Page advances the printer one page
/PPA	/Print Printer Align resets 1-2-3's line count to zero
/PPG	/Print Printer Go starts printing the current selected print area
/PPQ	/Print Printer Quit exits the sticky Print menu
/PPOH	/Print Printer Options Header sets the header that appears at the top of each page
/PPOF	/Print Printer Options Footer sets the footer that appears at the bottom of each page
/PPOM	/Print Printer Options Margin sets the top, bottom, left, and right margins, or removes all margins
/PPOB	/Print Printer Options Border selects the border columns and rows or the worksheet frame
/PPOS	/Print Printer Options Setup sets the setup string
/PPOP	/Print Printer Options Page-Length sets the page length
/PPOO	/Print Printer Options Other sets additional print formatting, such as printing the worksheet as it appears or printing the cell formulas, including the headers, footers, and page breaks, or suppressing them
/PPS	/Print Printer Sample prints a sample worksheet and graph to display how 1-2-3 prints your printer's features
/PPOQ	/Print Printer Options Quit exits the sticky Print Options menu
/PPOAF	/Print Printer Options Advanced Fonts selects the fonts for an area of the printed output
/PPOALL	/Print Printer Options Advanced Layout Line-Spacing sets the line spacing
/PPOALP	/Print Printer Options Advanced Layout Pitch sets the character spacing
/PPOALO	/Print Printer Options Advanced Layout Orientation sets whether the range is printed on the page top-to-bottom or left-to-right
/WP	/Worksheet Page inserts a page break into a worksheet
/WCH	/Worksheet Column Hide hides worksheet columns and does not print them

7

BASIC WORKSHEET FUNCTIONS

Built-In Function Basics
A Close-Up Look at Each of the Function Categories
Review Exercise
Review

Your 1-2-3 models have already shown you the importance of formulas. Formulas are actually the power behind a spreadsheet package like 1-2-3; they record your calculations and use them over and over again. However, there is a problem with formulas: it takes a long time to record them, and when you are recording a long series of calculations, it is easy to make a mistake. Fortunately, 1-2-3 has built-in functions to reduce these drawbacks. These functions are prerecorded formulas that have already been verified for accuracy. All you need to do is specify which data they should operate on each time you use them. The built-in functions also provide features that go beyond the capabilities of formulas, such as accessing the system date and calculating square roots and tangents.

In this chapter you will examine how 1-2-3's built-in functions are recorded on the worksheet. You will learn the syntax and the rules that provide a powerhouse of almost 102 prerecorded calculations that you can access easily. You will learn about six of the eight function categories into which all 1-2-3 functions are grouped. A seventh category, which allows you to add logical capabilities to your models easily, is covered in Chapter 8. The eighth category is data-management functions, which will be covered in Chapter 9 when data-management features are discussed. In this chapter, you will examine a variety of functions from the different categories and learn how to use them in application models.

BUILT-IN FUNCTION BASICS

A few general rules apply to all functions, regardless of their type, yet individual functions can differ from one another in how they expect you to convey the data with which you want them to work. You need to know the general rules and the individual exceptions, as well as which category of function is likely to handle the task you wish to address. This section provides such information. Read it before addressing the individual function categories; it is an important first step.

General Rules

Since built-in functions are formulas, they are value entries in worksheet cells. There are several rules for functions that do not apply to formulas, all of them pertaining to the syntax of recording the different components. A diagram of these components is shown in Figure 7-1.

The first rule for function entry is that all functions must start with an @ symbol. After entering the @ symbol, you must include the special keyword that 1-2-3 uses to represent the function. This keyword is the function's name. You can enter it in either upper- or lowercase, but it must follow 1-2-3's spelling exactly. With Release 3, you

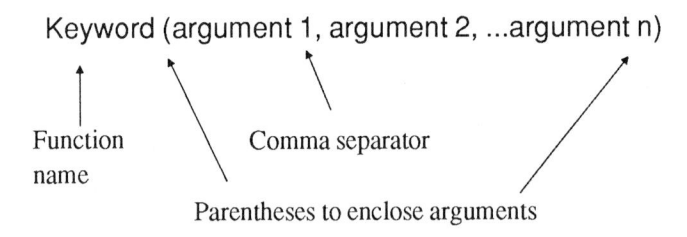

FIGURE 7-1.   Function format

can even have the package supply it for you. If you press the F3 (NAME) key after typing the @ symbol, 1-2-3 will display a list of all the @ function keywords. When you highlight the word you want and press ENTER, 1-2-3 adds the function keyword to your entry.

RULES FOR FUNCTION ARGUMENTS The next component within a function is its *arguments,* which specify the data with which the function will work. Arguments are required by most functions, since most functions must be defined exactly in order to be used. Arguments must be enclosed within parentheses, but if the function you are using does not require arguments you do not need to use parentheses.

When using a function that requires multiple arguments, use a comma (,) or a semicolon (;) to separate the arguments. Spaces cannot be used within a function, so they are not valid as separator characters.

Function arguments can be provided as cell addresses, a range name that you assign to one or more cells, constants, or even formulas or other built-in functions. The examples you enter in this chapter may include some constants in functions to expedite data entry. However, it is preferable to store the data needed by the function in worksheet cells and to reference these cells within the function, since a change in an argument's value will not require you to edit the function.

Much variety is possible with arguments. Look at these examples of the @SUM function, which totals the values you provide as arguments:

```
@SUM(9,4,8,7)
@SUM(A1;D3;Y6;Z10)
@SUM(Salaries,Rent_Exp,Equipment)
@SUM(A1..H4)
@SUM(A1,@SUM(B2..B3),Z2)
```

All five are valid function entries (although you need Release 2 or higher for the semicolons in the second example). As you progress through the exercises in this chapter, you will have an opportunity to use different types of arguments.

Most built-in functions expect value entries for arguments. Other built-in functions require string or character data for arguments. You cannot substitute a type of data for an argument that is different from what 1-2-3 is expecting. For example, if you use 1-2-3's @SUM function, you will need to provide value entries as arguments. @SUM will add these together to produce a total. If you substitute label entries for the arguments, @SUM will not be able to total them and will treat the labels as zeros.

DIFFERENT TYPES OF FUNCTION ARGUMENTS Different functions require different arguments and use them in different ways. The three basic types of functions are those that require no arguments, those that expect a list of arguments in any sequence, and those that require a specific number of arguments in a specific order.

Examples of functions that require no arguments are @RAND, @NA, and @PI. @RAND is used to generate a random number and does not require any input. @NA is used when data is missing and you want to mark its position as not available at the current time. @PI is used to represent the special mathematical constant 3.14159265, which is used in geometric problem solving.

There are also a number of functions that expect a list of values for arguments. The entries in the list can be single cells or ranges of cells and can be provided in any order you like. All of the statistical functions fall within this category of argument types. For example, these two functions are equivalent:

```
@SUM(A1,B4,C5,D2..D10,F1,H2..M4)
@SUM(F1,H2..M4,A1,C5,D2..D10,B4)
```

In both cases all individual values, as well as each of the values in the ranges, will be totaled to produce a single sum. Functions that allow this interchangeability of argument order specify *list* as their argument. For example, since @SUM accepts this type of argument, you can expect to see @SUM(*list*) when we discuss the syntax of this function in detail.

The last type of function argument is position-dependent. Functions that require arguments in a specific order cannot have their arguments reordered without erroneous results. For example, the @PMT function is designed to calculate the amount of a loan payment. The function requires three arguments: the principal, the interest, and the term of the loan. Later in the chapter you will see the functions specified like this:

@PMT(*principal,interest,term of loan*)

When using the function, you must provide the three arguments in this exact order.

A CLOSE LOOK AT EACH FUNCTION CATEGORY

There are seven categories of functions in 1-2-3, excluding the special database functions. The various function categories form the organizational structure of the rest of this chapter. You can use the remainder of the chapter in two ways. The preferred approach is to work through the exercises in each function category to become familiar with each function's use. There may be function categories that apply to your models, but unless you take an in-depth look at what they can do, you might not realize their potential. A second alternative, if your time is limited, is to focus on those function categories for which you have immediate use, and then to come back and take a look at the other categories as you need them.

Built-in functions are grouped into categories in which each of the functions within a category has some similarity of purpose. This logical grouping allows you to focus easily on the special requirements of a category. It can also help you increase your knowledge of a new function whose purpose might be similar to some functions you are already using. For example, if you are working with the @PMT and @FV functions from the financial category, it is wise to look closely at the other financial functions; many of them may provide useful features in your models. Although this chapter covers only a subset of the functions, a comprehensive list of all of the functions can be found at the end of Chapter 10.

As you work through this section you will find that Release 3 has functions that were not provided in earlier releases. Within individual categories and in Appendix C, the new Release 3 functions are appropriately marked.

Statistical Functions

"Statistics" is a word that causes many people to be apprehensive—they recall statistics as complicated mathematical procedures from a required college math course. 1-2- 3's statistical functions need not invoke this sense of alarm. They are simple to use, and they compute the most basic statistical measures, computations that you perform every day without even thinking about them as "statistical." They include computations for such operations as finding the average, summing, counting, and finding the minimum and maximum value.

1-2-3's statistical functions perform their magic on lists of values. These lists are often a contiguous range of cells on the worksheet. They can also be a series of individual values or a combination of a range and individual values. Blank cells can be included within the list, but all values in the blank range will count as zeros. When a range contains multiple blank cells, 1-2-3 will ignore the cells that contain blanks.

The @COUNT function is an exception to the others in the statistical category. It counts the number of non-blank entries in the list. It can accept string values in addition to numeric values within its argument list.

You will use one model to test all of the statistical functions. It will contain information on the monthly sales for all the High Profits Company sales personnel in region 4, as shown in Figure 7-2. Before continuing, you should follow these steps to create the basic model.

1. Enter /**Worksheet Global Format Currency**. Type **0** and press ENTER.

   This command establishes a Global format for the model before you enter data. Next, you will format a section of the model that requires whole numbers to be displayed without the dollar sign.

2. Enter /**Range Format Fixed**. Type **0** and press ENTER. Type **B6.C13** and press ENTER.

3. Move the cell pointer to column A and enter /**Worksheet Column Set-Width**. Press the RIGHT ARROW key four times, and press ENTER.

   This action widens this column to 13 positions in preparation for the data to be entered. There is one more column to be widened.

   You could have entered these commands, like the formatting command, after you entered the data in the worksheet. However, if you know what your final report will look like, it is often best to perform the housekeeping tasks first.

4. Move the cell pointer to column G and enter /**Worksheet Column Set-Width**. Press the RIGHT ARROW key twice for a width of 11, and then press ENTER.

   Once you have completed the housekeeping tasks, you are ready to begin entering the data for the model. You can use Figure 7-2 as a guide for the entries, or you can use the detailed entries in step 5.

A:G6: [W11] @SUM(D6..F6)   `READY`

A	A	B	C	D	E	F	G
1			High Profits Quarterly Sales Figures				
2			Region 4				
3							
4				Jan	Feb	Mar	Qtr.
5	Salesperson	District	Branch	Sales	Sales	Sales	Total
6	Jason Rye	1	1705	$95,800	$105,650	$114,785	**$316,235**
7	Paul Jones	3	3201	$56,780	$52,300	$48,750	$157,830
8	Mary Hart	1	1705	$89,675	$108,755	$135,400	$333,830
9	Tom Bush	2	4250	$91,555	$87,600	$92,300	$271,455
10	Gary Lowe	2	4250	$76,900	$82,600	$83,500	$243,000
11	Karen Stein	3	2950	$68,565	$76,500	$82,300	$227,365
12	Cindy Boyd	2	4590	$110,800	$153,400	$105,665	$369,865
13	Jim Rogers	1	1921	$98,000	$114,785	$114,785	$327,570
14							
15		TOTAL SALES		$688,075	$781,590	$777,485	$2,247,150

FIGURE 7-2.   Using the statistical functions

5. Place the following entries in the worksheet cells listed:

C1: High Profits Quarterly Sales Figures
D2: Region 4
A5: Salesperson
A6: Jason Rye
A7: Paul Jones
A8: Mary Hart
A9: Tom Bush
A10: Gary Lowe
A11: Karen Stein
A12: Cindy Boyd
A13: Jim Rogers
B5: District
B6: 1
B7: 3
B8: 1
B9: 2
B10: 2
B11: 3
B12: 2
B13: 1
B15: TOTAL SALES
C5: Branch
C6: 1705
C7: 3201
C8: 1705
C9: 4250
C10: 4250
C11: 2950
C12: 4590
C13: 1921
D4: Jan
D5: Sales
D6: 95800
D7: 56780
D8: 89675
D9: 91555
D10: 76900

D11: 68565
D12: 110800
D13: 98000
E4: Feb
E5: Sales
E6: 105650
E7: 52300
E8: 108755
E9: 87600
E10: 82600
E11: 76500
E12: 153400
E13: 114785
F4: Mar
F5: Sales
F6: 114785
F7: 48750
F8: 135400
F9: 92300
F10: 83500
F11: 82300
F12: 105665
F13: 114785
G4: Qtr.
G5: Total

6. Move the cell pointer to D4 and enter /**Range Label Right**. Move the cell pointer to G5 and press ENTER.

Your model should match the one in Figure 7-3. You are now ready to use it in testing the statistical functions.

@SUM   The @SUM function totals a list of values. The syntax for the function is @SUM(*list*), where *list* can be a range of values, a list of individual values separated by commas, or a combination of the two.

@SUM is one of the most frequently used functions. It easily performs the laborious task of adding each of the numbers in a range without your having to enter a long formula to add each value separately. It can be used just as easily to total a row of values. As with any other formula, once you have entered it for one row or column, you can easily copy it to other locations where you have similar needs.

```
A:D15:                                                      VALUE
@SUM(_

A        A         B        C       D        E       F        G
1                        High Profits Quarterly Sales Figures
2                                   Region 4
3
4                                   Jan      Feb     Mar     Qtr.
5   Salesperson District Branch    Sales    Sales   Sales   Total
6   Jason Rye        1     1705  $95,800 $105,650 $114,785
7   Paul Jones       3     3201  $56,780  $52,300  $48,750
8   Mary Hart        1     1705  $89,675 $108,755 $135,400
9   Tom Bush         2     4250  $91,555  $87,600  $92,300
10  Gary Lowe        2     4250  $76,900  $82,600  $83,500
11  Karen Stein      3     2950  $68,565  $76,500  $82,300
12  Cindy Boyd       2     4590 $110,800 $153,400 $105,665
13  Jim Rogers       1     1921  $98,000 $114,785 $114,785
14
15             TOTAL SALES      ██████████
```

FIGURE 7-3.   Right-aligning the labels

Using @SUM to Total Sales   You will use the @SUM function to compute the total sales in each month and the total sales for each salesperson during the quarter. Follow these steps to add the sum computations:

1. Move the cell pointer to D15 and type **@**. Press F3 (NAME), highlight SUM, and press ENTER.

   Your entry will match the one shown in Figure 7-4. You could have typed **@SUM(** rather than using the F3 (NAME) key to add the function keyword. If

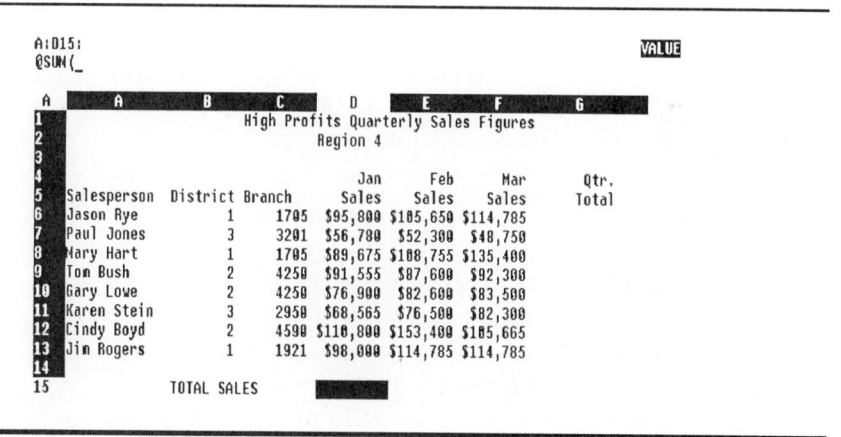

```
A:D15:                                                      VALUE
@SUM(_

A        A         B        C       D        E       F        G
1                        High Profits Quarterly Sales Figures
2                                   Region 4
3
4                                   Jan      Feb     Mar     Qtr.
5   Salesperson District Branch    Sales    Sales   Sales   Total
6   Jason Rye        1     1705  $95,800 $105,650 $114,785
7   Paul Jones       3     3201  $56,780  $52,300  $48,750
8   Mary Hart        1     1705  $89,675 $108,755 $135,400
9   Tom Bush         2     4250  $91,555  $87,600  $92,300
10  Gary Lowe        2     4250  $76,900  $82,600  $83,500
11  Karen Stein      3     2950  $68,565  $76,500  $82,300
12  Cindy Boyd       2     4590 $110,800 $153,400 $105,665
13  Jim Rogers       1     1921  $98,000 $114,785 $114,785
14
15             TOTAL SALES      ██████████
```

FIGURE 7-4.   Entering @SUM

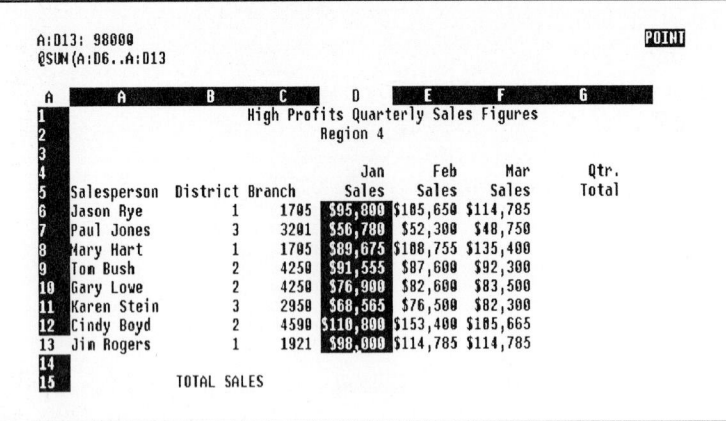

FIGURE 7-5.   Highlighting the range

you are not certain of the spelling of the keyword, the F3 (NAME) option is the best strategy; otherwise, typing may be the quickest approach.

2. Move the cell pointer to D6 and type a period to lock the beginning of the range in place. Then move the cell pointer to D13 to highlight all the entries, as shown in Figure 7-5.

3. Type) and press ENTER to display the results shown in Figure 7-6.

```
A:D15: @SUM(D6..D13)                                              READY

A      A           B         C        D        E        F        G
1                             High Profits Quarterly Sales Figures
2                                       Region 4
3
4                                       Jan      Feb      Mar      Qtr.
5  Salesperson  District  Branch        Sales    Sales    Sales    Total
6  Jason Rye          1     1705      $95,800 $105,650 $114,785
7  Paul Jones         3     3201      $56,780  $52,300  $48,750
8  Mary Hart          1     1705      $89,675 $108,755 $135,400
9  Tom Bush           2     4250      $91,555  $87,600  $92,300
10 Gary Lowe          2     4250      $76,900  $82,600  $83,500
11 Karen Stein        3     2950      $68,565  $76,500  $82,300
12 Cindy Boyd         2     4590     $110,800 $153,400 $105,665
13 Jim Rogers         1     1921      $98,000 $114,785 $114,785
14
15              TOTAL SALES           $688,075
```

FIGURE 7-6.   @SUM completed

You have just entered your first @SUM function using the pointing method for specifying the range. If you prefer, you can always type the range address rather than pointing to it, but the pointing method helps prevent errors. As you point to the beginning of the range you want to sum, you get visual verification that this is the correct beginning location for the calculation. The same is true when you point to the end of the range, since 1-2-3 highlights everything in the range. Either way you choose to enter the @SUM function, this function is a lot quicker than typing +D6+D7+D8+D9+D10+D11+D12+D13—the alternative for computing the desired result.

4. With the cell pointer in D15, enter /**Copy**. Press ENTER, move the cell pointer to E15, and type a period before moving the cell pointer to G15 and pressing ENTER.

   This /Copy command totaled all the columns for you, giving you maximum use from the one function you entered.

5. Move the cell pointer to G6. Type **@SUM(** and then move the cell pointer to D6. Type a period and move the cell pointer to F6. Type) and press ENTER.

   This formula produced a quarterly sales figure for Jason Rye.

6. Enter /**Copy** and press ENTER. Move the cell pointer to G7 and type a period. Then move the cell pointer to G13 and press ENTER.

   This last instruction copies the totals down the column so that you now have a total sales figure for each salesperson for the quarter, as in the model shown earlier in Figure 7-2.

Allowing for Expansion   The example you just completed computes the monthly sales totals correctly; but if you want to add another salesperson to the bottom of the list, you need to revise the @SUM formulas at the bottom of the columns so they include a reference to the cell containing the figure for the new employee. You don't need to do this, however, if you insert the blank row in the middle of the sum range and enter the new data there. The new row would then be included automatically, since 1-2-3 would expand the range. The problem is that most of your additions are at the very top or bottom of the range and 1-2-3 does not stretch the range to include these new rows. However, you can overcome this revision requirement by entering your initial sum formula a little differently.

Leaving a blank row at the top and the bottom of the column you are summing will give you the expansion capability you need. If your original @SUM range includes a blank row at the top and bottom of the range, you can insert blank rows at the top or bottom and 1-2-3 will adjust the range for you. The blank rows do not affect the @SUM

```
A:A6: [W13]                                                      READY
```

A	A	B	C	D	E	F	G
			High Profits Quarterly Sales Figures				
1				Region 4			
2							
3							
4				Jan	Feb	Mar	Qtr.
5	Salesperson	District	Branch	Sales	Sales	Sales	Total
6							
7	Jason Rye	1	1705	$95,800	$105,650	$114,785	$316,235
8	Paul Jones	3	3201	$56,780	$52,300	$48,750	$157,830
9	Mary Hart	1	1705	$89,675	$108,755	$135,400	$333,830
10	Tom Bush	2	4250	$91,555	$87,600	$92,300	$271,455
11	Gary Lowe	2	4250	$76,900	$82,600	$83,500	$243,000
12	Karen Stein	3	2950	$68,565	$76,500	$82,300	$227,365
13	Cindy Boyd	2	4590	$110,800	$153,400	$105,665	$369,865
14	Jim Rogers	1	1921	$98,000	$114,785	$114,785	$327,570
15							
16		TOTAL SALES		$688,075	$781,590	$777,485	$2,247,150

FIGURE 7-7.   Inserting a blank row to facilitate expansion

results, since 1-2-3 treats them as zero. To alter the original @SUM formula and then copy it across again in preparation for adding a new salesperson, follow these steps:

1. Move the cell pointer to A6 and enter /**Worksheet Insert Row**. Then press ENTER to produce a display like the one shown in Figure 7-7.

2. Move the cell pointer to D16, type **@SUM(D6..D15)**, and then press ENTER.

3. Enter /**Copy** and press ENTER. Move the cell pointer to E16, type **.**, and then move the cell pointer to G16 and press ENTER.

   These new @SUM entries will allow you to expand your entries at either the top or the bottom of the database by placing the cell pointer in either row 6 or row 15 and then using /Worksheet Insert Row to add a new blank row for the new employee information.

4. Move the cell pointer to A7, enter /**Worksheet Insert Row**, and press ENTER.

5. Make these entries to add the new salesperson:

   A7: Jane Hunt
   B7: 2
   C7: 4590
   D7: 87650
   E7: 92300
   F7: 93415
   G7: @SUM(D7..F7)

```
A:G7: [W11] @SUM(D7..F7)                                              READY
```

	Salesperson	District	Branch	Jan Sales	Feb Sales	Mar Sales	Qtr. Total
	High Profits Quarterly Sales Figures						
	Region 4						
7	Jane Hunt	2	4590	$87,650	$92,300	$93,415	$273,365
8	Jason Rye	1	1705	$95,800	$105,650	$114,785	$316,235
9	Paul Jones	3	3201	$56,780	$52,300	$48,750	$157,830
10	Mary Hart	1	1705	$89,675	$108,755	$135,400	$333,830
11	Tom Bush	2	4250	$91,555	$87,600	$92,300	$271,455
12	Gary Lowe	2	4250	$76,900	$82,600	$83,500	$243,000
13	Karen Stein	3	2950	$68,565	$76,500	$82,300	$227,365
14	Cindy Boyd	2	4590	$110,800	$153,400	$105,665	$369,865
15	Jim Rogers	1	1921	$98,000	$114,785	$114,785	$327,570
17	TOTAL SALES			$775,725	$873,890	$870,900	$2,520,515

FIGURE 7-8. Total for the quarter

The worksheet shows that the totals for each month have been adjusted to show the new results. This means that you will be able to add new entries in any location within the data and have the formula updated for you automatically. Notice that the district and branch values in this new line are formatted as currency, since the original ranges that were formatted did not include these cells.

6. Move the cell pointer to B7 and enter /**Range Format Fixed**, type 0, and press ENTER. Move the cell pointer to C7 and press ENTER. The worksheet looks like Figure 7-8.

@COUNT The @COUNT function returns the number of non-blank entries in a list. Its syntax is @COUNT(*list*), where *list* can represent a range. You will not want to use a series of individual cell references because @COUNT will increment the count by one for each of these references even if they are blank. Unlike the other statistical functions, @COUNT does not require value entries. It can count employee names as well as entries in the sales column.

Entries that contain zero are not equivalent to blanks and will be counted. You must carefully choose which column or row of a worksheet to count, since you want to select data where mandatory entries are required for each record. Otherwise, the computed count may be artificially low due to the blank values in certain fields.

Follow these steps to count the number of sales personnel for region 4 of High Profit:

1. Move the cell pointer to B18 and type '# **SALES PERSONNEL.**

2. Move the cell pointer to D18, type **@COUNT(A6.A16)**, and press ENTER.

   The name field was chosen for counting the number of entries because it is assumed that all sales personnel have a name entry. It is possible that some salespeople who were not employed for the full quarter might not have all the months of sales data and that counting other fields might cause results to be computed lower than they should be.

3. Enter **/Range Format Fixed**, type **0**, and press ENTER twice.

   Your model should match the display in Figure 7-9.

4. Enter **/File Save**, type **SUMCOUNT**, and press ENTER.

The @COUNT function has widespread applicability. You can use it to count the number of loan payments that have been received. You can count the number of items in your inventory. Once you have mastered the basics, you will find you have many worksheets in which the @COUNT feature will be useful.

@MIN   The @MIN function searches a list of values and returns the smallest value in the list. Its syntax is @MIN(*list*). You could use this function to find the lowest contract bid if all your bid figures were listed on a worksheet. You could also use it

---

A:D18: (F0) @COUNT(A6..A16)   `READY`

A	A	B	C	D	E	F	G
1			High Profits Quarterly Sales Figures				
2			Region 4				
3							
4				Jan	Feb	Mar	Qtr.
5	Salesperson	District	Branch	Sales	Sales	Sales	Total
6							
7	Jane Hunt	2	4590	$87,650	$92,300	$93,415	$273,365
8	Jason Rye	1	1705	$95,800	$105,650	$114,785	$316,235
9	Paul Jones	3	3201	$56,780	$52,300	$48,750	$157,830
10	Mary Hart	1	1705	$89,675	$108,755	$135,400	$333,830
11	Tom Bush	2	4250	$91,555	$87,600	$92,300	$271,455
12	Gary Lowe	2	4250	$76,900	$82,600	$83,500	$243,000
13	Karen Stein	3	2950	$68,565	$76,500	$82,300	$227,365
14	Cindy Boyd	2	4590	$110,800	$153,400	$105,665	$369,865
15	Jim Rogers	1	1921	$98,000	$114,785	$114,785	$327,570
16							
17		TOTAL SALES		$775,725	$873,890	$870,900	$2,520,515
18		# SALES PERSONNEL		9			

FIGURE 7-9.   Using @COUNT

```
A:G19: [W11] @MIN(G6..G16)                                          READY
```

A	A	B	C	D	E	F	G	
1				High Profits Quarterly Sales Figures				
2				Region 4				
3								
4				Jan	Feb	Mar	Qtr.	
5	Salesperson	District	Branch	Sales	Sales	Sales	Total	
6								
7	Jane Hunt	2	4590	$87,650	$92,300	$93,415	$273,365	
8	Jason Rye	1	1705	$95,800	$105,650	$114,785	$316,235	
9	Paul Jones	3	3201	$56,780	$52,300	$48,750	$157,830	
10	Mary Hart	1	1705	$89,675	$108,755	$135,400	$333,830	
11	Tom Bush	2	4250	$91,555	$87,600	$92,300	$271,455	
12	Gary Lowe	2	4250	$76,900	$82,600	$83,500	$243,000	
13	Karen Stein	3	2950	$68,565	$76,500	$82,300	$227,365	
14	Cindy Boyd	2	4590	$110,800	$153,400	$105,665	$369,865	
15	Jim Rogers	1	1921	$98,000	$114,785	$114,785	$327,570	
16								
17		TOTAL SALES		$775,725	$873,890	$870,900	$2,520,515	
18		# SALES PERSONNEL		9				
19				LOWEST QTR SALES FIGURE			$157,830	

FIGURE 7-10.   Using @MIN

to find the lowest recorded temperature, the lowest-price supplier for an item, the individual who is paid the lowest salary, or in the High Profit model, the lowest sales amount for a month or the quarter.

Add a label and a calculation to show the sales for the worst performer in region 4 for the quarter:

1. Move the cell pointer to D19, type **LOWEST QTR SALES FIGURE**, and move the cell pointer to G19.

2. Type **@MIN(G6.G16)** and press ENTER to produce the results shown in Figure 7-10.

    You could use this low sales amount to help you establish incentive programs or minimum sales standards.

The @MIN function will ignore blank cells. Cells that contain characters are evaluated as zero and could therefore erroneously be considered the lowest value in a list. Unfortunately, the function does not highlight the entry that produced the lowest value; it only returns it. If you want to find the entry that matches the returned value, you must visually scan the values in the cells that comprise the list.

@MAX   The @MAX function examines a list of values and returns the largest value in the list. It returns the exact opposite of @MIN but uses an identical syntax of

A:G20: [W11] @MAX(G6..G16)   `READY`

```
A      A           B         C        D         E         F          G
              High Profits Quarterly Sales Figures
1
2                       Region 4
3
4                              Jan       Feb       Mar      Qtr.
5   Salesperson  District Branch   Sales     Sales     Sales     Total
6
7   Jane Hunt         2      4590  $87,650   $92,300   $93,415  $273,365
8   Jason Rye         1      1705  $95,800  $105,650  $114,785  $316,235
9   Paul Jones        3      3201  $56,780   $52,300   $48,750  $157,830
10  Mary Hart         1      1705  $89,675  $108,755  $135,400  $333,830
11  Tom Bush          2      4250  $91,555   $87,600   $92,300  $271,455
12  Gary Lowe         2      4250  $76,900   $82,600   $83,500  $243,000
13  Karen Stein       3      2950  $68,565   $76,500   $82,300  $227,365
14  Cindy Boyd        2      4590 $110,800  $153,400  $105,665  $369,865
15  Jim Rogers        1      1921  $98,000  $114,785  $114,785  $327,570
16
17           TOTAL SALES        $775,725  $873,890  $870,900 $2,520,515
18           # SALES PERSONNEL      9
19                      LOWEST QTR SALES FIGURE        $157,830
20                      LARGEST QTR SALES FIGURE       $369,865
```

FIGURE 7-11.   Using @MAX

@MAX(*list*). You can use it to find the amount sold by the top performer, the highest hourly wage or annual salary, or the highest temperature in the month of August (assuming that the worksheet contains appropriate data values for these items). Use @MAX now to determine the highest sales for the quarter by making the following entries:

1. Move the cell pointer to D20, type **LARGEST QTR SALES FIGURE**, and move the cell pointer to G20.

2. Type **@MAX(G6.G16)** and press ENTER.
   Like the @MIN function, @MAX ignores blank cells. It also treats labels as zeros. The results are shown in Figure 7-11.

3. Enter /**File Save**, type **MIN_MAX**, and press ENTER.

@AVG   The @AVG function returns one value: the arithmetic average of all the values in a list. The average is computed by summing all of the values in the list and then dividing the sum by the number of entries in the list. @AVG is equivalent to the calculation @SUM(*list*)/@COUNT(*list*), and it uses the syntax @AVG(*list*).
   You can use this new function to determine the average sales for each month. Follow these steps:

1. Enter /**File Retrieve**, type **SUMCOUNT**, and press ENTER.
   This will bring the original @SUM example into memory.

2. Move the cell pointer to B19 and type **AVERAGE SALES**. Then move the cell pointer to D19.

3. Type **@AVG(D6.D16)** and press ENTER.

4. Enter /**Copy** and press ENTER. Move the cell pointer to E19 and type a period. Then move the cell pointer to G19 and press ENTER.
   You should now have the average for all three months and the quarter total in your model, as shown in Figure 7-12.

5. Enter /**File Save**, press ENTER, and type **R**.
   1-2-3 will replace the copy of the model on disk with the current copy.

6. Enter /**Worksheet Erase Yes** to clear memory.

@SUMPRODUCT   This function is new in Release 3. It allows you to perform a series of multiplication operations and add the results of each individual operation. The function expects two ranges of identical size as its arguments. It matches the corresponding entries in the ranges and multiplies one value by the other. The function

---

A:D19: @AVG(D6..D16)   READY

	A	B	C	D	E	F	G
1			High Profits Quarterly Sales Figures				
2			Region 4				
3							
4				Jan	Feb	Mar	Qtr.
5	Salesperson	District	Branch	Sales	Sales	Sales	Total
6							
7	Jane Hunt	2	4590	$87,650	$92,300	$93,415	$273,365
8	Jason Rye	1	1705	$95,800	$105,650	$114,785	$316,235
9	Paul Jones	3	3201	$56,780	$52,300	$48,750	$157,830
10	Mary Hart	1	1705	$89,675	$108,755	$135,400	$333,830
11	Tom Bush	2	4250	$91,555	$87,600	$92,300	$271,455
12	Gary Lowe	2	4250	$76,900	$82,600	$83,500	$243,000
13	Karen Stein	3	2950	$68,565	$76,500	$82,300	$227,365
14	Cindy Boyd	2	4590	$110,800	$153,400	$105,665	$369,865
15	Jim Rogers	1	1921	$98,000	$114,785	$114,785	$327,570
16							
17		TOTAL SALES		$775,725	$873,890	$870,900	$2,520,515
18		# SALES PERSONNEL	9				
19		AVERAGE SALES		$86,192	$97,099	$96,767	$280,057
20							

FIGURE 7-12.   Using @AVG

adds each result to a counter and provides the total in this counter after all multiplication operations are complete.

You can use @SUMPRODUCT to compute a total invoice amount when an invoice includes several products in varying quantities. This eliminates the need for individual price extensions (unit price times the number of units) if you do not need them. This same concept can be used to compute the total number of parts needed for an assembly operation, when the same part number is used in varying quantities in several phases of the assembly.

Follow these instructions to create an invoice with a total computed by @SUMPRODUCT:

1. Type **Invoice as of March 10, 1990** in B2. Move the cell pointer to B4.

2. Enter **/Worksheet Column Set-Width**, type **18**, and press ENTER.

3. Complete the following entries in the cells shown:
   B4: ITEM
   B5: Chair 8740
   B6: Desk 1180
   B7: Credenza 9876
   B8: File cabinet 5643
   B10: Invoice Total
   C4: QUANTITY
   C5: 4
   C6: 2
   C7: 1
   C8: 3
   D4: PRICE
   D5: 100
   D6: 500
   D7: 500
   D8: 200

4. Move the cell pointer to column, enter **/Worksheet Column Set-Width**, type **12**, and press ENTER.

5. Move the cell pointer to D10 and type **@SUMPRODUCT(C5..C8,D5..D8)**.
   Your worksheet will look like Figure 7-13. 1-2-3 will multiply C5 times D5 and add 400 to a counter. It will then multiply C6 times D6 and add another 1000 to the counter. Next, C7 is multiplied by D7, adding another 500 to the counter. The last multiplication is C8 times D8, adding 600 to the counter. The

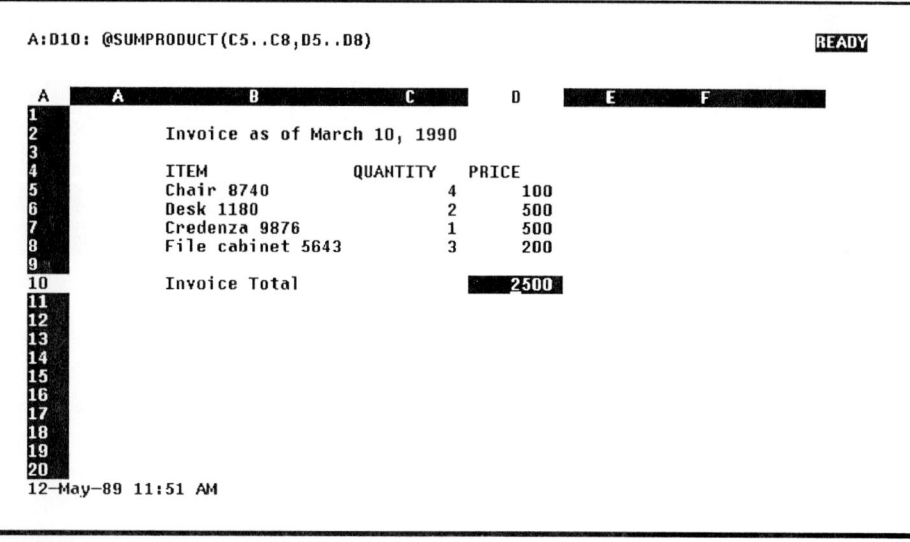

```
A:D10: @SUMPRODUCT(C5..C8,D5..D8)                                    READY

A    A          B          C          D      E       F
1
2           Invoice as of March 10, 1990
3
4           ITEM          QUANTITY    PRICE
5           Chair 8740          4     100
6           Desk 1180           2     500
7           Credenza 9876       1     500
8           File cabinet 5643   3     200
9
10          Invoice Total              2500
11
12
13
14
15
16
17
18
19
20
12-May-89 11:51 AM
```

FIGURE 7-13.   Using @SUMPRODUCT

total number in the counter is 2500, and this is returned as the result of the function.

Date and Time Functions

Date and time information are important parts of many business decisions. You need date information to know if a loan is overdue or if there is still time remaining in the discount period for an invoice. Time information can be used to calculate the service time for various tasks or to log the delivery time for various carriers. Release 3 has time functions that allow you to time-stamp a worksheet and perform calculations that involve time differences.

WORKING WITH DATES   1-2-3 can work with dates between January 1, 1900, and December 31, 2099. A unique serial number is assigned to each date. The number for January 1, 1900, is 1, and the number for December 31, 2099, is 73050. This serial date number represents the number of days since December 31, 1899. Although representing every date in terms of its distance from the previous century may seem strange, this method provides the date arithmetic features of the package. Since all dates have the same comparison point, you can subtract one date from another to determine how many days apart they are. If a loan is due on a date whose serial date number is 32980 and today's serial date number is 32990, then it is obvious that the loan is overdue—the serial number for the due date is less than today's serial date number.

All of this may seem a little confusing, but 1-2-3 can reduce some of the difficulty. You will not need to calculate or enter serial date numbers. 1-2-3 does that for you with its date functions. 1-2-3 also provides a command that formats serial date numbers so they look presentable. You can choose from a variety of Date formats that are familiar to you in the Range Format menu.

Date-Stamping the Worksheet　All releases of 1-2-3 provide a way for you to put a *date stamp* on the worksheet. With Release 3, you have two choices. First you can use the @TODAY function. This function does not require arguments; when you enter it in a worksheet cell, it always accesses the system date and displays the serial date number for the system date in the worksheet cell where you entered the function. Second, you can use /Range Format to change the appearance of this serial date number to something more familiar.

Release 3 also supports the @NOW function. You will learn some additional features of @NOW later, but for the moment, the only important information about @NOW is that it enters a serial number in the worksheet cell. This serial number contains two parts, a whole number and a decimal fraction. The whole number represents the serial date number, and the decimal fraction represents the current time. Both the date and the time will be updated every time the current model is recalculated. If you save your worksheet file after entering the @NOW function, it will be available the next time you use the worksheet. Every time you boot your system, you will want to ensure that the correct date is being used so that your models can be time-stamped accurately.

You can try out this date-stamping feature with these instructions:

1. Enter /**Worksheet Erase Yes Yes**.

2. Type **@NOW** and press ENTER.

   If you are using Release 3, you should see a serial date number display that looks something like this:

Your display will be slightly different because it will be based on the date when you are using the worksheet. Once entered, this function will be updated every time the worksheet is recalculated, so if you work with the spreadsheet past midnight you will see the date change. If you save the worksheet to disk, the next time you retrieve the worksheet an updated date will appear in the cell that contains @NOW.

3. Enter /**Worksheet Column Set-Width** and press the RIGHT ARROW key. Then press ENTER.

   This instruction widens the display so that you can view date and time display in this column.

4. Enter /**Range Format Date** to produce this display:

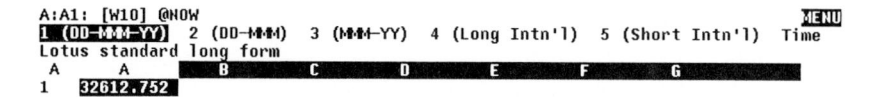

This shows the various date formatting options.

5. Use the RIGHT ARROW key to move to each of the menu options, and view the date pattern that would be produced by selecting each option. Then select option 1 by typing **1** and pressing ENTER.

   The serial date number should now be formatted with a pattern like this:

Your display will look a little different; your date is probably different from the one used for this example.

If you include @NOW in an area of your worksheet that you normally print, you will have an automatic date-stamp on every printed report you create. Since you must retrieve the worksheet in order to print it, the date will be updated automatically every time the worksheet is printed.

Time-Stamping the Worksheet   A *time stamp* accessed with the @NOW function is available only for Release 2 and above. The difference between using @NOW to date-stamp the worksheet or to time-stamp it is the format you place on the result of the function. @NOW returns both a whole number and a fractional decimal. The whole number represents the number of days; the fractional decimal represents the portion of the current day that has already elapsed. For example, if the decimal is 0.25, that would represent a quarter of the day as having elapsed, or 6:00 A.M.. A decimal fraction of 0.5 represents noon, and 0.75 represents 6:00 P.M..

To see these time displays as other than decimal fractions, you will need to format the entries by using /Range Format Date Time. The display is

```
A:A1: (D1) [W10] @NOW                                              MENU
1 (HH:MM:SS AM/PM)  2 (HH:MM AM/PM)  3 (Long Intn'l)  4 (Short Intn'l)
Lotus standard long form
A     A          B         C         D         E         F         G
1   14-Apr-89
```

The variety of time displays will allow you to create a report that closely matches the organizational standards you are currently using.

You can time-stamp your worksheet by following these steps:

1. Move the cell pointer to A2, type **@NOW**, and press ENTER.

2. Enter **/Range Format Date Time 2** and press ENTER.
   Your display will be formatted like the following one:

```
A:A2: (D7) [W10] @NOW                                              READY

A     A          B         C         D         E         F         G
1     14-Apr-89
2     06:05 PM
```

Entering Dates   Often, when you work with dates, you do not want to use the current date—you want to record the date of hire, a loan due date, or an upcoming anniversary date. 1-2-3 provides a way for you to record this date information in the worksheet; You use the @DATE function and supply arguments that represent the year, month, and day.

The @DATE function is the first one you have worked with for which the arguments need to be supplied in a specific order, as shown in this syntax:

@DATE(*YR,MO,DA*)

The first argument, *YR,* can be any number from 0 to 199, with 1900 represented by 0, 1988 by 88, and 2099 by 199. The month argument, *MO,* can be any number from 1 through 12. The day argument, *DA,* can be a number from 1 to 31 but it must be a valid day number for the month you select. For example, September cannot have 31, because 30 is the largest number of days in September. Since you will want the function to generate the correct serial date number for you, you must adhere exactly to the order shown for the three arguments.

You can put the @DATE function to work in a model that calculates the charges for video rentals. In this example, the charges depend on the number of days that a patron has had the video. You will enter the customer number in column A, the video number in column B, the date the video was checked out in column C, and the date it

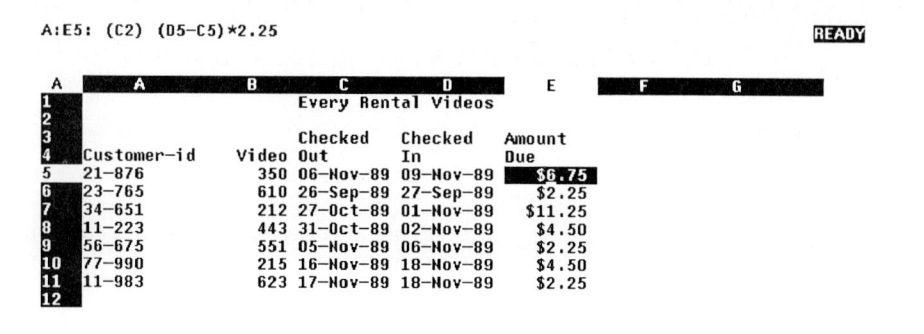

FIGURE 7-14.   Result of subtracting two dates

was returned in column D. These last two entries will be used to compute the charges. The formula you use will subtract the date when the video was checked out from the date when it was returned and multiply the number of days by $2.25. Follow these steps to make the entries and apply the formats shown in Figure 7-14:

1. Enter /**Worksheet Erase Yes Yes** and make these entries in the worksheet cells listed:

    A4: Customer-id
    A5: '21-876
    A6: '23-765
    A7: '34-651
    A8: '11-223
    A9: '56-675
    A10: '77-990
    A11: '11-983
    B4: Video
    B5: 350
    B6: 610
    B7: 212
    B8: 443
    B9: 551
    B10: 215
    B11: 623
    C1: Every Rental Videos

C3: Checked
C4: Out
D3: Checked
D4: In
E3: Amount
E4: Due

Since you are using Release 3, there is another way to enter the labels in column A: you can format the cells with /Range Format Other Label, and you will not need to enter the label indicator with each entry.

2. Now enter these dates using the @DATE function:

C5: @DATE(89,11,6)
C6: @DATE(89,09,26)
C7: @DATE(89,10,27)
C8: @DATE(89,10,31)
C9: @DATE(89,11,5)
C10: @DATE(89,11,16)
C11: @DATE(89,11,17)
D5: @DATE(89,11,9)
D6: @DATE(89,09,27)
D7: @DATE(89,11,1)
D8: @DATE(89,11,2)
D9: @DATE(89,11,6)
D10: @DATE(89,11,18)
D11: @DATE(89,11,18)

As a new feature of Release 3, the dates in columns C and D can be entered without the need for @ functions by entering them in a date format such as 6-Nov-89.

3. Move the cell pointer to E5 and type **(D5-C5)∗2.25**.

This entry computes the cost of the rental, which is the number of days times the daily charge of $2.25. But first you must calculate the number of days by subtracting the two dates.

4. Enter /**Copy**, press ENTER, move the cell pointer to E6, and type a period. Then move the cell pointer to E11 and press ENTER.

5. Move the cell pointer to column A, and enter /**Worksheet Column Set-Width**. Then type **12** and press ENTER.

6. Move the cell pointer to C5. Enter /**Range Format Date 1**. Type **C5.D11** and press ENTER.

7. Enter /**Worksheet Column Column-Range Set-Width**, press the RIGHT ARROW key to include columns C and D, and press ENTER. Press the RIGHT ARROW key so that the dates display properly. Then press ENTER.

8. Move the cell pointer to E5. Enter /**Range Format Currency**. Press ENTER, type **E5.E11**, and press ENTER to produce the completed model shown in Figure 7-14.

Your model is now complete. You may be thinking that it would be just as easy to type in the date just as you want to see it by using a label entry such as Apr-14-90. This is a new feature of Release 3. Release 3 will automatically convert a date entered in one of its acceptable formats into a serial date number. This is unlike previous releases that required a function like @DATE to create date serial numbers you could use in computations.

Extracting a Portion of a Date   Three functions allow you to extract part of a date. You have the choice of extracting the year, month, or day from a serial date number. The syntax for the three functions is as follows:

@YEAR(*serial date number*)
@MONTH(*serial date number*)
@DAY(*serial date number*)

Try all three functions by adding new columns to the existing model for the video rentals:

1. Move the cell pointer to H5. Type **@YEAR(D5)** and press ENTER.
   The year number 89 should now be displayed in this cell.

2. Move the cell pointer to I5. Type **@MONTH(D5)** and press ENTER.
   The month number should now appear in the cell.

3. Move the cell pointer to J5. Type **@DAY(D5)** and press ENTER.
   The day number should now appear in the cell, as shown in Figure 7-15.

4. Move the cell pointer to H5, enter /**Copy,** and press the RIGHT ARROW key twice to move the cell pointer to J5. Then press ENTER. Move the cell pointer to H6 and type a period. Then move the cell pointer to H11 and press ENTER.
   The model should match the data shown in Figure 7-16.

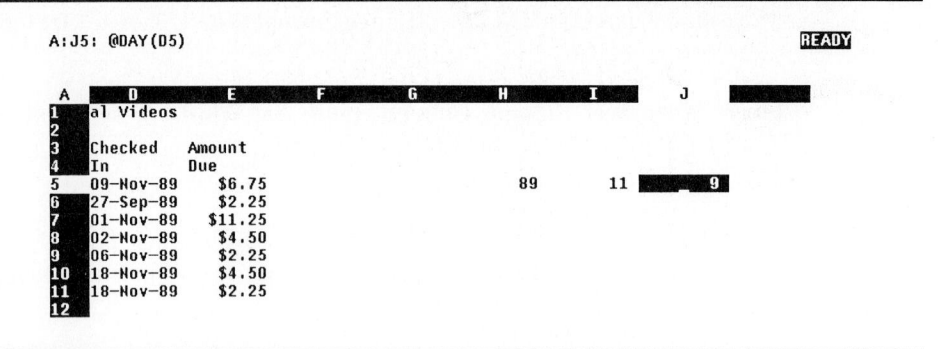

FIGURE 7-15.   Extracting date components

5. Press HOME, enter /**File Save**, type **VIDEOS**, and press ENTER.

6. Enter /**Worksheet Erase Yes**.

Entering Times   Just as you need to use a function to enter dates, you must also use one for making time entries on the worksheet. If you enter time representations without using the special time function, you will not be able to use it in time computations. The function used to make a time entry on the worksheet is @TIME. Its syntax is

@TIME(*hour,minute,second*)

```
A:H5:  @YEAR(D5)                                                    READY

A     D          E        F        G        H        I        J
1     al Videos
2
3     Checked    Amount
4     In         Due
5     09-Nov-89    $6.75                              89       11       9
6     27-Sep-89    $2.25                              89        9      27
7     01-Nov-89   $11.25                              89       11       1
8     02-Nov-89    $4.50                              89       11       2
9     06-Nov-89    $2.25                              89       11       6
10    18-Nov-89    $4.50                              89       11      18
11    18-Nov-89    $2.25                              89       11      18
12
```

FIGURE 7-16.   Copy the date functions

In this function, *hour* is a number between 0 and 23, with 0 representing midnight and 23 representing 11:00 P.M.; *minute* is a number between 0 and 59; and *second* has the same acceptable value range as *minute*.

Follow these instructions to create a worksheet that determines the time elapsed from when a vehicle is logged in for repair and when it leaves the service facility:

1. Make these entries:

   A3: Job
   A4: Number
   A5: 1
   A6: 2
   A7: 3
   A8: 4
   B1: QUICK CAR REPAIR November 12,1989
   B3: Time
   B4: In
   C4: Repair
   C5: Tire
   C6: Brakes
   C7: Steering
   C8: Lube
   D3: Time
   D4: Out
   E3: Elapsed
   E4: Time

   Your model should now look like this:

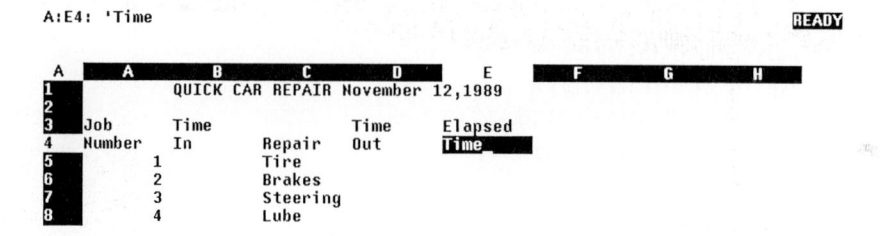

2. Move the cell pointer to B5, and enter **/Range Format Date Time 2**. Move the cell pointer to B8 and press ENTER.

3. Move the cell pointer to D5 and enter **/Range Format Date Time 2**. Move the cell pointer to D8 and press ENTER.

4. Move the cell pointer to E5 and enter **/Range Format Date Time 4**. Move the cell pointer to E8 and press ENTER.

5. Move the cell pointer to B5, type **@TIME(8,5,0)**, and press the DOWN ARROW key.

   Notice the zero entry for seconds. It is used as a place marker even when you do not have a special value to enter. With Release 3, you have an option for entering times that eliminates the need for @ functions. You can enter the times in a format like 09:17 AM or 12:52, and 1-2-3 will convert the entries into time serial numbers.

6. Move the cell pointer to B6, type **@TIME(8,10,0)**, and press the DOWN ARROW key.

7. Move the cell pointer to B7, type **@TIME(8,30,0)**, and press the DOWN ARROW key.

8. Move the cell pointer to B8, type **@TIME(8,32,0)**, and press ENTER to produce this display:

```
A:B8: (D7) @TIME(8,32,0)                                          READY

A       A        B         C         D         E        F      G      H
1                QUICK CAR REPAIR November 12,1989
2
3    Job      Time                Time      Elapsed
4    Number   In        Repair    Out       Time
5         1 08:05 AM Tire
6         2 08:10 AM Brakes
7         3 08:30 AM Steering
8         4 08:32 AM Lube
```

9. Finish the remaining time entries for the times the vehicles were completed by making these entries in column D:

   D5: @TIME(9,17,0)
   D6: @TIME(10,34,0)
   D7: @TIME(13,18,0)
   D8: @TIME(9,44,0)

Notice the use of a 24-hour clock representation in these entries, with the number 13 used to represent 1:00 P.M.: yet the time is displayed as "01:18 PM" due to the format of D7 for the time entries:

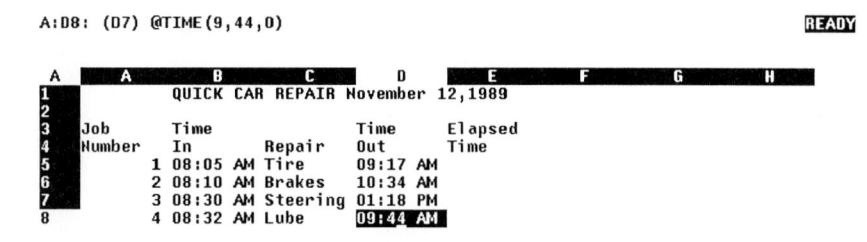

10. Move the cell pointer to E5, type **+D5-B5**, and press ENTER.

    This computes the elapsed time for the repair of the first vehicle. When you copy this formula for the remaining entries, your job will be finished.

11. Enter **/Copy** and press ENTER. Move the cell pointer to E6, type **.**, move the cell pointer to E8, and press ENTER to produce these results:

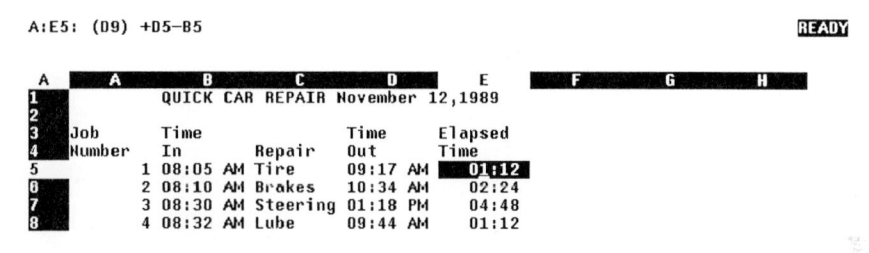

12. Enter **/File Save**, type **TIME**, and press ENTER.

13. Enter **/Worksheet Erase Yes**.

Extracting Part of a Time Entry Three functions can extract any part of a time serial number. They are @HOUR, @MINUTE, and @SECOND. All three use a time serial number as their argument, as in @HOUR(*time serial number*). Since all three follow the same pattern, you will only need to take a close look at one to understand how each of them works.

Use the @HOUR function whenever you wish to work with only the hour portion of a time entry. The function always returns a value between 0 and 23. You can use this function to track the delivery hour for packages if the @TIME function was used to record the time of receipt. Follow these steps to enter the information about the packages and extract the delivery hour:

1. Complete these entries:

   A1: Time
   A2: Received
   A3: @TIME(8,4,6)
   A4: @TIME(9,11,0)
   A5: @TIME(9,30,0)
   A6: @TIME(9,45,0)
   B1: Package
   B2: Number
   B3: 1761
   B4: 3421
   B5: 2280
   B6: 7891
   C2: Recipient
   C3: B. Jones
   C4: R. Gaff
   C5: J. Bowyer
   C6: J. Kiger
   D2: Hour

2. Move the cell pointer to A3 and enter /**Range Format Date Time 1**. Press the END key followed by the DOWN ARROW key, and then press ENTER.

3. Enter /**Worksheet Column Set-Width**, type **14**, and press ENTER.

4. Move the cell pointer to column C. Enter /**Worksheet Column Set-Width**, type **16**, and press ENTER.

5. Move the cell pointer to D3, type **@HOUR(A3)**, and press ENTER.
   This extracts the hour number, which is 8.

6. Enter /**Copy** and press ENTER. Move the cell pointer to D4, type **.**, move the cell pointer to D6, and press ENTER.
   This produces the following display:

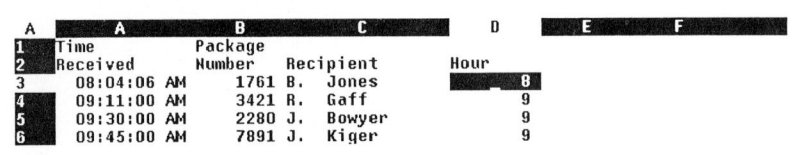

```
A:D3: @HOUR(A3)                                              READY

A       A            B            C            D       E       F
1  Time         Package
2  Received     Number       Recipient        Hour
3     08:04:06 AM     1761 B.   Jones               8
4     09:11:00 AM     3421 R.   Gaff                9
5     09:30:00 AM     2280 J.   Bowyer              9
6     09:45:00 AM     7891 J.   Kiger               9
```

7. Enter **/File Save**, type **HOUR**, and press ENTER.

8. Enter **/Worksheet Erase Yes**.

String Functions

String functions provide a variety of character-manipulation formulas that give you flexibility in rearranging text entries. With string functions, you can work with the entire label entry for a cell or with just a part of it. The functions in this category can be real life-savers when you have to correct data-entry errors. You will work in this chapter with abbreviated examples that correct errors in one or two entries, but the same formula you create for one entry could be copied down a column to correct a large portion of a worksheet. You will have the opportunity to work with functions that change the case of an entry from upper- to lowercase or even to proper case (with the first letters of words capitalized as in proper names). You will also learn how to extract one or more characters from the beginning or the end of a character string.

When the string values you are working with are used as arguments for string functions, they must be enclosed in quotation marks ("). However, when the same entries are referenced by a cell address, no quotation marks are required. For example, the @UPPER function converts text entries to uppercase. If you want to include the string **jim smith** as an argument in this function, you need to record it as **@UPPER("jim smith")**. However, if you store **jim smith** in A5, you can write **@UPPER(A5)** without quotation marks.

Some string functions produce another string as a result of the function. Other string functions produce numeric results that are equivalent to a position number within the string.

@UPPER   The @UPPER function will change all the characters to uppercase. This feature allows you to convert worksheet text data to all capital letters if that is your preference. The syntax of the function is @UPPER(*string*).

Make these entries to try the function:

1. Move the cell pointer to A1, type **jim smith**, and move the cell pointer to A2.

2. Type **Bill Brown** and move the cell pointer to A3.

3. Type **JANE JONES** and move the cell pointer to B1.

4. Enter **/Worksheet Global Col-Width**, type **12**, and press ENTER.

5. Type **@UPPER(A1)** and press ENTER.

6. Enter **/Copy** and press ENTER. Move the cell pointer to B2, type **.**, move the cell pointer to B3, and press ENTER.

    The converted data appears like this:

@LOWER The @LOWER function converts text entries to all lowercase. Regardless of whether the text is uppercase, lowercase, or proper case, the @LOWER function produces a string that is guaranteed to be in lowercase.

You can use the example you created to test the @UPPER function for the @LOWER function. Follow these steps to add a new column to the model:

1. Move the cell pointer to C1, type **@LOWER(A1)**, and press ENTER.

2. Enter **/Copy** and press ENTER. Move the cell pointer to C2, type **.**, move the cell pointer to C3, and press ENTER to produce this display:

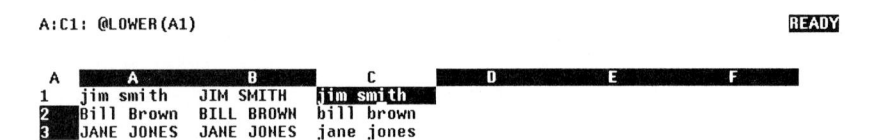

@PROPER The @PROPER function converts text into the format you expect to see for proper nouns. The first letter in each word is capitalized, and the remaining letters of the word are displayed in lowercase. This is another function you can use to establish consistency in the data on your worksheet. The model that was used to test the @UPPER and @LOWER functions can be used with @PROPER. Add another column to this model by following these instructions:

1. Move the cell pointer to D1, type **@PROPER(A1)**, and press ENTER.

2. Enter **/Copy** and press ENTER. Move the cell pointer to D2, type **.**, move the cell pointer to D3, and press ENTER to produce this display:

A:D1: @PROPER(A1)   `READY`

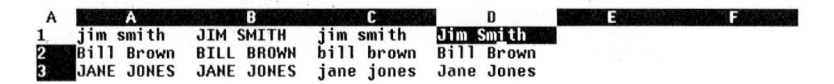

3. Enter /**File Save**, type **CASE**, and press ENTER.

4. Enter /**Worksheet Erase Yes** to clear the worksheet.

@RIGHT   The @RIGHT function extracts one or more characters from the right of a string entry. The function has two arguments: the function you want to extract from, and the number of characters to extract. The syntax of the function is

@RIGHT(*string,number of characters*)

Examples of this function and the results it produces are shown here:

@RIGHT("Lotus 1-2-3",5)	Equals 1-2-3
@RIGHT("ABC COMPANY ",8)	Equals Y with seven trailing blanks

You can use this function to extract a warehouse location represented by the last three characters in every part number. Make these entries on your worksheet to see how this function works:

1. Enter the following:

   A1: Part No.
   A2: TY-3452-DAL
   A3: ST-67-CHI
   A4: JV-893-DAL
   B1: Warehouse

2. Move the cell pointer to column A, enter /**Worksheet Column Set-Width**, type **12**, and press ENTER.

3. Move the cell pointer to B2, type **@RIGHT(A2,3)**, and press ENTER.

4. Enter /**Copy**, press ENTER, and move the cell pointer to B3. Type ., move the cell pointer to B4, and press ENTER to produce this result:

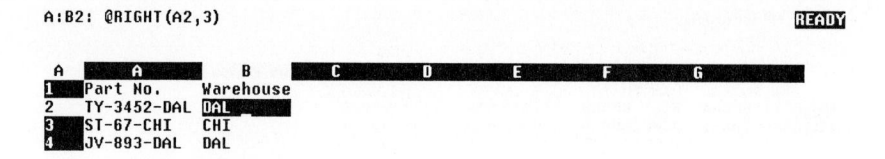

The warehouse locations have been filled with the result of the @RIGHT function. The last three characters of each part number represent the location, which is now displayed in column B. This feature is useful if you need to create a report that displays the warehouse locations but does not require the full display of the part numbers. Because the warehouse location is extracted from the longer entry, it is now much easier to focus on the information of interest (assuming that it is the warehouse location).

5. Enter /**File Save**, type **RIGHT**, and press ENTER if you want to save this model.

@LEFT   The @LEFT function removes characters from the front of a string. You can use it to reference strings in separate first-name, last-name, and middle-initial columns of the worksheet, and to combine the result of these three functions with the string operator for concatenation (&). Concatenation will join all three into a set of initials. Make these entries to try the @LEFT function:

1. Enter /**Worksheet Erase Yes**.

2. Make the following entries on the worksheet:
   A1: F Name
   A2: Sally
   A3: Joe
   A4: Sam
   A5: Kim
   B1: M Init
   B2: T.
   B3: L.
   B4: P.
   B5: D.
   C1: L Name
   C2: Smith
   C3: Harris
   C4: Polk
   C5: Jackson
   D1: Initials

2. Move the cell pointer to D2 and type this line:

   @LEFT(A2,1)&@LEFT(B2,1)&@LEFT(C2,1)

   Then press ENTER to see the first set of initials displayed:

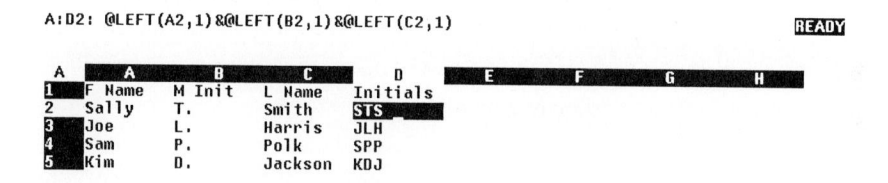

```
A:D2: @LEFT(A2,1)&@LEFT(B2,1)&@LEFT(C2,1)                              READY

A       A        B        C          D        E        F        G        H
1   F Name   M Init   L Name     Initials
2   Sally    T.       Smith      STS
3   Joe      L.       Harris
4   Sam      P.       Polk
5   Kim      D.       Jackson
```

In this string formula the & symbol serves as a means of combining strings, just as a + is used with numbers.

3. Enter **/Copy** and press ENTER. Move the cell pointer to D3, type ., and move the cell pointer to D5. Press ENTER to complete the copy operation.
   The results look like this:

```
A:D2: @LEFT(A2,1)&@LEFT(B2,1)&@LEFT(C2,1)                              READY

A       A        B        C          D        E        F        G        H
1   F Name   M Init   L Name     Initials
2   Sally    T.       Smith      STS
3   Joe      L.       Harris     JLH
4   Sam      P.       Polk       SPP
5   Kim      D.       Jackson    KDJ
```

4. Enter **/File Save**, type **LEFT**, and press ENTER.

@REPEAT   The @REPEAT function duplicates a character string a specified number of times. The primary purpose of this function is to improve the appearance of the worksheet. @REPEAT can create dividing lines between the assumptions of a report and the display of the final results. In one sense, @REPEAT is similar to the backslash character (\) because it repeats labels. However, \ is restricted to filling a single cell, whereas @REPEAT can extend across many worksheet cells. In addition, @REPEAT can complete the dividing line with the entry of one function, while the \ character normally requires repeated entries or copying.

If you wish, you can go back to the sales projections you entered in an earlier chapter and replace the asterisks with the backslash, using a new character sequence. For now, let's use @REPEAT in a worksheet cell to see how it works:

1. Move the cell pointer to A7.

2. Type **@REPEAT("+-",36)** and press ENTER.

Your display should match this:

```
A:A7: @REPEAT("+-",36)                                              READY

A      A            B        C        D        E      F      G      H
1    F Name    M Init   L Name   Initials
2    Sally     T.       Smith    STS
3    Joe       L.       Harris   JLH
4    Sam       P.       Polk     SPP
5    Kim       D.       Jackson  KDJ
6
7    +-+-+-+-+-+-+-+-+-+-+-+-+-+-+-+-+-+-+-+-+-+-+-+-+-+-+-+-+-+-+-+-+-+-+
```

Notice that quotation marks were required in the function, since a string value was placed in the function as an argument.

Math Functions

1-2-3's math functions perform both simple calculations and more complex operations suited to an engineering or manufacturing application. Rather than looking at the trigonometric functions and more complex operations, you will benefit most from the general-purpose examples emphasized by the exercises in this section. You will learn how to overcome rounding problems, look at the absolute value of a number, and work with only the integer portion of a number.

@ABS   The @ABS function returns the positive or absolute value of a number, without regard to whether the number is positive or negative. This function is useful when you are concerned with the relative size of numbers and do not care if the numbers are positive or negative.

An example of this function is illustrated by the need of retail establishments to monitor cash surpluses and shortages in their registers. Consistent cash surpluses and shortages indicate a cash-control problem that should be corrected. Simply adding the surpluses and shortages doesn't always work: they might cancel each other out. However, examining the absolute value of the surpluses and shortages reveals the total amount of the differences.

Follow these instructions to set up a model for the Hot Dog House Register:

1. Enter **/Worksheet Erase Yes Yes** and then **/Worksheet Global Format Currency**. Press ENTER to accept the default of two decimal places.

2. Place these entries in worksheet cells:

    A5: Monday
    A6: Tuesday
    A7: Wednesday
    A8: Thursday
    A9: Friday
    A10: Saturday
    A11: Sunday
    A13: TOTAL DIFFERENCE FOR THE WEEK:
    C1: Hot Dog House Register
    C2: Week of November 10, 1989
    C4: Over/Under
    C5: 42
    C6: -35
    C7: 22.78
    C8: -57
    C9: 12.58
    C10: .58
    C11: -2.10
    E4: Absolute Value

3. Move the cell pointer to E5, type **@ABS(C5)**, and press ENTER.
This step computes the absolute value of the entry in C5.

4. Enter **/Copy** and press ENTER. Move the cell pointer to E6, type **.**, move the cell pointer to E11, and press ENTER.
Once you have completed this step, all the daily cash differences have been converted to their absolute values and stored in column E.

5. Move the cell pointer to E13, type **@SUM(E5.E11)**, and press ENTER to produce the results shown in Figure 7-17.
This step computes a total of the cash differences, without regard to whether they were positive or negative, by using the absolute value of each day's total in the sum calculation. This method prevents the cash differences from partially canceling each other out and seeming like less of a problem than they actually are.

A:E13: @SUM(E5..E11)   READY

```
  A       A        B        C        D       E      F       G       H
  1                      Hot Dog House Register
  2 °                    Week of November 10, 1989
  3
  4                      Over/Under           Absolute Value
  5  Monday                $42.00               $42.00
  6  Tuesday              ($35.00)               $35.00
  7  Wednesday             $22.78               $22.78
  8  Thursday             ($57.00)               $57.00
  9  Friday                $12.58               $12.58
 10  Saturday              $0.58                 $0.58
 11  Sunday               ($2.10)                $2.10
 12
 13  TOTAL DIFFERENCE FOR THE WEEK:        $172.04
 14
```

FIGURE 7-17.   Using @ABS

@INT   The @INT function lets you truncate the decimal places in a number to produce a whole number or integer. You can use it when you work with date computations and wish to truncate the decimal fraction that represents the time portion of the current date. You can also use it when calculating the number of complete items that can be produced on a production line.

To see how this function works, create a model that determines how many complete items can be produced from a given volume of raw material. The raw material is cowhide, and the product being produced is wallets. It has been determined that one wallet will require 0.6789 square feet of cowhide. Partially completed items will not be considered, since they cannot be shipped. It does not work to round the calculated result; the decimal fraction computed could be rounded upward and would no longer represent completed items. The only solution is to truncate the decimal portion of the number. The @INT function that you will use when creating your model has this syntax:

@INT(*number*)

Follow these steps to create your model:

1. Enter **/Worksheet Erase Yes Yes** and make the following entries:

    A1: Cowhide needed for 1 wallet -
    A3: Available sizes
    A4: 1
    A5: 5

A6: 10
A7: 15
A8: 20
A9: 25
D3: Wallets Produced
E1: .6789
F1: Sq. ft.

2. Move the cell pointer to D4 and type **@INT(A4/$E$1)**.

Notice that the argument for the @INT function is the formula A4/$E$1. This formula divides the size of the piece of raw material by the square-footage requirements. The reference to the requirements of one piece is absolute; this one value will be referenced in all the calculations and should not change if the formula is copied. The second part of the formula adds the @INT function, which will cause any decimal fraction resulting from the computation to be truncated, representing the actual number of wallets that can be produced.

3. Enter **/Copy** and press ENTER. Move the cell pointer to D5, type **.**, move the cell pointer to D9, and press ENTER.

You now have the integer portion of each of the calculations, as shown here:

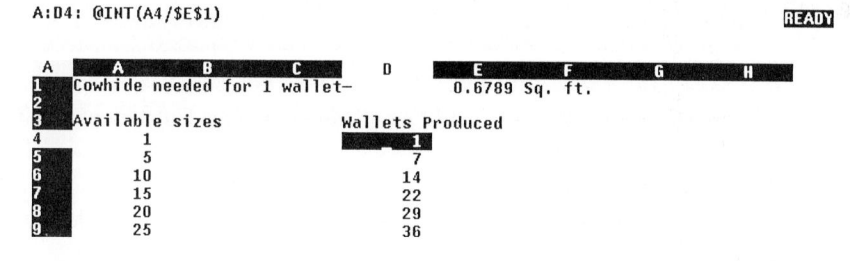

4. Enter **/File Save**, type **INTEGER**, and press ENTER.

5. Enter **/Worksheet Erase Yes**.

@ROUND   The @ROUND function actually alters the way a number is stored internally by letting you specify the number of decimal places you want. This function can solve some of the problems caused by the discrepancy between how numbers are stored and the format you use to display them. In Chapter 3, you learned that you could use the format commands (/Worksheet Global Format and /Range Format) to display numbers with a varying amount of decimal places. But the problem with these changes is that the full internal accuracy is still maintained despite the change in the display appearance. This can cause totals at the bottom of a column to appear as though they are not added up properly, because of the greater internal storage accuracy of the numbers being added.

Use the following steps to create a model that shows this discrepancy and then applies the @ROUND function to the formulas in the model so that the internal accuracy is equal to the numbers that are displayed:

1. Make these entries:

   A2: Product 1 Sales
   A3: Product 2 Sales
   A4: Product 3 Sales
   C1: Price
   C2: 33.3333
   C3: 67.5068
   C4: 3.3335
   D1: Quantity
   D2: 100
   D3: 50
   D4: 100
   E1: Total $

2. Move the cell pointer to C2, enter /**Range Format Currency**, type **4**, and press ENTER. Press the END key followed by the DOWN ARROW key, and then press ENTER.

3. Move the cell pointer to E2 and enter /**Range Format Currency**, type **0**, and press ENTER. Type **E2.E5** and press ENTER.

   The END and DOWN ARROW sequence will not work for this format operation, since the cells are empty at this time and the sequence would format to the bottom of the column.

4. Type **+C2*D2** and press ENTER.

   This formula computes the total cost of the purchase. A whole number is displayed; however, there is a decimal fraction in the number stored internally because of the decimals in the price.

5. Enter /**Copy** and press ENTER. Move the cell pointer to E3, type **.**, move the cell pointer to E4, and press ENTER.

6. Move the cell pointer to E5 and type **@SUM(E2.E4)**. Press ENTER to produce these results:

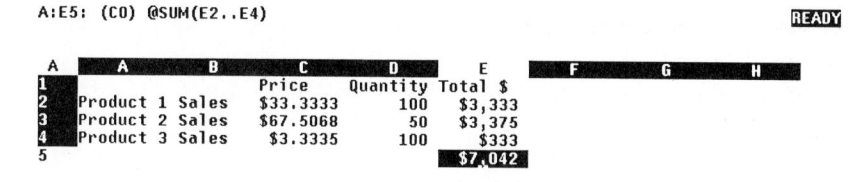

```
A:E5: (C0) @SUM(E2..E4)                                          READY
```

Looking at the column E figures suggests that the total should be $7,041, not the $7,042 shown. The difference of $1 is due to the rounding discrepancy that occurs when the total dollar numbers are displayed. The @SUM function is computed from the numbers that are stored, not those that are displayed.

The @ROUND function can solve this problem. Its format is

@ROUND(*number to be rounded,place of rounding*)

The number to be rounded can be a number, a reference to a cell that contains a number, or a formula that evaluates as a number. The place of rounding is a positive or negative number that specifies the place of rounding. Rounding to the nearest whole number uses 0 as the place of rounding. Rounding to decimal places to the right of a whole number uses positive integers for each place further to the right. Rounding to the left of the whole-number position is represented by negative integers. Table 7-1 shows the effect of some of the rounding options on a number.

You can apply this @ROUND function to the total dollar computations with these steps:

1. Move the cell pointer to E2 then press F2 (EDIT).

2. Press the HOME key to move to the front of the entry. Press DEL to delete the + sign.

Number	Rounded Number	Formula for Rounding
12345.678123	12345.6781	@ROUND($A$3,4)
	12345.68	@ROUND($A$3,2)
	12345.7	@ROUND($A$3,1)
	12346	@ROUND($A$3,0)
	12300	@ROUND($A$3,-2)
	10000	@ROUND($A$3,-4)

TABLE 7-1.   Effects of Various Rounding Options

3. Type **@ROUND(**.

4. Press the END key, type **,0)**, and press ENTER.

5. Enter **/Copy** and press ENTER. Move the cell pointer to E3, type **.**, move the cell pointer to E4, and press ENTER to produce these results:

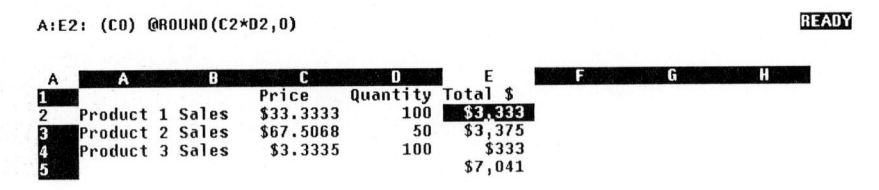

```
A:E2: (C0) @ROUND(C2*D2,0)                                    READY
```

The addition of @ROUND to each formula makes the column total agree with the numbers displayed. This is because you altered the internal accuracy of each of the numbers to make it match the display.

6. Enter **/File Save**, type **ROUND**, and press ENTER.

7. Enter **/Worksheet Erase Yes**.

Many worksheets will have @ROUND added to most of the formulas. To use it, follow the same procedure used in this example, making each formula an argument to the @ROUND function.

Special Functions

1-2-3's special functions are grouped together because they do not fit neatly into any of the other function categories. Some of them are used to trap error conditions; others count the number of rows in a range or allow you to choose a value from a list of options. Still others let you examine the contents of worksheet cells closely, thus providing information about a cell's value or other attributes. For the most part, this group can be thought of as a smorgasbord of sophisticated features. Because these special functions are so complex, only one of them will be introduced at this time. More sophisticated examples will be discussed in Chapter 10.

@NA   This function causes the letters "NA" (for "not available") to appear in the cell where @NA is entered. Its impact does not stop there: all worksheet cells that reference this cell will also have the value NA. There are no arguments for this function; its syntax is simply @NA.

@NA is used as a flag to remind you to complete missing entries before finalizing a report. Since cells that reference this cell take on the value NA, there is no way for you to erroneously assume that a total reflects all data entries. The presence of "NA" in the total area acts as a flag to remind you to enter the missing value before you finalize a report.

Create a model that uses the @NA feature to flag missing grades for an instructor. All students who miss an exam have their grades entered as @NA rather than as a test score. This means that the students' final grade-point average will be NA, since it will reference each of the exam grades, including the one recorded with @NA. An instructor could use this model at the end of a semester to identify students who have not yet made up missing exams. The instructor would have the option to change the missing exam grade to a 0, or to record an incomplete for the student's final grade. Follow these steps to complete the model:

1. Make these entries to add a heading for each category and to place the students' names in the model:

    C1: Fall Semester - 1989
    A3: Student
    A4: B. Black
    A5: S. Conners
    A6: F. Dalton
    A7: G. Limmer
    A8: S. Melton
    A9: P. Stock
    A10: J. Zimmer
    B3: Exam 1
    C3: Exam 2
    D3: Exam 3
    E3: Final
    F3: Average

2. Record these grades for the first exam:

    B4: 75
    B5: 67
    B6: 78
    B7: 88
    B8: 67
    B9: 67
    B10: 91

3. Record these entries for the second exam:

C4: @NA
C5: 78
C6: 90
C7: 81
C8: 55
C9: 89
C10: 82

Since B. Black did not take exam 2, @NA was entered for that student's score. Entering just the letters "NA" will not give you the same effect. @NA is a value entry that will affect calculations referencing the cell; "NA" is a label entry and cannot be used in arithmetic calculations.

4. Record these grades for exam 3 and the final exam:

D4: 82
D5: 72
D6: 89
D7: 93
D8: 40
D9: @NA
D10: 75
E4: 88
E5: 81
E6: 92
E7: 87
E8: 60
E9: 78
E10: 89

5. Move the cell pointer to F4, type **@AVG(B4.E4)**, and press ENTER.

6. Enter **/Copy** and press ENTER. Move the cell pointer to F5, type **.**, and move the cell pointer to F10. Then press ENTER.

   The results are shown in Figure 7-18. Notice that the average for B. Black and P. Stock is displayed as "NA." These averages are not available, since one of the values needed to compute them is missing.

7. Enter **/File Save**, type **NA**, and press ENTER.

8. Enter **/Worksheet Erase Yes**.

```
A:F4: @AVG(B4..E4)                                                    READY

A    A         B        C        D        E       F         G        H
             Fall Semester - 1989
  Student  Exam  1  Exam 2  Exam 3  Final    Average
  B. Black       75      NA      82      88       NA
  S. Conner      67      70      72      81      74.5
  F. Dalton      78      90      89      92     87.25
  G. Limmer      88      81      93      87     87.25
  S. Melton      67      55      40      60      55.5
  P. Stock       67      89      NA      78       NA
  J. Zimmer      91      82      75      89     84.25
```

FIGURE 7-18.   Using @NA

Financial Functions

1-2-3 provides an entire category of functions to use in investment calculations and other calculations concerned with the time value of money. You can use these financial functions to monitor loans, annuities, and cash flows over period of time. Depreciation calculations are also included. You can quickly compare various financial alternatives, since you can rely on the function to supply the correct formulas. As with the other functions, all you need to supply are arguments to tailor the calculations to your exact needs.

When you use financial functions, it is very important that all of the arguments and the result both use the same unit of time. For example, a function to compute a loan payment amount will require you to decide whether you want to calculate the payment amount on a yearly, quarterly, or monthly basis. Once you decide on one of these or some other unit of time, you must apply it consistently across all arguments. If you choose to compute a monthly payment amount, the interest rate must be expressed as a monthly rate. Likewise, the term should be expressed as a number of months. You will work with three of the built-in functions in this section.

@DDB   The @DDB function computes the depreciation expense for a specific period using the double declining balance method. The format of the function is

@DDB(*cost,salvage,life,period*)

Here, *cost* is the amount you paid for the asset you are depreciating. It must be a value or a reference to a cell that contains a value. The value of the asset at the end of its useful life is *salvage*. Like the cost, this argument must be a value or a reference to a cell that contains one. The expected useful life of the asset is represented by *life;* this is the number of years needed to depreciate the asset from its cost to its salvage value. Normally, the life of the asset is expressed in years, but it must always be a value or a reference to a value. The *period* argument is the specific time period for which you are computing the depreciation. Since the double declining balance method of depreciation is an accelerated method that allows you to depreciate more in the early years of an asset's life, it is important to specify the correct period for your calculations. Like the other arguments, *period* must be a value or a reference to one.

Use the @DDB function to build a model that calculates the depreciation expense for each year in an asset's five-year life:

1. Make these entries:

    A1: Depreciation Expense Using the Double Declining Balance Method
    A3: Cost:
    A4: Salvage Value:
    A5: Useful Life:
    A6: Year 1:
    A7: Year 2:
    A8: Year 3:
    A9: Year 4:
    A10: Year 5:
    A12: Total Depreciation:
    C3: 11000
    C4: 1000
    C5: 5

2. Enter /**Worksheet Global Format Currency** and press ENTER.

3. Move the cell pointer to C3, enter /**Range Format Currency**, type **2**, and press ENTER. Move the cell pointer to C4 and press ENTER.

4. Move the cell pointer to C5 and enter /**Range Format Fixed**. Type **0** and press ENTER twice.

5. Enter /**Worksheet Column Set-Width**, press RIGHT ARROW twice, and press ENTER. Move the cell pointer to column A, enter /**Worksheet Column Set-Width**, type **11**, and press ENTER.

6. Move the cell pointer to C6, type **@DDB($C$3,$C$4,$C$5,1)**, and press ENTER.

```
A:C6:  [W11] @DDB($C$3,$C$4,$C$5,1)                              READY
```

A	A	B	C	D	E	F	G
1	Depreciation Expense Using the Double Declining Balance Method						
2							
3	Cost:		$11,000				
4	Salvage Value:		$1,000				
5	Useful Life:		5				
6	Year 1:		$4,400.00				
7	Year 2:						
8	Year 3:						
9	Tear 4:						
10	Year 5:						
11							
12	Total Depreciation:						
13							

FIGURE 7-19.   Depreciation for Year 1

This formula computes the depreciation expense for the first year, as shown in Figure 7-19. The dollar signs were used so that the formula could be copied, even though it will need to be edited to change the year number.

7. Enter /**Copy** and press ENTER. Move the cell pointer to C7, type ., move the cell pointer to C10, and press ENTER.

   The formula has been copied, but each formula needs to be edited to reference the proper year.

8. Move the cell pointer to C7 and press F2 (EDIT). Press the LEFT ARROW key and then press the BACKSPACE key to delete the 1. Type **2** and press ENTER.

9. Use the same editing technique to change the formulas in A8..A10 to reference the proper year.

10. Move the cell pointer to A12, type **@SUM(C6.C10)**, and press ENTER to produce the results shown in Figure 7-20.

11. Enter /**File Save**, type **DEPREC**, and press ENTER.

12. Enter /**Worksheet Erase Yes**.

@PMT   The @PMT function calculates the appropriate payment amount for a loan. The syntax for this function is

@PMT(*principal,interest,term of loan*)

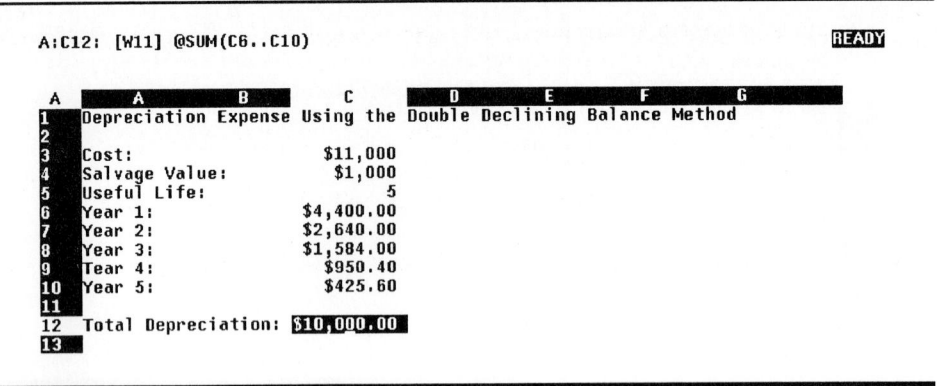

FIGURE 7-20.   Copying @DDB

The *principal* argument is a numeric value that represents the amount of money borrowed, and *interest* is a numeric value that represents the interest rate. To specify a nine-percent interest rate, you can use 9% or .09. The *term* argument is the number of payments for the loan. It is a numeric value and should be expressed in the same time period as *interest*.

You can test this function by building a model that determines whether you can afford the monthly payments on your dream home. This model will also utilize range-name references for the function arguments. You learned how to apply these names to cell in Chapter 3, but the process will be reviewed in this example as you apply range names to the principal, interest, and term for the loan before entering the function.

1. Make the following entries:

    A1: Principal:
    A2: Interest:
    A3: Term:
    A5: Monthly Payments:
    C1: 150000
    C2: .09
    C3: 20
    D3: years

2. Move the cell pointer to C1. Enter **/Range Name Create**, type **PRINCIPAL**, and press ENTER twice.

    This step applies the range name PRINCIPAL to C1.

3. With the cell pointer still in C1, enter /**Range Format Currency** and press ENTER twice.

4. Move the cell pointer to C2, enter /**Range Name Create**, type **INTEREST**, and press ENTER twice.

    This step applies the range name INTEREST to C2.

5. With the cell pointer in C2, enter /**Range Format Percent**. Press ENTER twice.

6. Move the cell pointer to C3, enter /**Range Name Create**, type **TERM**, and press ENTER twice.

    This step applies the range name TERM to C3.

7. With the cell pointer in C5, enter /**Range Format Currency** and press ENTER twice.

8. Enter /**Worksheet Column Set-Width**, type **12**, and press ENTER.

9. Type **@PMT(**.

10. Press F3 (NAME), highlight PRINCIPAL, and press ENTER. Type a comma (,).

11. Press F3 (NAME), highlight INTEREST, and press ENTER. Type /**12** to convert the annual interest rate to a monthly rate. Type a comma.

12. Press F3 (NAME), highlight TERM, and press ENTER. Type *12) to convert the number of years to the number of months. Press ENTER to finalize the entry.

    This function shows the use of formulas for function arguments, since the interest rate must be divided by 12 to convert the annual percentage to a monthly figure, and the term must be multiplied by 12 to be expressed as months. 1-2-3 does not object to the use of these formulas, because they return value entries needed for each of the function arguments. The result is shown here:

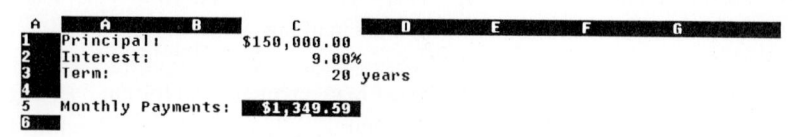

```
A:C5: (C2) [W12] @PMT(PRINCIPAL,INTEREST/12,TERM*12)                    READY
A      A        B         C          D        E        F        G
1    Principal:          $150,000.00
2    Interest:                9.00%
3    Term:                   20 years
4
5    Monthly Payments:    $1,349.59
6
```

13. Enter /**File Save**, type **PAYMENT**, and press ENTER.

14. Enter /**Worksheet Erase Yes**.

Logical Functions

1-2-3's logical functions allow you to build conditional features into your models. The functions in this category return logical values (true or false) as the result of the condition tests they perform. They are a powerful addition to 1-2-3 because they allow you to alter calculations based on conditions in other locations of the worksheet. This flexibility lets you construct models patterned after "real world" business conditions, where exceptions are prevalent.

Logical functions let you have more than one calculation for commission payments, purchase discounts, FICA tax, or any other computation requiring multiple calculations that depend on other values in the worksheet. Because these functions frequently use both simple and compound operators and because they are frequently used in combination when making an entry, none of them are covered in this chapter. However, many logical functions will be introduced in Chapter 10, when advanced functions are discussed.

REVIEW EXERCISE

Apply your new skill with 1-2-3 @ functions to building a model that computes total payments for the month, given three different loans. A car loan, a tuition loan, and a home mortgage will comprise the borrowings, but three different formulas will be needed, because the principal is borrowed for a different amount of time in each case and at different interest rates. Figure 7-21 gives you a look at the end result.

1. Enter the labels in C1, B3..E4, B9, and A5..A7. *Hint:* After entry, the /Range Label Right command was used for the labels in B3..E4.

2. Enter the appropriate principal, interest, and term amounts. *Hint:* Interest rates are entered as decimal fractions, as in .022. The /Range Format command is used twice, once to format B5..B7 as Currency with 0 decimal places, and once to format C5..C7 as Percent with 2 decimal places.

3. Enter the formula to compute the car loan payment, and format it as Currency with two decimal places. *Hint:* Use @PMT(B5,C5/12,D5*12) and then copy the formula for the other payment computations.

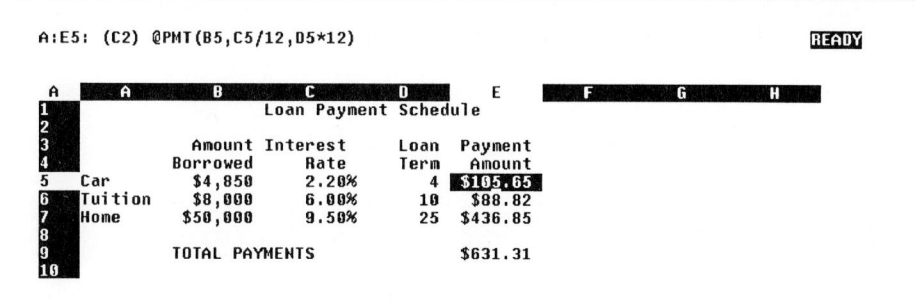

A:E5: (C2) @PMT(B5,C5/12,D5*12)   READY

	Loan Payment Schedule						
	Amount	Interest	Loan	Payment			
	Borrowed	Rate	Term	Amount			
Car	$4,850	2.20%	4	$105.65			
Tuition	$8,000	6.00%	10	$88.82			
Home	$50,000	9.50%	25	$436.85			
	TOTAL PAYMENTS			$631.31			

FIGURE 7-21.   Model for computing payments

4. Total the payments with the @SUM function, and format the total as Currency with two decimal places. Notice that the total does not seem to match the sum of each of the individual entries—the format you selected rounds the display to two decimal places, but the numbers are still stored with all their decimal accuracy. You can solve this problem by using the @ROUND function with each @PMT function.

5. Edit the first payment function and add @ROUND to it to round to two decimal places. *Hint:* Press the F2 (EDIT) key, press HOME to move to the front of the entry, type **@ROUND(**, press the END key, type **,2)**, and press ENTER. Copy this formula to E6 and E7. The resulting model will look like Figure 7-22 and the sum will match the total of each of the displayed entries; the extra decimal digits have been eliminated.

REVIEW

- Functions are prerecorded formulas. They are accessed by using an @ symbol followed by a keyword. Most functions also have arguments that define your specific needs to 1-2-3. These arguments are enclosed in parentheses and separated by commas.

- Release 3 allows you to use the F3 (NAME) key instead of typing the function keyword. After typing the @ symbol, press F3 (NAME), highlight the desired keyword in the list, and press ENTER.

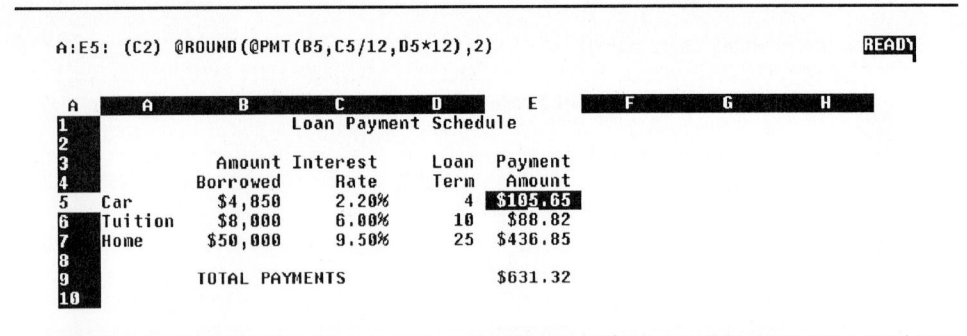

FIGURE 7-22.   Using the @ROUND function to display the correct total

- There are eight categories of 1-2-3 functions. Statistical functions perform basic statistical computations. Date and time functions allow you to record dates and times in worksheet cells and work with these special entries in other ways. String functions are designed to provide a way to work with character strings. Math functions perform simple mathematical operations and access to trigonometric calculations. Financial functions compute depreciation and computations involving the time value of money. Special functions are miscellaneous functions that do not fall into any of the other categories. Logical functions allow you to test conditions. Data-management functions allow you to perform computations on entries in a 1-2-3 database.

Functions

@ABS(x)	Computes the absolute value of the number represented by x
@AVG(*list*)	Computes an average of the value provided
@COUNT(*list*)	Provides the number of non-blank entries in the list
@DATE(*year, month,day*)	Records the date serial number for the date specified
@DAY(*date-number*)	Extracts a day number from a date serial number
@DDB(*cost, salvage,life, period*)	Computes the double declining balance for an asset
@HOUR(*time-number*)	Extracts the hour number from a time serial number
@INT(x)	Returns the integer portion of the number represented by x

@LEFT *(string,n)*	Returns a specified number of characters in a string, with *n* determining the number of characters returned
@LOWER *(string)*	Converts a string to lowercase
@MAX*(list)*	Returns the maximum value in the list
@MIN*(list)*	Returns the minimum value in the list
@MINUTE *(time-number)*	Extracts the minute number from a time serial number
@MONTH *(date-number)*	Extracts the month number from a date serial number
@NA	Marks the entry as not available
@PMT*(principal,interest, term)*	Computes a loan payment
@PROPER *(string)*	Converts the string to proper case
@REPEAT *(string,n)*	Duplicates a character string a specified number of times
@RIGHT *(string,n)*	Extracts a specific number of characters from the right side of a string, with *n* determining the number of characters
@ROUND*(x,n)*	Rounds the number x to the number of decimal places specified by n
@SECOND *(time-number)*	Extracts the second number from a time serial number
@SUM*(list)*	Totals the value entries in the list
@TIME*(hour, minute,second)*	Records the specified time serial number in a worksheet cell
@UPPER *(string)*	Converts the entry to uppercase
@YEAR*(date-number)*	Extracts a year number from a date serial number

8

CREATING GRAPHS

Creating a Graph
Saving a Graph
Printing a Graph
Review Exercise
Review

The worksheet provides an excellent way to *perform* all your financial projections, but it is not always the best way to *present* the results from these calculations. Important numbers that you want to highlight often get lost in a sea of other figures. How can you make sure that you and others who read your report, which contains hundreds of numbers, will focus on those conditions and trends that you think are important?

One solution is to use 1-2-3's graphics features, which let you present your data in an easy-to-interpret format. Graphs do not present all of the specific numbers; instead, they summarize your data in a way that lets you focus on general patterns and trends. When you find something in a graph that warrants more detailed analysis, you can still return to the supporting worksheet for a closer look.

You do not have to reenter your 1-2-3 data to use the graphics features; you can use the data already entered for your spreadsheet application without making any changes. Nor do you need to learn a new system to create your graphs; you access 1-2-3's graphics features through menus that are just like 1-2-3's other menus. You only need to learn a few new commands. Once you have entered your worksheet data, you make only a few menu selections to present the data in a graph format. (Incidentally, any changes you make to your data will be reflected in your graph.)

To view your graphs on the screen, you need a color or monochrome monitor with a graphics card. If you do not have a monitor that will support graphics, you can still make the menu selections that define the graph and save it to disk for later printing.

Release 3 significantly improves the quality of the graphs that you can display and print. The display is designed to take advantage of today's high-resolution monitors, providing significantly enhanced professional-looking images suitable for the creation of slides and transparencies for important business meetings. Release 3 also provides direct printing features so you can print a graph directly from 1-2-3's menus without the need for a separate program like PrintGraph. Another new graphics feature is splitting the display to view the worksheet on one half and a graph in the other half.

This chapter will introduce you to the basic commands for defining a graph. You will learn about some of the special options that produce a more professional product. You will find out how to create and save multiple graphs in a single worksheet file. You will also learn how to obtain a printed copy of a graph with 1-2-3's Print menus.

CREATING A GRAPH

Creating a basic graph is really quite simple. There are three basic steps: first, decide what type of graph you wish to see; second, tell 1-2-3 what data to place in this graph; and third, tell 1-2-3 to display the graph for you. Once you have completed these basics, you may want to add further enhancements.

Basic Graphics Terminology

Before you can begin to create your first graph, there are a few basic terms to understand. A sample graph, with the key terms and components marked, is shown in Figure 8-1. A discussion of each of the basic terms is presented here; more specialized terms are covered along with the implementation of specific features later in the chapter.

DATA SERIES   1-2-3's graphs are designed to show from one to six sets of data values, depending on the type of graph that you select. A set of data values is referred to as a *series* and must consist of a range of contiguous cells on the worksheet. A series can represent sales of a product for a period of 6 months, the number of employees within the company each year for the last 10 years, or the number of rejects on a production line for each of the last 16 weeks.

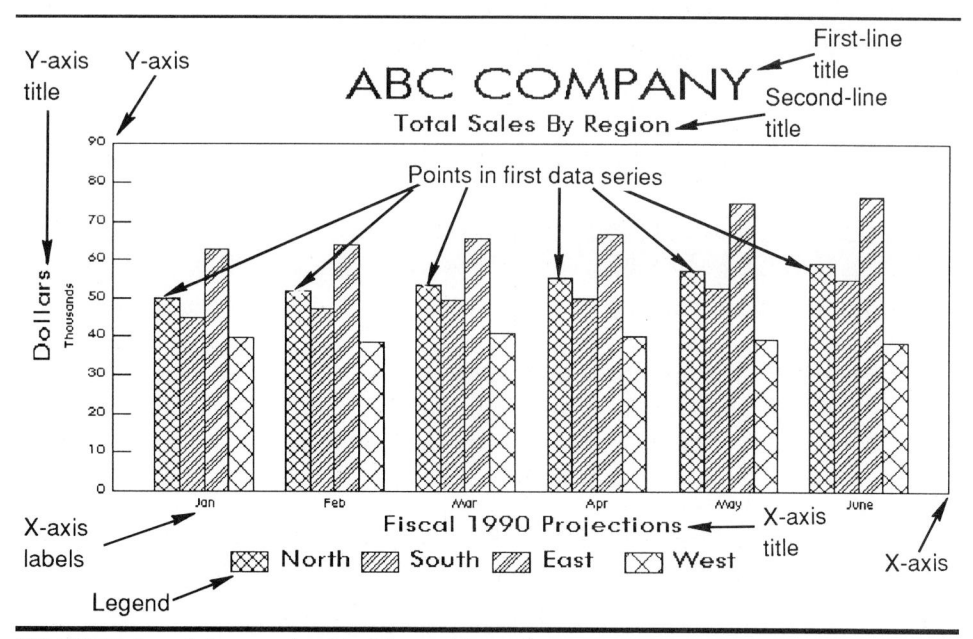

FIGURE 8-1.   A bar graph with titles and legend

X AXIS   The individual values in the series are represented as data points along the *X axis,* which is the horizontal axis at the bottom of the graph. Each point along this axis might represent a year, a month, or a quarter. It could also represent a division, a product, or a project. The points along the X axis can be labeled to make it clear what they represent. In addition, a title can be placed along the X axis to describe the general category of data it shows. For example, if each of the points on the X axis represents a month between January and December, an appropriate title for the X axis might be "Fiscal 90 Projections" to describe the category to which each of these months belongs.

Y AXIS   The *Y axis* is the vertical axis found on most of the graphs that 1-2-3 produces. It is used to measure the relative size of each value within a series. Once you tell 1-2-3 which data to display on the graph, the Y axis is labeled automatically. 1-2-3 will sometimes represent graph data in thousands or millions and label the Y axis appropriately. You can also make a title for this axis; you might describe the units of measure as dollars, number of employees, or some other appropriate unit of measure for the quantities shown on this axis.

LEGENDS If you choose to show more than one data series on a graph, you can describe each of the series with a *legend* at the bottom of the graph. The legend will show the symbol or pattern used to represent each series in the graph and will describe the data represented by that symbol or pattern.

Entering Data for a Graph

If you have worked through the examples in this book from Chapter 1 onward, you already have a number of worksheets that 1-2-3's graphics features could represent nicely. Even though you have some data for a graph, you will enter a short new worksheet designed to let you work with a small amount of data yet still experience the maximum number of graphics features. Follow these steps to enter the required data for the examples in this chapter:

1. Make the following entries in the worksheet cells shown:

    D1: '   ABC COMPANY
    D2: SALES BY REGION
    A5: North
    A6: South
    A7: East
    A8: West
    B4: Jan
    B5: 50000
    B6: 45000
    B7: 62800
    B8: 39550
    C4: Feb
    C5: +B5*1.035
    C6: +B6*1.05
    C7: +B7*1.02
    C8: +B8*.98
    D4: Mar
    E4: Apr
    F4: May
    G4: June

2. Enter **/Worksheet Global Format Currency**, type **0**, and press ENTER.

3. Move the cell pointer to B4 and enter **/Range Label Right**. Move the cell pointer to G4 and press ENTER.

This aligns the labels on the right side of the cell as the numbers are aligned.

4. Move the cell pointer to C5, enter /**Copy**, and move the cell pointer to C8. Press ENTER, move the cell pointer to D5, type ., move the cell pointer to G5, and press ENTER again.

5. Move the cell pointer to the following cells and type these numbers:

   D8: 41000
   E6: 50000
   F7: 75000

   Adding these numbers overlays the formulas in those cells and provides more variety in the graph than a growth at a constant rate.

6. Move the cell pointer to C5.

Your entries should look like those in Figure 8-2. Notice that the original formula is not altered by the addition of several numeric constants to the model.

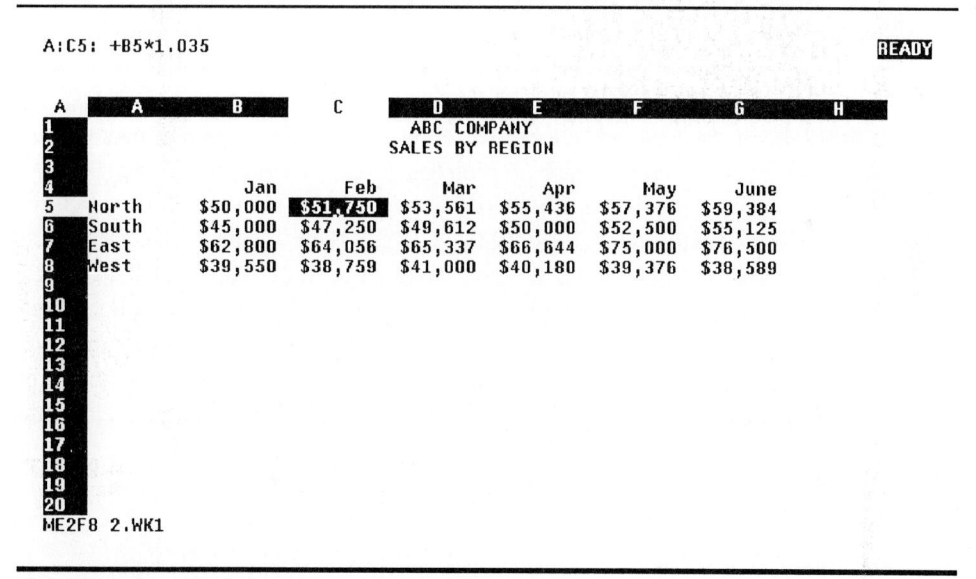

FIGURE 8-2.   Worksheet for using graph features

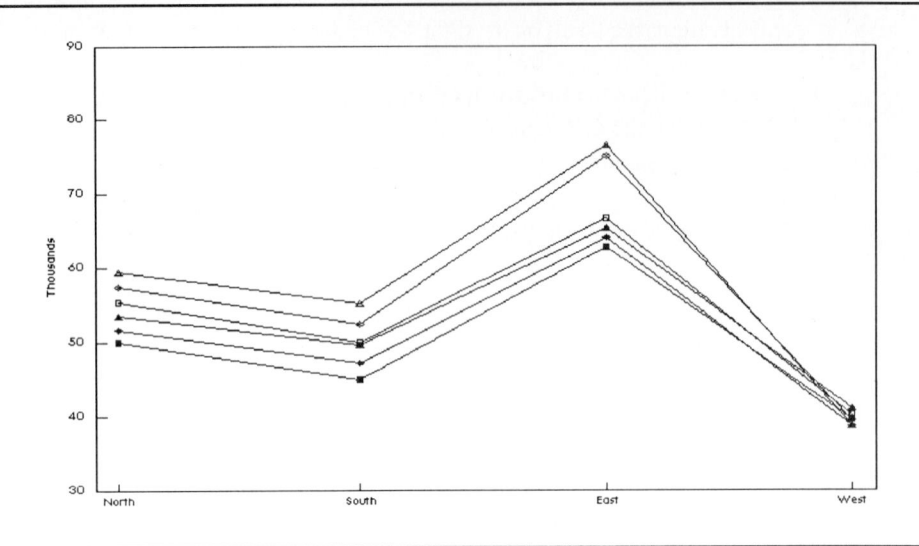

FIGURE 8-3.   An automatic graph

Creating an Automatic Graph

You are now done entering the data you will use with the graph examples, so it is time to create the graph. 1-2-3 offers a quick method for creating a graph: you can create an *automatic graph* if the worksheet data is in the proper format. Basically, all of the data you want graphed must be segregated from the surrounding worksheet data. The worksheet that you have just created is a good example of the kind of data you can use for an automatic graph—each division has its data on contiguous rows.

To create an automatic graph of this data, move the cell pointer to B4, the first cell of data you want in the graph. Press the F10 (GRAPH) key. The automatic graph 1-2-3 creates is shown in Figure 8-3. 1-2-3 uses the first row in the data to label the X axis. Each row in the worksheet afterwards is a data series. 1-2-3 creates a line graph, although if you select a graph type (as discussed next), 1-2-3 will use that graph type to create an automatic graph. 1-2-3 will only create an automatic graph if the cell pointer is in the correct position for an automatic graph. You can use an automatic graph to quickly see how 1-2-3 will graph your data.

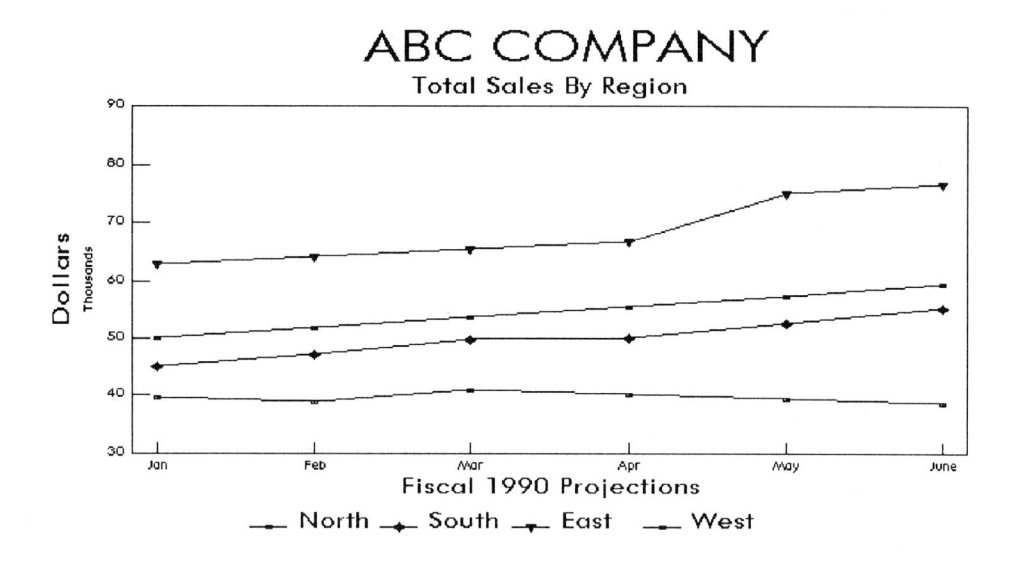

FIGURE 8-4.   A line graph

Deciding on a Graph Type

1-2-3 offers you seven different graph types: line, bar, stacked bar, XY, pie, HLCO, and mixed graphs. The menu from which you select the graph type also offers other options, but these options provide enhancements to the basic graph types.

A *bar graph* looks like the one shown in Figure 8-1. It uses bars of different heights to represent the data ranges you wish to graph. Bar graphs are especially appropriate when you wish to contrast the numbers in several series.

A *line graph* shows the points in the data range you specify, plotted against the Y axis. The points may be connected with a line, shown as symbols, or both. This type of graph is an excellent choice for plotting data trends over time, such as sales or expenses. An example of a line graph is shown in Figure 8-4.

A *stacked bar graph* places the values in each of the series you select on top of each other for any one point on the X axis. A stacked bar graph is a good choice when

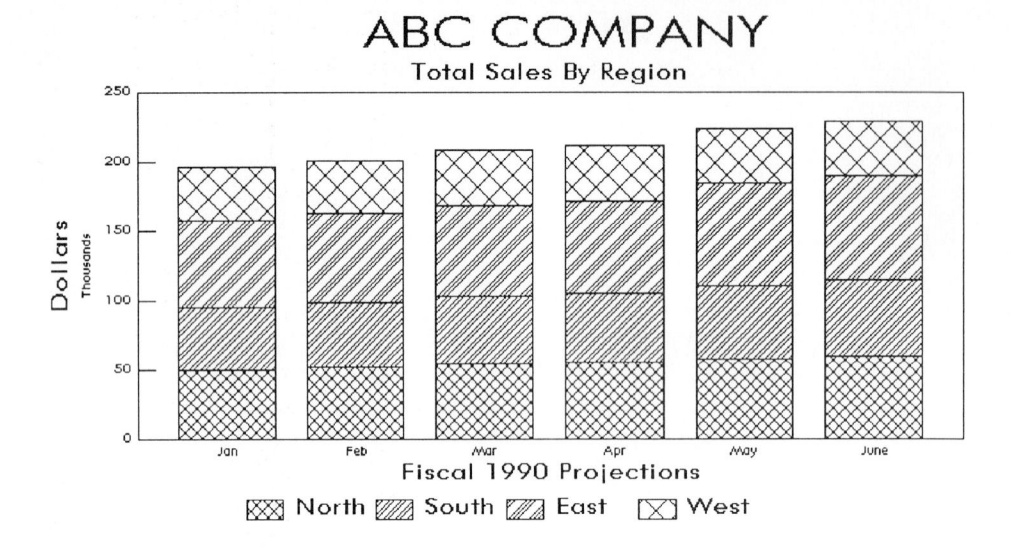

FIGURE 8-5.   A stacked bar graph

you wish to see the level of the total as well as each of its components. You might use this type of graph to show the contribution to profit from each of the company's subsidiaries, as shown in Figure 8-5.

An *XY graph* plots the values in one series against the values from a second series. You might use this graph type to plot age against salary, time against temperature, or machine repairs against the age of the machinery. Figure 8-6 shows an example of an XY graph.

A *pie graph* shows only one range of values. It represents each value as a percentage of the total, using a pie wedge to show the comparative size of the value. A pie chart is an effective way to show the relative size of different components of a budget or the contribution to profit from different product lines. An example of a pie chart is shown in Figure 8-7.

An *HLCO graph* can display as many as six data ranges, but it plots each data range differently. This graph type is used for plotting such financial and statistical data as the change in a stock's price. The data in the first range starts a line that continues to the data in the second range. The data in the third data range appears as a horizontal bar to the left of the lines between the high and low values for each first and second data series values. The data in the fourth data range appears as a horizontal bar to the

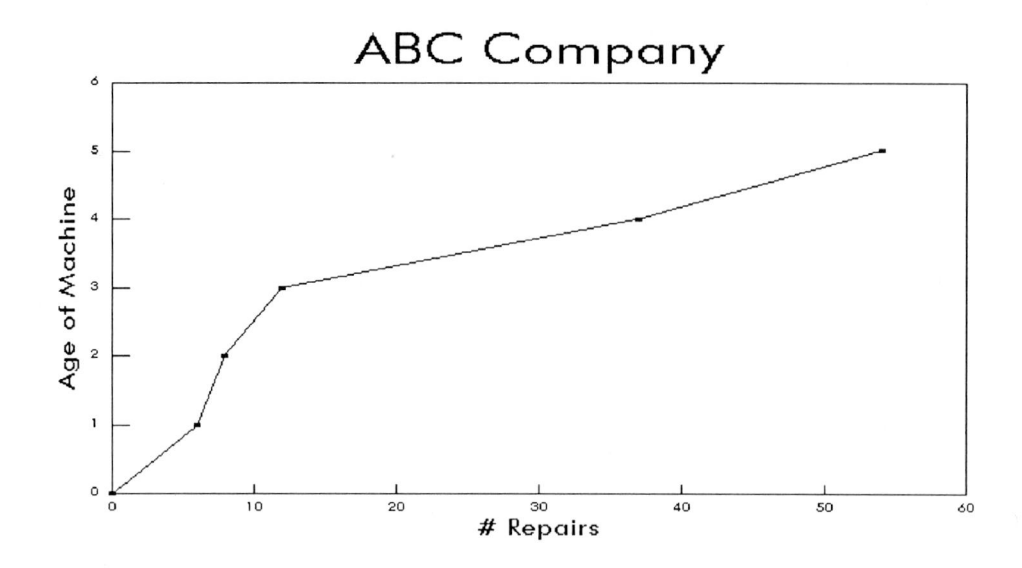

FIGURE 8-6.   An XY graph

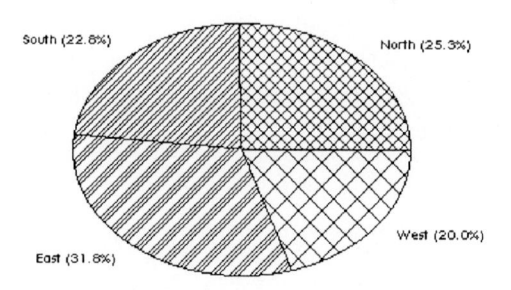

FIGURE 8-7.   A pie chart

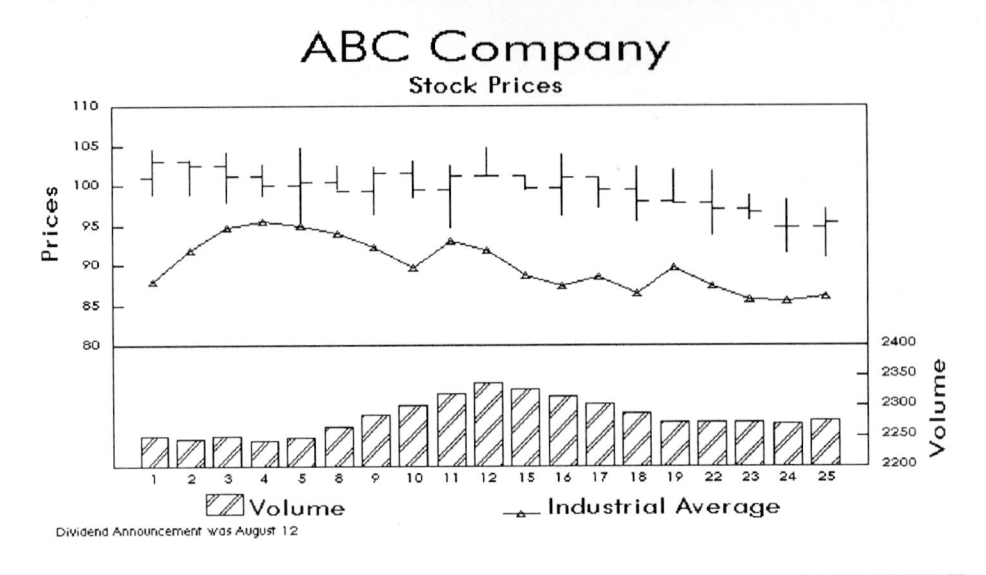

FIGURE 8-8.　An HLCO graph

right of the lines between the high and low values for each first and second data series values. The fifth data series appears below the first four data series as a bar graph. The sixth data series is a line graph plotted with the first four data series. Figure 8-8 shows and example of an HLCO graph.

A *mixed graph* graphs the first three data ranges as bar graphs and the last three data ranges as line graphs. This type of graph is useful for combining different types of data. Figure 8-9 shows a mixed graph.

If you do not choose one of the graph types for your graph, 1-2-3 will use the default type of a line graph. Your first example will be of a bar graph, so use the following steps to make that selection:

1. Enter **/Graph**.

    This will display the main Graph menu:

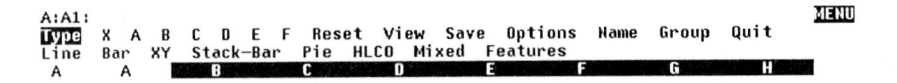

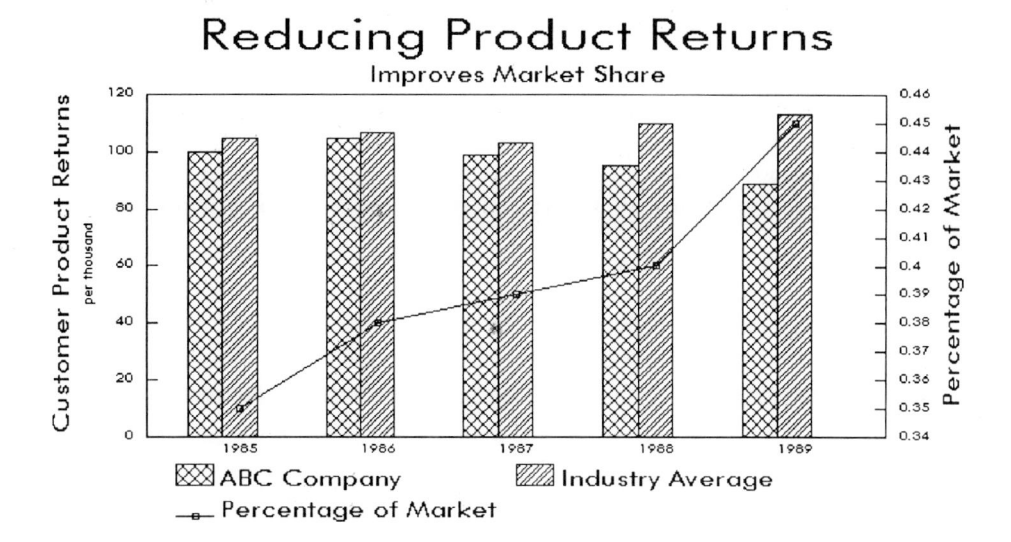

FIGURE 8-9. A mixed graph

2. Enter **Type** to see the following submenu:

```
A:A1:                                                          MENU
Line  Bar  XY  Stack-Bar  Pie  HLCO  Mixed  Features
Line graph
```

3. Enter **Bar**.

Notice that once you have made the type selection, you are returned to the main Graph menu, not READY mode. The Graph menu is another "sticky" menu like the Print menu; it will stay around so you can make additional selections for defining your graph, disappearing only when you choose Quit.

Specifying the Data for the Graph

There are no defaults for the data to be shown in a graph. If you forget to tell 1-2-3 which data to display on the graph, your graph will be blank. All graph types except pie charts can each show up to six data series or ranges. These graph types can have data assigned to graph range A, B, C, D, E, and F in the Graph menu. (Pie charts are special; a pie chart can only show one data range. In a pie chart, data is assigned to graph range A.) To select the data ranges to use in a graph, you can select one data range at a time or you can select multiple data ranges if the data for the data ranges are in contiguous ranges.

Follow these steps to assign data to graph ranges A through D in the current graph:

1. Enter **A** to produce this display:

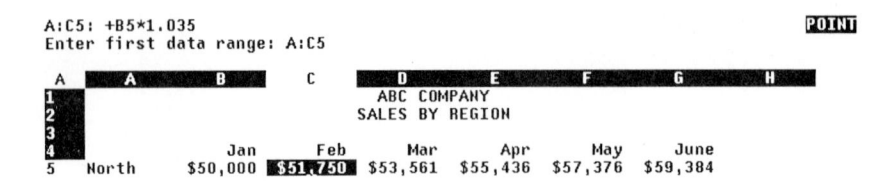

There is no need to enter /Graph, since the Graph menu is already on the screen.

2. Move the cell pointer to B5 and type a period. Then move the cell pointer to G5 and press ENTER.

   This step assigns the range B5..G5 to range A of the graph so that it will now represent the sales for the North region in the months of January through June.

3. Enter **B** and move the cell pointer to B6. Type ., move the cell pointer to G6, and press ENTER.

   This assigns the data for the South region to range B of the graph.

4. Enter **C** and move the cell pointer to B7. Type ., move the cell pointer to G7, and press ENTER.

   This assigns the data for the East region to range C of the graph.

5. Enter **D** and move the cell pointer to B8. Type ., move the cell pointer to G8, and press ENTER.

   This assigns the data for the West region to range D of the graph. This is the last region for ABC Company, so the E and F ranges are currently unassigned.

Notice that all the assigned ranges have the same unit of measure—dollars. If some ranges were measured in units of products sold and others in dollars, both could not be shown on the same Y axis, since the Y axis can measure units or dollars but not both. The unit of measure should be the same for all of the data shown on a graph. If a graph uses two units of measure, you need to create a second Y axis for the data ranges that use the second unit of measure.

Viewing the Graph

Although the graph is not quite finished, you can still view it to see how the various data ranges stack up against each other. Sometimes if one range is either extremely large or small in comparison to the others, it is not practical to graph the data together; the values in the smaller range will seem to blend with the X axis.

To view your graph and return again to the menu, follow these steps:

1. Enter **View**.

    If your monitor can display graphics, this command will produce an image like the one in Figure 8-10. All four data ranges are shown on the graph; the A range values are represented by the leftmost bar in each grouping. There are six different points on the X axis, each representing one month in the range. If

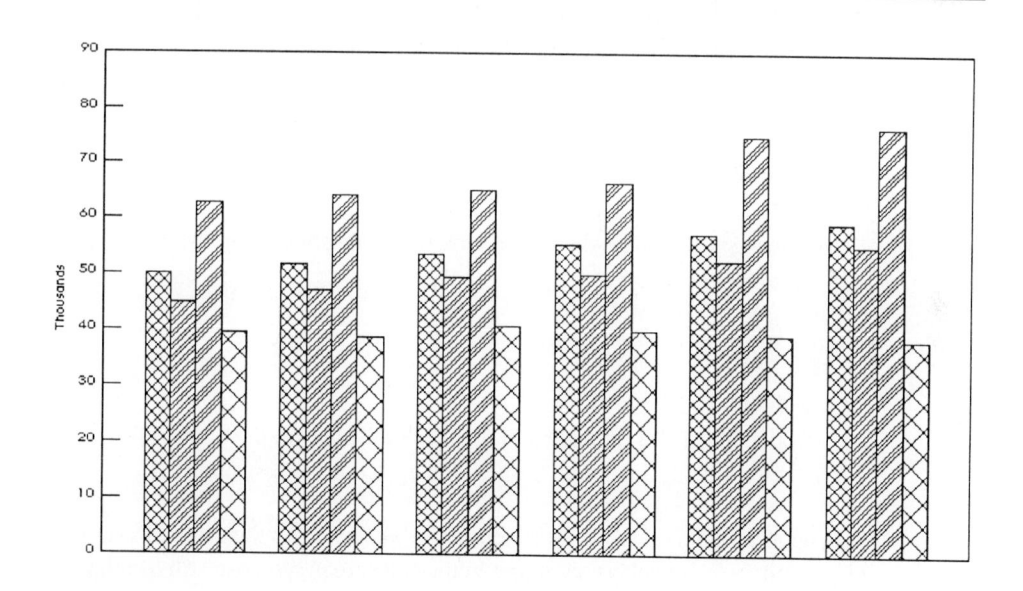

FIGURE 8-10.   Displaying the data in a bar graph

your monitor can display colors, each range may appear in a different color instead of a different hatch pattern.

2. Press any key to return to the menu display.

1-2-3 offers you another method for viewing the current graph—the F10 (GRAPH) key. To try this feature, press the F10 (GRAPH) key. 1-2-3 displays the graph in Figure 8-10. To return to READY mode, press any key. Unlike previous releases of 1-2-3 in which this function key only worked from READY mode, you can use F10 (GRAPH) at any point, even while you are in 1-2-3's menus or while you are entering information for graph settings. You can also use it when you change the worksheet data a graph uses and you want to see the effect on the graph. Throughout this chapter, when the examples tell you to select View to look at the current graph, you can press F10 (GRAPH) for the same results.

Viewing the Graph and Worksheet Simultaneously

Release 3 has a new feature so you can view the graph as you work on the worksheet. As you change the data 1-2-3 uses in the graph, 1-2-3 updates the graph on the screen. To see this new method of viewing the graph and how 1-2-3 keeps the graph up to date, follow these steps after pressing ESC to return to Ready mode:

1. Move the cell pointer to E5.

2. Enter /**Worksheet Window Graph**.
     1-2-3 splits the screen in half at the cell pointer's position. The left side of the screen shows the worksheet and the right side shows the current graph, as in Figure 8-11.

3. Move to B8.

4. Type **70000** and press ENTER.
     Notice that 1-2-3 immediately updates the values in the other cells in row 8 and also updates the graph to show the effect of the new numbers.

5. Type **39550** and press ENTER to return the worksheet to the original values.
     While 1-2-3 displays the graph in the full screen, you can still use the full screen to display the graph.

6. Press F10 (GRAPH). 1-2-3 displays the current graph, using the full screen.

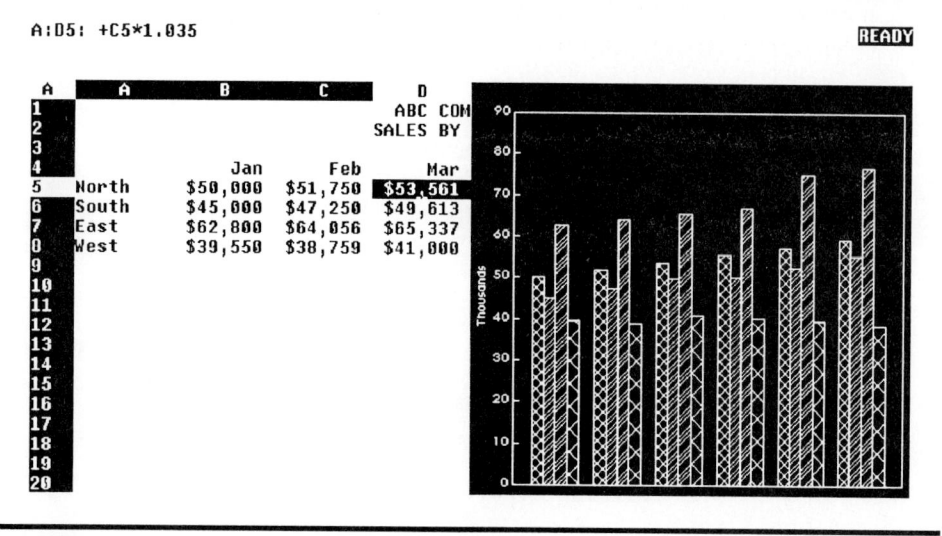

A:D5: +C5*1.035   READY

A	A	B	C	D
1				ABC COM
2				SALES BY
3				
4		Jan	Feb	Mar
5	North	$50,000	$51,750	$53,561
6	South	$45,000	$47,250	$49,613
7	East	$62,800	$64,056	$65,337
8	West	$39,550	$38,759	$41,000

FIGURE 8-11.   Worksheet with graph window

7. Press any key to return to the original display.

8. Enter /**Worksheet Window Clear** to remove the graph window.

Enhancing the Display

The current graph is not very useful—the bars are all hatch-marked or color-coded to distinguish them, but the only way to tell which set of bars represents which data is by remembering the sequence in which the different regions were assigned to the graph ranges. Nor can you tell whether the points on the X axis represent years, months, or days and whether the graphed numbers are sales, expenses, or number of employees. Obviously, some additional information must be added to the graph. In this section you will learn how to add titles to the graph, label the X-axis points, and add legends and grid lines.

LABELING THE X-AXIS DATA POINTS   Without labels along the X axis, it is impossible to tell what each group of values represents. You can overcome this problem easily by assigning a range of labels to be displayed along this axis. The range of labels should correspond to the values in the data ranges and should have the same number of entries in the range. You usually will already have values like this in a column or row of the worksheet.

For the current example, the labels that you need for the X axis are in B4..G4. You can assign these labels to the X axis with the X range option from the Graph menu. Follow these steps to make the assignment:

1. Enter **X**.

   This will produce a display similar to the one used for the graph's data ranges:

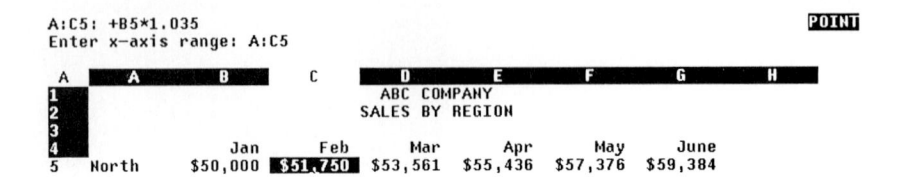

   You must enter the range address you want to use either by typing it or by using the pointing method.

2. Move the cell pointer to B4, type **.**, and move the cell pointer to G4 before pressing ENTER.

3. Enter **View** to see the graph with the addition of labels along the X axis.
   Your display should match the one shown in Figure 8-12.

4. Press any key to return to the Graph menu.

Using Release 3's
Shortcut Approach

With Release 3, you can consolidate range assignments into one easy step. Your data must be in tabular form for this to work with the data used to label the X axis at the top or left side of the detail entries. Follow these steps to assign all of the data ranges with one command:

1. Enter **Group**. 1-2-3 displays this prompt:

```
A:C5: +B5*1.035                                    POINT
Enter group range: A:C5
```

2. Move to B4, type ., press END, press HOME, and press ENTER to select B4..G8 as the worksheet data range for the data ranges.

1-2-3 displays this prompt:

```
A:C5: +B5*1.035                                              MENU
Columnwise  Rowwise
Use columns as data ranges
```

This selection determines whether 1-2-3 divides the worksheet data into graph data ranges according to rows or columns.

3. Enter **Rowwise**.

1-2-3 automatically assigns the first row to data range X, the second row in the worksheet range to data range A, and so on. By using the /Graph Group command, you can assign all of the graph data ranges instead of assigning the worksheet data to data ranges one at a time.

4. Enter **View** to create the display shown in Figure 8-12.

5. Type any key to return to the graph menu.

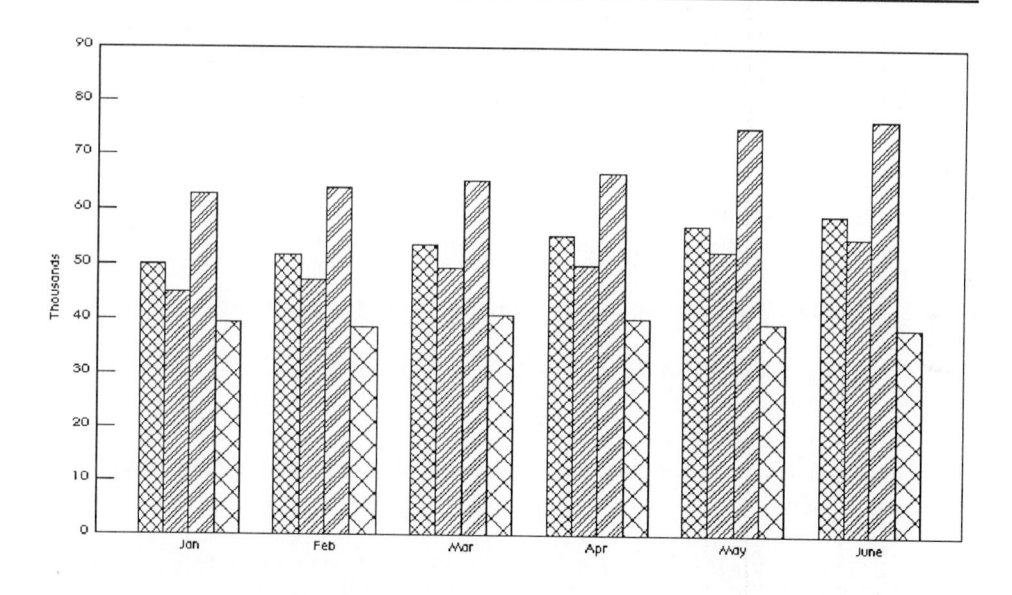

FIGURE 8-12.   Adding X-axis labels to the bar graph

ADDING TITLES   You can add titles to your graph in seven different locations to improve its appearance. You can add a title along either of the axes or at the top of the graph in one or two lines. With a new Release 3 feature, you can add two lines to the bottom of the graph as well. The menu you will see when you select /Graph Options Titles looks like this:

```
A:C5: +B5*1.035                                                    MENU
First  Second  X-Axis  Y-Axis  2Y-Axis  Note  Other-Note
Assign first line of graph title
```

Once you select the option you want, 1-2-3 prompts you for the text for the title. The title is limited by the number of characters 1-2-3 can display or print on your graph. You can use data that is already stored in a worksheet cell for the title. Follow these steps to enhance your current graph with titles in four locations:

1. Enter **Options** to produce the following menu:

```
A:C5: +B5*1.035                                                    MENU
Legend  Format  Titles  Grid  Scale  Color  B&W  Data-Labels  Advanced  Quit
Create data-range legends
```

2. Enter **Titles First** to add a title at the top of the graph.

3. Type **\D1** and press ENTER.
     This makes the current entry in D1 the title at the top of the graph. Notice how the Options menu returns to the screen. It too is a sticky menu: you must choose Quit in order to leave.

4. Enter **Titles Second**, type **Total Sales by Region**, and press ENTER.
     This time, the title was added by typing, since there was no entry on the worksheet that exactly matched the desired title.

5. Enter **Titles X-Axis**, type **Fiscal 1990 Projections**, and press ENTER.

6. Enter **Titles Y-Axis**, type **Dollars**, and press ENTER.

7. Enter **Quit**.
     This will exit the Graph Options menu and place you in the main Graph menu.

8. Enter **View** to produce a display with four titles like the one shown in Figure 8-13.

9. Press any key to return to the Graph menu.

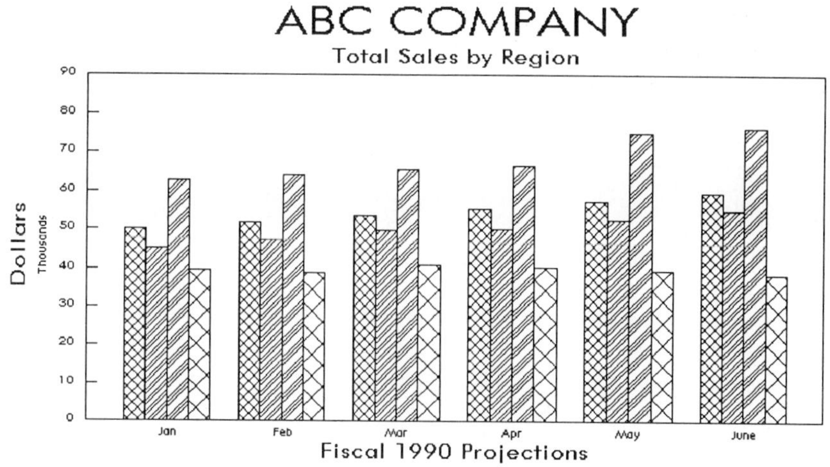

FIGURE 8-13.   Adding titles to the bar graph

ADDING LEGENDS   Legends add clarity to any graph that presents more than one data series by identifying how each data series is represented on the graph. If symbols are used to distinguish the different data series, the legend will consist of the series indicator and the text describing the data shown by that series. If color or hatch patterns are used, a small square of the color or pattern is placed at the bottom of the screen along with the the text description of the series. In Release 3, you can add all of the legends at once with a new menu option. Also, 1-2-3 will automatically adjust the legend display to use more than one line if the legend text needs it.

Selecting Legend presents the Legend submenu, as shown below:

```
A:C5: +B5*1.035                                          MENU
A  B  C  D  E  F  Range
Assign first data-range legend
```

You can choose from the same six letters you used to assign worksheet ranges to the different data series for the graph. A new Range option selects a worksheet range for all of the data range legends. To select a legend for a single range, select each of the data series that you assigned and enter a legend for it. You can either type the text or type a backslash and the cell address containing the text you want to use for the legend. You will need to select Legend and the appropriate letter each time until you have assigned a legend entry to each of the data series you used in the graph.

Follow these steps to assign the legends for the current graph:

1. Enter **Options Legend A**, type **\A5**, and press ENTER.

   The label stored in cell A5 will be used for the legend. Your other option is to type **North** and press ENTER. The advantage of using the label entry in the cell is that if you decide to update it later, the graph title will automatically be updated for you the next time the graph is created.

2. Enter **Legend B**, type **\A6**, and press ENTER.

3. Enter **Legend C**, type **\A7**, and press ENTER.

4. Enter **Legend D**, type **\A8**, and press ENTER.

5. Enter **Quit**.

6. Enter **View** to create the display shown in Figure 8-14.

7. Press ESC to return to the Graph menu.

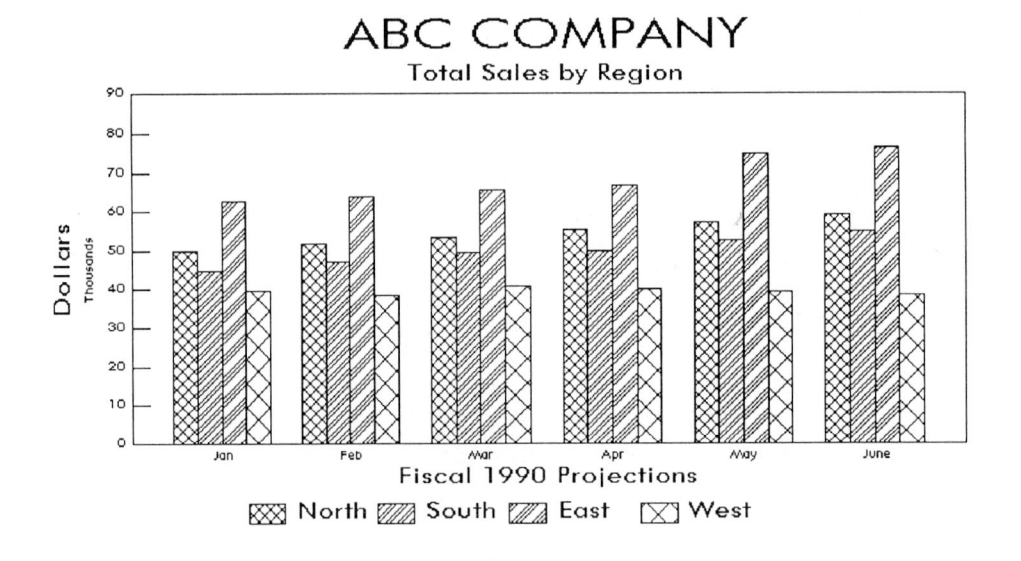

FIGURE 8-14.   Adding legends to the bar graph

By using the Range option, you can follow these simpler steps to assign worksheet data as the legend text for the data ranges:

1. Enter **Options Legend Range**.

   1-2-3 displays this prompt:

```
A:C5: +B5*1.035                                            POINT
Enter legend range: A:C5
```

2. Move to A5, type ., press the DOWN ARROW key three times, and press ENTER to select A5..A8 as the worksheet data range for the data range legends.

   1-2-3 automatically assigns the first worksheet cell as the A data range legend, the second worksheet cell as the B data range legend, and so forth.

3. Enter **Quit**.

4. Enter **View** to create the display shown in Figure 8-14 again.

5. Type any key to return to the Graph menu.

ADDING GRID LINES   *Grid lines* are lines that are parallel to either the X axis or the Y axis and that originate from the markers on the axis. They help you interpret the exact value of data points by extending either up or to the right from these markers. Using gridlines in both directions at once will create a grid pattern on your graph.

To get to the Grid menu, you enter /**Graph Options Grid**. The Grid options can be used with all graph types except pie charts; grid lines across a pie chart would detract from your ability to interpret the graph. The Grid menu contains these options:

```
A:C5: +B5*1.035                                            MENU
Horizontal  Vertical  Both  Clear  Y-Axis
Draw grid lines across the graph
```

The first option, Horizontal, is appropriate with a bar graph only; it lets you interpret the top of each of the bars more accurately. Try it now on the current graph:

1. Enter **Options Grid Horizontal**.

2. Enter **Quit** to leave the options menu.

3. Enter **View** to produce the graph shown in Figure 8-15.

4. Press any key to return to the Graph menu.

5. Enter **Options Grid Clear Quit**.

   This will remove the horizontal grid lines and return to the graph menu. If you wish to verify that the lines have been removed, you can use the View option.

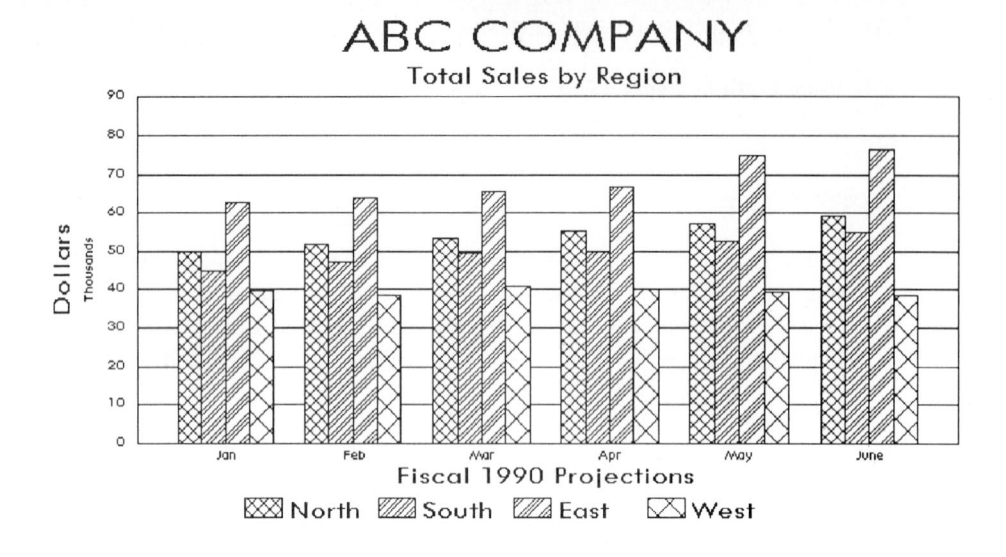

FIGURE 8-15.   Adding horizontal grid lines to the bar graph

VIEWING THE GRAPH IN COLOR   If you have a monitor that shows a single color, your only option is to view the graph with the B&W (black and white) option. If you have a color monitor, you can select Options Color, and different colors will be used for the various data ranges. The colors used in the graph depend on the graphics support supplied by your system.

The B&W option distinguishes the various data series by replacing colors with hatch patterns. If you are able to view the system in color, you will want to use the B&W option to switch back to black and white to see how the graph will print if you are not printing it in color. Although the color Option uses color to distinguish the various data ranges, these color differences are lost when the graph is printed on a standard black-and-white printer.

Naming the Current Graph

1-2-3 can only maintain one set of graph definitions at a time unless you assign a name to these definitions. Now that you have completely defined a graph, you should assign a name to these specifications before you create a second graph. The command to use is /Graph Name Create. Once you have used this command to assign a name, you are free to reset the current graph settings. This lets you start fresh to define a new graph or make a few changes to create a second graph that has many of the same options as the first graph.

Follow these steps to assign a name to the current graph settings so you can create additional graphs:

1. Enter **Name Create**.

    You do not need to enter /Graph, since you are already in the Graph menu.

2. Type **Sls_bar** and press ENTER.

Using Other Graph Types

Working with several additional graph types will give you a close-up look at how easy it is to create additional graphs or to change the type for the existing graph. In this section you will use the current data series to create a line graph, an area graph, a stacked bar graph, and a rotated graph. Then you will create a pie graph with a subset of this data. Follow these steps to create the three additional graphs:

1. Enter **Type Line**.

2. Enter **View** to display a graph like the one shown in Figure 8-16.

    Notice that different symbols are used for each series shown on the graph. The legend changes automatically from the hatch patterns to these symbols.

3. Press any key to return to the Graph menu.

4. Enter **Name Create**, type **Sls_line**, and press ENTER.

5. Enter **Options Format**. 1-2-3 prompts you to select the data series that you will select to format.

6. Enter **Graph** to select all data ranges. You will see these options:

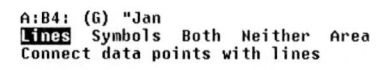

```
A:B4: (G) "Jan                                              MENU
Lines  Symbols  Both  Neither  Area
Connect data points with lines
```

7. Enter **Area**.

    The Area option stacks the data ranges on top of each other and fills the area between the data ranges with different hatch patterns.

8. Select **Quit** two times to return to the main Graph menu.

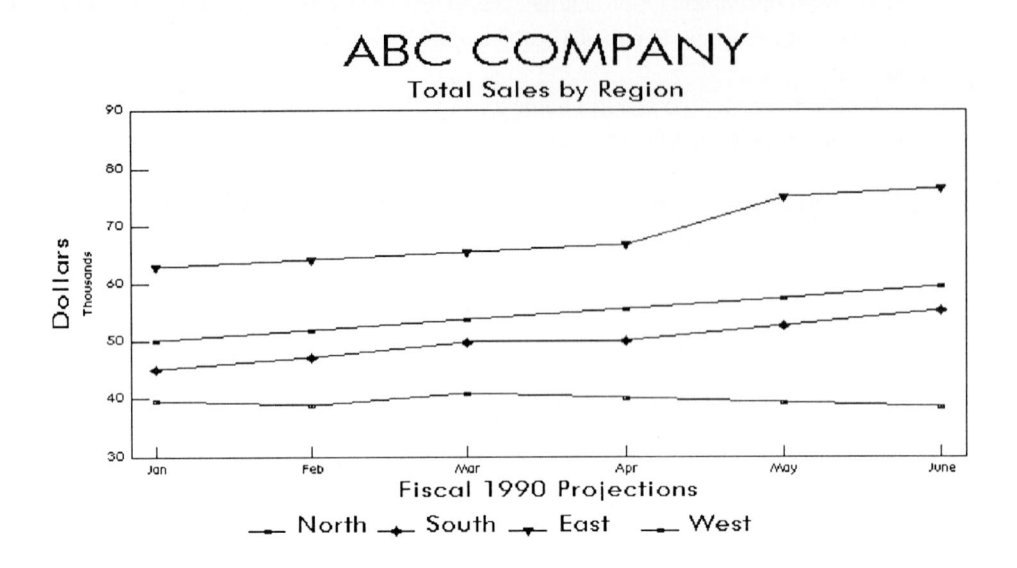

FIGURE 8-16.   The same data as a line graph

9. Enter **View** to see the graph shown in Figure 8-17.
   Notice how the hatch patterns identify the area each data range represents.

10. Press a key to return to the menus.

11. Enter **Type Stacked-Bar.**

12. Enter **Options Titles Second**, press ESC to remove the existing title, type **Total Company Sales**, and press ENTER.
    You can use this technique when you want to change any of the current graph specifications.

13. Enter **Quit** and **View** to display a graph like the one shown in Figure 8-18.
    Notice that the legend is automatically changed back to the hatch patterns.

14. Press any key to return to the Graph menu.

15. Enter **Name Create**, type **Sls_sbar**, and press ENTER.

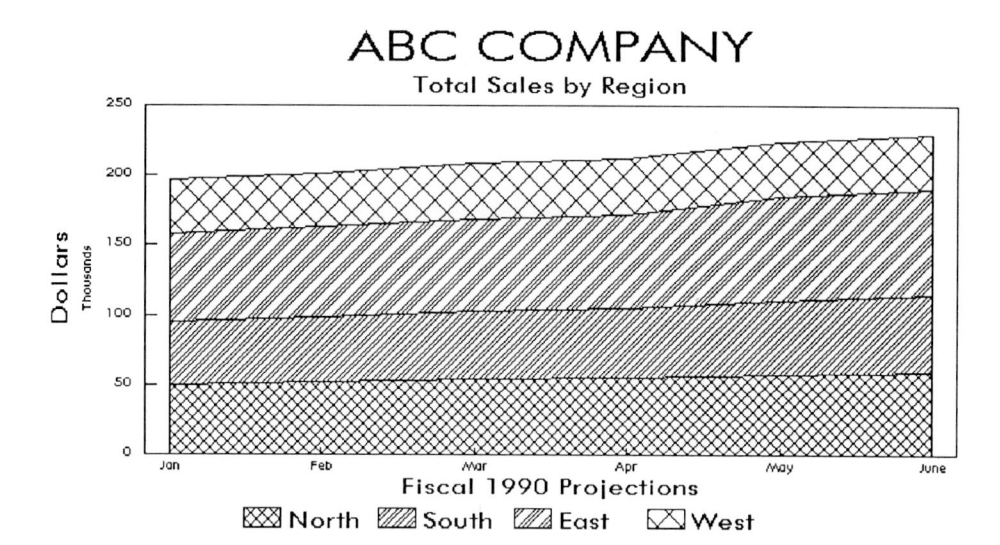

FIGURE 8-17. The same data as an area graph

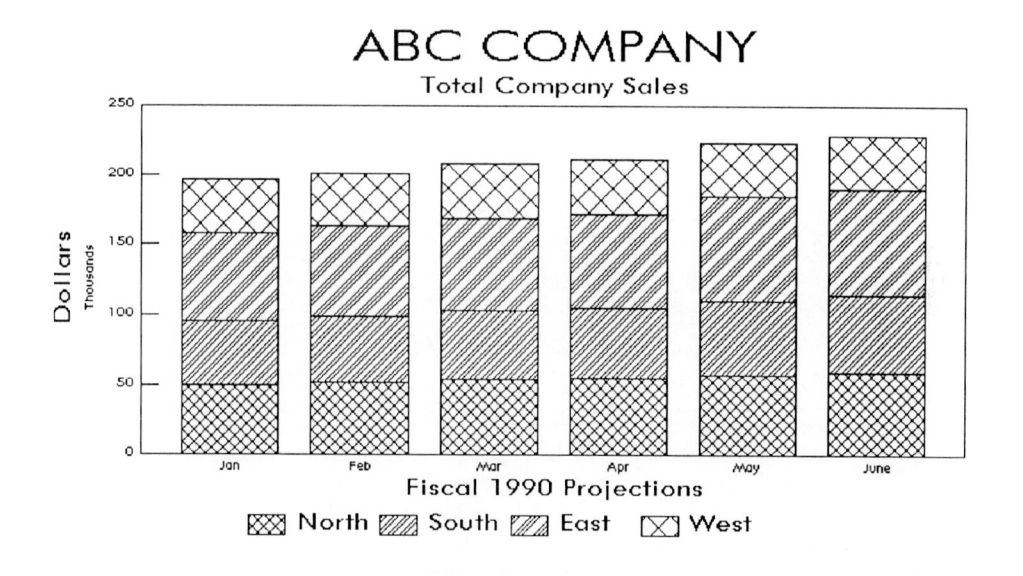

FIGURE 8-18. The same data as a stacked bar graph

16. Enter **Type Features** to display these options:

```
A:B4: (G) "Jan                                                    MENU
Vertical  Horizontal  Stacked  100%  2Y-Ranges  Y-Ranges  Quit
Draw the graph upright
```

The first two options, Vertical and Horizontal, set the orientation of axes. The other options are beyond the scope of this book.

17. Enter **Horizontal** and press F10 (GRAPH) to see how this option affects the graph. The results are shown in Figure 8-19.

    The Horizontal option rotates the axis of the graph so the X axis is vertical and the Y axis is horizontal.

18. Press any key to return to the menus, and enter **Vertical** to return the axes to the default.

19. Enter **Quit** to return to the main Graph menu.

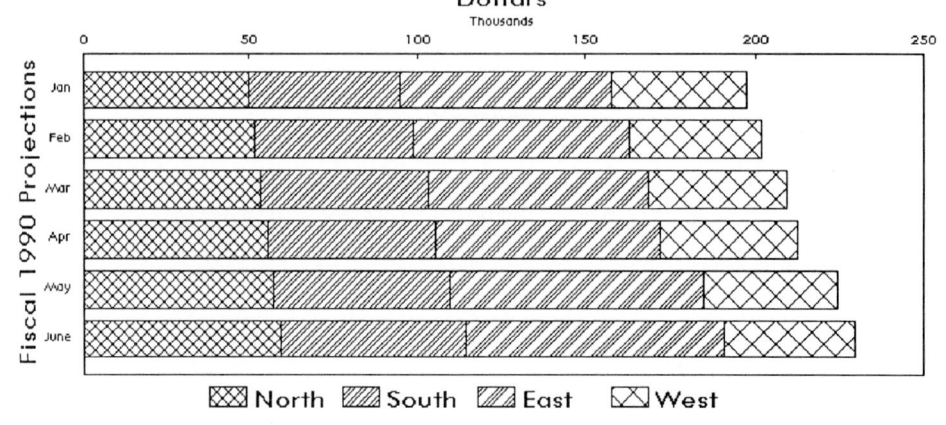

FIGURE 8-19.   The same data as a rotated graph

20. Enter **Reset** to produce this display:

```
A:C5: +B5*1.035                                                    MENU
Graph  X  A  B  C  D  E  F  Ranges  Options  Quit
Clear all current graph settings
```

21. Enter **Graph**.
    This will eliminate all the previous graph settings.

22. Enter **Group**, select **A5.B8**, and press ENTER. Enter **Columnwise** to divide the
    data into data ranges by columns.

23. Enter **Type Pie**.

24. Enter **Options Titles First**, type **ABC COMPANY**, and press ENTER.

25. Enter **Titles Second**, type **January Sales by Region**, and press ENTER.

26. Enter **Quit View** to view a graph like the one in Figure 8-20.

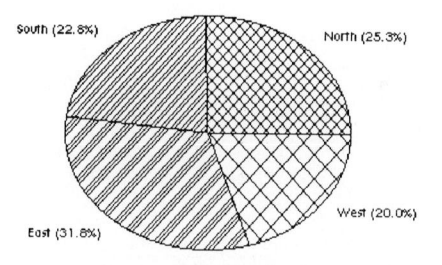

ABC COMPANY
January Sales by Region

FIGURE 8-20. A pie chart

27. Press any key, enter **Quit**, move your cell pointer to A12, and make these entries:

    A12: 1
    A13: 102
    A14: 3
    A15: 4

    With Release 3, you can use these codes to change the appearance of the graph. First create a range with the same number of value entries as the range shown on the graph. Numbers 0 to 14 are used, each representing a unique hatch pattern or color, depending on if the graph appears in color or monochrome. Adding 100 to any one of these entries will explode that piece from the pie (that is, split it off from the pie sections that remained joined).

    These values will show as currency, since that is the Global format. This will not affect their impact on the graph; however, if you find the dollar signs confusing, you can eliminate them with /Range Format General.

28. Enter **/Graph B**, type **A12.A15**, and press ENTER.

29. Enter **View**.

    Notice how the new graph shown in Figure 8-21 differs from the previous one. It is much easier to read and emphasizes the South's contributions.

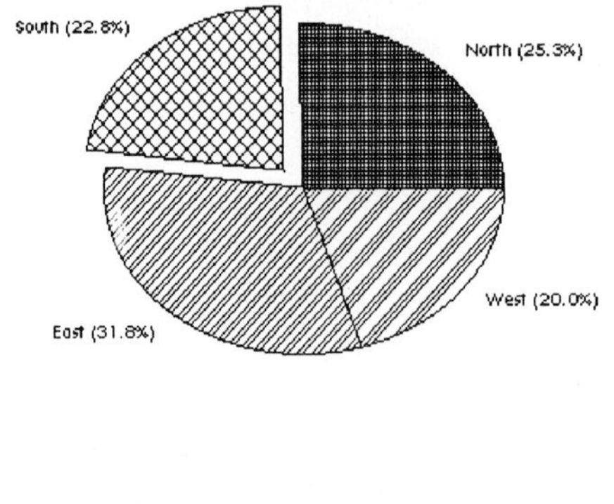
ABC COMPANY
January Sales by Region
South (22.8%)
North (25.3%)
West (20.0%)
East (31.8%)

FIGURE 8-21. A pie chart using hatch-pattern codes

30. Press any key to return to the Graph menu.

31. Enter **Name Create**, type **Jan_pie**, and press ENTER.

32. Enter **Quit** to return to READY mode.

SAVING A GRAPH

Several aspects of graphs must be saved. You must save the graph definition if you plan to use the graph the next time you work with the current worksheet. Since the graphic images are separate from the worksheets, you must also save the graph if you want to use the graphic image in another program such as Freelance or WordPerfect.

Saving the Worksheet File

Once you have created graph definitions, you will want them to be available the next time you work with the current worksheet. To save the graph definitions, save the worksheet file to disk after defining the graphs. To save the graphs for the Profit file, enter **/File Save**, type **Profit**, and press ENTER.

Saving the Graph Image

When you save the worksheet file, the graph is an integral part of the worksheet. If you want to use a graph in another package such as Freelance or WordPerfect, you must use /Graph Save. This menu option saves the file under the name that you specify and adds the filename extension .CGM (or .PIC if you change the default extension with the /Worksheet Global Default Graph PIC command) to distinguish the file from a worksheet file. The .CGM extension means the image is saved using the ANSI standard, which allows other programs to use the image.

To save a graphic image, you must save the graph as the current graph, even though the graph is defined on the current worksheet. To save a graph, use /Graph Name Use followed by Save.

Follow these steps to save the Sls_line graph created for the PROFIT worksheet:

1. Enter **/Graph Name Use**, point to Sls_Line, and press ENTER.

   The line graph you created will now be the active graph. Since you exited the Graph menu to save the worksheet, you now must reenter it. The current graphic image was not saved along with the graph definition stored in the worksheet file.

2. Press ESC, enter **Save**, type **Sls_line**, and press ENTER.

Although you are using the same name as you used for the graph specifications on the worksheet, the step you just took creates a unique file. The file that is created with this instruction will be named SLS_LINE.CGM as it is stored on disk. To use this file in a program that accepts files in a .CGM format, the ANSI standard for graphic images, you must follow the instructions that the other program provides for using these images.

PRINTING A GRAPH

Release 3 can print 1-2-3 graphs directly through 1-2-3's Print menus. In earlier releases, you had to save your file to a PIC file with the /Graph Save command and use the PrintGraph program to print your graphs. By printing with 1-2-3's menus, you only have to learn a few commands to print graphs. Also, you can print a worksheet and a graph on the same page. As with printing worksheets, 1-2-3 must be configured for your printer. This should have been completed when 1-2-3 was configured in the installation process. If not, return to Install to add the necessary information. This process is described in Appendix A.

Selecting Graphs to Print

Once you have created a graph, you can print it. Since printing a graph takes longer than printing a worksheet, you should view the graph before printing it to ensure that the graph contains the information you want to print. To print the Sls_bar graph you created earlier, follow these steps:

1. Enter **Quit** to leave the Graph menus.

2. Enter /**Print Printer** to print to the printer.
   You can also print to an encoded (.ENC) file, but you cannot print a graph to a .PRN file.

3. Enter **Image Named-Graph** and select **Sls_bar**.
   If you wanted to print the current graph, you would enter **Current** instead of **Named-Graph** and not select a graph name.

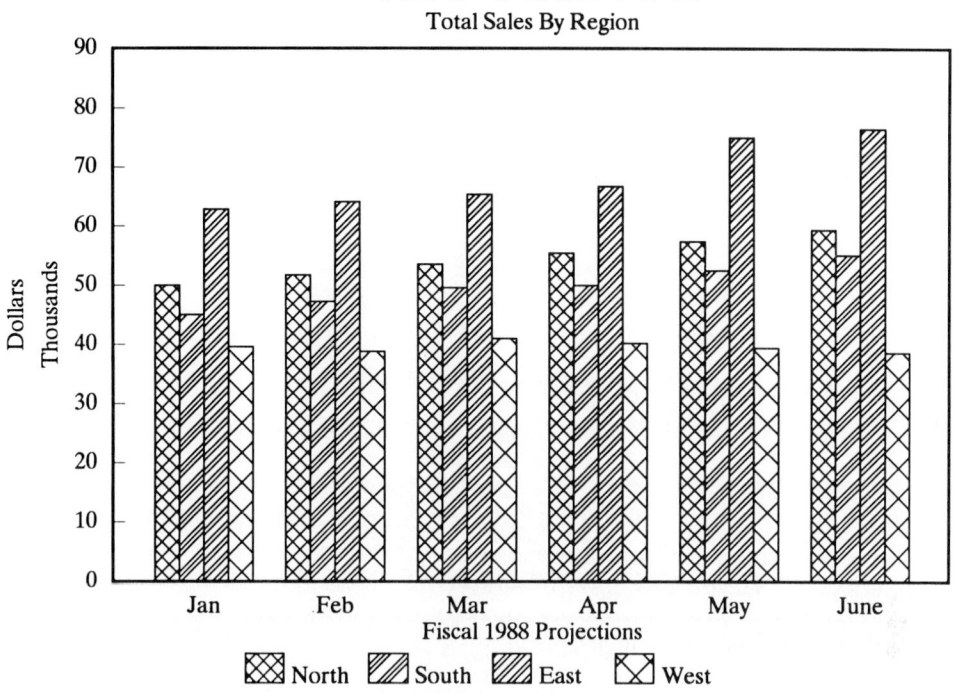

FIGURE 8-22.   Printout of Sls_bar graph

4. Enter **Align Go Page** to print a graph that looks like the one in Figure 8-22.
   Since you have not given 1-2-3 other directions about how you want to print the graph, 1-2-3 uses the full page to print the graph and uses other default settings that you can change.

Another option for printing a graph is to use the /Print Printer Range command and include the graph name in the print range. To print the Jan_pie graph you created earlier, follow these steps:

1. Enter **Range**, type **∗JAN_PIE**, and press ENTER.
   The asterisk before the graph name tells 1-2-3 to print the named graph, Jan_pie.

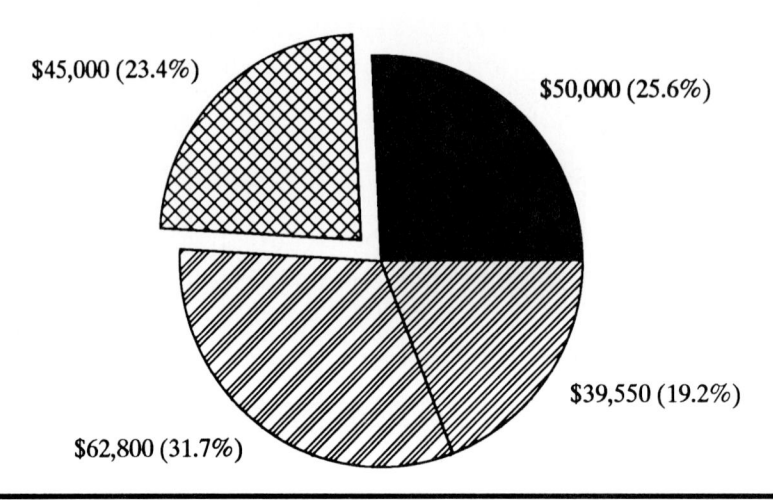

ABC COMPANY
January Sales By Region

$45,000 (23.4%)

$50,000 (25.6%)

$39,550 (19.2%)

$62,800 (31.7%)

FIGURE 8-23.   Printout of Jan_pie graph

2. Enter **Align Go Page** to print a graph that looks like the one in Figure 8-23.

One use of graphs named with the /Print Printer Range command is combining graphs and worksheet ranges in a single printing task. For example, you can use this feature to print part of a worksheet on the same page as a graph. To print the worksheet in this example with the line graph of the same data, you must first change the size in which 1-2-3 will print the graph.

Controlling the Settings

1-2-3 has a wide variety of settings that allow you to tailor the printing of a graph. Many of these settings are advanced features, best explored once you have mastered the basics. This section presents the basic settings that you can work with to make basic changes in how 1-2-3 prints your graph. The following menu shows the various options that can be changed when you enter /Print Printer Options Advanced Image:

```
A:C5: +B5*1.035                                    MENU
Rotate  Image-Sz  Density  Quit
Print the graph sideways on the page
```

CHANGING THE SIZE OF THE GRAPH   When 1-2-3 prints your graph, it tries to make the graph as large as possible. If you want to print two graphs on the same page or print a graph and a worksheet range, you will want to reduce the size of the graph. Changing the size is easy—you can tell 1-2-3 how wide or tall you want the graph on the page, and 1-2-3 resizes the graph within the width or height you select using the same dimensions. Try this feature to print the Sls_line graph and the data the graph uses:

1. Enter **Clear All**.

2. Enter **Range**, select **A1.G8**, type a semicolon, type **∗SLS_LINE**, and press ENTER.

   The selected print range prints the worksheet range and then prints the named graph, Sls_line.

3. Enter **Options Advanced Image Image-Sz**.

   1-2-3 displays this menu:

```
A:C5: +B5*1.035                                    MENU
Margin-Fill  Length-Fill  Reshape
Fill the page from left to right margin with the printed graph
```

   The first option prompts you for the width; 1-2-3 determines the height. The second option prompts for the height; 1-2-3 determines the width. The third option prompts for the width and height. The last option changes the height-to-width proportion 1-2-3 uses.

4. Enter **Length-Fill**, type **33**, and press ENTER. Since this is half of the current value, the graph height will be reduced by half.

5. Enter **Quit** three times to return to the main Print menu.

6. Enter **Align Go Page**.

   1-2-3 prints the worksheet and graph like the output shown in Figure 8-24.

ROTATING THE GRAPH   Another commonly used method for printing a graph is rotating the graph. If you set the size of the image, 1-2-3 uses the size that you provided to limit the size of the graph, although the height limit you provide will apply to the graph's width and the width limit you provide will apply to the graph's height. To see how this changes the way 1-2-3 prints a graph, follow these steps:

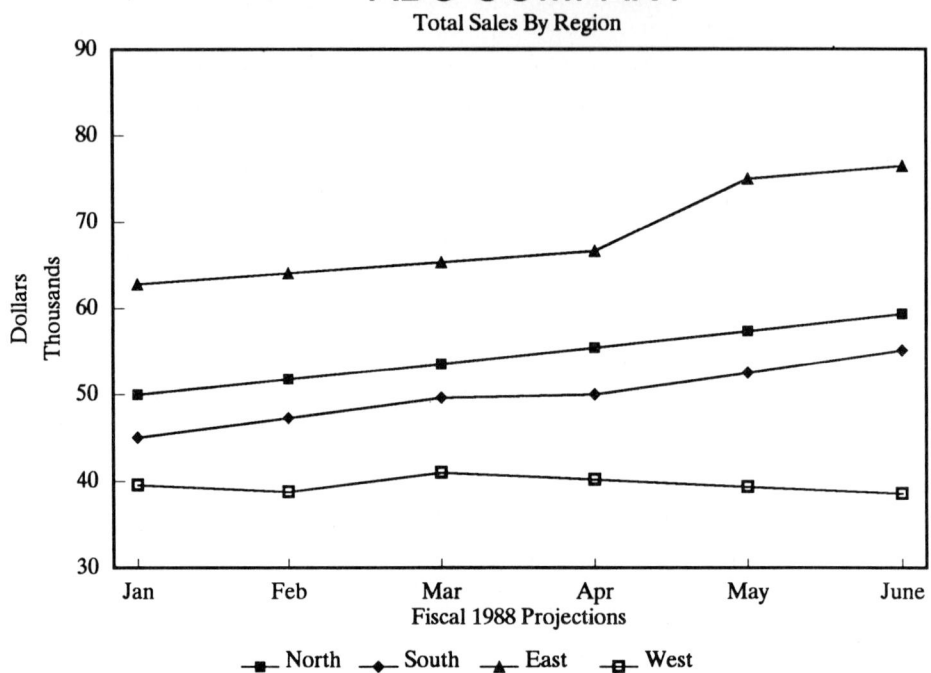

ABC COMPANY
SALES BY REGION

	Jan	Feb	Mar	Apr	May	June
North	$50,000	$51,750	$53,561	$55,436	$57,376	$59,384
South	$45,000	$47,250	$49,612	$50,000	$52,500	$55,125
East	$62,800	$64,056	$65,337	$66,644	$75,000	$76,500
West	$39,550	$38,759	$41,000	$40,180	$39,376	$38,589

FIGURE 8-24.   Printout of a worksheet range and a graph

1. Enter **Clear All**.

2. Enter **Image Current**.

3. Enter **Options Advanced Image Rotate Yes**.

4. Enter **Quit** three times to return to the main Print menu.

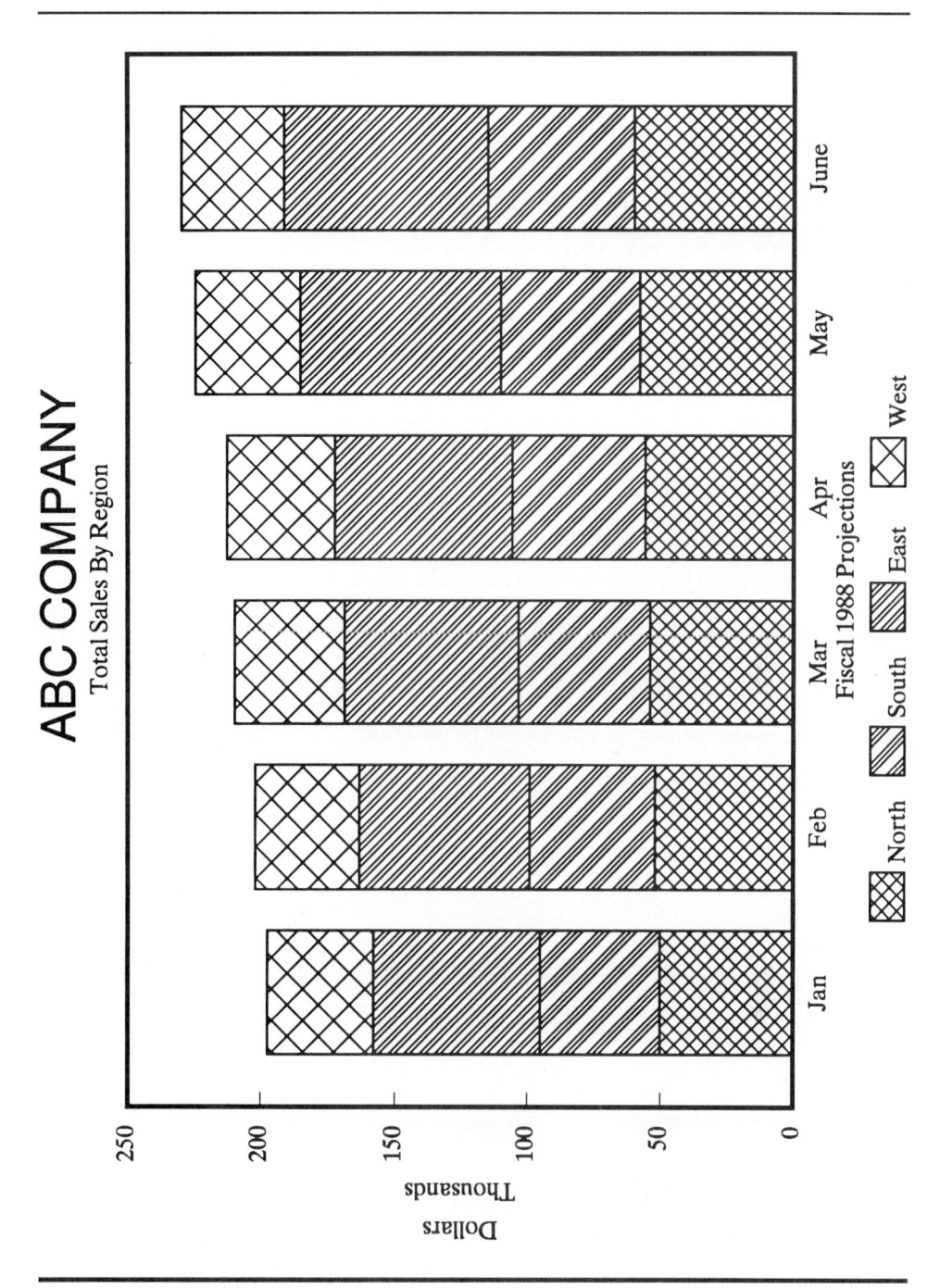

Figure 8-25.   Printout of rotated graph

5. Enter **Align Go Page** to print a graph that looks like the one in Figure 8-25.

6. Enter **Options Advanced Image Rotate No** to return the rotation to the default setting.

REVIEW EXERCISE

In this chapter you learned how to use 1-2-3's graphics features. The following exercises offer you an opportunity to try these features, using the data from the SALESPRJ file that you created in Chapter 5.

1. Retrieve the SALESPRJ file. If it is unavailable, enter the data in Figure 8-26 in an empty worksheet.

2. Assign the data in B3..G3 to range X. Assign the data in B4..G4 to data range A. Assign the data in B5..G5 to data range B. Assign the data in B6..G6 to the data range C. View the graph. Notice how 1-2-3 creates a line graph because you have not selected a graph type. *Hint:* Use /Graph Group, select the range B3..G6, and enter **Rowwise** to divide the worksheet range by rows into graph data ranges.

3. Make the current graph a bar graph. (*Hint:* Select Type and Bar.) View the graph.

4. Use the labels in A4, A5, and A6 for the legends for the A, B, and C data ranges. (*Hint:* Use Options Legend Range and select the range A4..A6.) View the graph.

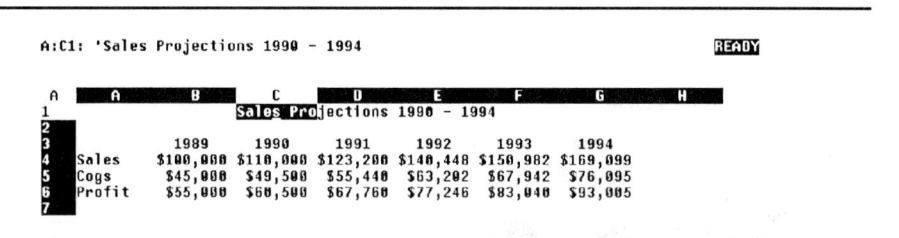

FIGURE 8-26. SALESPRJ worksheet

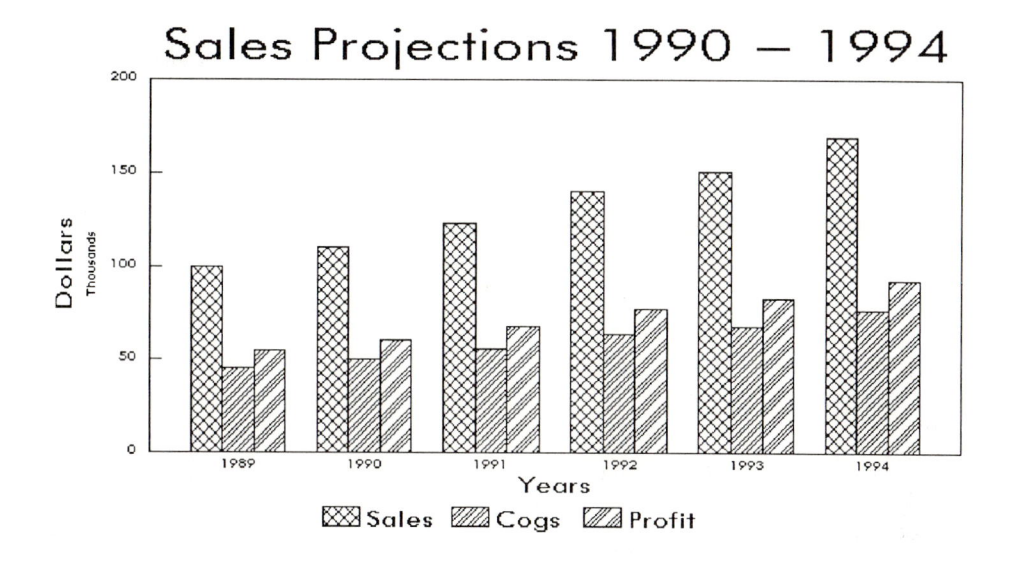

FIGURE 8-27. Graph with X- and Y-axis titles

5. Use the contents of C1 as a graph title. Label the X axis "Years" and the Y axis "Dollars." View the graph, which looks like Figure 8-27. *Hint:* To title the graph, use Options Titles First and enter **\C1**. To label the X axis, use Titles X-Axis and enter **Years**. To label the Y axis, use Titles Y-Axis and enter **Dollars**. Then use Quit to return to the main Graph menu.

6. Save the graph settings as Sales_bar. *Hint:* Use Name Create, type **Sales_bar**, and press ENTER.

7. Save the graphic image in the file SALE_BAR.CGM. *Hint:* Use Save, type **Sale_bar**, and press ENTER.

8. Make the current graph a line graph. (*Hint:* Use Type and Line.) View the graph.

9. Save the graph settings as Sales_line. *Hint:* Use Name Create, type **Sales_line**, and press ENTER.

10. Print the Sales_line graph. *Hint:* Use /Print Printer Image Current Go.

11. Clear all print settings. *Hint:* Use Clear All.

12. Print the worksheet range A1..G6 and the Sales_bar graph. Do not change the size of the graph. The graph will print on a separate sheet, since you have not changed the size of the graph. *Hint:* Use Range, type **A1..G6;∗Sales_bar**, press ENTER, and use Align Go Page.

13. Save the file so the current and named graph settings you have created remain with the worksheet. *Hint:* Use /File Save, press ENTER, and select Replace.

REVIEW

- 1-2-3 can create seven different graph types from your worksheet data. It can create bar, line, pie, stacked bar, XY, HLCO, and mixed graphs.

- 1-2-3 can plot up to six series of data in a graph.

- A graph can contain legends to identify the data ranges, grid lines, and titles to enhance a graph's appearance.

- A worksheet has only one current graph at a time. Once you name a graph, you can make a different graph current and still be able to use the named graph at a later time.

- You can save the graph settings by saving the worksheet.

- Saving the graphic image with /Graph Save saves the image to a file that other programs can use.

- 1-2-3 Print menus let you print 1-2-3 graphs with a variety of print enhancements. You can select the graph to print with the Image or Range option from the main Print menu.

Commands and Keys

F10 (GRAPH)	Displays the current graph
/GA	Assigns worksheet data to data range A
/GB	Assigns worksheet data to data range B
/GC	Assigns worksheet data to data range C
/GD	Assigns worksheet data to data range D
/GE	Assigns worksheet data to data range E
/GF	Assigns worksheet data to data range F
/GG	Assigns worksheet data to all data ranges

Command	Description
/GG	Assigns worksheet data to all data ranges
/GNC	Makes the current graph a named graph
/GNU	Makes a named graph the current graph
/GOB	Displays current graph in black and white (monochrome)
/GOC	Displays current graph in color
/GOFGA	Displays the data ranges as area graphs
/GOGB	Displays horizontal and vertical grid lines in the current graph
/GOGC	Removes grid lines in the current graph
/GOGH	Displays horizontal grid lines in the current graph
/GOGQ	Returns to the Graph Options menu
/GOGV	Displays vertical grid lines in the current graph
/GOL	Assigns legends to data ranges A through F
/GOTF	Provides the first line title for the current graph
/GOTS	Provides the second line title for the current graph
/GOTX	Provides the title for X axis in the current graph
/GOTY	Provides the title for Y axis in the current graph
/GS	Saves the graphic image to a .CGM file
/GT	Selects the current graph type
/GTFH	Displays X axis vertically and Y axis horizontally
/GTFV	Displays X axis horizontally and Y axis vertically
/GV	Views the current graph
/GX	Assigns worksheet data to the X data range
/PPI	Selects a graph to print
/PPOAII	Sets the size of a printed graph
/PPOAIR	Rotates a printed graph

9
DATA MANAGEMENT BASICS

Setting Up a Database
Sorting the Database
Searching the Database
Special Features
Using the Database Statistical Functions
Review Exercise
Review

All the work you have done with 1-2-3 until now has been concerned with calculating some type of numeric result, which is the usual application for the 1-2-3 program. However, 1-2-3 also has other features that are oriented more toward the management of information than toward calculations. These data management features are a special group of commands that provide capabilities for the design, entry, and retrieval of information, with or without additional calculations. You can use these commands to keep track of information about your suppliers, clients, or employees.

Since this is a new area of 1-2-3 for you, the first step is to learn some new terms. A *database* is a collection of all the information you have about a set of things. These things can be customers, employees, orders, parts in your inventory, or anything else. If you created a database of employee information, you would place the information about each of your employees in it. All the information about one employee would be in one *record* of the database. A record is composed of all the pieces of information you want to record about each thing in the set, such as one employee. These individual pieces of information in the record are referred to as *fields*. Fields you might include in each record in an employee database would contain name, job classification, salary, date of hire, and social security number. Every time you design a new database, you need to decide what fields will be included in each record.

A 1-2-3 database is a range of cells on the worksheet. The database can be in any area of the worksheet you want, but you must put the fields' names in the top row of the range. The records in the database, which contain data for each field, must go in the rows beneath the field names.

SETTING UP A DATABASE

To create a new database, you first create a list of the fields you plan to use, and then estimate the number of characters required for each field. To make this estimate, total the characters required to store one record in the database. Then estimate the number of records that you will place in the database, and multiply this number by the size of one record to get an estimate of how much memory is required for the database. Next, load 1-2-3 and enter **/Worksheet Status** to see how much memory is available. If the total you need exceeds the amount of available memory, another alternative is required—for example, splitting the database into two sections. With Release 3, this limitation is less of a factor. However, you still have a limit of 8192 rows in the database range in the worksheet, which may limit the number of records that you store in a worksheet.

Try this process for the employee file you will create:

1. Take a piece of paper and write down this list of field names:

    Last Name
    First Name
    SS#
    Job Code
    Salary
    Location

2. Write the size of each field next to the field name.

    For this example, use 12 characters for the last name, 12 characters for the first name, 11 for the social security number, 4 for the job code, 8 for the salary, and 3 for the location. This makes a total of 50 characters for one record. In addition, you need to add 4 for each cell used to store information for the record. This would make the total 74 for this example.

STAT

```
Available memory: 2404720 of 2404720 Bytes (100%)

Processor: 80286
Math coprocessor: None

Recalculation:
   Method.......... Automatic
   Order........... Natural
   Iterations...... 1

Circular reference: (None)

Cell display:
   Format.......... (G)
   Label prefix.....  '
   Column width..... 9
   Zero setting..... No

Global protection: Off
```

FIGURE 9-1.   Using the /Worksheet Status command to check available memory

3. Estimate the number of records you plan to eventually enter into the database, and multiply this number by the size of one record.

   For this example, 100 records is a good estimate. Multiplying 100 by 74 results in 7400, which should be well within the limit of any system. However, for those occasions on which this estimate is larger, you can take a look at how to verify this calculation.

4. Enter /**Worksheet Status** and check the amount of available memory.

   The amount of memory shown in the worksheet status display in Figure 9-1 is 2,404,720 bytes—more than enough to accommodate 7400 characters, plus some extra for special options such as formatting. If the amount of available memory exceeds the size requirements of the database, it is safe to proceed. Press any key to return to READY mode.

When the size of the database is larger than available memory, you must develop an alternative plan before beginning data entry. You may also want to consider disabling the Undo feature since it requires additional memory. This is not likely to solve your entire problem, however, so you may need to consider more than one database table to meet your needs.

Choosing a Location

Any area of the worksheet can be used for a database. Normally, when your worksheet serves a dual purpose (both calculations and a database), you should place the database below the calculations so it can expand easily. If nothing else is stored on the worksheet, row 1 is as good a starting location as any other. Chapter 13 will introduce multilevel worksheets, which are worksheet files that contain multiple worksheets. When you learn how to use multiple worksheets, you can use one worksheet for the database table and another worksheet for other data.

Entering Field Names

Whatever area you select for your database, record your field names across the top row. Always choose *meaningful* names; they will be used again to invoke the data-management features. Meaningful names can be self-documenting in that they can help clarify what you are doing. Each field name must be contained within a single cell. Field names that span two cells are not acceptable. Neither are spaces at the end of a field name. Spaces or special characters in the cell immediately beneath the field name can also cause a problem with some of 1-2-3's data-management features.

To enter the field names in the chosen area, simply type them in their respective cells and adjust the column widths:

1. Enter the field names for the employee database in these cells now:

    A1: Last Name
    B1: First Name
    C1: "SS#
    D1: Job Code
    E1: "Salary
    F1: Location

    Pay special attention to the spelling of field names. When you use the field names in later tasks, they must match exactly if the job is to be completed properly.

2. Move the cell pointer to column A and enter /**Worksheet Column Column-Range Set-Width**. Move the cell pointer to column E. Figures later in the chapter display salary as having [W12]. Press ENTER, type **12**, and press ENTER.

    The label entries require a width equal only to the number of characters in the field. The Salary field has been estimated at 8 digits; however, 12 is allowed in the column width for the addition of a dollar sign, a comma, a decimal point, and one extra space to separate the entry from the adjacent fields.

3. Move to column D and enter /**Worksheet Column Reset-Width**. After widening the columns, the entries look like this:

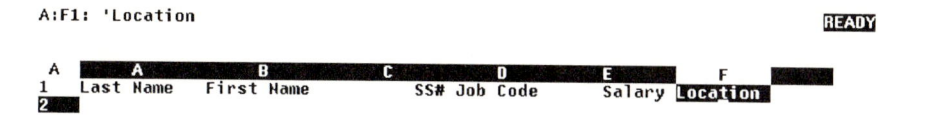

A:F1: 'Location   READY

A	A	B	C	D	E	F
1	Last Name	First Name	SS#	Job Code	Salary	Location
2						

Entering Data

Now that you have entered the field names, you can begin entering the data beneath them. The first record should be entered immediately beneath the field names. Each record will occupy one row; do not skip rows as you begin to enter records.

Make sure that the data you enter in each field is the same type. If a field contains value entries, the entries in all records for this field should contain value entries. If you do not have all the data for a record, you can leave the field blank as long as you do not leave the entire row blank. Except for these few simple guidelines, everything is exactly the same as entering data in the worksheet environment.

You will need to complete the data entry for the database used throughout the rest of this chapter. The normal procedure for entering records in a database is to enter a complete record at once; however, since it might be easier to complete the entries in one column before moving to the next one, the directions in this chapter are written from that perspective. You can either work from the screen display shown in Figure 9-2 or follow these directions to complete the entries:

A:A1: [W12] 'Last Name   READY

A	A	B	C	D	E	F
1	Last Name	First Name	SS#	Job Code	Salary	Location
2	Larson	Mary	543-98-9876	23	$12,000	2
3	Campbell	David	213-76-9874	23	$23,000	10
4	Campbell	Keith	569-89-7654	12	$32,000	2
5	Stephens	Tom	219-78-8954	15	$17,800	2
6	Caldor	Larry	459-34-0921	23	$32,500	4
7	Lightnor	Peggy	560-55-4311	14	$23,500	10
8	McCartin	John	817-66-1212	15	$54,600	2
9	Justof	Jack	431-78-9963	17	$41,200	4
10	Patterson	Lyle	212-11-9090	12	$21,500	10
11	Miller	Lisa	214-89-6756	23	$18,700	2
12						
13						
14						
15						
16						
17						
18						
19						
20						

MEFG9 2.WK3

FIGURE 9-2.   The employee database

1. Place these entries in the Last Name field:

   A2: Larson
   A3: Campbell
   A4: Campbell
   A5: Stephens
   A6: Caldor
   A7: Lightnor
   A8: McCartin
   A9: Justof
   A10: Patterson
   A11: Miller

2. Make these entries in the First Name field:

   B2: Mary
   B3: David
   B4: Keith
   B5: Tom
   B6: Larry
   B7: Peggy
   B8: John
   B9: Jack
   B10: Lyle
   B11: Lisa

3. Move the cell pointer to C2, enter **/Range Format Other Label**, move the cell pointer to C11, and press ENTER.

   This step makes labels of the social security numbers that you enter in the next step without having to enter a label prefix character.

4. Make the following entries in the SS# field:

   C2: 543-98-9846
   C3: 213-76-9874
   C4: 569-89-7654
   C5: 219-78-8954
   C6: 459-34-0921
   C7: 560-55-4311
   C8: 817-66-1212
   C9: 431-78-9963
   C10: 212-11-9090
   C11: 214-89-6756

5. Enter the following Job Codes:

    D2: 23
    D3: 23
    D4: 12
    D5: 15
    D6: 23
    D7: 14
    D8: 15
    D9: 17
    D10: 12
    D11: 23

6. Move the cell pointer to E2, enter /**Range Format Currency**, type **0** and press ENTER, move the cell pointer to E11, and press ENTER.

7. Make the following salary entries:

E2:	22000
E3:	23000
E4:	32000
E5:	17800
E6:	32500
E7:	23500
E8:	54600
E9:	41200
E10:	21500
E11:	18700

8. Enter the following Location codes:

F2:	2
F3:	10
F4:	2
F5:	2
F6:	4
F7:	10
F8:	2
F9:	4
F10:	10
F11:	2

    This completes the entries required to create a database with 10 records.

```
A:E2: (CO) [W12] 22000                                              READY

A        A              B              C           D         E         F
1    Last Name      First Name            SS# Job Code      Salary Location
2    Larson         Mary         543-98-9846        23     $22,000         2
3    Campbell       David        213-76-9874        23     $23,000        10
4    Campbell       Keith        569-89-7654        12     $32,000         2
5    Stephens       Tom          219-78-8954        15     $17,800         2
6    Caldor         Larry        459-34-0921        23     $32,500         4
7    Lightnor       Peggy        560-55-4311        14     $23,500        10
8    McCartin       John         817-66-1212        15     $54,600         2
9    Justof         Jack         431-78-9963        17     $41,200         4
10   Patterson      Lyle         212-11-9090        12     $21,500        10
11   Miller         Lisa         214-89-6756        23     $18,700         2
12
13
14
15
16
17
18
19
20
MEFG9 3.WK3
```

FIGURE 9-3.   Updating the database

Making Changes

Making changes to entries in the database is no different from making changes in the worksheet data you use. You have two good choices: retype any entry to replace it, or use the F2 (EDIT) technique to make a quick correction. To feel at home with making changes, just as if you were still making worksheet entries, carry out the following steps to change the salary and social security number for Mary Larson:

1. Move the cell pointer to C2, press the EDIT key (F2), and move with the LEFT ARROW key until the small cursor is under the 7. Press the DEL key, type **4**, and press ENTER to correct the SS number.

2. Move the cell pointer to E2, press the EDIT key (F2), and press the HOME key. Next, press the DEL key, type **2**, and press ENTER to produce the display shown in Figure 9-3.

The other way to update the entries in the database is to retype them, if changes are extensive.

SORTING THE DATABASE

1-2-3 provides a Sort feature that can alter the sequence of the records in your database to any sequence you need. If you decide that you would like an employee list in alphabetical order, 1-2-3 can do this for you. If you decide that you want the records in order by job code, salary, or location, 1-2-3 can make this change easily. Release 3 lets you use up to 255 fields for sorting your database. You will find 1-2-3's Sort commands easy to work with, and you will be amazed at how rapidly 1-2-3 can rearrange your data.

All the commands that you will need for specifying the sort are located on this menu, which you can activate by entering /**Data Sort**:

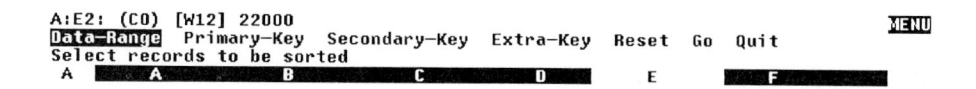

Defining the Database Location

The first step in resequencing your database is to tell 1-2-3 where the data is located. When you are sorting data, 1-2-3 is not interested in the field names, only in the data values that you expect it to sort. If you accidentally include the field names in this range, 1-2-3 will sort them just as if they were intentionally included as data values.

In defining the area to be sorted, you have the choice of defining some of the records or all of them. Always include all of the fields, even if you want to exclude some of the records. Excluded fields remain stationary and do not remain with the other portion of the record to which they belong, thus jeopardizing the integrity of your file. Therefore, it is a good idea to save the file before sorting, in case you accidentally exclude some of the field names. Having Undo enabled is another safeguard, although it is only effective if you reverse the result of the sort operation before entering another command.

Follow these steps to tell 1-2-3 where the employee records are located:

1. Enter /**File Save**, type **EMPLOYEE**, and press ENTER.

2. Enter /**Data Sort**.

3. Enter **Data-Range** to produce this display:

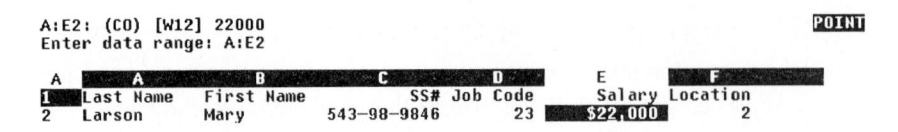

```
A:E2: (CO) [W12] 22000                                              POINT
Enter data range: A:E2
```

A	A	B	C	D	E	F
1	Last Name	First Name	SS#	Job Code	Salary	Location
2	Larson	Mary	543-98-9846	23	$22,000	2

4. Press the HOME key. Press the DOWN ARROW key.

   This will position you in A2, right below the first field name. If you had sorted this database previously, you would first have to press ESC to free the beginning of the range before moving the cell pointer.

5. Type **.** and press the END key followed by the HOME key.

   At this point the database range should be highlighted like the one shown in Figure 9-4.

6. Verify that the range you wish to sort is highlighted, and press ENTER.

Defining the Sort Sequence

You can sort your data in sequence based on any of the database fields. If you sort by the contents of column D, the database will be in sequence by job code. If you sort by column C, the social security numbers will determine the sequence. Whichever field you choose to sort on, you will also have to decide whether you want the entries to be sequenced from highest to lowest (descending order) or lowest to highest (ascending order).

1-2-3 refers to the field that determines the sequence of the records after the sort as the *primary key*. It also allows you to establish a *secondary key* and up to 253 additional keys. The secondary key is a precaution against duplicates in the primary key. The extra keys, which are also optional, are a precaution against duplicates in the primary and secondary keys. 1-2-3 ignores the secondary key except when the primary key contains duplicate entries. It ignores the extra keys except when the primary and secondary keys contain duplicate entries. The secondary key and extra keys are used to break the tie.

CHOOSING A PRIMARY KEY   There are three ways to specify the sort sequence. One is to enter /**Data Sort Primary-Key** and point to a cell that contains an entry for the field you want to control the order of the records. Another is to type the address of this cell. The third option will work if you have named the first cell in each of the data-entry columns. An easy way to apply these names is to use the /Range Name Label Down command and specify the range of labels that represent the field

```
A:F11: 2                                                    POINT
Enter data range: A:A2..A:F11
```

A	A	B	C	D	E	F
1	Last Name	First Name	SS#	Job Code	Salary	Location
2	Larson	Mary	543-98-9846	23	$22,000	2
3	Campbell	David	213-76-9874	23	$23,000	10
4	Campbell	Keith	569-89-7654	12	$32,000	2
5	Stephens	Tom	219-78-8954	15	$17,800	2
6	Caldor	Larry	459-34-0921	23	$32,500	4
7	Lightnor	Peggy	560-55-4311	14	$23,500	10
8	McCartin	John	817-66-1212	15	$54,600	2
9	Justof	Jack	431-78-9963	17	$41,200	4
10	Patterson	Lyle	212-11-9090	12	$21,500	10
11	Miller	Lisa	214-89-6756	23	$18,700	2
12						
13						
14						
15						
16						
17						
18						
19						

```
MEFG9 3.WK3
```

FIGURE 9-4.   Highlighting the range to sort

names. If you use this approach, you can press F3 when prompted for a field or a column and select a range name from the list provided. 1-2-3 will display the cell address of the entry on the settings sheet and follow it with the name assigned to the range. The first time the data is sorted, the named cell may be shuffled to a record other than the first record, but this will not affect the use of it later, since the sort accepts any of the entries with a field.

Regardless of the method chosen for specifying the cell, the next prompt you will see asks for the sort order. A and D are the only acceptable choices. The A represents ascending sequence, and D represents descending sequence. When 1-2-3 asks for the sort order, a default choice is present on the screen. If you want to use it, just press ENTER.

Follow these steps to see /Data Sort Primary-Key in action:

1. Enter **Primary-Key** to create this prompt:

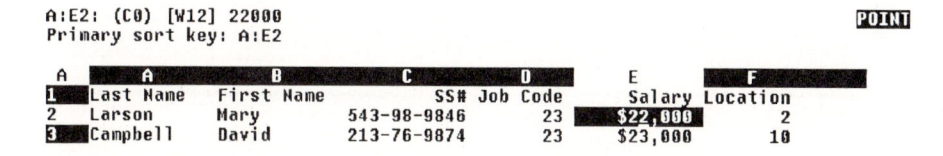

```
A:E2: (C0) [W12] 22000                                      POINT
Primary sort key: A:E2
```

A	A	B	C	D	E	F
1	Last Name	First Name	SS#	Job Code	Salary	Location
2	Larson	Mary	543-98-9846	23	$22,000	2
3	Campbell	David	213-76-9874	23	$23,000	10

2. Move the cell pointer to C2 and press ENTER.

This selects the social security number as the primary sort key.

3. Type **D** to create this display:

```
A:E2: (C0) [W12] 22000                                                    EDIT
Primary sort key: A:C2              Sort order (A or D): D
```

A	A	B	C	D	E	F
1	Last Name	First Name	SS#	Job Code	Salary	Location
2	Larson	Mary	543-98-9846	23	$22,000	2
3	Campbell	David	213-76-9874	23	$23,000	10

4. Press ENTER to request descending sequence.

5. Enter **Go** to activate the sort and change the sequence of the records to match Figure 9-5.

Just defining the sort key does not change the data sequence. You must enter **Go** to tell 1-2-3 that you are ready for the sort to take place.

CHOOSING A SECONDARY KEY   The secondary key is the primary tie breaker. It resolves duplicate entries and determines which one of the duplicates should be listed first, based on the value of the secondary field. In situations like the

```
A:E2: (C0) [W12] 54600                                                    READY
```

A	A	B	C	D	E	F
1	Last Name	First Name	SS#	Job Code	Salary	Location
2	McCartin	John	817-66-1212	15	$54,600	2
3	Campbell	Keith	569-89-7654	12	$32,000	2
4	Lightnor	Peggy	560-55-4311	14	$23,500	10
5	Larson	Mary	543-98-9846	23	$22,000	2
6	Caldor	Larry	459-34-0921	23	$32,500	4
7	Justof	Jack	431-78-9963	17	$41,200	4
8	Stephens	Tom	219-78-8954	15	$17,800	2
9	Miller	Lisa	214-89-6756	23	$18,700	2
10	Campbell	David	213-76-9874	23	$23,000	10
11	Patterson	Lyle	212-11-9090	12	$21,500	10
12						
13						
14						
15						
16						
17						
18						
19						
20						

```
ME2F9 5.WK1
```

FIGURE 9-5.   Records in SS# sequence

last example, where the social security number was the controlling sequence, a secondary key is not needed. The SS# field does not contain legal duplicates, so there is no need for a tie breaker. On the other hand, if you want to sort the employee file by last name, a secondary key is appropriate—last names sometimes are duplicated.

The process for specifying the secondary key is the same, except that you enter **/Data Sort Secondary-Key**. Try this feature by sorting the employee database by name:

1. Enter **/Data Sort Reset**.

    This cancels the current settings for the options in the Data Sort menu.

2. Enter **Data-Range**, type **A2.F11**, and press ENTER.

3. Enter **Primary-Key**, type **A2**, press ENTER, type **A**, and press ENTER.

    The top cell in the Last Name field was selected as the sort key.

4. Enter **Secondary-Key**, type **B2**, press ENTER, type **A**, and press ENTER.

    The top cell in the First Name field was selected as the secondary key. This key will be used to resolve the tie only when more than one employee has the same last name. In that case, the first name field will determine which record is placed first.

5. Enter **Go** to resequence the data as a name list in alphabetical order, as shown in Figure 9-6.

    There is no need to quit the Sort menu. Using Go to execute the sort will place you back in READY mode after the data has been resequenced. The Quit option is available for occasions when you want to exit the menu without performing the sort.

When you save the worksheet with /File Save, 1-2-3 will save the sort specifications you just entered. The next time you use the worksheet, you can execute the sort and change only those options that are different. Be particularly careful when updating the data range if you add more fields to the end of the database; if you do not adjust the range, the new fields will remain stationary while the rest of the record is shifted to a new row.

CHOOSING AN EXTRA KEY   Release 3 can have up to 253 extra keys. This new feature gives you up to 253 other fields that /Data Sort can use as a tie breaker. It resolves duplicate entries with the primary key, secondary key, and other extra keys and determines which one of the duplicates should be listed first, based on the value of the extra key field. In the last example employees had the same last name but

A:E2: (C0) [W12] 32500   READY

A	A	B	C	D	E	F
1	Last Name	First Name	SS#	Job Code	Salary	Location
2	Caldor	Larry	459-34-0921	23	$32,500	4
3	Campbell	David	213-76-9874	23	$23,000	10
4	Campbell	Keith	569-89-7654	12	$32,000	2
5	Justof	Jack	431-78-9963	17	$41,200	4
6	Larson	Mary	543-98-9846	23	$22,000	2
7	Lightnor	Peggy	560-55-4311	14	$23,500	10
8	McCartin	John	817-66-1212	15	$54,600	2
9	Miller	Lisa	214-89-6756	23	$18,700	2
10	Patterson	Lyle	212-11-9090	12	$21,500	10
11	Stephens	Tom	219-78-8954	15	$17,800	2
12						
13						
14						
15						
16						
17						
18						
19						
20						

123R3MEF.WK3

FIGURE 9-6.   Records in sequence by name

different first names, so extra keys were not needed; a secondary key was sufficient. On the other hand, if you want to sort the employee file by job code and location, an extra key is appropriate—some employees have the same information for both fields, and you may want to use a third field to order these duplicate entries.

The process for specifying an extra key is similar to specifying the other keys. Try the Extra-Key feature by sorting the employee database by social security number within job code and location, following these steps:

1. Enter **/Worksheet Global Default Other Undo Enable**. This will let you "unsort" the database so you can sort the database by last name, which is more convenient.

2. Enter **/Data Sort Reset**.
   This cancels the current settings for the options in the Data Sort menu.

3. Enter **Data-Range**, type **A2.F11**, and press ENTER.

4. Enter **Primary-Key**, type **D2**, press ENTER, type **A**, and press ENTER.
   The top cell in the Job Code field is selected as the primary sort key.

5. Enter **Secondary-Key**, type **F2**, press ENTER, type **A**, and press ENTER.

The top cell in the Location field is selected as the secondary key. This key will resolve a tie when more than one employee has the same job code. In this case, the Location field will determine which record is placed first.

6. Enter **Extra-Key**.

   1-2-3 prompts you for a key number for the first extra key used after the secondary key.

7. Press ENTER to accept **1**.

8. Type **C2**, press ENTER, type **A**, and press ENTER.

   The prompt now looks like this:

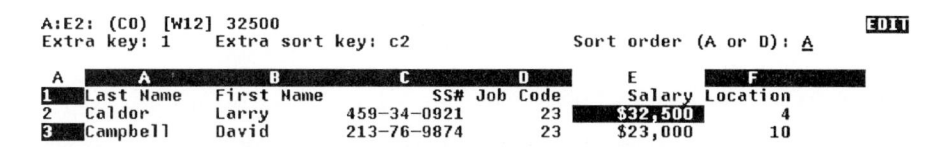

```
A:E2: (CO) [W12] 32500                                          EDIT
Extra key: 1    Extra sort key: c2              Sort order (A or D): A

A        A          B            C        D        E         F
1    Last Name   First Name         SS# Job Code    Salary Location
2    Caldor      Larry       459-34-0921      23    $32,500        4
3    Campbell    David       213-76-9874      23    $23,000       10
```

9. Press ENTER. The top cell in the SS# field is selected as the first extra key. This key will resolve a tie when more than one employee has the same job code and location. When this happens, the employee with the lower social security number will be placed first.

10. Enter **Go** to resequence the data as shown in Figure 9-7.

11. Press ALT-F4 (UNDO) and type **Y** to return the database to the last- and first-name sequence.

SEARCHING THE DATABASE

As your database increases in size, it becomes increasingly important to review the information it contains selectively. Once the employee file contains 500 records, it becomes extremely time-consuming to locate all the records that have a job code of 23 by scanning the Job Code column visually.

1-2-3 gives you a way to work with information in your database selectively by means of an *exception reporting* capability. This means you will have a method of selectively presenting information that falls outside of a norm you establish. This selective review feature can also provide an easy way to clean up the database or to create reports in response to unexpected requests.

```
A:E2: (CO) [W12] 32000                                          READY
```

A	A	B	C	D	E	F
1	Last Name	First Name	SS#	Job Code	Salary	Location
2	Campbell	Keith	569-89-7654	12	$32,000	2
3	Patterson	Lyle	212-11-9090	12	$21,500	10
4	Lightnor	Peggy	560-55-4311	14	$23,500	10
5	Stephens	Tom	219-78-8954	15	$17,800	2
6	McCartin	John	817-66-1212	15	$54,600	2
7	Justof	Jack	431-78-9963	17	$41,200	4
8	Miller	Lisa	214-89-6756	23	$18,700	2
9	Larson	Mary	543-98-9846	23	$22,000	2
10	Caldor	Larry	459-34-0921	23	$32,500	4
11	Campbell	David	213-76-9874	23	$23,000	10
12						

FIGURE 9-7.   Records in sequence by job code, location, and social security number

Working with 1-2-3's Selective Reporting feature requires that you enter your specifications for record selection on the worksheet. These specifications are known as *criteria* and must be entered on the worksheet before you invoke 1-2-3's commands.

Once the criteria are entered, you must make various menu selections. All commands required for working with 1-2-3's Selective Reporting feature are found in the Data Query menu, shown here:

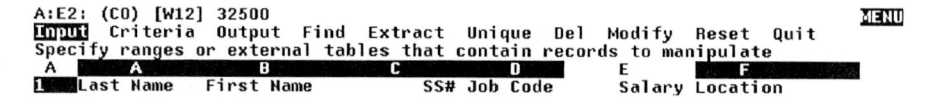

```
A:E2: (CO) [W12] 32500                                            MENU
Input  Criteria  Output  Find  Extract  Unique  Del  Modify  Reset  Quit
Specify ranges or external tables that contain records to manipulate
 A     A         B              C          D        E       F
 1   Last Name  First Name        SS# Job Code   Salary Location
```

Like the Sort menu, the Data Query menu is a sticky menu; in most situations, you must make more than one selection from it before 1-2-3 completes your task.

Since the /Data Query commands have a number of steps, the best approach is to look at each step and then try a few examples that combine all of the features. You will begin by exploring the rules for entering your criteria on the worksheet.

Entering Criteria

You enter criteria on the worksheet to tell 1-2-3 which records you want to work with. 1-2-3 will ignore records that do not match these criteria when you use the Data Query menus to perform a task with the database.

The first step in creating criteria is choosing a blank area on the worksheet in which to enter them. The rules for entering criteria differ, depending on whether you are working with label data or value data. Regardless of which type of data you want to enter, the criteria will represent the field name you are attempting to match against in the existing records. If you want to search against the Job Code field, you enter **Job Code** in the blank area that you chose. You must enter the field name exactly as it is in the database, with identical spelling. You will then place the criteria specification immediately beneath this field name. If you want to ensure that you have the field names spelled correctly, copy the field names from the database table.

CRITERIA FOR VALUE DATA   You can enter two different types of criteria for matching records when you use a field that contains value entries. One option is to use *exact-entry match criteria,* which places a value that could occur in the field beneath the field name. If you want to search for all records with the number 23 in the Job Code field, all you need to do is place **23** beneath the entry "Job Code" in the criteria area.

Make the following entries to set up the exact-match criteria:

1. Move the cell pointer to A13 and type **Job Code**. Then move the cell pointer to A14 to finalize.

    Although it takes a few seconds more, you might want to use /Copy to copy the field name from the database to ensure that you do not spell the name incorrectly.

2. Type **23** and press ENTER to create the criteria entry shown in Figure 9-8.

A:A14: [W12] 23   `READY`

A	A	B	C	D	E	F
1	Last Name	First Name	SS#	Job Code	Salary	Location
2	Caldor	Larry	459-34-0921	23	$32,500	4
3	Campbell	David	213-76-9874	23	$23,000	10
4	Campbell	Keith	569-89-7654	12	$32,000	2
5	Justof	Jack	431-78-9963	17	$41,200	4
6	Larson	Mary	543-98-9846	23	$22,000	2
7	Lightnor	Peggy	560-55-4311	14	$23,500	10
8	McCartin	John	817-66-1212	15	$54,600	2
9	Miller	Lisa	214-89-6756	23	$18,700	2
10	Patterson	Lyle	212-11-9090	12	$21,500	10
11	Stephens	Tom	219-78-8954	15	$17,800	2
12						
13	Job Code					
14	23					
15						
16						
17						
18						
19						
20						

MEFG9 7.WK3

FIGURE 9-8.   Entering cirteria to select records with a job code of 23

=	Equal
>	Greater than
>=	Greater than or equal to
<	Less than
<=	Less than or equal to
<>	Not equal to

TABLE 9-1.   Logical Operators for Building Criteria Formulas

These entries do not select any records; they only enable you to use the /Data Query commands to select the records you want. Before moving on to the remaining steps, look at the other types of criteria that are available. In fact, you can set up examples of some of these on the worksheet. You can make multiple-criteria entries in different locations on the worksheet as long as you use them one at a time.

The other type of value criteria is a *comparison formula*. This can be more powerful because it not only performs an exact match, but also identifies records with values less than, greater than, and not equal to an established value. The variety of logical operators that can be used to express these conditions is shown in Table 9-1.

You can still place the field name on the worksheet at the top of the criteria area, although 1-2-3 really does not care what field name you use when you are entering formula criteria. However, it is worth entering the correct field name even though it is not required; this helps document the basis of your selection.

The second entry is the formula. The formula is designed to compare the values in a field against another value. For example, to select those records in which the salary is greater than $25,000 you could enter the formula **+SALARY>25000**. You can either use the field name, as in SALARY, or the cell address of the first field value, as in E2. You can also use a short-cut approach and enter **'>25000** as long as you enter it as a label. You can use column C for this criteria by following these directions:

1. Move the cell pointer to C13, type **Salary**, and move the cell pointer to C14 to finalize.

   Actually, any field name would work equally well. However, Salary is the recommended entry because it clarifies which field you are using in the comparison.

2. Type **+E2>25000** and press ENTER.

   Do not be alarmed that your entry is displayed as the numeral 1 (if you enter **+E2>25000**) or ERR (if you enter **+SALARY>25000**) rather than the formula.

The 1 means it is true—E2 is greater than 25,000. If you are intent upon seeing it displayed as you entered it, you can use /Range Format Text on the cell. However, that is not really necessary.

CRITERIA FOR LABEL DATA There are both similarities and differences between value and label criteria. Exact-match entries work the same way as for value entries. You can place a field name in the criteria area and place the label entry you are looking for immediately beneath it. 1-2-3 is not concerned with differences in either capitalization or alignment between the two entries.

Wildcard characters are a new option with label entries. You can make a partial entry and use the asterisk (*) to tell 1-2-3 that you do not care which characters come at the end of the entry as long as the characters you have specified match. For example, to find all records in which the last name begins with "C," you would enter **Last Name** for the field name in the criteria area and immediately beneath it you would enter **C***. To find all the records where the last name starts with "Camp," you would enter **Camp***. Enter a sample for this type of criteria:

1. Move the cell pointer to A16, type **Last Name**, and move the cell pointer to A17 to finalize.

2. Type **Camp* and press** ENTER.

There is one additional type of label criteria. The last type uses string formulas. Since this is an advanced topic, we will address the use of the criteria you have already entered.

Defining the
Database Location

You must tell 1-2-3 where your data is stored before it can search the database for the information you need. In this case, you must include the field names in the range that you provide, since they are an integral part of identifying the information you want to select.

The command by which you specify the location of the database is /Data Query Input. After you enter this command, you can point to your data range or type the required cell references as a range address. In both cases the field names must be included. You can select the employee database with these steps:

1. Enter **/Data Query Input**.

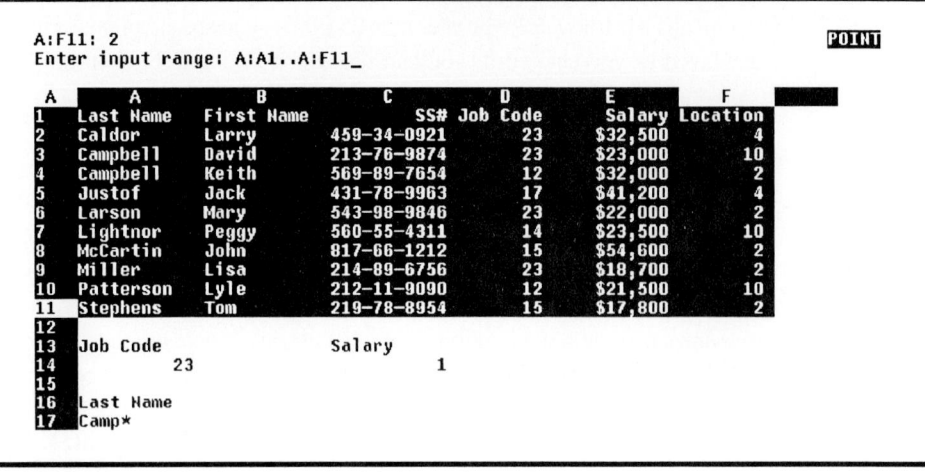

FIGURE 9-9. Selecting the area with /Data Query Input

2. Press HOME to move the cell pointer to A1, type ., press the END key followed by the DOWN ARROW key, and then press the END key followed by the RIGHT ARROW key.

   The database area should be highlighted as shown in Figure 9-9. Notice that the field names are included in this area.

3. Press ENTER to finalize.

   The menu will remain on the screen for additional selections, such as the criteria location and the type of selection you want performed.

Telling 1-2-3 Where You Have Stored the Criteria

1-2-3 uses criteria to determine which records from the database will be used to fill your request. You have already entered several sets of criteria on the worksheet. Now you need to choose one set that 1-2-3 can use to check each record in the database. 1-2-3 will reject records that do not meet these criteria.

To define the location of your criteria on the worksheet, use /Data Query Criteria. Remember that the criteria must already be stored on the worksheet from READY mode before you can use this command effectively. First, use the criteria that searches all of the records to find those that contain a job code of 23:

1. Enter **Criteria**.

2. Move the cell pointer to A13, type ., press the DOWN ARROW key once, and press ENTER.

Now all you need to do is tell 1-2-3 to highlight records that match the criteria.

Finding Matching Records

1-2-3's /Data Query Find command highlights records that match the criteria you have defined. If there are multiple entries that match, the records are highlighted one at a time. 1-2-3 begins at the top of the database, highlighting the first record that matches, and lets you use the UP and DOWN ARROW keys to move to other records that match the criteria. If the number of fields exceeds the width of the screen, you can also use the RIGHT and LEFT ARROW keys to view other fields within a highlighted record. As you highlight a matching record, you can edit the record's contents just as you can from READY mode by pressing F2 (EDIT) when the cell pointer is on the field you want to edit. You cannot move to records that do not match the criteria; the highlighted bar automatically skips over them.

You already completed the preliminary steps for the Find procedure when you entered your criteria on the worksheet and then defined its location as well as the location of the data. Now, whenever you enter **Find**, the criteria that was defined and referenced with Criteria will be used. The data referenced with the input range will be searched for matching records. Since the preliminaries have been completed, only one step is needed to highlight the first record:

1. Enter **Find** to produce the display shown in Figure 9-10.
   Notice that the first record containing a job code of 23 was classified as matching the criteria, and that it is currently highlighted.

2. Press the DOWN ARROW key to move to the next record with a job code of 23, as shown in Figure 9-11.

3. Press the UP ARROW key to move back to the previous record.

4. Press ESC to return to the Data Query menu.

A:A2: [W12] 'Caldor   FIND

	A	B	C	D	E	F
1	Last Name	First Name	SS#	Job Code	Salary	Location
2	Caldor	Larry	459-34-0921	23	$32,500	4
3	Campbell	David	213-76-9874	23	$23,000	10
4	Campbell	Keith	569-89-7654	12	$32,000	2
5	Justof	Jack	431-78-9963	17	$41,200	4
6	Larson	Mary	543-98-9846	23	$22,000	2
7	Lightnor	Peggy	560-55-4311	14	$23,500	10
8	McCartin	John	817-66-1212	15	$54,600	2
9	Miller	Lisa	214-89-6756	23	$18,700	2
10	Patterson	Lyle	212-11-9090	12	$21,500	10
11	Stephens	Tom	219-78-8954	15	$17,800	2
12						

FIGURE 9-10.   Finding the first matching record

Extracting Matching Records

The Find option is useful when you need to answer a question quickly or to take a quick look at someone's record. You can specify the criteria to have these records selectively highlighted for you. The problem with Find is the data does not stay on the screen. Often, when you move to the second record, the first record disappears from

A:A3: [W12] 'Campbell   FIND

	A	B	C	D	E	F
1	Last Name	First Name	SS#	Job Code	Salary	Location
2	Caldor	Larry	459-34-0921	23	$32,500	4
3	Campbell	David	213-76-9874	23	$23,000	10
4	Campbell	Keith	569-89-7654	12	$32,000	2
5	Justof	Jack	431-78-9963	17	$41,200	4
6	Larson	Mary	543-98-9846	23	$22,000	2
7	Lightnor	Peggy	560-55-4311	14	$23,500	10
8	McCartin	John	817-66-1212	15	$54,600	2
9	Miller	Lisa	214-89-6756	23	$18,700	2
10	Patterson	Lyle	212-11-9090	12	$21,500	10
11	Stephens	Tom	219-78-8954	15	$17,800	2
12						
13	Job Code		Salary			
14	23		1			
15						
16	Last Name					
17	Camp*					
18						
19						
20						

123R3ME3.WK3

FIGURE 9-11.   Finding the second matching record

view (the database is probably larger than your small example). The Extract option can solve this; it permits you to selectively copy fields from the database to a new area on the worksheet. As you extract this information, you can also use the fields in any sequence in the output area you are building.

To use Extract, you must complete a preliminary step from READY mode. This step involves constructing an output area in a blank area of the worksheet. You create the output area by placing the field names you wish recorded in this area at its top. Any sequence is acceptable as long as the names exactly match the ones in the top row of the database in terms of spelling, capitalization, and alignment.

SETTING UP AN OUTPUT AREA   You must choose a location for the output of the Extract option and prepare it to receive data. One approach is to leave some blank rows at the bottom of the database and place the output area beneath this area. This way you will not find yourself moving the output area as the database expands. Another approach is to place the output area to the right of the database so you do not need to worry about the amount of expansion that will be required.

Once you have selected the location, enter the names of the fields you want copied from matching records. Remember, you will not need to include every field, and the fields you choose do not need to be in the same sequence as in the database. You may want to copy the field names to the output area from above the database. This strategy eliminates all possibilities of differences in spelling, capitalization, and alignment. Complete this task now for the employee file:

1. Enter **Quit** to return to READY mode.
   You cannot build the output area from the Data Query menu. You must exit it and return after you have completed the needed cell entries.

2. Move the cell pointer to A41, type **First Name**, and move the cell pointer to B41 to finalize the entry.

3. Enter **Last Name** and move the cell pointer to C41.

4. Enter **"Salary** and move the cell pointer to D41 to finalize.

5. Enter **Job Code** and press ENTER.

This is all that is required to set up the output area like the following:

```
A:D41: 'Job Code                                                    READY

   A        A            B            C          D          E          F
  41    First Name   Last Name        Salary  Job Code
```

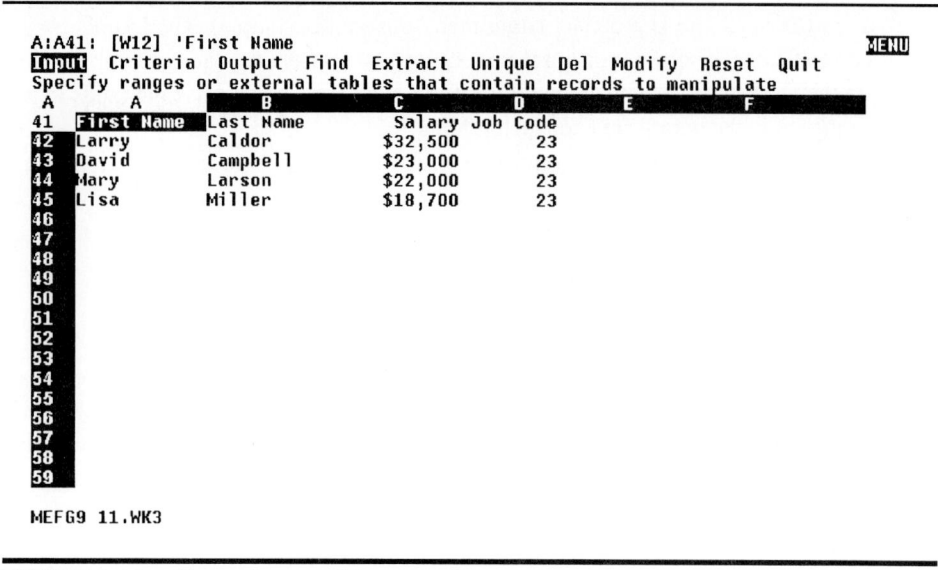

```
A:A41: [W12] 'First Name                                                    MENU
Input Criteria Output Find Extract Unique Del Modify Reset Quit
Specify ranges or external tables that contain records to manipulate
   A        A           B            C         D          E          F
41  First Name  Last Name      Salary Job Code
42  Larry       Caldor        $32,500      23
43  David       Campbell      $23,000      23
44  Mary        Larson        $22,000      23
45  Lisa        Miller        $18,700      23
46
47
48
49
50
51
52
53
54
55
56
57
58
59

MEFG9 11.WK3
```

FIGURE 9-12.   Extracting matching records

You are ready to take a look at the remaining menu commands required to complete the extract operation. The first command you need is /Data Query Output, which tells 1-2-3 where the output area is located. You can define the row containing the field names you just entered as the output area (row 41 in the current example). Be aware that 1-2-3 will use all rows from this point to the end of the worksheet to write matching records. You can also select the row containing the field names and an appropriate number of rows beneath it. If you choose the latter approach, the output area you choose must be large enough to contain all of the selected records or you will get an error message rather than the results you are looking for.

PERFORMING THE EXTRACT   Once you have completed the preliminaries, you have done all the difficult work. Now all that is required is selecting Extract from the menu. Try it now with your data:

1. Enter **/Data Query Output**. Move the cell pointer to A41, type ., press END, and then press the RIGHT ARROW key. Press ENTER.

2. Enter **Extract**.
      Move the cell pointer so you can view the entries that have been copied to the extract area. They should look like the ones in Figure 9-12.

```
A:A41: [W12] 'First Name                                          MENU
Input  Criteria  Output  Find  Extract  Unique  Del  Modify  Reset  Quit
Copy to output range all records that match criteria
  A       A            B            C        D        E         F
 41  First Name  Last Name       Salary  Job Code
 42  Larry       Caldor          $32,500      23
 43  Keith       Campbell        $32,000      12
 44  Jack        Justof          $41,200      17
 45  John        McCartin        $54,600      15
 46
 47
 48
 49
 50
 51
 52
 53
 54
 55
 56
 57
 58
 59
 60
MEFG9 11.WK3
```

FIGURE 9-13.   Extracting records with a salary greater than $25,000

3. Enter **Quit**.

Trying a Few More Examples

You entered more than one set of criteria as you looked at some of the ways that criteria could be entered in worksheet cells. You can try an extract with the remaining two sets of criteria, using just a few easy steps. First use the criteria that selects records in which the salary is greater than $25,000, and then use the criteria that selects records in which the last name begins with "Camp." Follow these steps:

1. Enter **/Data Query Criteria**, type **C13.C14**, and press ENTER.
   This is where you stored the criteria to select records by the salary field. You can use the same input area and the same output area as your previous request without making another entry.

2. Enter **Extract** to write the records shown in Figure 9-13 to the extract area. Enter **Quit** and move the cell pointer to A41 to view the list.

3. Enter **/Data Query Criteria**, type **A16.A17**, and press ENTER.

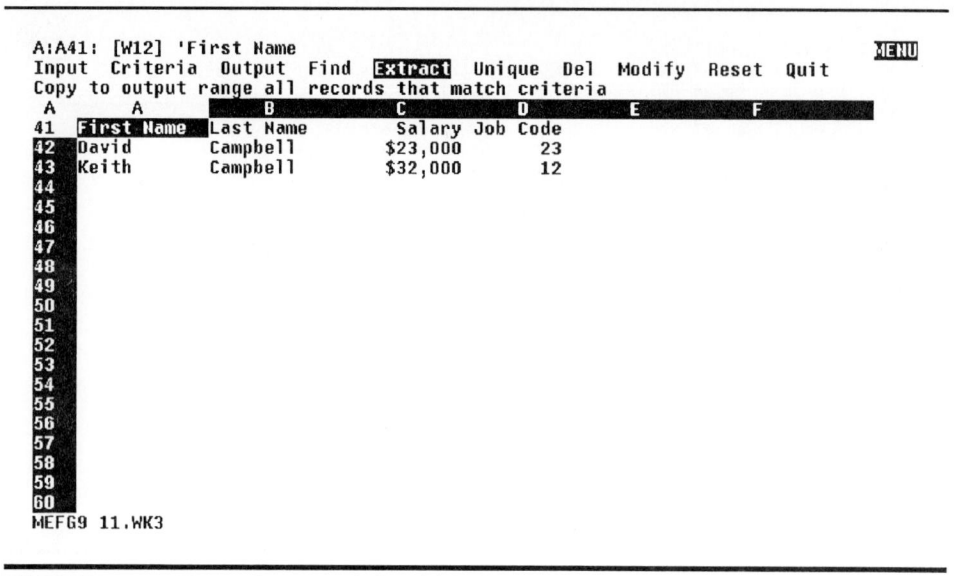

```
A:A41: [W12] 'First Name                                              MENU
Input  Criteria  Output  Find  Extract  Unique  Del  Modify  Reset  Quit
Copy to output range all records that match criteria
   A        A           B              C        D         E        F
41 First Name   Last Name         Salary Job Code
42 David        Campbell          $23,000      23
43 Keith        Campbell          $32,000      12
44
45
46
47
48
49
50
51
52
53
54
55
56
57
58
59
60
MEFG9 11.WK3
```

FIGURE 9-14.   Extracting records in which the last name begins with "Camp"

This will use the criteria you entered earlier, which selects last names that begin with "Camp." If you choose to point to this criteria rather than typing the range address, press ESC first.

4. Enter **Extract** to produce the data shown in Figure 9-14.

5. Enter **Quit** to return to READY mode, and move the cell pointer to A41 to view the data.

SPECIAL FEATURES

Now that you have completed the basics of data management, you may want to take a look at some of 1-2-3's data-management features. These include a short-cut approach to executing a query operation, referencing the database with a range name, and using powerful database statistical functions.

A:A17: [W12] 'L*   READY

A	A	B	C	D	E	F
1	Last Name	First Name	SS#	Job Code	Salary	Location
2	Caldor	Larry	459-34-0921	23	$32,500	4
3	Campbell	David	213-76-9874	23	$23,000	10
4	Campbell	Keith	569-89-7654	12	$32,000	2
5	Justof	Jack	431-78-9963	17	$41,200	4
6	Larson	Mary	543-98-9846	23	$22,000	2
7	Lightnor	Peggy	560-55-4311	14	$23,500	10
8	McCartin	John	817-66-1212	15	$54,600	2
9	Miller	Lisa	214-89-6756	23	$18,700	2
10	Patterson	Lyle	212-11-9090	12	$21,500	10
11	Stephens	Tom	219-78-8954	15	$17,800	2
12						
13	Job Code		Salary			
14	23		1			
15						
16	Last Name					
17	L*					
18						
19						
20						

FIGURE 9-15.   Changing criteria to select records in which last names begin with "L"

Using a Short-Cut Approach

There is a short-cut approach to reexecuting a /Data Query command. However, it requires that certain conditions be met. The first condition is that the database be exactly the same size and at the same location as when the last query was executed. The second condition is that you must be certain that your criteria are the same size and shape. They can have new values or check new fields, just as long as the location of these criteria is the same. The third condition is that if you are performing extract operations, the output area must be the same size and shape. The fourth and last condition is that you must be performing the same data query operation; if you performed an extract last time, you must perform an extract this time. If all of these conditions are met, you can reexecute the last query operation by pressing F7 (QUERY).

Try this by carrying out the following directions to update the criteria:

1. Move the cell pointer to A17 and type **L***, as shown in Figure 9-15.

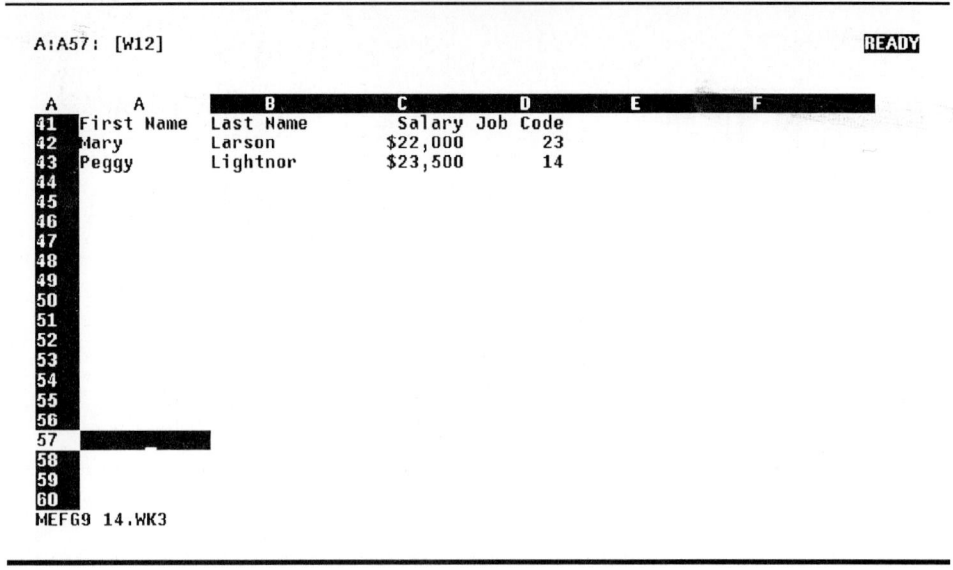

A:A57: [W12]   READY

A A	B	C	D	E	F
41 First Name	Last Name	Salary	Job Code		
42 Mary	Larson	$22,000	23		
43 Peggy	Lightnor	$23,500	14		
44					
45					
46					
47					
48					
49					
50					
51					
52					
53					
54					
55					
56					
57					
58					
59					
60					

MEFG9 14.WK3

FIGURE 9-16.   Extracting records with last names that begin with "L"

2. Press F7 (QUERY) and then press PGDN twice to produce the display shown in Figure 9-16.

   This is a handy feature if you need to perform multiple query operations. You only need to use the menu the first time; then you can type new values in the criteria area if you wish and press F7 to have 1-2-3 use the new criteria.

Naming the Database

Using a name rather than a range address to refer to the database can provide flexibility. 1-2-3 permits you to assign a name to a range of cells. If you expand this range of cells by inserting blank rows or columns in the middle, the range referenced by the name will be expanded automatically. If a built-in function or formula references the name rather than an address, the built-in function is automatically adjusted for any change in the range.

You can assign names with the /Range Name Create command you first used in Chapter 3. Try it now with the employee database:

1. Enter **/Range Name Create**, type **EMPLOYEE**, and press ENTER.

2. Press ESC, press HOME, type ., and press END followed by DOWN, END followed by RIGHT, and ENTER.

You will now be able to reference the range A1..F11 by the name EMPLOYEE. If you insert blank rows or columns in the middle of your database and make entries, the reference to EMPLOYEE will make these available immediately.

USING THE DATABASE STATISTICAL FUNCTIONS

The database statistical functions are a special category of built-in functions designed to work exclusively in the data-management environment. Like other built-in functions, they are prerecorded formulas that can perform calculations for you with a minimum of work on your part. Unlike other built-in functions, they operate on a database and require that you establish criteria to designate the records that are to be included in the calculations they perform.

All of the database statistical functions except @DQUERY have the same format for their arguments, as follows:

@DFUNCTION(*database, field in database,criteria location*)

The first argument in all of these functions is the location of the database. The range that you use to identify the location should include the field names as well as the data. The second argument, the field, is the field name in quotes that you want used in the calculations. You can also select the field by providing its *offset,* which is the number of columns it is away from the left side of the database table. The offset is always one less than what you would expect with the ordinary way of counting. The first column has an offset of zero, and each column to the right has its offset incremented by one. The last argument is the location of the criteria. The criteria are defined in the same way as the ones you used with Extract and Find in the Data Query menu. You must record them on the worksheet before you include their location in the function. Putting a few of these to work will clarify exactly how you work with them.

Using @DAVG

The @DAVG function allows you to compute the average for a field in a selected group of database records. You can use this function to determine the average salary for employees with a job code of 23. You can use the criteria you entered for the data query operations. Just follow these steps:

1. Move the cell pointer to A21 and type **Average Salary for Job Code 23:**. Move the cell pointer to D21 to finalize your entry.

2. Type **@DAVG(EMPLOYEE,"Salary",A13.A14)** and press ENTER.

Notice that the database reference uses the range name, EMPLOYEE, which includes the field names, all records, and all fields. The field name is Salary; this field contains the values you want to average. The criteria location uses the entries in A13 and A14 to select the records whose salary entries will be included in the average. The results are shown here:

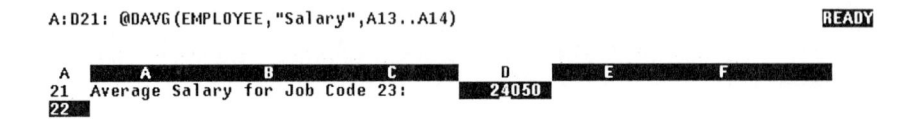

Using @DSUM

The @DSUM function follows the same pattern as the @DAVG function. If you want to total one of the fields in the database for all records with a job code of 23, you can use it without entering criteria again. Follow these steps:

1. Move the cell pointer to A22, type **Total Salaries for Job Code 23:**, and move the cell pointer to D22 to finalize your entry.

2. Type **@DSUM(EMPLOYEE,"Salary",A13.A14)** and press ENTER. The results of this calculation are as follows:

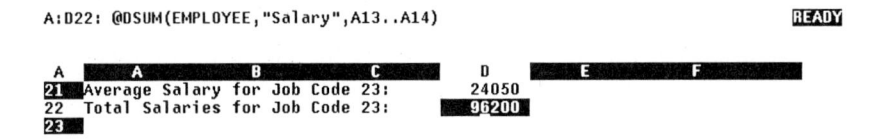

Using @DCOUNT

The @DCOUNT function is used to selectively count the number of non-blank entries in records that match your criteria. It follows the same pattern as the other database functions and operates on the entries in the column specified by the field name. You can use this function to count the number of employees with a job code of 23. Follow these steps to enter the function:

1. Move the cell pointer to A23, type **Number of Employees in Job Code 23:**, and then move the cell pointer to D23 to finalize your entry.

2. Type **@DCOUNT(EMPLOYEE,"Job Code",A13.A14)** and press ENTER. The results of this calculation are as follows:

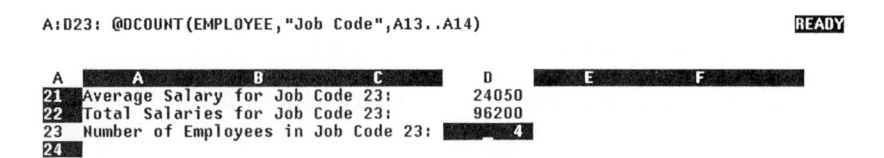

```
A:D23: @DCOUNT(EMPLOYEE,"Job Code",A13..A14)                    READY

A        A            B            C         D        E          F
21  Average Salary for Job Code 23:          24050
22  Total Salaries for Job Code 23:          96200
23  Number of Employees in Job Code 23:            4
24
```

The count operation is performed on the Job Code field. This will effectively give you a count of the records with a job code of 23. If the Job Code field is blank, the records will not be selected as matching the criteria for job code 23, making the count match exactly with the number of records that match.

Using @DMIN

The @DMIN function searches for the minimum value in the column specified. Only records that match your criteria are eligible for this minimum comparison. This provides a convenient way to determine the lowest salary paid to an individual in location 2, or the lowest salary paid to someone with a job code of 23. This time, you will change the criteria and then enter the formula to determine the lowest salary in location 2:

1. Move the cell pointer to A16 and type **Location**.

2. Move the cell pointer to A17 and type **2**.

3. Move the cell pointer to A24 and type **Minimum Salary for Location 2:**. Then move the cell pointer to D24 to finalize your entry.

4. Type **@DMIN(EMPLOYEE,"Salary",A16.A17)** and press ENTER to produce these results:

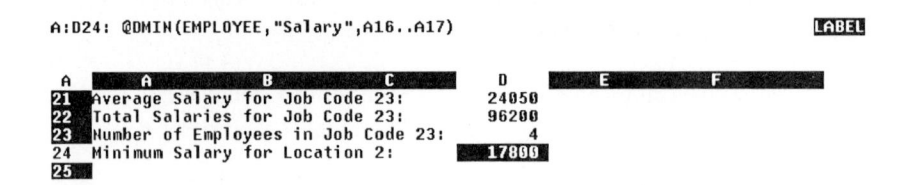

```
A:D24: @DMIN(EMPLOYEE,"Salary",A16..A17)                              LABEL

A        A            B            C         D        E          F
21  Average Salary for Job Code 23:        24050
22  Total Salaries for Job Code 23:        96200
23  Number of Employees in Job Code 23:        4
24  Minimum Salary for Location 2:         17800
25
```

REVIEW EXERCISE

You can try out your new skills with 1-2-3's data-management features by creating the database shown in Figure 9-17. You will use the data shown in this figure to guide your entries. Follow these steps to format the entries and try out the sort, query, and database statistical operations:

1. Clear screen and format range C2..C6 as currency with 2 places. Format E2..E6 as Date 1. Widen the column width for column E to 14. *Hint:* Use the /Range Format and /Worksheet Column commands.

2. Make the entries shown in Figure 9-17. You can enter the dates by typing the entries in the figure and letting 1-2-3 convert the entries to serial date numbers.

3. Establish criteria for the vendor ABC in A18..A19, and use the Find option to highlight records in which the vendor is ABC. *Hint:* Enter the criteria on the worksheet first by placing "Vendor" in A18 and ABC in A19. Next, use /Data Query, specify the input as A1..E6, specify the criteria as A18..A19, and choose Find from the menu. Choose Quit to exit from the Query menu.

4. Sort the database by part number within vendor (that is, the vendor will be the primary key and the part number will be the secondary key. *Hint:* Use /Data Sort Data-Range to define A2..E6 as the range. Choose Primary-Key and select D2. Use ascending order. Choose Secondary-Key and select B2. Select Go to sort the data.

5. Use the database statistical functions to compute the average cost of purchases from ABC and Royston. You can use the locations shown in Figure 9-18 for the additional criteria B18..B19 or choose another location. Labels were added

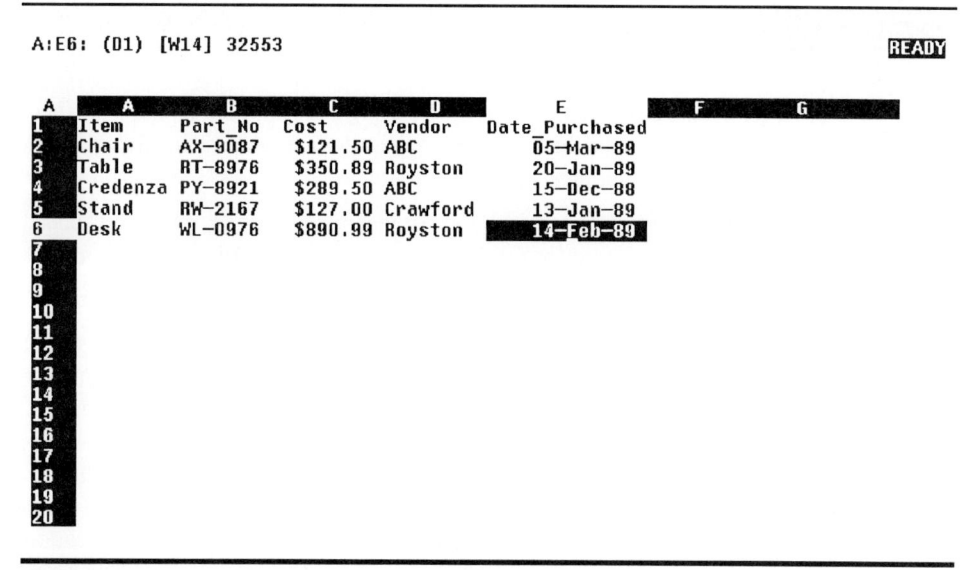

FIGURE 9-17.   A database to record purchases

in A11..A12 to describe the computations placed in E11..E12. The cells containing the formulas were formatted as currency with two decimal places.

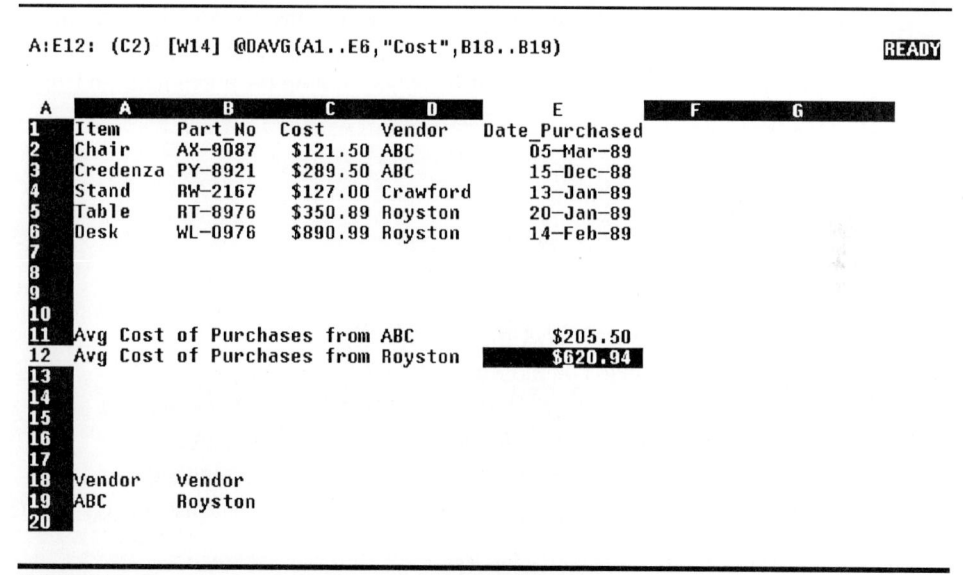

FIGURE 9-18.   A sorted database with @DAVG functions

REVIEW

- You can create a database with 1-2-3 by using a tabular area on the worksheet. Your first step should be comparing your storage needs with the available memory in your computer.

- Field names are placed one per cell across the top row of the table. Rows beneath the field names are used for the data in the database records.

- You can resequence the records in a 1-2-3 database with the /Data Sort command. The records are specified as the data range for the sort. Primary, secondary, and extra keys can be selected to control the sequence of the records. Once your specifications are defined, the Go option will sort the records.

- 1-2-3's /Data Query command allows you to specify conditions for selecting the records in the database. You can highlight matching records with the Find option or copy them out to a new area on the worksheet if you set up an output area and then use Extract. Only records that match your criteria or specifications are highlighted or copied.

- You must enter your specifications for records that you want 1-2-3 to work with when using the /Data Query commands. You can use exact-match criteria for label or value data. With label data you can use the * and ? wildcard characters to eliminate the need for entering an exact match. Logical formulas are another option. They allows you to describe acceptable entries for fields containing either label or value data.

- The database statistical functions are @ functions that work with the records in a 1-2-3 database and the criteria you have established to select records of interest. You can obtain a total, average, minimum, maximum, and other statistical computations on a selected group of your records with these functions.

Commands, Keys, and Functions

/DQC	/Data Query Criteria defines for 1-2-3 the specification you have entered on the worksheet
/DQE	/Data Query Extract writes copies of records meeting the specifications in the criteria area to the output area
/DQF	/Data Query Find highlights records matching the criteria
/DQI	/Data Query Input defines for 1-2-3 the database records for the query operation

/DQO	/Data Query Output defines the output area for a data query extract operation
/DSD	/Data Sort Data-Range defines the records to be sorted
/DSE	/Data Sort Extra-Key allows you to define as many as 253 additional sort keys
/DSG	/Data Sort Go executes the sort operation
/DSP	/Data Sort Primary-Key defines for 1-2-3 the primary sort sequence
/DSS	/Data Sort Secondary-Key defines for 1-2-3 the secondary sort sequence
@DAVG	Computes an average of a specified field in the records matching your specifications
@DCOUNT	Computes a count of the non-blank entries in a specified field for the records matching your specifications
@DMIN	Determines the minimum value in a specified field in the records matching your specifications
@DSUM	Computes a sum of a specified field in the records matching your specifications
F7 (QUERY)	Repeats the most recent query operation

10

USING ADVANCED FUNCTIONS

Adding Logic to Your Calculations
Turning Label Entries into Serial Date and Time Values
Manipulating Labels
Review Exercise
Review

You have already learned how to use some of the basic built-in functions that 1-2-3 has to offer. These provide an excellent way of performing everyday tasks, such as totaling a column of numbers and rounding the results of a calculation to two decimal places. In addition to these built-in functions, 1-2-3 offers a number of more sophisticated and specialized functions that can help you handle complex business needs. This chapter will show you how to use a number of these functions.

In Chapter 7, the functions were organized by category. In this chapter, although a particular category of functions is addressed, the focus is on the integration of the functions with an application example. In many instances, several functions are combined to resolve a specific application example. This is especially important for the more complex functions; new users need to understand how to apply them to the business problems they face.

ADDING LOGIC TO YOUR CALCULATIONS

According to 1-2-3's rules, you can place only a single entry in a worksheet cell. Therefore, only one formula can be stored in each cell. This can be limiting when it comes to the many exception conditions and special rules that apply to the calculations performed every day in a business setting. For example, when you give a customer a purchase discount, you may not want to multiply the purchase amount by a fixed percentage. The amount of the discount might depend on the size of the sale, whether the sale is cash or credit, and the amount purchased by the customer on an annual basis.

Regular 1-2-3 formulas can calculate a discount based on a fixed percentage, but they cannot cope with all these conditions. Fortunately, 1-2-3 has a number of built-in functions that can step in to fill this need. These functions let you add *logic processing* to your calculations and let you make your calculations on the basis of any conditions you wish to apply.

Creating a Salary Projection Model

In this first example you will create a salary model that lets you estimate the various components of salary expense. After projecting a salary increase with a percentage growth factor, you can also estimate other salary expenses, such as your FICA contribution as an employer and the cost of the benefits you are supplying for different personnel classifications. You can easily adapt the model to meet other conditions and situations—either by adding new expense categories (patterning calculations after the examples provided) or by altering the formulas for the existing calculations. Since this model is dependent on the @IF function, it is a good idea to review how the @IF function works before starting the model.

USING @IF   The @IF function lets you test a condition to determine the appropriate value for a cell. @IF is one of the most powerful built-in functions because it frees you from the limitation of deciding on one formula for a cell. You can set up two different values for a cell and determine which one to use, based on other conditions in the worksheet. You can create two or more discount levels, payroll deductions, commission structures—any calculation that involves more than one alternative.

The @IF function uses three arguments in this sequence:

@IF(*condition to test,value if true,value if false*)

The first argument is the condition to be tested. It can be any logical expression that can be evaluated as true or false. Examples are A1>9, C2=G10, and A2+B6>C3*H12. The expression returns a value of true only if the specified condition is met. For example, in the first expression, true will be returned only if A1 is greater than 9. If this expression evaluates as true, the cell will take on the value specified in the second argument of the function.

The second argument for the @IF function, the value the cell will use if the condition is true, can take several forms. It can be an actual numeric value, a formula that needs to be calculated, or another @IF statement to be checked if multiple levels of conditions must be met before an action is determined. This argument can be a string value as long as it is enclosed in double quotation marks.

The third argument is the value the cell containing the @IF statement will assume if the condition in the function is false. All the conditions mentioned above for *value if true* also apply here.

1-2-3 also allows strings to be used with the logical IF condition. For example, you could create an entry such as @IF(A10="Chicago",F2,G2). If A10 contains Chicago, the cell containing this entry will take on the value of F2. If A10 contains anything else, the cell containing the function will be equal to G2.

MAKING THE ENTRIES IN THE SALARY MODEL   You only need to enter data for a few employees; then a simple copy operation and additional data entry allow you to expand this model to include as many employees as you want. The model you will be building is shown in Figure 10-1. You can follow these instructions for your entries:

1. Enter /**Worksheet Erase Yes** to clear the worksheet. A second Yes will be needed if the file has not been saved.

2. Enter /**Worksheet Column Set-Width**, type **13**, and press ENTER.
   This will widen column A to accept the name entries.

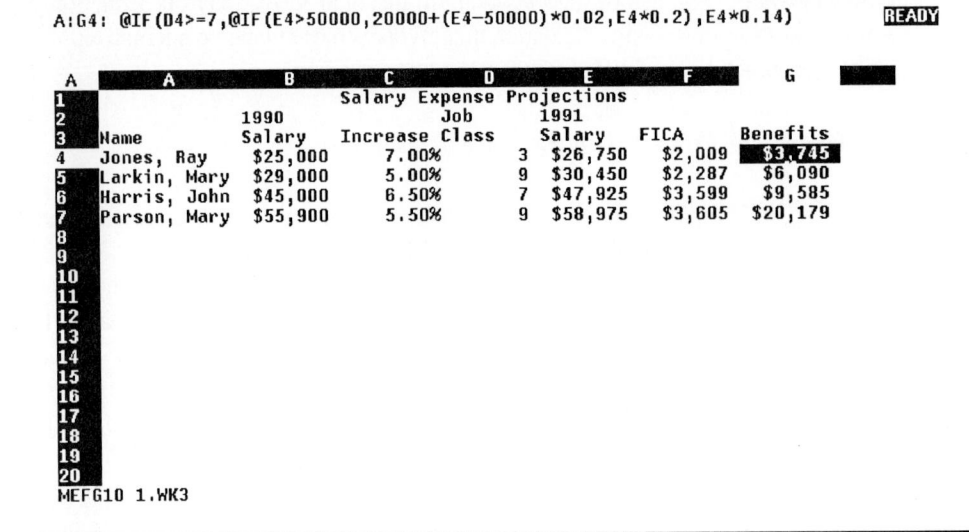

A:G4: @IF(D4>=7,@IF(E4>50000,20000+(E4-50000)*0.02,E4*0.2),E4*0.14)   READY

A	B	C	D	E	F	G
		Salary Expense Projections				
	1990		Job	1991		
Name	Salary	Increase	Class	Salary	FICA	Benefits
Jones, Ray	$25,000	7.00%	3	$26,750	$2,009	$3,745
Larkin, Mary	$29,000	5.00%	9	$30,450	$2,287	$6,090
Harris, John	$45,000	6.50%	7	$47,925	$3,599	$9,585
Parson, Mary	$55,900	5.50%	9	$58,975	$3,605	$20,179

MEFG10 1.WK3

FIGURE 10-1.   Completed salary model

3. Make these entries on the worksheet:

A3: Name
A4: Jones, Ray
A5: Larkin, Mary
A6: Harris, John
A7: Parson, Mary
B2: '1990
B3: Salary
B4: 25000
B5: 29000
B6: 45000
B7: 55900
C1: Salary Expense Projections
C3: Increase
C4: .07
C5: .05
C6: .065
C7: .055
D2: Job
D3: Class

D4: 3
D5: 9
D6: 7
D7: 9
E2: '1991
E3: Salary
F3: FICA
G3: Benefits

4. Move the cell pointer to C4, enter **/Range Format Percent**, press ENTER, move the cell pointer to C7, and press ENTER again.

5. Move the cell pointer to D4, enter **/Range Format Fixed**, type **0**, and press ENTER. Move the cell pointer to D7 and press ENTER again.

6. Enter **/Worksheet Global Format Currency**, type **0**, and press ENTER to produce the display shown in Figure 10-2.

   All the remaining entries in this model must be calculated. Standard formulas will not work; various factors affect the computed results, and a regular formula cannot deal with these exceptions. After analyzing each of the required conditions, enter an @IF statement that captures the essence of how you would perform these calculations manually under all circumstances.

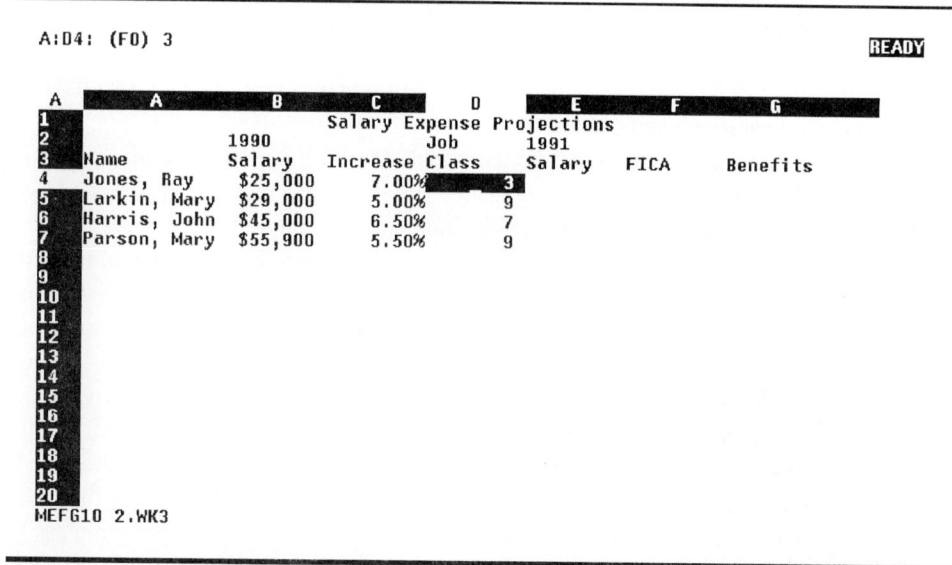

FIGURE 10-2.   Salary model before adding formulas

FICA is not computed by the same method for all wage levels. It is calculated at 7.51% unless the individual earns more than the established cap amount for FICA. If earnings exceed the cap amount, you will only pay an employer's FICA contribution on the cap amount. You can record this with the @IF function if the condition to be tested is recorded in the function and the two different methods for performing the FICA computation are recorded as the values for true and false conditions.

Follow these directions for making your entries:

7. Move the cell pointer to E4, type **+B4∗(1+C4)**, and press ENTER.

    This formula calculates the projected salary for 1991, based on the increase percentage.

8. Enter **/Copy**, press ENTER, move the cell pointer to E5, type ., move to E7, and press ENTER.

9. Move the cell pointer to F4 and type

    @IF(E4<48000,E4∗.0751,48000∗.0751)

    Then press ENTER.

    This function checks whether the salary is less than $48,000, and if it is, multiplies the salary by 7.51%. If it is not less than $48,000, the rate will be applied to $48,000, the amount chosen for this example as the arbitrary limit for FICA payments. You now have the rules for two different ways to perform the FICA calculation, depending on the amount of the salary.

10. Enter **/Copy**, press ENTER, move the cell pointer to F5, type ., move the cell pointer to F7, and press ENTER.

    The results will look like the worksheet in Figure 10-3. Naturally, if you had more records on your worksheet, you could copy this formula further down the worksheet than cell F7 before finalizing the copy.

    In this example, the @IF function provided just the solution you needed. The next problem for the salary expense model involves calculating the cost of benefits. You can also solve this calculation with @IF, but because of its complexity you will require multiple levels of @IF statements.

    The hypothetical model you are creating requires an answer to two different conditions concerning benefits. According to the company's specifications, the first question concerns the job class of the employee. Executives have a job class greater than or equal to 7, and their benefits are calculated by different rules than those for nonmanagement employees. Even when the job class is

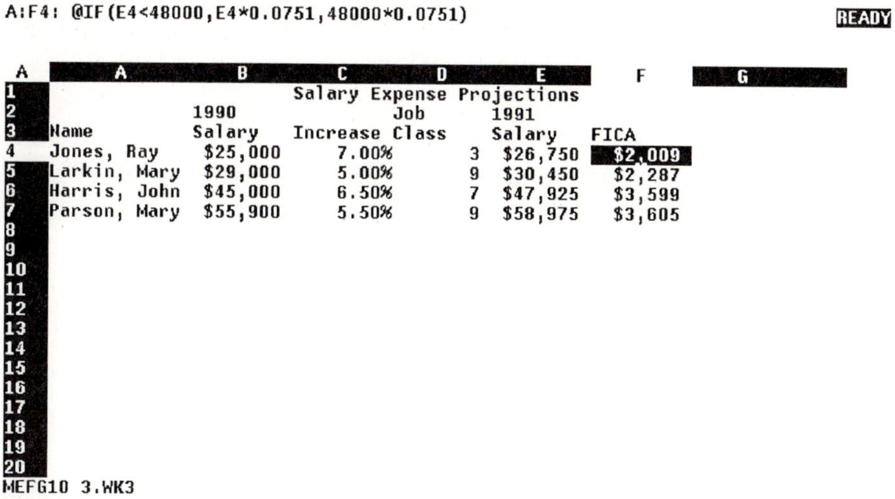

```
A:F4:  @IF(E4<48000,E4*0.0751,48000*0.0751)                    READY
```

```
  A         A          B         C        D        E        F          G
1                          Salary Expense Projections
2                    1990               Job       1991
3          Name      Salary    Increase Class     Salary   FICA
4          Jones, Ray  $25,000   7.00%      3     $26,750   $2,009
5          Larkin, Mary $29,000  5.00%      9     $30,450   $2,287
6          Harris, John $45,000  6.50%      7     $47,925   $3,599
7          Parson, Mary $55,900  5.50%      9     $58,975   $3,605
8
9
10
11
12
13
14
15
16
17
18
19
20
MEFG10 3.WK3
```

FIGURE 10-3.   Salary model with @IF formula for FICA calculation

decided, however, there is still the salary factor, which can affect the estimated benefit amount.

In the current example, benefits for executive employees are calculated as 20% of the executive's salary unless the executive makes more than $50,000, which classifies the person as senior executive management. In this case, the computation is $20,000 plus 2% of the excess over $50,000. For nonexecutive employees, the calculation is a little different; it is always computed as 14% of the projected salary.

All this may sound a little complex at first; but if you stop and think about it for a minute, you realize that you have no difficulty making these computations by hand. The trick is to record all these conditions in a worksheet cell:

11. Move the cell pointer to G4 and type

    @IF(D4>=7,@IF(E4>50000,20000+(E4-50000)*.02,E4*.2),E4*.14)

This formula examines all of the necessary conditions. The condition in the first @IF checks if the job class is greater than or equal to 7. If this condition is true, the second @IF becomes the value of this cell and must be evaluated. The second @IF condition checks the salary to see if it is greater than $50,000 and, depending on the result of this test, computes the benefit expense to be either $20,000 plus 2% of the excess over $50,000 or 20% of the salary. Another condition occurs when the job class is less than 7. In this case, the benefit expense is 14% of the salary.

Multiple levels of conditions are frequently referred to as *nested @IF statements*. They are a little complicated but are worth your time for the flexibility they offer.

12. Enter **/Copy**, press ENTER, and move the cell pointer to G5. Type **.**, move the cell pointer to G7, and press ENTER.

Your salary model is now complete and should match the model shown earlier in Figure 10-1. If you have other salary expenses, you can alter the model to include them and then save it.

13. Enter **/File Save**, type **SALARY**, and press ENTER.

If you do not wish to save this model, you can clear it by entering **/Worksheet Erase Yes**.

Calculating the Net Purchase Price

The next model you will build also needs the flexibility of logic incorporated in worksheet cells. Since calculating a net purchase price involves calculating varying purchase discounts and applying shipping costs, many conditions must be considered. In such a case, the @IF function would be a cumbersome solution; many levels of nesting would be required to solve the problem. There are several additional functions within 1-2-3 that offer a wide range of options. The two that you will examine now are the @VLOOKUP function, which builds a table of codes and associated values on the worksheet for reference, and the @INDEX function (available in Release 2 or higher), which also builds a table of values but uses a different approach for finding the correct entry. You will first examine each of the functions and enter the basics of the model. Then you will apply the information you have obtained on the inner workings of the two functions to complete the model.

USING @VLOOKUP   The @VLOOKUP function allows you to search a table you have entered on the worksheet for an appropriate value to use in your worksheet. When you create the table that @VLOOKUP will be referencing, you must store the codes that will be looked up in a column on the worksheet. The values that you wish to correspond to each of these codes will be stored in the columns to the right of the

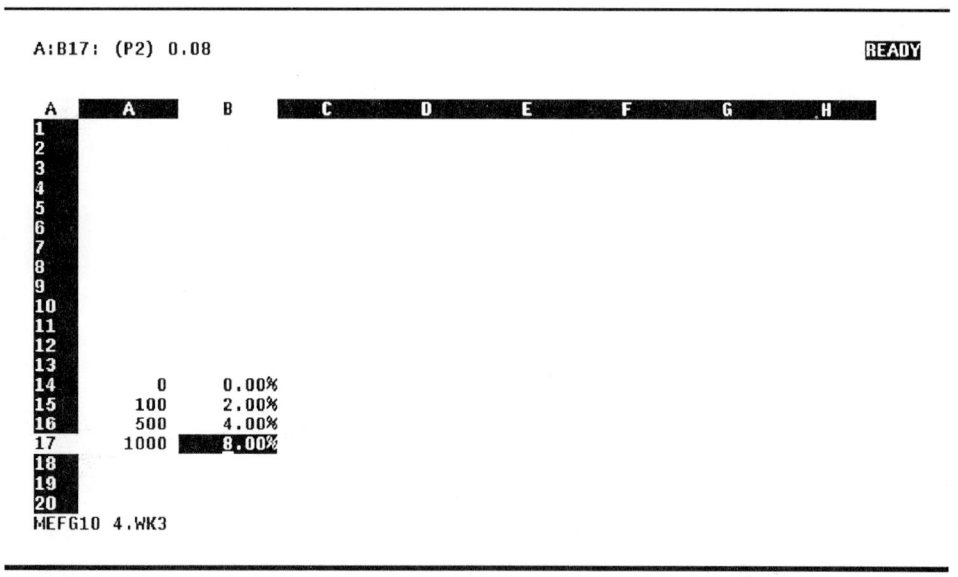

A:B17: (P2) 0.08   READY

	A	B	C	D	E	F	G	H
1								
2								
3								
4								
5								
6								
7								
8								
9								
10								
11								
12								
13								
14	0	0.00%						
15	100	2.00%						
16	500	4.00%						
17	1000	8.00%						
18								
19								
20								

MEFG10 4.WK3

FIGURE 10-4.   Entering the lookup table's codes and values

codes. Figure 10-4 shows a table of codes in column A and the associated return values
for each code in column B.

You must understand the way that @VLOOKUP works before you enter the codes
and associated values in the table. The @VLOOKUP function expects three arguments
in this sequence:

@VLOOKUP(*code to be looked up,table location,offset*)

The first argument is *code to be looked up*—the entry in your worksheet, which will
be compared against the column of table values. When numeric values are used, 1-2-3
looks for the largest value in the table that is not larger than the code you have supplied.
The codes should be in ascending order. If the first code in the column is larger than
the code you supply, you will get an ERR condition. When string values are used, the
search is always for an exact match. This means that the case of the entries is important;
for example, CLEVELAND would not match Cleveland.

Since a table must be at least two partial columns on the worksheet, the second
argument, *table location,* will always be a range reference to at least two partial
columns on the worksheet. This reference must include the table codes as well as the
return values.

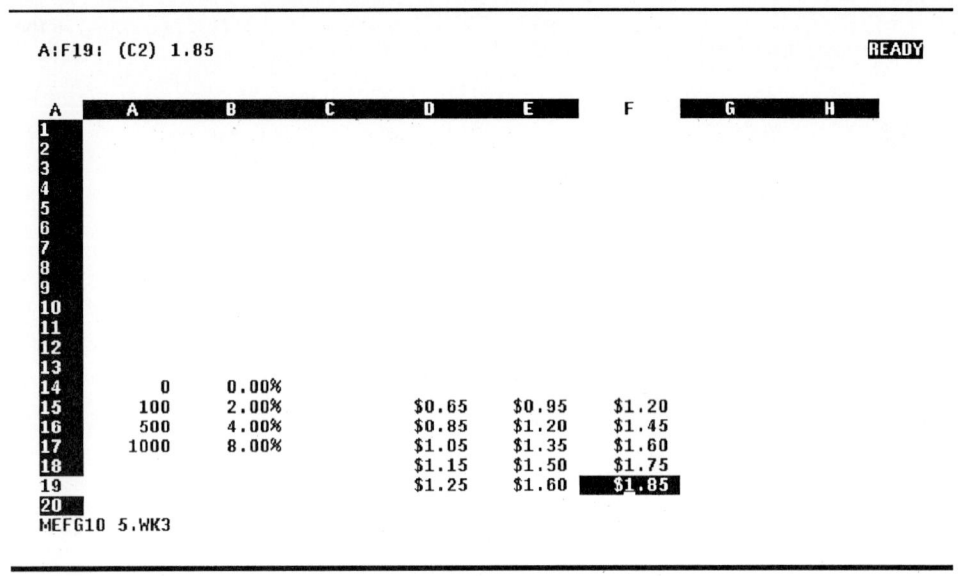

A:F19: (C2) 1.85   READY

	A	B	C	D	E	F	G	H
14	0	0.00%						
15	100	2.00%		$0.65	$0.95	$1.20		
16	500	4.00%		$0.85	$1.20	$1.45		
17	1000	8.00%		$1.05	$1.35	$1.60		
18				$1.15	$1.50	$1.75		
19				$1.25	$1.60	$1.85		

MEFG10 5.WK3

FIGURE 10-5.   Entering the index table values

The third argument, *offset,* tells 1-2-3 how many columns to the right of the code column it should use when obtaining the return values. This function allows you to create tables that are more than two columns wide.

USING @INDEX   The @INDEX function also requires you to enter a table on the worksheet, but you do not enter values for matching. Every entry in the table is designed to be a return value. Which of these return values to use is determined by the row and column number you specify. You make your specifications known to 1-2-3 through this function:

@INDEX(*table location,column number,row number*)

The *table location* argument is the address of all the codes in the table. For example, the table location of the entries shown in the lower middle of Figure 10-5 is D15..F19. The *column number* argument is the number of the offset column, which contains the value you wish to use. The leftmost column in the table has a column offset of 0, with the column offset number increasing by 1 for each column as you move to the right. The *row number* argument is the number of the row you wish to use. The same numbering scheme is used: the upper row is row 0, and each row further down in the table is incremented by 1.

@INDEX is ideal for the type of application in which your data values can be used to access the correct value in the table. Computing shipping costs is a good example, if the cost is determined by weight and distance and values can be assigned for each. You will soon put the @INDEX function to work computing shipping costs.

CREATING THE PURCHASE MODEL   To compute a net purchase price, you need to know the basic components: the item purchased, a purchase price and quantity, a purchase discount amount, the shipping weight of the item, and the customer's shipping zone. All items weigh between 1 and 5 pounds and all customers are assigned a shipping zone from 1 to 3, depending on their distance from a regional warehouse.

Purchase discounts are computed on the extension of the item's cost—the number of units multiplied by the unit price. Shipping costs are added after purchase discounts are calculated. The discount rate applied increases with the size of the purchase. For a purchase of $100, a 2% discount is given; for $500, a discount of 4%; and for $1000 or more, an 8% discount.

You can construct the @VLOOKUP table with these entries:

1. Move the cell pointer to A14, type **0**, and press ENTER.

   Normally, you would use a location further away from the data to allow for expansion, but you will find it easier for now to view the entries while building your formulas.

2. Enter these table codes and their associated values:

   A15: 100
   A16: 500
   A17: 1000
   B14: 0
   B15: .02
   B16: .04
   B17: .08

   This completes the table entries for the @VLOOKUP table. You still need to enter the values for shipping costs, but this time you will use an index table. For purchase discounts, the index table is not an option because of the wide gap between entries. You would need an index table with 1000 entries, even though only three discounts needed to be stored. All these extra entries would be due to the @INDEX function's method of finding a return value based on the row and column location. Continue with the entries for the shipping table:

3. Move the cell pointer to D15, type **.65**, and press ENTER.

This is the value that will be used for the shipping cost of a one-pound item shipped to zone 1.

4. Complete the entries as follows:

D16: .85
D17: 1.05
D18: 1.15
D19: 1.25
E15: .95
E16: 1.20
E17: 1.35
E18: 1.50
E19: 1.60
F15: 1.20
F16: 1.45
F17: 1.60
F18: 1.75
F19: 1.85

Once you have entered the tables, enter the data in the main section of your model.

5. Move the cell pointer to A1 and begin making these entries:

A1: Item
A2: Number
A4: X5401
A5: YT45
A6: CF514
A7: RT908
A8: R4312
B1: Units
B2: Purchd
B4: 3
B5: 7
B6: 12
B7: 5
B8: 10
C1: Unit
C2: Cost
C4: 25.50
C5: 38

```
C6: 47.50
C7: 150
C8: 12.50
D2: Weight
D4: 1
D5: 3
D6: 4
D7: 1
D8: 2
E2: Zone
E4: 2
E5: 0
E6: 1
E7: 2
E8: 1
F2: Discount
G1: Shipping
G2: Cost
H1: Net
H2: Price
```

6. Move the cell pointer to C4, enter **/Range Format Currency**, press ENTER, move the cell pointer to C8, and press ENTER again.

7. Move the cell pointer to F4, enter **/Range Format Currency**, press ENTER, move the cell pointer to H8, and press ENTER.

8. Move the cell pointer to D15, enter **/Range Format Currency**, press ENTER, move the cell pointer to F19, and press ENTER.

9. Move the cell pointer to B14, enter **/Range Format Percent**, press ENTER, move the cell pointer to B17, and press ENTER.

   This completes the data entry. The model is ready for the formulas and should now look like Figure 10-6. Naturally, other fields like customer name and shipping address still need to be added. However, these are not important for your purposes at this time.

   The formula for the purchase discount will use the @VLOOKUP function. The first argument will be the purchase amount, which must be computed by multiplying the units times the cost per unit. This value will be looked up in the table stored in A14..B17. 1-2-3 does not attempt to find an equal match. Instead, it searches for the largest value in column A that is not greater than the purchase amount. It then returns the value in column B from the same row.

A:B14: (P2) 0   **READY**

A	A	B	C	D	E	F	G	H
1	Item	Units	Unit				Shipping	Net
2	Number	Purchd	Cost	Weight	Zone	Discount	Cost	Price
3								
4	X5401	3	$25.50	1	2			
5	YT45	7	$38.00	3	0			
6	CF514	12	$47.50	4	1			
7	RT908	5	$150.00	1	2			
8	R4312	10	$12.50	2	1			
9								
10								
11								
12								
13								
14	0	0.00%						
15	100	2.00%		$0.65	$0.95	$1.20		
16	500	4.00%		$0.85	$1.20	$1.45		
17	1000	8.00%		$1.05	$1.35	$1.60		
18				$1.15	$1.50	$1.75		
19				$1.25	$1.60	$1.85		
20								

MEFG10 6.WK3

FIGURE 10-6.   Purchase model without formulas

The table location will be specified as the second argument. The third argument instructs 1-2-3 which column in the table to use for the return value. In the current example, this number is 1, indicating that 1-2-3 should use the values in column B, since they are one column to the right of the table codes.

10. Move the cell pointer to F4 and type **@VLOOKUP(**.

11. Move the cell pointer to B4, type *, move the cell pointer to C4, and type a comma.

12. Move the cell pointer to A14 and press F4 (ABS).
    This will place dollar signs in front of the row and column portion of the address, making it an absolute reference to the beginning of the table. You need an absolute reference, since you want the table reference to remain the same regardless of where you copy the formula.

13. Type a period and move the cell pointer to B17.

14. Type **,1)*(B4*C4)** and press ENTER.

A:F4: (C2) @VLOOKUP(B4*C4,$A$14..$B$17,1)*(B4*C4)   READY

A	A	B	C	D	E	F	G	H
1	Item	Units	Unit				Shipping	Net
2	Number	Purchd	Cost	Weight	Zone	Discount	Cost	Price
3								
4	X5401	3	$25.50	1	2	$0.00		
5	YT45	7	$38.00	3	0	$5.32		
6	CF514	12	$47.50	4	1	$22.80		
7	RT908	5	$150.00	1	2	$30.00		
8	R4312	10	$12.50	2	1	$2.50		
9								
10								
11								
12								
13								
14	0	0.00%						
15	100	2.00%		$0.65	$0.95	$1.20		
16	500	4.00%		$0.85	$1.20	$1.45		
17	1000	8.00%		$1.05	$1.35	$1.60		
18				$1.15	$1.50	$1.75		
19				$1.25	$1.60	$1.85		
20								

MEFG10 7.WK3

FIGURE 10-7.   Computing purchase discounts

This formula will look up a discount percentage appropriate for the purchase amount and multiply it by the amount of the purchase. In this case the discount is 0, since the purchase amount is $76.50.

15. Enter /**Copy**, press ENTER, and move the cell pointer to F5. Type ., move the cell pointer to F8, and press ENTER.

    The purchase discount has been computed for all entries on the model, as shown in Figure 10-7.

16. Move the cell pointer to G4 and type **@INDEX(**.

17. Move the cell pointer to D15 and press F4 (ABS).

    This will make the table reference absolute, which will allow the formula to be copied.

18. Type . and move the cell pointer to F19.

19. Type ,, move the cell pointer to E4, type another ,, and move the cell pointer to D4.

In this step you have specified E4, the zone, as the column to use for the return value and D4, the weight, as the row.

20. Type)∗, move the cell pointer to B4, and press ENTER.

    This completes the formula, which will find the cost of shipping one item from the index table and then multiply it by the number of items.

21. Enter /**Copy**, press ENTER, move the cell pointer to G5, type ., move the cell pointer to G8, and press ENTER.

22. Move the cell pointer to H4, type +**B4∗C4-F4+G4**, and press ENTER.

    This formula calculates the net purchase price by extending units times unit cost, subtracting the discount, and adding the shipping cost. Once it is copied to the other rows, your model is complete.

23. Enter /**Copy**, press ENTER, move the cell pointer to H5, type ., move the cell pointer to H8, and press ENTER.

    Figure 10-8 shows the resulting calculations in column H.

24. Enter /**Worksheet Erase Yes Yes** to clear memory, or use /File Save to create a copy of the model on disk before clearing memory.

A:H4: (C2) +B4∗C4-F4+G4   `READY`

A	A	B	C	D	E	F	G	H
1	Item	Units	Unit				Shipping	Net
2	Number	Purchd	Cost	Weight	Zone	Discount	Cost	Price
3								
4	X5401	3	$25.50	1	2	$0.00	$4.35	$80.85
5	YT45	7	$38.00	3	0	$5.32	$8.05	$268.73
6	CF514	12	$47.50	4	1	$22.80	$19.20	$566.40
7	RT908	5	$150.00	1	2	$30.00	$7.25	$727.25
8	R4312	10	$12.50	2	1	$2.50	$13.50	$136.00
9								
10								
11								
12								
13								
14	0	0.00%						
15	100	2.00%		$0.65	$0.95	$1.20		
16	500	4.00%		$0.85	$1.20	$1.45		
17	1000	8.00%		$1.05	$1.35	$1.60		
18				$1.15	$1.50	$1.75		
19				$1.25	$1.60	$1.85		
20								

MEFG10 8.WK3

FIGURE 10-8.   Completed purchase model

Checking Entries for Errors

Data-entry errors can cause serious problems in worksheet accuracy. There are no facilities for validity checks; you make entries directly into each worksheet cell. However, a group of logical functions can be used in combination with the @IF function to alert you to potential errors in certain fields. These functions can check a cell to see if it contains a number or a string value. They can also check for NA, which indicates that an entry is not available, or ERR, which indicates an error condition in a formula.

These are the functions and the checks they perform:

@ISERR(*value*)	Checks for a value of ERR in a cell
@ISNA(*value*)	Checks for a value of NA in a cell
@ISNUMBER(*value*)	Checks for a numeric value in a cell
@ISSTRING(*value*)	Checks for a string value in a cell

In all four functions, the *value* argument is normally a cell address that references a cell you want checked. In the first function, a 1 representing true is returned if the cell has a value of ERR. In the second, 1 is returned if the cell has a value of NA. The function @ISNUMBER returns 1 if the cell contains a number. @ISSTRING returns 1 if the cell contains a string.

Although these functions can be used alone, they are most frequently combined with the @IF statement, as in

@IF(@ISNUMBER(A6),"A6 is numeric","A6 is not numeric")

This @IF statement checks to see if @ISNUMBER(A6) returns 1 for true or 0 for false. If the result of this test is true, "A6 is numeric" will be placed in the cell containing the function. If the condition tests false because A6 does not contain a numeric value, the phrase "A6 is not numeric" will be placed in the cell that contains this function.

You will build two short models to look at the effects of two of these functions. You will see from these examples that it is easy to enter an error-checking formula once and copy it down the column. You can visually scan data for errors, but it is much easier to scan a special column in which messages flag error conditions.

CHECKING FOR MISSING DATA   The first example you will enter works with the @NA function. This function serves as a place keeper for missing data. The model records the order number, order date, quantity, and price, and computes a total. If the price is missing, NA is inserted in its place. The order total is computed by multiplying quantity by price, and if the value for a price is NA, the total for that item is NA. To prevent this, insert a message that is more noticeable. Complete these steps to create the model:

1. Move the cell pointer to A1, enter /**Worksheet Column Set-Width**, type **13**, and press ENTER.

2. Make these entries on the worksheet:
   A2: Order Number
   A3: 12760
   A4: 12781
   A5: 12976
   B2: Date
   B3: '01-Oct-89
   B4: '01-Oct-89
   B5: '02-Oct-89
   C2: Quantity
   C3: 3
   C4: 4
   C5: 12
   D2: Price
   D3: 3.5
   D4: @NA
   D5: 12.25
   E2: Total

   Notice that the dates in column D were entered as labels. This is not the usual approach to take with dates, since the @DATE function will create a serial date number that can be used in calculations. However, label entries were used because there is no need to use them in calculations. Later in this chapter, you will look at the features of another built-in function that can convert these labels to serial date numbers.

3. Move the cell pointer to D3, enter /**Range Format Currency**, and press ENTER. Move the cell pointer to E5 and press ENTER.

   Now that you have completed the preliminary entries, it is time to enter a formula in E3 that will test the price for the first entry for a value of NA. If a true condition is returned, the cell should take on the value NA; if a false condition is returned, the cell will have the value that is computed by multiplying price times quantity. Follow these steps to have the error-checking formula placed in column E:

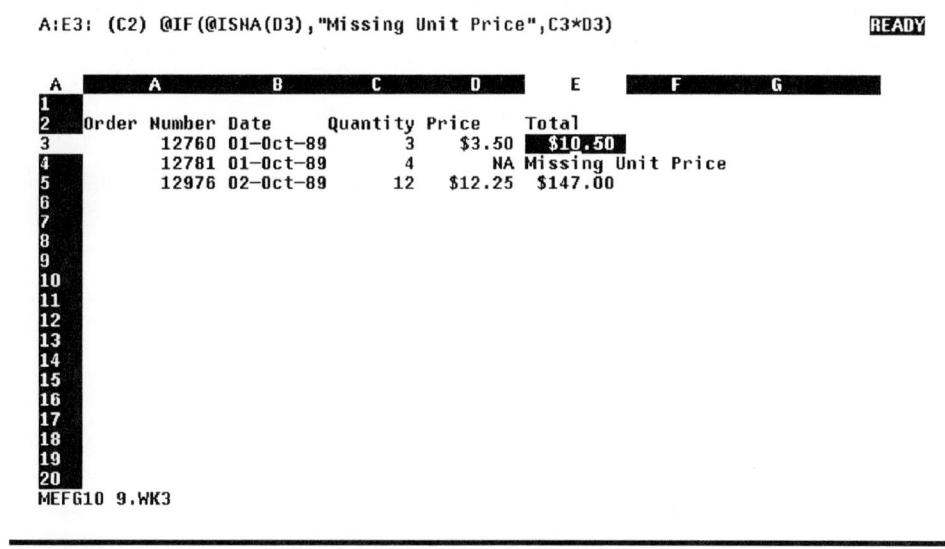

```
A:E3: (C2) @IF(@ISNA(D3),"Missing Unit Price",C3*D3)              READY

A        A          B          C       D        E          F        G
1
2  Order Number Date       Quantity Price    Total
3          12760 01-Oct-89         3    $3.50  $10.50
4          12781 01-Oct-89         4       NA Missing Unit Price
5          12976 02-Oct-89        12   $12.25 $147.00
6
7
8
9
10
11
12
13
14
15
16
17
18
19
20
MEFG10 9.WK3
```

FIGURE 10-9.   Order data with @ISNA to locate missing information

4. Move the cell pointer to E3 and enter

    @IF(@ISNA(D3),"Missing Unit Price",C3*D3)

    Then press ENTER.

5. Enter /**Copy** and press ENTER. Move the cell pointer to E4, type ., move the
    cell pointer to E5, and press ENTER.

    The worksheet looks like the one in Figure 10-9. Notice how the message
    "Missing Unit Price" flags the record that has no price entry. This is not
    necessary when you have only three records, but when you have hundreds, it
    could save you a significant amount of time.

6. Enter /**Worksheet Erase Yes Yes** to clear memory.

    Remember to first use /File Save if you want to retain a copy of this example.

CHECKING FOR NON-NUMERIC DATA   You may have an application in
which you want to require your computer operators to enter numeric values in certain
key fields. Although there is no direct way to lock out unacceptable input, you can
display an error message if non-numeric data is entered. Use a combination of
@ISNUMBER and @IF to handle this task for you. First, make a few entries in an
address file. Then add a formula that checks the first ZIP code field to see if it contains

a number, since the application is designed to accept a five-digit ZIP code for individuals living in the U.S. If the field does not contain a numeric entry, a message will be printed.

Follow these directions to make the entries in the file:

1. Move the cell pointer to A1, enter **/Worksheet Column Set-Width**, type **15**, and press ENTER.

2. Move the cell pointer to B1, enter **/Worksheet Column Set-Width**, type **20**, and press ENTER.

3. Make these entries in the worksheet cells shown:

    A3: Name
    A4: John Smith
    A5: Jill Brown
    A6: Harry Olson
    A7: Mary Greene
    B3: Address
    B4: '1215 East 11th St.
    B5: '41 S. Main St.
    B6: '1111 G St. NW
    B7: '42 Stone Ct.
    C1: Client Listing
    C3: City
    C4: Towson
    C5: Akron
    C6: Austin
    C7: Berea
    D3: State
    D4: New York
    D5: Ohio
    D6: Ohio
    D7: Michigan
    E3: Zip Code
    E4: 98765
    E5: 45321
    E6: r567w1
    E7: 44040
    F3: Zip Code Errors

Notice that a single quotation mark was used at the front of the address entries to ensure that the entries were treated as labels. The only task remaining is to enter the error-checking formula:

4. Move the cell pointer to F4, type

   @IF(@ISNUMBER(E4)," ","ERROR - Zip Code Must be numeric")

   and press ENTER.

   It is possible that in your own models you might want to require label entries for the ZIP code to accommodate the ten-digit ZIP codes or entries for the northeast states that start with a zero, but for this model you do not want to allow labels. The formula bases the result of the @IF test on whether or not the referenced cell contains a number. If it does, a blank (enclosed with the set of quotation marks) is placed in the cell. If the entry is not numeric, an error message is placed at that location.

5. Enter **/Copy**, press ENTER, move the cell pointer to F5, type **.**, move the cell pointer to F7, and press ENTER again.

   The worksheet looks like the one in Figure 10-10.

6. Enter **/Worksheet Erase Yes** to clear memory.

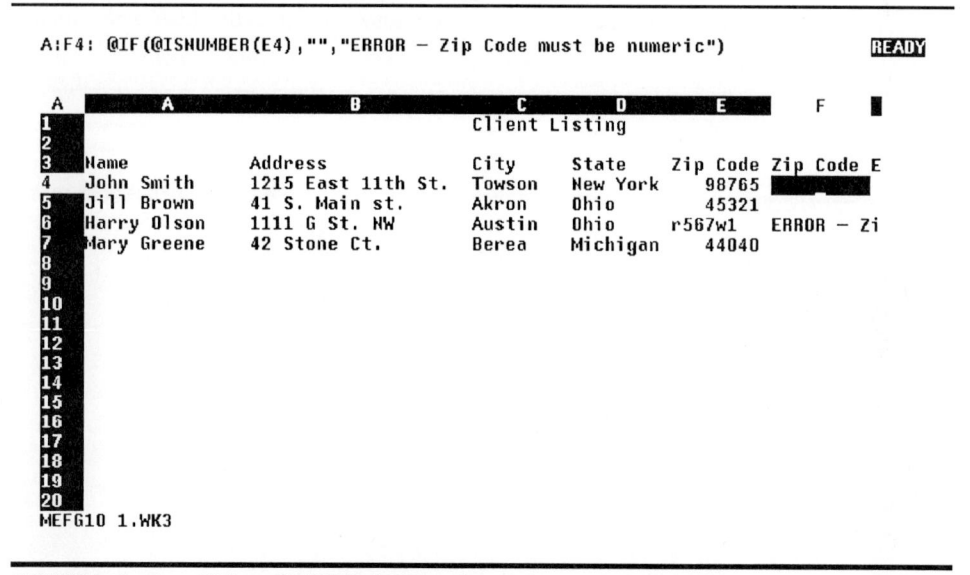

FIGURE 10-10.   Using @ISNUMBER to locate incorrect ZIP codes

TURNING LABEL ENTRIES INTO SERIAL DATE AND TIME VALUES

Both date and time entries can require extra effort, especially when you have an entire column of date entries to make. The @DATE and @TIME functions that you used in Chapter 7 each require three arguments. In addition, many users find the sequence of the date arguments to be different from their normal entry sequence, since the year, month, and day sequence is not normally used. Two functions allow you to enter either the date or time as a label in one of the date or time display formats and then have another function convert the entry to a valid date or time serial number. @TIMEVALUE changes a label entry in a valid time format to a time serial number, and @DATEVALUE converts a label that looks like a date to a valid date serial number.

Using Dates from Label Entries to Compute Rental Fees

Figure 10-11 shows a few records that were entered with the dates stored as labels in columns C and D. As the entries in column E show, the fact that all the calculations are erroneously displaying as zeros suggests a problem with the calculation of the amount due. The cause of this problem is the manner in which the dates were entered.

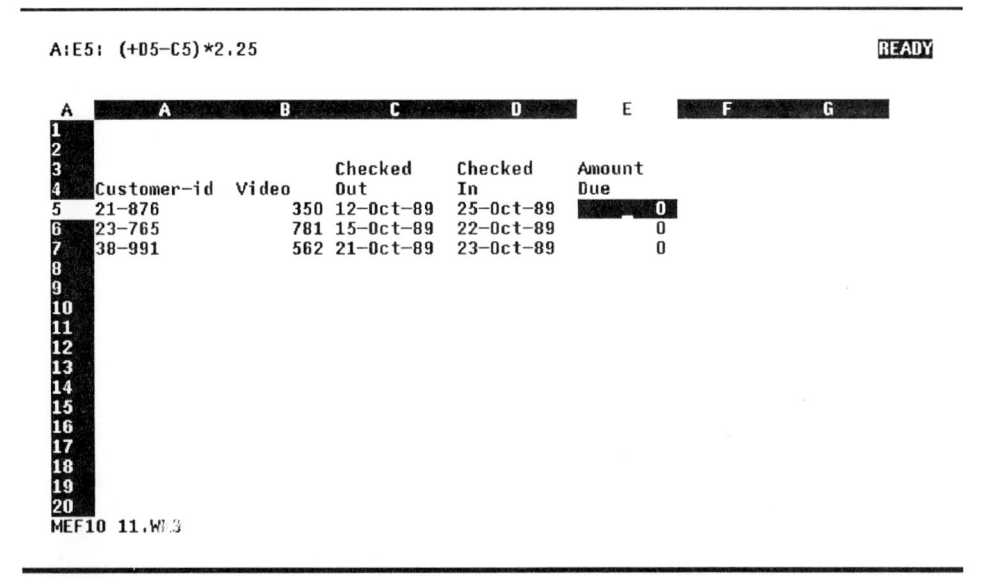

FIGURE 10-11.   Dates stores as labels

Since the formula for amount due subtracts the date in D5 from the date in C5, 1-2-3 is expecting values in these cells. A serial date number would meet this requirement, but label entries do not unless the cells were formatted with 1-2-3's new Other Automatic format before your entries were made. These dates were entered as labels and the Automatic format was not in effect at the time of entry, which means that they cannot be used in arithmetic calculations.

You can correct this problem with a few modifications to the formula, but let's first enter the basic data that the model will use:

1. Move the cell pointer to column A, enter **/Worksheet Column Set-Width**, type **13**, and press ENTER. Use this same procedure to widen column C and column D to 11.

2. Make these entries:

   A4: Customer-id
   A5: '21-876
   A6: '23-765
   A7: '38-991
   B4: Video
   B5: 350
   B6: 781
   B7: 562
   C3: Checked
   C4: Out
   C5: '12-Oct-89
   C6: '15-Oct-89
   C7: '21-Oct-89
   D3: Checked
   D4: In
   D5: '25-Oct-89
   D6: '22-Oct-89
   D7: '23-Oct-89
   E3: Amount
   E4: Due

   The formula for the amount due in Figure 10-11 was entered as **(D5-C5)∗2.25**. That figure already showed you that a different solution is required.

3. Move the cell pointer to E5, type

   (@DATEVALUE(D5)-@DATEVALUE(C5))∗2.25

   and press ENTER.

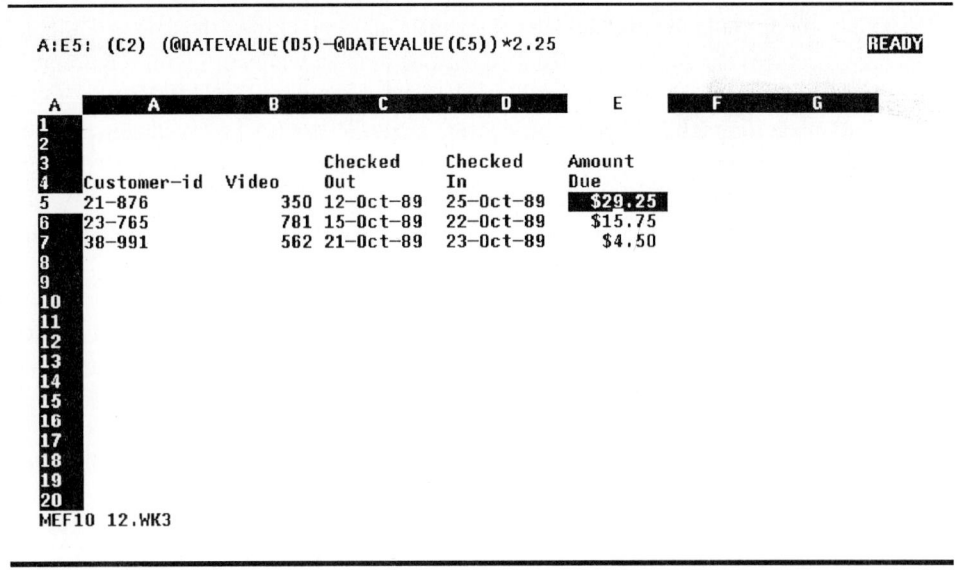

A:E5: (C2) (@DATEVALUE(D5)-@DATEVALUE(C5))*2.25   READY

	A	B	C	D	E	F	G
1							
2							
3			Checked	Checked	Amount		
4	Customer-id	Video	Out	In	Due		
5	21-876		350 12-Oct-89	25-Oct-89	$29.25		
6	23-765		781 15-Oct-89	22-Oct-89	$15.75		
7	38-991		562 21-Oct-89	23-Oct-89	$4.50		
8							
9							
10							
11							
12							
13							
14							
15							
16							
17							
18							
19							
20							

MEF10 12.WK3

FIGURE 10-12.   Using @DATEVALUE for dates in labels found in formulas

4. Enter /**Range Format Currency** and press ENTER twice.

    This format will be copied when you copy the formula to other cells in the range.

5. Enter /**Copy** and press ENTER. Move the cell pointer to E6, type ., move the cell pointer to E7, and press ENTER.

    Now that the label entries are converted to actual date serial numbers, they can be used in formulas without causing an error, as the worksheet in Figure 10-12 shows.

6. Use /**Worksheet Erase Yes Yes** to clear memory or save the worksheet with the /**File Save** command.

Turning Time Labels into Hours For Billing Clients

The @TIMEVALUE function converts labels that look like time entries into numeric time representation, which is suitable for use in any calculation. The format of the function is @TIMEVALUE(*time string*). You can use it to convert time entries that are labels to numbers that can be involved in calculations. This conversion is one way to avoid the need for the three arguments that @TIME requires. It can also correct mistakes in data entry in which times were accidentally entered as labels. To try this function with a short example, follow these steps:

1. Move the cell pointer to column C, enter **/Worksheet Column Set-Width**, type **13**, and press ENTER.

2. Move the cell pointer to E5, enter **/Range Format Date Time**, type **4**, move the cell pointer to E7, and press ENTER.

3. Make these worksheet entries:

   A3: Job
   A4: Number
   A5: 1
   A6: 2
   A7: 3
   B3: Time
   B4: In
   B5: '8:05 AM
   B6: '8:10 AM
   B7: '8:30 AM
   C4: Repair
   C5: Tires
   C6: Brakes
   C7: Steering
   D3: Time
   D4: Out
   D5: '9:17 AM
   D6: '10:34 AM
   D7: '1:18 PM
   E3: Elapsed
   E4: Time

   It is possible to enter these times without the AM or PM designation for the entries before 1:00 P.M. It is also possible to enter these designations in lowercase, as in **9:05 am** or **10:16 pm**.

4. Move the cell pointer to E5, type

   @TIMEVALUE(D5)-@TIMEVALUE(B5)

   and press ENTER.

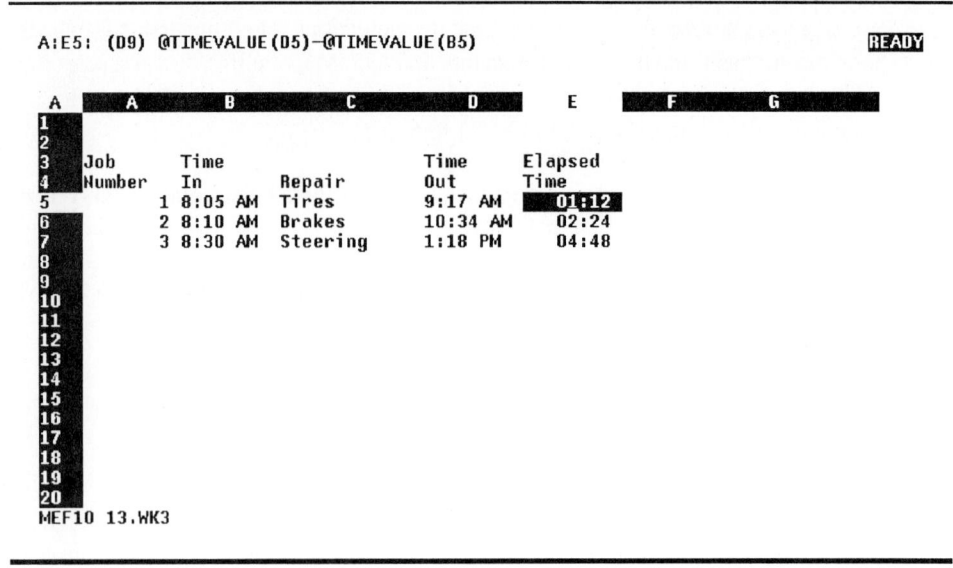

A:E5: (D9) @TIMEVALUE(D5)-@TIMEVALUE(B5)   READY

A	A	B	C	D	E	F	G
1							
2							
3	Job	Time		Time	Elapsed		
4	Number	In	Repair	Out	Time		
5	1	8:05 AM	Tires	9:17 AM	01:12		
6	2	8:10 AM	Brakes	10:34 AM	02:24		
7	3	8:30 AM	Steering	1:18 PM	04:48		
8							
9							
10							
11							
12							
13							
14							
15							
16							
17							
18							
19							
20							

MEF10 13.WK3

FIGURE 10-13.   Using @TIMEVALUE for times in labels found in formulas

5. Enter **/Copy**, press ENTER, move the cell pointer to E5, type ., move the cell pointer to E7, and press ENTER.

   The final results look like the worksheet in Figure 10-13.

6. Enter **/Worksheet Erase Yes Yes** to clear memory.

MANIPULATING LABELS

1-2-3 has an entire category of built-in functions that only operate on label or string entries. The string functions provide a variety of character-manipulation formulas that give you flexibility in arranging your text entries. They are extremely useful for correcting data-entry errors and for restructuring worksheet data for a new application.

The unique feature of the string functions is that many of them work with individual characters in the string. When 1-2-3 works with individual characters, its numbering system is different from yours. 1-2-3 considers the first character in the string to be in position 0 of the string. Since 1-2-3 will not adjust its numbering scheme, in order to work 1-2-3's numbering method you will have to adjust your method of counting.

Replacing Incorrect Characters

You can replace characters with a text string without having to retype the entire string. You can use this feature to change slash symbols to dashes or to manipulate a part number into a warehouse location. The function is extremely flexible; you can replace multiple characters with one character, or you can replace one character with multiple characters.

The function you will use to make these replacements is @REPLACE. It uses four different arguments:

@REPLACE(*original string,start location,# characters,new string*)

The first argument, *original string* is a reference to the cell containing the original string. The second argument is the position number in the original string where you want to begin the replacement. Remember that 1-2-3 calculates the position number, beginning with position 0 for the first character in the string.

The third argument is the number of characters to remove from the string. This argument offers considerable flexibility. You can specify 0 characters to have the new string inserted in the original string. When the number of characters is greater than the length of the new string, the string that is returned by this function will be shorter than the original. When the number of characters is the same as the number of characters in the original string, the entire string will be replaced.

The last argument is a series of characters enclosed in quotation marks, or a reference to a cell that contains a string. When *new string* is empty (that is, " ") @REPLACE will simply delete the characters from the original string.

You will work here with an example that will alter a series of part numbers on the worksheet. The existing part numbers have three sections, each separated by slashes. @REPLACE will change the first slash to a dash and will delete the middle section of the entry. Follow these steps to take a look at @REPLACE in action:

1. Make the following entries:

    A1: Part Number
    A2: AB/567/8907
    A3: VB/907/6754
    A4: JK/675/8752
    A5: LK/999/5544
    C1: Altered Part Number

    Your worksheet should now look like this:

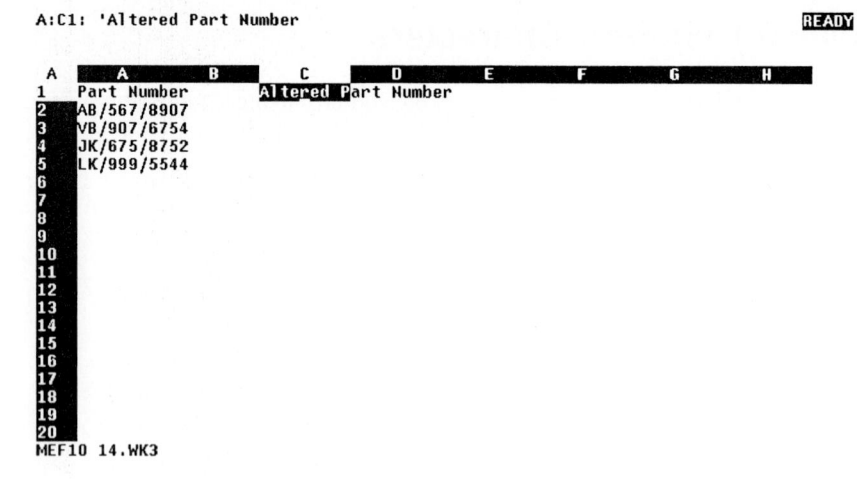

```
A:C1:  'Altered Part Number                                              READY

A      A         B         C         D         E         F         G         H
1   Part Number         Altered Part Number
2   AB/567/8907
3   VB/907/6754
4   JK/675/8752
5   LK/999/5544
6
7
8
9
10
11
12
13
14
15
16
17
18
19
20
MEF10 14.WK3
```

2. Move the cell pointer to C2, type **@REPLACE(A2,2,5,"-")**, and press ENTER.

   The character in position two is a slash, since position two refers to the third character in the string. The next argument tells the function to remove the / symbol and the next four characters from the string. This removes both slashes and the three characters between them. These five characters are replaced with a single dash.

3. Enter **/Copy**, press ENTER, move the cell pointer to C3, type **.**, move the cell pointer to C5, and press ENTER.

   The final results are as follows:

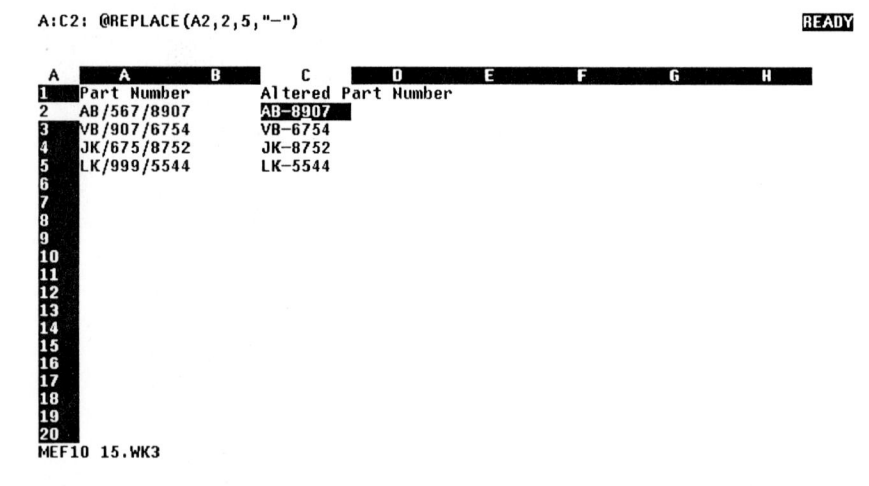

```
A:C2:  @REPLACE(A2,2,5,"-")                                              READY

A      A         B         C         D         E         F         G         H
1   Part Number         Altered Part Number
2   AB/567/8907         AB-8907
3   VB/907/6754         VB-6754
4   JK/675/8752         JK-8752
5   LK/999/5544         LK-5544
6
7
8
9
10
11
12
13
14
15
16
17
18
19
20
MEF10 15.WK3
```

4. Enter /**Worksheet Erase Yes Yes** to clear memory.

Using Part of a Name Entry

Some string functions allow you to dissect a string entry and restructure the original entry into a string that looks quite different. This can be useful for altering names entered as "John Smith" to "Smith, John," or just "Smith" if you are only interested in the last name. Unfortunately, unless you have worked with string functions for a while, you may have to experiment a bit to come up with the correct solution. Creating the correct formula is difficult partly because meaningful activities with these functions frequently require the use of a number of functions in one formula.

You will create a string formula that extracts the last name from an entry that looks like "John Smith." This will require three built-in functions: @MID, @FIND, and @LENGTH. First you need to take a look at these functions and the arguments you will use with them.

USING @FIND   Use the @FIND function whenever you wish to locate the position of a string within a string. You can use it to locate the position of a blank space between the first and last name, for example. When you combine the position of the blank space with the result of other functions, you can switch a name that is sequenced as *first name/last name* to a name that is sequenced as *last name, first name.*

The @FIND function has three arguments and looks like this:

@FIND(*search string,string to be searched,starting location*)

The search string is a character sequence or a reference to a cell that contains a character sequence to be found in the second argument. As with the other string functions, when the characters are entered directly into the function, they must be enclosed in quotation marks. The length of the search string must be at least one less than the length of the string you plan to search. The function is case-sensitive when it completes the search, so you must differentiate carefully between uppercase and lowercase. One option is to store the string directly within the function. The string can also be stored in a cell, and the cell address where it is stored can be used as a function argument. The maximum length of this string is 512 characters.

The last argument, *starting location,* is the position at which you want to begin your search in the string to be searched. 1-2-3 counts the leftmost character in the string as 0, causing you to make a mental adjustment as you specify the place to begin.

If you were to enter @**FIND("-","213-28-7865",4)**, the result 6 would be returned. (Remember that 1-2-3 begins counting with position 0.) Even though 1-2-3 begins at position 4 when it determines what location the search string matches, it determines the position number based on its position from the far left of the string. You will use @FIND in the following example to build the formula that extracts the last name.

USING @MID   You can use the @MID function whenever you want to extract a portion of a string. Unlike @RIGHT and @LEFT, which only extract from the beginning or the end of a string, @MID can be used to extract a portion from the center of a string. This function offers the ultimate in flexibility; you can start anywhere in the string and extract as few or as many characters as you want.

The function looks like this:

@MID(*string,start number,number of characters*)

The first argument, *string,* is any group of characters, a reference to a group of characters, or a string formula. The *start number* argument is the first character position you wish to extract from the string. If you choose to extract the first letter in the string, this is referred to as position 0. The last argument, *number of characters,* is a number representing how many characters to extract from the string. An upper limit of 512 and a lower limit of 0 are the range of acceptable values. The entry @MID("abcdefghi",3,3) would return "def."

USING @LENGTH   The @LENGTH function returns a count of the number of characters in a string. This is not the same as the position number of the last character, which will always be one less than the string length. @LENGTH is written as @LENGTH(*string*). For example, @LENGTH("Profit") equals 6, while the position number of the "t" is 5.

Since this is the last function needed for your formula, you are ready to put all three together to access the last name.

COMBINING THE THREE FUNCTIONS   Extracting the last name from entries that look like "John Smith" can be quite a challenge. The @RIGHT function cannot handle the task, because last names have varying numbers of characters. You can use the three functions just discussed in combination to handle the task. Follow these steps to test the process:

1. Make these worksheet entries:

    A1: John Smith
    A2: Jim Pearson
    A3: Rob Smithfield
    A4: Ken Horn

2. Enter /**Worksheet Column Set-Width**, type **15**, and press ENTER.

3. Move the cell pointer to A10, press the spacebar once, and press ENTER.

   This step will not appear to have an effect on the cell, but it alters it to contain one blank space. This is quite important: it is the character you will be searching for within the name to identify the end of the first name.

4. Move the cell pointer to B1 and type

   @MID(A1,@FIND($A$10,A1,0)+1,@LENGTH(A1))

5. Enter /**Copy**, press ENTER, move the cell pointer to B2, type **.**, move the cell pointer to B4, and press ENTER.

   Each of the entries in column B shows the last name of the individual listed in column A like this:

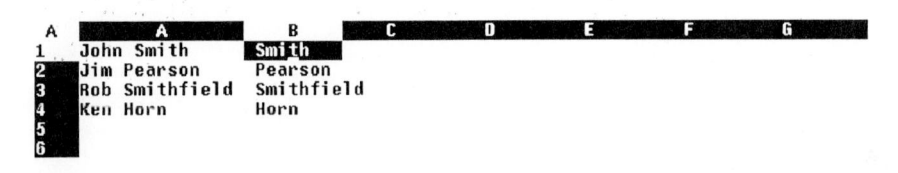

```
A:B1: @MID(A1,@FIND($A$10,A1,0),@LENGTH(A1))                          READY

A          A              B          C        D        E        F      G
1    John Smith     Smith
2    Jim Pearson    Pearson
3    Rob Smithfield Smithfield
4    Ken Horn       Horn
5
6
```

The formula will work for all first and last name entries, regardless of the length of each component. If the entries in column A contained middle names, a different formula would be required.

Combining Numbers And Strings

String and number entries cannot be combined into one cell, because string and numeric data have different attributes. String data cannot be used to perform calculations; numeric data is not affected by changes in label alignment. Although you cannot negate any of the basic attributes of strings or values, you can change one type of entry to the other type with built-in functions. One built-in function turns string entries into numeric values, and another function that converts values into strings. You can use them when you want to perform arithmetic operations on a string that looks like a number. After conversion with the @VALUE function, you will be able to perform the desired operation. These functions are also useful when you want to concatenate (combine) a numeric branch number or a date with some text data to produce a heading for a report. After conversion with the @STRING function, this is possible.

The @STRING function uses two arguments; one represents the number to be converted, and the other represents the number of decimal places that the string will display. It looks like this:

@STRING(*number,number of decimal places*)

The first argument, *number,* can be an actual numeric value or a reference to a value. The second argument, *number of decimal places,* is the number of decimal places that you want the converted string to display. If the original number has more decimal places than the number you specify, a string will be created by a rounded representation of the original number. If the number of decimal places in the original number is shorter, zeros will be used for padding.

You will make entries that allow you to test the workings of the @STRING function as it converts numeric data, so that it can be concatenated with character data to produce the report heading. These are the required steps to complete the example:

1. Make these entries:

    A3: Dept:
    A4: Headcount:
    B3: 400
    B4: 50

2. Move the cell pointer to column A, enter /**Worksheet Column Set-Width,** type **10,** and press ENTER.

3. Move the cell pointer to B1 and type

    +"January Budget Report for Department "&@STRING(B3,0)

    Press ENTER to produce these results:

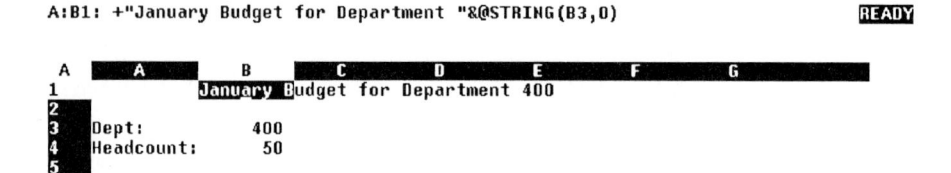

```
A:B1: +"January Budget for Department "&@STRING(B3,0)                    READY

    A         A           B         C         D         E         F         G
    1                  January Budget for Department 400
    2
    3        Dept:           400
    4        Headcount:       50
    5
```

This formula starts with a plus sign to make 1-2-3 use the entry as a value. This may seem contradictory, but all formulas are value entries even if they are string formulas. The string that is included in the formula is enclosed within quotation marks, which are required for all text not stored in a cell. The ampersand (&) joins (or concatenates) the two components of a string, and the @STRING function creates a string from the value in B3. The arguments for this function tell 1-2-3 to show zero decimal places when the conversion is made.

As you work with additional string entries, keep in mind that the conversion can take the opposite approach and turn strings that look like values into value entries.

REVIEW EXERCISE

This chapter has introduced you to several powerful functions that can enhance your models. Trying another example that utilizes these powerful functions will help give you the confidence to use them in your own models. The following example creates a property comparison model.

1. Erase the current worksheet so you can start with an empty worksheet. *Hint:* Use /Worksheet Erase Yes.

2. Set the width of column A to 14, column B to 8, column C to 6, column D to 23, and column E to 21. *Hint:* For each column use /Worksheet Column Set-Width, type the column width, and press ENTER.

3. Change 1-2-3's default display format to Currency format with zero decimal places. *Hint:* Use the /Worksheet Global Format Currency, type **0**, and press ENTER.

4. Make these entries on the worksheet:
   A2: Address
   A4: '513 Curtis
   A5: 5234
   A6: '11335 West
   A7: '110 Main
   B2: Cost
   B4: 65000
   B5: 74000
   B6: 78000
   B7: "$70,000
   C2: Taxes
   D1: "Error Checking
   D2: Address
   E1: Cost

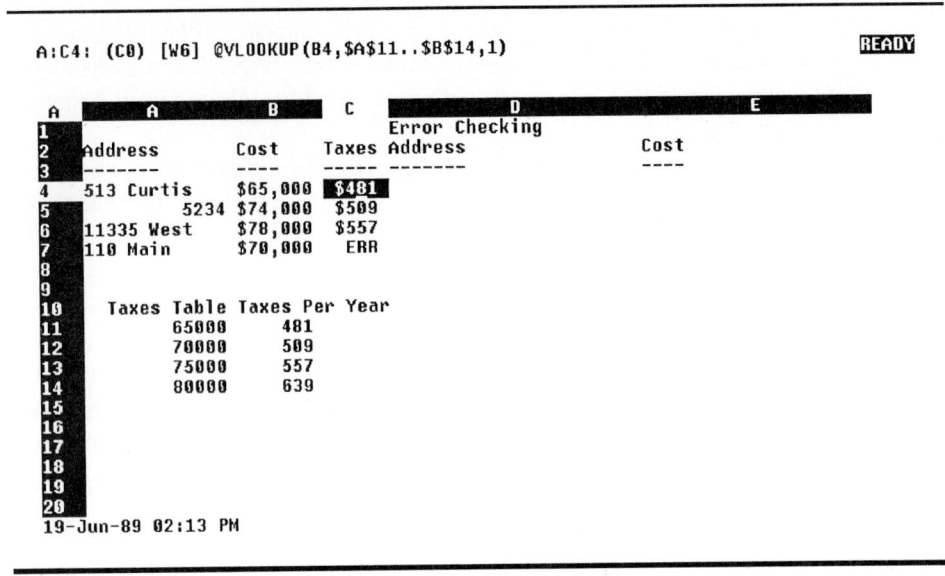

A:C4: (C0) [W6] @VLOOKUP(B4,$A$11..$B$14,1)   READY

```
  A          A            B       C         D                    E
                                          Error Checking
1
2  Address      Cost    Taxes Address           Cost
3  --------     ----    ----- -------           ----
4  513 Curtis  $65,000  $481
5        5234  $74,000  $509
6  11335 West  $78,000  $557
7  110 Main    $70,000  ERR
8
9
10    Taxes Table Taxes Per Year
11         65000      481
12         70000      509
13         75000      557
14         80000      639
15
16
17
18
19
20
19-Jun-89 02:13 PM
```

FIGURE 10-14.   Property listing with @VLOOKUP for property taxes

5. Use the @REPEAT and @LENGTH functions to make a hyphenated line below the column headings in row 2 that is the same length as the column headings. *Hint:* Enter **@REPEAT("-",@LENGTH(A2))** in A3. Then select /Copy, press ENTER, select the range B3..E3, and press ENTER.

6. Add the following data that lists the property taxes for different property values:

```
Taxes Table Taxes Per Year
      65000      481
      70000      509
      75000      557
      80000      639
```

7. Use the @VLOOKUP function and the property tax table you created to compute the property tax in column C for each property. The worksheet is shown in Figure 10-14. (*Hint:* Enter **@VLOOKUP(B4,$A$11..$B$14,1)** in C4. Then copy the formula by selecting /Copy, press ENTER, select the range C5..C7, and press ENTER again.) Notice that 1-2-3 returns an ERR value for the last property. While you can visually check the Address and Cost entries with a small worksheet like this, you will want to use formulas. Formulas allow you to apply these concepts to your own worksheets when there are too many entries to manually check each one.

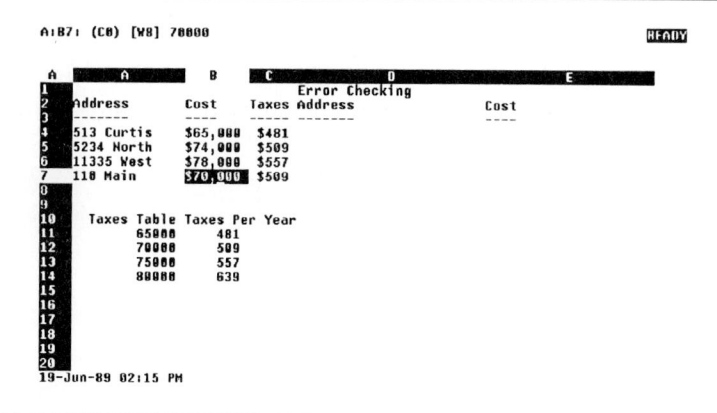

FIGURE 10-15.   Property listing with @ISSTRING and @ISNUMBER to detect errors

8. Add the formula

    @IF(@ISSTRING(A4)," ","Address must be a label")

    in column D for the rows containing addresses to check that all addresses are entered correctly. (*Hint:* After entering the first formula in A4, select /Copy, press ENTER, select the range D5..D7, and press ENTER.) Notice that the @IF formula returns an error message in D5 because you entered a number in A5.

9. Move to A5 and enter **'5234 North**.

10. Add the formula

    @IF(@ISNUMBER(B3)," ","Cost must be a number")

    in column E for the rows containing entries, to check that all costs are entered correctly. (*Hint:* Then select /Copy, press ENTER, select the range E5..E7, and press ENTER.) Notice that the @IF formula returns an error message in E7 because you entered a label in B7.

11. Move to B7 and enter **70000**. The final worksheet looks like Figure 10-15.

12. Save this model as PROPERTY, or erase the worksheet if you do not wish to save this model. *Hint:* Select /File Save, type **PROPERTY**, and press ENTER, or use /Worksheet Erase Yes.

REVIEW

- The @IF function lets you create a formula that can provide more than one result. The result returned by the formula depends on a condition, which is an expression that evaluates as true or false. You can includes strings in the condition, or you can choose to return a string rather than a value.

- You can place one @IF statement inside another @IF statement by using the second @IF as the entry used when the condition evaluates as either true or false. The process of using one @IF inside another @IF is referred to as nesting @IF statements.

- @VLOOKUP allows you to search a vertical table for an entry stored in the worksheet. @VLOOKUP searches the first column of the table for the entry stored in the worksheet. Once it locates a matching entry, it returns a value from the same row of the table.

- @INDEX also returns a value from a table. @INDEX does not search for a matching entry. You must supply the row and column offset from the beginning of the table. The @INDEX function returns the entry in the cell with the specified offset in the table.

- 1-2-3 provides several functions that check for errors. They let you check entries in other worksheet cells and plan appropriate actions. These functions can also be used with @IF to return different results, depending on whether on not the special functions return true or false. The @ISERR function determines if a cell contains an @ERR value. @ISNA tests to determine if a cell equals NA. The @ISNUMBER function determines if a cell contains a number, and @ISSTRING determines if a cell contains a string.

- Other 1-2-3 functions convert one type of data to another. @DATEVALUE converts a string containing a date to a serial date number. @TIMEVALUE converts a string containing a time to a serial time number. @VALUE converts a string containing a number to a value. @STRING converts a value to a string.

- The string functions manipulate and return strings. @REPLACE replaces part of one string with another. @FIND finds the position within a string that contains another string. @MID returns a portion of a string. @LENGTH returns the length of a string.

Functions

@IF	Returns one value if the condition tested is true and another value if it is false
@INDEX	Returns a value from the specified row and column of a table
@ISNA	Returns 1 if a value equals NA or 0 otherwise
@ISERR	Returns 1 if a value equals ERR or 0 otherwise
@ISNUMBER	Returns 1 if a value is a number or 0 otherwise
@ISSTRING	Returns 1 if a value is a string or 0 otherwise
@MID	Returns characters from a string, starting at any position in the string
@FIND	Returns the position at which a character string starts in another character string
@REPLACE	Replaces characters in one string with another character string
@LENGTH	Returns the length of a string
@STRING	Converts a value entry to a string
@VALUE	Converts a string of numeric digits stored as a label to a value
@VLOOKUP	Compares a worksheet entry against table entries and returns a value from the same row in the table

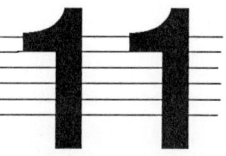

ADVANCED FILE-MANAGEMENT TECHNIQUES

Saving a Section of the Worksheet
Combining Data from Other Files with Your Worksheet
Using Links to Incorporate Data from Other Worksheets
Importing Text Data
Review Exercise
Review

By now you are probably an expert at the basic file-management features for saving and retrieving your worksheet files. These commands are the workhorses of the file commands because they play a central role in every worksheet session. A number of other file-management commands are used less commonly but provide powerful options that you will want to incorporate into your set of skills.

In this chapter you will learn to use the Extract feature to save a small portion of the worksheet in a worksheet file. This feature will let you transfer account names or end-of-period totals to another worksheet without having to reenter any of the data. You will also learn to use 1-2-3's Combine feature, which lets you combine an entire file or a range of data with the file currently in memory. This means that you can bring data into memory from disk without wiping out the current entries in the worksheet, as /File Retrieve does. Finally, you will explore a feature that lets you import text data from a word processing program or other source into your 1-2-3 worksheet. This feature brings the lines of your word processing document into the current worksheet as a column of long label entries. If you prefer, you can use one of the Data menu selections to split these long labels into individual cell entries.

Together, these new commands provide ways to increase productivity by letting you reuse existing data rather than having to reenter it. The commands also let you consolidate the numbers in individual worksheets to compute a total automatically.

SAVING A SECTION
OF THE WORKSHEET

This section examines the commands that let you save a range on a worksheet to a file without having to save the entire worksheet. You have complete control over the amount of data that is saved to a file, and you can use it to start a new worksheet application. You can also add the data in a file to an existing application with the 1-2-3 commands covered later in this chapter.

Why You Would Want to
Save Part of a Worksheet

You may be wondering what purpose can be served by saving a portion of a current worksheet to a file. One of the advantages is that this approach lets you continue very large applications when you are running out of memory. Suppose that you have a model in which you are recording the detailed expenses by department for 1990. You have been monitoring the amount of available memory month by month and have come to the realization that you will not be able to fit an entire year's worth of information in memory at once. One approach open to you is to record expenses for the first quarter or six months in one worksheet and use other worksheets for the remaining periods. However, this strategy alone will not provide all the information you need. You will have all the detailed expenses, but you will not have a total of all the expenses for the year, which is likely to be just as important as the detailed expenses.

1-2-3's /File Xtract command will let you total each expense category on the worksheet that contains the expenses for the first quarter, and to save these totals separately in a worksheet file. The worksheet containing the totals can be used as the basis for the second-quarter worksheet. The same process can be used at the end of the second and third quarters so that the worksheet with the fourth-quarter figures will be able to present a total for the entire year.

The same capability can be used in the data-management environment when a database begins to grow too large for the worksheet. You can sort the worksheet and save one or more categories of data with the /File Xtract command. This data can be used as the basis for a second database, containing only those categories of data that you have saved with /File Xtract.

In Chapter 12, you will learn how to create multiple worksheets within one worksheet file. The /File Xtract command will copy one of these worksheets to another file. You can retrieve the new file and save it with a .WK1 extension if you want to use it with Release 2.0 or 2.01.

You could use the /File Xtract feature on the employee database discussed in Chapter 9 to split the database by an alphabetical break if it became too large. Perhaps you could divide records by placing records in which last names begin with the letters "A" through "M" in one database, and placing the others in a separate database. Other possible divisions would be by location or job codes.

The ability to extract information from a worksheet can also be useful when you wish to save data-entry time. You can use a worksheet containing a list of all your account names to save these names into a file by themselves. Anyone starting a new application requiring these names can retrieve the extract file.

Different Options for Saving

There is more than one way to create the extract file: you can save just the values in the selected range, or if you prefer, you can save the formulas. This chapter examines both prospects so that you can become familiar with some of the potential sources of problems encountered when you save formulas.

Whether you plan to save formulas or values, the command that you will use is /File Xtract. The spelling is a little different than you might expect, because of 1-2-3's commitment to having only one command that begins with a given letter in a menu. The "E" is already used for the Erase command, so "extract" become "Xtract."

The menu that Xtract presents looks like this:

You can try each of these options in the next two sections.

SAVING VALUES   When you choose to save cells with the Values option, 1-2-3 will save the current values of the cells you select in a worksheet file. This file will have the filename extension .WK3. The extracted data is placed in the new file beginning in cell A1. The portion of the new file that contains data will be determined by the size and shape of the extracted data, which will retain its original size and shape, although each cell's address will be determined by its offset from the beginning of the range. The same offset will be used in the new file, but the origin is always A1.

When you select the Values option, calculated results and labels will be retained in the new file. All formulas are replaced by the result of the formula calculations. This is a convenient way to carry the result of calculations forward to a new worksheet without bringing the data forward, as is required when saving formulas.

When you enter **/File Xtract Values**, 1-2-3 asks for the name of the file to store the data in, using a prompt message like this:

You have the same options as you do with the /File Save command. 1-2-3 will provide a default name that you can use, or you can type another filename instead. The default filename is FILE followed by a four-digit number starting with 0001 and increasing by 1 for each default filename used. You can type the name of a new file and 1-2-3 will store your data in that file. You can type the name of an existing file, specify the range to be saved, and 1-2-3 will prompt you with this message:

Building a small model is a good way to test the operation of the /File Xtract command. The model will present the detailed sales data for each month in the first quarter and sum this data to provide an end-of-quarter figure. Although there is not enough data to cause a condition of insufficient memory, the concept and potential actions required are exactly the same as you would need with much larger models. Follow these steps to create this practice example:

1. Enter **/Worksheet Erase Yes** to ensure that the worksheet is blank.

2. Enter **/Worksheet Column Set-Width**, type **18**, and press ENTER.

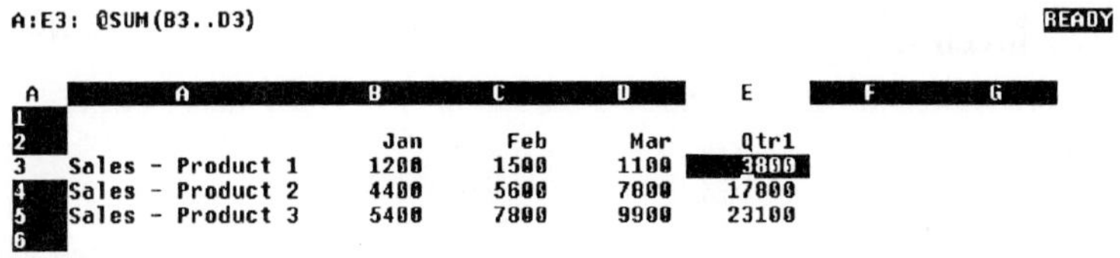

```
A:E3:  @SUM(B3..D3)                                                    READY

A            A             B        C        D        E        F        G
1
2                          Jan      Feb      Mar      Qtr1
3   Sales - Product 1      1200     1500     1100     3800
4   Sales - Product 2      4400     5600     7800     17800
5   Sales - Product 3      5400     7800     9900     23100
6
```

FIGURE 11-1.   Data for the first quarter

3. Complete these entries:

    A3: Sales - Product 1
    A4: Sales - Product 2
    A5: Sales - Product 3
    B2: "Jan
    B3: 1200
    B4: 4400
    B5: 5400
    C2: "Feb
    C3: 1500
    C4: 5600
    C5: 7800
    D2: "Mar
    D3: 1100
    D4: 7800
    D5: 9900
    E2: "Qtr1
    E3: @SUM(B3.D3)
    E4: @SUM(B4.D4)
    E5: @SUM(B5.D5)

These entries will produce the results shown in Figure 11-1.

4. Move the cell pointer to E3.

5. Enter **/File Xtract Values**.

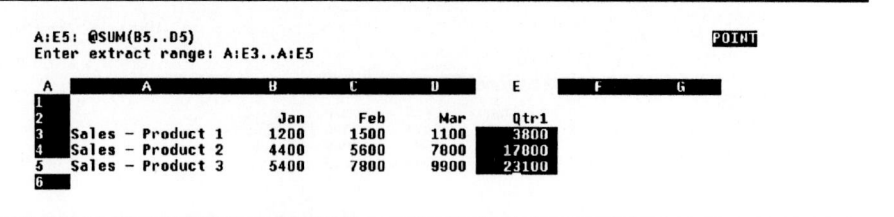

```
A:E5:  @SUM(B5..D5)                                              POINT
Enter extract range: A:E3..A:E5

 A        A          B        C        D      E       F      G
1
2                   Jan      Feb      Mar    Qtr1
3    Sales – Product 1   1200     1500     1100    3800
4    Sales – Product 2   4400     5600     7000   17000
5    Sales – Product 3   5400     7800     9900   23100
6
```

FIGURE 11-2.   Selecting an extract range

6. Type **QTR1VALU** and press ENTER.
   QTR1VALU will be the name of the file used for this extract.

7. Expand the range by moving the cell pointer to E5 so that it looks like the highlighted range in Figure 11-2.

8. Press ENTER to finalize.
   The current value of these three cells will be written to the specified file.

9. Enter /**File Save**, type **1ST_QTR**, and press ENTER to save the original file.

10. Enter /**File Retrieve**, type **QTR1VALU**, and press ENTER.
    This will place the three values in cells A1, A2, and A3. Your screen will look like this:

```
A:A1:  3800                                              READY

 A        A        B      C      D      E      F      G      H
1       3800
2      17800
3      23100
4
```

You will have an opportunity to work with this extract file again later. You will learn how to place its contents anywhere you like in the worksheet by combining it with an existing worksheet.

SAVING FORMULAS   Saving formulas is just as easy as saving values, but before you use the Formulas option you must consider how you will use the file and what it will contain. If you save the formulas without the data they need, will there be data on the new worksheet for them to operate on? Do they contain relative references that will be adjusted when they are placed in the new worksheet? Will the adjustments that are made be logical? In many cases, the answer to these questions is no, indicating that another approach would be preferred, but there are situations in which it is convenient to save the formulas.

You will want to save the quarter totals as values to look at the differences. Follow these steps to complete the exercise:

1. Enter **/File Retrieve**, type **1ST_QTR**, and press ENTER to recall the original worksheet.

2. Move the cell pointer to E3.

3. Enter **/File Xtract Formulas**.

4. Type **QTR1FORM** and press ENTER.
   QTR1FORM will be the name of the file used for this extract.

5. Expand the range by moving the cell pointer to E5, and press ENTER to finalize.
   The formulas or values in these three cells will be written to the specified file.

6. Enter **/File Retrieve**, type **QTR1FORM**, and press ENTER to produce this display:

Notice that the formulas were adjusted for the new worksheet. This situation has a high potential for error, since the formulas might not be adjusted as you would expect. In this particular case, the Values option meets your needs better. Later, you will see the package work with formulas when you use the /File Combine Add feature and only the current value of the formula. Another option is to reference the cells in the other worksheet by creating an external file link, as this chapter later discusses.

COMBINING DATA FROM OTHER FILES WITH YOUR WORKSHEET

The /File Retrieve command has a Worksheet Erase feature built right into it. Every time you use the /File Retrieve command, the current file in memory will be replaced with the contents of the file you are bringing in from the disk. In many cases this is exactly what you need, but in many others, you might prefer to retain the current contents of memory and bring information into memory from disk to *add* to the current data. The /File Combine command provides this capability.

This section examines each of the /File Combine options separately in order to illustrate the functions they serve. Each of these components will then be joined in examples to help you understand their sequence and their relationship with the File Combine menus.

Applications for The Combine Feature

There are many applications for the Combine feature. This feature has three options, with a menu like this:

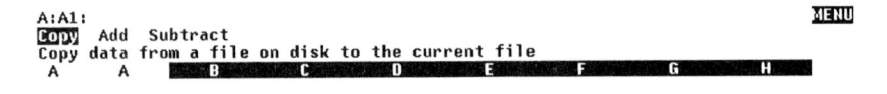

One option copies data from disk to an area of the worksheet and replaces the contents of this area with what is on the disk. This option would be useful for adding a list of account names that were stored in a file created with the Xtract command. The second option adds the data on the disk to the data already in memory. Each value in the file will be added to a corresponding value in the current worksheet. The corresponding value is determined by the cell-pointer location at the time the command is invoked. This option lets you automate the consolidation of sales or expenses for all units within a company to produce a total company report. The third option can be used to remove the results for a subsidiary from the total company reports.

Deciding How Much Data to Combine

You have two options when combining a file with the current worksheet—to combine everything in the file, or to combine a range from the file.

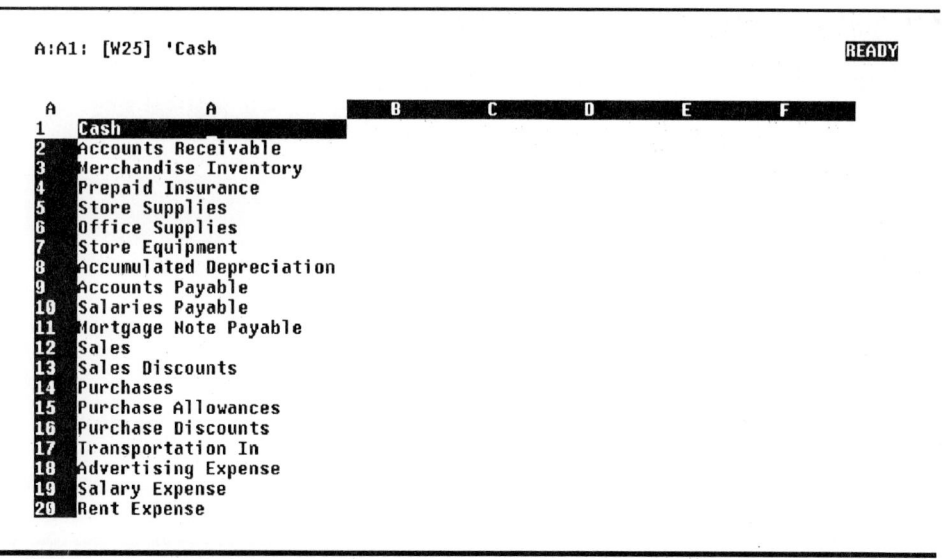

FIGURE 11-3. Account names

USING AN ENTIRE FILE When you combine an entire file, everything in the file will be placed within the current worksheet. Which combining method you should use depends on which selections you make. Figure 11-3 shows a list of account names

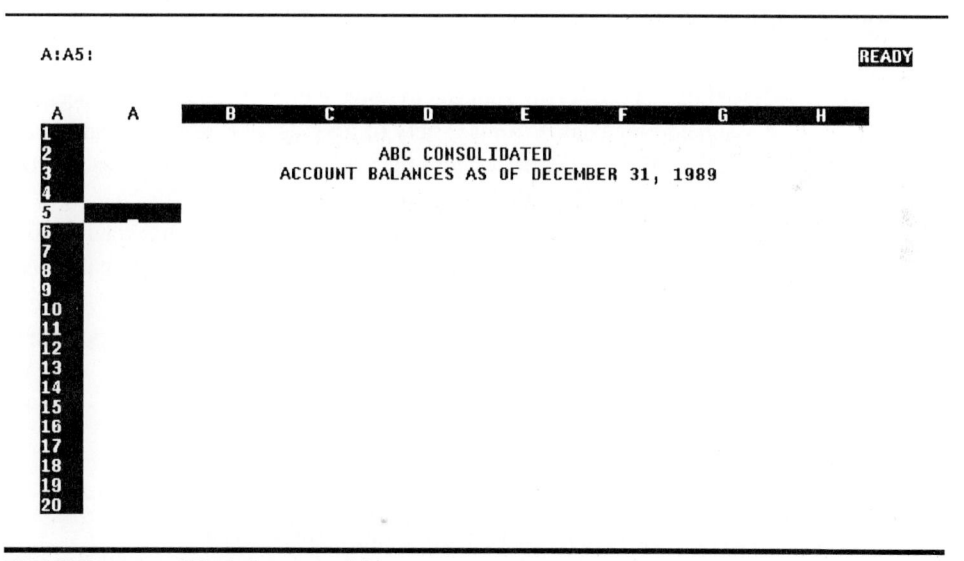

FIGURE 11-4. Worksheet requiring account names

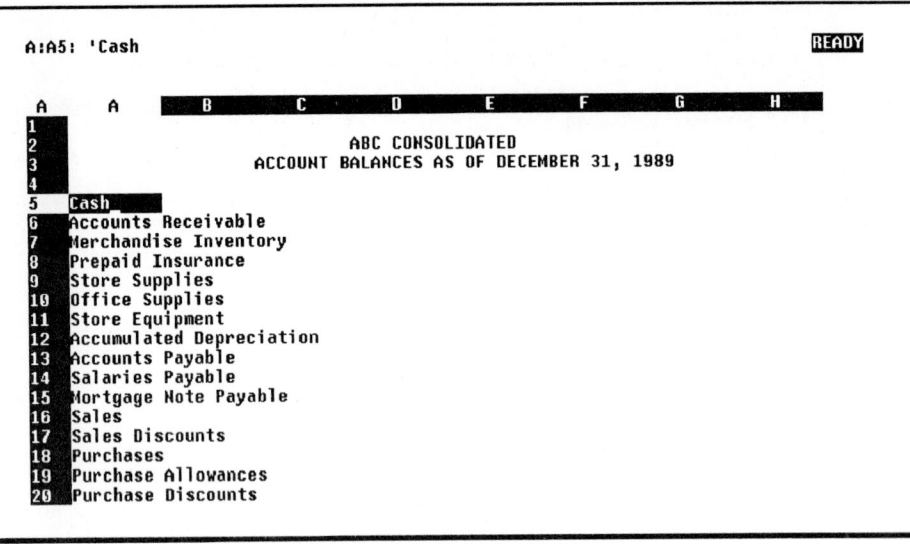

A:A5: 'Cash   READY

```
   A    A        B       C       D       E       F       G       H
1
2                              ABC CONSOLIDATED
3                      ACCOUNT BALANCES AS OF DECEMBER 31, 1989
4
5       Cash
6       Accounts Receivable
7       Merchandise Inventory
8       Prepaid Insurance
9       Store Supplies
10      Office Supplies
11      Store Equipment
12      Accumulated Depreciation
13      Accounts Payable
14      Salaries Payable
15      Mortgage Note Payable
16      Sales
17      Sales Discounts
18      Purchases
19      Purchase Allowances
20      Purchase Discounts
```

FIGURE 11-5.   Worksheet with account names added

that are stored in a file named ACCOUNTS. The current worksheet shown in Figure 11-4 can use this list of names. The results of combining ACCOUNTS with the current worksheet is shown in Figure 11-5. The accounts were placed just where they were needed by means of the placement of the cell pointer in A5 before the combine operation was invoked with the menu.

USING A RANGE   You were introduced to range names in Chapter 2. Ranges of cells can be assigned range names for a variety of reasons. For example, names can be added to improve the readability of formulas; they can also be used to let you combine less than an entire file with the current worksheet.

If you want to use numbers in another worksheet, you can create an extract file for each group of numbers you wish to transfer. However, a far easier approach is to use the /Range Name command in the sending file, save that file, and use the /File Combine command with the Named/Specified-Range option to obtain the data you need in a receiving file.

To try with the 1ST_QTR file you created earlier, follow these steps:

1. Enter **/File Retrieve**, type **1ST_QTR**, and press ENTER.

2. Move the cell pointer to E2 and enter **/Range Name Create**.

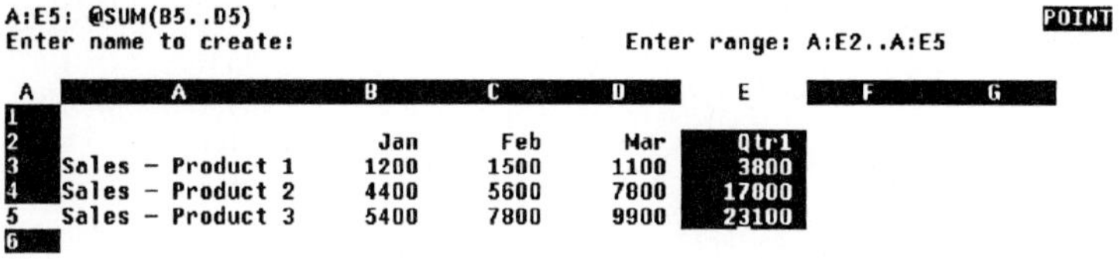

```
A:E5: @SUM(B5..D5)                                              POINT
Enter name to create:              Enter range: A:E2..A:E5

A            A          B       C       D      E         F       G
1
2                      Jan     Feb     Mar    Qtr1
3  Sales - Product 1   1200    1500    1100   3800
4  Sales - Product 2   4400    5600    7000   17000
5  Sales - Product 3   5400    7800    9900   23100
6
```

FIGURE 11-6.   Naming a range to use later with /File Combine

You are including the label "Qtr1" in this range so you can see how the label is handled.

3. Type **Total** and press ENTER.

4. Move the cell pointer to E5 to produce the display shown in Figure 11-6.

5. Press ENTER.

   Both the label and formulas are now named Total. If you later use this named range with /File Combine, the combination method you select will determine whether the current value of the formula or the formula itself is used. The option you select will also determine whether the label at the top of the formulas is used. This will be more clear after you have examined the options for combining in more detail.

6. Enter /**File Save**, press ENTER, and enter **Replace**.

   This is required to save the assigned range names on the disk.

Methods for Combining

There are three methods for combining data in a file with the current contents of memory. Each method has a completely different effect on the current worksheet, so be sure that you understand each one clearly before using them on your own applications. You should also save the current worksheet before you begin so if you use the wrong method, you can retrieve the worksheet from disk and try again.

You will need to build a new worksheet model to use with the Combine feature. Follow these directions:

1. Move the cell pointer to B2, enter /**Range Erase**, move the cell pointer to E5, and press ENTER.

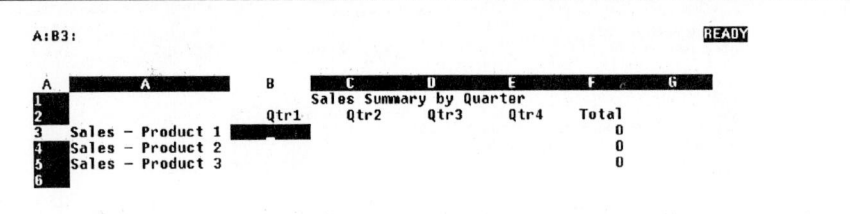

FIGURE 11-7.   Worksheet before /File Combine

This is a short-cut approach to creating the new model, since you need the same entries and width for column A.

2. Make these worksheet entries:

    B2: "Qtr1
    C1: Sales Summary by Quarter
    C2: "Qtr2
    D2: "Qtr3
    E2: "Qtr4
    F2: "Total
    F3: @SUM(B3.E3)
    F4: @SUM(B4.E4)
    F5: @SUM(B5.E5)

The model shell is now ready to receive data from the various quarters and looks like the worksheet in Figure 11-7.

The /File Combine options provide the perfect solution because they do not destroy the current model as you bring the quarter totals in from other files. The data that you will be bringing in must be on disk, either as range names in a complete model or as an extract file that contains only the data you need.

COPYING TO THE CURRENT WORKSHEET   Use the /File Combine Copy command when you have data stored on disk and you want to replace a section of the current worksheet. To bring the data into the current worksheet, position the cell pointer carefully; it will control the placement of the data. Use the values you stored in QTR1VALU for your first look at this command:

1. Move the cell pointer to B3.

2. Enter /**File Combine Copy.**

```
A:B3: 3800                                                               READY

  A         A            B       C         D         E        F       G
1                                Sales Summary by Quarter
2                        Qtr1      Qtr2     Qtr3      Qtr4    Total
3     Sales - Product 1  3800                                 3800
4     Sales - Product 2  17000                                17000
5     Sales - Product 3  23100                                23100
6
```

FIGURE 11-8.   Copying data to the worksheet with /File Combine Copy

   3. Enter **Entire-File**.

   4. Type **QTR1VALU** and press ENTER to produce the results shown in Figure
      11-8.

Notice that each of the values in this small file are placed on the model, and the entries
are included in the total.

Try the same exercise with the formulas you stored in QTR1FORM, using these
steps:

   1. Move the cell pointer to B3, enter **/Range Erase**, move the cell pointer to B5,
      and press ENTER.

   2. Enter **/File Combine Copy**.

   3. Enter **Entire-File**.

   4. Type **QTR1FORM** and press ENTER to produce the results shown in Figure
      11-9.

Notice that everything seems the same at first glance, but looking at the formula in
the control panel shows that everything is not the same—it includes entries from most
of the columns. These formulas have the potential to cause trouble, as the CIRC status
indicator at the bottom of the screen tells you. It indicates that the worksheet contains
a formula reference to itself.

   Another problem to be on the lookout for is incorrect cell-pointer placement or a
lack of knowledge of the exact contents of an extract file or range name. If you were
to position the cell pointer in the wrong place and use the Combine option, you could
wind up with results like those in the worksheet shown in Figure 11-10; everything is
shifted by one row, making the resulting model useless.

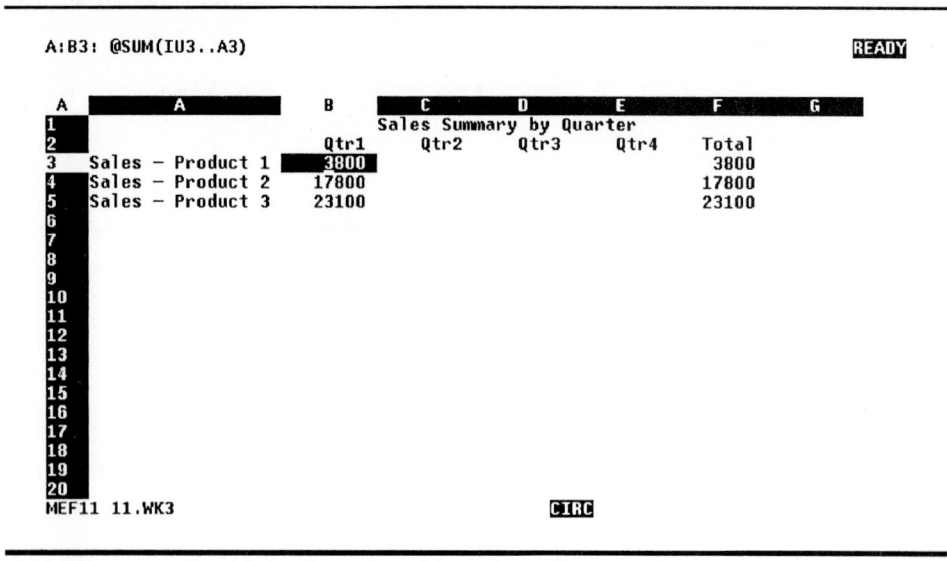

FIGURE 11-9.   Combining formulas without the cells they reference

ADDING TO THE CURRENT WORKSHEET   The /File Combine Add command lets you add values to the existing values. Which values are added is determined by cell-pointer position and the placement of the file values within the file. If the worksheet cells are blank, the differences between Copy and Add are that Add ignores labels, leaves formulas in the current worksheet intact, and copies the results of formulas to the current worksheet. Follow these steps to try the Add option:

1. Move the cell pointer to B3, enter **/Range Erase**, move the cell pointer to B6, and press ENTER.

2. Move the cell pointer to B2.

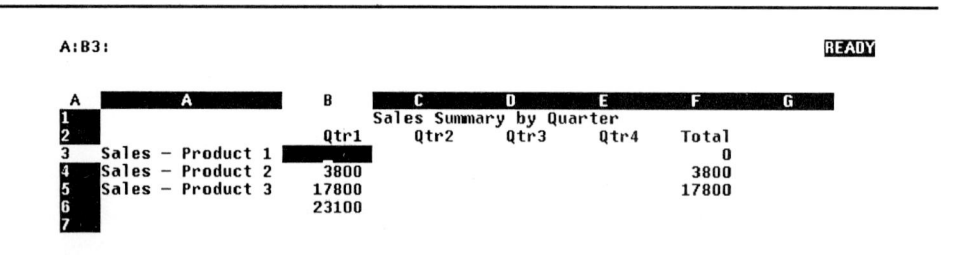

FIGURE 11-10.   Misjudging the cell pointer's position for /File Combine

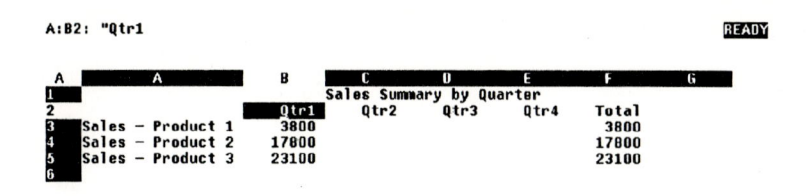

FIGURE 11-11.   Copying data to the worksheet with /File Combine Add

You will be using the named range Total in the 1ST_QTR file this time. Since the Qtr1 label is included in the range, you need to position the cell pointer to B2 so the first value in the file will be matched with B3.

3. Enter **/File Combine Add Named/Specified_Range**.

4. Type **Total** and press ENTER.

5. Type **1ST_QTR** and press ENTER to produce the results shown in Figure 11-11. Try this again to see if it really adds.

6. Enter **/File Combine Add Named/Specified_Range**.

7. Type **Total** and press ENTER.

8. Type **1ST_QTR** and press ENTER. Move the cell pointer to B3 to see the value 7600 in B3, as in Figure 11-12.

   You can see that each of the numbers in the current worksheet doubled as the numbers on the file were added to the current worksheet again.

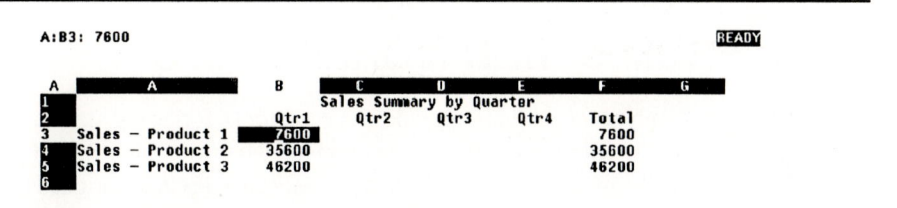

FIGURE 11-12.   Adding a range to the worksheet twice

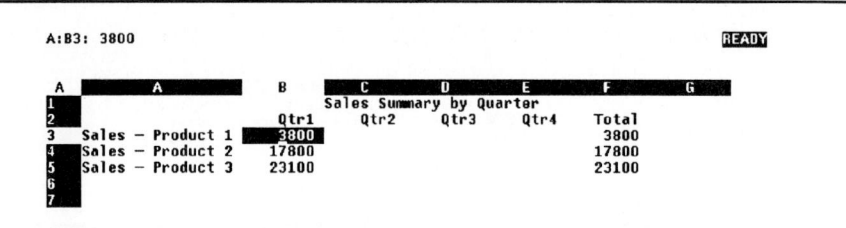

FIGURE 11-13.   Subtracting data from the worksheet with /File Combine Subtract

SUBTRACTING FROM THE CURRENT WORKSHEET   The /File Combine command's Subtract option is the exact opposite of the Add option. It subtracts the values stored on disk from the current worksheet cells. This option depends on the cell-pointer location and the offset within the file that controls which numbers will be subtracted from which entries. You can try this by subtracting the last entry you added to the worksheet:

1. Enter /**File Combine Subtract Entire-File**.

    Since you will use the QTR1VALU file, leave the cell pointer in B3; there is no need to have the cell pointer in B2. This file does not have a label before the numeric values the way the named range did.

2. Type **QTR1VALU** and press ENTER to produce the results shown in Figure 11-13.

    Each of the entries returned to original value as the subtract operation was completed.

3. Enter /**File Save**, type **QTRTOTAL**, and press ENTER to save the new file.

USING LINKS TO INCORPORATE DATA FROM OTHER WORKSHEETS

The /File Combine commands provide a set of tools for using data from other worksheets in the current one. When you combine data from other files, 1-2-3 does not automatically update these values when there are changes in the original files from which you obtained the data. When you use the /File Combine command to reference the data in other worksheet files, you must continually repeat the /File Combine commands every time you use the worksheet to check that the data is still current.

Release 3 offers another solution that allows 1-2-3 to update the worksheet data. The updating is accomplished by establishing *links* to data in other worksheet files. 1-2-3 will update the links that you establish every time you tell it to do so.

As an example of the File Link feature, the summary worksheet that you create to combine expenses can contain formulas that reference the totals in the supporting worksheets. The summary worksheet is referred to as the *target file;* it will contain data stored in the other files. The files that contain the data are referred to as the *source files;* they are the source of the data you need. If the data in the source worksheets change, 1-2-3 updates the values in the target files when the /File Admin Link-Refresh command is used.

Release 3 supports file links that are single cells or ranges. You can use the external file links as you would other single and multiple cell references from the current worksheet. For example, the QTRTOTAL worksheet could contain an @SUM function that sums the values in the TOTAL range in the 1ST_QTR worksheet. Another possibility is to reference the single values of the 1ST_QTR worksheet in the QTRTOTAL worksheet. As the values in the 1ST_QTR worksheet change, the /File Admin Link-Refresh command will update the values in the QTRTOTAL worksheet.

Using External File Links

To include a value from another file, you must specify the worksheet file from which you want to obtain the value, as well as the worksheet cell address or range address or name. If the file is not on the current drive or in the current directory, you will need to specify this information along with the filename. If the filename has an extension other than .WK3, as in .WK1 for a link to a Release 2 worksheet, you must specify the filename extension. The filename must also be enclosed in a set of double angle brackets, as in +<<BUDGET.WK3>>A2, to link the current cell in the target worksheet to cell A2 in the BUDGET worksheet.

Follow these easy steps to establish a link from the current cell to a cell in a source worksheet:

1. Type + to tell 1-2-3 that you are starting a formula.

2. Type << to enter the left side of a set of double angle brackets. Use the less-than symbol (<) to create these brackets.

3. Enter the filename.

    Although 1-2-3 does not require you to include the directory name or the file extension unless you are using a directory other than the current directory or an extension other than .WK3, you may want to develop the habit of entering it anyway. Then you will not need to worry about which directory is current when you establish the link. 1-2-3 assumes that the file has a .WK3 extension unless you provide another extension.

4. Enter the closing right-angle brackets by typing >>. Use the greater-than sign (<) for this entry.

5. Enter a reference to the cell or range that contains the values you want to link to, as in B10 or TOTAL.

   This reference can be entered as a cell address, range address, or range name.

6. Press ENTER to finalize the entry.

   1-2-3 finds the value in the source worksheet file and displays the current value in the cell containing the link in the target worksheet.

A cell that references an external worksheet cell can include other formula features of 1-2-3. This means that a cell can have a formula such as

+<<BUDGET.WK1>>A2*<<BUDGET.WK1>>B3

Also, the external worksheet cell reference can be an argument for a function in the cell, as in

@PMT(<<FINANCE.WK1>>A3,B3,C7)

If 1-2-3 cannot find the values in the other file, it treats the external file link as an undefined range name; the formula displays when the cell pointer highlights it, but the formula evaluates to ERR.

1-2-3 computes the values of an external file link two times. First, it computes the value when the formula is entered or edited. Second, it updates the values of an external file link when the /File Admin Link-Refresh command is executed. This confirms that external file links are using the most up-to-date values of the cells in the other worksheets. In a network environment this command should be performed frequently, since other users may be updating entries in the source file while you are working in the target file. Before printing or making decisions based on the information in the target file, you may want to refresh the links to data in the source file. To refresh the values of the external file links, use /File Admin Link-Refresh, which checks all external file links. If any have changed, 1-2-3 updates the value in the current worksheet.

USING EXTERNAL FILE LINKS FOR A CONSOLIDATED WORKSHEET

Consolidating quarterly sales data provides a practical application for the use of external file links. Follow these steps to create a consolidated worksheet by using external file links:

1. Enter **/File Retrieve**, type **1ST_QTR**, and press ENTER.

   This contains the first quarter of data that you want to consolidate. Notice that the data that you will include in the consolidation is stored in E3, E4, and E5. You can use this worksheet as the basis for the second quarter's data.

2. Complete these entries:

   B2: "Apr
   B3: 1400
   B4: 6000
   B5: 8900
   C2: "May
   C3: 1100
   C4: 5600
   C5: 7600
   D2: "Jun
   D3: 1300
   D4: 6400
   D5: 8000
   E2: "Qtr2

   These entries produce the results shown in Figure 11-14.

3. Enter **/File Save**, type **2ND_QTR**, and press ENTER to save the new file.

   Notice that the data you will include in the consolidation is stored in E3, E4, and E5.

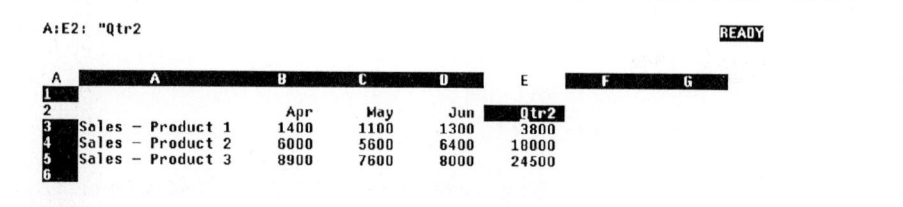

FIGURE 11-14.   Worksheet containing second-quarter data

4. Enter **/File Retrieve**, type **QTRTOTAL**, and press ENTER.

5. Enter **/Range Erase**, select B3..B5, and press ENTER.

Since you can use external file references instead of the /File Combine commands, you will want to remove the old data first.

6. Enter **+<<1ST_QTR.WK3>>E3** and press ENTER. The formula looks like this:

```
A:B3: +<<1ST_QTR.WK1>>A:E3..A:E3                                    READY
```

```
A          A          B        C         D        E        F        G
1                              Sales Summary by Quarter
2                     Qtr1     Qtr2      Qtr3     Qtr4 Total
3    Sales - Product 1  3800                               3800
```

1-2-3 adds .WK3 to the filename for you. The file 1ST_QTR.WK3 has stored the value 3800 in E3. If the values in 1ST_QTR.WK3 later change, you can use the newer values by executing the /File Admin Link-Refresh command. Since this external file link is a formula, you can use the /Copy command to copy it for the other products.

7. Enter **/Copy**, press ENTER, move to B4, type a period, move to B5, and press ENTER to copy the formula from B3 to B4..B5.

Notice that 1-2-3 automatically adjusts the cell reference in the formula as you copy it. You cannot copy the formula to the next column because the second-quarter column uses a different worksheet file, making it easier to type the external reference in the correct way rather than editing it.

8. Enter **+<<2ND_QTR.WK3>>E3** in C3 and press ENTER.

1-2-3 adds .WK3 to the filename for you. The file 2ND_QTR.WK3 has stored the value 3800 in E3. If the value in E3 in 2ND_QTR.WK3 later changes, you can use the newer values by executing the /File Admin Link-Refresh command. Since this external file link is a formula, you can use the /Copy command to copy it for the other products.

9. Enter **/Copy**, press ENTER, move to C4, type a period, move to C5, and press ENTER to copy the formula from C3 to C4..C5. The worksheet now looks like the one in Figure 11-15.

The real advantage of using external file links instead of /File Combine commands is that the external links use the newer values when the data changes. To see the effect of changing the data, follow these steps:

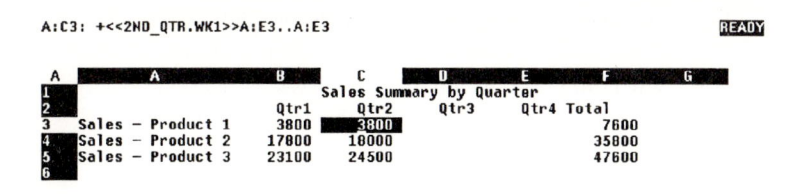

FIGURE 11-15.   External file links to obtain data from another worksheet

1. Enter /**File Save**, press ENTER, and enter **Replace** to save the QTRTOTAL file.

2. Enter /**File Retrieve**, type **2ND_QTR**, and press ENTER.

3. Move to D3 and enter **1700**.

   The new value automatically updates the Product 1 total in E3. If you used /File Combine commands to consolidate data, the QTRTOTAL worksheet would not contain the updated number. When you create a file link between the consolidated worksheet and the supporting worksheet, 1-2-3 will update the values for you.

4. Enter /**File Save**, press ENTER, and enter **Replace** to save the 2ND_QTR file.

5. Enter /**File Retrieve**, type QTRTOTAL, and press ENTER.

   The last step is to update the new values.

6. Enter /**File Admin Link-Refresh**.

   The worksheet looks like the one in Figure 11-16. 1-2-3 updated the external file links when you executed the /File Admin Link-Refresh command.

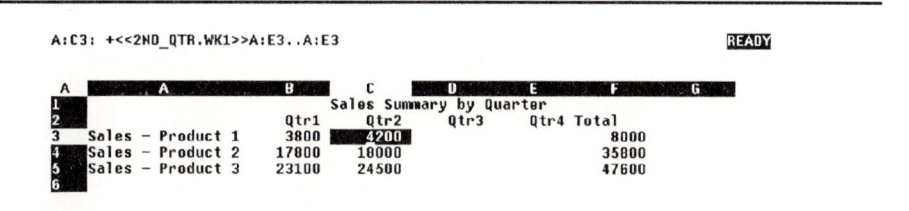

FIGURE 11-16.   File links refreshed to show updated data

LISTING EXTERNAL FILE LINKS   As you develop models with external file links, it can become difficult to remember all the source files to which a worksheet is linked. To quickly remind you which files the current worksheet uses, 1-2-3 offers the /File List Linked command, which displays this result for the QTRTOTAL file:

```
A:C3: +<<2ND_QTR.WK1>>A:E3..A:E3                                          FILES
Enter names of files to list: C:\123NEW\
          1ST_QTR.WK1     29-Apr-89        12:41 PM        1811
1ST QTR.WK1
2ND QTR.WK1
```

The screen shows the file information for the files to which QTRTOTAL is linked. From this display, you can press ENTER to return to the worksheet.

IMPORTING TEXT DATA

1-2-3 provides a feature that allows you to transfer data from a word processor or any other program that can create ASCII text files. The data will be brought into 1-2-3 as a long label. Each line in the word processing document will be one label, with the end result of the transfer being an entire column of long labels. Although the entries seem to reside in separate fields because of the alignment of the data in the original word-processed document, this is not the case. There is no automatic way to use a portion from the center of the long label without 1-2-3's string functions. For large amounts of data, this is not an effective solution. Instead, the /Data Parse command, which you will examine later, can break long labels into separate cells.

Why You Would Want to Put Text Data in the Worksheet

The worksheet seems to be the place for calculations and other methods of rigorous analysis. Why would anyone want to put word processing data on the worksheet? One reason is a significant savings in data-entry time. If you have account names, employee numbers, inventory items, or other lists of text data in a word processing document and find that the same information is required in the spreadsheet environment, why retype it when you can have the package duplicate it for you? You will be assured of data consistency between the two applications.

```
C:TRANS123.PRN L5        C35         Insert
                ═ N O N D O C U M E N T   E D I T   M E N U ═
  CURSOR        SCROLL          DELETE      OTHER              MENUS
^E up        ^U up          ^G char     ^J help          ^O onscreen format
^X down      ^Z down        ^T word     ^I tab           ^K block & save
^S left      ^R screen up   ^Y line     ^V turn insert off ^P print controls
^D right     ^C screen      Del char    ^M split the line ^Q quick functions
^A word left    down        ^U undo     ^L find/replace  Esc shorthand
^F word right               ^B top bit     again

Smith, John    500      2500     12                              <
Brown, Jill    330      1200     18                              <
Stick, Jim     600      9000     12                              <
Parks, Mal     120      5600     18                              <
Appel, Jon     900      1350     12                              ^
                                                                 ^
                                                                 ^
                                                                 ^
                                                                 ^
                                                                 ^
                                                                 ^
```

FIGURE 11-17.   Text data entered with WordStar

Bringing Data into
The Worksheet

Bringing data into the worksheet involves several steps. Before you can enter 1-2-3 commands, you must complete preliminary tasks. The data you wish to access must be saved in a word processing file before you attempt the import operation.

If you have a word processing program, use it for this exercise. You should check your word processor's documentation to ensure that you use the correct option for creating an ASCII text file without edit characters. Some word processors create the document and require you to strip off special characters to create an ASCII file; others have an option for creating it directly.

If you do not have a word processor to try this exercise with, you can still practice by entering the data shown in Figure 11-17 into the worksheet and printing the worksheet to a file with the command /Print File. Specify the range just as if you were printing it to your printer. In fact, the only differences are that you must specify a file name for saving the data, and you should choose Options Other Unformatted and Margins None from the Print menu before printing to disk. This process will create a text file for you that will automatically have the filename extension .PRN that you need to import the data.

Figure 11-17 shows some data that was entered with WordStar. You can duplicate these entries with your word processor, and then import the data into 1-2-3. Follow these steps:

1. Enter /**Quit Yes** to exit 1-2-3. Load your word processor, enter the data shown in Figure 11-17 into your word processor, and save the file as a text file with the filename extension .PRN and the name TEXT (TEXT.PRN).

   If your word processor assigns its own filenames, you will have to rename the file in step 3. If you print a 1-2-3 file to disk rather than the printer, 1-2-3 creates an ASCII text file on the disk with a filename extension .PRN. It is unlikely that your word processor follows the same naming convention; it is very likely that you will have to rename the text file to change the extension name.

2. Exit your word processor.

3. Use the DOS RENAME command if you do not have a filename extension of .PRN.

Using the /File Import command is the next step. This command can bring up to 8192 lines of text data into the worksheet. Each line of the file can have a maximum of 512 characters.

You have two basic options for importing text data into your worksheet. After using /File Import, you can choose either Text or Numbers. Your selection will affect the manner in which the data is placed on the worksheet. Use the Text option when you want to import the entire file, including all label entries. Use Numbers when you want to strip away everything but the numbers and the label data enclosed in quotes.

If you import the data in Figure 11-17 with the Text option, each line of the word processing document will become one long, left- aligned label. You will have an entire column of left-aligned labels. You can use the /Data Parse command to split these long labels into entries for individual cells.

If you select the Numbers option, only characters enclosed in double quotes and numbers will be imported. Characters not inside quotation marks, as well as blanks, will be eliminated in the import process. Each number in a line of the text file will generate a numeric cell entry, and each quote-enclosed label will create a left-justified label cell. Entries from the same line of a text file will produce entries in the same row of the worksheet, proceeding from the left to the right of the row with each new entry.

You will want to try both /File Import options with the data you entered a few minutes ago. Continue with these steps:

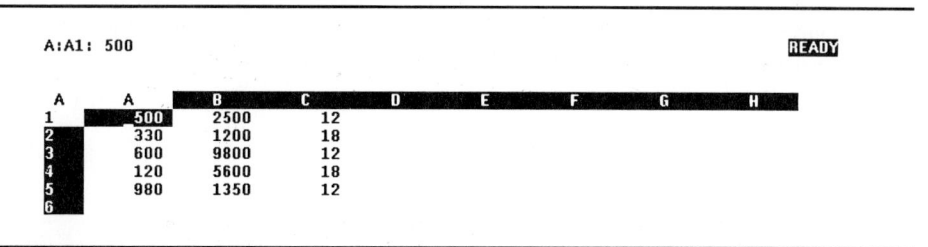

FIGURE 11-18.   WordStar data imported as numbers

1. Reload 1-2-3 or enter **/Worksheet Erase Yes** to ensure that memory is clear.

2. Enter **/File Import Numbers** to produce these results:

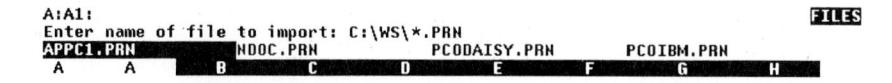

3. As 1-2-3 searches the disk for all files with the filename extension .PRN, select a text file from the list presented to produce the display shown in Figure 11-18. Notice how the quantity figures are in column A, and the prices are stored in column B.

4. Clear memory by entering **/Worksheet Erase Yes.**

5. Enter **/File Import Text** and select TEXT.PRN to produce the results shown in Figure 11-19.

Notice the difference between this example and the earlier one. All these entries are stored in column A as long labels. There is no automatic way to work with the

FIGURE 11-19.   WordStar data imported as text

quantity in the first row because it is not easily accessible; it is buried in the middle of a long label entry. (If you used tabs to separate the columns in your word processing document, 1-2-3 will expand these tabs correctly.)

Separating Text Data into Fields with /Data Parse

It is nice to be able to display data from your word processor in the worksheet environment, but the data imported with the Text option is not especially useful in its current format. Importing the data as numbers does not solve the problem, since only numeric entries and labels enclosed in quotation marks are brought over to the spreadsheet application.

You cannot use the data imported as text in calculations and cannot reference any of the individual pieces of information separately. The /Data Parse command offers a solution to this problem. *Parse* is a fancy word that has been used by programmers for a long time. In 1-2-3 it means splitting the long label entries into smaller pieces. You can use it to split the long labels created by /File Import into separate cell values. Using /Data Parse to accomplish this task is a multiple-step process. You must create a pattern that will be used for the parsing operation, define the labels to be parsed, define the area where the newly generated cell values should be stored, and tell 1-2-3 to begin the parse operation. The menu that provides these options is accessed by entering **/Data Parse** and is shown here:

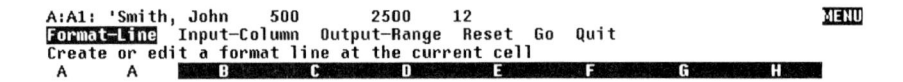

CREATING A FORMAT LINE   The *format line* is an edit pattern that will be used against each long label to determine how it should be split into its component parts and what each component should look like. Each cell in the column of long labels will have the format line applied to it until another format line is encountered within the column. At that point, the new format line will be used until the end of the labels or until another format line is encountered.

1-2-3 makes its best guess at the format that should be used for each component, using the symbols shown in Table 11-1 to present each of the options. It makes its determination from the entries in the line in which you place your cell pointer, and it inserts a new line and positions the format line immediately above this. When it encounters a space in the label, it assumes that a field has ended.

Character	Meaning
D	Marks the first character of a date block.
L	Marks the first character of a label block.
S	Indicates that the character below should be skipped during the parse operation. This character is never generated by 1-2-3, but you can enter it when you are editing a format line.
T	Marks the first character of a time block.
V	Marks the first character of a value block.
>	Indicates that the block started by the letter that precedes it is continued. The entry that began with a letter will be placed in one worksheet cell until a skip or another letter is encountered.
*	Represents a blank space immediately below the character. This position can become part of the block that precedes it if additional space is required.

TABLE 11-1.   Format Line Characters for Data Parse

If you want, you can create many format lines for one column of labels; however, each of them must be generated separately. Despite the fact that you can create multiple format lines, some consistency in the organization is required. You would not want to create a format line for each line that is parsed.

Try this by moving the cell pointer to the column of long labels you imported. Follow these steps:

1. Move the cell pointer to A1.

    This is the top entry in the column of long labels generated with /File Import.

2. Enter **/Data Parse**.

3. Enter **Format-Line**.

    This produces the following menu of Format-Line options:

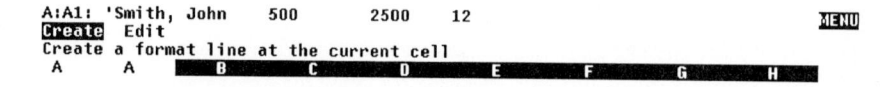

```
A:A1: 'Smith, John     500      2500     12                              MENU
Create  Edit
Create a format line at the current cell
   A       A        B          C          D        E          F          G          H
```

4. Enter **Create**.

    1-2-3 will insert a blank line above the cell pointer's location and generate a format line at this location that looks like this:

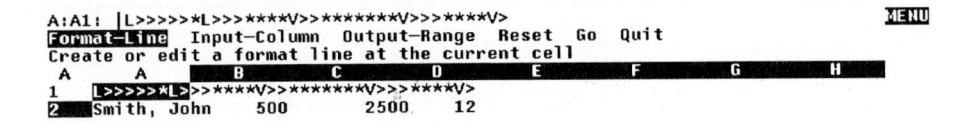

If you were to continue with /Data Parse and use this format line, five fields would be generated. A separate field would be generated for both the first and last names. If you want both the first and last names within the same cell, you will need to modify the format line.

MODIFYING THE FORMAT LINE   You can modify the format line you have generated by selecting Format-Line again, since the Data Parse menu remains on the screen for further selections. This time you will choose Edit to make your changes. Try this technique to alter the two name fields to make them one field:

1. Enter **Format-Line**.

2. Enter **Edit** to produce the display shown in Figure 11-20.
   The OVR indicator is turned on to indicate that you are in overstrike mode. Any character you type will replace a character in the existing format line. You can use the UP and DOWN ARROW keys to change which rows appear, although the format line always appears in the first line.

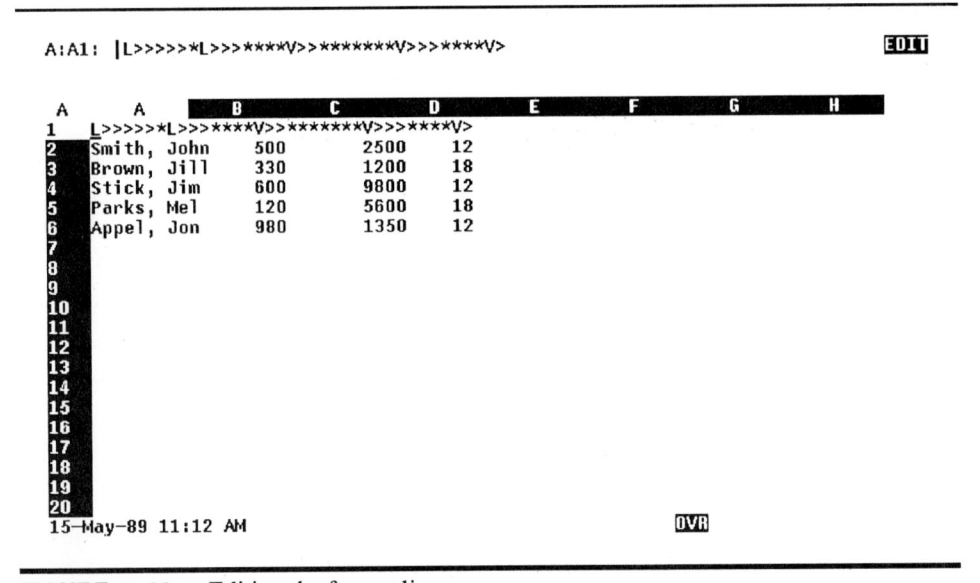

FIGURE 11-20.   Editing the format line

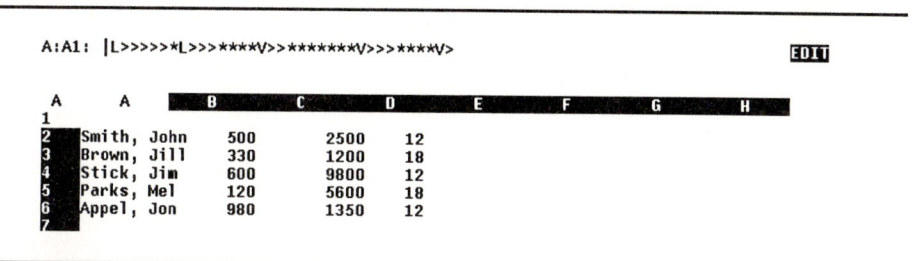

A:A1: |L>>>>>*L>>>****V>>********V>>>****V>   EDIT

FIGURE 11-21.   Edited format line

3. Move the cell pointer to the asterisk that precedes the second "L," and type >>
   to change the display so it looks like the worksheet in Figure 11-21.
   This will cause the two name fields to be combined into one field.

4. Press ENTER to finalize.

PRODUCING THE FINAL PRODUCT   There are still a few more steps. You
have to tell 1-2-3 where the input is located and where you would like to store the
output of the parse operation. Your last step is to select Go from the menu so that 1-2-3
will apply the information entered in the preliminary steps to your column of long
labels, producing individual entries.

Follow these steps to define the input and output areas and create the finished
product:

1. Enter **Input-Column** and then highlight A1..A6 with the cell pointer as in
   Figure 11-22. You must include the format line in the input column.

2. Press ENTER.

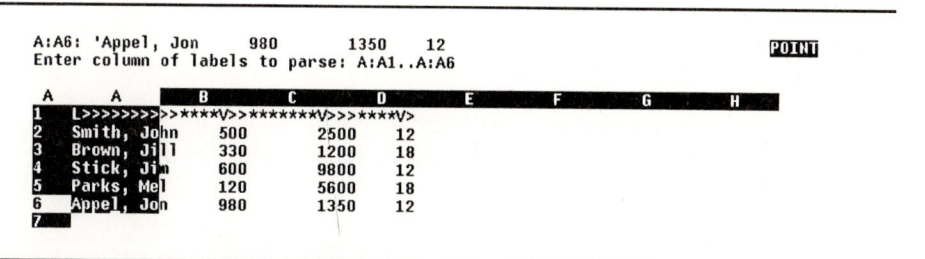

A:A6: 'Appel, Jon   980   1350   12   POINT
Enter column of labels to parse: A:A1..A:A6

FIGURE 11-22.   Selecting the data to parse

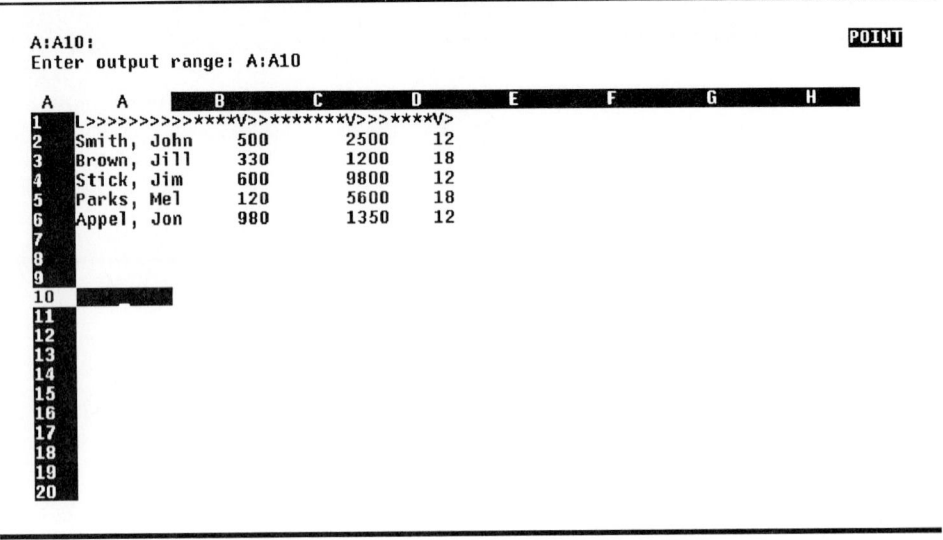

```
A:A10:                                                          POINT
Enter output range: A:A10

    A      A         B          C          D      E      F      G      H
1          L>>>>>>>>>>****V>>*******V>>>****V>
2          Smith, John   500        2500      12
3          Brown, Jill   330        1200      18
4          Stick, Jim    600        9800      12
5          Parks, Mel    120        5600      18
6          Appel, Jon    980        1350      12
7
8
9
10
11
12
13
14
15
16
17
18
19
20
```

FIGURE 11-23.   Selecting where 1-2-3 places the parsed data

3. Enter **Output-Range** and move the cell pointer to A10 as in Figure 11-23.
   You can position the cell pointer in the upper-left corner of the range, rather than calculating the exact space requirements and making a mistake.

4. Press ENTER and enter **Go** to produce the results in Figure 11-24.

5. Enter **/Worksheet Column Set-Width**, type **11**, and press ENTER to expand the column width, as shown in Figure 11-25.

This conversion required a number of steps and would not be a worthwhile investment of time for so little data. With volumes of data, however, this command can provide a real enhancement that can save hours of time.

REVIEW EXERCISE

This chapter has taught you several new skills that you will use for your worksheets. To further enhance your advanced file-management skills, try this exercise to create price and sales projection worksheets:

1. Erase the current worksheet. *Hint:* Use /Worksheet Erase Yes.

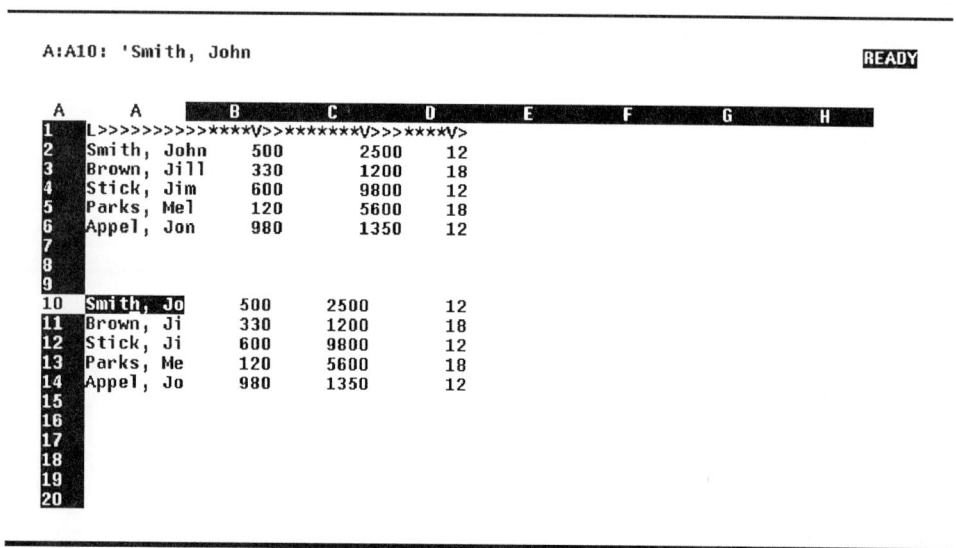

FIGURE 11-24.   Imported data that has been parsed

2. Set the column width for all columns to 15. *Hint:* Use /Worksheet Global Col-Width, type **15**, and press ENTER.

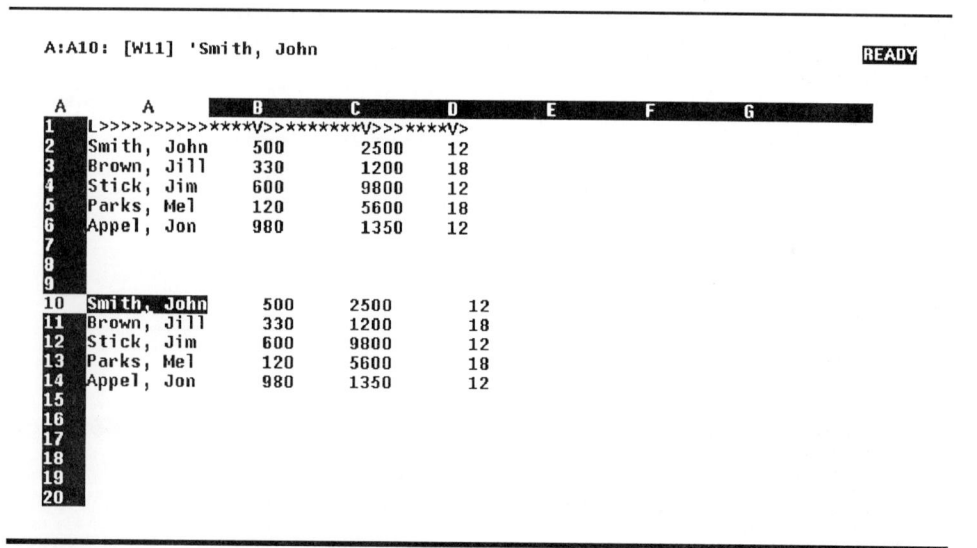

FIGURE 11-25.   Widening column A

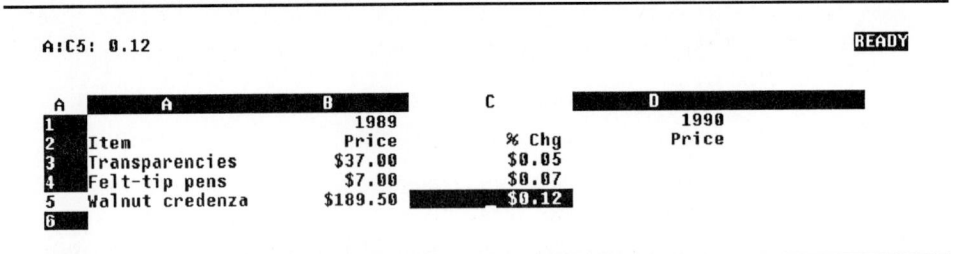

FIGURE 11-26.   Worksheet entries for price projection model

3. Set the format for all cells to currency with two decimal digits. *Hint:* Use /Worksheet Global Format Currency, type **0**, and press ENTER.

4. Make the entries shown in Figure 11-26. Enter the years as right-aligned labels.

5. Enter the formula +**B4**∗**(1**+**C4)** in D4. Copy this formula to C5..C6. *Hint:* Enter +**A4**∗**B4** in C4. Then select /Copy, press ENTER, select C5..C6, and press ENTER again.

6. Set the format for the percentage change to show the numbers as percentages with two digits after the decimal point. The results appear in Figure 11-27. *Hint:* Use /Range Format Percent, type **2**, and press ENTER.

7. Name the cells containing the item names ITEM_NAMES. *Hint:* Use /Range Name Create, type **ITEM_NAMES**, press ENTER, highlight A3..A5, and press ENTER again.

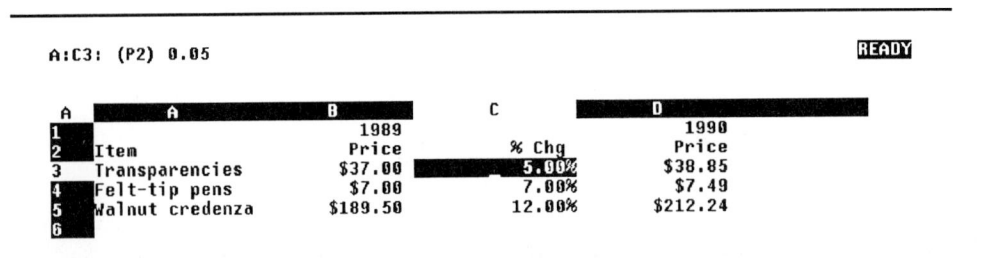

FIGURE 11-27.   Completed price projection model

8. Name the cells containing the 1990 prices 1990_PRICE. *Hint:* Use /Range Name Create, type **1990_PRICE**, press ENTER, highlight D3..D5, and press ENTER again.

9. Save the values of the cells containing the 1990 prices as PRICE_90. Since you have named the range containing the 1990 prices, you can provide the range name instead of the range address. *Hint:* Use /File Xtract Values, type **1990_PRICE**, press ENTER, type **1990_PRICE**, and press ENTER again.

10. Save this file as PRICES. *Hint:* Use /File Save, type **PRICES**, and press ENTER.

11. Erase the PRICES worksheet from 1-2-3's memory. (*Hint:* Use /Worksheet Erase.) At this point you are ready to create a new worksheet that uses the information in the PRICE_90 worksheet. To make the new worksheet easier to create, you can use the data from the PRICES worksheet in your new worksheet.

12. Set the column width for all columns to 15. *Hint:* Use /Worksheet Global Col-Width, type **15**, and press ENTER.

13. Move to A4.

14. Copy the ITEM_NAMES range from the PRICES worksheet into this worksheet. *Hint:* Use /File Combine Copy Named/Specified Range, type **ITEM_NAMES**, press ENTER, type **PRICES**, and press ENTER again.

15. Make the entries shown in Figure 11-28.

16. Set the format of B4..B6 and D4..D6 to Currency with 2 decimal digits. *Hint:* Use /Range Format Currency, type **2**, press ENTER, select B4..B6, and press ENTER again. Then perform the same steps for the D4..D6 range.

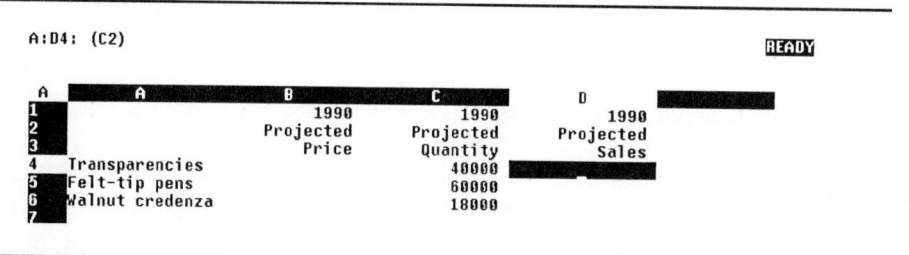

FIGURE 11-28.   Worksheet entries for sales projection model

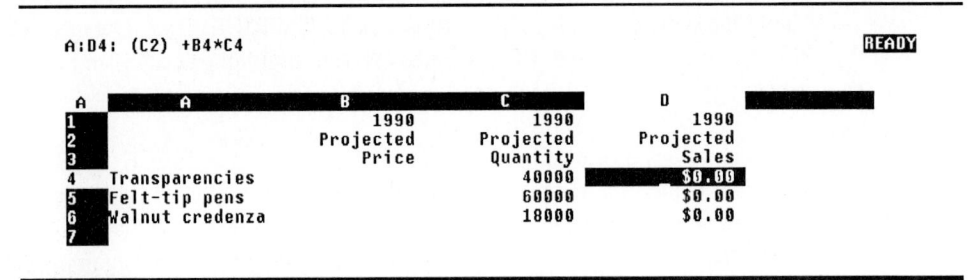

A:D4: (C2) +B4*C4   READY

A	A	B	C	D	
1		1990	1990	1990	
2		Projected	Projected	Projected	
3		Price	Quantity	Sales	
4	Transparencies		40000	$0.00	
5	Felt-tip pens		60000	$0.00	
6	Walnut credenza		18000	$0.00	
7					

FIGURE 11-29.   Sales projection model without prices

17. Enter the formula +**B4*C4** in D4. Copy this formula to D5..D6. The worksheet now looks like the one in Figure 11-29. (*Hint:* Enter +**B4*C4** in D4. Then select /Copy, press ENTER, select D5..D6, and press ENTER again.) At this point, all that is missing is the price data. After saving the file, you can try several methods of entering the price data into the worksheet.

18. Move to B4.

19. Copy the price values in the PRICE_90 file. (*Hint:* Use /File Combine Copy Entire-File, type **PRICE_90**, and press ENTER.) Notice that the worksheet contains the values for the 1990 prices, since the values were extracted to the PRICE_90 file.

20. Erase the 1990 prices. *Hint:* Use /Range Erase, select B4..B6, and press ENTER.

21. Add the price values in the PRICES file. (*Hint:* Use /File Combine Add Named/Specified Range, type **1990_PRICE**, press ENTER, type **PRICES**, and press ENTER.) The worksheet now contains the values for the 1990 prices instead of the formulas that the PRICES worksheet has, since the values are added to the PRICE_90 file. Try the next two steps to create a external file link to incorporate the 1990 prices from the PRICES worksheet file into this worksheet.

22. Erase the 1990 prices. *Hint:* Use /Range Erase, select B4..B6, and press ENTER.

23. Enter +**<<PRICES.WK3>>D3** in B4 and copy this formula to B5..B6. The results are shown in Figure 11-30. 1-2-3 adjusts the row in the address of these formulas for the external file link used as 1-2-3 copies the formula to B5 and B6.

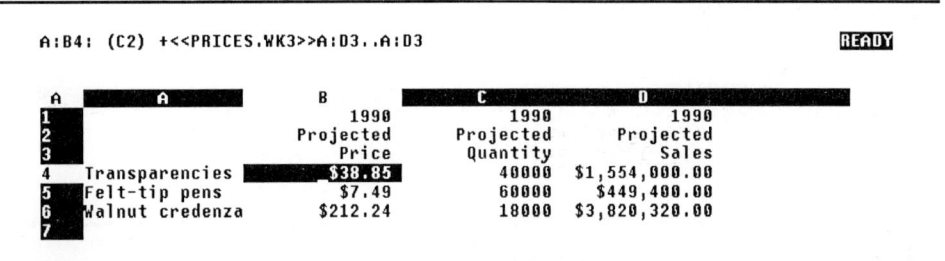

A:B4: (C2) +<<PRICES.WK3>>A:D3..A:D3   READY

	A	B	C	D
1		1990	1990	1990
2		Projected	Projected	Projected
3		Price	Quantity	Sales
4	Transparencies	$38.85	40000	$1,554,000.00
5	Felt-tip pens	$7.49	60000	$449,400.00
6	Walnut credenza	$212.24	18000	$3,820,320.00
7				

FIGURE 11-30.   Sales projection model with prices added

24. Save this worksheet as SALES_90. *Hint:* Use /File Save, type **SALES_90**, and press ENTER.

    This chapter also introduced the /Data Parse command for breaking long labels into smaller cells. You can use this worksheet to try these features by printing this worksheet to a file and importing it.

25. Print the range A4..D6 to a file called PARSE with no margins, headers, footers, or page breaks. *Hint:* Press HOME. Select /Print Printer, type **PARSE**, and press ENTER. Select Range, press HOME, type a period, press END-HOME, and press ENTER. Use Options Margin None to remove the margins. Then use Other Unformatted Quit Go Quit to print the file.

26. Erase the SALES_90 worksheet from 1-2-3's memory. *Hint:* Use /Worksheet Erase.

27. Import the PARSE.PRN file into the new 1-2-3 worksheet as long labels. The worksheet looks like the one in Figure 11-31. *Hint:* Use /File Import Text, type **PARSE**, and press ENTER.

28. Create a format string that looks like this:

	A	B	C	D	E	F	G	H
1	L>>>>>>>>>>>>> *********V>>>> *********V>>> *V>>>>>>>>>>>>							
2	Transparencies	$38.85		40000	$1,554,000.00			
3	Felt-tip pens	$7.49		60000	$449,400.00			
4	Walnut credenza	$212.24		18000	$3,820,320.00			
5								

    Hint: Use /Data Parse Format-Line Create.

29. Select the imported rows to parse. *Hint:* Use Input-Column, select A1..A4, and press ENTER.

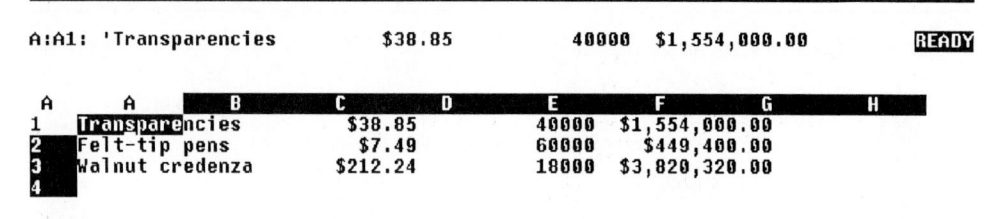

A:A1: 'Transparencies $38.85   40000 $1,554,000.00   READY

A	A	B	C	D	E	F	G	H
1	Transparencies		$38.85		40000	$1,554,000.00		
2	Felt-tip pens		$7.49		60000	$449,400.00		
3	Walnut credenza		$212.24		18000	$3,820,320.00		
4								

FIGURE 11-31.   1-2-3 print file imported into a new worksheet

30. Select A10 as the destination for the parsed data. *Hint:* Use Output-Range, select A10, and press ENTER.

31. Parse the data using the settings you have entered. The results appear in Figure 11-32. *Hint:* Use Go.

REVIEW

- You can extract a portion of a worksheet to another worksheet file with the /File Xtract command. This command copies either values (formulas are converted

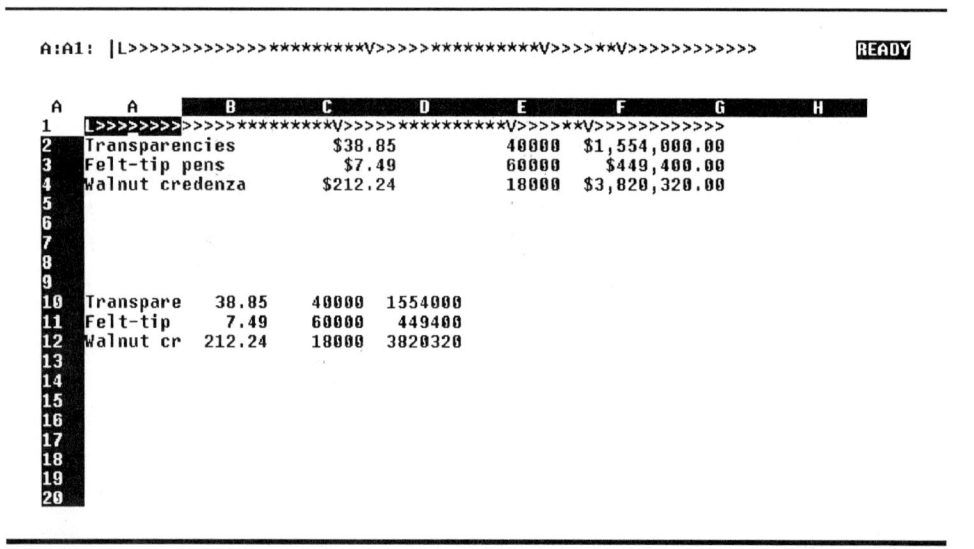

A:A1: |L>>>>>>>>>>>>>>*********V>>>>>**********V>>>>**V>>>>>>>>>>>>   READY

A	A	B	C	D	E	F	G	H
1	L>>>>>>>>>>>>>*********V>>>>>**********V>>>>**V>>>>>>>>>>>>							
2	Transparencies		$38.85		40000	$1,554,000.00		
3	Felt-tip pens		$7.49		60000	$449,400.00		
4	Walnut credenza		$212.24		18000	$3,820,320.00		
5								
6								
7								
8								
9								
10	Transpare	38.85	40000	1554000				
11	Felt-tip	7.49	60000	449400				
12	Walnut cr	212.24	18000	3820320				
13								
14								
15								
16								
17								
18								
19								
20								

FIGURE 11-32.   Parsed data

to their value in the new worksheet) or formulas (formulas remain intact). The Formulas option should only be used if the cells the formulas reference are part of the range extracted to the new file. Once a file is extracted, you can retrieve it and use it just as you do other worksheet files.

- You can combine the values of a range or an entire worksheet file into the current worksheet file with the /File Combine command. You must be careful where the cell pointer is when you use this command, because the cells copied into the current worksheet have the same relative distance to the cell pointer's position as the cells have in their original file to the upper-left corner of the range or worksheet. The /File Combine options let you copy (incoming data replaces current worksheet data), add (incoming numbers are added to the current worksheet data), or subtract (incoming numbers are subtracted from the current worksheet data).

- A cell formula can contain external file links that refer to a cell or a range in another worksheet. The cell formulas containing an external file link must have the filename in double angle brackets (<< >>) and the cell address or range name of the other worksheet the link refers to. The links are updated when you use the /File Admin Link-Refresh command.

- 1-2-3 can import, or bring in, data from other computer programs if the other computer program can produce a text file (which does not contain any special characters). The imported data can be separated into long labels with each line in the imported data converting into a cell's entry, or into individual cell entries for each line if the data is separated by commas or spaces and the text data is enclosed in quotes.

- The /Data Parse command can break labels into smaller cell entries. It also converts the label data into numbers, dates, and times if the appropriate format line characters are used. The format line determines how 1-2-3 divides the text into cells.

Commands and Keys

/DPFC	Creates a format line to parse label data
/DPFE	Edits a format line to parse label data
/DPG	Parses the data using the other /Data Parse command selections
/DPI	Selects the format line and input labels to parse
/DPO	Selects the area where 1-2-3 copies the parsed data
/FAL	Refreshes external file links
/FCA	Adds range or worksheet data from another file to the current worksheet

/FCC	Copies a range or worksheet from another file to the current worksheet
/FCS	Subtracts range or worksheet data that is from another file from the current worksheet
/FIN	Brings data into 1-2-3 and stores numbers and characters enclosed in quotes in individual cells
/FIT	Brings data into 1-2-3 and stores the data as long labels
/FXF	Copies the formulas in a worksheet range to a new worksheet file
/FXV	Copies the values in a worksheet range to a new worksheet file

12

USING THE MULTILEVEL SPREADSHEET FEATURES

Adding Worksheets
Adding Other Worksheet Files
Review Exercise
Review

When you perform tasks without the computer, paper is the normal medium for organizing your information. You usually need more than one sheet of paper for each task or activity. With Release 3, you can use multiple sheets in one worksheet file to help you organize your information. You might store salary information on one sheet and travel expenses on another. Or perhaps you are overseeing several branch operations and want to organize the data for each branch separately. Release 3 provides the solution with multiple-sheet capabilities. Once you have added the extra sheet, you can access information in all of the sheets as if it was on one sheet by specifying the sheet level in which you are interested. You can also open more than one worksheet file in memory at one time. This allows you to bring together the information in these files and move between them for comparison purposes.

The limitation on your electronic desktop is 256 sheets at one time. These sheets can all be in the same file, or they can be from different files. Realistically, the true limit is likely to be the amount of memory in your machine; you may run out of memory in which to store the sheets before you reach the absolute limit if 256 sheets.

ADDING WORKSHEETS

Adding a worksheet to a worksheet file is like adding another sheet to a folder: you flip to the current sheet at which you want to add the new sheets and then add one or more sheets before or after the current sheet. If you have multiple sheets already in the file, you move to the worksheet where you want to add the new worksheets, and then tell 1-2-3 that you want to add worksheets, specifying whether you want them before or after the current sheet.

To try this out, you will make some entries to a new worksheet file and then add worksheets. Use the following steps to create a multilevel worksheet:

1. Use Figure 12-1 as your guide to complete the entries for a short worksheet example.

2. Enter /**Worksheet Insert Sheet** after completing the entries shown in Figure 12-1.

   1-2-3 displays this prompt:

```
A:D10: @SUM(D4..D8)                                          MENU
Before  After
Insert blank worksheets in front of the current worksheet
```

3. Enter **Before**.

   1-2-3 prompts you for the number of worksheets to enter, like this:

```
A:A1:                                                        POINT
Enter number of worksheets to insert: 1
```

4. Press ENTER to accept the default of 1. Enter **1**.

   The top of your screen looks like this:

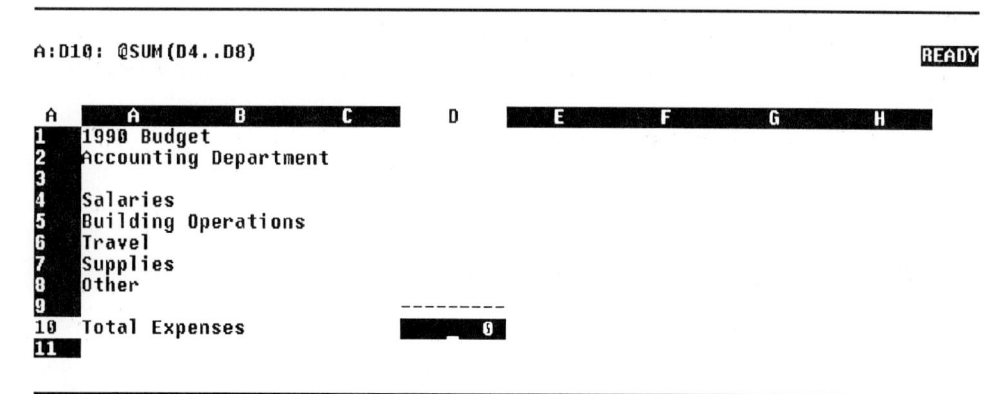

FIGURE 12-1.   Worksheet for multilevel example

This is the new empty worksheet you have inserted. You entered it before the worksheet in which you made the entries, so the data that you entered is now on the second worksheet. Notice that the new worksheet has an "A" at the intersection of the row and column names—this is the sheet level indicator. "A" stands for the first sheet.

To see your entries again, you must tell 1-2-3 you want to switch to the next worksheet, sheet B:

5. Press CTRL-PGUP.

Your data looks like this:

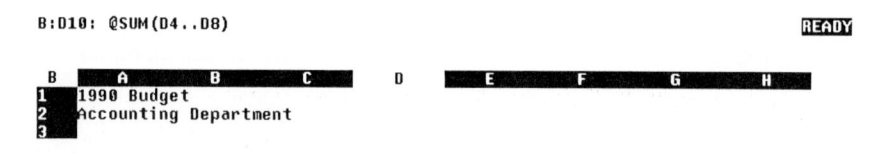

Notice that the corner of the worksheet no longer contains an "A" as it did before you inserted the new worksheet. The worksheet letter consistently appears in the upper-left corner of the worksheet and in cell addresses as the letter before the colon, as in B:B1. 1-2-3 labels worksheets just like it labels columns. The first 26 worksheets are labeled A through Z. After the twenty-sixth worksheet, 1-2-3 uses two-letter combinations starting with AA and ending with IV. As this step describes, you can press CTRL-PGUP to move to the next worksheet. CTRL-PGDN will move you to the previous worksheet.

6. Press CTRL-PGDN. 1-2-3 returns to the first worksheet.

   At this point you can only see one worksheet at a time. You can look at two or three worksheets at a time by using 1-2-3's window features.

7. Press CTRL-PGUP to return to worksheet B.

   You can add other worksheets to try other /Worksheet Insert Sheet options:

8. Enter /**Worksheet Insert Sheet After**, type **3**, and press ENTER.

   1-2-3 inserts three blank worksheets after worksheet B.

9. Press CTRL-PGUP and CTRL-PGDN to move through new worksheets labeled C, D, and E.

Creating Windows to See Other Worksheets

When you are working with multiple sheets, you will want to see more than one at a time. However, the full screen display only shows one worksheet at a time. The /Worksheet Window command introduced in Chapter 5 lets you look at two or three worksheets at once. To look at the worksheets you have added, follow these steps:

1. Press CTRL-PGUP until you are on worksheet A. Move to A6, which is where you want to split the worksheet into windows.

2. Enter /**Worksheet Window Horizontal**.

   The screen now looks like Figure 12-2.

3. Press CTRL-PGUP. Your worksheet now looks like the one in Figure 12-3.

1-2-3 moved the cell pointer to the next worksheet while keeping the second window on worksheet A. You can use horizontal and vertical windows to look at two different worksheets within the same worksheet file, just as you used horizontal and vertical windows to look at two different areas of the same worksheet. You can always tell which worksheet is current by looking at the cell address in the control panel. The /Worksheet Window Vertical command can also be used to view two worksheets.

1-2-3 has another /Worksheet Window option that displays three windows at once. To see how 1-2-3 will display your worksheet file, follow these steps:

1. Enter /**Worksheet Window Clear** to remove the existing window.

A:A5:   `READY`

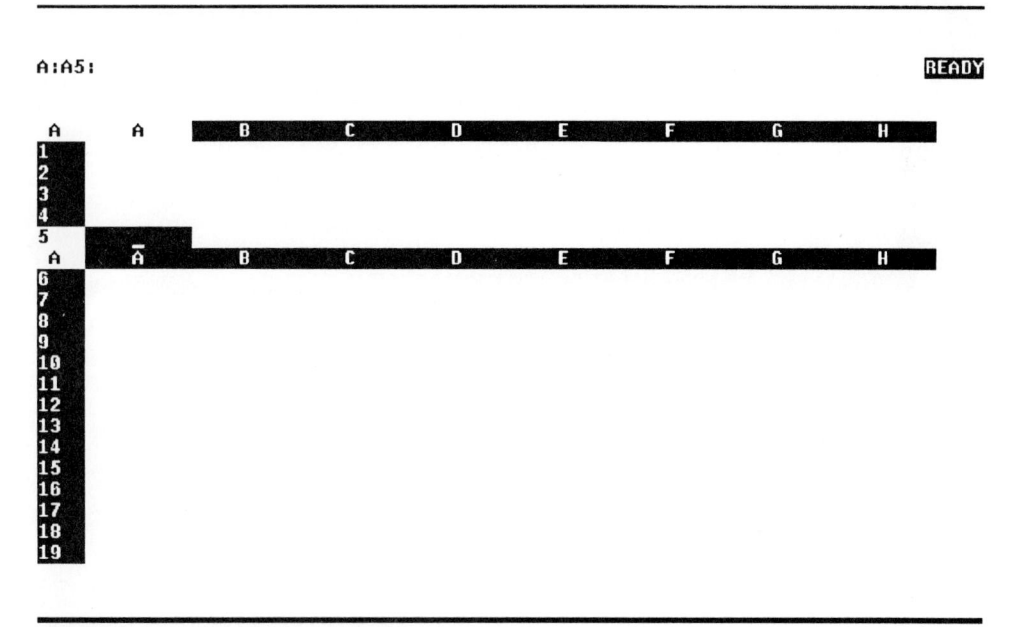

FIGURE 12-2.   Horizontal window

B:A5: 'Building Operations   `READY`

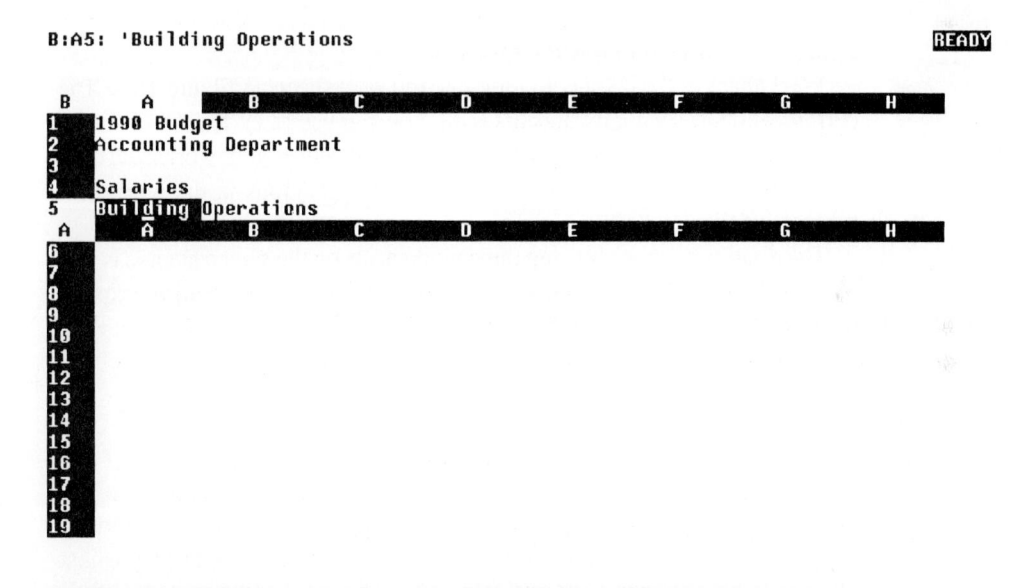

FIGURE 12-3.   Using a horizontal window to view two worksheets

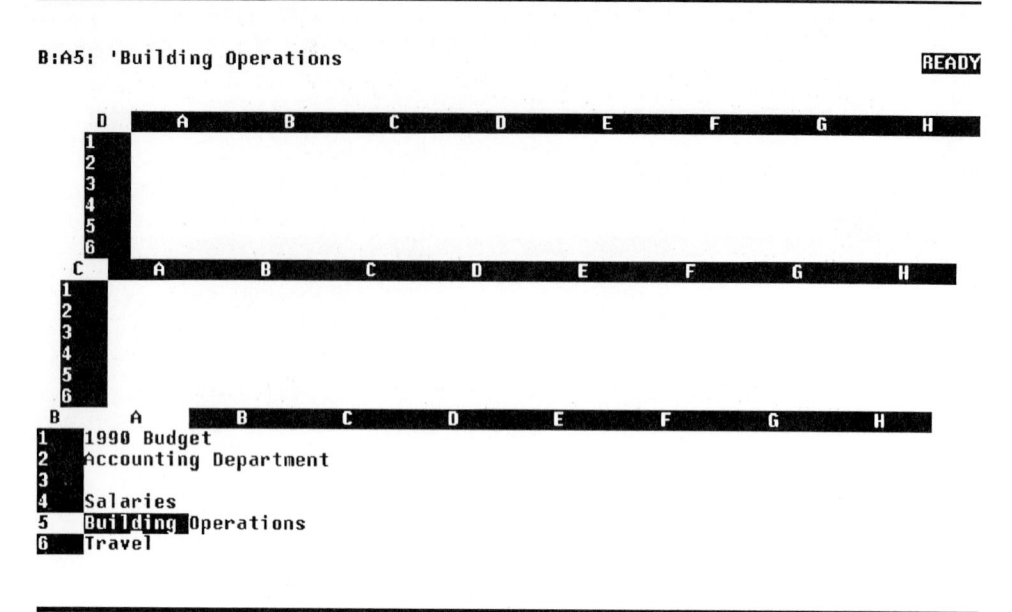

FIGURE 12-4. Using /Worksheet Window Perspective to view three worksheets

2. Enter /**Worksheet Window Perspective**.

1-2-3 changes the display to look like the worksheets in Figure 12-4. The current worksheet initially appears first. You can use F6 (WINDOW), CTRL-PGUP, and CTRL-PGDN to move through the worksheets. If your worksheet only has one or two worksheets, the last one or two positions in the worksheet perspective view will appear empty.

The disadvantage of showing three worksheets on the screen at once is you only see six lines of each worksheet. If you want, you can temporarily expand one of the worksheets to use the full screen and then contract it when you want to return to the window display.

3. Press ALT-F6 (ZOOM) to make worksheet B fill the screen.

4. Press ALT-F6 (ZOOM) to return the display to the three worksheets.

Now that you have created this perspective window, you can return to displaying only the current worksheet. Removing this window display is just like removing a horizontal or vertical window display.

5. Enter **/Worksheet Window Clear**.

   1-2-3 now only displays worksheet B, although you can go to the others by pressing CTRL-PGUP and CTRL-PGDN.

Deleting Worksheets In a Worksheet File

Just as you can create and delete worksheet files, you can also create and delete worksheets within a worksheet file. The previous steps described how easily you can add a worksheet to a file. The steps for deleting a worksheet are just as easy. The worksheet you have created has more worksheets than you need for three departments and a summary sheet, so follow these steps to remove one of the worksheets:

1. Press CTRL-PGUP until the cell pointer is in worksheet D.

2. Enter **/Worksheet Delete Sheet**.

   1-2-3 prompts you for the worksheet range to delete:

```
D:A5:                                                      POINT
Enter range of worksheets to delete: D:A5..D:A5
```

   If you wanted to delete multiple worksheets, you would press CTRL-PGUP or CTRL-PGDN to highlight at least one cell in each sheet that you wanted to delete. To delete a single worksheet, you want to position the cell pointer on the worksheet you want to delete before executing this command (to prevent accidentally deleting the wrong one).

3. Press ENTER to select worksheet D.

   When 1-2-3 returns to READY mode, you might think it has not deleted the worksheet. When 1-2-3 deletes a worksheet, it reassigns letters to the remaining worksheets. The worksheet now labeled worksheet D was worksheet E before you deleted the worksheet. You can test this by trying to move to the next worksheet.

4. Press CTRL-PGUP.

   1-2-3 beeps to indicate that the worksheet file does not contain any more worksheets after D.

5. Enter **/File Save**, type **DEPTS**, and press ENTER.

Designing Multilevel Applications

1-2-3 will let you include up to 256 worksheets in one file, but you want to ensure that multiple sheets are providing you benefits. Application planning lets you decide how to arrange the worksheet data so you can easily access the information you want. While you have unlimited possibilities for arranging your worksheet, this chapter considers two different arrangements of information. The same considerations that determine how the information is divided into worksheets will determine how you split your own data into multiple worksheets.

STORING THE SAME TYPE OF INFORMATION   When you created models that used the /File Combine commands, the models that you used contained the same type of information, but the information was for different branches, regions, or departments within the same company. The /File Combine operation was used to provide a consolidated view of the company's performance.

Multiple sheets with similar information might be useful in expense reports for different departments, where each department uses the same format and worksheet design but the department numbers and expenses differ. Figure 12-5 shows an example of multiple worksheets that contain the same type of data. The worksheet A contains the summary information for all of the departments. The worksheets B and C contain

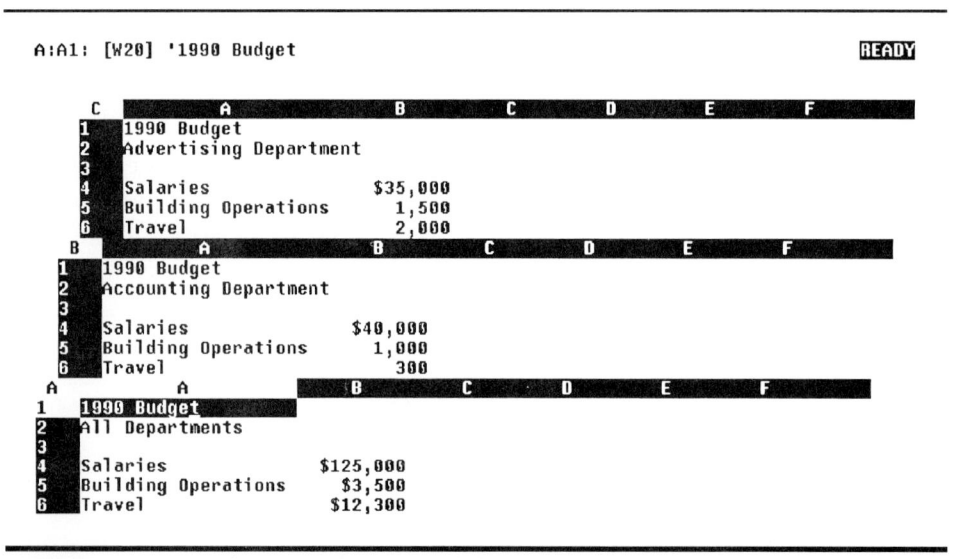

FIGURE 12-5.   Multiple worksheets containing same type of data

the detailed information for the accounting and advertising departments. The worksheet file can also contain the same type of information for all of the remaining departments in the company. As numbers are entered in the worksheets for the individual departments, the formula in the summary worksheet immediately updates the values for department expense. Consider how much easier this is than using the /File Combine Add command, where you must remember to invoke the /File Combine operation for each of the departmental sheets.

STORING DIFFERENT TYPES OF INFORMATION   When you create databases like the ones in Chapter 9, you store the data, the criteria, and the output area for database queries on the same worksheet. This works well when the database is small, but as the database grows, the database, criteria, and output area will need more room. The additional room required makes it trickier for you to position these three areas without having them interfere with each other. Also, with these three areas on a single worksheet, you have to be careful as you add and delete rows and columns not to destroy part of your work.

By using multiple worksheets and storing these three different types of information on separate worksheets, you can work on one area and not have to consider the effect of deleting or inserting rows or columns on the other worksheets. Try this with the employee database you created in Chapter 9 by following these steps:

1. Enter **/File Retrieve**, select EMPLOYEE, and press ENTER. Your screen looks like Figure 12-6. The records may be in a different order, which will not matter for this example. If you do not have this file available, enter the field names and the first three records.

2. Enter **/Worksheet Insert Sheet After 2** to add two worksheets.

3. Enter **/Worksheet Window Perspective** to display all three worksheets.

4. Make the following entries in worksheets B and C:
    B:A1: Criteria
    B:A2: Last Name
    B:A3: Camp*
    C:A1: Last Name
    C:B1: First Name
    C:C1: "SS#
    C:D1: Job Code
    C:E1: "Salary
    C:F1: Location

A:A1: [W12] 'Last Name

A	A	B	C	D	E	F
1	Last Name	First Name	SS#	Job Code	Salary	Location
2	Larson	Mary	543-98-9876	23	$12,000	2
3	Campbell	David	213-76-9874	23	$23,000	10
4	Campbell	Keith	569-89-7654	12	$32,000	2
5	Stephens	Tom	219-78-8954	15	$17,800	2
6	Caldor	Larry	459-34-0921	23	$32,500	4
7	Lightnor	Peggy	560-55-4311	14	$23,500	10
8	McCartin	John	817-66-1212	15	$54,600	2
9	Justof	Jack	431-78-9963	17	$41,200	4
10	Patterson	Lyle	212-11-9090	12	$21,500	10
11	Miller	Lisa	214-89-6756	23	$18,700	2
12						
13						
14						
15						
16						
17						
18						
19						
20						

FIGURE 12-6.   Employee database

5. Press HOME, enter /**Worksheet Column Column-Range Set-Width**, press RIGHT ARROW twice, press ENTER, type **12**, and press ENTER again to set the width of columns A, B, and C to 12.

6. Move to worksheet A.

7. Enter /**Data Query Input**, select A1..F11, and press ENTER.

8. Enter **Criteria**, press CTRL-PGUP, select A2..A3, and press ENTER.

9. Enter **Output**, press CTRL-PGUP twice, select A1..F1, and press ENTER.

10. Enter **Extract**.
      The three worksheets look like the ones in Figure 12-7.

11. Select **Quit** to return to READY mode.

While this example describes an application that only applies to databases, you will encounter other situations that will suggest the use of multiple worksheets for different

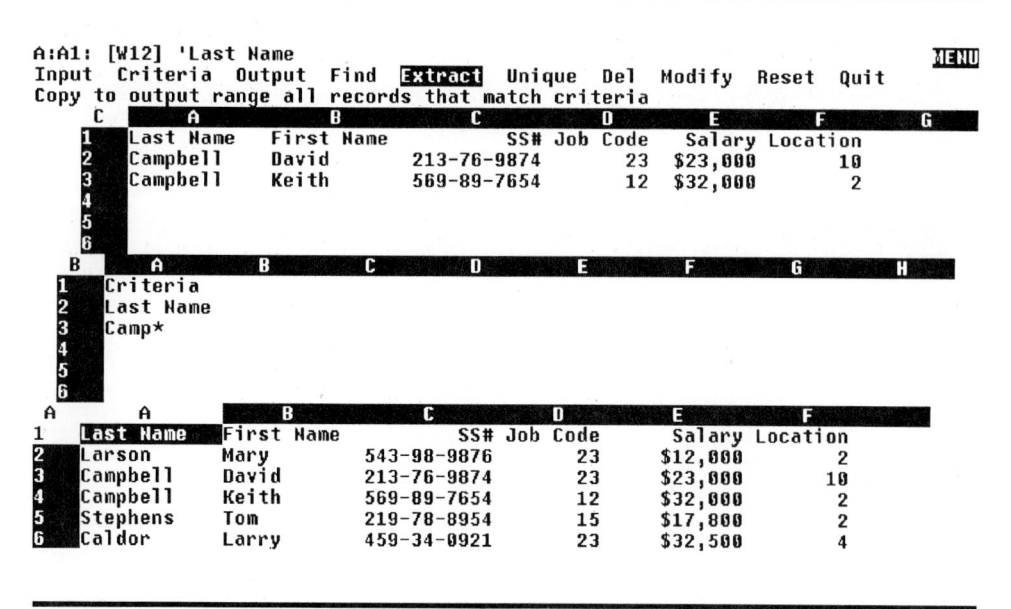

FIGURE 12-7.   Employee database using multiple worksheets

types of data. Another example is a worksheet file containing various types of reports. Since each report may use a different format, you do not want them too close to each other to prevent your actions in one report affecting another. You can put each report on a separate worksheet, and then each worksheet can have its own default format and label prefix. If you want to further enhance your worksheet, you could design the first worksheet as a data-entry screen. After data was entered in the first screen, 1-2-3 would automatically use that data in the other worksheets to create the reports. Figure 12-8 shows such a worksheet, which minimizes the chance that a user will accidentally enter data in the wrong place.

Copying Across Worksheets

You can copy data across worksheets as easily as you can copy it across one sheet. Copying across worksheets is an ideal solution when you are storing similar types of data on multiple worksheets. To try it, follow these steps:

1. Enter **/File Retrieve**, type **DEPTS**, and press ENTER.

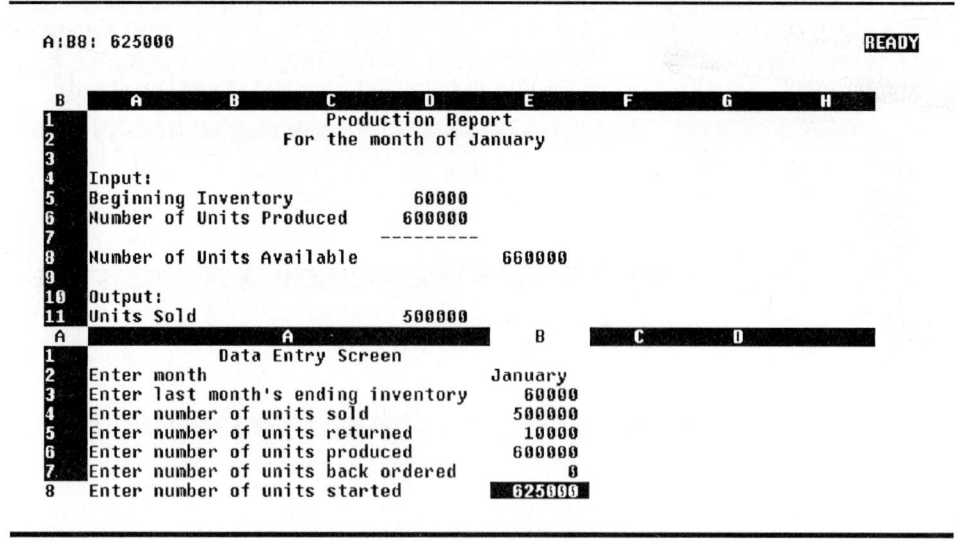

FIGURE 12-8.   Worksheets containing different types of data

2. Enter /**Worksheet Window Perspective** to see three worksheets at once.

3. Press CTRL-PGUP to move to worksheet B, which contains the data you entered earlier in the chapter.

4. Enter /**Copy.**

5. Select A1..D10 as the range to copy, and press ENTER.

6. Press CTRL-PGDN to move to worksheet A.

7. Highlight A1 and press ENTER. Press CTRL-PGDN to see the data you copied.
    1-2-3 copied all of the information in worksheet B to worksheet A. Just as in copying cells in a single worksheet, you can select a range to copy and make several copies:

8. Press CTRL-PGUP to return to worksheet B.

9. Enter /**Copy**, select A1..D10 as the range to copy, and press ENTER.

10. Press CTRL-PGUP to move to worksheet C.

`A:A1: '1990 Budget`   `READY`

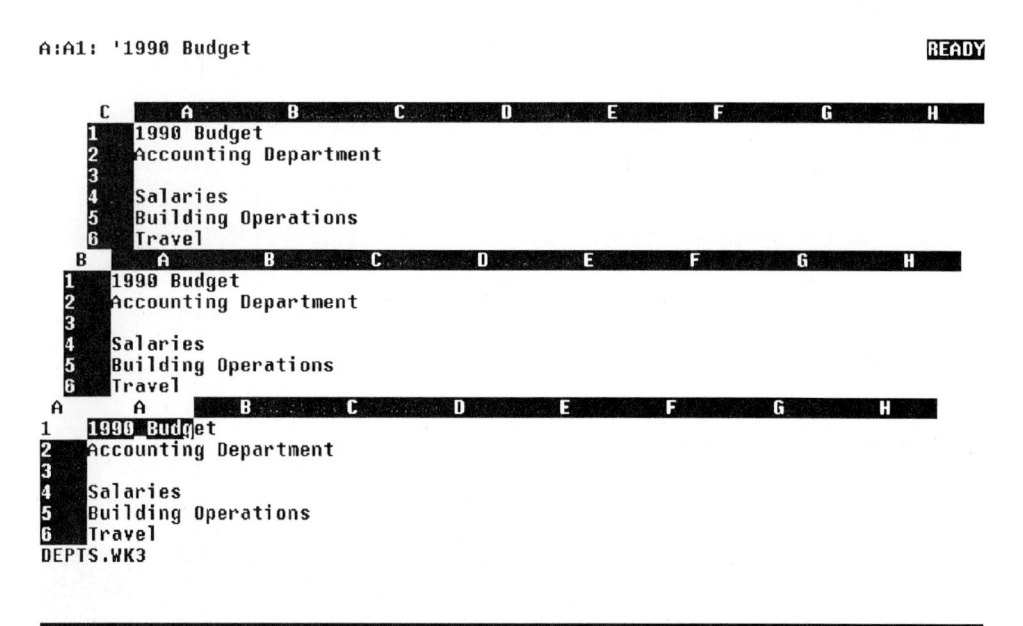

FIGURE 12-9.   Worksheets after data has been copied between worksheets

11. Type a period to anchor the destination range for copying, and press CTRL-PGUP so the to range is C:A1..D:A1. Press ENTER.

12. Press CTRL-PGUP and CTRL-PGDN to flip through the worksheets.

    Figure 12-9 shows three of the worksheets you created. Just as when you make multiple copies of a range, you only have to select the upper-left corner of the cells to which you want the range copied. Now the only remaining step is entering the data that customizes each sheet.

13. Enter the following values:

    A:A2: All Departments
    B:D4: 40000
    B:D5: 1000
    B:D6: 300
    B:D7: 500
    B:D8: 200
    C:A2: Advertising Department

C:D4: 35000
C:D5: 1500
C:D6: 2000
C:D7: 700
C:D8: 3000
D:A2: Marketing Department
D:D4: 50000
D:D5: 1000
D:D6: 10000
D:D7: 200
D:D8: 450

Using GROUP Mode
To Format Worksheets

When you are creating a worksheet file that has several worksheets that contain the same type of information, you will make some changes that are the same on each worksheet. It would be convenient if you could change one worksheet and have the changes apply to the other worksheets. Release 3 offers this feature through GROUP mode, which changes the effects of several commands so that instead of affecting only the current worksheet, they affect every worksheet in the current file. When GROUP mode is enabled, it does not matter which sheet is current—the command causes 1-2-3 to apply the changes to all sheets. The following commands are affected by the use of GROUP mode:

/Range Format
/Range Label
/Worksheet Column
/Worksheet Delete Column
/Worksheet Delete Row
/Worksheet Global Col-Width
/Worksheet Global Format
/Worksheet Global Label
/Worksheet Insert Column
/Worksheet Insert Row
/Worksheet Page
/Worksheet Titles

The following commands are beyond the scope of this book but also affect all worksheets when GROUP mode is enabled:

/Range Prot
/Range Unprot
/Worksheet Global Prot
/Worksheet Global Zero

When you use GROUP mode, it offers significant time savings. You must be careful when enabling GROUP mode, however; if you have one worksheet in a worksheet file that you do not want affected by the listed commands, you cannot enable GROUP mode to change the appearance of the other worksheets in the file.

GROUP mode is used when you first set up a multiple-sheet model with sheets having identical formats in 1-2-3. You can try GROUP mode with the DEPTS worksheet file to see how this mode works:

1. Enter /**Worksheet Global Group Enable**.

    The GROUP indicator appears at the bottom of the screen, as in Figure 12-10.

2. Move to B:D4.

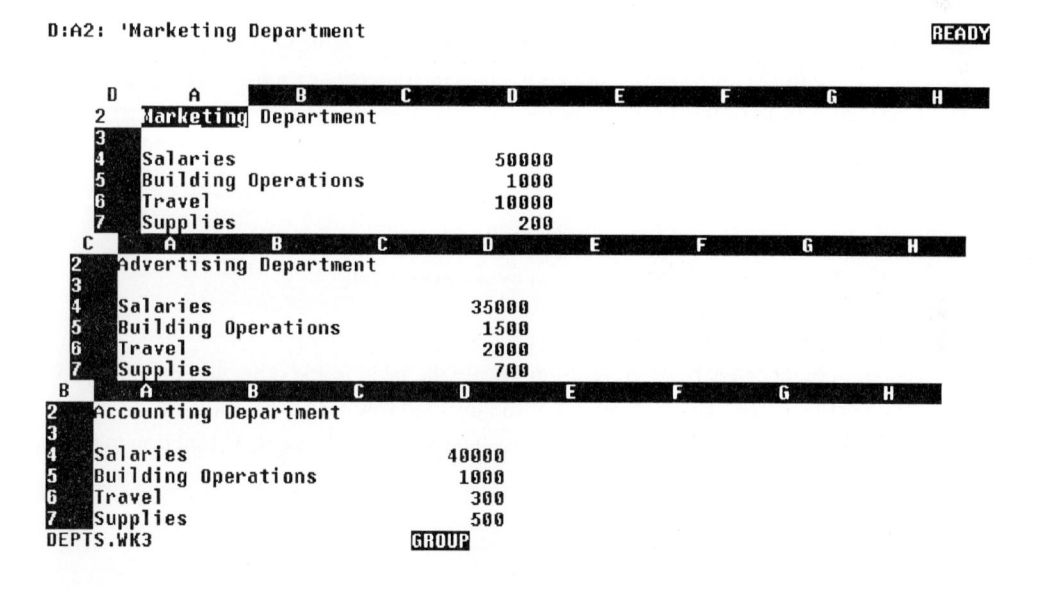

FIGURE 12-10.   GROUP mode enabled

3. Enter **/Worksheet Global Format Currency**, type **0**, and press ENTER.

   All of the numbers in all worksheets change to the Currency format with 0 decimal places.

4. Enter **/Range Format Currency**, type **0**, and press ENTER twice.

   All of the numbers in D4 in all worksheets change to the Currency format with 0 decimal places.

5. Move to D10.

6. Enter **/Range Format Currency**, type **0**, and press ENTER twice.

7. Enter **/Worksheet Column Set-Width**, press RIGHT ARROW twice, and press ENTER.

8. Move to column A.

9. Enter **/Worksheet Column Set-Width**, type **20**, and press ENTER.

   This expands column A to allow the full display of all the expense titles that you entered earlier in the chapter. Columns B and C will no longer be necessary.

10. Move to column B.

11. Enter **/Worksheet Delete Column**, press RIGHT ARROW, and press ENTER.

    After deleting the column, insert a row for a new expense to see how 1-2-3 adjusts all of the worksheets.

12. Move to A7.

13. Enter **/Worksheet Insert Row** and press ENTER.

    1-2-3 inserts the new row on every worksheet.

14. Type **Insurance** and press ENTER.

    Notice that 1-2-3 does not duplicate the label in the other worksheets; you will have to copy it. Also, since the inserted row is in the middle of the range the formula in B11 uses, you do not have to adjust the @SUM function in B11 in the worksheets.

15. Enter **/Copy** and press ENTER to select the current cell to copy.

16. Press CTRL-PGDN to move the cell pointer to A:A7, type a period, and press CTRL-PGUP until the cell pointer is in D:A7. Press ENTER.

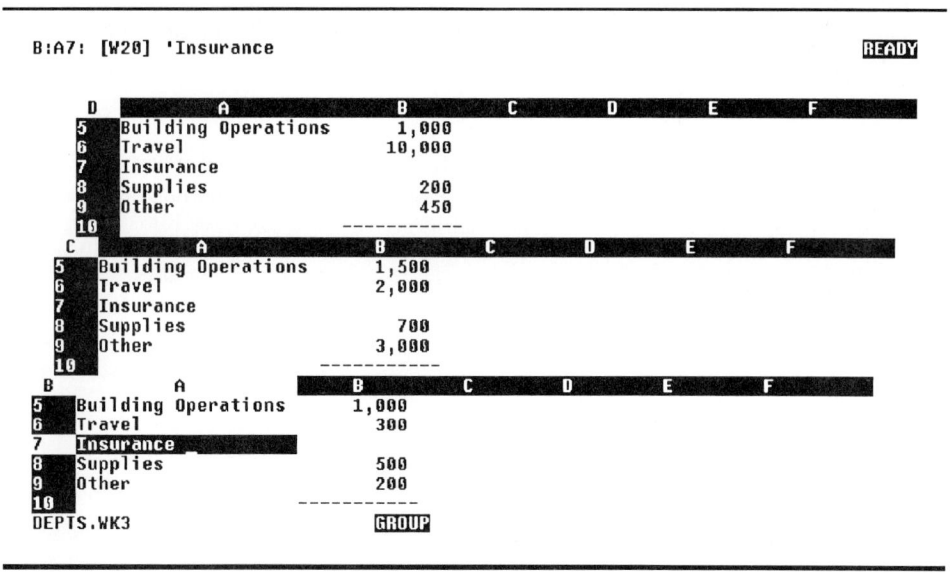

FIGURE 12-11.   Worksheets modified with GROUP mode enabled

Three of the worksheets appear in Figure 12-11. For all of the steps except entering **Insurance** in A7, you only executed the commands for one worksheet and they affected all the sheets. Since this completes the changes affecting all the sheets, you are ready to leave GROUP mode:

17. Enter /**Worksheet Global Group Disable**.

The GROUP indicator disappears as 1-2-3 disables GROUP mode.

18. Enter **400** in B:B7, **800** in C:B7, and **700** in D:B7.

Using Worksheet Functions
With Multiple Worksheets

Although you have used multiple sheets for both similar and dissimilar data, you have not as yet used any of the information from the various sheets together. The need for consolidating information is often the need that prompts the use of multiple sheets files, since it is so easy to perform computations like sums or averages on data from various entities by referring to a range that spans sheets. You can reference cells outside the current sheet by pointing to them or by typing the address, making sure that you include the worksheet letter.

To create formulas in the DEPTS worksheet file that uses multiple worksheets, follow these steps:

1. Move to A:B4.

    This worksheet only has formulas to total the expenses in column B, so it needs a formula that adds the expenses for each type and puts the result in worksheet A.

2. Type **@SUM(** to start the formula you want to use.

3. Press CTRL-PGUP.

    The control panel looks like this:

```
B:B4: (C0) [W11] 40000                                          POINT
@sum(B:B4
```

4. Type a period to anchor the cell reference.

5. Press CTRL-PGUP twice to include the range B:B4..D:B4.

6. Type) and press ENTER to complete the formula, which now looks like this in the control panel:

```
A:B4: (C0) [W11] @SUM(B:B4..D:B4)                               READY
```

Pointing to cells from other worksheets is just like pointing to cells in the current worksheet. 1-2-3 will automatically include the worksheet letter with the cell address. Another option is typing the addresses.

7. Press DOWN ARROW to move to A:B5.

8. Type **@SUM(B:B5.D:B5)** and press ENTER.

    Typing the cells in the formula is just like typing cell addresses, except that you must explicitly enter a worksheet letter; 1-2-3 assumes you want to use the current worksheet when a worksheet letter is not provided. Now that you have created a formula using multiple worksheets, you can copy the formula for the remaining expenses:

9. Enter **/Copy**, press ENTER to select A:B5 to copy, press DOWN ARROW, type a period, and press DOWN ARROW three times to highlight the range A:B6..A:B9. Press ENTER.

    This copies the formula for the remaining expenses. 1-2-3 automatically adds the total expenses using the @SUM formula you copied to the worksheet

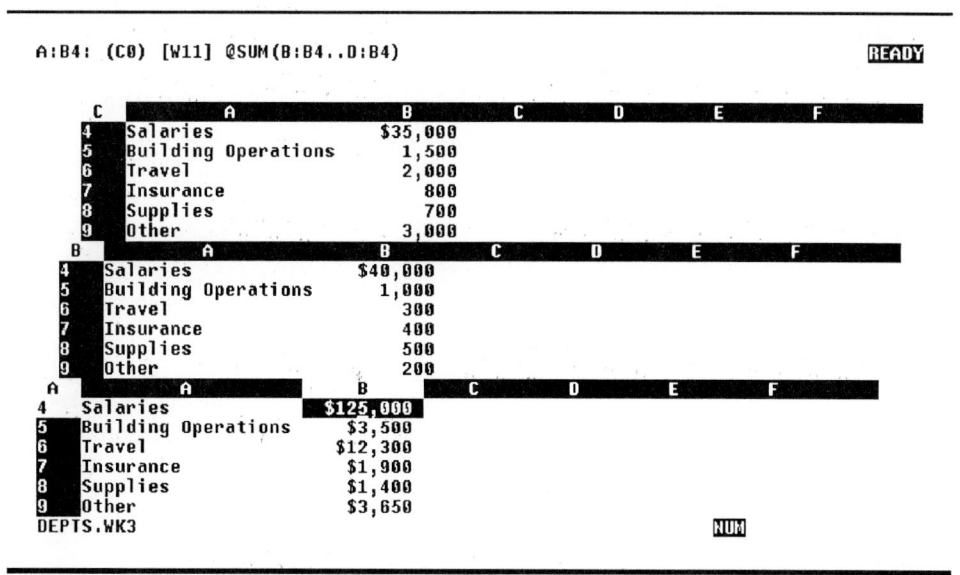

FIGURE 12-12.   Using @SUM across worksheets

earlier in the chapter. The first three worksheets will look like the ones shown in Figure 12-12.

ADDING OTHER WORKSHEET FILES

Creating multiple worksheet files expands the applications for which it is practical to use 1-2-3. You can expand them even further with applications that access multiple files. For example, suppose that the data in the worksheets in the DEPTS file you created earlier is entered by different people. It may be difficult to keep this information in the same file, since each person needs the worksheet for his or her own department. Instead, you may want separate worksheets for each department. When you are ready to combine the data into a summary worksheet, you can use another separate worksheet to combine the file data and use external file links, which allow you to obtain the data for a cell from the contents of cells in a disk file or another file in memory. Rather than having to remember the cells or range names you want from each worksheet, you can place several worksheets in memory at once if you have sufficient memory and then point to the data you want to access. 1-2-3 helps you create the external file links.

Use the DEPTS sheets as the basis for multiple worksheets, and then create a summary sheet with Release 3's multiple-file features. To create multiple worksheets with the DEPTS worksheet file data, follow these steps:

1. Press HOME to move to A1.

2. Enter **/File Xtract Formulas**, type **DEPT_SUM** for the filename, and press ENTER. Press END and HOME to select all of the cells in the worksheet, and press ENTER to select this as the range to extract.

   Do not worry about copying the formulas without copying the cells they reference; in the new file, these formulas will evaluate to ERR. Later, you will replace them with formulas that reference cells in other worksheets.

3. Press CTRL-PGUP to move to worksheet B.

4. Enter **/File Xtract Formulas**, type **DEPT_ACC** for the filename, and press ENTER. Press END and HOME to select all of the cells in the worksheet, and press ENTER to select this as the range to extract.

5. Repeat steps 3 and 4 for the C and D worksheets, using DEPT_ADV and DEPT_MKT as the filenames.

6. Enter **/File Save**, press ENTER, and select **Replace** to save the worksheet.

   With the separate files for the different departments, you are ready to use multiple worksheet files.

Opening Additional Worksheet Files

1-2-3 provides two commands that can open additional worksheet files. The /File New command creates a new worksheet file that is added before or after the current worksheet file. The /File Open command opens an existing file before or after the current worksheet file. The name of the current worksheet file appears at the bottom of the screen after it is saved for the first time.

When you execute the /File New command, 1-2-3 prompts you for a filename and, like the /File Save command, displays a FILE*nnnn* default filename. You can accept this name or enter a new filename before pressing ENTER. The new file is created on disk. Since you have not made any entries, it is empty; the file will not contain any information until you save it at a later point. If you use the /System command while this file is active, you will see a file that contains 0 bytes. If you do not save the file, 1-2-3 deletes the 0-byte file.

Try the /File New command now:

1. Enter **/File New Before** to produce this display:

```
D:A1: [W20] '1990 Budget                                              EDIT
Enter name of file to create: C:\123FILES\FILE0001.WK3
```

The Before and After options are similar to the Before and After options for the /Worksheet Insert Sheet command. The difference is that 1-2-3 does not insert a new worksheet file in the middle of another worksheet file. The /File New (and /File Open) commands insert a worksheet file either before the first or after the last worksheet in the current worksheet file.

The default filename that 1-2-3 suggests is identical to the filename suggestion for the /File Save command: FILE followed by the lowest unused four-digit number.

2. Type **NEW_FILE** and press ENTER for the filename.

The worksheet looks like the one in Figure 12-13. 1-2-3 opens the new worksheet file before worksheet A of the DEPTS worksheet file. Your disk contains a worksheet file called NEW_FILE.WK3. You can press CTRL-PGDN

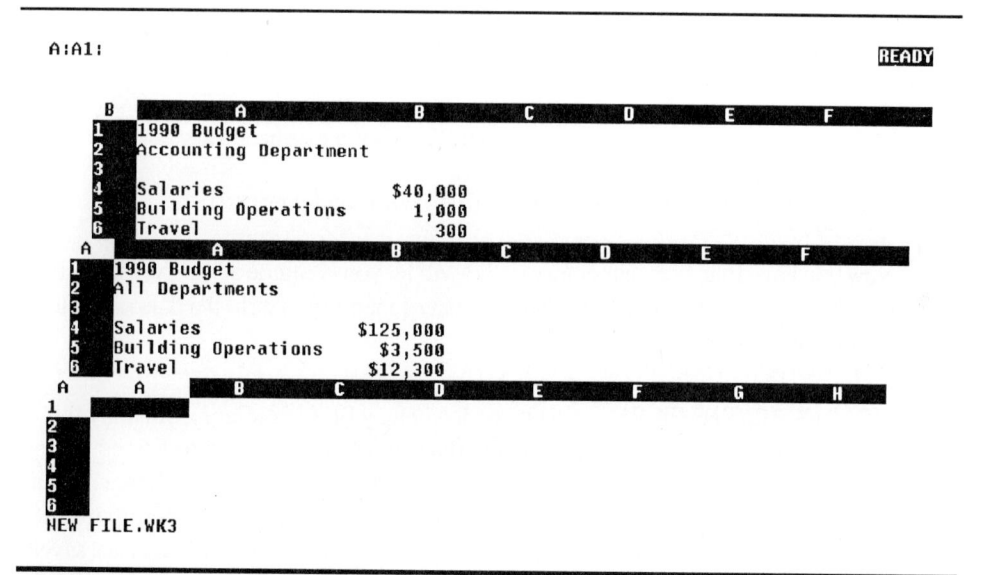

FIGURE 12-13.   New file opened

and CTRL-PGUP to switch between the files and between the worksheets in the files. You can always tell which worksheet file is current by looking at the filename at the bottom of the screen if the Clock option is set to display filenames there.

With multiple worksheet files in memory, you will want to try adding data from several files. Follow these steps to load the department files into memory:

1. Move to the NEW_FILE worksheet.

2. Enter /**File Retrieve**, select DEPT_SUM, and press ENTER.

   As you learned in Chapter 4, the /File Retrieve command replaces one file with another. When you have multiple files open, the /File Retrieve command only affects the current file.

3. Press CTRL-PGUP to move to the DEPTS worksheet.

4. Enter /**File Retrieve**, select DEPT_ADV, and press ENTER.

5. Enter /**File Open Before** with the cell pointer in the DEPT_ADV worksheet file.

   The Before and After options are identical to those of the /File New command. Except for selecting the Before or After option, executing the /File Open command is also identical to executing the /File Retrieve command.

6. Select DEPT_ACC and press ENTER.

   The perspective view of these three files is shown in Figure 12-14.

7. Press CTRL-PGUP to move to the DEPT_ADV worksheet file.

8. Enter /**File Open After**, select DEPT_MKT, and press ENTER.

Now you have four files in memory. 1-2-3 will let you continue adding worksheets or files to memory until your computer runs out of memory to hold the data or the total number of worksheets in memory is 256.

LISTING ACTIVE FILES   When you load many files in memory, you may find it difficult to keep track of the files. Release 3 has a new option in the /File List command that lists the active files. The list is different than the ones produced by other options for this command, since it has three additional columns. Like the other options for /File List, the Active option lists the filename, the date and time the file was last saved, and the file size. The three additional columns display the number of worksheets in

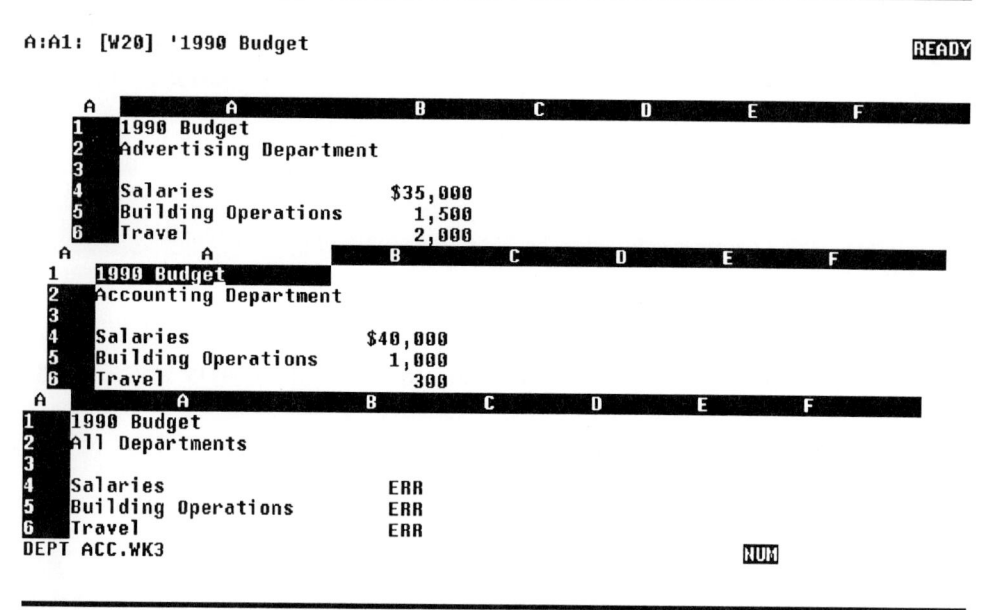

FIGURE 12-14. Multiple worksheet files active

the file, if it has been modified since you loaded it into 1-2-3's memory (MOD means it has, UNMOD means it is unchanged), and if you have the file reservation (only applicable in network environments and under OS/2). To see this file list, enter **/File List Active**. 1-2-3 creates a display like this:

```
A:B6: [W11] 10000                                                    FILES
Enter names of files to list: C:\123FILES\DEPT_SUM.WK3
DEPT_SUM.WK3  25-May-89    03:54 PM     2503          1    UNMOD
DEPT_SUM.WK3          DEPT_ACC.WK3    DEPT_ADV.WK3       DEPT_MKT.WK3
```

Using Multiple Worksheet Files in Formulas

The DEPT_SUM worksheet file contains formulas that contain ERR, since the cells the formulas reference were omitted from the extract range. You want to change the formula so it uses the values in the other files. To create a new formula, follow these steps:

1. Move the cell pointer to A:B4 in the DEPT_SUM worksheet file.

2. Type +.

3. Press CTRL-PGUP and move to A:B4 in the DEPT_ACC worksheet file. The formula in the control panel looks like this:

```
A:B4: (C0) [W11] 40000                                            POINT
+<<C:\123FILES\DEPT_ACC.WK3>>A:B4
```

1-2-3 automatically adds the file reference for you.

4. Type +.

5. Press CTRL-PGUP twice and move to A:B4 in the DEPT_ADV worksheet file.

6. Type +.

7. Press CTRL-PGUP and move to A:B4 in the DEPT_MKT worksheet file.

8. Press ENTER to finalize the formula.
   The formula looks like the one in Figure 12-15. Pointing is one way to include the external file links in the formulas; typing is another:

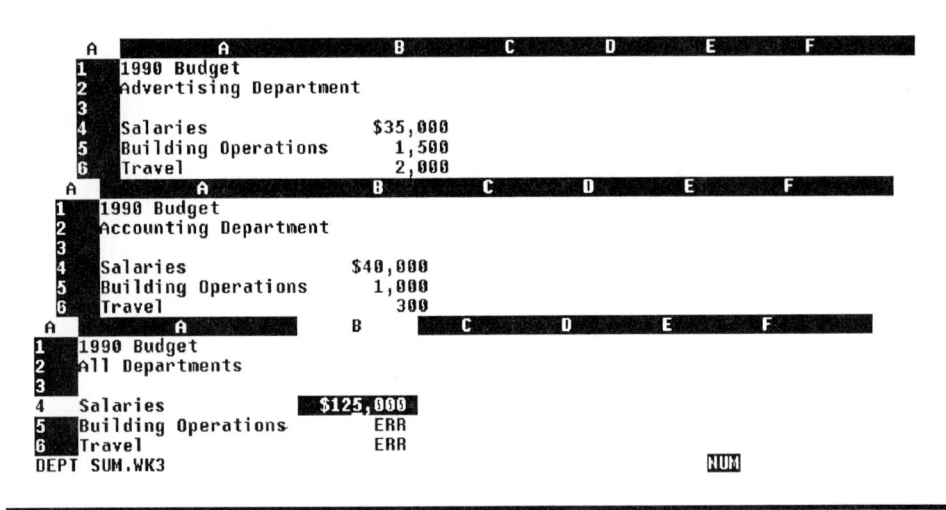

FIGURE 12-15.   Formula referencing multiple files

9. Move to A:B5.

10. Type

    +<<DEPT_ACC.WK3>>A:B5+<<DEPT_ADV.WK3>>A:B5+
    <<DEPT_MKT.WK3>>A:B5

    and press ENTER. You should also include the directory before the filename so
    1-2-3 can find the file if it is not in the current directory.

Another option is using the F3 (NAME) key. Pressing this key when multiple files
are open causes 1-2-3 to list the active filenames as well as the range names of the
current file. Selecting an active filename then displays the range names in the other
file. Using range names in multiple-file formulas prevents problems if you move cells
in the file that the formula references. 1-2-3 does not adjust external file links for
moved cells the way it adjusts cell and range addresses that move within the same
worksheet or worksheet file.

To try using range names and the F3 (NAME) function key, follow these steps:

1. Press CTRL-PGUP to move to the DEPT_ACC file. Move to A6.

2. Enter /**Range Name Labels Right**, select the A6..A9 range, and press ENTER.

3. Repeat steps 1 and 2 for the DEPT_ADV and DEPT_MKT files.
      1-2-3 requires that range names be unique within a file. You can use the
   same range names again in a different file, as in using Sales to name a range
   containing sales figures in each of your files. Since 1-2-3 commands will not
   accept ranges that span files, you must name the ranges separately for each
   file. Also, the /Range Name and GROUP mode commands only affect the
   current file, so you cannot use GROUP mode to name cells in all of the
   worksheet files at once.

4. Move to A:B5 in the DEPT_SUM worksheet file.

5. Type + to tell 1-2-3 you are starting a formula.

6. Press F3 (NAME) to produce this display:

```
A:B5: (C0) [W11] @SUM(ERR)                                          NAMES
Enter name:
<<DEPT ACC.WK3>> <<DEPT ADV.WK3>>  <<DEPT MKT.WK3>>
```

7. Highlight <<DEPT_ACC.WK3>> and press ENTER.

1-2-3 produces this display:

```
A:B5: (C0) [W11] @SUM(ERR)                                              NAMES
Enter name: <<C:\123FILES\DEPT_ACC.WK3>>
BUILDING OPERAT  INSURANCE         OTHER              SALARIES
```

8. Highlight BUILDING OPERAT and press ENTER.

   F3 (NAME) lists the filenames and range names for you. Use this key to complete the rest of this formula.

9. Type +, press F3 (NAME), select <<DEPT_ADV.WK3>>, and select BUILD-ING OPERAT to include the BUILDING OPERAT range from the DEPT_ADV worksheet file.

10. Type +, press F3 (NAME), select <<DEPT_MKT.WK3>>, and select BUILD-ING OPERAT to include the BUILDING OPERAT range from the DEPT_MKT worksheet file.

11. Press ENTER to finalize the formula.

    Rather than entering this formula for the rest of the cells in the DEPT_SUM worksheet, copy the formula and let 1-2-3 adjust the cell reference.

12. Enter /**Copy**, press ENTER, highlight A:B7..A:B9 as the to range, and press ENTER.

Saving Multiple Worksheet Files

Saving multiple worksheet files is different from saving a single worksheet file; you can specify which file to save or elect to save all of them. When you enter /**File Save**, 1-2-3 displays [ALL MODIFIED FILES]. If you press ENTER, 1-2-3 saves all files changed since the last /File Save command. Another option is saving the current file. When 1-2-3 displays [ALL MODIFIED FILES], you can press F2 (EDIT) to change the display from all modified files to the name of the file you wish to save. Saving one file at a time requires that you position the cell pointer on the file that you want to save.

Try saving the files that you are using with these steps:

1. Enter /**File Save** to produce this display:

```
A:B6: (C0) [W11] +<<C:\123FILES\DEPT_ACC.WK3>>TRAVEL+<<C:\123FILES\DEPT_ADV  EDIT
Enter name of file to save: [ALL MODIFIED FILES]
```

2. Press ENTER.

   1-2-3 displays the same Cancel, Replace, and Backup options that you see when you save a single file.

3. Select **Replace**.

1-2-3 replaces the files DEPT_SUM, DEPT_ACC, DEPT_ADV, and DEPT_MKT with the files currently in memory.

To save a single file when multiple files are open, you use similar steps:

1. Enter **/File Save**.

2. Press F2 (EDIT) to change [ALL MODIFIED FILES] to DEPT_SUM.WK3.

3. Press ENTER to accept this filename.

4. Enter **Replace**.

Removing a File from Memory

So far, the only way you have tried to remove a worksheet file in memory is by retrieving another one. 1-2-3 has other options. An obvious one is /Quit, which removes everything from 1-2-3's memory and returns you to your operating system. Another option is the /Worksheet Erase command, which removes all worksheet files from 1-2-3's memory so you can start again. The /Worksheet Delete File command, new to 1-2-3, also removes files from memory. Unlike the /File Erase command, /Worksheet Delete File leaves the worksheet that you have saved with /File Save intact.

You can try these commands by following these steps:

1. Enter **/Worksheet Delete File**.

1-2-3 displays this selection list:

```
A:B6: (C0) [W11] +<<C:\123FILES\DEPT_ACC.WK3>>TRAVEL+<<C:\123FILES\DEPT_ADV FILES
Enter name of file in memory to delete: C:\123FILES\DEPT_SUM.WK3
DEPT_SUM.WK3          DEPT_ACC.WK3        DEPT_ADV.WK3         DEPT_MKT.WK3
```

2. Select DEPT_SUM.

1-2-3 removes the DEPT_SUM worksheet file from memory. You can still see the DEPT_ACC, DEPT_ADV, and DEPT_MKT worksheet files.

3. Enter **/Worksheet Erase Yes**.

1-2-3 removes all of the worksheet files from memory. You have a blank worksheet that you can start a new model with.

REVIEW EXERCISE

This chapter has introduced you to a wealth of commands that you can use to design and create multiple worksheets within one file. You have also learned techniques that allow you to work with multiple files at once. Try these commands so you can approach your own models with ease and confidence:

1. Retrieve the DEPTS worksheet file. *Hint:* Use /File Retrieve and select DEPTS.

2. Add a new worksheet before the Marketing Department worksheet. *Hint:* Press CTRL-PGUP until the cell pointer is on worksheet D. Then use /Worksheet Insert Sheet Before and press ENTER.

3. Copy the contents of the Advertising Department worksheet to the new worksheet. *Hint:* Press CTRL-PGDN and HOME. Use /Copy, press END and HOME, and press ENTER. Then press CTRL-PGUP and ENTER.

4. Make the following entries in the new worksheet:

   A2: Inventory Department
   B4: 150000
   B5: 12000
   B6: 0
   B7: 5000
   B8: 50000
   B9: 100000

5. Move to worksheet C and enable GROUP mode so the new worksheet has the same formats and column widths as the other worksheets. Disable GROUP mode. *Hint:* Press CTRL-PGUP. Use /Worksheet Global Group Enable. Then use /Worksheet Global Group Disable.

6. Move sheet C. Enable GROUP mode to apply the format from this sheet to the new worksheet.

7. Add the word "Averages" in A:C3.

8. Add a formula in column C that averages each of the expenses for the four departments. The final result will look like Figure 12-16. *Hint:* In C4, enter the formula @SUM(B:B4..E:B4) by pointing or typing. Then copy the formula from C4 to C5..C9.

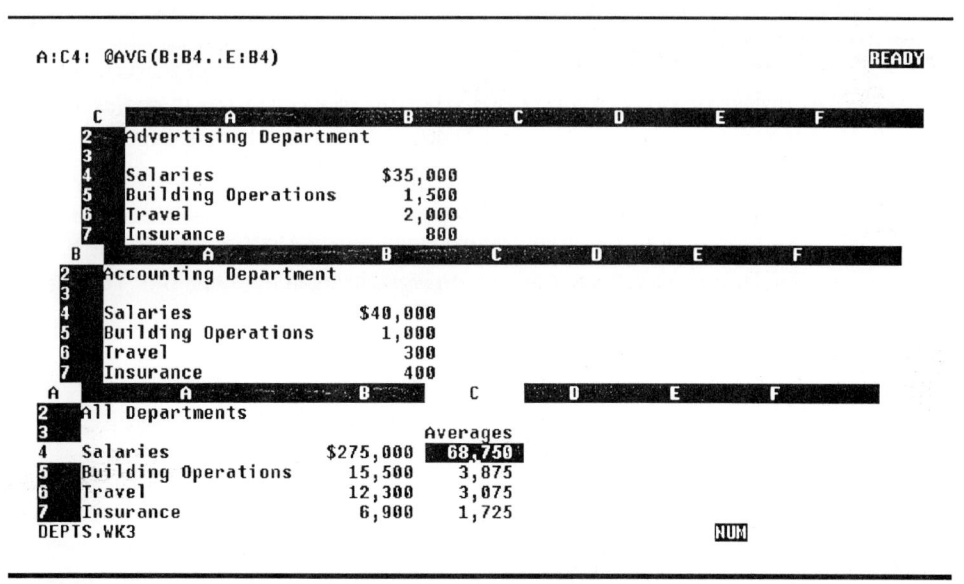

FIGURE 12-16.   Summary worksheet showing totals and averages

9. Retrieve the DEPT_ADV file. Change the value of Travel in the DEPT_ADV worksheet file to 1000. *Hint:* Use /File Open After and select DEPT_ADV. Then change the value of B6 in this file to 1000.

10. Copy the new travel expense from the DEPT_ADV file to the Travel expense for the advertising department in the DEPTS worksheet. *Hint:* Use /Copy, press ENTER, press CTRL-PGDN three times, and press ENTER again.

11. Save both of the modified files. *Hint:* Use /File Save, press ENTER to accept [ALL MODIFIED FILES], and select Replace.

REVIEW

• A worksheet file can contain up to 256 worksheets. You may be limited to fewer files; the number of worksheets is also determined by your computer's memory. Sheets are added with /Worksheet Insert Sheet and removed with /Worksheet Delete Sheet.

- Release 3 lets you load multiple worksheet files in memory at once. You can switch between these files just as you would use multiple worksheets in a single worksheet file. 1-2-3 limits the worksheets in memory to 256, regardless of how many files make up the 256 worksheets. The limit may be less, depending upon the worksheet file contents and the computer's memory.
- You can use windows to look at two or three worksheets at once. You can move in each window just as if you are using windows to look at the same file.
- 1-2-3 lets you select ranges that span worksheets in the same file. You cannot select ranges that span worksheets in different files.

Commands

/FLA	/File List Active provides information about all active files.
/FN	/File New opens a new file in memory, leaving the other files in memory intact.
/FO	/File Open opens an existing file in memory, leaving the other files in memory intact.
/WDF	/Worksheet Delete File removes a worksheet file from 1-2-3's memory, leaving the file on disk intact.
/WDS	/Worksheet Delete Sheet removes a sheet from a file.
/WGG	/Worksheet Global Group enables or disables GROUP mode, causing some /Range and /Worksheet commands to affect all worksheets in a file.
/WIS	/Worksheet Insert Sheet adds a sheet to a file.
/WWP	/Worksheet Window Perspective splits the screen in perspective view to display three worksheets.

13

CREATING 1-2-3 MACROS

Keyboard Alternative Macros
Macro Building Blocks
Creating a Few More Macros
Special Macro Topics
Review Exercise
Review

Many 1-2-3 users are intimidated by macros. They have heard about the failures that others have experienced when attempting to use them. However, failure is not inevitable; in fact, if you use the step-by-step approach presented in this chapter, you will have no need for concern. There is no reason why you cannot be just as successful with macros as you are with 1-2-3's /Range Format and /File Save commands.

In their simplest form, macros are nothing more than a way to automate the selections you have been making from 1-2-3's menus. Such macros are referred to as *keyboard alternative macros*. In their most complex form, macros provide an entire programming language with the special 1-2-3 command-language instructions. Attempting to use the most sophisticated form of macros without mastering the keyboard variety is a little like practicing diving before you have learned to swim— you would find yourself well over your head and doomed to failure.

Using command-language macros before mastering the keyboard alternative variety is asking for problems. This chapter introduces macros in a logical sequence to help you avoid such problems. It introduces you first to a step-by-step approach to the creation of keyboard alternative macros that can ensure your success. You will learn how to enter menu selections and special keyboard entries in worksheet cells for later execution. You will also learn 1-2-3's rules for naming macros and how you can execute the macro instructions you have stored. You will also learn how to use Release 3's Record feature to significantly reduce the effort involved in the creation of keyboard alternative macros. You will create several ready-to-use macros, which will be your foundation for creating macros that fit your particular needs. Since macros are based on a series of building blocks, you will need to learn something about each of them before creating a macro. In this chapter you will be introduced to the building blocks and then combine them in your first macro example before making your entries.

KEYBOARD ALTERNATIVE MACROS

Keyboard alternative macros are nothing more than a column of label entries that have a special name assigned to them. The contents of the label entries are the sequence of 1-2-3 keystrokes that you want 1-2-3 to execute for you. Once the keystrokes are entered in the column of worksheet cells, you use the /Range Name Create command to assign a name to the top cell in the macro. You can use a backslash (\) and a single letter for the macro name or use a longer entry of up to the 15-character limit for range names. If you choose the \ and the single letter, you can execute the macro by holding down the ALT key and typing the letter used in the macro name, or you can press ALT-F3 (RUN) and select the name from the list of macro names. If you use the longer entry option for the name, your only alternative is to press ALT-F3 (RUN) and select the macro name.

When you save the worksheet on which you entered the macro, you save the macro for later use. A macro can be used on any worksheet that allows you to create a macro on one worksheet and use it on another. In addition, the worksheet containing the macro and the worksheet that uses the macro can be in different worksheet files. This allows you to create a library of macros in a worksheet file that you can use with all your other worksheets.

Keyboard alternative macros provide a wealth of time-saving features. You can use them to automate printing, formatting, or any other 1-2-3 task that can be handled with menu selections. After you have learned the basics, you will want to examine the tasks you execute repeatedly. The more frequently a task is performed, the greater the potential reward of automating it with macro instructions. Some users find that data-management tasks such as sorting and extracting are most important to automate; other users feel that printing and formatting have the highest priority because they use these commands most frequently. Although the macros in the remainder of the chapter have widespread application, only you can decide which tasks offer you the greatest payback when automated.

MACRO BUILDING BLOCKS

The secret to creating macros that run correctly the first time you try them is having a structured approach that you use consistently for each new macro you create. At first glance, the steps recommended here might seem unnecessarily time-consuming; however, you will find that they guarantee immediate success and thereby save debugging time.

The first step for successful macros is to lay out a road map of where you want to go with the macro. Whether you type the macro entries or use the Record feature to place them on the worksheet, you need to test the instructions that you hope will get you there. If you are not using the recorder, you may want to test the instructions before recording them. Once the instructions are stored on the worksheet, you will need to name them. Documenting the workings of the macro is an often overlooked step, but it can guarantee continued trouble-free execution. Complete this step for every macro. Only then will you be ready to try your new macro.

You can examine each of these steps more closely in the sections that follow.

Knowing Where You Are Going Before You Begin

If you are typing the macro entries, the only way to guarantee first-try success for every macro is to try the 1-2-3 instructions that you want to store in a macro and to monitor their effect on the worksheet. This happens automatically when you use the recorder, since 1-2-3 is executing and recording the instructions as you enter them.

If you are typing the macro entries, write each command on a piece of paper as you enter them. If the results meet your needs, you can enter the keystrokes you have written on your sheet of paper as a series of label entries on the worksheet. If the commands do not perform the required tasks, you can alter them and try again. Once you discover the correct combination of menu requests, you have a guarantee (if you enter them carefully) that they will function; you have already tried them and ensured their correct operation before recording them. The other objective of this phase is to ensure that you have not forgotten any of the requirements. For example, you must understand the path of the specific commands that you will need. Planning is required if you use the recorder approach.

Recording Menu Selections

You will want to select an out-of-the-way location on the worksheet for recording your macros commands. With Release 3, you have the option of adding the commands in a worksheet that contains other data, as long as the macros are positioned so they will not interfere with the data, or you can add a new worksheet to contain all of the macros you want for the file. Another possibility is to place the macro in a different worksheet file. This option requires you to open the worksheet file containing the macros before you execute them on the current worksheet. In earlier releases, macros were often stored to the right of the other worksheet data.

To prevent 1-2-3 from executing the menu commands you want to record, begin the macro sequence with an apostrophe so that it is treated as a label. Indicate each request for the menu with a slash, and record each menu selection as the first letter of the selection. To record the keystrokes necessary to obtain a worksheet status display, type '/ws or '/WS in the cell (case is never important when you are entering menu selections).

In addition to entering the menu selections, you sometimes have to indicate that the ENTER key would be pressed if you were entering the command sequence from the keyboard. In a macro, this key is represented by the tilde (~). When you are entering data other than menu selections, such as a filename or a range name, enter the names in full. For example, to record the keystrokes necessary to retrieve a file named Sales, you would enter '/frSales~ in the macro cell.

Menu selections should always be recorded with the first letter of the selection. Typing the full name of the command is not a substitute for the first letter and will cause errors in the macro. While it is possible to select commands by pointing to the menu selections through the successive use of the RIGHT ARROW key and the ENTER key, this should be avoided in macros. In subsequent releases of the product, Lotus might alter the sequence of the menu selections, causing this menu selection method to fail. This same problem can occur if you are using the macro in an earlier release of the product. Also, a macro that uses arrow keys is harder to understand, and it is difficult to confirm its accuracy. However, you can be sure the first letters of the selections are not likely to change, which means your macros are more likely to be compatible with future releases of the 1-2-3 product.

Recording Special Keys

There are a number of special keyboard keys, such as the function keys and cursor-movement keys, that you will want to include in your macros. These keys and the macro keywords that stand for them are shown in Table 13-1. Notice that all the special keywords are enclosed in curly braces ({}). You will find it easy to remember most

Special Keys	Keywords
Cursor-Movement Keys	
UP ARROW	{UP} or {U}
DOWN ARROW	{DOWN} or {D}
RIGHT ARROW	{RIGHT} or {R}
LEFT ARROW	{LEFT} or {L}
HOME	{HOME}
END	{END}
PGUP	{PGUP}
PGDN	{PGDN}
CTRL-RIGHT	{BIGRIGHT}
CTRL-LEFT	{BIGLEFT}
Editing Keys	
DEL	{ESCAPE} or {DEL}
INS	{INSERT} or {INS}
ESC	{ESCAPE} or {ESC}
BACKSPACE	{BACKSPACE} or {BS}
Function Keys	
F1 (HELP)	{HELP}
F2 (EDIT)	{EDIT}
F3 (NAME)	{NAME}
F4 (ABS)	{ABS}
F5 (GOTO)	{GOTO}
F6 (WINDOW)	{WINDOW}
F7 (QUERY)	{QUERY}
F8 (TABLE)	{TABLE}
F9 (CALC)	{CALC}
F10 (GRAPH)	{GRAPH}
ALT-F6 (ZOOM)	{ZOOM}
ALT-F7 (APP1)	{APP1}
ALT-F8 (APP2)	{APP2}
ALT-F9 (APP3)	{APP3}
ALT-F10 (APP4)	{ADDIN} or {APP4}

TABLE 13-1.   Special Keys in Macro Commands

of these words; they are the same words you probably connect with the special keys—for example, EDIT represents F2. The only thing you will need to remember is to use the braces like this:

{EDIT}

Without the braces, 1-2-3 will not recognize the entry as a special key.

Several special keys cannot be represented in a macro. The NUM LOCK key has no representation and must be turned on by the operator if a macro requires it. The SCROLL LOCK key requires the same procedure, since it too cannot be represented. CAPS LOCK also has no representation, although this is less important than the other two keys; you will be able to control capitalization if you are requested to input directly during a macro. If macro instructions include cell entries for other parts of the worksheet, you will get to choose whether to make these entries in upper- or lowercase when building the macro. The case you choose will be maintained when the macro is executed.

CURSOR-MOVEMENT KEYS   When you are creating a macro, movement of the cell pointer to the right will be represented by {RIGHT} or {right}. (Case is never important for the special macro words, although uppercase will be used throughout this chapter.) Movement to the left is {LEFT}, movement down is {DOWN}, and movement up is {UP}.

If you have to move in a direction more than once, there is a short-cut approach. Include a space and the number of times you want the cell-pointer movement performed before you enter the closing curly brace. For example, {UP 3} moves the cell pointer three cells up.

When you are working from the keyboard, the effect of the HOME key depends on whether you are in READY or EDIT mode. This is also true in the macro environment. If you record {HOME} in a macro, its effect will depend on what you are having the macro do for you. If you have placed 1-2-3 in EDIT mode, the instruction will take you to the left side of the entry in the current cell; otherwise, it will place you in A1.

The END and arrow key combinations are supported in macros. You can enter {END}{RIGHT} to have the cell pointer moved to the last occupied cell entry on the right side of the worksheet. To specify paging up and down, you can use {PGUP} and {PGDN}.

FUNCTION KEYS   All function keys can be represented by special macro keywords. To use F2 (EDIT), you use {EDIT}. The F5 (GOTO) key is another key that is used frequently. Release 3 adds {HELP} for F1 (HELP). To record the fact that you wanted the cell pointer moved to D10, you would make this entry in a macro:

{GOTO}D10~

Notice that the cell address you want the cell pointer moved to is placed outside the braces and is followed by a tilde (~). Remember that the tilde represents the ENTER key and is required to finalize the request, just as you would press ENTER if you were executing the command directly.

Other keys required frequently are the representation for F6 (WINDOW) and F9 (CALC). As you might expect, {WINDOW} is the macro representation for F6 and {CALC} is the representation for F9. The remaining function keys are shown in Table 13-1.

THE EDIT KEYS   In addition to F2 (EDIT), which places you in EDIT mode, several other keys are used frequently for correcting cell entries. The ESC key can remove an entry from a cell and can delete a menu default, such as a previous setup string. This lets you to cancel the default and make a new entry. When ESC is used in a macro, everything works the same, except that braces are required, as in {ESC}.

To delete a character to the left of the cursor while in EDIT mode, or to delete the last character entered, use either {BS} or {BACKSPACE} in your macro. To delete the character above the cursor from EDIT mode, use {DEL} or {DELETE}. For example, you could create a macro that requests a change in the label prefix to center justification. The sequence of entries in the macro would be

{EDIT}{HOME}{DEL}^~

This is the same sequence of keys you would press if you were typing the request to be executed directly, rather than storing the keystrokes in a macro.

In Release 3, repeat factors can also be used with these keys. {DELETE 4} is equivalent to pressing the DEL key four times. {BACKSPACE 7} will delete seven characters to the left of the cursor on the edit line.

Creating the Macro

We promised you not the fastest path to macro entry, but the fastest path to a macro that would run correctly the first time you tried. Your first step in creating a macro will be to make a plan and to try your plan before recording your first keystroke. This step is critical if you want to ensure success.

PLANNING THE MACRO   If you are thinking of creating a macro, you must have a task that you want to automate. For your first example, you will automate a request for formatting, based on the assumption that you need to format data as currency frequently and would like to create a macro that will save you a few keystrokes. Your first step is to ask yourself which 1-2-3 commands you normally use to handle this task. The answer should be the /Range Format Currency command sequence. Also ask yourself if you want the macro to specify the number of decimal places and the range for formatting, or whether you want the operator to complete the instruction from the keyboard. For this example, the number of decimal places will be supplied but the range will be controlled by the operator at execution.

Once your decisions are made, you will want to test the series of instructions you plan to use before typing them. If you are using 1-2-3's Record feature (covered later in this chapter), you can use your trial run to capture the keystrokes. Either way, you will need some test data on the worksheet before beginning. Follow these steps for creating test data to see if the formatting commands and subsequent macro function correctly:

1. Make the following worksheet entries:

   A1: 2
   A2: 5
   A3: 4
   A4: 9
   A5: 7
   C6: 8
   C7: 9
   C8: 3

   There is nothing special about these entries. They are just a few numbers that will be stored in the default format of General and that will provide practice entries for formatting. Copy them across the worksheet to create additional entries.

2. Move the cell pointer to A1 and enter /**Copy**. Press the END key followed by the DOWN ARROW key. Press ENTER, move the cell pointer to B1, type ., move the cell pointer to F1, and press ENTER.

3. Move the cell pointer to C6, enter /**Copy**, move the cell pointer to C8, and press ENTER. Move the cell pointer to E6, type ., move the cell pointer to F6, and press ENTER to create the display shown in Figure 13-1.

   This provides a little variety in the length of the column of numbers you will be formatting with your macro once it is created.

   Now you are ready for a trial run of the instructions you plan to record:.

4. Move the cell pointer to A1.

   This is the first cell you will format. The movement of the cell pointer could be incorporated in the macro, but it would eliminate some of the macro's flexibility and is probably not desirable.

5. Enter / and write down a slash on the piece of paper where you are recording the keystrokes from the trial.

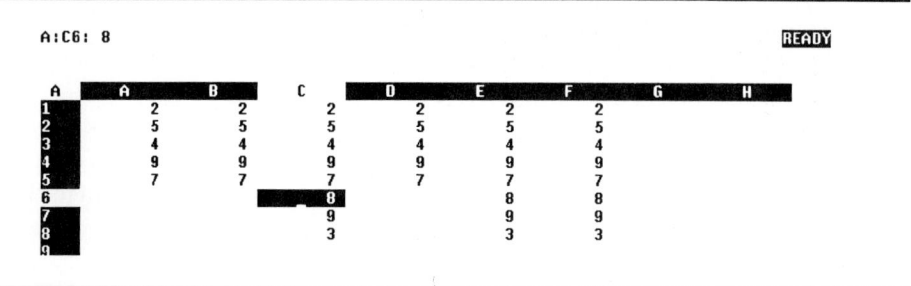

FIGURE 13-1.   Numbers ready for formatting

6. Enter **Range** and record an "R" on the piece of paper.

7. Enter **Format** and record an "F" on the piece of paper.

8. Enter **Currency** and record a "C" on the piece of paper.

9. Type **0** and record a 0 on the piece of paper.

10. Press ENTER and record the tilde (~) on the piece of paper. Press ESC to return to READY mode.

    Every keystroke you enter, whether it is from the menu or just a keyboard entry, should be written on the piece of paper. Most beginners would skip steps 5 through 10, which is why their macros fail. Once you become a 1-2-3 expert and have all the menu selections committed to memory, you can skip the writing, but until you reach that point, the importance of these steps cannot be overemphasized.

11. Press ENTER again to record the range selection. However, do not record this; you are leaving the range selection up to the user when the macro is executed.

12. Enter **/File Save**, type **NUMBERS,** and press ENTER.

    This will save a copy of the numeric entries in the file NUMBERS. You can retrieve it at a later time to practice with this or other macros.

MAKING THE MACRO ENTRIES   The macro entries you need to make are recorded on your sheet of paper. All you need to do now is record these entries on the worksheet. You can record them all in one cell or you can split them into more than one cell—as long as the cells are in the same column on the worksheet. With such a short macro it will not make much difference, but as your macros become longer, you may want to split them well before you reach the 512-character limit for a cell entry. Keeping the length of an individual cell entry to a minimum will allow you to document each step in the macro.

Normally, you would place your macro away from the other worksheet data. However, since this is your first macro, you will want to keep it in view as it executes, so place it in the lower portion of column B. Follow these steps to record the macro keystrokes you have written down on your sheet of paper:

1. Move the cell pointer to B15.

2. Type '/r and then move the cell pointer to B16.
   The single quotation mark prevents the immediate execution of your entries. The slash represents the request for the menu, and the "R" is used to invoke the Range commands (the "R" can be either upper- or lowercase).

3. Press the DOWN ARROW key, type **fc0~**, and press ENTER.
   These entries tell 1-2-3 that you want to use the Format option and have selected Currency with 0 decimal places as the format you want to use.

This is all that is required for entering any macro. The only mandatory step that remains is naming the macro.

Naming the Macro

Now that you have recorded all the keystrokes, you are ready to name the macro. Before doing this you will want to position the cell pointer in the top cell in the macro, as this is the only cell that you will name. You will use the /Range Name Create command to apply the name to this cell. You must assign to the cell a name of not more than 15 characters or use a special name consisting of a backslash and a single letter. The backslash identifies your entry as a macro name, which will allow you to execute the macro with the ALT key and letter used in the macro name. This naming convention lets you create 26 unique, quickly executable macros on one worksheet, since 1-2-3 does not distinguish between upper- and lowercase letters in a macro name.

If you follow the recommendation of positioning the cell pointer before you begin, the process is really quite simple. You will only need to press ENTER after typing the name to have the name applied to the macro. Saving a macro after you name it will save both the macro entries and the name, so they will be available when you use the worksheet.

Follow these steps to name the formatting macro you just entered:

1. Move the cell pointer to B15.

2. Enter /**Range Name Create**.

3. Type \c and press ENTER twice.

This will apply the name to the current cell. Theoretically, you can now execute the macro; however, it is best to document it first. If you do not take the time to document your work now, you will never do it; later, it will be difficult to remember what name you chose for the macro and what each step accomplishes.

Documenting the Macro

You will want to develop a few easy documentation rules for yourself so that your documentation is always stored in the same place. A good strategy is to place the macro name in the cell immediately to the left of the top cell in the macro. If the macro is named \a, you would enter '\a in this cell. The single quotation mark prevents the backslash from being interpreted as a repeating label indicator and filling your cell with the letter "a."

A good area to use for documenting the macro is the column of cells to the right of the actual macro instructions. Depending on the length of the macro instructions, this documentation may extend one or more cells to the right of the macro column. Entering a brief description of every command can make the purpose of the macro much clearer when you go back to examine it at a later time.

Follow these steps to document the formatting macro:

1. Move the cell pointer to A15, type '\c, and press ENTER.

2. Move the cell pointer to C15, type

    request Range command

    and press ENTER.

3. Move the cell pointer to C16, type

    select Currency format with 0 decimal places

    and press ENTER.

    The macro is now ready to execute.

Executing the Macro

Once you have entered and named a macro, you can use it whenever you wish. Whenever you have a macro that requires the cell pointer to be positioned in a certain cell, you will need to put the cell pointer there before you execute the macro. The cell pointer does not need to be on the macro itself in order to execute it. After you have positioned your cell pointer, you can execute the macro by holding down the ALT key and, while the key is pressed, pressing the letter key you used in your macro name. Another option is pressing ALT-F3 (RUN) and selecting the macro name. The macro will begin executing immediately.

Follow these instructions to try your new formatting macro:

1. Move the cell pointer to B1.

2. Press the ALT key and, while holding it down, type **c**.

   The macro executes. This particular macro requests formatting and ends in time for you to complete the range that should be formatted.

3. Move the cell pointer to B5 and press ENTER.

   The entries in B1..B5 should now be formatted as Currency with 0 decimal places. You will want to try this again to see how flexible the macro is.

4. Move the cell pointer to C1, press the ALT key, and type **c**. Move the cell pointer to C8 and press ENTER to create the display in Figure 13-2.

   This time the entries in C1..C8 are formatted. The same macro can format one cell or a large range of cells. You can try the other method of executing a macro to format column D's entries.

5. Move the cell pointer to D1, press ALT-F3 (RUN), and press ENTER to select \c. Move the cell pointer to D8 and press ENTER to format entries in column D.

   This time the entries in D1..D8 are formatted. While pressing ALT and typing **C** is quicker than using the ALT-F3 (RUN) key, ALT-F3 (RUN) is the only way you can execute macros with names that do not start with a backslash. You can try the macro several more times with the remaining numeric entries on the worksheet.

6. Enter /**File Save**, press ESC, type **FORMAT**, and press ENTER to save this example.

7. Enter /**Worksheet Erase Yes** to clear the worksheet from memory.

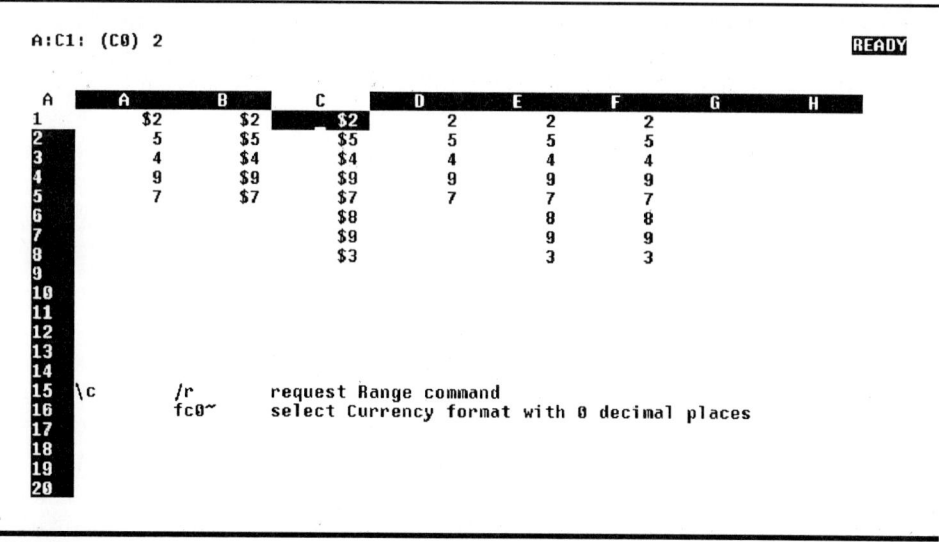

FIGURE 13-2.   Numbers formatted with keyboard alternative macro

Using 1-2-3's Macro Recorder

You can use Release 3's Record feature to record keyboard alternative macros, rather than typing them. This approach offers a couple of major advantages. First, you can try out your plan for a macro and have 1-2-3 record your entries. If you make a few mistakes, you do not need to start over; you can edit the entries that 1-2-3 places on the worksheet with the same techniques you use for changing any entry. Second, when you have 1-2-3 record the keystrokes, you do not need to remember the keywords that 1-2-3 uses for the function keys and other special keys. All you need to do is press the proper key and 1-2-3 will record them in the macro cells correctly.

Unlike the macro recorders for earlier versions of 1-2-3, you do not have to tell 1-2-3 to record your keystrokes. 1-2-3 has a 512-byte buffer that constantly records your keystrokes. As you make entries in a worksheet, 1-2-3 is recording them in case you want to copy the keystrokes to a worksheet range.

To use 1-2-3's Record feature you must follow several steps. First, you should clear 1-2-3's recording buffer so your earlier keystrokes will not be confused with the macro keystrokes you want to record. Then you need to perform the steps you want 1-2-3 to record. Finally, you must copy the keystrokes to the worksheet. Since the buffer that stores your keystrokes is 512 bytes, you may perform these three steps repeatedly for a lengthy macro.

You can try out this procedure with a macro that will correctly format three date entries. First, place the date entries on the worksheet that 1-2-3 converts into serial date numbers:

1. Type **15-JUL-89** in A1 and press the DOWN ARROW key.

2. Type **15-APR-90** in A2 and press the DOWN ARROW key.

3. Type **9-MAY-89** in A3 and press the DOWN ARROW key.

Now you are ready to explore the Record feature.

CLEARING THE RECORDER BUFFER   Since 1-2-3 records every keystroke you make, you want to clear 1-2-3's buffer, or storage area, where 1-2-3 records your keystrokes before you perform the steps that you want in a macro. Clearing the buffer prevents you from accidentally copying keystrokes that you do not want in the macro. Since clearing the buffer separates your other keystrokes from the keystrokes you want in the buffer, you should position your cell pointer where you want to begin recording the keystrokes for the macro before doing this. To clear the recorder buffer, follow these steps:

1. Press HOME. This is a step you want to perform before recording a macro.

2. Press ALT-F2 (RECORD). 1-2-3 displays the following menu:

```
A:A1: 32704                                                          MENU
Playback  Copy  Erase  Step
Select keystrokes to play back
```

3. Select **Erase**.
    The buffer is empty and ready to store your next set of keystrokes.

RECORDING A MACRO   Once you have cleared the buffer, you are ready to record the macro. To record the macro, perform the steps that you want recorded in the macro. For the current worksheet follow these steps:

1. Enter **/Range Format Date 1** to select Date format 1.

2. Press the DOWN ARROW key twice to highlight the range of the three dates, and press ENTER.
    You will not see 1-2-3 record anything while you perform these steps.

3. Enter /**Worksheet Column Set-Width**, type **10**, and press ENTER.

COPYING THE KEYSTROKES TO THE WORKSHEET   Once you execute
the steps for the macro, you are ready to transfer the keystrokes from 1-2-3's recorder
buffer to the worksheet. After the keystrokes are copied to the worksheet, you can
name the range, and the macro is ready to run just as if you entered the macro onto
the worksheet yourself. For the date-formatting macro, follow these steps:

1. Press ALT-F2 (RECORD).

2. Enter **Copy**.
    1-2-3 displays the contents of the recorder buffer:

```
A:A1: (D1) [W10] 32704                                    EDIT
Press TAB to anchor cursor, then highlight keystrokes to copy:
/RFD1{D 2}~/WCS10~_
```

While the macro is displayed like this, you can edit the keystrokes 1-2-3 has
recorded; use the same keys that you use for editing cell entries. For example,
if you want to reformat four cells instead of three, you could change {D 2} to
{D 3}. To copy keystrokes from the buffer to the worksheet, you must select
the keystrokes you want. It is just like selecting text in a word processing
document.

3. Press HOME to move to the beginning of the recorder buffer.

4. Press TAB to anchor the beginning of the text you want to copy.

5. Press END to move to the end of the recorder buffer.

6. Press ENTER to select the highlighted keystrokes.

```
A:A1: (D1) [W10] 32704                                    POINT
Select range to copy TO: A:A1
```

1-2-3 prompts you for a worksheet location in which to copy the keystrokes:
1-2-3 will copy the keystrokes to the buffer, using the selected range to define
the area where the keystrokes are copied. 1-2-3 uses the number of columns
selected to determine how wide the entries in the output area should be. You
have set columns D and E, so the cells containing the keystrokes will be no
wider than the combined width of columns D and E. If only one row is included
in the output area, 1-2-3 uses as many cells in the first column of the output

area. If multiple rows are selected, 1-2-3 uses only the rows included in the output area.

7. Select E1.

The copied keystrokes look like this:

8. Move the cell pointer to D1, type **format_3dates**, and press ENTER.

9. Enter **/Worksheet Column Set-Width** and type **14** and press ENTER to widen the column.

10. Enter **/Range Name Label Right** to use this entry to name the top cell in the macro. Press ENTER.

The /Range Name Label Right command is a different version of the /Range Name Create command. It assigns the labels in the range you specify to the entries in the cells immediately to the right of the cell containing the label. This command is often used when you have several cells to name that have their names in labels in adjacent cells.

11. Type three more date serial numbers, as shown here:

B1: 31-DEC-89
B2: 8-JUN-90
B3: 2-APR-90

12. Move the cell pointer to B1 and try the macro by pressing ALT-F3 (RUN). Highlight the name of the macro as shown here:

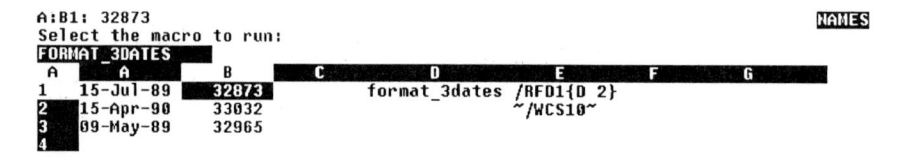

13. Press ENTER.

1-2-3 will format the cells as dates:

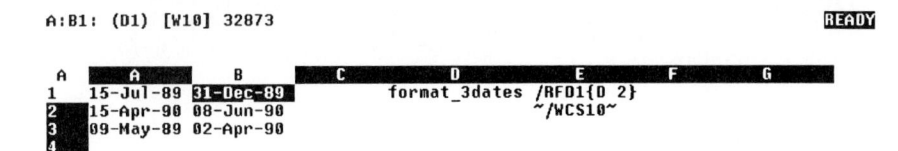

```
A:B1: (D1) [W10] 32873                                              READY

A        A        B          C          D          E          F          G
1    15-Jul-89 31-Dec-89              format_3dates /RFD1{D 2}
2    15-Apr-90 08-Jun-90                        ~/WCS10~
3    09-May-89 02-Apr-90
4
```

If you plan to use this macro later, you will want to document the tasks the macro executes and then save the worksheet.

CREATING A FEW MORE MACROS

You have now created your first two macros, but you have not begun to experience the variety that macros can offer. You can follow the instructions in this section to create two more macros. This practice should help you improve your macro skills

Creating a Print Macro

Print macros are useful because printed output must be created from most worksheets periodically. In addition, by adding instructions in a print macro you can add any special form feeding, range printing, headers, footers, borders, or extra copies. Make these entries to provide a few lines of data to print:

1. Enter **/Worksheet Erase Yes Yes**, enter **/Worksheet Column Set-Width**, type **15**, and press ENTER.

2. Place these entries on the worksheet:
   A1: Name
   A2: John Smith
   A3: Bill Brown
   A4: Karen Hall
   A5: Janice Gold
   B1: Salary
   B2: 25600
   B3: 45300
   B4: 18900
   B5: 42500

C1: Location
C2: Dallas
C3: Chicago
C4: Dallas
C5: Chicago

Your worksheet should look like this:

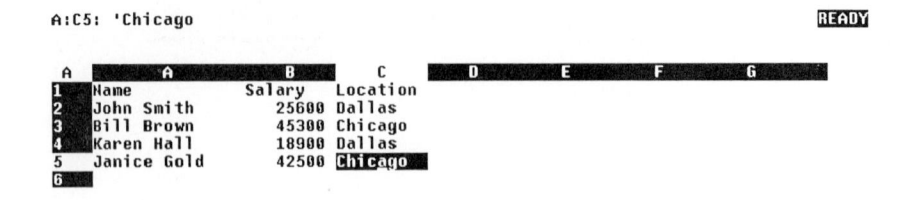

```
A:C5: 'Chicago                                                    READY

 A         A            B         C        D        E        F        G
1   Name         Salary    Location
2   John Smith     25600  Dallas
3   Bill Brown     45300  Chicago
4   Karen Hall     18900  Dallas
5   Janice Gold    42500  Chicago
6
```

Now you are ready to create a print macro. It will print two copies of the data you just entered on the worksheet.

3. Make these entries to create the macro:

H2: '\p
I2: '/pp
J2: Invoke print printer command
I3: rA1.C5~
J3: Specify range
I4: g
J4: Begin printing
I5: pa
J5: Page and align
I6: g
J6: Print a second copy
I7: pa
J7: Page and align
I8: q
J8: Quit the print menu

4. Move the cell pointer to I2, enter **/Range Name Create**, type **\p**, and press ENTER twice. The macro looks like the one in Figure 13-3.
    Make sure your printer is on and online before following the directions in the next instruction.

5. Press ALT and **P** to execute the macro and print the worksheet.

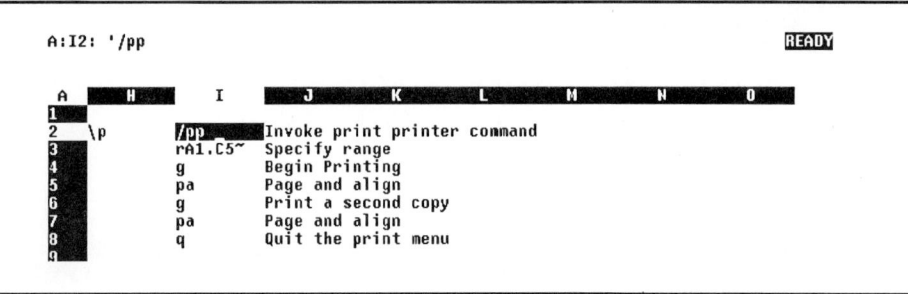

```
A:I2: '/pp                                                    READY

  A     H        I      J     K      L      M      N      O
1
2   \p           /pp     Invoke print printer command
3              rA1.C5~    Specify range
4              g          Begin Printing
5              pa         Page and align
6              g          Print a second copy
7              pa         Page and align
8              q          Quit the print menu
9
```

FIGURE 13-3.   Macro for printing a worksheet

Creating a Macro
To Insert Rows

You can create a macro to insert one or more blank rows in a worksheet, and use it with the print data you entered for the last example. A macro like this will be useful if you work frequently in the data-management environment and want to have some blank rows between field names. Since blank rows can cause problems for Query commands, you can have one macro to add them when you need them and another macro to remove them again. In this section, you will create a general-purpose macro: it will insert blank rows anywhere. If you wish, you can add a {GOTO} instruction to position the cell pointer right below the field names, so the blanks are inserted automatically at the correct location for a database.

To create a macro to insert blank rows, follow these instructions:

1. Place the following entries in the cells listed, using a single quotation mark in front of the entry for S2 and T2:

   S2: \i
   T2: /wi
   U2: Request worksheet insert
   T3: r
   U3: Specify rows
   T4: {DOWN}~
   U4: Move down to insert 2 rows

2. Move the cell pointer to S2 and enter /**Range Name Label Right**. Then press ENTER to name the top cell in the macro.

3. Move the cell pointer to A2.

4. Press ALT and **I** to execute the macro.

The macro will insert blank rows in the worksheet, and it will look like this:

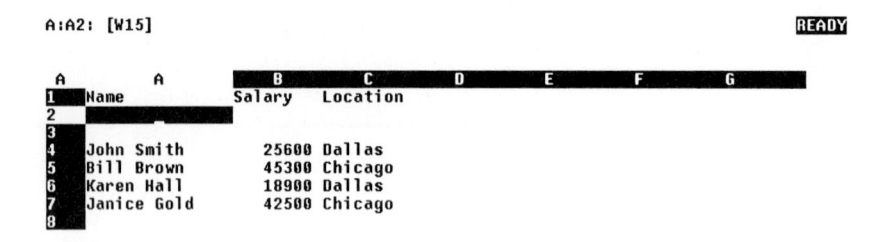

5. Enter /**Worksheet Erase Yes Yes**.

When you have a macro that inserts and deletes rows, you must be sure that it does not insert or delete rows of the macro instructions. If rows are inserted into macro instructions, the macro stops when it reaches a blank cell and omits the second half of the macro instructions. When rows are deleted from macro instructions, the macro is missing part of instructions it uses to complete its task.

SPECIAL MACRO TOPICS

There are many macro options—so many, in fact, that complete books are written on the subject. This chapter cannot cover all possible options, but it can show you a few of particular interest that go beyond the simpler keyboard alternatives to add command-language ability, minus all the complexity. In this section you will take a look at a few of the special options as well as several command-language instructions.

Creating Automatic Macros

1-2-3 has a unique feature that lets you create an *automatic macro*. Every time a worksheet containing an automatic macro is retrieved, 1-2-3 immediately executes this macro without requiring you to press any keys as long as /Worksheet Global Default Autoexec has not been set to No. Once you begin to use the advanced commmand language features, there are numerous applications for such a macro. For now, there are still a few applications for an automatically executing keyboard macro. For example, you might want to create a worksheet in which the input area is immediately erased. This means that even if the file is saved with previous data, the slate will be wiped clean with each new retrieval and you will be ready for data input.

The only difference between an automatic macro and one that you must execute is the name that you assign to the macro. An automatic macro must have a name of \0 (zero).

You can put the automatic macro to use with a model that calculates the monthly payments on a loan. The model is designed to function regardless of the principal, interest, or time. So that you can easily tell what data elements have been entered for each use of the model, the old data fields will be erased and new entries will be made.

Follow these directions to set up the basic model and then set up the automatic macro:

1. Move the cell pointer to column E, enter **/Worksheet Column Set-Width**, type **1**, and press ENTER.

2. Move the cell pointer to column G, enter **/Worksheet Column Set-Width**, type **1**, and press ENTER.

3. Move the cell pointer to B3, type **Enter desired borrowings:**, and move the cell pointer to E2.

4. Type **************.

5. Enter **/Copy**, press ENTER, move the cell pointer to E4, and press ENTER. Move the cell pointer to E3 and type *****.

6. Move the cell pointer to B6, type **Enter interest rate:**, and move the cell pointer to B10.

7. Type **Enter term in years:** and move the cell pointer to B13.

8. Type **** Your Payments Will Be **** and move the cell pointer to F13.

9. Type **@PMT(F3,F6/12,F10*12)** and press ENTER.
   Everything is now entered for this model, except for the data and a few more asterisks to form boxes on the data-entry form.

10. Move the cell pointer to E2, enter **/Copy**, move the DOWN ARROW key to E4, and press ENTER. Move the cell pointer to E5 and press ENTER.

11. Keeping the cell pointer in E2, enter **/Copy**, move the DOWN ARROW key to E4, and press ENTER. Move the cell pointer to E9 and press ENTER.

12. Add the remaining three asterisks to complete the boxes by placing an asterisk in G3, G6, and G10.

13. Move the cell pointer to F13, enter **/Range Format Currency**, and press ENTER twice.

    You have already completed quite a bit of work, but you have yet to enter the automatic macro. Follow these instructions to create the macro:

14. Move the cell pointer to B21, type **'/reF3~**, and move the cell pointer to B22.

15. Type **'/reF6~** and move the cell pointer to B23.

16. Type **'/reF10~** and move the cell pointer to B24.

17. Type **{GOTO}F3~** and move the cell pointer to B25.

    The tilde (~) is a very important part of the last three steps. It is easy to forget, but problems will occur if you leave it off.

18. Enter **{?}~{DOWN 3}{?}~{DOWN 4}** and move the cell pointer to B21. This will move the cell pointer to where the user needs to enter information.

19. Enter **/Range Name Create**, type **\0**, and press ENTER twice.

20. Move the cell pointer to A21, type **'\0**, and press ENTER.

21. Make the following documentation entries:

    C21: Erases previous borrowing entry
    C22: Erases previous interest rate
    C23: Erases previous term
    C24: Positions the cell pointer for the first entry
    C25: Moves cell pointer for entries

22. Make these entries to perform the first payment calculation:

    F3: 65000
    F6: .1025
    F10: 30

    Your display should now match Figure 13-4.

23. Enter **/File Save**, type **PAYMENT**, and press ENTER.

24. Enter **/File Retrieve**, point to PAYMENT in the list of filenames, and press ENTER.

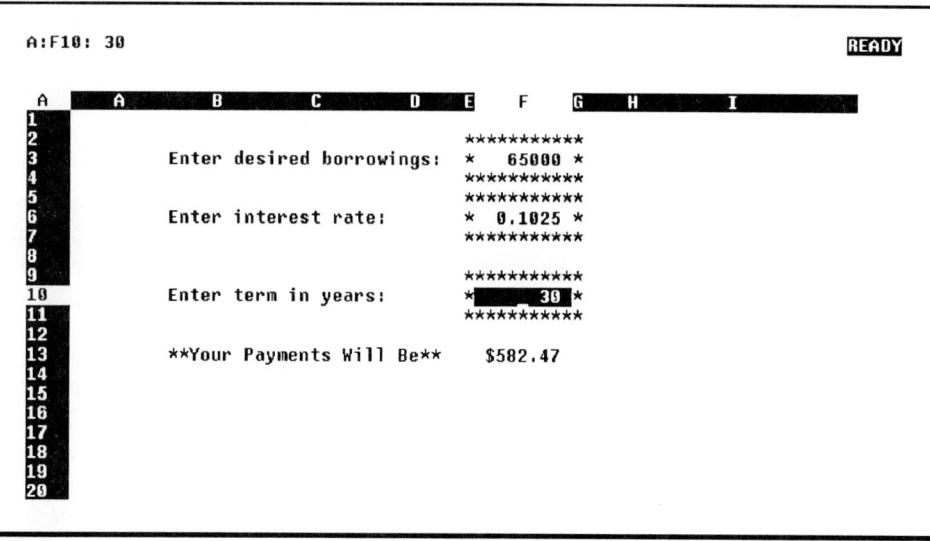

FIGURE 13-4.   Calculating a payment amount

If the macro does not begin executing immediately, enter **/Worksheet Global Default Autoexec Yes Update** and retrieve the worksheet again.

25. Complete entries in F3, F6, and F10 to calculate a new payment with different numbers.

Adding Sophistication with Command-Language Instructions

You have already explored the workings of the keyboard alternative macros. The command-language instructions make up a complete programming language for 1-2-3 instructions. However, you can look at just a few that can add power to your macros.

Each of the special command-language commands uses braces around the keyword entry for the command, as in the {QUIT} command that ends a macro. Some command-language commands also use arguments similar to the built-in functions' use of arguments. These arguments refine the use of the command to a specific situation. They look something like this:

{BRANCH End}

This command will cause the macro to begin executing the instructions stored at the range named End. Notice that the command-language argument is also enclosed within the braces.

BRANCHING WITHIN A MACRO   The {BRANCH} command allows you to change the flow of execution within a macro to another location on the worksheet. This location can be specified as a cell address or a range name. The command's format is {BRANCH *location*}. This command is seldom used alone; normally, it is combined with a condition test that will cause the macro to branch only if a certain condition is true.

The {BRANCH} command does not alter the location of the cell pointer. It is not related to the {GOTO} command, which is designed to position the cell pointer rather than to alter the execution flow of a macro.

ADDING A COUNTER   A *counter* will permit you to count the number of times you have executed a group of instructions. To use it for such a task, however, you must combine it with other instructions. For now, you will find out how counters are established; then, later in this section, you will see how a counter is combined with other instructions to create a macro that executes certain instructions repetitively. As you learn more about the macro, you will find that 1-2-3 has a {FOR} instruction that automatically initializes a counter and increments it for you. You may want to use this option later; while you are beginning with macros, however, you will find it more beneficial to establish your own counter so you can understand exactly what is happening.

A counter can be a cell address or a range name that you have assigned to a cell address. Once you decide on a location to use for a counter, you should reserve the location's use for this counter.

The {LET} command is used to set the value for a counter. When used in a macro with repetitive processing, {LET} must be used in two different ways: first, to initialize the value of the variable at the start of the macro, and second, to increment the variable each time you process the repetitive instructions within the macro. To use A1 as a counter and initialize it to 0, you could use this instruction at the beginning of the macro:

{LET A1,0}

To increment this counter within a macro after completing an iteration of the processing, you could use this instruction:

{LET A1,A1+1}

This will work regardless of the current value of A1, as long as it contains a value entry.

The two instructions affecting the value of the counter might be incorporated like this in a macro that performed repetitive processing:

```
\m       {Let A1,0}
         ...
         ...
Top      ...
         ...
         {LET A1,A1+1}
         ...
End      {QUIT}
```

You would enter the instructions to be executed repetitively in the section between Top and End. "Top" represents the beginning of the repetitive section. "End" marks the first instructions following the section that would be executed repetitively. Naturally, other instructions must be added to control the execution flow.

ADDING A CONDITION CHECK   Just as the @IF function is one of the most powerful built-in function tools, the {IF} macro instruction is one of the most powerful command-language instructions. It serves a similar purpose because it also allows you to deal with logical conditions. Its power is far more extensive because it lets you perform any other macro instruction, depending on the result of the condition test. It is not limited to controlling the value of a single cell in the way that @IF is. In fact, the {IF} command is normally combined with {BRANCH} to completely change the execution flow within a macro.

Any condition can be tested. In macros where you have established a counter to control processing, the condition that is normally checked is the value of the counter. If the condition tested is true, the command on the same line as {IF} will be executed. You might find a line like this within a macro:

{IF A1>10}{BRANCH End}

This line checks the value of A1. If A1 is greater than 10, the macro will branch to the range named End and execute the macro instructions it finds at that location.

ACCEPTING INPUT FROM THE KEYBOARD   Several commands let you accept data from the keyboard while a macro is executing. The simplest of these is {?}. When a macro encounters this special entry, it suspends execution and waits for input from the keyboard. When the operator presses ENTER, the macro continues where it left off.

You can use this feature to create a macro that removes the repetition involved in entering a series of built-in functions. You can supply the variable portion of the function and have the macro automate the entry of the portion that is the same.

A macro like the following rounds a number for you; all you need to supply is the original number and the number of places you want the number rounded:

X	Y	Z
1 \r	@ROUND(	Start rounding function
2	{?}	Wait for original number to be rounded
3	,	Add comma after number
4	{?}	Wait for number of places to round
5	)~	End function and finalize with ENTER
6	/wcs15~	Widens column to 15

Make sure that you place a single quotation mark in front of the entries in X1 and Y6 to ensure that the contents of these cells are interpreted as labels.

If you like, you can enter this macro and give it a name. The following section provides a version of this macro that is a bit more sophisticated. It incorporates several advanced macro features into the macro and creates a macro that will enter ten rounded numbers. You will take a different strategy with this macro and document each instruction immediately after entering it. This will help you understand what each step is doing. A macro like this would be used in a model in which you want to automatically use rounded numbers so someone looking at the worksheet will not think the arithmetic is incorrect.

BUILDING A MACRO TO ROUND NUMBERS   This section combines the advanced features just discussed into a working macro example. It uses the concept of a counter, branching, and keyboard input all in one macro, since it is common to include multiple advanced instructions in a macro. Follow these directions to create the macro:

1. Enter **/Worksheet Erase Yes Yes**, move the cell pointer to J1, enter **/Worksheet Column Set-Width**, type **23**, and press ENTER. Type **{LET A1,0}** and move the cell pointer to K1.

2. Type **Initialize A1 to 0 as a counter** and move the cell pointer to J2.

3. Type **{IF A1=10}{BRANCH End}** and move the cell pointer to K2.

4. Type **Check for max value in the counter** and move the cell pointer to J3.

5. Type **{LET A1,A1+1}** and move the cell pointer to K3.

6. Type **Increment counter** and move the cell pointer to J4.

7. Type **'@ROUND(**, and move the cell pointer to K4.
   The single quotation mark is required to prevent 1-2-3 from interpreting the @ as a value entry in the cell.

8. Type **Enter first part of function** and move the cell pointer to J5.

9. Complete the remaining entries like this:
   J5: {?}
   K5: Pause for original number to be rounded
   J6: ,
   K6: Enter the comma separator
   J7: {?}
   K7: Pause for number of places to round
   J8:)~
   K8: Generate function close & finalize entry
   J9: {DOWN}
   K9: Move the cell pointer down one cell
   J10: {BRANCH Top}
   K10: Begin Loop again
   J11: '/wcs15~
   K11: Expand column width to 15
   J12: {QUIT}
   K12: End macro after 10 entries

   The {QUIT} command is the only one that has not been discussed. It is used to end the execution of a macro just as a blank cell will do. Using {QUIT} rather than a blank cell makes it clearer that you intended the macro to end at that point.

10. Enter these labels in the specified cells:
    I1: '\z
    I2: Top
    I11: End

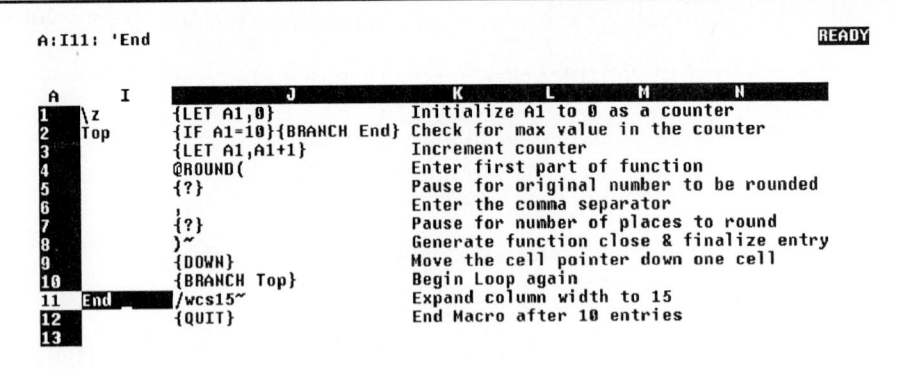

FIGURE 13-5.   A maccro for entering rounded numbers

The macro should now match Figure 13-5.

11. Move the cell pointer to I1, enter /**Range Name Label Right**, expand the range to I13, and press ENTER.

   The Range Name Label Right command saves you from having to use the /Range Name Create command three times. It assigns the labels in the range you specify to the entries in the cells immediately to the right of the cell containing the label.

12. Move the cell pointer to D1 and press the ALT key and **Z** to execute the macro.

   You can enter anything you want in this macro for the original number and the number of digits you want rounded as long as the entries are valid and you press ENTER after each entry. Figure 13-6 shows one set of entries that were completed with the macro.

Debugging Macros

The debugging process involves testing and correcting macros to ensure that you are obtaining the desired results. One of the most common mistakes users make in creating keyboard macros is forgetting to enter the tilde to represent each time the ENTER key is pressed. When you add command-language commands to a macro, you do not have the ability to test it completely before entering it.

   1-2-3's STEP mode lets you execute a macro one keystroke at a time. This allows you to follow its progress and spot the area of difficulty if problems are encountered. To activate STEP mode, press ALT-F2 (RECORD) and select Step. Since this is a toggle

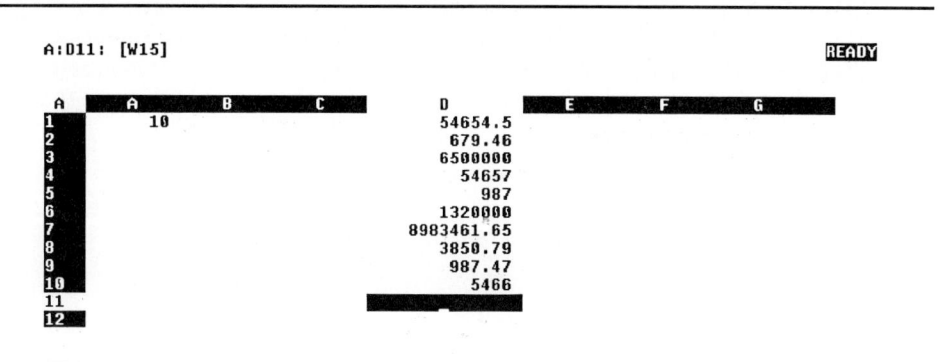

```
A:D11: [W15]                                                              READY

    A    A        B        C        D          E      F       G
    1        10                  54654.5
    2                            679.46
    3                           6500000
    4                             54657
    5                               987
    6                           1320000
    7                         8983461.65
    8                           3850.79
    9                            987.47
   10                              5466
   11
   12
```

FIGURE 13-6. Numbers entered and rounded with the macro

process, repeating the action disables STEP mode. When this mode is operational, you will see the STEP indicator at the bottom of your screen, as shown in Figure 13-7.

When STEP mode is on, any macro you invoke will be executed one step at a time. You will press the spacebar each time you are ready for the next keystroke. The menu selections invoked will be displayed in the control panel to provide information on the operation of the macro. You will not be able to enter direct commands while the macro is executing. "SST" will flash at the bottom of the screen while the macro is executing.

```
A:C1: (C0) 2                                                             READY

   A    A        B        C        D       E       F       G       H
   1       $2       $2       $2       2       2       2
   2        5       $5       $5       5       5       5
   3        4       $4       $4       4       4       4
   4        9       $9       $9       9       9       9
   5        7       $7       $7       7       7       7
   6                         $8               8       8
   7                         $9               9       9
   8                         $3               3       3
   9
  10
  11
  12
  13
  14
  15  \c       /r         request Range command
  16           fc0~       select Currency format with 0 decimal places
  17
  18
  19
  20
FORMAT.WK3                                  STEP              NUM
```

FIGURE 13-7. Placing the macro in STEP mode

To stop a malfunctioning macro, press the CTRL and BREAK keys simultaneously. This cancels the macro operation immediately and presents an error indicator at the upper-right corner of the screen. Pressing ESC will return you to READY mode so you can make the necessary corrections to your macro.

Follow these instructions to try a macro in STEP mode:

1. Enter /**File Retrieve**, type **FORMAT**, and press ENTER.

2. Press ALT-F2 (RECORD) and select Step.

3. Move the cell pointer to F1, and press ALT and **C**.

4. Press the spacebar to execute a keystroke.

5. Continue pressing the spacebar until you are asked to supply the range to format.

6. Press the END key followed by the DOWN ARROW key. Then press the ENTER key.

7. Execute step 2 again to toggle STEP mode into the off position.

8. Enter /**Worksheet Erase Yes Yes**.

REVIEW EXERCISE

Although practice will improve your skills with all 1-2-3 tasks, it is especially important with macros because a number of steps are required to achieve successful results. For practice, you will create a macro that enters the month names in a column beginning at the cell pointer. You can use the same approach to enter account names or part numbers if you need to use them in a number of places within one model. These steps even include a deliberate mistake and its correction.

1. Clear the macro recorder buffer. *Hint:* Press ALT-F2 (RECORD) and select Erase.

2. Start recording the keystrokes as you start a trial run in A2. Make a deliberate mistake in typing "November" by entering **Novemv**. Press the BACKSPACE key and type **ber**. Press ENTER.

3. Copy the macro recorder buffer to E1. *Hint:* Press ALT- F2 (RECORD) and select Copy. Then press HOME, TAB, END, and ENTER. Move to E1, and press ENTER.)

4. Widen column D so you can see the entire macro name. *Hint:* Use /Worksheet Column Set-Width, press RIGHT ARROW four times, and press ENTER.

5. Enter **enter_months** in D1 for the macro name, and name the macro. *Hint:* Use either /Range Name Create or type **enter_months** in D1, and use /Range Name Label Right to name the top cell in the macro. The macro will look like this:

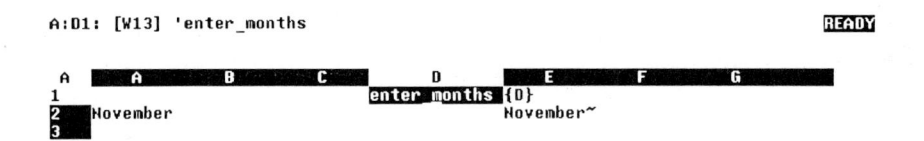

Notice that 1-2-3 automatically made the correction in your entry.

6. Move to B5 and execute the enter_month macro. *Hint:* Move to B5, press ALT-F3 (RUN), and select enter_month.

REVIEW

- 1-2-3's keyboard alternative macros allow you to perform repetitive tasks with ease. You can type the keystrokes in a cell or use 1-2-3's macro recorder to record them. Once a macro is named, you can execute it.

- Macros are saved with the file that contains them. However, they execute on the current worksheet.

- To record function keys and special keys you must use 1-2-3's keywords enclosed in braces ({}). To record menu selections, use the first character in each command name. To record entries, type them as you would without a macro.

- Macros are entered in a group of contiguous cells in a column of the worksheet. If you are typing the entries, each one must be a label entry.

- You can use two different methods for naming macros. In both cases, only the top cell in the macro is named. Your selection will determine how you can execute the macro. If you use \ and a single letter, you can press ALT and the letter to execute the macro. If you use a regular range name, you will need to use ALT-F3 (RUN) to execute the macro.

Commands and Keys

ALT-*letter*	Executes a macro
ALT-F2 (RECORD)	Accesses the macro recorder
ALT-F3 (RUN)	Executes a macro
/RNLR	/Range Name Label Right applies names to cell immediately to the right
/WGDA	/Worksheet Global Default Autoexec determines if 1-2-3 tries to execute a macro called \0 when a file is retrieved

INSTALLING 1-2-3

Your Equipment
Installing 1-2-3
Using Install After Installing 1-2-3

This appendix is designed to serve as an introduction to installing Lotus 1-2-3 on various types of equipment. Whether you use a hard disk or a floppy disk, you will find detailed instructions to ensure that the installation process proceeds smoothly.

If your copy of 1-2-3 has already been installed by your computer dealer or someone else in your organization, you do not need to read this appendix. If your copy of 1-2-3 is still covered in shrink wrap, you will need to install the package, and you will find this appendix to be a valuable reference for the steps that you must take. It will also provide some information on various equipment options to help you make intelligent selections during the installation process.

Before beginning with 1-2-3 specifics, this appendix introduces the hardware options for 1-2-3 and the various system components. You cannot install 1-2-3 if you do not have at least some general knowledge about the system you will be using. In order for the Install program to configure your copy of 1-2-3 to run with your specific hardware, you must be able to tell the program what those components are.

YOUR EQUIPMENT

1-2-3 Release 3 is designed to run on a DOS- or OS/2-based 80286 or 80386 IBM-compatible computer. This includes AT's and the newer PS/2 machines. Since the compatible market is constantly changing, you will need to check with your dealer for the most up-to-date list of certified compatibles. In case of doubt, have the dealer demonstrate 1-2-3 on the machine you are considering.

Throughout this appendix, it is assumed that you have an IBM AT or PS/2.

Minimum Configuration

Release 3 has different minimum system requirements than its predecessors. Release 3 requires a minimum of 1 megabyte (1Mb) of RAM. Most AT's that use 640K RAM for DOS applications have 1Mb of RAM that 1-2-3 can use. If you are planning to use OS/2, you should have 4Mb of RAM, which is the minimum that OS/2 Version 1.1 needs. Release 3 can use expanded and extended memory, allowing you to take full advantage of the memory in a PS/2 as well as memory added to an AT with a card like Intel's Above Board card.

Unlike earlier versions, 1-2-3 Release 3 must be run from a hard disk. The hard disk needs at least 4Mb of available space to hold the 1-2-3 files if the DOS or OS/2 operating system is used. If you plan to use both DOS and OS/2, 5Mb of disk space is required.

The models you create are limited by the amount of memory on your system. If you are operating 1-2-3 at the lowest memory level possible you can use all of its features, but you are restricted in the size of your data files, spreadsheet applications, and the number of files you have in memory. If you plan to build large models, you should consider expanding the memory of your machine. The DOS protected-mode extension technology is built into the 1-2-3 product to allow the software to take advantage of all the memory on a machine. Network and TSR software can still be used within the conventional 640K limit for DOS while 1-2-3 utilizes extended memory. Release 3 can use up to 16Mb of extended memory and 32Mb of LIM4 memory. With the LIM4 memory board option and DOS, you can use up to 48Mb of memory for 1-2-3 and your models. Under OS/2, the limit is 16Mb of extended memory.

Release 3 also supports the addition of a math coprocessor. Both the 80387 and the 80287 coprocessor chips are supported and are automatically recognized once they are installed. Spreadsheet models with a significant number of calculations are calculated much faster with one of these chips added to the motherboard of your machine.

KEYBOARD   You will begin using the keyboard in this appendix as you work with the Install program. Any directions given here will refer to key names on the enhanced keyboard. The enhanced keyboard offers a second set of movement keys as well as a numeric keypad, so you can use the numeric keypad for numbers as you use the second set of movement keys for moving in 1-2-3. Pressing the NUM LOCK key switches the numeric keypad between movement keys and number keys. Other keyboard types usually have the same keys, but you must find where these keys are located.

MONITOR   Monitors are described in terms of two features: color and resolution. Monitors can be either color or monochrome. Monochrome can display one color; this may be white, green, or amber on black. A monochrome monitor usually displays only text, although you can add cards such as an enhanced graphics adapter or a Hercules card. Even with the graphics adapter, a monochrome monitor will display one-color graphs. A color monitor can display graphs in color as well as utilize color for highlighting some of the 1-2-3 screens; for example, it can use red for the error indicator and blue to highlight menu choices.

The second feature of a monitor, the resolution, refers to how many dots of light your monitor can display across the screen—the more dots your monitor uses to fill the screen the sharper the images the monitor can display. The different types of monitor resolution are described with acronyms like CGA, EGA, and VGA. With Release 3, the installation program will automatically detect which type of a display you have and suggest the type for you. Unless you know the suggestion is wrong, you will use it when you install 1-2-3. With earlier releases you had to note the type of display you had before installing 1-2-3.

PRINTERS   If you have both a dot-matrix and a letter-quality printer, you may want to use the letter-quality device for text and use the dot-matrix device to print graphics. If you have both a dot-matrix printer and a laser printer, you can use the dot-matrix printer for draft copies and the laser printer for the final output. On a network, you may have a variety of output devices from which to select, including a plotter for graphics and a laser printer for professional-looking text and graphics output.

To connect any of these printers to your system, you will also need a cable and an available port. It is possible to connect printers to both parallel and serial ports as long as they are compatible, but there are some special settings if you use a serial connection. First, you must set the printer's baud rate to control the speed of data transfer. At any baud rate except 110 you should also set 1 stop bit, 8 data bits, and no parity. With a speed of 110 there should be 2 stop bits. Once the program is loaded, use the /Worksheet Global Default Printer Interface command and select the baud rate matching your printer's rate. This is done by typing **/WGDPI**, pointing to the baud rate you need, and pressing ENTER. This change is saved with the /Worksheet Global Default Update command (/WGDU). If you are purchasing your system at the same time you acquire 1-2-3, your dealer will normally assist you with this installation.

A plotter provides another option for producing graphs. With most devices you can use either paper or transparencies in your plotter with the appropriate pens to create the display medium of your choice. Since 1-2-3 supports only a limited number of plotters, you should be sure the one you are considering is on the "acceptable" list; otherwise, it may not function with 1-2-3.

ADDING DISK DRIVES   Although Release 3 can be used with a hard disk, you have the option of storing your data to a hard disk or a floppy disk. Hard drives offer the advantage of storing large amounts of information. A hard drive that holds 100Mb of information is equivalent to 278 floppy disks.

Your computer may have one or two disk drives. When two disks are next to each other, the one to the left or above the other is usually referred to as drive A. The one to the right or below the other is usually referred to as drive B. If your computer only has one drive, it is drive A.

Before you can store data on a floppy disk, the disk needs to be prepared. Use the FORMAT command described in your operating system manual, or review the section "Using /System to Prepare a Disk" in Chapter 4 before storing data on floppy disks.

The Operating System

The operating system is the control program that resides in the memory of your computer regardless of the software you are working with. It controls the interface between the various devices and establishes the format for data storage on disk. Release 3 can use the DOS or OS/2 operating system, or both. To use Release 3 with DOS, you must use at least a 3.0 version of DOS. For OS/2, you must use at least the 1.1 version of IBM OS/2.

Noting Your Equipment

You are now ready to proceed with the steps needed to install your 1-2-3 disks. First, however, make a note of your monitor, your graphics card, and printer. For your monitor, you must notice the type of screen it uses. For the printer, you must note the manufacturer and the model number.

INSTALLING 1-2-3

Installation tailors your 1-2-3 disks to run with your specific hardware configuration. If 1-2-3 only ran with one type of hardware, this step would not be necessary. Since it is, you should remember that it offers you an advantage: you can continue to use the package even if you change your hardware configuration to include a plotter, a new printer, or a different monitor.

Preliminary Steps

When you purchase 1-2-3, the package you receive contains an envelope with several floppy disks, depending on the disk size. With 3 1/2" disks, you receive an Install Disk, a System Disk for DOS, a System Disk for OS/2, two Driver Disks, a Font Disk, and a Translate Disk. With 5 1/4" disks, you receive different disks, but they contain the same information.

The *Install Disk* contains the installation program, Install, which copies the necessary files to your computer. The *System Disks* for DOS or OS/2 contain the program files 1-2-3 runs to execute 1-2-3. The *Font Disks* contain information 1-2-3 uses to print and display fonts. The *Driver Disks* contain the driver files for all the equipment Lotus supports, including printer drivers, plotter drivers, and display drivers. When you run the Install program and indicate your equipment selection, the drivers will be copied from the driver disks to your computer. The *Translate Disk* contains 1-2-3's translation programs and sample files to use with 1-2-3. The translation programs allow you to maximize the benefit from data recorded in another program such as dBASE III or VisiCalc by translating the data to a format that 1-2-3 can use.

Installing 1-2-3
On a Hard Disk

The Install program for 1-2-3 uses the same steps for the DOS operating system, the OS/2 operating system, or both DOS and OS/2. The instructions for this section assume that DOS or OS/2 is on your hard drive and that you are using Release 3 of 1-2-3.

The first step in installing 1-2-3 is determining if the free disk space is adequate. To install 1-2-3 for DOS or OS/2, the computer must have 4Mb of free disk space. To install 1-2-3 for both DOS and OS/2, the computer must have 5Mb of free disk space. To start the Install program, insert the Setup/Install disk into drive A. Type **A:** and press ENTER to make the drive current. Then type **INSTALL** and press ENTER to start the program. If you need to use drive B to install 1-2-3, replace "B" with "A" when it appears for the drive selection. If you need to leave the Install program for any reason, press ESC until the Install program asks if you want to exit it, and select Yes.

In the next step, Install prompts you to register your name and the company's name. In the first line, enter your name. In the second line, enter your company name. If you do not have a company name to supply, reenter your name. Then press INS to finalize the entries. The Install program ask you for confirmation, which you can supply by typing **Y**.

Install displays the opening menu. After reading it, press ENTER. Then Install displays a menu to select the type of installation. Type **1** to select Both DOS and OS/2, **2** to select DOS, or **3** to select OS/2. Press ENTER.

Once 1-2-3 knows the operating system you will use with 1-2-3, Install displays a menu that allows you to have the translation files copied. Type **Y** to copy the translation files or **N** to skip copying these files. Press ENTER. Since 1-2-3 compresses the files, you want to use Install to copy these files. Install expands them as it copies them. If you copy them directly from the disk, you must later use the Inflate program to expand them, since the programs are compressed. When you copy the translation files, the Install program copies the sample files that the Tutorial section of the 1-2-3 manual uses to illustrate 1-2-3 features.

Next, 1-2-3 prompts you for the disk drive and displays drive C as the default. If you want to use 1-2-3 on a hard disk other than drive C, enter the drive letter. Press ENTER to accept the default of C or your new entry.

The Install program prompts you for the directory that 1-2-3 will use. This can be an existing directory or one that Install will create for you; either use 1-2-3's suggested directory of \123R3, or supply a subdirectory name. Subdirectories have the same name conventions as file names and are limited to eight characters. Press ENTER to finalize the entry and continue with the next step.

If the directory does not exist, the Install program displays a confirmation box prompting you to type **Y** to continue and create the subdirectory or **N** to return to the screen to select a new directory. After typing either letter, press ENTER to return to the previous screen or to advance to the next installation step.

If the directory exists and contains files, the Install program prompts you for confirmation. Type **Y** and press ENTER if the file contains Release 3.0 program files that the Install program will replace. Type **N** and press ENTER if the directory contains other files. You do not want Install to copy over files you will later need. If you type **N** and press ENTER, 1-2-3 returns to the screen for entering the file directory name.

If you provide an existing empty directory, 1-2-3 does not prompt you for a confirmation but immediately starts copying files from the Setup/Install Disk.

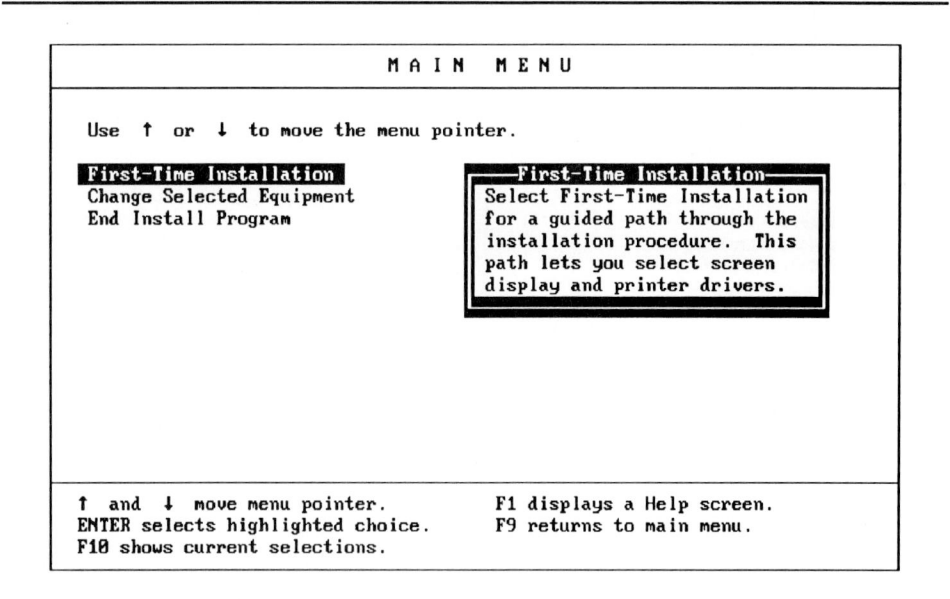

```
┌──────────────────────────────────────────────────────────────────────┐
│                          M A I N   M E N U                             │
├──────────────────────────────────────────────────────────────────────┤
│                                                                        │
│   Use  ↑  or  ↓  to move the menu pointer.                             │
│                                                                        │
│   ┌─────────────────────────┐  ┌─First-Time Installation─┐            │
│   │First-Time Installation  │  │Select First-Time Installation │       │
│   Change Selected Equipment    │for a guided path through the  │       │
│   End Install Program          │installation procedure.  This  │       │
│                                │path lets you select screen    │       │
│                                │display and printer drivers.   │       │
│                                └───────────────────────────────┘       │
│                                                                        │
│                                                                        │
│                                                                        │
│                                                                        │
│   ┌──────────────────────────────────────────────────────────────┐    │
│   ↑ and ↓ move menu pointer.          F1 displays a Help screen.       │
│   ENTER selects highlighted choice.   F9 returns to main menu.         │
│   F10 shows current selections.                                        │
└──────────────────────────────────────────────────────────────────────┘
```

FIGURE A-1.   Install's main menu

After you confirm an existing name or instruct 1-2-3 to create the directory, 1-2-3 starts copying files from the Setup/Install Disk.

Most of the installation process involves copying files from the 1-2-3 disks to your computer. 1-2-3 prompts you for the following disks: the Translate Disk if you are copying translation or sample files, Driver Disk 1, 1-2-3 System Disk (DOS) if you are installing for DOS or DOS and OS/2, and 1-2-3 System Disk (OS/2) if you are installing for OS/2 or DOS and OS/2. If you are using the 5 1/4" disks, Install will instruct you to insert different disks. For each of the disks the Install program requests, insert the disk in drive A and press ENTER. Make sure you close the disk drive door or insert the disk fully into the disk drive. Also, do not remove a disk from the drive until the Install program prompts you for the next disk.

When the Install program has finished copying files to your hard drive, it displays a screen for the second part of installation, in which you tell 1-2-3 the type of monitor and printer you will use. Press ENTER to continue to the next step.

The next screen is the main menu of the Install program, shown in Figure A-1. Since you are installing 1-2-3 for the first time, press ENTER to select First-Time Installation. Later, if you use the Install program, you will use the Change Selected

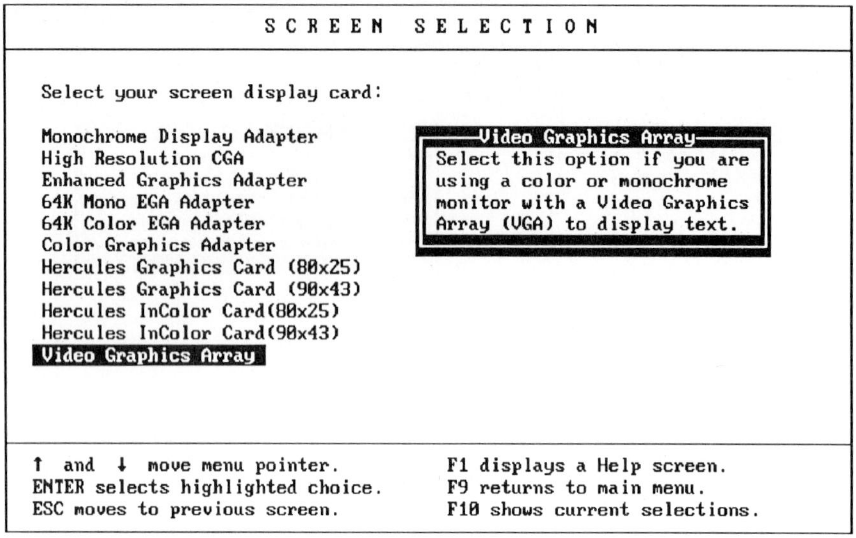

```
┌──────────────────────────────────────────────────────────────────┐
│                  S C R E E N   S E L E C T I O N                   │
├──────────────────────────────────────────────────────────────────┤
│                                                                    │
│   Select your screen display card:                                 │
│                                                                    │
│   Monochrome Display Adapter     ┌─────Video Graphics Array────┐   │
│   High Resolution CGA            │ Select this option if you are│  │
│   Enhanced Graphics Adapter      │ using a color or monochrome  │  │
│   64K Mono EGA Adapter           │ monitor with a Video Graphics│  │
│   64K Color EGA Adapter          │ Array (VGA) to display text. │  │
│   Color Graphics Adapter         └──────────────────────────────┘  │
│   Hercules Graphics Card (80x25)                                   │
│   Hercules Graphics Card (90x43)                                   │
│   Hercules InColor Card(80x25)                                     │
│   Hercules InColor Card(90x43)                                     │
│  ▐Video Graphics Array▌                                            │
│                                                                    │
├──────────────────────────────────────────────────────────────────┤
│   ↑ and ↓ move menu pointer.        F1 displays a Help screen.     │
│   ENTER selects highlighted choice. F9 returns to main menu.       │
│   ESC moves to previous screen.     F10 shows current selections.  │
└──────────────────────────────────────────────────────────────────┘
```

FIGURE A-2.   Selection of monitor display options

Equipment option. At the end of the installation process, you may use the last option, End Install Program, to return to the system prompt.

Next, the Install program displays a screen describing how to select a screen display. The Install program displays what it has identified as the correct screen display. For most monitors, it is correct. Unless you know that the suggestion is incorrect, write down this suggestion. Press ENTER to see the the available screen displays, as shown in Figure A-2.

Move the highlight to the video display that you want. In most cases this is the suggestion from the previous screen. Press ENTER. Some monitor selections have a second menu that offers additional options for the resolution 1-2-3 will use when displaying to your screen. The options can include available colors and the number of lines 1-2-3 uses; for example, 1-2-3 can display 25, 34, or 60 lines with a video graphics array monitor. For each of the selections, 1-2-3 can display the worksheets in color or monochrome. You can select two display drivers by highlighting the one you want most of the time and pressing the spacebar. A 1 appears next to this selection. Then highlight the other one you want to use and press the spacebar. A 2 appears next to this selection. When you are in 1-2-3, you can use the /Worksheet Window Display command to select the first or second display driver.

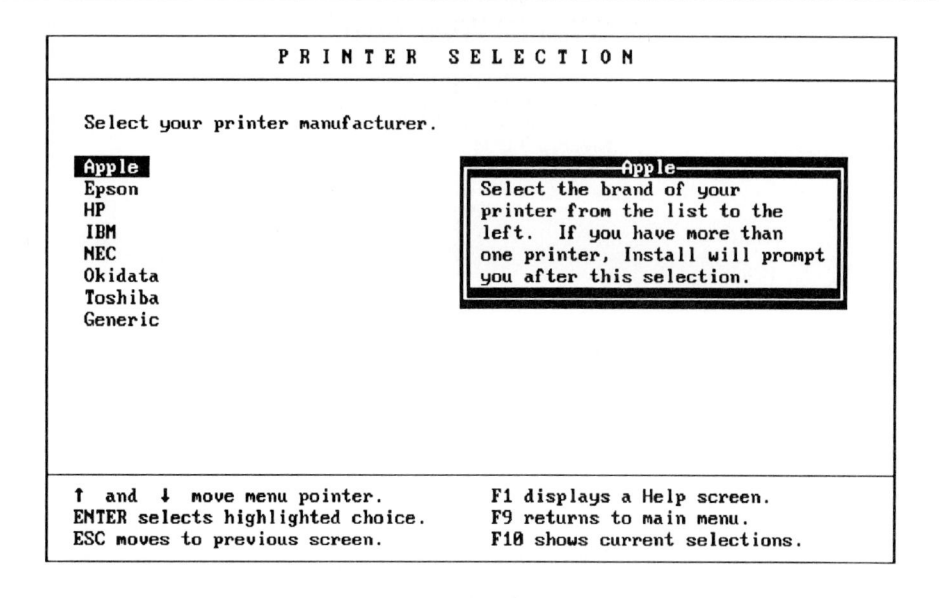

```
          P R I N T E R    S E L E C T I O N

  Select your printer manufacturer.

    Apple                        ┌─────────Apple─────────┐
    Epson                        │ Select the brand of your│
    HP                           │ printer from the list to the│
    IBM                          │ left.  If you have more than│
    NEC                          │ one printer, Install will prompt│
    Okidata                      │ you after this selection.│
    Toshiba                      └─────────────────────────┘
    Generic




  ↑ and  ↓ move menu pointer.      F1 displays a Help screen.
  ENTER selects highlighted choice. F9 returns to main menu.
  ESC moves to previous screen.     F10 shows current selections.
```

FIGURE A-3.   Selection of printer manufacturers

Press ENTER to advance to the next menu. 1-2-3 wants to know the printer that you want to use. This lets 1-2-3 print graphs directly and to include printer enhancements such as fonts in your graphs and worksheets. Unless you do not have a printer, select Yes. Then select the printer manufacturer from the list like the one in Figure A-3. The Install program lists most major manufacturers. If yours is not listed, select one that is identical to yours or select Generic. If you must select Generic, you will not be able to print graphs. For each of the printer models, the Install program prompts you for additional information. Highlight the option that is appropriate for your printer, and press ENTER.

After all the selections for the first printer are made, the Install program prompts you to determine if you will use a second printer with 1-2-3. You may want to select a second printer if your computer has two printers or if the type of printer connected to your computer varies. If you select Yes, 1-2-3 repeats the same steps that you performed for selecting the first printer. If you select No, 1-2-3 skips the second printer information requests.

After the printers are selected, 1-2-3 prompts you to determine the name you want to use for the configuration file. The configuration file contains the information about the screen display, printer, and other information that 1-2-3 uses to execute. If you do

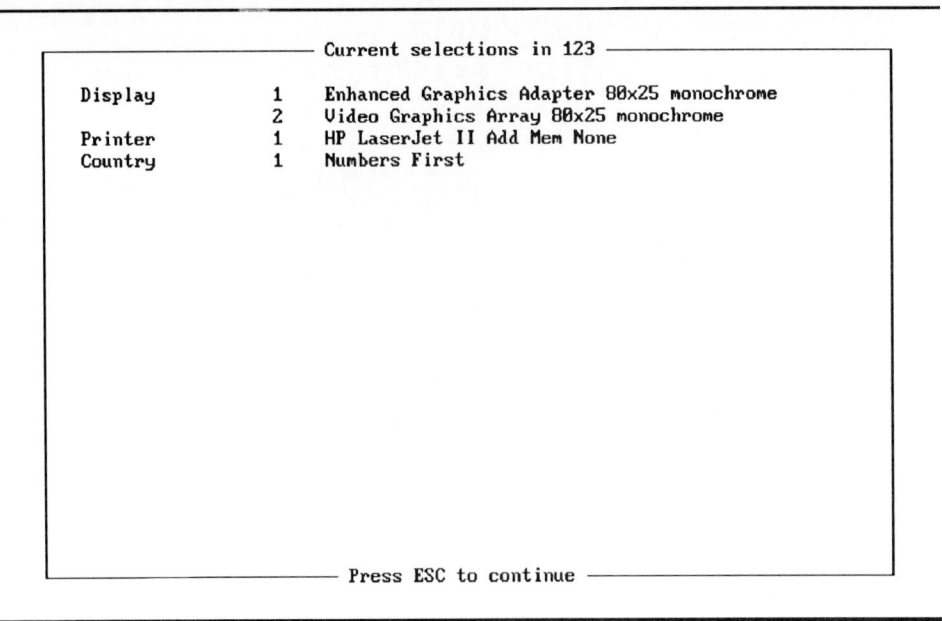

FIGURE A-4.   Install listing current selections

not name the configuration file, Install names it 123.DCF. If you name the configuration file, you must provide a filename of up to eight characters. At any time you may want to press F10 to view your current selections; you will see something like Figure A-4.

Now that the Install program knows the printer and the screen display, it needs to copy additional files to your computer. 1-2-3 again asks for the disk drive letter, displaying A as a possible selection. For most cases, press ENTER; if the drive that Install will read the files from is incorrect, type the new letter and press ENTER. 1-2-3 prompts you for the Driver Disks, depending on the selections made. For each of the disks that Install requests, insert the disk in drive A and press ENTER.

Once 1-2-3 has copied the files, it tells you that 1-2-3 is successfully installed. To continue, press ENTER. 1-2-3 displays a screen that asks you if you want to leave Install. If you select Yes, you are returned to the system prompt. If you select No, you return to the Install program main menu.

With Install completed, you are ready to use 1-2-3. You can display graphs and interface with your printer or plotter. Changing between 1-2-3 programs will be easy, since all the Lotus files are stored on your disk.

USING INSTALL AFTER
INSTALLING 1-2-3

Once you have installed 1-2-3, you can continue to use the Install program. You can use it to create more than one driver set, or to change the hardware configuration to include another printer or screen display. You may also want to change the sort order 1-2-3 uses for the /Data Sort command.

Creating More Than
One Driver Set

If you frequently alter the configuration of your system, you will want more than one driver set. This will allow you to switch from one driver set to another without having to change the installation parameters each time.

If you use more than one driver set, pick a meaningful driver name for each, such as 2MONITOR, PLOTTER, or HOME. You can use up to eight characters for the first part of the name. You must avoid the following symbols:

, . ; : / ? * ^ + = < > [ ] \ '.

1-2-3 adds a .DCF extension for the filename, as in COLOR.DCF.

Use the First-Time Installation option to create each driver set. Save each driver set under a different name. You may want to store these multiple drivers on a separate disk if you want to use different drivers with the files in different directories.

Modifying the Current Driver

Install has two options for modifying the 1-2-3 driver files: First-Time Installation and Change Selected Equipment. The First-Time Installation option creates driver files. The Change Selected Equipment option changes a driver file. To change a driver file, select Change Selected Equipment. To select the driver file to modify, select Choose Another DCF to Modify and enter the driver name that you want to modify. If you do not select a driver file, Install uses 123.DCF. Then select Modify Current DCF. This selection has the following options: Return to Menu, Change Selected Display, Change Selected Printer, and Change Selected Country. Selecting one of them can change the display driver, printer driver, or sort sequence for the current driver file. When you are finished with this menu, select Return to Menu.

Changing the Display   The display driver may need to be changed if you want to change the initial display driver or if you want to add a second one. Several monitors can use more than one display driver. For example, if you are using a monitor with a VGA display, you may want to see how your graphs will look to someone with an EGA monitor. You can have two display drivers for a driver file.

To add or change a display driver, select Change Selected Display. The Install program lists the possible display drivers, with a 1 next to the display driver name that is selected. To add a second display driver or replace the first one, select the display driver you want to add or substitute (for some selections you will need to make an additional choice). This selects the display driver that you added as the secondary display driver. To replace the first display driver with the second display driver, select Change Selected Display again and highlight the display driver you want to remove. Press the spacebar. The 1 next to the highlighted selection disappears and the 2 next to the selection you added becomes a 1. Press ESC to return to the Change Selected Equipment menu.

To select which display driver 1-2-3 uses, use the /Worksheet Window Display command. Then type **1** or **2** to select the display driver.

CHANGING THE PRINTER   The printer driver may need to be changed if you change the printer or you want to add a second one. 1-2-3 allows up to 16 printer drivers in a driver configuration file. To add or change a printer driver, select Change Selected Printer. The Install program lists the possible printer manufacturers. When you select a printer manufacturer, Install displays a number (1-9) or letter (a-g) next to a printer driver that has been selected. To add another printer driver, select the printer driver you want to add. Then make the additional menu selections appropriate for the printer. This selects the printer driver that you added as the next available printer driver. To remove a printer driver, select Change Selected Printer again, select the manufacturer, and highlight the printer driver you want to remove. Press DEL. You may have to press DEL again in a second menu, depending on the printer driver you are removing. The number or letter next to the highlighted selection disappears. Install reassigns numbers and letters to the remaining printer drivers.

To select which printer driver 1-2-3 uses, use the /Worksheet Global Default Printer Name command. Then type the letter or number to select which printer driver to use.

CHANGING THE SORT ORDER   The Change Selected Country option allows you to change the collating sequence for the existing driver set. Release 3 provides three options: Numbers First, Numbers Last, and the standard ASCII sequence. If you

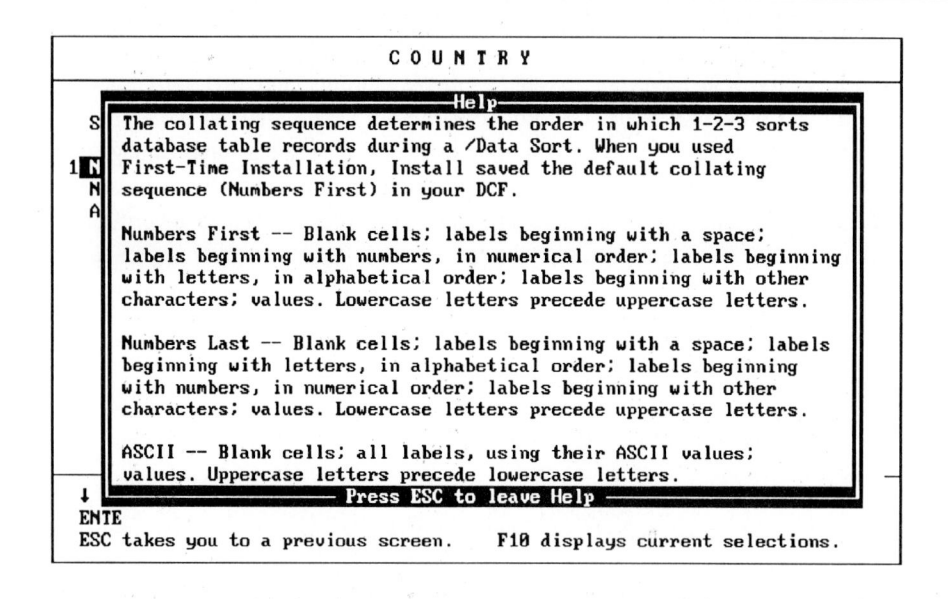

FIGURE A-5. HELP screen illustrating different sort options

are not familiar with sorting sequences, look at the Install HELP screen shown in Figure A-5 for a sample of the three options. These selections sort in this order:

- Numbers Last: Blank cells, label entries with letters in alphabetical order, label entries beginning with numbers in numeric sequence, labels beginning with special characters, and then values.

- Numbers First: Blank cells, labels beginning with numbers in numeric sequence, labels beginning with letters in alphabetical order, labels beginning with special characters, and then values.

- ASCII: Blank cells, followed by labels and values in ASCII order. Capitalization will affect the sort order with this choice. This selection also makes @ functions case-sensitive and can have serious implications for formulas containing string functions that are used in computations or the criteria area with /Data Query commands.

To change the collating sequence, select Change Selected Country from the menu and then select the sort order you want from the submenu.

Saving the Driver Files

Once you have changed your driver file's display, printer, and sort configurations, you need to save the driver file so it will contain your new selections. To do so, use the main menu's Change Selected Equipment option and select Save Changes. When 1-2-3 displays the filename, you can edit it if you want the new settings saved with a different filename. When the filename is correct, press ENTER to save the updated changes. When you return to the Change Selected Equipment menu, you can select End Install Program to leave Install or continue using the other menu options.

Changing Other Configuration Parameters

Most of the hardware configuration options are specified in the installation process. However, two additional options that could require frequent change are changed directly from 1-2-3. One is the disk drive assignment for data files, and the other is the printer settings.

The disk drive assignment can be changed from the default drive of C:\123R3 to another drive. The command to do this within 1-2-3 is /Worksheet Global Default Dir. Printer options can be changed with /Worksheet Global Default Printer. The changes made with this command can be saved with /Worksheet Global Default Update.

B
GLOSSARY

@Function XT = A prerecorded formula that is already stored internally in 1-2-3. You can access @ functions by following set rules; the @ followed by a keyword and, in most cases, a set of parentheses encasing specific arguments that provide the values the function will use. Functions have different areas of applications such as statistical, mathematical, and financial applications. For example, @SUM(A1..B10) totals all the values in the cells within the range A1..B10. You can use functions as part of another formula or function, as in @PMT(@SUM(A4..A10),C5,D10).

3-D *See* Multilevel.

Absolute A type of reference used in a worksheet formula. An absolute cell reference always refers to the original cell, regardless of where the formula is copied. An absolute reference is distinguished from other types of references by the $ in front of both the row and the column portion of the address, as in $A:$A$2, $A:$D$50, and $A:$Z$3.

Alignment The placement of a label entry within a cell. 1-2-3 allows left, right, or center alignment for label entries within a cell. Special label indicators are used to control the alignment. The caret (^) is used for center alignment, an apostrophe (') represents left alignment, and the double quotation mark (") represents right alignment.

Arguments   Individual values, quote-enclosed labels, range references, or range names that define how you wish to use a built-in function or command-language instruction. The number and type of arguments supplied will depend on the function or command-language instruction selected. When cell references are included in your arguments, you have the option of typing the reference or pointing to the cell or range you wish to select.

Arithmetic Operators   Symbols used within 1-2-3 formulas to define the type of mathematical operation to be performed. When more than one arithmetic operator is included in a formula, the operators are evaluated from left to right, using an order of precedence for the operators. The valid arithmetic operators and their order of precedence is

^	Exponentiation
+, -	Positive, negative number
*, /	Multiplication, division
+, -	Addition, subtraction

Parentheses can be used to override the order of precedence.

ASCII   A format for file storage in which text and special characters are assigned code numbers. This standard coding system facilitates the exchange of information between programs, since standard codes represent each character. 1-2-3 is able to bring ASCII data into the worksheet with the /File Import command. The characters in the acronym ASCII represent American Standard Code for Information Interchange.

Axes   The horizontal (X axis) and vertical (Y axis) lines, that provide the framework for the construction of most types of graphs. The Y axis functions as a scale for a quantitative measurement of the data shown on the graph. The X axis is used to represent the categories in the data series that are being plotted.

Background Printing   How 1-2-3 sends information to the printer and at the same time allows you to continue to work with other 1-2-3 features. This is unlike previous releases, which displayed the WAIT mode indicator until 1-2-3 completed the printing task.

Background Recalculation   How 1-2-3 performs minimal recalculation and at the same time allows you to continue to work with other 1-2-3 features. This feature lets you continue to make data entries while 1-2-3 updates the rest of the worksheet for the new values.

Backup   An additional copy of a file (with a slightly different name so the operating system can tell the two files apart) that is used to store data in case you lose the newest version. 1-2-3's /File commands provide this option when you try saving a file with an existing filename. The backup copy of the file has a .BAK extension.

Built-in Function   *See* @ Function.

Cell   A single location on the worksheet. You have the option of storing a number, a label, or a formula in a worksheet cell. Other characteristics, such as label alignment and formatting, can also be specified for one or more worksheet cells.

Cell Pointer   The highlighted bar that marks the current cell on the worksheet. The cell pointer can be moved with the arrow keys and with other special keys such as HOME, PGUP, PGDN, and the F5 (GOTO) key.

Cell Reference   A reference to a worksheet cell in a formula. There are three types of cells references that you can use: a relative reference (A:A1), an absolute reference ($A:$A$3), and a mixed reference ($A:A$4 or A:$A4).

Circular Reference   A reference that depends on itself to calculate a result; for example, a formula stored in A1 as +A3/A1*2, which directly uses a reference to the cell itself. In many circular references, the dependence on itself is indirect. 1-2-3 places a CIRC indicator at the bottom of the screen when a worksheet contains a circular reference. You can use the /Worksheet Status command to identify the first cell causing the circular reference.

Column   The vertical division of the worksheet, consisting of one cell from each row of the worksheet in a vertical column. A column of cells on the worksheet can be widened or narrowed as well as hidden.

Column Width   The number of characters that can be stored in a column. You can change this number globally or for an individual column. The default column width is 9 characters. You can widen a column to 240 characters. The narrowest width permissible is 1 character.

Command Language   The advanced macro commands that make up the 1-2-3 macro command language. These commands provide a full programming language with which 1-2-3 users can extend the usefulness of the macro features beyond a duplication of 1-2-3 menu commands. Command-language instructions are all encased in braces ({}) and many use one or more arguments to refine their task. For example, {LET A1,0} is a command-language instruction.

Configuration File   The file that contains the default parameters for 1-2-3. Some of the options can be set with the /Worksheet Global Default command. Choosing the Update option from the same menu updates this file so your changes are present in subsequent 1-2-3 sessions.

Control Panel   The area consisting of three lines at the top of the 1-2-3 screen. The top line displays the current cell address, cell contents, and cell characteristics. The top line also displays a mode indicator in the right corner, which tells you that 1-2-3 is ready to process a new task or shows 1-2-3's current task. The second line serves a dual purpose. In EDIT mode it functions as the edit line for altering your data. In MENU mode the current menu is displayed in this line. The third line provides a description of the current menu selection in MENU mode.

Criteria   Specifications for searching the database. Criteria are entered on the worksheet and the /Data commands are invoked to either copy, highlight, or delete records that match them.

Database   A collection of individual pieces of data about a group of objects. In 1-2-3, a database is an organized structure for storing items of information (fields) about objects on the worksheet. Taken together, all the data about one object in the set is considered to be a record, which is stored across a row of the worksheet. Fields are stored vertically in columns of the worksheet, with a record having one value in each field. Numerous 1-2-3 commands can be used to select records from the database, as well as to sort it into a new sequence. Release 3 also lets you access a database created with another program using 1-2-3 commands (not covered in this book).

Data Series   A set of related data that is included in a graph that 1-2-3 takes from a worksheet. An example of data series is sales for each month of several products where each product is a different series. 1-2-3 can include up to six data series in a graph.

Debugging   The process of removing errors from a computer program. Since macros can be used to write a program within 1-2-3, it is also appropriate to refer to the process of testing and eliminating errors from a macro as debugging.

Directory   The current location for 1-2-3's data files. The /File Dir command allows you to change the current disk drive and subdirectory. The /File commands use this disk unless another one is provided.

Edit   The process of making corrections to an entry without needing to completely reenter the data.

Edit Line   The second line of the control panel. This is the line on which 1-2-3 displays your data as you enter it. 1-2-3 also uses this line to display data that is being edited.

Encoded File   A file containing data that you want to print and the printer-specific codes 1-2-3 adds to invoke printer features. These files include characters that make the file unusable for applications other than printing.

END   In READY mode, this indicates that you want to move your cursor to the last entry in a specific direction. After pressing END, you always press a direction arrow to indicate the direction you want to move. In EDIT mode, END takes you to the last character in a cell.

Erase   To remove from the worksheet or disk file. There are several Erase options in 1-2-3's menus. The /Range Erase command removes the entries from the cells you specify. The /Worksheet Erase option removes the current worksheet files from memory completely; it requires your confirmation. The /File Erase command makes the space a file is using available for the storage of new files and alters the entry within the file directory.

Error Message   A message that appears at the lower-left corner of the screen when an error condition is encountered. This message will appear when the printer is not ready or when the disk is full. Press F1 (HELP) to see a more complete description.

Expanded Memory   Memory above the 640K that can be added to the motherboard of a standard PC. This memory is added on an expansion card.

Extended Memory   Memory in the newer model PS/2 machines that provides more RAM beyond the original 640K limit. 1-2-3 can use this memory to store your worksheets so you can work with more data.

External File Links   A formula that references data in another 1-2-3 worksheet file. Release 3 formulas can use values from other files in most cases, just as they would use values in the same worksheet file. 1-2-3 updates these links with the /File Admin Link-Refresh command.

Extract   The process of pulling selected information from a database. Before you can use the /Data Extract command to accomplish this, you will need to set up output and criteria areas on the worksheet.

Field Names   Names used for the types of data stored in a database. In an employee database, some of the field names you might have are Last Name, Job Code, and Salary. In 1-2- 3, field names are always stored at the top of a column, with the values for each record placed beneath them.

File   An organized collection of data on the disk. 1-2-3 uses filename extensions to distinguish between the various types of files it stores on disk. Print files have the extension .ENC or .PRN, worksheet files the extension .WK3, and graph files the extension .CGM or .PIC.

Filename   The name used to access data stored on a disk. This name must follow standard DOS rules and consist of from 1 to 8 characters in the name portion of the entry. It may also include an optional 1- to 3-character filename extension. If this extension is used, a period will separate it from the filename. 1-2-3 will provide most file extensions for you.

Fonts   A set of characters in a specific format. 1-2-3's printing and graphics features support various fonts for use in printing graphs and worksheet ranges.

Format   The type of display used to present values. The format displayed may portray less internal accuracy than the package can support. Some of the permissible formats are Currency, Percent, Scientific, and Date. A new Release 3 feature can automatically format your data based upon the formatting characters you enter.

Formula   An entry in a worksheet cell that performs a calculation. A formula in 1-2-3 can be up to 512 characters long.

Function Keys   Special keys at the left or top of the keyboard that give you quick access to some of 1-2-3's features. 1-2-3 may use these keys differently than other packages, since each software vendor may use them in any way it chooses.

Graph   A representation of numeric worksheet data in a graphic format, which permits easy interpretation of results. 1-2-3 supports seven graph types: pie charts, line graphs, XY graphs, bar charts, stacked bar charts, HLCO graphs, and mixed graphs.

Grid-Lines   Horizontal and vertical lines that can be added to a graph to aid interpretation of the data points. These lines extend from the points on one or both axes.

Header   A line that can be printed at the top of every page. This line can include a report name, the preparer's name, the date, the page number, or any other information you would like to include at the top of each page of a report.

Home   The A1 location on the worksheet screen of the current worksheet. In EDIT mode, the home position is the first character in the entry being edited.

Import   The process of bringing text into the worksheet. Text can be imported with the /File Import command as numbers or text. The Text option brings in the complete line in the text file as a long label. The Numbers option only brings in the numeric values and character data enclosed in quotes from a line of text, but stores each one as a separate cell entry across a row of the worksheet.

Label   A series of up to 512 characters you want treated as text. Label entries cannot be used in arithmetic formulas. You can use labels in special string formulas and functions.

Label Indicator   The special character at the beginning of a cell entry that identifies the entry as a label. If you enter a non-numeric character in a cell, 1-2-3 will generate this indicator for you. If you enter a numeric character as the first character in a cell, you will have to enter the label indicator unless you want 1-2-3 to treat the entry as a label. The default label indicator is an apostrophe, indicating that the entry should be left aligned within the cell. A double quotation mark can be used for right alignment, a caret symbol can be used for center alignment, a backslash can be used to repeat a label for the length of the cell, and a vertical bar can be used to include printer codes and page breaks within a worksheet.

Legend   A description, added to the bottom of a graph, that distinguishes one set of data on the graph from other data series that may also be shown. If a hatch pattern is used to shade bars, the legend identifies which data set each pattern represents. If symbols are used to mark the various points on a line graph, the legend identifies the symbol that represent each series.

Logical Operator   Used when you want 1-2-3 to evaluate an expression to determine whether the expression is true or false. The simple logical operators and their meanings are

=	Equal to
>	Greater than
>=	Greater than or equal to
<	Less than
<=	Less than or equal to
<>	Not equal

In addition, three compound logical operators are used to join logical expressions: #AND, #OR#, and #NOT#. An example is @IF(A1>7 #AND# B3=6,0,12).

Macro   A form of shorthand that allows you to record 1-2-3 formulas in worksheet cells easily and to execute the same entries as commands at a later time with equal ease. Macros also allow you to create complete applications with your own menus and other features, using the extensions that the command-language instructions provide.

Macro Keyword   An instruction from 1-2-3's macro command language. The keyword is enclosed in braces and used with arguments to make your specific needs known to 1-2-3. A macro keyword within a macro might look something like {LET A1,1}.

Macro Recorder   1-2-3 stores all of your keystrokes in a buffer reserved for storing keystrokes. You can use this buffer to record keystrokes and copy them into a worksheet so you can include the keystrokes in a macro.

Map   A display of the types of data in worksheet cells. When 1- 2-3 displays the map of a worksheet, it uses ", #, and + to mark which cells contain labels, numbers, and formulas.

Margin   The amount of white space that you wish to leave around a printed document. 1-2-3 has default settings for a top, bottom, right, and left margin but allows you to change any of them.

Math Coprocessor   A special chip that can be added to your computer to enhance the processing speed.

Menu   A selection of features presented in a horizontal line at the top of the screen. You can activate each menu option by pointing to it and pressing ENTER or by typing the single letter beginning the selection.

Minimum Recalculation   How 1-2-3 recalculates the values in your worksheet, recalculating the value of the cell only when it contains a formula that references a cell that has changed. This feature reduces the time between entering a value and having 1-2-3 update the cells in the worksheet to reflect the new value.

Mode Indicator   The indicator in the upper-right corner of the 1-2-3 display screen that lets you know what 1-2-3 is doing at any point in time. 1-2-3 will be waiting to process your next request only when this indicator reads READY.

Multilevel   A worksheet that contains multiple worksheets. Each worksheet is referenced with a different letter (or two letters and a colon) that precedes the column address.

Operator Precedence   The order in which operators are processed. The following list is from the highest to the lowest priority. Formulas containing multiple operators with the same priority level are evaluated from left to right.

( )	Parentheses for grouping
^	Exponentiation
+-	Positive and negative indicators
/*	Division and multiplication
+-	Addition and subtraction
< > <= >= <>	Logical operators
#NOT#	Complex NOT operator
#AND#	Complex AND operator
#OR#	Complex OR operator
&	String operator

Parse   Dividing up long pieces of data into smaller pieces of data. You can use the /Data Parse command to break long labels into smaller ones.

Pointing   A method for building worksheet formulas. With the pointing method, you type the special characters and arithmetic operators but you point to the cell addresses of interest.

Protected Mode   A mode of memory addressing used on 80286 and 80386 machines that have more than 640K of memory.

RAM   Random access memory. This is where your computer stores temporary information, such as programs as they execute and the data the program uses. RAM can also be used as a temporary disk to store information until the computer is rebooted.

Range   A group of cells on the worksheet. Many commands in 1-2-3's menus operate on ranges, including /Range Erase, /Range Format, and /Range Name.

Range Name   A name that you assigned to a group of cells on the worksheet. This name can be from 1 to 15 characters in length. It can be used anywhere you would have used a range address to refer to the same cells. If you assign names to all ranges used in formula calculations, your formulas will be self-documenting.

Range Reference   A reference to one or more cells on the worksheet. To specify a range reference, use two cells at opposite corners of the range. For example, A1..A10, A2..B4, B4..A2, A1..A1 are all valid ranges. Just as a cell reference can be relative, absolute, or mixed, a range reference has the same options. To span multiple worksheets, include the beginning and ending worksheet letters in the range address, as in A:B5..G:H10.

Recalculation   The process of reevaluating all the formulas on the worksheet. The default for 1-2-3 is to use automatic recalculation, which means that every time you make a change to a cell entry, every formula on the worksheet will be reevaluated. If you disable automatic recalculation, you will need to press F9 (CALC) when you want to recalculate the worksheet. Release 3 uses minimal and background recalculation so your worksheets are updated quickly.

Relative   A type of cell reference used in formulas. A relative reference is entered as a reference to a specific cell in the original formula, but when this formula is copied the reference is updated based on the new location. It will still represent a cell with the same relative direction and distance as the original cell reference, but the reference will not be to the same cell as the original. A relative reference to a cell might look like A1, M2, or B5. It is the default reference type placed into a formula that you build with the pointing method, unless you take a special action to override this default.

Rounding   The process of affecting the internal precision of a number in memory. You can use 1-2-3's @ROUND function to reduce the internal precision. A number stored as 123.567 will be stored as 123.57 after being rounded to two decimal places. If this same number is rounded to a whole number, it will be 124. You can control which numbers are rounded and the place at which you would like rounding to occur. This is different from formatting, which changes the number's appearance but does not change how 1-2-3 stores the value and uses it in calculations.

Row   A horizontal line of consecutive cells on the worksheet. Release 3 has 8192 rows in each worksheet.

Setup String   A series of characters transmitted to the printer to activate certain printer features. Each printer has its own set of characters for its features. On a Hewlett Packard LaserJet Series II printer, the print font is returned to Courier from another font with a setup string of \027(s10H.

Sheet   *See* Worksheet.

String   A series of characters. 1-2-3 has several features that work with strings. You can use the concatenation character & to join two strings. Release 3 also has a number of built-in functions that focus on string manipulation.

Titles   The text characters that are used to provide description on a graph. They can be placed at the top of the graph or along the X or Y axis. In the worksheet environment, titles can also refer to the data that you want to freeze on the top or left side of the screen as you scroll the cell pointer down or to the right.

Undo   Removes the effect of the last change that you made since 1-2-3 was in READY mode. This feature is enabled and disabled with the /Worksheet Global Default Other Undo command. Enabling Undo reduces the memory available for your worksheet files.

Value   A number or formula entry on the worksheet.

Window   A portion of the screen used to show another part of the same worksheet, a different worksheet, or a graph while the remaining portion of the screen contains one or two other parts.

Worksheet   The entire electronic sheet of paper that 1-2-3 creates in the memory of your computer system. This worksheet is composed of many cells organized into rows and columns. Release 3 lets you have worksheet files that contain several sheets.

Worksheet File   A file that contains the data you enter in 1-2- 3. A worksheet file can contain more than one sheet.

X Axis   The horizontal axis on a graph. This is the axis on which the categories of a data series are shown.

Xtract   A file menu selection that creates a worksheet file containing a subset of the current worksheet. Only the range you specify will be saved to the worksheet file with this operation. You will have the option of saving formulas or values to this file. If you choose, you can create this file as a snapshot of the current worksheet with only labels and values stored in the new file. Xtract should be distinguished from Extract, which is used in the data-management environment to copy information from the database to another area of your worksheet.

Y Axis   The vertical axis on a bar, line, or XY graph that measures quantitative units such as dollars, units sold, or number of employees.

1-2-3's BUILT-IN FUNCTIONS

Function	Type	Release 3
@@(*cell*)	Special	
@ABS(*number*)	Math	
@ACOS(*number*)	Math	
@ASIN(*number*)	Math	
@ATAN(*number*)	Math	
@ATAN2(*number*)	Math	
@AVG(*list*)	Statistical	
@CELL(*attribute string,range*)	Special	
@CELLPOINTER(*attribute string*)	Special	
@CHAR(*code*)	String	
@CHOOSE(*number,list*)	Special	
@CODE(*string*)	String	
@COLS(*range*)	Special	
@COS(*number*)	Math	
@COORD(*worksheet,column,row,absolute*)	Special	*
@COUNT(*list*)	Statistical	
@CTERM(*interest,future value,present value*)	Financial	
@DATE(*year,month,day*)	Date & Time	
@DATEVALUE(*date string*)	Date & Time	
@DAVG(*input range,offset column,criteria range*)	Database	
@DAY(*serial date number*)	Date & Time	

Function	Type	Release 3
@DCOUNT(*input range,offset column,criteria range*)	Database	
@DDB(*cost,salvage,life,period*)	Financial	*
@DGET(*input range,offset column,criteria range*)	Database	
@DMAX(*input range,offset column,criteria range*)	Database	
@DMIN(*input range,offset column,criteria range*)	Database	
@DQUERY(*function,list*)	Database	*
@DSTD(*input range,offset column,criteria range*)	Database	
@DSTDS(*input range,offset column, criteria range*)	Database	*
@DSUM(*input range,offset column,criteria range*)	Database	
@DVAR(*input range,offset column, criteria range*)	Database	
@DVARS(*input range,offset column,criteria range*)	Database	*
@D360(*start date,end date*)	Date & Time	*
@ERR	Special	
@EXACT(*string1,string2*)	String	
@EXP(*number*)	Math	
@FALSE	Logical	
@FIND(*search string,entire string,starting location*)	String	
@FV(*payment,interest,term*)	Financial	
@HLOOKUP(*code to be looked up,table location,offset*)	Special	
@HOUR(*serial time number*)	Date & Time	
@IF(*condition to be tested,value if true,value if false*)	Logical	
@INDEX(*table location,column number,row number[,worksheet number]*)	Special	
@INT(*number*)	Math	*
@INFO(*attribute string*)	Special	
@IRR(*guess,range*)	Financial	
@ISERR(*value*)	Logical	
@ISNA(*value*)	Logical	
@ISNUMBER(*value*)	Logical	
@ISRANGE(*string*)	Logical	*
@ISSTRING(*value*)	Logical	

Function	Type	Release 3
@LEFT(*string,number of characters to be extracted*)	String	
@LENGTH(*string*)	String	
@LN(*number*)	Math	
@LOG(*number*)	Math	
@LOWER(*string*)	String	
@MAX(*list*)	Statistical	
@MID(*string,start number,number of characters*)	String	
@MIN(*list*)	Statistical	
@MINUTE(*serial time number*)	Date & Time	
@MOD(*number,divisor*)	Math	
@MONTH(*serial date number*)	Date & Time	
@N(*range*)	String	
@NA	Special	
@NOW	Date & Time	
@NPV(*discount rate,range*)	Financial	
@PI	Math	
@PMT(*principal,interest,term of loan*)	Financial	
@PROPER(*string*)	String	
@PV(*payment,periodic interest rate, number of periods*)	Financial	
@RAND	Math	
@RATE(*future value,present value,number of periods*)	Financial	
@REPEAT(*string,number of times*)	String	
@REPLACE(*original string,start location, # characters,new string*)	String	
@RIGHT(*string,number of characters to be extracted*)	String	
@ROUND(*number to be rounded,place of rounding*)	Math	
@ROWS(*range*)	Special	
@S(*range*)	String	
@SECOND(*serial time number*)	Date & Time	*
@SHEETS(*range*)	Special	
@SIN(*number*)	Math	
@SLN(*cost,salvage value,life of the asset*)	Financial	
@SQRT(*number*)	Math	
@STD(*list*)	Statistical	*
@STDS(*list*)	Statistical	
@STRING(*number,number of decimal places*)	String	
@SUM(*list*)	Statistical	

Function	Type	Release 3
		*
@SUMPRODUCT(*list*)	Statistical	
@SYD(*cost,salvage value,life,period*)	Financial	
@TAN(*number*)	Math	
@TERM(*payment,interest,future value*)	Financial	
@TIME(*hour,minute,second*)	Date & Time	
@TIMEVALUE(*time string*)	Date & Time	*
@TODAY	Date & Time	
@TRIM(*string*)	String	
@TRUE	Logical	
@UPPER(*string*)	String	
@VALUE(*string*)	String	
@VAR(*list*)	Statistical	
@VARS(*list*)	Statistical	*
@VDB(*cost,salvage,life,period[,depreciation factor]*)	Financial	*
@VLOOKUP(*code to be looked up,table location,offset*)	Special	
@YEAR(*serial date number*)	Date & Time	

* Indicates this function is new to Release 3.

TRADEMARKS

COMPAQ®	COMPAQ Corporation
HAL™	Lotus Development Corporation
IBM®	International Business Machines Corporation
IBM® PC AT	International Business Machines Corporation
IBM® PC XT	International Business Machines Corporation
Intel®	Intel Corporation
Lotus®	Lotus Development Corporation
Microsoft®	Microsoft Corporation
MS-DOS®	Microsoft Corporation
1-2-3®	Lotus Development Corporation
OS/2™	International Business Machines Corporation
Zenith™	Zenith Data Systems

Index

{?} command, 476
* wildcard, 327
@functions. *See* Functions

A

@ABS function, 250-52
Absolute addresses, 136, 142
Active cell, 6
Addition operator, 37
Alignment
      in headers and footers, 192-93
      of labels, 20-21, 99-101
ALT-F2 (RECORD) key, 465-67, 478
ALT-F3 (RUN) key, 452, 462
ALT-F4 (UNDO) key, 19, 32
ALT-F6 (ZOOM) key, 426
ALT key, 452
AND operator, 52-53
ANSI standard, 297
Area graphs, 291-92
Arguments, 217
Arithmetic formulas, 37-49
Arithmetic operators, 49
Arrow keys, 10-13
Ascending order, 318, 319
ASCII order, 494-95
ASCII text files, 179, 404, 405
Automatic format, 75, 83-85
Automatic graphs, 274
Automatic macros, 470-73
Automatic recalculation, 161
Averages, finding, 230-31
@AVG function, 230-31

B

Background recalculation, 160
BACKSPACE key, 16-18
Backups, 112, 116, 117-19
.BAK extension, 46, 112
Bar graphs, 275
Baud rates, 485
Beep feature, 13
Billing-by-hour model, 368-70
Boldface, 198, 201
Borders, 194-95
Boxing text, 156-57
{BRANCH} command, 474

C

Calculations. *See* Formulas
CAP indicator, 9
Case
      converting, 245-47
      in formulas, 39
      in keywords, 216
      in macro instructions, 456
      in menu selections, 72
      in range names, 60
      in search strings, 166
      in string values, 353
Cell addresses, 6, 38-39, 63, 136
Cell pointer, 5-6
Cell ranges. *See* Ranges
Cell references, 60, 62-63
Cells, 5-6
      default width of, 23
      entering labels in, 20-25

Essential 1-2-3 Release 3 Commands

Worksheet Commands

Alters format of all worksheet cells

Alters width of all worksheet columns

Sets recalculation to automatic

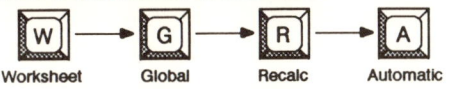

Sets recalculation to manual

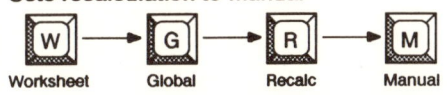

Determines whether \O macros are executed

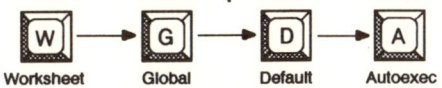

Treats all sheets in a worksheet as a group

Inserts rows, columns, or sheets in worksheet

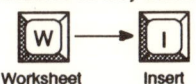

Deletes worksheet rows, columns,
files, or sheets from memory

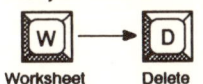

Alters width of a single column

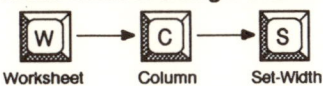

Hides a worksheet column

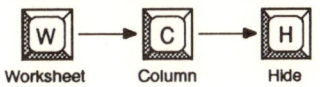

Alters width of a range of columns

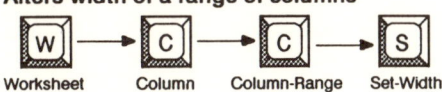

Worksheet Commands

Erases worksheet even if
worksheet has not been saved

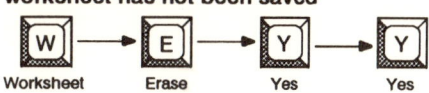

Sets and clears worksheet titles

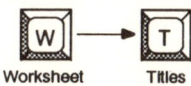

Sets and clears worksheet windows

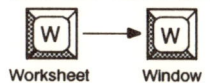

Creates map of worksheet entries

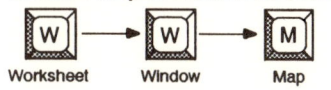

Creates perspective view of three sheets

Adds page break at the cell pointer location

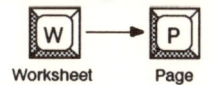

Range Commands

Assigns format to a range

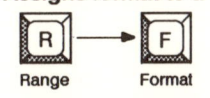

Changes label alignment of a range of labels

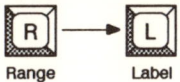

Erases contents of a range

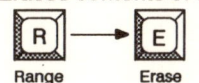

Creates and deletes range names

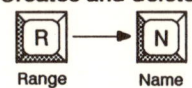

Range Commands

Applies entry in worksheet cell
to the cell immediately to its right

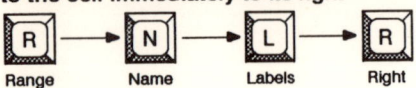

Alters orientation of a range of entries

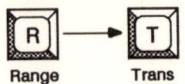

Allows you to search for an entry in a range

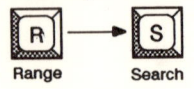

Copy Command

Copies worksheet entries and formats

Move Command

Moves worksheet entries

File Commands

Retrieves file from disk

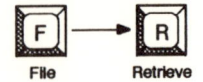

Saves file to disk

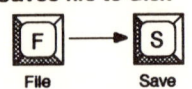

Cancels save request

Tells 1-2-3 to replace disk file
with current contents of memory

Creates .WK3 file and .BAK file

File Commands

Combines information from disk
with the current worksheet

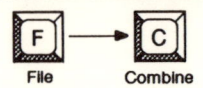

Saves part of a worksheet to disk

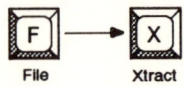

Erases a file on disk

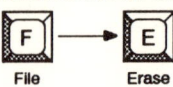

Creates list of files
in the current directory

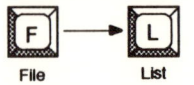

Imports data into worksheet

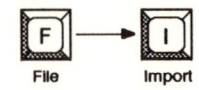

Changes current directory

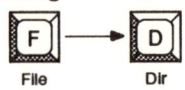

Creates new worksheet file in memory

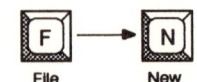

Opens worksheet file in memory

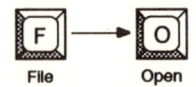

Refreshes links to external files

Print Commands

Directs print output to printer

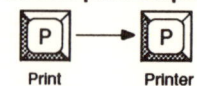

Establishes range for printing

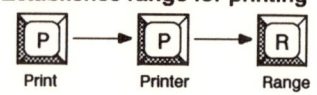

Print Commands

Advances one line

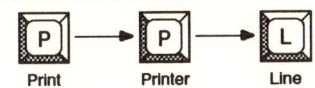

Advances one page

Allows you to enter a header line

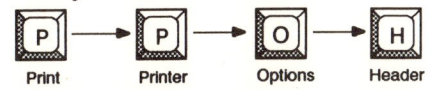

Allows you to enter a footer line

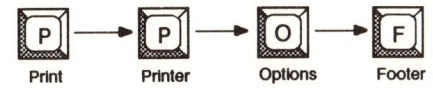

Allows you to set top, bottom, right, left margins

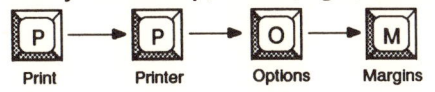

Allows you to establish border rows or columns

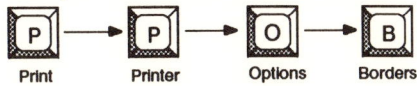

Allows you to enter a setup string to control print output

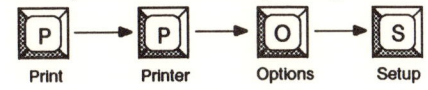

Allows you to set page length

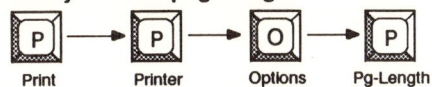

Provides access to other print settings

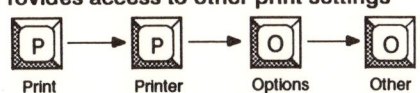

Allows you to use advanced print options like font

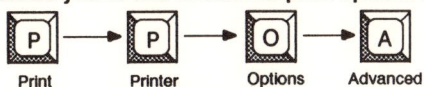

Quits the Print Options menu

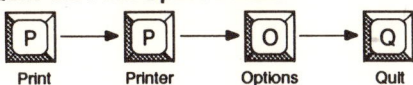

Print Commands

Clears print settings

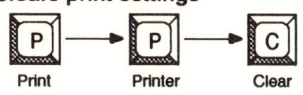

Zeroes line count and tells 1-2-3 you're starting a new page

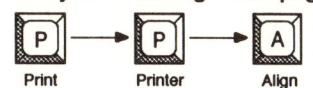

Starts printing

Allows you to print a graph

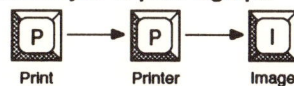

Lets you view print selections

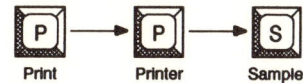

Directs print output to a disk file

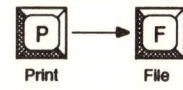

Directs print output to an encoded file

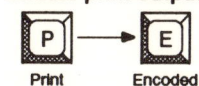

Suspends printing

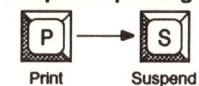

Resumes printing

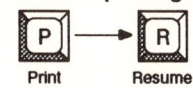

Cancels print request

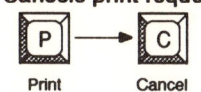

Quits printing and returns to READY mode

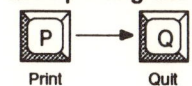

Allows you to select a graph type

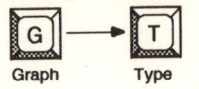

Sets the X graph range

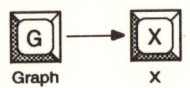

Sets the A graph range

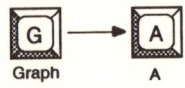

Sets the B graph range

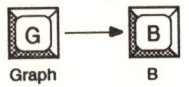

Sets the C graph range

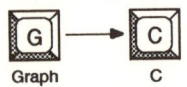

Sets the D graph range

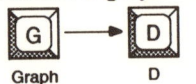

Sets the E graph range

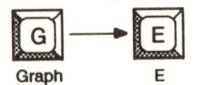

Sets the F graph range

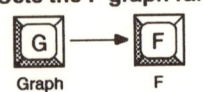

Lets you view the graph

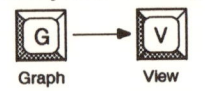

Saves the graph image file

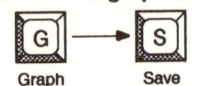

Allows you to establish legends for each graph data range

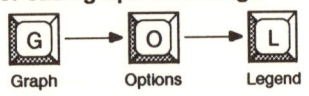

Sets format for an area graph

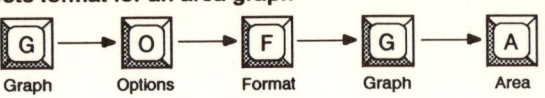

Allows you to create graph titles

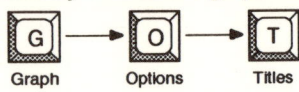

Allows you to establish and clear grid lines

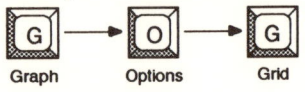

Sets display to color

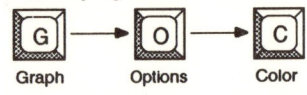

Sets display to black and white

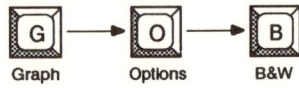

Allows you to create and use graph names

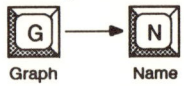

Allows you to set all graph ranges with one command

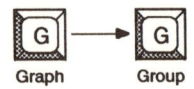

Data Commands

Generates series of evenly spaced numbers

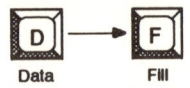

Specifies range for sorting

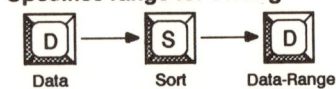

Specifies main sort key

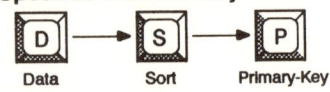

Data Commands

Specifies secondary sort key

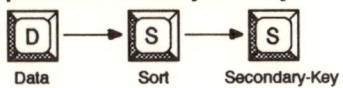

Data → Sort → Secondary-Key

Sorts data

Data → Sort → Go

Specifies input range for query

Data → Query → Input

Tells 1-2-3 which record to use

Data → Query → Criteria

Specifies output range for query

Data → Query → Output

Highlights matching records

Data → Query → Find

Extracts matching records

Data → Query → Xtract

**Allows you to create and edit
a format line for parsing data**

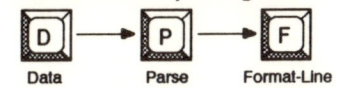

Data → Parse → Format-Line

Defines input for data parse operation

Data → Parse → Input-Column

Defines location for output of data parse

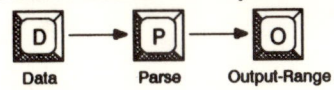

Data → Parse → Output-Range

**Splits long label according to definition
and data parse format line**

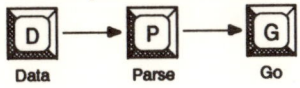

Data → Parse → Go

System Command

Temporarily exits to the operating system

System

Quit Command

**Quits 1-2-3 even if the worksheet
hasn't been saved**

Quit → Yes → Yes

You're important to us...

We'd like to know what you're interested in, what kinds of books you're looking for, and what you thought about this book in particular.

Please fill out the attached card and mail it in. We'll do our best to keep you informed about Osborne's newest books and special offers.

YES, SEND ME A FREE COLOR CATALOG
of all Osborne/McGraw-Hill computer books.

Name:_____ Title:_____

Company:_____

Address:_____

City:_____ State:_____ Zip:_____

I'M PARTICULARLY INTERESTED IN THE FOLLOWING*(Check all that apply)*

I use this software:
- ❏ Lotus 1-2-3
- ❏ Quattro
- ❏ dBASE
- ❏ WordPerfect
- ❏ Microsoft Word
- ❏ WordStar
- ❏ Others_____

I use this operating system:
- ❏ DOS
- ❏ OS/2
- ❏ UNIX
- ❏ Macintosh
- ❏ Others_____

I rate this book:
- ❏ Excellent   ❏ Good   ❏ Poor

I program in:
- ❏ C
- ❏ PASCAL
- ❏ BASIC
- ❏ Others_____

I chose this book because...
- ❏ Recognized author's name
- ❏ Osborne/McGraw-Hill's reputation
- ❏ Read book review
- ❏ Read Osborne catalog
- ❏ Saw advertisement in _____
- ❏ Found while browsing in store
- ❏ Found/recommended in library
- ❏ Required textbook
- ❏ Price
- ❏ Other_____

Comments_____

_____

Topics I would like to see covered in future books by Osborne/McGraw-Hill

include:_____

_____

ISBN# 541-X

BUSINESS REPLY MAIL

First Class   Permit NO. 3111 Berkeley, CA

Postage will be paid by addressee

Osborne McGraw-Hill

2600 Tenth Street
Berkeley, California 94710-9938